This volume amply fulfils the promise of its title by surveying the vast range of religious revivals enjoyed in Scotland down to 1857. Tom Lennie has identified them with care and chronicled them with great sympathy.

David Bebbington
Professor of History, University of Stirling, Scotland
Author of *Evangelicalism in Modern Britain: A History from the 1730s to the 1980s* and *Victorian Religious Revivals*

Tom Lennie has provided us with a thoroughly researched and referenced treatment of the history of evangelical revivals in Scotland from the early 16th century to the mid 19th century. I know of no work covering the same ground at the same depth. Whilst enthralling us with the reality of spiritual revival, he cautiously and sympathetically investigates the counterfeits. At the same time it is challenging, inspiring and informative. This book is a classic to be added to any literature on the subject of revival.

Brian H. Edwards
Lecturer & Theologian,
Author of *Revival: A People Saturated With God* and *Can We Pray For Revival?*

Tom Lennie's work on the history of revivals is a welcome addition to the literature. It is a wonderful story, and Tom tells it well. The historical evidence is judiciously assessed and carefully written. Beginning with the Scottish Reformation, which the author rightly sees as an example of revival, we are treated to a thrilling re-telling of three centuries of God's work in Scotland. It is a reminder to those of us who are called to work in Scotland that we have a good inheritance; it is a reminder to every reader that we have a glorious God. May the same divine work which shaped the church in the past continue to come in power to revive us again.

Iain D. Campbell
Minister, Point Free Church of Scotland, Isle of Lewis

In a day when many of us long for a much needed Gospel awakening, Tom Lennie has provided a historically accurate, theologically framed and inspirationally written page turner documenting the multiple and varied Holy Spirit sent and Gospel saturated revivals in the land of Scotland.

Harry L. Reeder, III
Pastor Teacher
Briarwood Presbyterian Church, Birmingham, Alabama

Tom Lennie treats us to a careful and well-written chronicle of thirty-three decades of God's amazing grace manifested in revival power in Scotland between 1527 and 1857. Tom shows how, in all but one of these decades, a revival movement of some significance arose in some corner of Scotland. Throughout the period covered, every single county of Scotland was touched by the Spirit of God at least once and most counties were touched on numerous occasions. Check out from the contents pages when and where God was at work in revival power in your area and be encouraged to pray for further outpourings of the Spirit in these spiritually needy days.

Hector Morrison
Principal, Highland Theological College
(University of the Highlands & Islands)

In these days in Scotland I know that many churches are experiencing encouraging signs of the Lord at work. However, I also meet many ministers and believers who feel that the times are dark and less encouraging. Whatever the reasons for such differences, the distance between the encouraging and discouraging situations pale into almost complete insignificance compared with the distance between what the Lord is doing now, and what He has done in times past. We are a long way from the scenes described in this book, when the land of Scotland has witnessed crowds of 55,000 gathering for a communion service, or crowds of 20,000 children gathering to hear the Word of the Lord – and this at a time when the population was much smaller than it now is. Numbers may not always be significant but they are not always insignificant. At the same time you will read here of small out-of-the-way places which may seem insignificant in terms of the nation's life but matter in God's Kingdom and were on the agenda of heaven for a visitation of the Holy Spirit. Since reading this book I can hardly find myself in any part of the land where my mind does not think with longing of what happened when God came there in times past. Wherever you live or worship you will probably find facts here about what God once did in or near that very place. Do not find comfort in nostalgia, but rather as you read these pages may they be an instrument in the hand of Almighty God by which we are 'made to wrestle with God for His promised presence, for his Spirit and blessing' (Ralph Erskine).

Kenny Borthwick
Minister, Holy Trinity Church
Wester Hailes, Edinburgh

Dr J. Edwin Orr, historian of revivals around the world, adopted the Scriptural policy that the great works of God should not be forgotten (Psalm 78). As a result, his writings strove to note and comment upon every revival about which he could find a record. But he did not write a book specifically on Scotland.

Many books have been published on Scottish revivals through the years, including several in which the authors have tried to make a complete Survey. Mr Lennie's researches reveal that none of these Surveys are complete. By looking even more thoroughly, more widely, and by using modern bibliographic aids, he has uncovered a good number of revivals not mentioned in earlier Surveys.

I found the Table of Contents at the front of the book to be the most forceful demonstration of this, where these revivals, large and small, are specified. Not only are more revivals that occurred within Presbyterian churches listed, but our author has also taken great trouble to include revivals mentioned in Baptist, Congregational and Methodist records. Especially is this apparent in his coverage of the revivals occurring within a decade or so of the Disruption in 1843.

Thus the book gives us a better view of the great works of God seen in the outpouring of the Holy Spirit in Scotland; it provides us with more reasons to praise the Lord for His wonderful works in saving sinners and in improving Scottish society morally and spiritually, and it inspires us as we turn to God in our present needs. I recommend this book wholeheartedly.

Robert Owen Evans
Revival historian, astronomer and
retired minister of the Uniting Church in Australia

Tom Lennie has produced an invaluable and extensive resource in his scholarly and inspiring survey of the history of revivals in Scotland in his 500 page work, Land of Many Revivals.

The approach of the author is a wise one from two standpoints. First, the decision to try to give a history of every known revival over a period of three hundred plus years is a mammoth, yet significant one, providing for the first time a comprehensive collection of all known revivals in Scotland's history up to 1857 in one volume.

Second, because of the broadness of the subject matter, the amount of material on each revival is necessarily limited. Lennie paints a broad canvas with small strokes of the pen. This approach provides a very readable history and gives a clear picture of the great heritage of God's gracious works in Scotland.

For any student of historic revival and Christian biography this book is a must read and will yield extensive knowledge of God's works of grace in that great land of the Reformation, as well as inspiration to cry out to God to do such great works again.

Mack Tomlinson
Pastor, Providence Chapel, Denton, Texas
Author of *In Light of Eternity: The Life of Leonard Ravenhill*

Three hundred years, five hundred pages, a small country, many souls converted – this book is alive with the sound and news of revival. How I long to see revival again. Reading this will whet your appetite and renew your desire for God to do a new work in our day.

R.T. Kendall
Writer, Speaker and Teacher;
former Senior Minister of Westminster Chapel

Sin is always a barrier. It not only separates humans from humans but men and women from their God. As the presence and severity of sin increases in a society, the true worship of God wanes. Fortunately, God Himself, when entreated by a believing remnant, manifests Himself afresh by drawing near to His floundering people. These seasons of God's nearness are called revivals. Scotland has experienced many of these precious visitations as Tom Lennie has so carefully shown. Surely, it is not idle hope that another great revival will sweep this ancient land.

Richard Owen Roberts
President, International Awakening Ministries
and Author of *Revival* and *Revival Literature: An Annotated Bibliography With Biographical and Historical Notices*

Land of Many Revivals is an exceptional work and will rank as one of the greatest research resources available on revivals in Scotland. It will certainly become a mandated book in the newly-established Kalibu University of Divinity and Revival. Tom Lennie is to be highly commended for tremendous insight and thoughtfulness in presenting this amazing masterpiece. Speaking as a revivalist who holds a passion for intercession for revival, and having personally experienced powerful revivals in Africa, I am greatly blessed to see that Mr Lennie has not only presented the facts of revivals in Scotland, but has done so with real passion. This is evident as I read through his truly professional presentation, and it makes for exciting rather than dull factual reading.

To ignore the way in which revivals have shaped the history and destiny of Scotland is virtually to ignore her true history altogether. We are looking at a nation that has been fashioned by the hand of God through revivals, and at considerable personal cost to so many. What a mandate this is for the future of Scotland. Though she has descended into the abyss of the wicked modernity of liberal humanism, yet the Lord will never forget this land of many revivals, which means that revivals in Scotland are far from over. All the Lord needs is for somebody to believe and step out in that belief and the Lord will make it happen. Each of the revivals recorded in this work is a God-event made manifest in response to the out-poured hearts of a few men and women.

This stirring work simply has to provoke even the hardest sceptic to think again about the intervention of an Almighty God in the affairs of the nations, particularly Scotland.

Certainly, this is a noteworthy and timely work.

Michael T. Howard
Founder and Principal of The Kalibu University of Divinity and Revival;
International revivalist; Author of *Intercession: Your Power To Possess The Nations*

Land of Many Revivals

Scotland's Extraordinary Legacy of
Christian Revivals over Four Centuries
(1527–1857)

Tom Lennie

hardback ISBN 978-1-78191-520-2

epub ISBN 978-1-78191-542-4

mobi ISBN 978-1-78191-547-9

First published in 2015
by
Christian Focus Publications Ltd,
Geanies House, Fearn, Ross–shire
IV20 1TW, Scotland

www.christianfocus.com

CIP catalogue record for this book is available from the British Library.

Cover design by Daniel Van Straaten
Cover photo: Glen Nevis by Leighton Pritchard

Livonia
Printed and bound by Livonia Print, Latvia

MIX
Paper from
responsible sources
FSC   FSC® C002795
www.fsc.org

CONTENTS

CHAPTER 2

'The Evangelical Revival' 1729–50

ABBREVIATIONS

BHMS	Baptist Home Missionary Society
DSCHT	*Dictionary of Scottish Church History and Theology* (Ed. Nigel M. de S. Cameron), Edinburgh, 1993
FCSRSRM	Free Church of Scotland Report on the State of Religion and Morals
GSS	Gaelic School Society
SCHSR	Scottish Church History Society Records
SCM	*Scottish Congregational Magazine*
SPGH	Society for Propagating the Gospel at Home
SSPCK	Society in Scotland for the Propagation of Christian Knowledge

ACKNOWLEDGEMENTS

I wish to express my deep gratitude to the many people who have in ways large or small provided help or encouragement in the ongoing research and writing of this labour of love over a considerable period of time. Especial thanks are due to Andrew T. N. Muirhead, President of the Scottish Church History Society, who graciously agreed to read through a draft version and went on to provide many helpful recommendations. Responsibility for all matters of historical accuracy and for opinions expressed of course rests entirely with myself.

DEDICATION

I dedicate *Land of Many Revivals* to the memory of all those whose heart-felt, persistent prayers and intercessions and bold, selfless endeavours helped lead to the innumerable seasons of spiritual outpouring outlined within these pages; and further, to all those in present day Scotland who know from ongoing experience what it means to bend the knee and cry to the living God for a fresh, mighty move of his holy Spirit to sweep across this dry, thirsty land.

Tom Lennie
February 2015

tom@linnadale.fsnet.co.uk

Lord Have Mercy

Lord, have mercy on our country
Turn our hearts to You again,
Though we've grieved Your Holy Spirit
By our deeds of sin and shame:

Though our sins rise like a dark cloud
May our prayers rise even higher,
Pleading for divine forgiveness
Pleading for the heavenly fire.

Bold Reformers, Covenanters
Interceded with their blood,
For the land they loved so dearly
For the freedom of Your word:

May the heart cries of our fathers
Now be mingled with our own,
As we intercede for Scotland
As we bow before Your throne.

May Your Spirit move in power
Until all the land is blessed,
From the North Isles to the Borders,
From Kinnaird Head to the West:

Bring the day for which we're waiting
And to which our hearts aspire,
Visit Scotland with revival
Send the fire, Lord, send the fire!

(Words: Alex Muir)

Introduction

This book, researched and documented over many years, takes in a broad sweep of Scottish Church history, from the revolutionary events of the Protestant Reformation of the 1500s to the early Victorian era of peace and prosperity of the sixth decade of the nineteenth century.[1] It seeks to show that throughout this period of often complicated, fast-changing and at times turbulent political history, spiritual revivals have typically appeared as features of the nation's religious and social setting.

Not that they have been regular in their appearance. Quite the reverse. The second decade of the seventeenth century, for example, is to be noted for the absence of revival activity almost anywhere in Scotland, whereas by contrast, during the two short years, 1839 and '40, revival was widespread throughout much of the land.

Nor have revivals been equal in their geographic spread. The names of some regions crop up repeatedly within these pages, such as Easter Ross-shire, the Breadalbane district of Perthshire, and the island of Skye. Specific towns and villages, such as Kilsyth and Grantown-on-Spey also feature recurrently. Then again other areas rarely or never get a mention, such as western Galloway or several of the Orkney isles.

Great variation is to be found, too, in both the magnitude and effect of revivals. Some are loud, bursting in on a community like a tornado, and sweeping up men, women and children by the score into their life-transforming throes. Such might be said of some places affected by the Breadalbane revival of 1814–19, or when 'the Spirit descended' on Kilsyth in 1839. Others are quieter affairs, such as the gradual awakening

---

1. It is not in any sense, however, a history of the Scottish Church per se, and generally refers only to events in Scotland's ecclesiastical history that have a direct bearing on times of revival blessing.

that spread through the Lewis parishes of Knock and Lochs under the ministry of Robert Finlayson in the 1830s.

As to effect, a small minority of spiritual movements burn out quickly and sadly leave little in the way of observable fruit in their aftermath. A great many others have long-lasting positive impact. Hugh Miller said that the effects of the revival that overtook communities in Easter Ross in the 1740s were still making themselves felt in these places more than eighty years later.

Taking all these variables into account, it is nevertheless the case that religious revivals have been remarkably recurring, pervasive features of the Scottish social and religious landscape throughout recent history. Indeed, in the 330 years covered in this book, there is barely a single decade in which a revival movement of some significance has not arisen in one part of the country or another (the 1610s, as previously noted, may constitute a notable exception). Nor, during the same period, is there a single county in which has not occurred a spiritual revival on at least one occasion, and in most counties, on manifold occasions, affecting numerous parishes or townships within its bounds.

So revivals are highly variable, quite unpredictable events, that have from time to time graced our land. They are uncommon, ethereal happenings, which although can be partially explained by natural circumstances (see page 483), cannot be engendered by the use of means, as American revivalist Charles Finney controversially taught. (If they could, would the past century have been so devoid of heaven-sent revival in the Western world as it has been?)

Indeed, of all their truly captivating, multifaceted features, it is the mystique of community revivals that grips me most. Their otherworldly qualities, their sheer improbability, even after all practical explanations have been exhausted, such as dire personal or social needs steering neighbourhoods in search of spiritual solace, forceful preaching from charismatic personalities, or even mass hysteria.[2]

Given the recurring appearance of religious revivals in Scotland's journey since the Reformation, it is to be regretted that they are largely ignored

---

2. Forms of hysteria may indeed be present on a few specific occasions during some revival scenarios, but virtually never feature through the larger part of their progress, and are entirely absent in most revival settings. In any case hysteria can hardly explain the utter transformation of the lifestyles of large numbers of individuals for the better, and with long-lasting effect.

in most secular accounts of Scottish history. Even many church histories of Scotland fail to note the frequency, magnitude or impact of evangelical revivals in the life of the nation. If they're mentioned at all, it's usually only one or two of the more powerful and widespread movements, such as the Cambuslang 'wark', or the dawning of Highland awakening in the early nineteenth century. Thus, even among Scottish Christians there is little appreciation of the remarkable revival legacy of the nation in which we live. Therefore, the extent to which evangelical revivals have played in Scotland's past as detailed in these pages may surprise many readers.

Neighbouring countries have also had their share of religious awakenings. Wales has the enviable and merited reputation of being 'the land of revivals', although its revival heritage started later than Scotland's, being especially prominent in the century-and-a-half from 1762 to the early twentieth century, and of course taking in the renowned 1904–05 awakening, perhaps the most famed single evangelical revival in the world. It would undoubtedly be most interesting to compare Scotland's revival narrative with that of its closest neighbour, England, which has also enjoyed a remarkably rich heritage of spiritual awakening dating back to the Puritan era. While this may be done in part, detailed comparisons cannot at present be properly achieved, for no comprehensive history of revivals south of the border has yet been compiled. The same is true of spiritual awakenings in America. Yet, other than Scotland, it is these two countries above all others that have seen the highest number of evangelical awakenings through the centuries (be they localised, regional or national).

This notwithstanding, taken alongside my previous book, *Glory In The Glen* – which uncovers a remarkable proliferation of revivals across the Scottish nation in the sixty short years between 1880 and 1940 – the present volume goes a long way in substantiating the claim that no nation on earth has a richer, more colourful, and more long-standing heritage of evangelical awakenings than Scotland. Scotland is, unquestionably, a Land of Many Revivals.

Establishing a Theory of Revivals

The term 'evangelical revival' did not find common usage until the nineteenth century, from which time it has commonly been employed to describe spiritual awakenings dating at least as far back as the 1740s. For the sake of simplicity and continuity I loosely use the phrase for movements of earlier periods still, by so doing implying that they contain similar essential attributes to revivals of later eras.[3] It is almost universally emphasised in textbooks on the subject that revival is not a series of special evangelistic meetings, whether in a local congregation or on a mass crusade-type scale. Nor is it mere emotional extravaganza. Rather, revival is seen as an extraordinary movement of the Holy Spirit, something that is 'prayed down', not 'worked up'.

Revivalism, on the other hand, is initiated, encouraged and prolonged by the methodology of man. Throughout the last thirty years, especially, the Church in the West has known far too much of revivalism, and next to nothing of heaven-sent revival.[4] No doubt it may in part be an elusive longing for the real thing that has led some promoters in desperate attempt to 'create' by any means possible a 'revival' scenario, full of hype but little else. This pattern has been observed again and again, notably in the States, over a number of years, and is now virtually standard practise.

This said, there will always be a mixture of the human and divine in revivals. As Nigel Wright has shown, 'Divine agency is mediated agency. When God acts, God acts in and through the natural that has been created and given.'[5] One obvious effect in regard to a move of the Spirit is to lessen its truly 'divine' nature, as both God and fallible humans are involved.

There is general consensus that the term 'revival' refers to the quickening of spiritual life among believers, whereas 'awakening' has to do with the conversion of non-Christians in the community. Generally, however, both these scenarios occur together during a move of the Spirit, hence I use both terms, along with various others, interchangeably.

---

3. See Michael A. G. Haykin & Kenneth J. Stewart (Eds.), *The Emergence of Evangelicalism: Exploring Historical Continuities*, Nottingham 2008 for an exploration of the origins of Evangelicalism. David Bebbington notes a thread of continuity in revivals from the 1620s onwards, but states that with the mushrooming of awakenings from the 1740s 'expectation of further revival emerged as a novelty' (p. 431).

4. There have of course been exceptions, though nearly always of a short-term, localised nature. Observe, for example the revival that moved Howard Payne University, Texas in 1995; or the small-scale revivals that characterised parts of the north of Scotland in the 1980s.

5. Nigel Wright, 'Does Revival Quicken or Deaden the Church?' in Walker & Aune (Eds), *On Revival*, p. 125.

Iain H. Murray states that 'Revivals are larger measures of the Spirit of God.'[6] Duncan Campbell calls revival 'A people saturated with God.'[7] Mark Stibbe regards revival as essentially 'a falling in love with Christ … like love, it is a mystical, even miraculous, phenomenon requiring more than a merely cerebral explanation.'[8] Arthur Wallis, in his inspiring study *In the Day of Thy Power*, suitably defines revival as

> divine intervention in the normal course of spiritual things. It is God revealing Himself to man in awful holiness and irresistible power. It is such a manifest working of God that human person-alities are overshadowed, and human programmes abandoned. It is man retiring into the background because God has taken the field. It is the Lord making bare His holy arm, and working in extraordinary power on saint and sinner … it has the stamp of Deity upon it, which even the unregenerate and uninitiated are quick to recognise.[9]

Of all definitions, I think that given by R. Tudor Jones is the fullest:

> A 'religious revival' involves a spiritual 'awakening' or 'revitali-sation' within churches or within an area which contrasts with the smooth flow of daily life. From the Christian perspective, it should be understood as the specific activity of the Holy Spirit deepening people's commitment to God and intensifying their concern about their eternal destiny. Individuals are converted often in large numbers, churches are revitalised and the excite-ment spreads to surrounding localities. These newly converted or revival Christians become infused with missionary spirit and dedicate themselves to a holy life and not infrequently to cultural and social service.[10]

---

6. Murray, *Pentecost Today*, p. 17.

7. Brian H. Edwards, *Revival: A People Saturated with God*, Darlington 1990, p. 26.

8. Mark Stibbe, 'Seized by the Power of a Great Affection' in Andrew Walker & Kristin Aune (Eds), *On Revival: A Critical Examination*, Carlisle 2003, p. 25.

9. Arthur Wallis, *In the Day of Thy Power*, Alresford 1956, pp. 20, 23.

10. R. Tudur Jones, *Faith and Crisis of a Nation: Wales, 1890–1914*, Cardiff 2004, p. 283.

Because the word 'revival' has so loose a meaning, and is constantly employed by Christians to describe events so diverse in duration, theological meaning and geographical spread, Steve Latham and Andrew Walker have identified six 'R' levels in understanding the term.

- R1: a spiritual quickening of the individual believer.

- R2: a deliberate meeting or campaign especially among Pentecostals to deepen the faith of believers and bring non-believers to faith.

- R3: an unplanned period of spiritual enlivening in a local church, quickening believers and bringing unbelievers to faith.

- R4: a regional experience of spiritual quickening and widespread conversions.

- R5: societal or cultural 'awakenings'.

- R6: the possible reversal of secularisation and 'revival' of Christianity as such.[11]

The revivals considered in this book all fit into categories R3, R4 or R5.

Revival in the Bible

The term 'revival' never appears in the Bible, although the verb 'revive' does appear, viz., Psalm 85:6: 'Will you not revive us again?' The concept of community 'revival', however, finds numerous biblical precedents. Old Testament writers attest to revival during the times of Samuel (1 Sam. 7:1-13:3), Elijah on Mount Carmel (1 Kings 18:1-46), Jonah in Nineveh (Jonah 1:1-4:11), the reforms of Kings Asa and Josiah (2 Chron. 15:1-18 and 2 Kings 22:8-23:3) and the combined post-exilic leadership of Ezra and Nehemiah (Neh. 8:1-11:2). However, it can be argued that while the Holy Spirit was certainly active among God's people in Old Testament times, the abundant outpouring of the Spirit lay in the future.

Hence a better appraisal of revivals in Scripture can be found in the New Testament, beginning with the events of Pentecost, when 'All of them were filled with the Holy Spirit and began to speak in other tongues as the Spirit enabled them' (Acts 2:4). The next few chapters of

---

11. Steve Latham, 'God Came from Taman', in Walker & Aune (Eds), *On Revival*, p. 172.

Acts depict a period in Jerusalem of 'vigorous life, sustained growth, new accessions of spiritual power through new infillings of the Holy Spirit, and the presence of God experienced in an unusual way in miracles of both blessing and judgement'.[12] It is with reason that Dr Martyn Lloyd-Jones noted that 'every period of revival is a returning to what you can read in the book of the Acts of the Apostles'.[13] The remainder of this action-packed biblical narrative is the story of one revival after another – with resulting persecutions – as the disciples spread out from Jerusalem to surrounding areas, where a dramatic turning to God was experienced throughout Judea, Galilee and Samaria, and, via Paul's tireless endeavours, through the areas of Galatia, Achaia and Macedonia.

Historical Revival Traditions

Central to the reasoning of Kenneth Jeffrey's excellent study of the 1858–62 revival in the north-east of Scotland is the proposal that revivals have evolved over time. He argues that three basic models of revival have appeared in Scottish Church history. In the earliest of these traditions – in rural seventeenth and eighteenth century Presbyterian Scotland – revivals were seen as spontaneous outbursts of divine favour. They were local community-based movements led principally by the parish minister, whose main tools of employment were the preaching of the Word and the infrequent and profoundly solemn Communion season.[14] Such revivals tended to be fairly protracted affairs (usually lasting many months or even a number of years), as too did the conversion process of individuals affected, which often involved physical manifestations such as weeping and prostrations, though generally in a fairly orderly manner. The typical convert within this tradition might be a church-attending, unmarried female in her early twenties.

A second genre of revival began to appear with the approach of the nineteenth century, and the accelerated growth of Independent congregations such as the Methodists, Baptists and Congregationalists.

---

12. Davies, '*I Will Pour Out My Spirit*', p. 50.

13. Dr Martyn Lloyd-Jones, *Revival – Can We Make It Happen?*, Basingstoke 1986, pp. 27-8.

14. Special times in the year when the sacrament of the Lord's Supper was celebrated. In Presbyterian churches, these generally biannual events were of great significance and were held over a number of days.

Awakenings in this category developed with the increased itinerant travels of lay, and often local, preachers among the largely superstitious people of remote districts, where little or no evangelical presence existed. Generally coming from the same social and intellectual background as their audiences, these evangelists often contextualised their message to fit with the particular conventions of the community. Though the process of conversion was still often a protracted affair, the actual experience of 'new birth' was increasingly viewed as sudden and climatic, based on a 'decision' made by the sinner. This type of revival was invariably short in duration and intense in nature, nearly always involving spontaneous and noisy outbursts of religious enthusiasm.

While the first two models of revival continued to co-exist, by the mid-nineteenth century a new form of evangelistic initiative had developed in Scotland, derived largely from Finney's controversial but incredibly popular 'revivalist' teaching and methodology in the United States. Finney wrote in his *Lectures on Revival of Religion* that, 'a revival is as naturally a result of the use of the appropriate means as a crop is of the use of its appropriate means … it consists entirely of the right exercise of the powers of nature.'[15] As such, the term 'revival' became increasingly synonymous with a special evangelistic crusade, centred in fast-expanding urban settings. Led by professional itinerant evangelists, these were highly organised affairs, tailor-made to fit in with the working patterns of city-dwellers, and often with special effort made to target specific groups of people. The movements were short in length, and involved the use of the 'anxious seat' at the front of the church, to which those concerned about their spiritual state were strongly encouraged to move towards; or an 'inquiry room', where, after the main meeting, they could be counselled individually or as a group. In Scotland, this modern form of revival found its expression in the larger towns and cities during the 1859–61 awakening, but gained almost universal acceptance following the visit of Moody in 1873–4.[16] It has been in vogue ever since. In fact claims of this form of revivalist activity in Scotland date from at least as early as 1839 (see page 397-8).

---

15. Murray, *Pentecost Today*, p. 8.

16. While, as we have seen, revivalism is essentially a different entity from revival, the two may nonetheless co-exist, as would appear to be the case in some Scottish locations during both the 1859–61 and 1873–4 periods.

Overview of Contents

Land of Many Revivals seeks to provide a chronological survey of Scotland's evangelical revival heritage from its very beginnings – the introduction of Protestantism to the land in the early 1500s. Chapter One examines events leading up to the epochal Scottish Reformation, evidence being provided to regard such movement as a genuine revival of religion. The strenuous Post-Reformation endeavours of men like Robert Bruce (Central Scotland & Inverness), John Davidson (Prestonpans) and John Welsh (Ayr), and the awakenings that accompanied them, are also noted, while the famed Stewarton and Kirk o'Shotts revivals are documented in some detail. Tokens of spiritual blessing following the signing of the National Covenant in 1638 are narrated, while further marks of divine blessing on groups of Covenanters amidst bitter persecution make for stirring reading. Again and again amidst the turbulent events of the century-and-a-half following the Reformation in Scotland one finds evidence of significant revival of spiritual life.

Chapter Two deals predominantly with a small-scale revival among a group of Secession churches in Lowland Scotland in the 1730s, constituting the first major separation from the Church of Scotland; and with a larger and more geographically diverse movement within the National Church during the following decade. Termed 'the Cambuslang Revival', this proved to be not only Scotland's first international awakening (due largely to the transatlantic role played by George Whitefield), but also its first national revival, given its spread across numerous counties of the Lowlands, affecting even large cities like Glasgow and Dundee, and extending as far north as Sutherland and Ross-shire. The second half of the eighteenth century is largely regarded by church historians as being the most barren evangelically, the entire land lying under something of a spiritual stupor. Somewhat counter to this, the examination of a choice assemblage of seemingly independent local revivals, confined mainly to Scotland's north, and each occurring between 1750 and 1800, will prove of considerable interest.

The essence of Chapter Three is a dramatic burst of evangelical witness, and the spiritual awakening induced by it, across the Highlands & Islands of Scotland in the dozen short years beginning 1797, much of it stemming from the zealous exertions of the *Haldane preachers*. Some of the main areas highlighted in this section are the northern outposts of Orkney and Caithness, Argyll and the Central Highlands, and the western isles of Arran and Skye.

Chapter Four shows this fledgling Highland awakening broadening in both magnitude and scope, with the works in Breadalbane, Arran and Skye intensifying, and fresh signs of spiritual revival developing in many other Highland regions, as well as in Shetland, Caithness and the Black Isle. Of particular interest here is detailed examination of the dawn of evangelical awakening in Outer Hebrides, from which locations springs of life-giving revival would flow recurrently over the course of the following century-and-a-half, most famously in the Lewis revival of 1949–51.

Chapter Five takes a close look at two unique revival movements that appeared in different parts of the country in the early 1830s. One was spurred by the deadly cholera epidemic that fast dispersed across the globe from 1831, causing thousands of Scots to flock to churches in search of spiritual solace. The second movement relates to Scotland's (and perhaps the world's) only pre-twentieth century charismatic revival, being marked by the practice of, and heated discussion around, the biblically-termed 'gifts of the Spirit'. In the same decade, and no less significant, denominational movements among three non-conformist groups – Congregationalists, Baptists and Methodists – are also recorded.

In Chapters Six and Seven I examine, region by region, what was hitherto by far the most widespread awakening in the nation, the 1839–42 revival, emerging as it did in central Scotland before diffusing all over the land in the four years prior to the fateful split within the National Church in May 1843, from which emerged the Free Church of Scotland. Chapter Six looks at the origins of the movement and the first signs of blessing, with the eruption of revival in Kilsyth, and soon after, Dundee. We follow the progress of the awakening as it weaves through the Scottish heartland (thanks largely to the labours of William Chalmers Burns) and other parts of central Scotland, and observe it's rapid spread into Ayrshire, Dumfries, Galloway and the Borders.

Chapter Seven continues to chart the procession of this most pervasive spiritual revival, as it travels northwards through Angus, Aberdeenshire and Moray, and right across the western expanse of Sutherland, Western Ross-shire and Argyll, also taking in many of the Inner Hebridean islands, and reaching as far-fetched a post as St Kilda, while by no means neglecting the northern isles of Orkney and Shetland.

Chapter Eight provides solid evidence that the Disruption was not only in part a consequence of the widespread awakening that preceded it, but was itself the cause of revival. The various locations where significant showers of blessing were experienced among congregations of the fledgling Free Church are highlighted in this section, from the Hebridean Islands of Lewis, Harris and Uist in the north to the Dumfries-shire communities of Kirkbean and Applegarth in the south. A surprising number of multifarious and apparently independent revivals of a highly localised nature is tracked down and detailed in the remaining pages of the chapter, these arising from such differing denominational streams as the Evangelical Union, the Baptists, the Congregational Church and others.

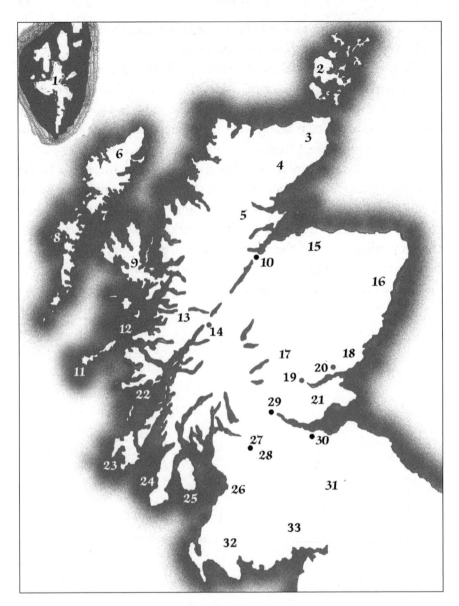

1 Shetland	12 Ardnamurchan	23 Islay
2 Orkney	13 North Argyll	24 Kintyre
3 Caithness	14 Fort William	25 Arran
4 Sutherland	15 Moray	26 Ayrshire
5 Ross-shire	16 Aberdeenshire	27 Glasgow
6 Lewis	17 Perthshire	28 Lanarkshire
7 Harris	18 Angus	29 Stirling
8 North Uist	19 Perthshire	30 Edinburgh
9 Skye	20 Dundee	31 Borders
10 Inverness	21 Fife	32 Galloway
11 Tiree	22 Mull	33 Dumfriesshire

CHAPTER 1

A Nation Awakened
1527–1728

The Reformation Period 1527–72[1]

Influences

Numerous were the factors that led to the Protestant Reformation in Europe. These included an emphasis by humanist thinkers on a more critical examination of the Bible; the translation of those Scriptures into vernacular languages; the development of printing, which disseminated new ideas more widely and more quickly; and the growth of nationalism, which sought to weaken papal jurisdiction within the states of Western Europe. However, the beginnings of the Reformation are popularly dated at October 1517 when German priest and theology professor, Martin Luther, nailed his ninety-five theses to the door of Castle Church in Wittenberg, denouncing many Church abuses, especially the sale of indulgences, whereby as a means of raising funds Church officials collected money in return for absolving the purchaser of his sins. Developments on the Continent progressed much more quickly than in Scotland. In Switzerland, the Reformation was initiated by Zwingli in Zurich in 1520, spreading to Basle, Berne, and Geneva, in which town the movement was led by John Calvin. Calvinism was adopted in France, the Low Countries, England and subsequently North America.

---

1. This is an approximate dating of the main period of the Reformation in Scotland, from Patrick Hamilton's return from Germany, when he began preaching Reformed doctrine, till the death of John Knox.

33

Lutheranism was espoused by Sweden in 1527 and Denmark in 1546, and also became the established religion of Norway, Finland, and Iceland.

It is widely accepted that the comparative smoothness with which the Reformation was effected in Scotland was due to such factors, among others, as the rich spiritual legacy left by the old Celtic church, with its centuries-long emphasis on education, and the teachings of men like French lawyer and pamphleteer, Peter Dubois (c. 1250–1312), English Franciscan friar and philosopher, William of Occam (c. 1288– c. 1348), and Czech priest and reformer John Huss (c. 1371–1415), all three of whose radical thoughts many Scottish travellers and students heard the reformers preach in various European centres, and which they brought back to their native land. Perhaps more significant was the influence of Lollardy, where through the safe passage granted by English monarchs to inhabitants of the northern kingdom, a continuous stream of Scottish students attended English Universities from 1357 to 1389, especially Oxford. It was during this period that the influence of theologian, preacher and translator, John Wycliffe (c. 1324–84) was most powerful, and Oxford was seething with his anticlerical and biblically-centred reforms.[2]

Though essentially an English movement, Lollardy thus made its presence felt north of the border. Building on Wycliffe's emphasis on biblical authority and on preaching, Lollards attacked the status of the papacy and the clergy, and denied the Roman Catholic doctrines of the mass and other sacraments. James Resby, an English Lollard, exercised an irregular preaching ministry in Scotland directed to the poor. Condemned and executed in Perth in 1407, he became the first of the Scottish proto-Protestant martyrs. The influence of Lollardy north of the border can be measured by the fact that after the founding of the Universities of Aberdeen, Glasgow and St Andrews in the fifteenth century, the ecclesiastical authorities made visitations to purge the teaching staff of Lollard errors. (It was at St Andrews also that the Hussite Paul Kravar was tried and burnt, c. 1413, for denying transubstantiation, prayers for the dead and the sacrament of confession – all of which Lollards had also denied).[3] A group of Ayrshire lairds known as the 'Lollards of Kyle' remained within the Roman Catholic

---

2. A. M. Renwick & A. M. Harman, *The Story of the Church*, Leicester 1958, p. 140.

3. T. M. Lindsay stated that archaeological research has brought out evidence of 'a closer connection between Scotland and Bohemia' than had before been suspected (*The Reformation in Scotland*, Edinburgh 1882 [reprinted 2006], p. 145).

Church despite their low view of Catholic errors (and were to be more receptive to Knox than most before 1560).

As early as 1525 the Scottish Parliament deemed it necessary to ban the importation of any works of Luther or his disciples, and attempts were made to suppress the recitation of 'his heresies or opinions' throughout the realm.[4] But Reformation literature continued to be smuggled in from the Continent to east coast ports such as Montrose, St Andrews and Leith, evidently having a ready market among scholars and the literate.[5]

Patrick Hamilton

The 'new' doctrines were also carried back to Scotland by men like Patrick Hamilton (*c.* 1504–28) and George Wishart (*c.* 1513–46). Hamilton, on a visit to Germany in 1527, became acquainted with Reformation leaders, by whom he was instructed in the knowledge of what he now saw as 'the true religion'. After only six months he was constrained to return to his homeland, taking up residence on the family estate at Kincavel, near Linlithgow. 'The bright beams of the true light', wrote John Knox, 'which by God's grace was planted in his heart, began most abundantly to burst forth as well in public as in secret.'[6] For during a few brief months at the close of 1527, this emboldened 23-year-old, 'inflamed with zeal to God's glory', began 'sowing the seed of God's work ... exposing the corruptions of the Romish church, and pointing out the errors which had crept into the Christian religion as professed in Scotland'. He was favourably received and followed by many, unto whom he readily 'shewed the way of God more perfectly'.[7] 'Linlithgow must have been stirred to no little excitement' by Hamilton's powerful and impacting preaching, noted one historian,[8] that it forced Archbishop Beaton to take notice and enforce measures to end it. Hamilton was invited to St Andrews, where for nearly a month he was allowed to

---

4. Nigel M. de S. Cameron (Ed.), *Dictionary of Scottish Church History and Theology* (hereafter *DSCHT*), Edinburgh 1993, p. 694.

5. A witness to Patrick Hamilton's execution was John Johnstone, who, as a Scottish exile, wrote pro-Reformation devotional literature, which was printed on the Continent in the early 1530s.

6. John Knox, *The Reformation in Scotland*, Edinburgh (1982 edition), p. 4.

7. John Howie, *The Scots Worthies*, Edinburgh 1870 (reprinted 1995), pp. 11-12.

8. Alexander Cameron (Ed.), *Patrick Hamilton: First Scottish Martyr of the Reformation. A Composite Biography*, Edinburgh 1929, pp. 37-8.

preach and dispute. At length he was arrested and tried as a heretic. He famously became the first martyr of the Scottish Reformation when he was burned at the stake on 29th February 1528.

George Wishart

The martyrdom of Hamilton served to stir up more widespread interest in the controversial ideas he taught, and in the 1530s a growing band of lairds and noblemen openly argued against clericalism and imbibed Lutheran views. At the same time more and more Scots were reading English translations of the Bible and discussing them. But it wasn't until the following decade that another Hamilton appeared on the scene. From 1544, after his return from England and the Continent, George Wishart made his controversial religious views known first in Montrose, where he taught in a school, then in Dundee. Here, he preached both day and evening for several weeks in St Mary's Cathedral, to which location towns-folk converged in huge numbers, keen to hear this fervent young preacher with his new ideas. Wishart's popularity in Dundee greatly worried the authorities, who forced him into exile to south-west Scotland, via Perth.

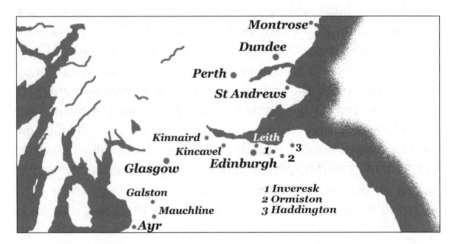

He preached the gospel in Ayr 'with great freedom and faithfulness' to a great concourse of people who crowded to his sermons.[9] Here, the Earl of Glencairn was one of his principal supporters. Everywhere, opposition was set against him, and in Mauchline the Sheriff of Ayr installed a garrison of soldiers in the church to keep him out. Constraining his supporters from entering by force, Wishart instead resorted to a muir

9. Howie, *The Scots Worthies*, p. 20.

on the edge of the town, saying, 'Jesus Christ is as mighty in the fields as in the church'. Here, he stood on a bank and preached to the great multitude who resorted to him for more than three hours. 'God wrought so wonderfully thereby', wrote Robert Fleming, 'as one of the wickedest men in all the country, the laird of Shield, was converted, and his eyes ran down with such abundance of tears, as all men wondered.'[10] While in this region, Wishart also often preached with remarkable success at the church of Galston and at other places. As a result of his ministry in the region over the course of around a month, one biographer writes, 'spiritual revival was sweeping through Ayrshire'.[11]

Hearing that the plague had broken out in Dundee, Wishart at once returned in order to comfort the dying. Here he again laboured for many weeks, preaching from the top of the Cowgate in the east wall of the city to both the living and healthy inside the city walls and the dying on the outside. His sermons were of much blessing to both groups of people, who 'thought themselves happy in having such a preacher'.[12] The reformer's last sermons were preached in East Lothian, where, in Leith, Inveresk and Haddington around Christmas time 1545, increasingly large crowds gathered to hear him. At Ormiston he was seized by the Earl of Bothwell and brought before Cardinal Beaton, Archbishop of St Andrews.

John Knox

Wishart was martyred in 1546 – semi-strangled then burned at the castle – but his passionate message found an echo in the heart of men like Haddington-born John Knox (c. 1514–72)[13], who had befriended the reformer, and even served for a time as his bodyguard. In St Andrews, Knox found himself among 'desperate outlaws, ardent Reformers and young lads' who followed him for the purpose of instruction.[14] His first sermon, preached in the parish church, drew a vast crowd, and he was unanimously declared their leader. 'Some men hew at the branches of

---

10. Robert Fleming, *The Fulfilling of the Scripture* (First published 1681). This edition: vol. 2, Glasgow 1801, p. 297.

11. James W. Baird, *Thunder Over Scotland: The Life of George Wishart, Scottish Reformer, 1513–1546*, California 1982, p. 121.

12. Howie, *The Scots Worthies*, p. 21.

13. Some sources claim his birthplace to have been the village of Gifford, four miles south of Haddington.

14. Richard Owen Roberts, *Scotland Saw His Glory*, Wheaton 1995, p. 36.

the Papacy', men said, 'but this man strikes at the root.'[15] Here also, a 'Reformed' communion service was held – the first of its kind in Scotland, as Knox dispensed the sacrament to over 200 people.

The next twelve years Knox spent variably as a prisoner/slave to the French navy, as an exile in England and in Europe, where he came under the strong influence of John Calvin in Geneva, and as a fugitive yet fiery and uncompromising preacher in various parts of lowland Scotland (1555–6), where his sermons deeply affected the poor and nobility alike. One English ambassador said that his preaching 'put more life into him than six hundred trumpets'.[16] Knox preached repeatedly in Edinburgh, where, from the pulpit of St Giles, he thundered forth his appeals, warnings and threats, and such was the force of his personality that in the eyes of many he was the real ruler of Scotland. Wrote James Burns:

> His convictions were maintained at white heat. His speech, which was rugged, impassioned, and majestic, especially when he assumed the role of prophet, swept away the timid opposition of other men. His sincerity, which none doubted, the transparent honesty of his motives, and his utter fearlessness of consequences appealed even to his enemies. His outstanding ability and his knowledge of affairs made him an ally which no party in the state could afford to disdain.[17]

Knox wrote that as he preached, he beheld 'the fervent thirst of our brethren, night and day sobbing and groaning for the bread of life. If I had not seen it with my own eyes, in my country, I could not have believed it ... The fervency here doth far exceed all others that I have seen.'[18]

As a result, the seeds of the Reformation were beginning to grow up in Scotland and to bring forth fruit. 'A great awakening was taking place among the people'[19] who were beginning to shake off the lethargy and bondage of centuries of serfhood, superstition and spiritual darkness. Thus the Protestant cause gained ground every day. 'God did so multiply

---

15. *Encyclopedia Britannica*, vol. XV, Cambridge 1911, p. 882.

16. Various Contributors, *Scottish Divines 1505–1872*, Edinburgh 1883, p. 11.

17. James Burns, *Revivals: Their Laws and Leaders*, London 1909, pp. 241-2.

18. Thomas McCrie, *The Story of the Scottish Church*, Edinburgh 1874 (reprinted 1988), p. 82.

19. Burns, *Revivals: Their Laws and Leaders*, p. 237.

our number', wrote Knox, 'that it appeared as if men had rained from the clouds.'[20] In May 1559 Knox returned from Europe to find that Ayr and Dundee were already officially Protestant through sanction of their town councils. In addition, that growing band of Scottish nobles and lords – now termed the 'Lords of the Congregation' – were more zealous than ever for reform, and were seeking to strengthen local Protestant congregations that were springing up here and there throughout mainly central Scotland.

Scotland was now in active revolt against the occupying French troops, who were becoming increasingly resented. It was, however, only with direct intervention of a ten-thousand-strong English army and naval fleet sent north by Queen Elizabeth that, finally, in July 1560 a decisive treaty was signed, whereby the French withdrew completely and Scotland was allowed to govern its own affairs. The following month an unauthorised Parliament met in Edinburgh and was found to be overwhelmingly Protestant. With almost incredible swiftness and unanimity, it declared for the Protestant faith, abolished Roman Catholicism, and called for a form of confession. This was drawn up and presented in four days and was accepted almost without a dissentient voice, being grounded upon 'the infallible truth of God's Word'. As early as the 1570s and '80s, claims Harry Reid, 'no one could deny the essential fact – Scotland was a Protestant country'.[21]

The triumph of Reformation opinions was almost immediately challenged, however, with the return from France of eighteen-year-old Mary (Queen of Scots) in 1561. Knox engaged in repeated conflicts with the monarch, who did all in her power to overawe him by her authority or move him by her charms. Following a scandal involving the murder of her husband, Lord Darnley, and her almost immediate re-marriage to James Hepburn, Earl of Bothwell, Mary's reputation was in tatters. Forced to abdicate, she fled to England, where lengthy captivity and untimely death awaited her. Meanwhile, the health of the great reformer began to break down. Knox preached for the last time in St Giles in November 1572. He had to be helped into the pulpit, but once there, 'the old fire which had

---

20. Iain H. Murray, 'The Puritans and Revival Christianity', in *Banner of Truth*, September 1969.

21. Harry Reid, *Reformation: The Dangerous Birth Of The Modern World*, Edinburgh 2009, p. 151.

set Scotland in a glow broke out once more. The cathedral rang with his trumpet notes. So vehemently did he preach that he was like to rend the pulpit in pieces.'[22] When the sermon was over, however, it was seen that his strength was spent and the end near. He died two weeks later.

Thomas Smeaton, a contemporary of Knox, said of him, 'I know not if God ever placed a more godly and great spirit in a body so little and frail. I am certain that there can scarcely be found another in whom more gifts of the Holy Ghost, for the comfort of the Church of Scotland, did shine.' French theologian Theodore Beza called him the 'great apostle of the Scots'.[23] Four centuries later, Harry Reid regards Knox as far more than a powerful preacher. He was 'an inspiration. Charismatic, energetic, resolute and zealous, he gave the Scotland cause substance and heart, and he helped bring about by far the most significant revolution in Scotland's long and turbulent history'.[24]

Extent of the Reformation

It would certainly be an exaggeration to suggest, as did church historian James Kirkton, that 'in Scotland the whole nation was converted by lump' ('a nation born in one day')[25], for much of the country beyond the Highland line remained in spiritual darkness for many years afterwards (not least because there was a chronic shortage of new ministers who could speak Gaelic).[26] The remark made regarding Scotland a decade later, that 'there were not ten persons of quality to be found in it who did not

---

22. Howie, *The Scots Worthies*, p. 63.

23. ibid.

24. Harry Reid, *Reformation: The Dangerous Birth Of The Modern World*, Edinburgh 2009, pp. 234, 185. In his academic yet accessible study of the Reformation to mark its 450th anniversary, Reid dissolves a number of popular and unsympathetic myths regarding the uncompromising reformer. He was, Reid reveals, a true Anglophile who 'loved and cherished England every bit as much as his native Scotland' (p. 189). He was, further, 'emphatically not the killjoy of popular caricature' (he was not against pastimes such as golf or dancing) and was 'always something of a ladies' man'. He also appreciated wine and fellowship (p. xxvi). Indeed, he had no objections to taverns and public houses being open on Sundays, as long as they were shut during the hours of public worship (p. 189).

25. James Kirkton, *The Secret and True History of the Church of Scotland from the Restoration to the year 1678*, Edinburgh 1817, pp. 21-2.

26. For the arrival of true Protestant reform to the Highlands and Islands, much of which was only nominally affected by the Reformation, see Chapters 3 and 4.

profess the true reformed religion', is equally inaccurate.[27] Nevertheless, it has been testified to that within just six or seven years of its genesis the Reformed church had 850 ministers serving nearly 1,200 parishes.[28]

Yet, clearly, all was not well. For even when the reformers obtained tacit conformity to Protestant beliefs and worship, the persistence of Catholic practices in many areas for decades to come showed that the Protestants did not have full hold on the people. In 1581 the Scottish Parliament issued a general lament that

> the dregges of idolatrie yet remain in diverse parts of the realme, by using of pilgrimages to some chappells, wels, croces, and suche other monuments of idolatrie, as also, by observing of the festivall dayes of sancts, sometimes named patrons, in setting forth of bone fires, singing of carrells, running about kirks at certane seasons of the yeere, and observing of suche other superstitious and Papisticall rites.[29]

However, by the turn of the seventeenth century, after little more than a generation of reform, the Protestants had largely succeeded in breaking up the religious pulse of late medieval Catholicism. Through the Reformation the heartland of Scotland had been won for what was regarded as the pure Gospel.

The Reformation certainly carried its share of overzealous accompaniment, such as the public humiliation of some Catholic priests who continued celebrating Mass, and the destruction, particularly in 1559, of altars, images and 'all monuments of idolatry' in many of the nation's monasteries. The first to be invaded was St Andrews; this was followed by the monasteries of Scone, Stirling, Cambuskenneth and Linlithgow.[30]

Yet the formal declaration of the nation as a Protestant country was a decisive development which accelerated the demise of medieval Scotland and spawned the rise of a new nation. Scottish historian, Professor Tom Devine, believes that the subsequent actions and policies of the Reformers transformed virtually every aspect of Scottish life; religious practice and authority, culture and education, the national mindset and

---

27. Kirkton, *The Secret and True History of the Church of Scotland*, pp. 21-2.

28. Reid, *Reformation*, p. 251.

29. David Calderwood, *The History of the Kirk of Scotland*, vol.3, p. 593; vol. 4, pp. 656-6.

30. McCrie, *Story of the Scottish Church*, pp. 36-9.

identity, and radical new relations with England. Notwithstanding some possible negative aspects,[31] Devine believes the Reformation had a lasting, profoundly positive influence on Scottish history, such as that of 'inspiring that great flowering of intellectual culture in the eighteenth century, the Scottish Enlightenment'.[32] Harry Reid, too, looks on the Reformation as 'the time when, belatedly, mediaeval Scotland vanished and Scotland finally entered the modern world'. The Scottish settlement, constantly modified over following centuries, laid down, Reid believes, 'the foundations of an extraordinary forward looking new state, away ahead of its time in matters such as education and welfare (a system of poor relief was to be introduced on a scale virtually unknown elsewhere in Europe, and there was to be a school in every parish)'[33] – all of this largely a reflection of Knox's highly adventurous personal vision. Knox had also longed for an age of ongoing friendship between Scotland and its auld enemy, England; this became largely realised in the Reformation, whereby many generations of suspicion and bloody hostility suddenly ended. In short, 1560 was, in Reid's view, 'indubitably the greatest year in Scotland's history'.[34]

While Reid acknowledges that some aspects of the Reformation were indeed negative, e.g. its 'oppressive emphasis on (the) pervasive and sometimes oppressive social discipline', he feels this was more than offset by its positive influences –

> the ameliorative emphasis on self-restraint, on self-improving, on education (discussion, argument and reading became much more prevalent), on democracy (politics and religion was devolved down to the individual), on social responsibility and on social inclusion.

---

31. The secular Scotland of the new millennium, Devine believes, views the Calvinist tradition as a malignant force which 'spawned intolerance, oppressive social disciplines, an aggressive and rapacious capitalism, sexual guilt and dysfunction, and warped attitudes to music, painting and the creative arts, which have only been changing in recent generations' (Tom Devine, 'Scotland: The Reformation and the Enlightenment', in *Life and Work*, January 2010, p. 11).

32. ibid.

33. Harry Reid, '1560: The Greatest Year in Scotland's History', in *Life and Work*, January 2010, pp. 14-15. Three centuries after the Reformation, James Burns could look back on its ongoing effects upon the national life of Scotland in terms of education as being 'incalculable' (Burns, *Revivals: Their Laws and Leaders*, p. 255).

34. ibid.

Scottish society was to progress from being feudal, ignorant and backward to being more cerebral and aspirational.[35]

While it was undoubtedly an intellectual and political movement, the Reformation in Scotland was primarily a religious awakening.[36] It was, from the beginning, explains James Burns, 'a religious movement set in motion by men who profoundly realised the corruption around them and who, having received light to their own souls, were willing to lay down their lives to hand on that light to others'.[37] It was a popular movement, affecting all classes, not least the poor, for whom it offered enormous benefits. It called into being a nation, awakening among the people a national consciousness. In perhaps no other country was the influence of the Reformation more immediate, deeper in character or more enduring, the rise of which in Scotland came with less bloodshed than in other nations. 'Whatever other countries lost through the Reformation', summed up Burns, 'it will be admitted by the most candid of observers that Scotland lost least and that the middle of the sixteenth century saw the outburst of a new spiritual and national life and the founding of a church in keeping with the genius and character of the people. In Scotland, perhaps, more than in any other country, the spiritual movement of the sixteenth century reaped its finest and most lasting fruits.'[38]

The Post-Reformation Period 1572–1600

Robert Bruce of Kinnaird

The closing years of the sixteenth century witnessed several notable cases of localised spiritual refreshing and awakening in mainly central Scotland. At the very outset of the ministry of Robert Bruce (c. 1554–1631) at John

---

35. Reid, *The Reformation*, pp. 246-8.

36. Revival historian, Brian Edwards claims that whereas reformation is primarily to do with doctrine – what we believe, revival is primarily to do with life – how we behave. Nevertheless, he states that ideally the two go hand in hand, with reformation often being accompanied by revival – 'this was certainly the case during the time of the Reformation across Europe in the 15th and 16th centuries' (Brian H. Edwards, *Can We Pray for Revival?*, Darlington 2001, pp. 22-3). See also Derek Frank, *The Jeremiah Diagnosis*, Godalming 2000, for a lively discussion on the distinction between reformation and revival.

37. Burns, *Revivals: Their Laws and Leaders*, p. 247.

38. ibid., pp. 255-6.

Knox's old pulpit of St Giles, Edinburgh in the late 1580s, there was, in the words of Robert Wodrow, an 'extraordinary effusion of the Spirit when he first dispensed the Sacrament of the Supper'.[39] From that day,

> he shined as a great light ... the power and efficacy of the Spirit most sensibly accompanying the word he preached ... some of the most stout-hearted of his hearers were ordinarily made to tremble, and by having these doors which formerly had been bolted against Jesus Christ, as by an irresistible power broke open, and the secrets of their hearts made manifest, they went away under convictions and carrying with them undeniable proofs of Christ speaking in him, and that God was with him of a truth.[40]

Scottish historian, James Kirkton said of Bruce in the pulpit: 'He made an earthquake upon his hearers and rarely preached but to a weeping audience.'[41]

A Mr Andrew Gray of Chryston, North Lanarkshire, 'an eminently pious old gentleman', was noted as being 'furnished with valuable materials relating to the success of the gospel in that part of the country'. He records, authoritatively: 'Two springs of the revival of religion in this corner of the country were the famous sermon at Kirk of Shotts (delivered by John Livingstone – see page 59); and the labours of Mr Robert Bruce.'[42] John Livingstone himself was of the firm opinion that 'no man in his time spake with such evidence and power of the Spirit (than Robert Bruce) ... yea, many of his hearers thought that no man since the apostles spake with such power'.[43]

The General Assembly of 1596

Yet all was not well. Before the sun had set on the sixteenth century, the generation that experienced the Reformation was nearly gone. With their disappearance the impetus the movement provided practically

---

39. Robert Wodrow, quoted in Iain H. Murray, *The Puritan Hope: A Study in Revival and the Interpretation of Prophecy*, Edinburgh 1971 (reprinted 1991), p. 22.

40. Fleming, *The Fulfilling of the Scripture*, pp. 365, 378.

41. Alex Muir, 'Revivals in Inverness: Robert Bruce, Fire in the North', quoted in *Sword* magazine, vol. 4, no. 5, p. 11.

42. John Gillies, *Historical Collections of Accounts of Revival*, Edinburgh 1845 (revised and enlarged 1981), p. 200.

43. John Laidlaw, *Robert Bruce's Sermons on the Sacrament*, Edinburgh 1901, p. lxxiii.

exhausted itself. In the words of W. J. Couper: 'A certain reaction in public manners and morals took place after the stress of conflict and uncertainty had been long enough removed … a grave state of affairs prevailed morally.'[44] Hill Burton, no admirer of the Reformation, wrote of 'the spirit of ferocity, rapacity and sensuality that was spreading moral desolation over the land' during the late sixteenth century.[45]

One man who deeply bemoaned the low ebb of spiritual life in the nation was John Davidson of Prestonpans, a small town to the east of Edinburgh. As early as 1591 this intrepid reformer had admonished his monarch sharply for his failure to punish evildoers, while not being slow to persecute God's servants. Two years later Davidson noticed how his congregation was deeply moved as he forewarned them of future dangers, and he freely rebuked their sins. Davidson, like his contemporary Andrew Melville, became increasingly concerned at the way the ministry had degenerated into a form of ecclesiastical politics, while at the same time he became ever more aware of the need for renewed spiritual life in the nation. He urged his Presbytery in Haddington to bring an overture to the General Assembly regarding the 'grosse sinnes' that prevailed in all aspects of the realm.[46] This was agreed as the Assembly's chief business in March 1596. Davidson read the solemnising document, which indicted everyone, from the King down to the meanest of his subjects.

The lengthy verdict against many ministers was both pungent and shocking. The communication deplored those who were 'light and wanton in behaviour, as in gorgeous and light apparrell, in speeche, in using light and profane companie, unlawfull gaining, as dancing, cairding, dyeing, and suche like … swearers or banners, profainers of the Sabbath, drunkards, fighters … leers, detractors, flatterers, breakers of promises, brawlers and quarellors …' as well as those who engaged in trading for 'filthie gain', keeping of public inns, and exacting excessive usury.[47]

---

44. Rev. W. J. Couper, *Scottish Revivals*, Dundee 1918, p. 7.

45. ibid., p. 16.

46. R. Moffat Gillon, *John Davidson of Prestonpans*, London 1938, p. 47.

47. Regarding sins of omission, sharp admonition was also urged upon those not given 'to their booke and studie of Scriptures, not careful to have bookes, not givin to sanctification and prayer, that studie not to be powerful and spirituall, not applying the doctrine to his corruptions, which is the pastoral gift, obscure and too scholastick before the people, cold and wanting zeale, negligent in visiting the sicke, caring for the poore, or indiscreit in choosing parts of the Word not meetest for the flocke, flatterers,

The Tuesday of the following week was fixed as a day of humiliation, led by Davidson. Four hundred men, 'all ministers or choice professors' assembled, and as Davidson led the Assembly through a prayer of confession, a sudden emotion took possession of the gathering, and for quarter of an hour,

> there were suche sighes and sobbs, with shedding of teares among the most part of all estats that were present, everie one provoking another by their example, that the Kirk resounded, so that the place might worthilie have been called Bochim; for the like of that day was never seen in Scotland since the Reformatioun, as everie man confessed. There have been manie dayes of humiliatioun for present or immanent dangers, but the like for sinne and defectioun was there never seen.[48]

At Davidson's earnest call, all present bar one [49] held up their hands to testify their entering into a new league with God.

Synods, presbyteries and congregations throughout Scotland responded readily to the call for repentance and reform, although McCrie perhaps exaggerated when he said: 'This ordinance was obeyed with an alacrity and ardour which spread from synod to synod, from presbytery to presbytery and from parish to parish, the inhabitants of one city saying to another, "come, and let us join ourselves to the Lord in a perpetual covenant that shall not be forgotten", until all Scotland, like Judah of old, "rejoiced at the oath".' [50] It was customary to join the taking of the Covenant with the dispensation of the Sacrament. Such covenant was renewed as early as 13th May by the Synod of Fife, then the stronghold of Presbyterianism in Scotland. Held in Dunfermline, the methodical two-day event was filled with Bible readings, sermons and admonitions from various church leaders. 'The Lord steirit upe sic a motioun of hart, that all war forcit to fall down befor the Lord, with sobbes and teares in aboundance, everie

---

and dissembling as publict sinnes, and speciallie of great personages in their congregations, for flatterie or for feare' (ibid., pp. 151-2).

48. ibid., pp. 155, 157.

49. This was Thomas Buchanan, whose heart had for some time 'been cold to the good cause', which he ultimately forsook. Some associated his early death with his scorn of the motion for spiritual reform (ibid., p. 158).

50. McCrie, *Story of the Scottish Church*, p. 37.

man mightelie commovit with the affectionnes of thair conscience in the presence of thair God, in privat meditatioun, rypping out thair wayes, confessing and acknawlaging thair unworthines and craving earnestlie grace for amendiment, and that for a lang space.' The brethren had come to the gathering fasting, and felt amply rewarded, for they left 'als full of spirituall joy in the saull as emptie of corporall fuid'.[51]

John Davidson in Prestonpans

Davidson's own ministry in Prestonpans from 1596 was, according to Couper, used by the Holy Spirit to stimulate an awakening in the district. Soon after his settlement there, the Presbytery minutes record:

> The haill gentlemen being required to reform their houses and use prayers at morn and evening, with reading of the Scriptures after dinner and supper, promised to obey; and for execution thereof every minister was ordered to visit their houses and see whether it was so or not; and for behoof of the unlearned Mr John Davidson was ordained to pen short morning and evening prayers, with graces before and after meat, to be communicated to each minister for behoof of his flock. These forms of prayer were approved by the Presbytery and ordered to be printed.[52]

Davidson's ministry in Prestonpans became so noted that his name became inseparably associated with the place.

Early Seventeenth Century Revivals 1600–35 [53]

Introduction

Lowland awakenings of the early seventeenth century – most notably the Stewarton revival and the Kirk o' Shotts movement that followed closely

---

51. Gillon, *John Davidson of Prestonpans*, p. 161.

52. Roberts, *Scotland Saw His Glory*, p. 84; Gillon, *John Davidson of Prestonpans*, p. 141.

53. Harry Stout has claimed (against extant evidence) that throughout the 17th and 18th centuries, revivals in Scotland, like those in New England towns such as Philadelphia and Boston, 'struck ... with a cyclic regularity'. He contrasts these Scottish revivals with those in pre-Whitefield America in that those in Scotland tended to be led by 'stranger preachers', or itinerant field preachers who 'toured the mountains and valleys, sowing the seeds for local revival' (Harry S. Stout, 'Whitefield in Three Countries', in Mark A. Noll, David B. Bebbington & George A. Rawlyk, *Evangelicalism:*

on its heels – have become especially renowned in Scottish religious history. Indeed, along with simultaneous revival across the Irish Sea in Ulster, they became, through the essential features that defined them – such as sudden awakenings and radical conversions, combined with unusual physical phenomena such as weeping, shouting, panting and swooning – a prototype of religious revival, establishing a tradition of emotional revivalism that would inform the course of religious history throughout the UK, and, through immigration, across America, for centuries to come. Bemoaning the state of the Scottish Church in the early eighteenth century, Patrick Walker expressed the hope that the Lord would 'pity this weather-beaten Sardis, Laodicean Church, and send forth a thaw-wind, and spring-tide day of the gospel, to thaw the frozen face of affairs, as was at Stewarton, and spread through the west of Scotland as muir-burn, a hundred years since, and at the kirk of Shotts five years thereafter … '.[54]

Not only were the Stewarton and Shotts revivals connected by their proximity in both time and location, but also by the involvement in both of them of two leading figures – David Dickson and John Livingstone. Few publications pertaining to religious revivals in Scotland fail to make note of these inaugural movements. They were seen as authentic by virtually all Presbyterians, and even the Secessionists of the early eighteenth century, in condemning the revivals of Cambuslang and Kilsyth, sought (unsuccessfully) to contrast them to the more 'authentic' revivals of Stewarton and Shotts, which they viewed as 'the return of strong Presbyterianism to the Church of Scotland, a precursor to the ecclesiastical reform of 1638'.[55]

John Welsh of Ayr

After a youth spent recklessly, the biblical story of the prodigal son was literally realised in dramatic fashion in the life of John Welsh (c. 1570–1622), son-in-law of John Knox, when he was, through the earnest entreaties of his aunt, received back into his father's house. His life totally transformed, Welsh shortly after entered the ministry, becoming the first graduate of Edinburgh University to be ordained. During his short

Comparative Studies of Popular Protestantism in North America, the British Isles, and Beyond, 1700–1990, New York 1994, p. 64).

54. Patrick Walker, *Six Saints of the Covenant*, vol. 1, London 1901, pp. 41-2.

55. Marilyn Westerkamp, *Triumph of the Laity: Scots-Irish Piety and the Great Awakening, 1625–1760*, Oxford 1988, p. 27.

period as minister in Kirkcudbright in the 1590s he reaped a harvest of converts which remained long after his departure, and were a part of Samuel Rutherford's flock, though not his parish, while he was minister at Anwoth. Welsh translated to Ayr (*c.* 1600), where he ministered until his banishment from the country in 1606.[56]

Described as 'one of the saintliest men who ever stood in a Scottish pulpit',[57] Welsh was known for the severe, Elijah-like devotion which he practised, commonly spending, for example, eight hours a day in private prayer. It was known to be his habit, even on the coldest winter nights, to rise early to pray, and his wife would sometimes get up in the middle of the night looking for him, only to find him prostrate in the garden or on the floor of the church, weeping and wrestling in intercession for the souls of his parishioners. On one such occasion, bowed down in prayer and overcome with grief, he answered his wife that he had that to press upon him what she did not – the souls of some 3,000 parishioners, and he knew not where many of them stood with the Lord. On another occasion, when she found him alone and in deep spiritual anxiety, Welsh informed his wife upon serious enquiry that the times that were soon to befall Scotland were heavy and sad on account of the people's contempt of the gospel. 'O God, wilt thou not give me Scotland! O God, wilt thou not give me Scotland!' was one of the expressions which he was overheard to utter in the course of those impassioned invocations.[58] As such, Welsh's devotional habits were censured as 'extravagant, unseasonable, puritanical, methodistical, enthusiastic'.[59]

Welsh regularly preached twice each week day, from nine to ten in the morning, and from four to five at night, besides his work on the Lord's day, and catechising and visiting of families and of the sick.[60] He also engaged wholeheartedly in social issues; settling brawls, warning

---

56. Welsh was first imprisoned and then banished to France, along with other ministers, for treason. He continued to minister with godly passion in various places until his death sixteen years later.

57. Donald Beaton, *Scottish Heroines of the Faith: Being Brief Sketches of Noble Women of the Reformation and Covenant Times*, London 1909, p. 45.

58. Fleming, *The Fulfilling of the Scripture*, vol. 1, pp. 361, 381.

59. Rev. James Young, *Life of John Welsh, Minister of Ayr*, Edinburgh 1866, p. 105.

60. Maurice J. Roberts, 'John Welsh of Ayr', in *Banner of Truth*, March 1978, vol. 174, p. 10.

the unruly, labouring to suppress Sabbath games and promoting decent sociality. In this way, little by little, Ayr grew more peaceful. His preaching was most effective – he spoke the truth with simplicity and earnestness, often accompanied with many tears. The impression produced was remarkable. James Kirkton said that he once heard one of his hearers, who was afterwards minister of Muirkirk in Kyle, say, 'Scarcely could any one hear him and forbear weeping, his utterance was so affecting … the consequence was, that he enjoyed an extensive popularity as a pulpit orator, and was importuned to preach wherever he went, his reputation surpassing in this respect that of any other minister in Scotland at that time, with the exception of that of Mr Robert Bruce'.[61]

Welsh's labours in Ayr were abundantly acknowledged and his popularity grew steadily. He took full advantage of the opportunity afforded by the plague which spread rapidly westwards to Ayr in 1604 and which alarmed many of the town's 3,000 inhabitants with the prospect of death. Referring especially to the last five years of his life at Ayr (up to 1606), Welsh spoke of 'many hundreds' whom he could look on as Christian confidants.[62] The last wills of a number in his congregation confirm other testimonies to the great spiritual good which Welsh achieved in the town. Wrote Kirkton: 'If his diligence was great, so it is doubted whether his sowing in painfulness or his harvest in success was greater; for if either his spiritual experiences in seeking the Lord, or the fruitfulness in converting souls be considered, they will be found unparalleled in Scotland.'[63] David Dickson of Irvine later graciously attested that Welsh's gleanings of grapes in Ayr were far above the vintage of Irvine in his own time.[64]

Perth and Sheens
But first we turn to events further north in Scotland, and to the very first light of the seventeenth century. An awakening began in Perth around the year 1600, five years after the Rev. William Cooper moved there from Bothkennar in Stirlingshire. (In this earlier charge, too, 'It pleased God to give such a blessing to the ministry of His Word' that within just six months the hearts of the people were so stirred as to begin a complete

61. Young, *Life of John Welsh*, p. 107.

62. ibid., pp. 134-5.

63. Gillies, *Historical Collections*, p. 168; Beaton, *Scottish Heroines of the Faith*, p. 46.

64. Couper, *Scottish Revivals*, p. 8.

restoration of their formerly desolate church building. Cooper enjoyed seven or eight years of 'very successful ministry in that place').[65] Apart from Sunday services, Cooper held public meetings three evenings per week, testifying that, 'It would have done a Christian's heart good to see those joyful assemblies, to have heard the zealous cryings to God among that people, with sighings, and tears, and melting hearts, and mourning eyes'. For nineteen years Cooper was 'a comfort to the best sort and a wound to the worst'. Speaking of himself the minister said: 'My witness is in Heaven, that the love of Jesus and His people made continual preaching my pleasure, and I had no such joy as in doing His work.'[66]

John Gillies, pastor, theologian and Scottish Church historian, received a letter from a ministerial friend in March 1753 in which the writer claimed to have 'seen a manuscript, in which there is an account of a remarkable pouring out of the Spirit of God on a company of ministers and Christians, at a private meeting at Sheens, near Edinburgh, on the day when the five articles of Perth were voted and passed in Parliament (1621),[67] particularly when Mr David Dickson (who was then only a young man) prayed.'[68]

Robert Bruce in Inverness

Further north still, considerable blessing attended the later ministry of Robert Bruce, especially during the four-year period of his second banishment from Edinburgh to Inverness in 1622.[69] Here, in a town rife

---

65. Clark's *Lives*, quoted in Roberts, *Scotland Saw His Glory*, p. 70.

66. ibid., pp. 70-1.

67. The Articles of Perth were a brazen attempt by King James VI of Scotland to impose practices on the Church of Scotland which would bring it into line with the Episcopal Church of England. Such policies included kneeling to pray, confirmation by a Bishop and the observance of Holy Days. Though the proposals incensed many Scottish believers, the Articles were reluctantly accepted by the General Assembly of the Church in 1618, though not approved by the Scottish Parliament till 1621.

68. Gillies, *Historical Collections*, p. 202.

69. His first period of banishment to Inverness, a result of his refusal to acquiesce to the King, was from 1605 to 1613. MacNicoll wrote of Bruce: 'he was ordained to be a pioneer apostle of the north. Nor did the King know, when he sent the great preacher to Inverness, that he was embarking upon a policy which should bring peace to the mountains and the glens, not through extermination, but through the instilling of a new principle of love' (Duncan C. MacNicoll, *Robert Bruce: Minister in the Kirk of Edinburgh*, London 1961, pp. 47, 197).

with violence and robbery, and scarcely touched by evangelical witness, Bruce faced many difficulties, including ill health, hostility from the local minister and magistrates, and even an attempt on his life. However, before leaving Edinburgh the preacher had foretold that the seed which he would plant in the north 'shall not be rooted out for many ages'.[70] And so it was.

Bruce's ministry in the north was singularly effectual. Fleming remarked that, 'While he was confined to Inverness, that poor dark country was marvellously enlightened, many were brought to Christ by his ministry, and a seed sown in these places which even this day is not wholly worn out.'[71] Findlater wrote of the 'remarkable revival of religion' which followed his active labours. Prayer and fellowship meetings were established and held every evening in town, with others held elsewhere in the neighbourhood.[72] It is noted in Robert Blair's autobiography that, 'The memory of that man of God, Mr Bruce, is sweet to this day (1700) in this place, Inverness. He in the days of James was confined in this town and country about, for multitudes of all ranks would have crossed several ferries every Lord's Day to hear him; yea they came both from Ross and Sutherland.'[73]

From the latter county we're told that it was not uncommon for people from Golspie and the districts around to walk all the way to Inverness, and to consider their labours and fatigue abundantly repaid if only they got within hearing distance of Mr Bruce on the Sabbath.[74] Opined his biographer: 'The capital of the Highlands must have been in those days, like Patmos or like the jail of Philippi, glorious with the very presence of God.'[75] Bruce regularly preached on Wednesday and

---

70. Gillies, *Historical Collections*, p. 179. Another presentiment of blessing came at a prayer meeting held near Edinburgh in 1621, when there was such an enlargement of heart that, at the end of it, the ministers felt certain that new days of gospel prosperity were coming (Alex Muir, 'Revival in Scotland: A Personal Perspective', in *Prophecy Today*, vol. 1, no. 4, 1985, p. 7).

71. Fleming, *The Fulfilling of the Scripture*, vol. 1, p. 366.

72. William Findlater, *Memoir of the Rev. Robert Findlater*, Glasgow 1840, p. 290.

73. T. McCrie (Ed.), *The Life of Mr Robert Blair, Minister of St Andrews, Containing His Autobiography, from 1593–1636*, Edinburgh 1848, p. 39.

74. D. P. Thomson, *Tales of the Far North West: A Sutherlandshire Miscellany*, Inverness 1955, p. 6.

75. MacNicoll, *Robert Bruce*, p. 232.

Sunday mornings, but crowds were largest when he spoke on fast days and communions. Another memorable occasion was when he preached at a conventicle in a hollow known as Lag na Bu, between Dunlichity and Balloan.[76]

Among the fruits of Bruce's ministry – some of whom were still alive at the Revolution (1688) – were the Earl of Sutherland, his Countess (a daughter of Lord Fraser of Lovat) and Alexander Munro – son of the Laird of Kitwell, Kiltearn, who after receiving several direct revelations calling him to enter the ministry, whereafter he would preach in Durness, went on to fulfil both parts of the divine message, becoming the first Protestant minister in that vast Sutherland parish.[77] A preacher of great power, Munro was used as the instrument of spiritual revival over a wide area, where he won 'a large harvest of souls', notices of which appear in the Presbytery records of Dingwall.[78] Soon Highland soldiers, previously dreaded for their savagery and revelry, were welcomed by the common people, and were given the epithet, 'Lions of the field, lambs in the house', for they earned a reputation for being well-mannered, even playing with the children in homes they entered. Writes one Highland minister: 'What kings of Scotland had failed to achieve by force of arms was brought about by one man armed only with the Gospel of Divine love.'[79]

On return from exile to Inverness, at a meeting in Edinburgh in 1626, a number of godly ministers met to discuss the plans the bishops had for Scotland and the action they ought to take. Bruce was asked to pray. He began to pray about these issues and the lamentable state of the Kirk, and in the urgency of his plea for God's help he unconsciously knocked upon the table at which they knelt. As he did so there was immediately 'such

---

76. Norman Campbell, *One of Heaven's Jewels: Rev. Archibald Cook of Daviot and the (Free) North Church, Inverness*, Stornoway 2009, p. 114.

77. L. M. McKinnon, *The Skye Revivals*, printed privately 1995, p. 5; Murdoch Campbell, *Gleanings of Highland Harvest*, Stornoway 1953 [reprinted 1989], pp. 136-8.

78. Adam Gunn, *Sutherland and Reay Country*, Glasgow 1897, p. 335. Munro's brilliant method of teaching the people of his parish – extremely difficult to traverse due to the lack of roads, the mountainous terrain and sheer size – was to compose a host of Scripture-based Gaelic hymns, which his flock would memorise and sing at their winter evening gatherings and at their work during other seasons, and which quickly passed from hamlet to hamlet around the district. Munro was succeeded by his son Hew, while another son, John, became minister at Alness.

79. Alex Muir, 'Revivals in Inverness: Robert Bruce, Exiled to Save!', in *Sword* magazine vol. 4, no. 6, 2009, p. 31.

an extraordinary motion on all present, so sensible a downpouring of the Spirit, as they could hardly contain themselves'. John Wemyss, a minister in attendance, afterwards exclaimed, 'O! how strange a man is this, for he knocked down the Spirit of God on us all'.[80] Equally remarkably, there were apparently some people in other parts of the house who knew nothing of the meeting, but who felt a deep sense of divine solemnity upon their spirits at the very moment Bruce knocked the table.

Even while on his own, noted Calderwood, Bruce sometimes 'felt God's presence so sensibly with him that he could not contain himself in the night from breaking out in these words, "I am the happiest man that ever was born; happy that ever I served God"'.[81] Calderwood spoke of Bruce as 'a man as noble by nature as he was by birth, who won so many thousands to Christ'.[82] For many generations after his departure, a 'chorus of testimonies ... handed down from sire to son', told of Bruce's worth,[83] and, regarding Inverness, James Haldane found the effects of his work still evident in the area at the turn of the eighteenth century. [84]

'The Stewarton Sickness' 1625

There is some contention over both the origin and timing of the Stewarton revival. Tradition has it that it began in 1625 in the north Ayrshire parish which gave its name to the movement, and that it spread from there eight miles down the Annick valley to Irvine, where it flourished under the ministry of David Dickson (c. 1583–1663).[85] Some writers however, while agreeing with this general flow of blessing, think it must have begun several years earlier, and certainly before May 1623,

---

80. Fleming, *The Fulfilling of the Scripture*, vol. 1, p. 367.

81. Murray, *A Scottish Christian Heritage*, Edinburgh 2006, p. 66.

82. ibid., p. 57.

83. McKinnon, *The Skye Revivals*, p. 5. As late as 1840 William Findlater could recall hearing, as a youth, 'traditional records of sayings and actings' of Bruce, which had descended orally through the generations (Findlater, *Memoir of Rev. Robert Findlater*, p. 290).

84. Angus Macdonald, *An Enduring Testimony: Inverness East Church*, Inverness 1998, p. 4.

85. Dickson was formerly Professor of Moral Philosophy at Glasgow University. Couper states that 'nothing is more conspicuous in the story of these early revivals than the weight of the men who led them, alike in preaching ability, scholarship, and personal impressiveness of character' (Roberts, *Scotland Saw His Glory*, p. 103).

for Covenanting minister Robert Blair engaged in it and by that date, having resigned as regent at Glasgow University, had crossed to Ireland.[86] At the other extreme, a few early historians, such as Wodrow and Crawford, suggest that the revival began as late as 1630.[87] Then there are those, like W. J. Couper, who see no valid reason for departing from the traditional date. Regarding Ulster, where spontaneous revival also ignited in this period,[88] there is greater unanimity in respect to 1625 being the year when emotional, enthusiastic outburst began under the ministry of James Glendenning. Thus, in view of controversy surrounding the date of the Stewarton movement, it remains a matter of debate as to whether it is in regard to Scotland or Ireland in this period that there began the first revival of its kind, at least the first recorded, to rise up in the British Isles, establishing a tradition of narrative that emphasised the providence of God, the spontaneity and inspiration of the preachers and the immediacy of the effects upon the hearers.[89]

---

86. This fact does not in itself preclude 1625 as being the correct date, for, as Westerkamp notes, both ministers and congregants carried revival enthusiasm back and forth from Ireland to Scotland as they travelled in both directions (*Triumph of the Laity*, p. 16). Nevertheless, Blair dates his Stewarton visit to as early as 1622, being a year before his departure for Ulster (W. Row (Ed.), *The Life of Mr Robert Blair*, Edinburgh 1848, p. 62; see also Murray, *The Puritan Hope*, pp. 27, 268; Rev. D. W. B. Somerset in *Free Presbyterian Magazine*, 2004/1, vol. 109, p. 13).

87. Couper, *Scottish Revivals*, p. 26.

88. This in the form of what became termed 'The Six Mile Water Revival' (c. 1625–33). The two primary promoters of this dramatic awakening were James Glendenning of Oldstone and Josias Welsh, son of John Welsh of Ayr (see page 48). These men, like numerous other Presbyterian ministers involved in the movement, such as Blair and Livingstone, had moved to Ulster from Scotland a few years previously. Glendenning was noted as a powerful hellfire and brimstone preacher who had the ability to strike terror in the hearts of his hearers but not to lead them to peace in Christ (Welsh proved providentially well-fitted to this latter ministry). Unfortunately, Glendenning developed some 'erroneous conceits and delusions' and had become almost completely ostracised by his ministerial colleagues well before his departure from Ireland in 1630 (W. D. Bailie, *The Six Mile Water Revival of 1625*, Belfast 1976, pp. 7-10).

89. Westerkamp, *Triumph of the Laity*, p. 27. Westerkamp goes on to describe the impact of this new expression of revivalism in Scotland and Ulster as going 'beyond an increase of power and authority accorded to the Established church, back to the new centrality of piety itself.' The people showed their deep interest in attending religious services of a revivalist nature. These services involved huge numbers of people coming together to partake in mainly outdoor communion sacraments, which continued over a number of days. Charismatic preachers delivered fiery sermons and prayers, created

As to the course the Stewarton revival took, Couper and several others held that it was 'usually described as being from Irvine up to the banks of the Annick'. Certainly the parish minister of Stewarton, William Castlelaw, is little mentioned in accounts of the movement, and very little is known of him, other than that he was popular and had 'the spiritual welfare of his flock very much at heart'.[90] Instead the revival appears to have centred around the fervent evangelical ministry of Dickson, who had only recently returned – in July 1623 – from forced exile in Turiff.

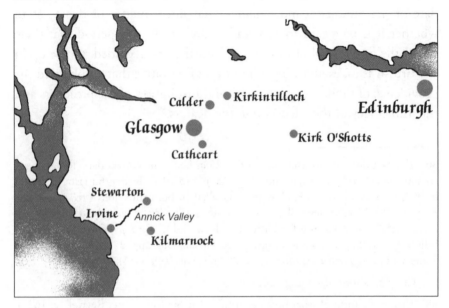

Whatever the exact details regarding the revival's beginnings, when Robert Blair visited the district, he reported: 'The Lord had a great work in converting many. Numbers of them were at first under great terrors and deep exercise of conscience, and thereafter attained to sweet and strong consolation.'[91] Encouraged by this demonstration of the work of

displays of emotionalism among their hearers, who were stricken with fear of God and a sense of their own depravity. The result was a profound personal awakening, often leading to dramatic conversion. Westerkamp suggests that lay participation was encouraged during these meetings, as it was also in the general spiritual life of the parish, and that the laity was loath to relinquish this power.

90. Row (Ed.), *The Life of Mr Robert Blair*, p. 19; Douglas MacMillan (Ed.), *Restoration in the Church: Reports of Revivals 1625–1839*, Glasgow 1839 (reprinted Fearn 1989), pp. 48-9.

91. Row (Ed.), *The Life of Mr Robert Blair*, p. 19.

the Spirit, Dickson began a 'lecture' in his church every Monday, the day of the weekly market, when the town was usually crowded with visitors from surrounding districts. The church became more packed for these services than it was on the Sabbath. Among those who came were many parishioners from Stewarton, who were encouraged by Castlelaw to feed from Dickson's table. Often, especially on Sunday evenings, in a large hall in the manse, scores of anxious souls would wait for Dickson when he came from church, and the learned minister would spend an hour or two answering their cases and speaking 'a word in season to the weary soul'.[92]

As a result of such meetings and the regular ministry, conversions were 'frequent and continuous'. Some even came to settle permanently in the town so they

> might be under the drops of ministry ... For a considerable time few Sabbaths did pass without some evidently converted, and some convincing proofs of the power of God accompanying his word; yea, that many were so choked and taken by the heart, that through terror (the Spirit in such a measure convincing them of sin in hearing the word) they have been made to fall over and thus carried out of the church, who after proved most solid and lively Christians.[93]

The occurrence of such prostrations led to the term 'The Stewarton sickness' being invoked by what Fleming calls 'the profane rabble of that time'. Others derided those affected as 'The daft people of Stewarton'. Yet some of these very scoffers, deliberately making their way to scenes of the revival, were effectually reached before their return home, with a visible, lasting change wrought upon their characters.[94] Expressions of emotion were largely kept in check, both by Dickson and by men who came to assist in the wark. So successful were they in putting down unseemly disturbances that, claims Wodrow, 'they were enabled to act so prudent a part as Satan's design was much disappointed'. Visiting helpers included the aforementioned Robert Blair, as well as Robert Boyd of Trochrigg, Principal of the College of Glasgow.[95] Additional help came

---

92. Howie, *The Scots Worthies*, p. 292.

93. Fleming, *The Fulfilling of the Scripture*, vol. 1, p. 355.

94. ibid.

95. Gillies, *Historical Collections*, pp. 157-233; Couper, *Scottish Revivals*, pp. 29-30; J. A. Wylie, *The History of Protestantism*, London 1879, vol. 3, Chapter 14.

from two ladies of the gentry, viz. Lady Robertland and Anna, Countess of Eglintoun, both of whom took a deep interest in those under the influence of the revival and did much to support them. The countess also persuaded her husband to 'forgo his hunting and hawking' to converse with the converts. The earl later 'protested that he never spoke with the like of them; he wondered at the wisdom they manifested in their speech'.[96]

For at least five years the general attention to religion continued in the valley and its neighbourhood. Marked changes took place in character and conduct. Stewarton and Irvine were made centres of pilgrimages for many believers over the whole country. The result was that 'solid, serious religion flourished mightily in the West of Scotland'. Writes Fleming, poetically: 'Like the spreading of a moor burn, increasing as it flows, and fertilising all within its reach, so did the power of godliness advance from one place to another, increasing in its progress, and throwing a marvellous lustre over those parts of the country.'[97]

Kirk o' Shotts Revival 1630

A remarkable revival commenced in Kirk o' Shotts, twenty miles east of Glasgow, in 1630.[98] Minister of the parish was John Home, who at that time was an elderly and infirm man. The Shotts manse being located on the highway which led through the parish, Home was in the habit of aiding travellers in their needs. Owing to the breakdown of her carriage in the vicinity, the minister invited the Marchioness of Hamilton and some companions to accept his hospitality. Seeing the dilapidated state of the manse, the marchioness made arrangements to procure the

---

96. Couper, *Scottish Revivals*, p. 30.

97. Fleming, *The Fulfilling of the Scripture*, vol. 1, p. 355. How long the effects of the revival remained in the community is unknown, but by the time Patrick Warner settled in Irvine in 1688 they had entirely disappeared. Indeed, Warner's heart was almost broken by the godlessness that was rampant around him, and he felt forced to retire early. Moral and spiritual abandon continued for some decades, though thankfully, during the time of the Cambuslang revival in 1742, many Ayrshire locations became participants of that blessing, including both Stewarton and Irvine (see page 128).

98. This movement may well have been influenced by that in Stewarton a few years earlier. Shotts lay on the high road of communication between Edinburgh and the west country and so connection could quickly have been transferred to the upland parish. In addition, John Livingstone, who had come under the influence of the Stewarton work, preached more than once in Shotts prior to 1630.

construction of a new one. In gratitude for such marvellous provision, Home asked what small favour he could offer in return. The ladies' sole request was permission to suggest the names of ministers to assist at the next dispensation of the Lord's Supper. This was readily granted.

Thus it was that such a worthy trio of preachers as David Dickson, Robert Bruce (then aged over seventy) and John Livingstone (1603–72) came to assist during the approaching Sacrament of the Lord's Supper, the latter two having arrived fresh from scenes of dramatic revival in Ulster,[99] where they had been labouring over a number of years. Livingstone was then aged twenty-seven and not ordained,[100] yet was a highly popular preacher at communions. He had spoken more than once previously at Kirk o' Shotts, where he had found 'more liberty in preaching than elsewhere'. On this occasion, in company with some other pilgrims, he spent the Sabbath night 'in conference and prayer'. Though Communion services up to that time normally ended on the Sabbath day, the ministers readily agreed to the wishes of the congregation that one of their number be invited to preach that Monday. At the suggestion of Lady Culross, Livingstone was requested at short notice to preach at the Monday service, the appointed preacher being unable to perform such duty. Filled with a sense of unworthiness and weakness, and overawed at the multitude and expectation of the people, Livingstone, for a time, considered hiding away for the day.[101] Then the words seemed to be spoken in his ear, 'Was I ever a barren wilderness or a land of darkness?', and he took courage.[102]

At an open-air service in the churchyard the next day, the young man preached from Ezekiel 36:25-6: '*Then I will sprinkle clean water upon you and you shall be clean.*' His 1½-hour sermon was followed by a further hour's exhortation, 'with such liberty and melting of heart', said Livingstone, 'as I never had the like in public all my life'. It began

---

99. Row (Ed.), *The Life of Mr Robert Blair*, p. 90.

100. Gillies incorrectly suggests he was only seventeen (*Historical Collections*, p. 199).

101. Donald Beaton wrote in 1909: 'The spot where Livingstone was engaged in meditation and prayer on the morning of this momentous day is still pointed out. The plough-share has not disturbed the coarse bent grass which grows as it must have grown in those far away days. The same rocks are there and the old churchyard – the only signs to connect the present with those days of power' (Beaton, *Scottish Heroines of the Faith*, p. 47).

102. Gillies, *Historical Collections*, p. 199.

to rain, and Livingstone, making the most of the opportunity, asked whether his hearers did not rather deserve that the Lord 'rain down fire and brimstone as He did on Sodom and Gomorrah'. At once there was a 'strange unusual motion of the hearers' – i.e. considerable manifestation of feeling took place – many shook, others fell down as if dead, and there were few present who were not profoundly affected. Robert Fleming spoke with surety that 'near five hundred had at that time a discernible change wrought on them, of whom most proved lively Christians afterward'.[103] Some of these were 'ladies of high estate, and others poor wastrels and beggars'.[104]

Of the few personal testimonies to have survived, one involves a coach-hirer who had driven a lady from Glasgow to the meeting. He was feeding his horse some distance from the tent when he apprehended – he knew not how – that something extraordinary was taking place in the churchyard. He rose up and ran with all speed into the congregation, and there became a partaker of the blessing which God was showering down on His people that day.[105]

An equally moving story involves 'three gay young gentlemen' from Glasgow who were travelling to Edinburgh for recreation purposes. They stopped at Shotts and, while their horse rested, went to hear the young man who was to preach. All three were riveted by the sermon, and when they later went to a public inn for a drink, not one could lift his tankard till a blessing was said, though this was not the custom of any. As they journeyed on to Edinburgh all were quietly under conviction, but none of them mentioned their concern to the others. In the capital city they engaged little in the amusements they had purposed but largely remained in their rooms. They returned home early, still speaking little to each other. Eventually one of the trio visited another and shared of the change wrought in his life by that sermon at Shotts. His friend frankly admitted that he had been similarly affected. They approached the third man, who

---

103. Fleming, *The Fulfilling of the Scripture*, p. 355. Murray argues that not only does Livingstone say nothing in his memoirs of the number converted at Shotts, but that nor does Fleming make any mention of 500 being actually *converted* under Livingstone's sermon, but rather coming under awakening influences (Murray, *The Puritan Hope*, p. 268).

104. Alexander Smellie, *Men of the Covenant: The Story of the Scottish Church in the Years of the Persecution*, London 1903, pp. 99-100.

105. William Grieve, *A Short History of Shotts Parish Church*, Shotts 1928, p. 13.

now made the same confession. Overjoyed at the mutuality of their experience, they at once started up a fellowship group and all three 'continued to have a practice suitable to their profession as long as they lived'.[106]

Like their brethren in Stewarton, a nickname, albeit not so derogatory, was quickly procured for converts of the Kirk o' Shotts revival; they being called 'The Puritans of the Muir of Bothwell'. Eight years later, when the National Covenant was being signed throughout the country, the Shotts district was one of the strongholds of the movement, while at the battle of Bothwell Bridge a banner inscribed 'For the Parish of Shotts' could be observed. Another influence of the revivals is related by a brother who spoke of 'Robert and Elizabeth Bruces, two old, solid, serious Christians, both my acquaintances, who got a hearty smack of the sweetness of the gospel in that good day at the Kirk of Shotts', soon after helping restore the faith of someone who had become involved in the frenzied cult begun by John Gibb, a sailor from Borrowstounness, who became known for ranting furiously against the Church, the State and almost everything that both stood for.

The Spread of Revival through West Scotland [107]
Just three days after his historic Kirk o' Shotts sermon, John Livingstone preached in Kilmarnock, where some little stamp of the inspiration he had been under remained.[108] The movement spread through other districts in the west of Scotland; acting, according to Fleming, as 'a sowing of the seed through Clydesdale, so as many of the most eminent Christians in that country could date either their conversion or some remarkable confirmation in their case from that day'.[109] A similar, though less well-known, effusion

---

106. Couper, *Scottish Revivals*, p. 38.

107. This appears to have been the first occurrence of revival in Scotland spreading across a significant geographical area. The localised nature of many early revivals has been seen as due in some measure to the lack of good communications (Callum G. Brown, *Religion and the Development of an Urban Society: Glasgow 1780–1914*, Unpublished Ph.D. Thesis, University of Glasgow 1981, vol. 1, p. 418).

108. However, being invited to speak in Irvine exactly a week after his Shotts experience, Livingstone felt so deserted that the message he had meditated upon and committed fully to memory he was utterly unable to get across. Thus, he wrote, 'it pleased the Lord to counterbalance his dealings and hide pride from man'. So discouraged was he by this experience that he resolved not to preach for a while, having to be urged by ministerial colleagues not to lose heart.

109. Fleming, *The Fulfilling of the Scripture*, vol. 1, pp. 355-6.

of divine grace occurred at a later date in Kirkintilloch, once again on the Monday after the Lord's Supper. The people being detained in church by a sudden fall of rain, John Carstairs, minister of Cathcart stepped into the pulpit, and in an extemporaneous discourse, described the nature of true faith. He warned the people against depending on 'a sort of faith that they had all their days and knew not how they came by', but rather declared faith to be a work of the Spirit of God with power. At this point 'there arose a mighty commotion in the congregation, many were brought into a deep concern about their souls' condition, the good fruit of which appeared in their after life and conversation'.[110]

Carstairs and Thomas Melvin, minister of Calder, were contemporaries of Bruce and Livingstone, but continued their ministries sometime after these men's passing. The two aforementioned, along with Messrs Bennett and Ramsay, were said to have been 'mutually helpful in promoting a lively work of grace in the west' by more ordinary means. It is said of Melvin's ministry that in a few years the worship of God was so generally set up in families in his parish that it was counted a scandal to such as neglected it. It is also reported that the number of praying societies rose from one to ten under his pastoral leadership.[111] On one occasion Carstairs came to officiate for Melvin at a communion at Calder, the latter having taken with a fit of sickness during the sacramental solemnities. While they were singing part of the 24th Psalm, 'Ye gates lift up your heads', and before the blessing of the elements, 'there was a mighty melting of heart seized the congregation, and the Spirit of God, like a mighty wind, burst open the everlasting doors, and took possession of the hearts of sinners', several people from that day dating their first soul-concern and conversion. In later days, Carstairs fondly reminisced about having experienced three days of heaven upon earth, and one of them was at Calder.[112]

George Barclay, a former covenanting preacher, is later quoted as saying that

above all places in Scotland he found the greatest gale upon his spirit upon the water Clyde, which he attributed much to the

---

110. Gillies, *Historical Collections*, p. 201.

111. ibid.

112. Wylie, *The History of Protestantism*, Ch. 14; Roberts, *Scotland Saw His Glory*, pp. 111-24.

plentiful, successful prayers of some of the old Christians and their offspring, who got a merciful cast of free grace, when casts were a dealing at the Kirk of Shotts, the 20th of June 1630, which perfumed and gave a scent to the overward of Clydesdale above all other places, but alas! is now much gone! [113]

Further south at this time, in the Kirkcudbrightshire parish of Anwoth, the saintly Samuel Rutherford was attracting large crowds from great distances to his Sabbath services and Communion occasions. So powerful and passionate were his sermon deliveries that a contemporary could record: 'Many times I thought he would hae flown out of the pulpit when he came to speak of Jesus Christ. He was never in his right elements but when he was commending Him.' [114]

The Covenanting Period 1638–88 [115]

The National Covenant 1638

That Great Day – 28th February 1638

When James VI became King of England in 1603 he quickly sought to exert his rule over Scotland's Presbyterian Church by extending episcopacy there. He used his powers to institute bishops, established an Act which acknowledged his authority over all estates, and gained control over the General Assembly, which now met only on rare occasions, such as to ratify a set of ritual innovations known as the Five Articles of Perth in 1618. His son, Charles I, though born in Scotland, was raised in England. He first travelled to Scotland in 1633, eight years after acceding to the throne. Largely ignorant of Scottish affairs and with a condescending attitude to its people and their opinions,

---

113. Walker, *Six Saints of the Covenant*, vol. 1, p. 337.

114. Rutherford's *Letters*, many of which were written during his banishment to Aberdeen from 1636, are marked by a profound depth of spirituality and poetic giftedness, and were hailed by Spurgeon as 'one of the best and most profitable volumes ever published' (Samuel Rutherford, *Letters of Samuel Rutherford*, 1664 [reprinted 1984], p. 5, flyleaf).

115. This period is broadly contemporaneous with the renowned Puritan movement in England. Rev. Maurice Roberts suggests that the 'glorious days of the seventeenth-century Covenanters' were 'a widespread and a mighty effusion of the Spirit of God', greater even than the 1859–61 revival in Scotland ('Remembering the 1859 Revival in Scotland', in *Banner of Truth* January 1993, vol. 352, p. 6).

Charles tactlessly replaced the service book central to Presbyterian worship (devised by John Knox) with an Anglican prayer book (termed 'Laud's Liturgy'). This created a great commotion when first used in St Giles Cathedral in July 1637. When Charles refused to compromise, further riots ensued, accompanied by two waves of petitions from right across the Lowlands, first mainly from ministers, then from lairds and nobles.

With the nation behind them, two learned Presbyterians – Alexander Henderson and Archibald Johnston of Warriston, a young lawyer of zealous puritan convictions – instituted another season of national reform when they drew up a lengthy document basically re-affirming the Covenant of 1560, listing the Acts of Parliament passed since that date against the Roman Church or in favour of the Reformed Church, and swearing loyalty to the Sovereign. This renewed National Covenant was written with the aim of having a wide appeal to all classes of the community. As such, it succeeded magnificently. After being well-publicised it was first read out to, and signed by, a concourse of nobles and barons in Greyfriars Kirk on 28th February 1638. The aged Earl of Sutherland was the first to sign his name to the parchment. Others followed in swift succession. Then the immense document was taken to the crowd in the churchyard – the size of which was estimated at a remarkable 60,000, consisting of townsfolk and those who flocked to the city from miles around – where it was spread before them on a flat grave-stone. The people listened with breathless attention to the prayers, addresses and reading of the Covenant, which was then signed by as many as could get near it. As they came forward, some wept aloud; some burst into shouts of exultation; some, after their names, added the words, 'till death'; and some, opening a vein, subscribed with their own warm blood. As the parchment became filled, they wrote their names in a contracted form, limiting them at last to their initials, till not a spot remained on which another letter could be inscribed.

That other main architect of the Covenant, Alexander Henderson, a convert of Robert Bruce's ministry, noted the remarkable scenes that accompanied that first 'great day';

> Zeal in the cause of Christ, and courage for the liberties of Scotland, warmed every breast. Joy was mingled with the expressions of some, and the voice of shouting arose from a few. But by far the

greater portion were deeply impressed with very different feelings. Most of them, of all sorts, wept bitterly, for their defection from the Lord. And in testimony of his sincerity every one confirmed his subscription by a solemn oath. With groans and tears streaming down their faces, they all lifted up their right hands at once. When this awful appeal was made to the Searcher of hearts at the day of judgement, so great was the fear of again breaking this Covenant, that thousands of arms which had never trembled even when drawing the sword on the eve of battle, were now loosened at every joint. After the oath had been administered the people were powerfully enjoined to begin their personal reformation. At the conclusion every body seemed to feel that a great measure of the Divine Presence had accompanied the solemnities of the day, and with their hearts much comforted and strengthened for every duty, the enormous crowd retired about nine at night.[116]

On the following two days, as the Covenant was carried around Edinburgh and signed by many unable to attend previously, a multitude of women and children followed behind, weeping and praying.

Edinburgh Districts

A couple of weeks after the events just described, on Sunday, 18th March, Archibald Johnston took his family to a church service in Currie, just south of Edinburgh. Here, after the sermon, they heard John Chartres remind his congregation that it was to be a day of fasting for subscription to the Covenant, for which he stressed a biblical precedent (based on Nehemiah 10 and 2 Chronicles 15). He proceeded to read aloud the Covenant in its entirety as he had done the previous Sabbath, explaining to all the details of it. The congregation sat motionless. Then the minister urged the people to stand, lift up their hands, and swear an oath to the living God. As they did so, noted Johnston,

> In the twinkling of an eye there fell such an extraordinary influence of God's Spirit upon the whole congregation, melting their frozen hearts, watering their dry cheeks, changing their very countenances, as it was a wonder to see so visible, sensible, momentous a change upon all, man and woman, lass and lad, pastor and

---

116. Thomas McCrie, *Life of Alexander Henderson*, Edinburgh 1846, pp. 255-6.

people, that Mr John, being suffocated almost with his own tears, and astonished at the motion of the whole people, sat down in the pulpit in amazement, but presently rose again when he saw all the people falling down on their knees to mourn and pray, and he and they for a quarter of an hour prayed very sensibly with many sobs, tears, promises, and vows to be thankful and fruitful in time-coming.[117]

A similar scenario was enacted exactly two weeks later when, back in Edinburgh, Johnston again heard the Covenant that he had helped design being read out to an eager congregation. After praying for 'the Lord's immediate presence, assistance and influence on the congregation', Mr Hery Rollo requested the people (beginning with the four noblemen present), to stand, hold up their hands and make an oath by the name of the living God. Immediately on so doing,

> There arose such a yell, such abundance of tears, such a heavenly harmony of sighs and sobs, universally through all the corners of the church, as the like was never seen nor heard of. The Spirit of the Lord so filled the sanctuary, warmed the affections, melted the hearts, dissolved the eyes of all the people, men and women, poor and noble, as for a long time they stood still with their hands up unto the Lord, till Mr Hery, after he recovered himself, scarce able to speak, after a short exhortation to thankfulness and fruitful-ness, closed all up in a heavenly prayer and praise, and announced the singing of Psalm 74 from verse 18.

Johnston personally wept his way through the entire service, especially when appeared a profound sense of divine presence, at which point his heart was 'liken to burst' and which he saw as a sign that God was 'testi-fying from heaven that he directed the work'. Apparently, that same day in Greyfriars Kirk, 'it pleased the Lord both forenoon and afternoon, at the swearing of the Covenant there, by the like motion, to show the like presence of his Spirit'.[118] The following Sunday, Communion was celebrated in both Edinburgh College Church and Greyfriars Church for the first time in twenty years.

---

117. George Morison Paul (Ed.), *Diary of Sir Archibald Johnston of Warriston 1632–1639*, Edinburgh 1911, pp. 327-8.

118. ibid., p. 331.

Lowland Counties

Such scenes of solemnity and zeal – which the Covenant's chief architect described as 'so wonderful in my eyes that I could scarce believe my own eyes, but was like a man in a dream' [119] – were repeated across the land as a result of copies of the Covenant being written out and sent by mounted despatch to every shire, bailiery and parish throughout the nation. From that day, according to Gillies, 'the influences of His grace were plentifully poured out upon multitudes through the nation',[120] although areas where the Covenant was not accepted, such as parts of Aberdeenshire and the Highlands, remained largely unaffected. In most places, however, the Covenant was received as a sacred oracle.[121] John Livingstone, describing scenes he personally witnessed at Lanark and several other parishes where the Covenant was read and sworn, said, 'excepting at the Kirk of Shotts, I never saw such motions from the Spirit of God. All the people generally and most willingly concurred. I have seen more than a thousand persons all at once lifting up their hands, and the tears falling down from their eyes as they entered into covenant with God.' [122]

The people of Galston, Ayrshire, signed the Covenant on 25th March 1638. John Fleming, local Session clerk, carefully noted his thankfulness to the Lord for

> sealling the renewing of our Covenant with strange and sensible motions of his spirit in the hearts of all people universallie throwh the land. And pouring upon us blessings of all sorts from that day forward … . being a day of solemne assemblie for that worke and docterin, with the wonderfull applause of all the congregatioun without exception, shewing that reddines of mynde by the elevatioun of heart and hand, cheirfulness of countenance,

---

119. ibid., p. 323.

120. Gillies, *Historical Collections*, p. 194; Rev. W. Taylor, *Memorials of Rev. C. C. Macintosh*, Edinburgh 1871, p. 8.

121. A few instances did arise (such as in Glasgow, St Andrews and Lanark) where personal compulsion was resorted to by a few over-zealous Presbyterians to obtain signatures. Similarly, some Highland clans, along with the Colleges of Glasgow, Aberdeen and St Andrews, were all reluctant to pledge their allegiance until a deputation was sent to personally garner their support. On the other hand one or two Jesuits resident in Scotland at the time independently recanted their faith and gladly signed the covenant.

122. McCrie, *Story of the Scottish Church*, pp. 149-50.

teares, and all expressioun of joy that the gravitie of the meitting could admit ...[123]

Northern Counties

It was recorded that virtually the whole of the towns of Forres, Elgin and Inverness subscribed the Covenant, excepting the ministers. It was said that the people of Sutherland, Easter Ross, Nairn and Moray, as well as of the town of Inverness, all entered the Covenant 'with alacrity', the way having been prepared a few decades previously by the ardent and extensive labours of Robert Bruce on his banishment to the north (see page 51). Of further advantage was the fact that the Sutherland family and the Rosses and Munroes of Easter Ross had been keen supporters of evangelical Presbyterianism ever since the Reformation. Thus it was that the Earl of Rothes could declare that over much of Sutherland, Ross-shire and Inverness-shire the day of the signing of the National Covenant was

> the joyfullest day that ever they saw, or ever was seen in the North; and it was marked as a special mark of God's goodness towards these parts, that so many different clans and names, among whom before was nothing but hostility and blood, were met together in one place for such a good cause, and in so peaceable a manner, as that nothing was to be seen and heard, but mutual embracements, with hearty praise to God for so happy a union.[124]

While there was considerably less covenant activity in the far north county of Caithness, three local gentry did support the cause and a body of men was recruited to fight for it. A severe famine is known to have prevailed around this time, and it is recorded that 'Caithness unitedly (like Nineveh) proclaimed a fast, and set themselves to confess their sin. The fast was held on October day in 1638, and it was this famine[125] and consequent penitence that explains why the National

---

123. Quoted in David Stevenson, *The Covenanters: The National Covenant and Scotland*, Edinburgh 1988, pp. 43-4.

124. Murdoch Macdonald, *The Covenanters In Moray and Ross*, Nairn 1875, pp. 16-17.

125. In particular, '1643 was noted for such a scarcity of seed that the land remained almost unsown. Multitudes died in the open field, while some, driven into a frenzy by the sight of their perishing relatives, committed suicide' (J. M. Baikie, *Revivals in the Far North*, Wick nd, p. 5).

Covenant was taken up in the far north ... the result was a spiritual awakening'.[126]

Attestations to Success of the Covenant

Johnston of Warriston hailed the Covenant's signing as 'the glorious marriage of the kingdom with God'.[127] Later in the century Robert Fleming wrote of the event:

> Many yet alive do know how their hearts were wrought on by the Lord. The ordinances were lively and longed after. Then did the nation own the Lord, and was visibly owned by him; much zeal and an enlarged heart did appear for the public cause; personal application was seriously set about; and then also was there a remarkable call of providence that did attend the actings of this people, which did astonish their adversaries, and forced many of them to feign subjection.[128]

'Never except among God's peculiar people, the Jews', wrote nineteenth-century historian, W. M. Hetherington, using similarly biblical imagery, 'did any national transaction equal in moral and religious sublimity that which was displayed by Scotland on the great day of her sacred National Covenant.'[129]

Patrick Walker wrote in the 1720s of his longing for the Lord to send 'a thaw-wind and spring-tide day of the gospel ... as was in our reforming covenanting days between the Thirty-eight and Forty-nine'.[130] The Rev. George Paxton posed – then proceeded to answer – the following probing question in the early nineteenth century, 'To what must our great and lasting prosperity be owing? We believe it has been greatly owing to the covenants of our fathers, to which a faithful and gracious God has hitherto had respect. It was not the ocean that surrounds us; it was not the number and prowess of our fleets and armies, nor the wisdom of our councils (when invasion was threatened) but the sword of the Lord, and the buckler of his favour that saved us.'[131]

---

126. ibid.

127. Paul (Ed.), *Diary of Sir Archibald Johnston*, p. 328.

128. Fleming, *The Fulfilling of the Scripture*, vol. 1, p. 357.

129. W. M. Hetherington, *History of the Church of Scotland*, Edinburgh 1848, p. 91.

130. Walker, *Six Saints of the Covenant*, vol. 1, pp. 41-2.

131. William Roberts, *Reformed Presbyterian Catechism*, Edinburgh 1853.

Fleming testified towards the end of the century that as a result of the National Covenant:

> What a solemn outletting of the Spirit has been seen; a large harvest, with much of the fruit of the gospel discernible; which has been proved in the bringing thousands to Christ, a part whereof are now in glory, and many who are yet alive who are a visible seal to this truth, of whom I am sure some will not lose the remembrance of those sweet refreshing times which the land for several years enjoyed, when a large blessing, with much of the Spirit and power of God was felt accompanying the ordinances. I could here point to many such remarkable times and places which would clearly demonstrate this.[132]

Indeed, such was the significance of the signing of the document throughout Scotland – which event soon became termed 'The Second Reformation' – that modern historians have similarly regarded it as being quite unique; 'a defining event in the development of Scottish national consciousness',[133] ... 'perhaps the most remarkable expression of national unity Scotland had seen in all its history',[134] ... 'another supremely important radical departure, not only in Scottish history, but conceivably also in European history ... a totally new exercise in civic humanism ... It marked, in a very real sense, the end of the medieval world'.[135]

Revival in the Army
But it wasn't only Scotland's civilian population that was subject to a wave of spiritual reviving at this time. Those serving in Scotland's armies similarly came under its gracious influence. In 1626 Sir Donald Mackay

---

132. Fleming, *The Fulfilling of the Scripture*, vol. 1, p. 357.

133. Open University, *A History of Scotland*, Milton Keynes, 2008, p. 18. George Gilfillan, a nineteenth-century United Presbyterian minister, regarded 'the Second Reformation' as 'a great religious revival, a time when sinners were saved and saints sanctified' (David Macrae, *George Gilfillan: Anecdotes and Reminiscences*, Glasgow 1891, p. 82). The Reformed Presbyterian Church of Scotland, a derivative of the Cameronian sect of the Covenanters, has always claimed to have had its historical and doctrinal roots in the 1638 covenant. A Cameronian presence still exists in Scotland at the time of writing, the number of congregations having recently increased from two to six.

134. Magnus Magnusson, *Scotland: The Story of a Nation*, London 2000, p. 424.

135. Ted Cowan, quoted in ibid., p. 425.

(who became the first Lord Reay), along with Munro of Foulis, mustered some 2,000 men from the northern counties to embark at Cromarty en route to the Continent as part of 'The Scots Brigade'. Here they fought the Protestant cause for the kings of Denmark and Sweden. Among the number were around 400 'as yet rude and irreligious' men from the Reay county of Sutherland, with Lord Reay as their chief. During their service under King Gustavus Adolphus of Sweden, 'a change was produced on their characters different from that which is usually the result of a camp life'. From their dealings with believers abroad these men returned to their own country enlightened, Christianised men, and from this is to be dated the high religious character for which the Reay district was so long renowned.[136]

In the Netherlands many soldiers were converted to Christ under the influence of English Puritan chaplains who had been enrolled, and large groups of them returned to their native counties as ardent Christians.[137] Having returned home, some Scots soldiers who lived a long distance from church began Sabbath evening meetings which were said to have been 'instrumental in the conversion of sinners and in the refreshing of God's heritage'.[138] It is claimed, remarkably, that as late as the nineteenth century many of Britain's most dependable regiments came from the counties of Sutherland and Ross-shire, consisting of a great number of men who, as well as being dedicated soldiers, were also eminent witnesses for their Saviour in distant parts of the world – men who often surprised locals by their godly conduct and a preference for Bible studies over public houses.[139] Indeed, of the 93rd Highlanders, or Sutherland Regiment, established in 1800, it is said that over a period of years not a single man warranted punishment.[140]

A policy developed to send an able minister of the gospel with every regiment of the army. Robert Blair of Irvine, former regent at Glasgow University, and an instrument in the Ulster revival of 1625–30, had

---

136. James Lumsden, *Sweden: its Religious State and Prospects: with Some Notices of the Revivals and Persecutions which are at Present taking place in that Country*, London 1855, p. 80.

137. Campbell, *Gleanings of Highland Harvest*, pp. 138-40.

138. Free Church of Scotland *Monthly Record*, 1918, p. 132.

139. Murray, *A Scottish Christian Heritage*, p. 153.

140. Donald Sage, *Memorabilia Domestica*, Wick 1889 (reprinted 1975).

become well-respected as the minister in St Andrews – but so important was the edification of soldiers deemed that he was summoned from
his charge in 1640 and posted with the regiment under Lord Lindsay's
jurisdiction. The chaplains jointly were vested with the powers of a presbytery. 'These were not', noted Mary Duncan, 'priests-errant, men of
inflamed passions, half insane with religious frenzy', as had been suggested, 'but men tried and found faithful in the private duties of the
ministry, selected carefully by the Church, and invested with the grave
powers of a church court'.[141] As the Scots advanced south in attempt to
overcome England, it became the duty of Blair to share the vicissitudes
of battles, as the army invaded and conquered Newcastle, then Durham,
before a treaty was signed with the English in Ripon. When this treaty
was set on foot, the committee of estates sent Blair up to assist the commissioners with his best advice. The chaplain was thoroughly impressed
with the religious condition of the Covenanting soldiers, for he noticed
that 'Amongst all the Scots army, there was scarce a man without a Bible;
a great part of them were devout and religious persons; so that when
they came to their quarters, there was little else to be heard but reading,
prayer, and solemn melody.' [142]

English Occupation 1651–60

Following the execution of Charles I in 1649, the Scots proclaimed
his son, Charles II, as King. This was in defiance of Oliver Cromwell's
English Commonwealth, and caused the Protector, no sooner returned
from his devastating conquest of Ireland in 1650, to advance north of
the border with an army of 16,000 horse and foot soldiers. Forced to
retreat to Dunbar, and on the brink of evacuating his troops by sea, an
unexpected opportunity allowed Cromwell to smash the Covenanter
army, killing 3,000, taking a further 10,000 prisoner, and also capturing
the capital city, Edinburgh. For the next nine years Scotland was kept
under military occupation. Cromwell admitted freedom of religion
except to Catholics and prelates. But such privilege was weakened by
almost constant infighting between the Protestors – the more radical
group of Covenanters – and the more moderate Resolutioners.

---

141. Mary Lundie Duncan, *History of Revivals of Religion in the British Isles, Especially
Scotland*, Edinburgh 1836, p. 198.

142. Row (Ed.), *The Life of Mr Robert Blair*, p. 95.

During these nine years, from 1651 until the Restoration of Charles II in 1660, according to James Kirkton, 'religion prospered in no ordinary measure ... There were more souls converted to Christ in that short period of time than in any season since the Reformation, though of triple its duration. Nor was there ever greater purity and plenty of the means of grace.'[143] Thomas McCrie, writing in 1874, added: 'There can be no question that the piety of that period was both more intense and more widely diffused than it has been ever since in Scotland.'[144] In his old age, following the Glorious Revolution, the Rev. Hutcheson of Killellan used to reminisce on the days prior to the Restoration of King Charles II, when, he claimed, 'there was far more of the power and efficacy of the Spirit and grace of God went along with sermons in those days ... and, for my own part (all the glory be to God) I seldom set my foot in a pulpit in those times, but I had notice of some blessed effects of the Word'.[145] A minister wrote in 1753 that he knew some older believers who often remarked that 'the period between 1650 and the Restoration was a very remarkable one in Scotland for the success of the gospel'.[146]

Protestors and Resolutioners

Success in this period was in no small measure due to the efforts of the Protestors. While political strife between them and the majority Resolutioners ran high, the discord did not dampen the religious zeal of the Protestors. In fact, the division only hardened their resolve to win the people over both to Christ and to their own party.[147] The sacramental

---

143. McCrie, *Story of the Scottish Church*, p. 246.

144. ibid., p. 247.

145. Gillies, *Historical Collections*, p. 201.

146. ibid., p. 202. Alexander Auld (*Life of John Kennedy*, London 1887, p. 83) believed that 'true godliness flourished in Lowlands of the kingdom during the last years of the Commonwealth, and especially about the year 1649, as it never did before, and probably has never done since'.

147. Opponents criticised the way the Protesters openly excluded any from the Lord's Supper who did not follow their rigid political line, and went out of their way to appeal to the people, evidently adopting at times a distinctively fervent style of prayer and preaching – 'a strange kind of sighing'– in attempt to add proselytes to their 'new refined congregation' of saints. (Leigh Eric Schmidt, *Holy Fairs: Scotland and the Making of American Revivalism*, Princeton, NJ 1989, p. 37). Nevertheless, these communion times were by no means wholly factional.

occasion would be one of their main instruments in this context. These communions were both powerful and popular, displaying revivalistic qualities. Kirkton gloried that 'If a man had seen one of their solemn communions, where many congregations met in great multitudes, some dozen of ministers used to preach, and the people continued, as it were, in a sort of trance (so serious were they in spiritual exercises) for three days at least, he would have thought it a solemnity unknown to the rest of the world'.[148]

John Livingstone reported in the mid-1650s, 'some reviving of the Work of God in the Land', noting in particular that 'in Teviotdale and the Merse, Communions were very lively and much frequented'.[149] Such events were not identified with the Protestors alone. Among the Resolutioners, Robert Blair was a chief actor and prime instrument at a number of sacramental gatherings in these years, as too was David Dickson. Blair wrote of some communion services he assisted at in northern districts of Fife between 1650 and '60, that they were 'sweet and soul-refreshing days of the gospel, and some solemn high Sabbaths'.[150] Blair's son-in-law commented that 'at these solemn occasions, many souls got much good by his ministry. It was the Lord's wonderful condescension and kindness to his own in Scotland, that, while they were under the feet of usurpers (Cromwell and the English), the Lord sweetened the bitterness of their bondage, by blessing the labours of his faithful servants of the ministry ... . in several parts of the kingdom'.[151]

A contemporary noted in his diary in 1654 that in Galloway there was 'never a greater outletting of God's presence in communions; two congregations, before dead, falling in great love of the ordinances'.[152] In the same year this diarist confided that 'Christ was at the communion in Fennick and that it was a refreshing day', and that in the 'north side of Fife' there was 'a great resort to communions, and ministers (speak) much of people getting good thereat'.[153]

---

148. Kirkton, *The Secret and True History of the Church of Scotland*, pp. 54-5.

149. ibid., p. 36.

150. Row (Ed.), *The Life of Mr Robert Blair*, p. 97.

151. ibid., pp. 322-3.

152. Schmidt, *Holy Fairs*, p. 36.

153. ibid.

Thomas Hogg of Kiltearn

The same could be said of Kiltearn, Ross-shire, where awakening attended the wholehearted labours of Thomas Hogg (1628–92) in the 1650s. 'The dry bones began to revive', noted Beaton, 'and pleasant blossoms and hopeful appearances displayed themselves everywhere through the parish'.[154] John Gillies wrote of Hogg: 'Few were favoured with so many testimonies of the Divine presence in the discharge of their ministry'.[155] These included Angus Macbean, later minister in Inverness; William Bulloch, Hogg's own servant; and 'the judicious and famous John Munro of Ross',[156] who being brought into a state of grace, did so excel in the virtues opposite to his former blemishes, that he became esteemed for solving disputes; numbers of people submitted their quarrels to him, acquiescing in his wise determinations. At one particularly solemn and successful Communion in Kiltearn, 'the Lord bowed his heavens and came down, and displayed his saving power on that occasion most comfortably and signally'.[157] Hogg's Ross-shire parish and the district around it – known as Ferindonald – produced such a number and such a succession of devoted believers that it became familiarly spoken of in the eighteenth century as 'The holy land'. More poetically still, a valley in the same county, from every house of which the voice of prayer and praise used to be daily heard, was known as '*Nead na smeorach*' – 'The land of thrushes'.[158] Further blessing occurred on Hogg's banishment to Knockgaudy, near Oldearn, Moray, where over a number of years, by preaching 'in his own private house, he became the happy instrument of converting or confirming many souls'.[159]

James Kirkton declared that by the time of the return to the throne of Charles II in 1660, every parish had a minister, every village had a

---

154. Donald Beaton, *Some Noted Ministers of the Northern Highlands*, Glasgow 1929 (reprinted 1985), p. 5. It was commonly accepted that Fellowship Meetings, which became popular in the Highlands, began during the ministry of Hogg in Kiltearn, originating, it is believed, from his student days in Aberdeen when 'he and some pious students had private meetings for prayer and conference and found them profitable' (J. Campbell Robinson, *The Rev. Alexander McIntyre*, Pharhan, Australia 1929, p. 29).

155. Gillies, *Historical Collections*, p. 194.

156. ibid., p. 195.

157. Schmidt, *Holy Fairs*, p. 36.

158. Taylor, *Memorials of Rev. C. C. Macintosh*, pp. 9-10.

159. Gillies, *Historical Collections*, pp. 194-5.

school and almost every family had a Bible. 'I have lived many years in a parish where I never heard an oath and you might have ridden many miles before you heard any', he said. 'Also, you could not for a great part of the country have lodged in a family where the Lord was not worshipped by reading, singing and public prayer'.[160]

The Restoration Period 1660–88

Presbyterianism Outlawed

Cromwell died of illness in 1658 and his son, Richard, was made Lord Protector. He quickly lost the confidence of his army, however, which removed him after just seven months. At the request of George Monck, governor of Scotland under the Cromwells, Charles II returned from exile and reclaimed his throne – being crowned at Westminster Abbey. He quickly sought to gain full control of the Church in Scotland, using a number of measures. He restored episcopacy under an Act of Parliament, and appointed bishops, who, under the rule of royal commissioners, wielded enormous influence. Lay patronage, abolished in 1648, was restored. Those holding public offices were forced to renounce the Covenants, and severe penalties were imposed for non-compliance as well as for not attending church.

The Covenanters were forced into hiding, as dragoons scoured the countryside, arresting these radicals, and breaking up their conventicles. Persecution continued throughout the Restoration period of 1660 to 1688, but was at its strongest during the infamous 'Killing Times' of 1680–88. But such pressure failed to stop the Covenanters holding their frequent clandestine meetings on hills and moors, to which many hundreds might eagerly gather to hear the gospel preached by fearless ejected ministers who were now fugitives from the law. In Kirkcudbrightshire, for example, when Gabriel Semple, the deprived minister of Kirkpatrick Irongray, began to preach in the hall of Corsock House, so great a number converged on the place that they were quickly required to resort to the open-air, where regular meetings were held. Further north, the banishment of Walter Pringle, laird of Greenknow, near Kelso, to Elgin in 1664 for imbibing non-conformist views, resulted not in desperate privations as he had expected, but in the comfort of being able to worship God without distraction and peace to write his inspirational

---

160. Quoted in Alex Muir, 'Revival in Scotland' in *Prophecy Today*, vol. 1, no. 4, 1985, p. 7.

memoirs. The forced exile of other Presbyterians to the north led to a healthy correspondence being kept between these (led by Pringle) and the noblemen of the region, and many people in the neighbourhood resorted to them for prayer and counsel. Indeed, so much good resulted that one historian called it 'a great revival of religion',[161] and the Bishop of Ross strongly feared that more evil was done by these men's exile north than if they had been left at home.

When persecution was at its strongest, many Presbyterian ministers were forced to cross the border to Northumberland in order to be able to continue their ministry without fear of harassment. Many Covenanters in the south of Scotland took advantage of any opportunity afforded them to cross into these north English districts to attend on exiled ministers' preaching. 'Such a blessing, indeed, rested on the non-conformist ministry in Northumberland', wrote J. Wood Brown, 'that a great revival of religion broke out there, … so that from Cheviot to Carter Fell, and even as far as the wilds of Kielderhead, Wheelcauseway and Deadwater in Cumberland, the country showed a flame of newly awakened interest'.[162] News of this spiritual movement even reached the ears of John Livingstone, then in exile in Holland, who at once wrote to his congregation in Ancrum, urging them if at all possible to make the journey across the border to partake firsthand of this mighty work of God in their neighbourhood.

In the wake of the Northumberland movement a fresh wave of spiritual fervour had begun to spread across the south-east of Scotland by 1669, extending as far north as Fife, the Lothians and Stirlingshire. This was evidenced by a mushrooming of field meetings led by ministers ejected from their charges – many open-air congregations now numbering in the hundreds or even thousands while parish churches stood empty.

Open-Air Communions in the North

Open-air Communions were especially blessed. In the Highlands, two locations in particular stand out as being sacred spots where the sacrament of the Lord's Supper was administered during these twenty-eight years' persecution, and several such seasons were long cherished. One was the Kinlochbervie district of Sutherland, the other Obsdale in Ross-shire.

161. J. Wood Brown, *The Covenanters of the Merse*, Edinburgh 1893, p. 77.
162. ibid.

In the parish of Kinlochbervie and Eddrachillis, the two places where the sacrament used to be held were considered too open and prominent for the purpose, so a secluded spot on a riverside was selected. Word went out privately, yet as many as five score parishioners gathered on one particular occasion, coming from the hamlets and clachans in the two adjoining peninsulas, and from the lonely scattered cottages on the hillsides, to celebrate the Supper with the outlawed George Squair.[163] Those who attended were said to have been the most devout and faithful in all the hamlets in Eddrachillis and Kinlochbervie. They approached

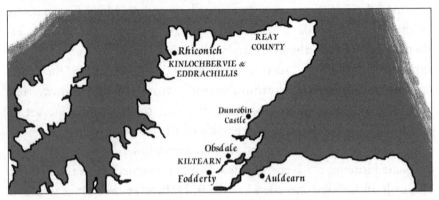

the place as if by stealth, with feelings greatly agitated, but with hearts rising in earnest prayer that the Lord might grant them His protection and His gracious presence. When they came to the place they found themselves in the centre of a glade overgrown with birchwood and sheltered by wild and beetling rocks. The pulpit desk was a birch tree, sawn off at a considerable height, and the tables were formed of turf covered with green, smooth sod.[164] Not only was there no interruption of the service, but all there felt so much of the Lord's presence, and their bonds were so loosened, and their fears so dispelled, that 'all, without a single exception, felt constrained to say with Thomas, "*My Lord and my God*", and without exception, commemorated the dying love of their

---

163. Squair was considered to be the only Presbyterian minister in the Reay country. He was eventually joined by three other persecuted ministers, and given that their presence there was now deemed precarious, they in time found refuge in a dry and commodious cave by Golspie burn and near Dunrobin Castle. Here they were served from the table of the castle until the day of their deliverance came (Alexander MacRae, *Kinlochbervie: Being the Story and Traditions of a Remote Highland Parish and its People*, Tongue 1932, p. 38).

164. ibid., p. 37.

Redeemer'.[165] Many years afterwards, during another time of spiritual blessing in the district, George Brodie, who had been settled in 1724 as the first minister of the newly formed parish of Eddrachilis, asked one of his elders whether he had ever before experienced a time of greater blessing and power. 'Only one', was the old man's reply, 'at the memorable communion at Rhichonnic, Eddrachilis' (of which he was the last survivor).[166]

Meanwhile, when John McKilligan, the fugitive but faithful minister of Fodderty, Ross-shire, who had been driven from his parish in 1662, administered the Lord's Supper to an attached people near Rosskeen in the same parish in September 1675, 'Many serious people were longing much to partake of the sacrament ... and having been at much pains in public preaching and from house to house to prepare them for it'. The sacrament was dutifully performed in the house of the lady Dowager of Fowlis at Obsdale. Two ministers assisted, for which one of them had to pay dearly. At the last sermon,

> there was a plentiful effusion of the Spirit upon a great many present; and the oldest Christians there declared that they had not been witnesses to the like. In short, there were so sensible and glorious discoveries made of the Son of Man, and such evident presence of the Master of Assemblies this day and the preceding, that the people seemed to be in a transport, and their souls filled with heaven, and breathing thither while their bodies were on earth; and some were almost at that (stage of) "whether in the body or out of the body, I cannot tell". Even some drops fell upon strangers.[167]

One such 'stranger to the gospel' was a poor man who came merely out of curiosity, but returned home full of the new-born joy of salvation. On learning at what outlawed event he had attended, his neighbour called him

---

165. Gunn, *Sutherland and the Reay Country*, p. 338.

166. Thomson, *Tales of the Far North West*, pp. 11-12.

167. Robert Wodrow, *The History of the Sufferings of the Church of Scotland, From the Restoration to the Revolution*, Edinburgh 1722, vol. 2, pp. 284-5; cf. John Kennedy, *Days of the Fathers in Ross-shire*, Edinburgh 1861 (reprinted 1979), pp. 37-40; See also Beaton, *Some Noted Ministers of the Northern Highlands*, pp. 16-17. The significant part played by sacramental occasions was to continue in the north counties over the following two centuries.

a fool, adding that all he owned – his cow and his horse – would surely be taken from him. The man replied that his neighbour was more to be pitied for not having had the pleasure of being at the conventicle, and that not only was he willing to give up his cow and horse, but his head too, if necessary. It was of course in the face of great danger that such conventicles were held, and in the Obsdale scenario Bishop Paterson, getting wind of the proposed communion, sent the county sheriff to search for McKilligan at his Alness manse. The minister wasn't there, of course, but his ripening apple trees were, and the soldiers could not resist their attraction. Providentially, before the officer in charge could draw his men away from their booty, and surround the house at Obsdale, the communicants had time to dispose of themselves and conceal the ministers.[168]

William Guthrie of Fenwick

Exceptionally, oppression escaped William Guthrie (1620–65) in his Ayrshire parish of Fenwick, to the north of Kilmarnock, in the early 1660s,[169] where his church, though a large country one, soon became overcrowded every Sabbath. Many came from Glasgow, Renfrewshire, Lanarkshire and all parts of Ayrshire to stay for the weekend, turning the corn field of Guthrie's glebe 'into a town, every one building a house for his family upon it, only that they might live under the drop of his ordinances and ministry'.[170] Arriving on Saturday, they would spend the greatest part of the night in prayer and conversation about the great concerns of their souls. After public worship on the Sabbath, the remainder of the day would be devoted to religious exercises, before returning home, five, ten or twenty miles on Monday, without grudging the long way or the lack of sleep or refreshment. Guthrie, a native of Angus, was said to have 'a strange way of persuading sinners to close

168. Macdonald, *The Covenanters in Moray and Ross*, pp. 122-3. McKilligan did not long escape his pursuers, however. He was apprehended the following year in the house of Rev. Hugh Anderson of Cromarty, who had been one of his assistants at the Obsdale communion. From the Tolbooth of Fortrose he was sent to the Bass Rock, where, during a long imprisonment, he contracted a disease from which he died.

169. This was partly through the favour of the Earl of Glencairn, then Chancellor. However, the crowds that came to hear Guthrie aroused the jealousy of Alexander Burnet, the Archbishop of Glasgow, and Guthrie was suspended from the ministry in 1664, dying a year later.

170. Kirkton, quoted in Roberts, *Scotland Saw His Glory*, p. 20.

with Christ, and answering all objections that might be proposed'.[171]
He also had the advantage of being able to speak to them in their own
dialect. As a result, great numbers were converted unto the truth, and
many built up in their faith.

Communion seasons were especially blessed occasions. 'Great numbers were converted unto the truth', noted Guthrie's biographer, 'and
many were built up in their most holy faith; a divine power animated
the gospel that was preached, and exerted itself in a holy warmth of
sanctified affections, a ravishing pleasure in divine fellowship, and a
noble joy and triumph in their king and Saviour which were to be visibly
discerned in the hearers.'[172] James Hutcheson of Killellan was assistant
at one communion and afterwards said, 'If there was a kirk full o' saints
in the world it was the Kirk of Fenwick that day'; not least the shining
faces he observed and the ecstasies which he shared – an experience to
him that was truly unforgettable. Even some of high rank were heard
saying they would have been heartily content to have lived upon Mr
Guthrie's ministry, even though they had to exchange their station for
that of poor ploughmen.[173]

Nor was the fruit of Guthrie's ministry confined to this one parish, for
the preacher travelled up and down the west coast, everywhere attracting
large and eager audiences. On one occasion a Glasgow merchant,
returning from Ireland, was forced to spend a Sabbath in Arran. He
reluctantly made his way to church, expecting not to understand a word
of the sermon which he was sure would be in Gaelic. But the man in the
pulpit was none other than William Guthrie, and through his prayer-
soaked message the wind of the Spirit moved in majestic, irresistible
power, carrying everyone along with Him. 'There was scarce a hearer
without tears, and many old people, in particular, were weeping', an old
source informs us.[174]

For years after his suspension by 'jealous and angry Prelates',
Guthrie's converts could never think of their spiritual father 'and

---

171. ibid., p. 19.

172. Quoted in Rev. W. K. Tweedie (Ed.), *Select Biographies*, Edinburgh 1847,
pp. 46-7.

173. Alexander Smellie, *Men of the Covenant: The Story of the Scottish Church in the
Years of the Persecution*, London 1903, p. 123.

174. ibid., pp. 123-4.

the power of that victorious grace which, in those days, triumphed so gloriously … without exultation of soul and emotion of revived affection'.[175] Indeed, for a long time the people of this parish were considered to be more civilised and religious than those of neighbouring areas.[176]

Conventicles in the South

The years 1677–80 were pivotal in this time of secrecy and danger, when, increasingly, communions were conducted in open defiance of the law. Robert Garnock of Stirling, himself influenced by a field sermon, recalled 'the three most wonderful days with the Lord's presence that ever I saw on earth' during a later open-air Sacrament at East Nisbet in the Borders in April 1677, when thousands came together. Garnock exulted, 'Glory to His sweet name that ever there was such a day in Scotland! Both good and bad were made to cry out … and I thought it was a heaven begun to be in that place'.[177]

By this time, however, the main focus of field preaching activity had moved from the east to the south-west of the country, which soon began to witness remarkable instances of spiritual power. Two particularly notable conventicles took place in 1678, both in the southern lowlands. At Irongray, Dumfriesshire, in a natural amphitheatre surrounded by high hills from which look-outs kept watch for troopers, local fugitive minister, John Welch (great grandson of John Knox) and John Blackadder officiated at meetings over three days to which an estimated 14,000 gathered, 3,000 of whom partook of the Lord's Supper. Meanwhile, a two-day conventicle, again with communion, held at Carrick, South Ayrshire, in August 1678 was attended by as many people (of which 600 were armed by way of defence).[178] Speakers

---

175. Howie, *The Scots Worthies*, p. 329.

176. ibid. Contemporaneous with Guthrie, and also from Ayrshire, John Brown of Priesthill (c. 1627–85) was a carrier and farmer who developed a remarkable ministry among children during the Covenanting period (J. D. Douglas suggests this might constitute the first traces of Sunday schools in Scotland). He conducted Sunday afternoon services to which people flocked on foot from miles around. Having regularly absented himself from Episcopalian worship, he was seized by Claverhouse's soldiers and shot in the presence of his pregnant wife and their children (*DSCHT*, p. 99).

177. Howie, *The Scots Worthies*, pp. 459-60.

178. Johannes G. Vos, *The Scottish Covenanters: Their Origins, History and Distinctive Doctrines*, Edinburgh 1998, p. 91.

included aforementioned John Welch, Richard Cameron, Archibald Riddell and Patrick Warner. Many received spiritual blessing at this convention, not least the above-noted Robert Garnock, and the youthful John Stevenson of Dailly, who was converted that day through Welch's sermon.[179] Around the same time, Robert Fleming of Glasgow witnessed 'the Lord's marvellous assistance and countenance at the two communions of Cathcart and Dunlop; with the great enlargement I had at the last of these places, at the last table'.[180]

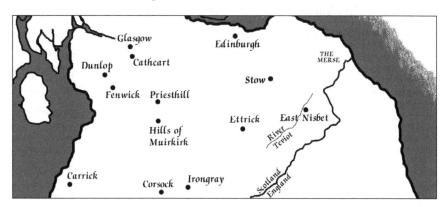

By 1678 Glasgow and Clydesdale were being deeply impacted by the spiritual revival that had overtaken other parts of the country. At the centre of the movement here was Donald Cargill, ejected minister of the Barony parish, to whose open-air addresses vast crowds were drawn week after week. At one point Cargill's voice, strained beyond endurance by preaching to such unusually large numbers, broke down completely, and he was reluctantly forced to keep silent for some weeks while others preached in his place. Regaining his vocal powers, Cargill preached outside Glasgow on eighteen consecutive Sabbaths to crowds so vast that the singing of the psalms could be heard in several parts of the city. The very size of the multitudes deterred the authorities from intervening, enabling the preacher to exhort freely without interruption.[181]

---

179. Stevenson was known thereafter for his life of godliness, testimonies of which can be gleaned from his own written memorial. He was known to spend as long as three days and nights at a stretch alone in prayer, and was likened to Alexander Peden in his predictive capacities (Rev. R. Lawson, *The Covenanters of Ayrshire*, Ayrshire 1887, pp. 30-1).

180. Gillies, *Historical Collections*, p. 187.

181. Maurice Grant, *No King But Christ: The Story of Donald Cargill*, Darlington 1988, pp. 72-3.

Further south, on 30th May 1680 Richard Cameron, the champion of Scotland's field preachers, delivered a sermon from a remote spot deep in the hills of Muirkirk, strategically located where four parishes converged – Crawfordjohn and Douglas in Clydesdale, and Muirkirk and Auchinleck in Ayrshire – so that hearers from as wide an area as possible might gather there. Choosing as his text John 5:40, Cameron confronted his audience with the claims of Christ as the only Saviour, his message coming over with extraordinary power. Indeed, such was the degree of outpouring of the Spirit that John Howie reckoned that with the possible exception of John Livingstone's sermon at Kirk o' Shotts fifty years previously, no sermon was 'more remarkably blessed with success from the Lord in Scotland since the primitive times'.[182] To many the occasion proved a veritable heaven on earth. One witness of Cameron's preaching testified that, 'as much of Christ and heaven were found as finite creatures on earth were able to hold. The streams of living waters ran through among his people at these meetings, like a flood upon the souls of many, who can witness if they were called to it that they would not have been afraid of ten thousands…The fathers will be telling the children of it, when they are old men, that in the year 1680 there were great days; upon the mountains up and down the west, it was then that I got the real impression of God on my soul'. Another wrote 'My soul has been refreshed to hear the voice and shouting of a king among these field-meetings, wherein the fountain of living waters has been made to run down among the people of God, in such a manner that armies could not have terrified us'.[183]

By this time vast swathes of the south and south-west of Scotland were under the influence of spiritual awakening. It was, in the words of one contemporary historian, 'a day of the power of the gospel, to the conviction and conversion of many souls, which made some to call in question if there had been a greater, since the apostles ceased out of the world, in so short a time and in so little bounds of the earth, as in the south and west of Scotland for some years after the standard of the gospel was publicly set up in the fields'.[184]

---

182. John Howie, 'A Collection of Lectures and Sermons', Edinburgh 1779, quoted in Maurice Grant, *The Lion of the Covenant: The Story of Richard Cameron*, Darlington 1977, p. 319.

183. Grant, *The Lion of the Covenant*, p. 224.

184. Patrick Walker, quoted in Grant, *No King But Christ*, p. 73.

The Glorious Revolution Period 1688–1728

Revolution Settlement

Charles II died in 1685, and his brother, James VII (II of England), succeeded him. Initially his dealings with the Covenanters were more ruthless than even those of his brother. While allowing complete freedom of worship to Catholics, he made attendance at a conventicle a hanging offence. Then, quite suddenly, in 1687, he allowed those of other religious persuasions the same freedom he had granted Catholics. While this brought the 'Killing Times' to a blessed and abrupt end, many Scots continued to distrust their Sovereign. As opposition grew the King fled, while his own Protestant son-in-law, William of Orange, his sights having been set on the throne of Scotland and England for some time, landed on British shores. In April 1689 the crown was offered jointly to William and his wife Mary. Presbyterianism was at once restored to Scotland and ministers previously deposed from their charges were reinstated. Additional measures under the Revolution Settlement in 1690 saw patronage once again abolished and the Westminster Confession of Faith confirmed.

Effusion of the Spirit

James Wodrow, personal friend of many famed Covenanters and later Professor of Divinity at Glasgow University, believed that the Church of Scotland,

> never enjoyed such a plentiful measure of the outpouring of the Spirit as since the Revolution; though the Lord has been pleased to bestow it in a different manner. In former times the gift (of the Spirit) was much more particular, confined, and restricted, to some particular persons here and there; but since the Revolution, I hope, and am persuaded, it is far more diffused, enlarged, and general … in the times of persecution … knowledge did much increase beyond what could have been expected … they had much converse with ministers in their wanderings and sufferings, and with Christians, and afterwards knowledge increased much by the field conventicles, and under the indulgence … at the liberty and Revolution, people had, after a long fast, a great appetite for the gospel; and considering the knowledge that has been since to be met with, and the orderly, regular lives and pleasant deaths of many … the gospel has done much good, and there has been a more plentiful

communication of the Spirit, though more diffusive, and consequently less observable as to particular persons, places, and times,
than even in any of our former times ... there was never such a set
of pious, painful, and diligent ministers that has been in Scotland as
at the liberty and since, and by far more numerous, than ever in any
of our former periods ... on the whole ... we were under a large,
yea larger, effusion of the Spirit than ever since the Reformation.[185]

Perthshire-born Thomas Halyburton, the son of an ejected covenanting minister of the 1660s, was ordained as minister of Ceres, Fife in
1700. A man of constant prayer and deep piety, his autobiographical
writings hold a high place among the great works of spiritual biography.
The conscientious pastor, after visiting between three and four hundred
people in his parish, learned that less than forty of these had not, at one
point or another, been more or less awakened by the Spirit through the
word of God, although in most cases little more came of it. All those
awakened further declared that their awakening came through the field-
preachers in the days of persecution, or since the Revolution. Many
confessed that prior to this new era their hearts were never touched
by the dry sermons of the Episcopal curates. Halyburton also testified that there was not one Presbyterian minister in the parish of Ceres
who, since the Revolution 'the Lord has not honoured to awaken many,
besides their being helped to beget some, through the gospel, to a new
and lively hope'. A number of these found their awakening through
the ministry of Halyburton personally, who was overjoyed that some
'seem to promise more than flowers, even fruits, and further, a general
acknowledgement from most that the word comes near them daily'.[186]

With the abundance of new liberties granted to Presbyterians, rights
they had been fighting for decades, one minister was able to write in
1753 that he had heard

old Christians speak of a remarkable reviving and uncommon power
attending the Word, immediately after the Revolution (1688), in

---

185. Robert Wodrow, *Life of James Wodrow*, Edinburgh 1828, pp. 171-4.

186. Thomas Halyburton, *Memoirs of the Life of the Rev. Thomas Halyburton*, Edinburgh 1847, pp. 189-90. After ten years at Ceres, Halyburton was appointed Professor
of Theology at St Andrews University, where, after a brief term of active professorial
life, he died from the effects of overwork in 1712.

the west and south of Scotland, Fife, Lothian, etc. Particularly, I have heard of a remarkable communion at Stow, near Galashiels, just about the time of the Revolution. The gospel was also attended with wonderful success by the ministrations of some particular ministers; such as Mr John Anderson, and Mr Thomas Forrester, at St Andrews; Mr Gabriel Semple at Jedburgh; Mr John Moncrief at College Kirk, Edinburgh; Mr William Moncrief at Largo; Mr John Flint at Lasswade, etc.[187]

Communion Seasons

More recently it was claimed that between 1688 and 1728, through-out much of Scotland, 'year in, year-out the communion season was a high point in the religious life of the community, and in one parish or another, in any given year, it was well-nigh certain to issue in "an extraordinary stir" among the people'. At a communion gathering in 1698, Elizabeth West reported 'a glorious work', with 'great weeping' and 'travailing of the new birth' among the people.[188] Elizabeth Cairns, in her memoirs, makes clear that communion events around the close of the seventeenth century were times of renewal, vision, illumination and transport. Similarly, Margaret Blackadder speaks of moments of bliss experienced at communions around this time, during which occasions, she wrote: 'I was so much ravished with His love, that I scarce knew where I was.'[189]

Such seasons of spiritual refreshment were not confined to the Low-lands. John Kennedy of Dingwall wrote:

A wave of blessing passed over the parishes bordering on the Cromarty Firth in the generation that arose after Prelacy. The Presbyterian ministers who succeeded the 'curates' were godly men, devoted in a marked way to their Master's service, and of unwearied diligence in instructing the people. At the Revolution in some parishes of Ross-shire many of the people were not far in advance of barbarism. As the 'curates', who turned Presbyterian to keep their places, were removed from the world, their parishes

187. Gillies, *Historical Collections*, pp. 201-2.

188. Schmidt, *Holy Fairs*; p. 45 'year in, year-out…'; p. 47 'a glorious work', with 'great weeping' …

189. ibid., pp. 47-8.

were supplied by men of prayer, who were not satisfied with a mere round of duties, but laboured to win souls, and they were not disappointed. [190]

Ebenezer Erskine of Portmoak, Fife

The Rev. Ebenezer Erskine (1680–1754) – later a founder of the Secession Church – was indebted to his wife, 'the partner of his bosom', for 'having been the instrument in the hand of God' in bringing him 'to the knowledge of the truth'[191] – this a few years after his settlement as minister of Portmoak, Fife, in 1703. From then on there was a marked unction in his preaching. Prayer meetings (superintended by elders) were established in every corner of his parish, for the management of which he drew up a set of rules. The pastor, too, 'abounded in secret prayer'. His Thursday lecture attracted many hearers, and even secular businesses ensured that their employees were given the freedom to attend.[192] Diets of examination, in like manner, also had their crowds of people. Erskine's flock regularly took notes of his sermons and discourses; indeed so common was this practice that Erskine occasionally referred to his congregation as his 'scribes'.[193]

Indeed, as a result of his labours, revival ensued, and from all the country around, as far as sixty miles distant, people flocked to Portmoak, especially at communion seasons. When he assisted at such occasions in neighbouring parishes, too, he was an object of great attraction to the people. One hearer, who travelled twenty miles to hear Erskine, replied to another who complained of drowsiness, 'O man, there is a savour coming out of that pulpit, which I think might help keep any person awake'.[194] After twenty-eight faithful years' service in Portmoak, Erskine was translated to Stirling in 1731.[195]

---

190. Kennedy, *Days of the Fathers*, p. 88, fn. 2.

191. John McKerrow, *History of the Secession Church*, Edinburgh 1839, p. 811.

192. John Ker & Jean L. Watson, *Lives of Ebenezer and Ralph Erskine*, Edinburgh 1882, pp. 67, 65-6.

193. *DSCHT*, p. 299.

194. Kerr & Watson, *Lives of Ebenezer and Ralph Erskine*, pp. 68, 67.

195. Erskine suffered a rapid succession of distressing bereavements in 1713, when, in the short space of three months three of his sons were snatched from him at an early period in life. Ralph, the first who died, was aged just one; Henry, who next departed, was eight, while in less than a fortnight he was followed by Alexander, aged five. The

Thomas Boston of Ettrick

Thomas Boston (1676–1732), a native of Duns, was converted through the ministry of Henry Erskine (father of Ebenezer and Ralph Erskine) at the age of eleven. Ordained in 1699 to Simprin, near Coldstream, he was transferred to the extensive parish of Ettrick, west of Selkirk, in 1707. Having been vacant for four years, immorality raged through the parish, which was additionally troubled with continuing Cameronian influences.[196] The first ten years were sorely trying to Boston, who felt they had been in vain. But gradually, through his diligent ministerial labours and written output, awakening spread throughout the district and beyond. Farmers and shepherds from the neighbourhood of Carnwath and Biggar went every Sabbath to Ettrick Church, which for twenty years became the centre of intellectual and spiritual stimulus to a vast area of countryside, especially during the preaching of his classic text, *The Fourfold State*.[197] Thus, amidst continuing trials – both personal (from 1724 he experienced various health problems, while of his ten children, several died in infancy, and only four survived him), and ecclesiastical (e.g. he refused to sign the Abjuration Oath, and he took an active part in the Marrow Controversy, a hotly-debated doctrinal controversy of that period) – Boston's ministry became so heartily received that it shaped the religious life of the parish for generations. It is noteworthy that whereas at his first dispensation of the Lord's Supper in Ettrick, conducted three years after his induction, only some sixty persons communicated, at his last communion, in 1731, the number of participants was 777.

---

death of his wife in 1720 inflicted still more pain on the beloved pastor (McKerrow, *History of the Secession Church*, p. 812).

196. It was said that every hamlet had its separatist. 'The common talk was all of separation, and of the lawfulness of attending service in the parish church; till Boston, ever eager to get to personal dealing with his people, was like to be wrestled out of breath with them, and almost dreaded his pastoral visiting' (Rev. George H. Morrison, 'Introduction' to *Memoirs of the Life, Time, and Writings of the Reverend and Learned Thomas Boston*, Edinburgh 1776, reprinted 2010).

197. It was not until November 1720 that Boston handled a bound copy of his work, *Human Nature in its Fourfold State*. 'Almost immediately it took a hold', wrote George Morrison over a century later. 'New editions were called for, and testimonies of its usefulness came pouring in. It was discussed in Edinburgh drawing-rooms. The shepherd read it on the hills. It made its way into the Highland crofts, where stained and tattered copies of the earlier editions may still be found. For more than 100 years its influence upon the religious life of Scotland was incalculable' (ibid.).

CHAPTER 2

'The Evangelical Revival' 1729–50

Introduction

The movement known as 'The Evangelical Revival' (generally referred to in America as 'The Great Awakening'), was the first example of a truly trans-Atlantic revival. It had its beginnings in the Pietist movement on continental Europe, the main emphasis of which was an internal and individual return of the soul to the authority of the Bible, to prayer and to piety. The Moravian community that emerged under the leadership of Count Nicholas von Zinzendorf developed largely under pietistic lines, as, too, did the ministry of Theodore Frelinghuysen, a German who studied theology in the Netherlands before moving to America in 1720. He served in several Dutch Reformed churches in New Jersey and many turned to the Lord in a revival that peaked in 1726 and spread elsewhere in the colony.

Pietistic as well as Scottish Calvinist influences helped ignite a revival in the church of Presbyterian minister, Gilbert Tennent in Brunswick, New Jersey in the 1730s. Gilbert had been taught in the 'Log College' set up by his Ulster-born father William Tennent. Two other Tennent sons, John and William, experienced revival in their church in Freehold, Jersey, in 1732. This was followed, two years later, by a deeply influential spiritual awakening in Northampton, Massachusetts, under the leadership of preacher, theologian and missionary to Native Indians, Jonathan Edwards, when over 300 were added to his church by May 1735, following which the revival began to die down. Because of

Edwards's universal esteem as a theologian and preacher, and because he wrote in detail of the movement he helped inaugurate, the Northampton movement has become renowned in eighteenth-century revival history.

Highly influential in the Great Awakening which was emerging in the American Colonies was George Whitefield, who crossed the Atlantic from England no fewer than seven times and itinerated widely. Whitefield was an important link in the trans-Atlantic revival chain, for he also played a significant role in the awakening which developed in England, Wales and Scotland. Wales had been stirred by the itinerant field preaching of Griffith Jones from 1709 and Daniel Rowland was converted at one of his later meetings. Rowland became one of a fresh generation of zealous preachers, along with the likes of Howell Harris and Howell Davis, both of whom experienced dramatic revival in various places they travelled to.

The Evangelical Revival also had a potent effect on Protestantism in England, where, in addition to the labours of Whitefield, the remarkable ministry of John Wesley (1703–91) over five decades had a mammoth impact. In his itinerant travels Wesley covered around 250,000 miles, mostly on horseback, and preached over 40,000 sermons. He also helped form scores of Methodist Societies in his native country between 1739 and 1791.[1] Also greatly effective during this period was the preaching of other outstanding ministers, such as William Grimshaw, John Cennick, William Romaine, Samuel Walker, John Berridge, Henry Venn and many more.[2]

In Scotland the Evangelical Revival occurred during a period of great political instability, just a couple of years prior to the Jacobite Rising of 1745. Meteorological storms of an almost unprecedented ferocity in 1739 resulted in a great many dwellings and outhouses being stripped of their thatch. The storms were followed by a period of intensely cold weather, when the frost was often too severe for peat to be dug and the waters so frozen that wood and coal could not be carried. The failure of essential crops throughout the country and the subsequent decimation

---

1. Regarding Wesley's ministry in Scotland, see page 147.

2. Believing that 'In the 1790s the Evangelical movement in Scotland was far behind the corresponding movement in England', Professor Burleigh makes the controversial claim that the Evangelical Revival north of the border really only began in the early part of the 19th century (J. S. H. Burleigh, *A Church History of Scotland*, London 1960, pp. 309-33).

of thousands of livestock resulted in widespread famine and untold misery, in which several thousand people perished.[3]

Disorder in the natural realm was reflected in the Church. The Patronage Act of 1712, which flagrantly violated the terms of the Treaty of Union of 1707, once again gave landowners the right to appoint ministers. The Act was bitterly opposed by evangelicals, and matters came to a head in 1733 when a band of dissatisfied ministers seceded from ministerial communion and started their own independent meetings. All this took place under the growing impact of the influential movement known as the Enlightenment, by which spirit of enquiry and criticism there gradually arose during the first half of the eighteenth century a number of Scottish University professors and church leaders who avowed theological views that appeared to be inconsistent with the Presbyterian Church government laid out in the Westminster Confession of Faith. By the second half of the century Moderatism had become a distinguishable movement and was dominant in the National Church, leading the way to increased dissension between evangelical and Moderate ministers.

To a considerable extent it was the rapid growth of Praying Societies, small independent groups of believers meeting together in private homes the length and breadth of Scotland throughout the eighteenth century, that kept evangelical religion alive in many districts of the country.[4] These had been popular in many areas from as early as the 1600s, when during the troubled 'Killing Times' the Covenanters advocated the use of such house meetings as a means of strengthening the faith and spiritual resolve of their people. In Ayrshire and other regions which proved particularly fertile ground for the planting of Secession congregations in the 1700s, the pre-existence of Praying Societies was thought to have helped greatly in preparing the soil. The absence of a minister in Cambuslang for a decade and a half prior to William McCulloch settling there in 1731 led to a huge number of praying societies rising up in the parish. As a result

3. S. Mechie, 'The Psychology of the Cambuslang Revival', in *SCHSR*, vol. 10 (1948–50), p. 181; Arthur Fawcett, *The Cambuslang Revival: The Scottish Evangelical Revival of the Eighteenth Century*, Edinburgh 1971, pp. 94-7.

4. e.g., see Donald Mackinnon, *Annals of a Fifeshire Congregation. Being the Story of the Original Associate (Burgher) Church at Kennoway, afterwards the United Original Secession Church at Kennoway, and since 1845 the Free Church at Kennoway – 1800–1945*, Perth 1946, p. 17.

of the revival that spread widely from Cambuslang from 1742, a group of Glasgow ministers commenced a prayer union in order that believers everywhere might earnestly intercede for an extensive outpouring of His Spirit on humanity (see page 128 fn 118). Soon there were forty-five prayer groups in Glasgow and thirty in Edinburgh, for young people alone. A vast number of new praying societies quickly proliferated throughout the country and continued to do so in the decades that followed.

The Momentum Gathers in the Far North

Easter Ross-shire

Revival broke through first in the far north. In the Ross-shire community of Nigg, as in many parishes in Scotland in the early 1700s, the majority of people lived in open and wilful profanation of the Lord's Day, which they devoted to all kinds of outdoor sports. About the year 1724 believers in the district began keeping diets of prayer and fasting. Shortly after, John Balfour, previously minister of Logie Easter and a man of eminent gifts and devoted piety, was appointed minister of Nigg. From around 1729 a gradual quickening 'with stops and intermissions' took place in the spiritual life of the parish.[5] In the populous district of Rosskeen, a neighbouring parish to Nigg, there was 'a pleasant appearance of good' from 1721, four years after the arrival of the Rev. Daniel Bethune (or Beaton – 1717–54), the first Presbyterian minister there since the Restoration. For nine or ten years Bethune saw 'the number of serious persons increasing, love and holiness maintained among them'.[6] From 1732 progress was very much at a standstill, comparatively, until a greater harvest issued in the early 1740s (see page 143). Also in Ross-shire, Walter Ross, minister of Kilmuir Easter, wrote in 1728 of large numbers of people travelling as far as fifty miles to share in the blessings of communion services in Sutherland.[7]

Sutherland

Further north still, Andrew Robertson settled into the parish of Farr in Sutherland in 1728. The population of this extensive district was over 3,000 and Robertson's work was an arduous one. But his heart was in the

---

5. Alexander MacRae, *The Life of Gustavus Aird, A.M., D.D., Creich, Moderator of the Free Church 1888*, Stirling 1908, pp. 4-5; John Gillies, *Historical Collections*, p. 453.

6. ibid., p. 455.

7. James Hutchison, *Weavers, Miners and the Open Book: A History of Kilsyth*, Kilsyth 1986, p. 28.

work; he laboured in season and out, and there arose a general awakening of souls through the parish, especially along the thirty-mile Strathnaver valley. The Presbytery of Tongue could report in 1729 that there were as many as 200 people in Farr who could repeat the whole catechism, with 140 others pretty far advanced.[8] The people were devastated when their minister was later translated to Kiltearn, Ross-shire, especially when a man 'not of the same spirit' became his successor. Some from Farr later travelled to Ross-shire to attend a communion, at which Robertson was assisting. One of the Farr men started sobbing aloud. When entreated to be silent by others in the crowd, he replied, 'How can I be silent, when I see the precious food that was rightfully mine richly dispensed to others, whilst my own soul is starving at home?'[9]

However, despite this short time of moderate incumbency, the strath was again blessed during the 1745 rebellion, when John Porteous of Kilmuir, being threatened by rebels, took refuge in its glens. He lived there for months, preaching the gospel as few could preach it, and during that short period his labours were manifestly blessed in turning sinners to God.[10] It is possible that this is the same movement mentioned in a Free Church Report of 1885, which records that 'Altnaharra in Sutherlandshire, a district of some 360 square miles in area, had a season of spiritual blessing, it appears, about the time of the Erskines'.[11] Soon the Rev. George Munro was settled in Farr, regarding whom one could see 'the eyes of old Christians kindle when they spoke of him, and the fruits of his ministry were great and permanent'.[12]

Secession Movement in Lowland Scotland

Introduction

Further south there were significant stirrings with the rise of the fledgling Secession movement, the first major secession from the Established Church. This denomination came about following a 1731 overture by

---

8. W. R. Mackay, 'Early Evangelical Religion in the Far North: A Kulturkampf', in *SCHSR* vol. 26, p. 124.

9. Angus MacGillivray, *Sketches of Religion and Revivals of Religion in the North Highlands During the Last Century*, Edinburgh 1859, p. 15.

10. ibid., pp. 14-16; Beaton, *Some Noted Ministers of the Northern Highlands*, p. 88.

11. *Free Church Report on the State of Religion and Morals* [hereafter *FCRSRM*], 1885, p. 3.

12. MacGillivray, *Sketches of Religion and Revivals of Religion*, p. 15.

the General Assembly of the Church of Scotland, whereby, as a result of several recent abuses of patronage – ministers whom parishioners did not wish to have thrust upon them – the Assembly sought to establish a greater degree of democracy by giving elders and heritors the right to fill a vacancy in cases where the patron had not exercised his right of appointment. Many evangelicals felt that the resulting Patronage Act of 1732 did not go far enough as it failed to give congregations the right of electing their own ministers. A number of seceding clerics, suspended from performing ministerial duties because of their public opposition to the Act, met at Gairney Bridge, Kinross-shire on 5th December 1733 to form the Associated Presbytery. Formal deposition from the Established Church only came in 1740.

Led by Ebenezer Erskine (see page 88), son of Henry Erskine, a persecuted Covenanter, the group strongly identified with covenanting principles. Indeed, the Covenanting tradition, with its emphasis on Scotland as a covenanted nation in a special relationship with God, resonated with popular piety in the seventeenth and eighteenth centuries. Like the Covenanting movement, the Secession movement was characterised by outdoor conventicles and fierce denouncements of unfaithful ministers, and thus brought the gospel message and the Covenanting tradition together in a powerful way, especially in areas of the country where that earlier tradition had been strongest. William Robertson, the leader of the Moderates in the late eighteenth century, referred to the Covenanting movement as banditry and unworthy of the new age of the Enlightenment. This, noted Kenneth Roxburgh, 'indicates the feeling of alienation that many ordinary Scots felt within the Established Church'.[13]

John Macpherson acknowledged that 'great spiritual quickening' took place throughout the country as a result of the Seceders' success. 'It cannot be doubted that their fervid evangelistic preaching did much to prepare the people for that remarkable period of revival in the years immediately following', he wrote (referring, presumably to the widespread movement known as 'The Cambuslang revival' – see page 104).[14]

---

13. Kenneth B. E. Roxburgh, 'Revival, An Aspect of Scottish Religious Identity', in Robert Pope (Ed.), *Religion and National Identity: Wales and Scotland c. 1700–2000*, Cardiff 2001, p. 205.

14. John Macpherson, *A History of the Church in Scotland From the Earliest Times Down to the Present Day*, Paisley 1901, p. 324.

Yet while the Secession brought a degree of revived spiritual interest to many people, the disputes surrounding it also created considerable unhealthy dissension within congregations. James Robe observed that in his Kilsyth parish the people 'were so bewitched as to incline to the separating side, and were so taken up with disputable things that little concern about these of the greatest importance could be observed among them'. This was easily recognisable, for example, in the fact that in Kilsyth parish all societies for prayer were then given up.[15]

Ayrshire

Ayrshire proved a particularly fertile ground for the development of the Secession, the soil having been steadily prepared by the existence of Praying Societies. Indeed, it was predominantly from Praying Societies that the leaders of the Secession movement obtained its support, and which eventually formed the basis of new congregations. The Society in the neighbourhood of Cumnock was the oldest in the country – having been formed in persecuting times. It met at a quiet spot on the waters of Glenmuir, near Airds Moss, where existed rich memories of those most worthy of Covenanters, Richard Cameron and Alexander Peden. One writer made comparisons to the exiles of Israel, in that, often, the faithful would 'weep by the rivers and streams, as they thought of the desolation of Zion' (the National Church).[16] The Society joined the Secession in 1739, a year before

15. Marilyn J. Westerkamp, *Triumph of the Laity: Scots-Irish Piety and the Great Awakening 1625–1760*, Oxford 1988, p. 130.

16. Hugh M. Agnew, *United Free Church West, Cumnock: Its History, 1773–1923*, Cumnock 1923, pp. 15, 23.

David Smyton became Ayrshire's first Secession minister at Kilmaurs
in November 1740.

Abernethy and Stirling

A communicant at a sacramental occasion in Abernethy in 1735 vividly
depicts events of that solemn and memorable weekend. On the Sabbath,
after the many tables had finally been served, Ralph Erskine (1685–
1752), without any interval, preached on Psalm 119:81. The meeting
concluded around midnight, after which the communicant had supper.
Some time later,

> having risen from private worship, I went out to the yards
> (gardens) of Abernethy on the north side of the town, to secret
> worship, about two in the morning, where I marvelled to hear
> the whole town ringing like a hive of bees, with prayer – the
> like I had never before heard, but my heart was lifted up with it.
> The people were so numerous that I could scarcely find a place,
> even although it was raining. I lay down, however, at the side
> of growing lint, and I really had in my own apprehension some
> liberty and freedom.[17]

Meanwhile, in April 1737, 3,000 communion tokens were made for the
celebration of the sacrament in Stirling. It was estimated that Erskine
drew about one-third of the population of St Ninians and one-half of
that of Stirling, together with a substantial number from other parishes.[18]

Commenting in general on the scenes that attended the commencement of the Secession Church, Ralph Erskine observed,

> All the outward appearances of peoples being affected among us in
> time of preaching may be reduced to two sorts; one is hearing with
> a close silent attention, with gravity and greediness, discovered by
> fixed looks, weeping eyes, joyful or sorrowful-like countenances,
> evidencing tenderness in hearing; another sort, where the word is
> so affecting to the congregation as to make them lift up their voices

---

17. John Kerr and Jean Watson, *The Erskines: Ebenezer and Ralph*, Edinburgh 1880,
p. 156.

18. Andrew T. N. Muirhead, 'A Secession Congregation in its Community: The Stirling Congregation of the Rev. Ebenezer Erskine, 1731–1754', in *SCHCR*, vol. XXII
(1986), pp. 221-2.

and weep aloud; some more depressed, and others more light; and at times the whole multitude in a flood of tears, till their voices be ready to drown out the ministers, so as he can scarcely be heard for the weeping noise which surrounds him.[19]

Kinclaven

John Fisher, another of the original Seceders, laboured faithfully from the time of his ordination at Kinclaven (Presbytery of Dunkeld) in 1725. After the Secession in 1733, his congregation received a considerable accession from nearby parishes such as Little Dunkeld, Redgorton, Moneidy, Caputh, Lethendy, Clunie and Cargill, as well as from Dundee. For communions pilgrims came from even further afield, particularly the west of Scotland, and even from Ireland. Many who thronged to this small parish could not be accommodated by locals, and were obliged to take up their abode, during the evening, in the parish church; and companies occasionally lodged in an adjacent wood called the Hill of Kinclaven. Ralph Erskine, when assisting the Rev. Fisher on one of these occasions, having gone out on a Sabbath morning, heard all around him the sounds of prayer and praise. When he returned to his brethren he stated with an air of anticipation, 'We shall have an excellent day, for the birds are singing very sweetly in the wood'.[20]

Dunfermline

Communion seasons had been important events in Ralph Erskine's parish of Dunfermline from an early point in his ministry there from 1711, but attendance grew significantly with the rise of the Secession movement. 'Dunfermline, on these occasions', wrote the Erskines' biographer, 'was crowded by strangers from all parts of the kingdom, many of whom, to the day of their death, spoke with transport of the enlargement of heart they had there experienced.'[21] The number of worshippers was such that it was impossible to find lodgings for them, and not a few spent the whole night in the churchyard, or on the banks of the adjoining burn, engaging in reverent conversation and prayer. In his diary, Erskine talks about 'having had my heart poured out in prayer'

---

19. John Brown, *Brief Account of a Tour in the Highlands of Perthshire, July 1818*, Edinburgh 1818, pp. 15-16.

20. McKerrow, *History of the Secession Church*, pp. 823-4.

21. Ker & Watson, *The Erskines*, p. 153.

during these sacramental observances. 'I was made to wrestle with Him for His promised presence, for His Spirit and blessing. I sought the presence particularly on this occasion, and that the Spirit might be sent to glorify Christ as the lamb of God in the midst of the throne, expressing my hope.'[22] A communion in the town in 1737 allegedly attracted between four and five thousand communicants, a number that surpassed even Cambuslang and Kilsyth, with tables being served from nine in the morning till about twelve at night. Erskine recorded modestly in his diary: 'The Lord owned the occasion. Ministers were well helped, and many people heartened.'[23]

Edinburgh

In March 1738 the Rev. William Wilson of Perth, another of the original Seceders, baptised ten children at a service on the Braid Hills just south of Edinburgh, some of the attendants having travelled twenty or thirty miles for the meeting. According to *The Caledonian Mercury*, there were about 5,000 hearers at each service (of which there were three in all), besides an 'ungodly audience consisting of many thousands, some of whom set fire to the furze'.[24] Similarly, John Willison of Dundee testified that considerable interest in spiritual things was shown throughout the Lothian region and beyond prior to Whitefield's first visit. He wrote: 'In the year 1740 and afterwards promising tokens began to appear of a revival of Christianity, for in Edinburgh and elsewhere some new praying societies were set up, and sundry students did associate with them.'[25]

Orwell

Ralph Erskine noted that on 'Sabbath, August 6th 1738, I was present at the sacrament in Orwell (near Kinross), where a vast multitude were gathered, and upwards of five thousand persons did communicate. I preached Saturday and Sabbath, on Romans 4:18, "*Who against hope believed in hope*". Ministers were helped, and many were refreshed.'[26] Meanwhile,

---

22. ibid., pp. 153-4.

23. Schmidt, *Holy Fairs: Scotland and the Making of American Revivalism*, p. 49.

24. Kenneth B. E. Roxburgh 'Revival: An Aspect of Scottish Religious Identity', p. 204 in Robert Pope (Ed.), *Religion and National Identity: Wales and Scotland c1700–2000*, Cardiff 2001, p. 217.

25. Couper, *Scottish Revivals*, p. 60.

26. McKerrow, *History of the Secession Church*, p. 840.

under the preaching of David Smyton of Kilmaurs, congregations at Orwell and Abernethy were so moved that the noise threatened to interrupt the services. The commotion was stopped only by the rebuke of Erskine who urged that nothing extravagant or disorderly could be supposed to proceed from divine influence.[27]

Increasingly, people were drawn to attend Secessionist services, whether out of curiosity, dissatisfaction with the lifelessness in their own churches or out of the earnest evangelical spirit they readily witnessed in the Secession assemblies. As a result, the success of this fledgling movement was considerable. It was estimated in 1766, within less than a quarter of a century of their origins, that there were 120 meeting houses and as many as 100,000 members throughout Scotland. Figures would in all probability have continued to steadily increase had it not been for the revival which dramatically arose within the Established Church in 1742, first in Cambuslang, before spreading throughout the land, rallying hesitating ministers and laity alike to remain within the borders of the national Church, which God was still clearly disposed towards and upon which He was still very ready to bestow showers of abundant blessing.

Whitefield in Edinburgh

English Anglican preacher, George Whitefield (1714–70)[28] paid a thirteen-week visit to Scotland in the summer of 1741 – the first of a remarkable fourteen journeys he was to make north of the border. From Edinburgh he conducted several preaching tours, west to Falkirk and Glasgow, north to Perth, Crieff and Aberdeen and south to Galashiels and the Borders. The Rev. James Ogilvie wrote regarding his Aberdeen visit: 'He answered our expectations so much that he has scarce more friends anywhere than here, where at first almost all were against him. The word came with much power ...'[29] Similarly, John Willison of Dundee testified that many were awakened in that city, and seven months later, 'still their numbers are increasing, and prayer meetings

---

27. Couper, *Scottish Revivals*, p. 76.

28. Gloucester-born Whitefield was converted in 1735 after reading *The Life of God in the Soul of Man* by Scottish Puritan and Professor at Aberdeen University, Henry Scougal.

29. Dugald Butler, *John Wesley and George Whitefield in Scotland, or, The Influence of the Oxford Methodists on Scottish Religion*, Edinburgh 1898, p. 33.

setting up so fast in all places of the town, that our difficulty is to get houses to accommodate them'.[30]

But the greatest impact was felt in Edinburgh itself, where, by August, the English evangelist questioned

> if there be not upwards of three hundred in this city seeking after Jesus. Every morning I have a constant levee of wounded souls … At seven in the morning, we have a lecture in the fields, attended not only by the common people, but persons of great rank. I have reason to think several of the latter sort are coming to Jesus … Congregations consist of many thousands. Never did I see so many Bibles, nor people look into them, when I am expounding, with such attention …. I preach twice daily, and expound at private houses at night, and am employed in speaking to souls under distress a great part of the day. [31]

On 24th September, Whitefield wrote: 'On Thursday evening I preached to the children of the city with a congregation of near twenty thousand in the park. It is remarkable that many children are under convictions, and everywhere great power and apparent success attend the word preached.' [32] Again, he recorded: 'The presence of God at the old people's hospital was really wonderful. The weeping of the people was like that in the valley of Hadad-Rimmon. They appear more and more hungry. Every day I hear of some good, wrought by the power of God. I scarcely know how to leave Scotland.' [33] In a letter written to Whitefield in November 1741, a correspondent tells that at the Tollbooth Church there were more than an extra hundred communicants at the most recent sacrament of the Lord's Supper, eighteen of whom were found to have been converted under his personal ministry. [34]

---

30. Duncan Macfarlan, *The Revivals of the Eighteenth Century, particularly at Cambuslang*, Edinburgh 1847, pp. 249-50.

31. 'The Works of the Reverend George Whitefield', quoted in Fawcett, *The Cambuslang Revival*, pp. 101-2.

32. George Whitefield letter, quoted in Harry Sprange, *Kingdom Kids: Children in Revival*, Fearn 1993, pp. 14-15.

33. Macfarlan, *The Revivals of the Eighteenth Century*, p. 257.

34. Kenneth B. E. Roxburgh, 'The Scottish Evangelical Awakening of 1742 and the Religious Societies', in *The Journal of the United Reformed Church History Society*, vol. 5 no. 5, November 1994, p. 272.

An even more prominent work was accomplished in three of Edinburgh's young people's (school) 'hospitals' (so called because both teachers and pupils ate, slept and lived there, the pupils receiving both their education and their maintenance free). Whitefield wrote that the inhabitants of the girls' school were 'exceedingly affected, and so were the standers-by. One of the mistresses told me that she is now awakened in the morning with the voice of prayer and praise'.[35] Heriot's Hospital, previously a 'den of vicious boys', had undergone 'a great reformation' and become 'a Bethel, for there God is worshipped'. Most of the boys, it was noticed, 'seem to be in love with their bibles and to delight in prayer'.[36] 'Through every corner of that large house you may hear little societies worshipping the God and Father of our Lord Jesus Christ, breathing from their souls a warm and holy devotion, till late at night'.[37] A letter written by a 'gentleman of Edinburgh' was printed in Whitefield's periodical, *The Weekly History*, describing 'a most excellent sermon by the evangelist in the city's orphan park, attracting, among others, 'people of the first Rank'.[38] On Whitefield's return to Edinburgh in 1742, he reported: 'The three little boys that were converted when I was last here came to me and wept and prayed with me before our Saviour. A minister tells me scarce one is fallen back that were awakened, both amongst old and young.'[39]

While several praying societies existed in Edinburgh prior to Whitefield's preaching in 1741 and '42, that number increased dramatically following it,[40] being further influenced by the wave of awakening that

---

35. Macfarlan, *The Revivals of the Eighteenth Century*, p. 257.

36. Sprange, *Kingdom Kids*, p. 18.

37. David Walters, *Children Aflame*, South Carolina, 1995, p. 38.

38. Harry S. Stout, 'George Whitefield in Three Countries' in Mark A. Noll, David B. Bebbington and George A. Rawlyk, *Evangelicalism: Comparative Studies of Popular Protestantism in North America, the British Isles, and Beyond, 1700–1990*, New York 1994.

39. Gillies, *Historical Collections*, p. 453. When George Muir, converted at Cambuslang in 1742, went to study in Edinburgh later in the 1740s, he found 'a great number of decidedly religious characters' in the city. Muir moved in such circles and became engaged in the erection and supervision of societies for prayer (*Edinburgh Christian Instructor*, April 1838, pp. 153-5).

40. Thomas Boston was noted for saying that 'in parishes where the gospel begins to thrive, these meetings are set up as naturally as birds draw together in spring' (Roxburgh,

was felt in the nation's capital as a result of the Cambuslang revival (see below), to which several hundred were estimated to have journeyed from the city to personally witness. At its peak the number of praying societies in Edinburgh grew to over thirty, several made up solely of boys and girls. One account mentions two particular societies, of twenty-five and twenty-six members each; one or two others consisted of upwards of thirty members. It was reported that as a consequence of hearing Whitefield preach 'two soldiers, a fiddler and an alehouse-keeper have now joined in a Society for Prayer'.[41] In October 1743, one who attended some of these meetings wrote: 'By all that I could see or hear, I am of the opinion that the success of the gospel, by the outpouring of the Holy Spirit at Edinburgh upon many of the young, and of the inferior sort, hath been extraordinary.'[42]

'The Cambuslang Revival'

The Wark in Cambuslang

Introduction

'The Cambuslang revival',[43] so called, is one of Scotland's most famous evangelical awakenings. Though often associated with George Whitefield, it in fact commenced more than four months before the evangelist's first visit to the district.[44] Its historical setting was amidst considerable turbulence and uncertainty. We have already noted the hardships caused by the failure of crops in 1739–40. Perhaps an even bigger issue facing the inhabitants of the parish of Cambuslang in the early 1740s was that of industrial change. Previously a rural agricultural hamlet, it became a growing centre for weaving in the 1730s, when a number of wealthy

---

'The Scottish Evangelical Awakening of 1742 and the Religious Societies', p. 269).

41. In February 1742 Willison wrote of 'a great increase of praying societies in Edinburgh and other towns and villages' (ibid.).

42. Gillies, *Historical Collections*, p. 453.

43. The term is used here to relate to the overall revival movement that began in Cambuslang and spread in ensuing weeks to other parts of central Scotland and well beyond.

44. One wonders, therefore, why, noting that there were no revivals in Ulster like those at Cambuslang and Kilsyth, Marilyn Westerkamp suggests that in Scotland, 'without Whitefield such revivalism would not have occurred' (Westerkamp, *Triumph of the Laity*, p. 133).

tobacco merchants from Glasgow, just five miles distant, began making substantial investments in such rural industries as the weaving of coarse and fine linens, mining and shoemaking. The change was dramatic, and the cloth industry in Cambuslang employed several dozen households by 1740 and soon involved almost half the inhabitants of the parish.[45]

Problems existed, not only in the parish generally, but also within the parish church. Cambuslang had had a notable connection with evangelical religion under the ten-year period of ministry there of Robert Fleming (author of *The Fulfilling of Scripture*) from 1653 to 1663, but having languished for nearly sixteen years without real supervision, had sunk, on the whole, to a pitiful state when the Rev. William McCulloch (1691–1771) took charge in 1731. It appears that McCulloch inherited a spirit of dissension and extremism on his induction and by 1740 a faction arose between himself and a group of five elders. The issues were complicated and were brought before the Presbytery of Hamilton, which eventually deposed the recalcitrant elders from their office. (After the revival began one of these men, Archibald Fyfe, expressed his dissatisfaction with what he had done and was reinstated as an elder.) Another concern for McCulloch was the growing attraction of Secessionist meetings, to which a number from his congregation were in the habit of travelling some distance to attend.

Precursors of Revival Blessing

Despite these very real concerns, McCulloch was encouraged by reports that came to his notice of revival being experienced in New England under the ministry of men like Jonathan Edwards and George Whitefield, and he took the opportunity to read to his congregation 'missives, attestations and journals' which he had received, outlining

---

45. Ned Landsman, 'Evangelists and their Hearers: Popular Interpretation of Revivalist Preaching in Eighteenth-Century Scotland', in *Journal of British Studies*, vol. 28, 1989, pp. 123-4. Landsman comments: 'The revival at Cambuslang resembled many other evangelical movements of the Anglo-American world in that it arrived at a time of prosperity and change.' Mechie, however, suggests that although improved forms of agriculture and new forms of industry were beginning to burgeon in districts such as Cambuslang, agriculture of a fairly primitive mode remained the main source of income, and the population lay to a great extent at the mercy of the weather. He concludes: 'At the time of the revival there was sufficient knowledge of new economic ways to break the bondage of custom and inspire men with hope of some improvement in their lot, but as yet not nearly enough to make the prospect of economic prosperity a central interest let alone an obsession' (Mechie, *The Psychology of the Cambuslang Revival*, p. 182).

the workings of the Spirit through these men.[46] In this way the minds and hearts of his parishioners were prepared to pray for and expect showers of blessing upon their own barren land. Several pre-sentiments of blessing became apparent prior to the dramatic outbreak of revival in February 1742, to which its origins are popularly dated. As early as 1738, Janet Jackson, a servant at the manse (who, like others in her family, was converted during the time of revival), observed, during a communion season, 'some young people coming to my master about the concerns of their souls, and they seemed to be very deeply impressed'.[47] Another encouraging sign were the societies of prayer, which were only three in number in 1731, but were now increasing (growing to over a dozen by 1742).

In the autumn of 1740 McCulloch recounted the course of awakenings in England and America under George Whitefield and Jonathan Edwards.[48] Throughout the following year he preached almost exclusively on the subject of the 'new birth', while in the autumn of that year Whitefield delivered a series of lectures in Glasgow, several folk from Cambuslang being among those deeply impressed. Two of these, Ingram More and Robert Bowman, a shoemaker and weaver respectively, were converted under Whitefield in the metropolis, and on their return to Cambuslang began organising prayer meetings, also circulating a petition from door to door with the aim of persuading their minister to add a regular Thursday lecture to the ordinary course

---

46. *The Statistical Account of Scotland*, vol. VII, pp. 107-9, quoted in Roxburgh, 'The Scottish Evangelical Awakening of 1742 and the Religious Societies', p. 266.

47. Macfarlan, *The Revivals of the Eighteenth Century*, p. 118.

48. Similarly, the revival that subsequently broke out in Cambuslang – being widely reported by interested parties, not least by Whitefield himself – had a considerable impact on movements in England, America and Germany. The important part played by 'skilful and enthusiastic religious promoters' in retelling these accounts of revival, particularly in printed form, has been the subject of considerable recent examination (e.g. Frank Lambert, *Inventing the Great Awakening*, Princetown, 1999; Harry S. Stout, *The Divine Dramatist; George Whitefield and the Rise of Modern Evangelicalism*, Grand Rapids 1991). In a later study, Stout compared the Scottish '*wark*' to the movements occurring simultaneously in America. But he also noted some striking differences. Extreme bodily emotions, including 'powerful out-of-body visions', were far more common in Scotland, due in part, Stout believed, to environmental factors such as the higher incidence of protracted late-night meetings held there, which more closely approximated 19th century American camp revivals than the more localised town revivals of the 18th century (Stout, *George Whitefield in Three Countries*, pp. 67-8).

of his preaching. McCulloch was only too happy to oblige. Then, in the first statistical account of the parish we get a glimpse of McCulloch preaching in good weather to crowded congregations out-of-doors (the church being both too small and out of repair) for about a year before the revival began. [49]

Outbreak of Revival

The first cases of extreme distress came less than two weeks later, in February 1742, at the weekly lecture (and just after the societies of prayer had held three consecutive evenings of prayer in the manse). Janet Jackson and her two sisters, daughters of a weaver and kirk elder, were taken out of the meeting-house in the middle of the sermon, and were later conversed with by McCulloch in the manse, along with numerous others, for over three hours. This paved the way for the 'day of days', just four days later – and commemorated annually for years afterwards – when, on Thursday, 18th February 1742, 'the church was filled with the sound of weeping … that night the manse was crowded with about fifty "wounded" souls'.[50] The Cambuslang revival had begun, and McCulloch was compelled to institute services on an almost daily basis for over six months. By May over 300 had been awakened, and as many as 9,000-10,000 were turning up for Sabbath services. During public addresses some clapped their hands or broke into cries, but McCulloch did little to restrain such outbursts. He was aware, however, of some 'gross counterfeits who crowded in among the really distressed, and observing and imitating their manner, pretended to be in a like condition'.[51]

One convert from well outwith the parish was George Muir of Haddington. Muir later became a Church of Scotland minister and was

---

49. Fawcett, *The Cambuslang Revival*, pp. 102-5.

50. Couper, *Scottish Revivals*, p. 44.

51. The Rev. Stuart Mechie regards this as possibly being unconscious imitation after intently observing another's behaviour, affecting the observer's motor-centres apart from the will and thence outworking itself through muscular activity. People's physical proximity in a crowd setting makes such unintentional copy-cat behaviour more likely, Mechie believes, for it reduces any sense of independence and individual responsibility, thus diminishing the inhibitions of normal behaviour. A yet more fundamental approach would be to view physical manifestations as products of instinct, particularly of self-preservation, given that many of the symptoms observed are based on attitudes psychologists associate with fear (Mechie, *The Psychology of the Cambuslang Revival*, p. 174).

known for his considerable writings of zealous evangelical content.[52] Claudius Buchanan, unlike Muir, was a native of Cambuslang. He became one of the first chaplains to go out to India and the man who, in 1813, shared with William Wilberforce the honour of getting Parliament to revoke legislation preventing evangelism under British rule in that country. At the time of the Cambuslang revival Alexander Buchanan, Claudius's father, was parish schoolmaster and apparently both Claudius and his future wife, the daughter of an elder in the Cambuslang Kirk, found new life in that spiritual movement.[53]

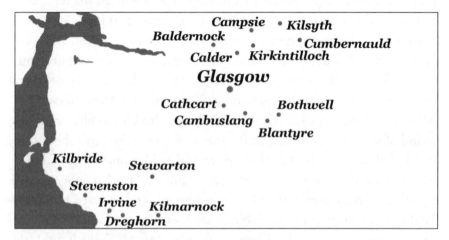

Many ministers from all over the land came to see the work for themselves and reported on the good fruit that was issuing forth. By now the church was seldom empty, and meetings sometimes continued till as late as six in the morning, while the manse, too, was oft-times crowded. By April a lull appeared in the work and McCulloch was about to tell his congregation that he would preach only on Thursdays and Sundays. But that very evening, 'such an extraordinary awakening came among the people that above thirty were convicted'. As a result, daily preaching was continued.[54]

Role played by George Whitefield

George Whitefield, aged just twenty-seven, paid a visit to Cambuslang at the beginning of July. He recorded that on the Tuesday of his arrival, he

52. Nigel M. de S. Cameron (Ed.), *Dictionary of Scottish Church History and Theology*, Edinburgh 1993, p. 610; see page 150.

53. Dallimore, *Whitefield and the Evangelical Revival in Scotland*, p. 23.

54. Fawcett, *The Cambuslang Revival*, p. 112.

preached at two to a vast body of people; again at six in the evening; and afterwards at nine. Such a commotion was surely never heard of, especially about 11 o'clock at night. It far outdid all that ever I saw in America. For about an hour and a half there was such weeping, so many falling into deep distress, and manifesting it in various ways, that description is impossible. The people seemed to be smitten by scores. They were carried off and brought into the house like wounded soldiers taken from a field of battle.[55]

McCulloch preached after Whitefield had finished, concluding after one o'clock in the morning, but even then the people could hardly be got to retire. Throughout the whole of the night the voice of prayer and praise could be heard from the fields.

Whitefield used strong imagery to touch the minds and consciences of his hearers. In one sermon he spoke of 'Toads of Corruption' that were crawling through sinners' hearts, which were also surrounded by 'Legions of Devils'. One woman told how this picture had a powerful impact on her mind after she got home. Out of body experiences were also not uncommon during Whitefield's preaching. One man noted how, on hearing the evangelist, he 'fell into a swoon', with 'a horror of great darkness coming over me'. He then saw a bright light shining around him, and a large scroll of papers which he found to list all the sins he had ever committed.[56]

The following Sabbath had been fixed as Communion weekend. Two tents were set up on the contoured hillside known as the 'braes', where throughout that long day preaching was continued (as it was, simultaneously, in the church and in the schoolhouse) and seventeen tables (1,700 communicants) were served. Between 20,000 and 35,000 people were gathered, and Whitefield witnessed scenes of which he had never before seen the like. 'The motion passed swift as lightening from one end of the audience to the other', he wrote. 'You might have seen thousands bathed

---

55. Mechie, *The Psychology of the Cambuslang Revival*, p. 171. At a later date McCulloch remarked regarding cases of prostration, 'By all that I can observe or hear, there are more of these that were under deep concern here in 1742 that appear still to persevere in a good way ... that never cried out aloud in time of public worship or that were never observably under these bodily agitations than of those that were under such outward commotions and that made the greatest noise' (Couper, *Scottish Revivals*, p. 72).

56. Stout, *George Whitefield in Three Countries*, p. 67.

in tears, some wringing their hands, some almost swooning, and others crying out and mourning over a pierced Saviour.'[57] McCulloch wrote of the occasion: 'The number present at the three tents on Sabbath was so great that, as far as I can hear, none ever saw the like in Scotland since the revolution, or anywhere else on a sacramental occasion. The lowest estimate I hear of with which Mr Whitefield agrees, makes them to have been upwards of thirty thousand.'[58]

One anxious enquirer who came to hear Whitefield preach in Cambuslang was Dugald Buchanan from Strathyre, Perthshire,[59] who had also been moved by hearing the Rev. Halley preach in Muthill a couple of weeks previously. Buchanan wrote of his time in Cambuslang: 'I was greatly comforted by hearing people narrate their religious experiences to one another. On the Sabbath there was a great multitude gathered. Such a sight I never saw. Mr Whitefield lectured from Matthew 19 and there was an uncommon concern among the people.'[60] Buchanan was finally converted two years later and went on to become an eminent teacher under the Society in Scotland for the Propagation of Christian Knowledge (SSPCK), as well as a celebrated Gaelic religious poet.

Unprecedentedly, a further sacrament of the Lord's Supper was arranged for the following month,[61] because, according to Session

---

57. Couper, *Scottish Revivals*, p. 47. Wrote Fitchett of Whitefield's preaching: 'His deep, melodious voice rang over vast crowds as with the vibrations of a great bell. His ardour, the note of passion that ran through his rhetoric, the trembling cadences of his eloquence, the visible tears running down his face, the flame-like zeal which burned in every syllable and gave energy to every gesture – these fairly carried away the Scottish crowds … there are fountains of feeling hidden deep in the rugged Scottish character, depths whose very existence is often unsuspected by their own possessors; and Whitefield somehow could reach these' (W. H. Fitchett, *Wesley and his Century: A Study in Spiritual Forces*, London 1906, p. 242).

58. Rev. A Sinclair, *Reminiscences of the Life and Labours of Dugald Buchanan, with his Spiritual Songs*, Edinburgh 1875, p. 26.

59. Buchanan received his first impressions through contact with a pious Highlander, who asked him his profession. 'I have none', replied Dugald, 'I am a sheet of white paper'. 'Take care', retorted the good man, 'lest the devil write his name on it' (Brown, *Brief Account of a Tour in the Highlands of Perthshire*, p. 8).

60. Sinclair, *Reminiscences of the Life and Labours of Dugald Buchanan*, pp. 25-6.

61. Traditionally among Presbyterians the sacrament was observed just once a year, but the occurrence of revival in a community increasingly led to more frequent observance. For other reasons also, men like John Brown of Haddington additionally argued for more frequent administration of the ordinance. 'If the prejudices of custom are

Minutes, 'many who had a design to have joined in partaking of that ordinance were kept back, through inward discouragements or outward impediments'.[62] At this, a dozen ministers officiated, and between 30,000 and 50,000 people, from all parts of Scotland and even from England and Ireland, gathered.

Fierce Opposition to the Wark

Intense opposition attended the movement throughout and long after its progress, both from within and without the Church. Some, including many Moderates, opposed the 'riot of irrational enthusiasm, whim and fancy', asserting that 'fanatical delusion explained everything'.[63] Yet stronger hostility was issued against the physical phenomena that accompanied the revival, which had never been seen and rarely if ever heard of before. The most strenuous opposition came from leaders of both the Cameronian Church and the larger Secession Church, at whose invitation Whitefield first came to Scotland, and who became deeply embittered when he refused to be bound by the rules they laid down for his conduct. A main offence, they stated, was the emotional manifestations exhibited by some participants. They attacked the conduct of Ingram More, who they claimed was holding his own private conferences, 'stirring up convictions in a great many, and by the lively description of his own feelings (which he was at all times ready to give) wrought up several to an earnest desire of the same pleasant sensations'. After three weeks of such gatherings, opponents claimed, some people began to cry out, saying they now saw hell open for them, and heard the shrieks of the damned, and expressed their agony not only in words, but by 'clapping their hands, beating their breasts, terrible shakings, frequent faintings and convulsions,

---

laid aside, is it any plainer from the Scripture that the Supper should be administered once a year only than it is that a man should pray only once a month?', Brown queried. His biographer additionally notes that sadly, a by-product of these great gatherings sometimes revealed itself in the outer fringes of the vast assemblies. 'All classes were brought promiscuously together, and there was conduct that was not worthy of the object for which they had met, and occasionally led to grave scandal. This grieved the hearts of many, and Burns swept it with the lightening fire of his keen satire, as in "*The Holy Fair*".' (Robert Mackenzie, *John Brown of Haddington*, London 1918 [reprinted 1964], p. 98).

62. Westerkamp, *Triumph of the Laity*, p. 133.

63. Couper, *Scottish Revivals*, p. 71.

the minister often calling out to them not to stifle or smother their convictions, but encourage them'.[64]

Other charges made were that conversion was seen as something immediate and complete – 'they are generally rais'd of a sudden from the deepest agony and grief to the highest joy and assurance' – and that the converted became arrogant fanatics who went round preaching presumptuously and insensitively to everyone they bumped into. The anxious, they observed, would sit at the front of meetings, and they invariably cried throughout the service, during psalms, sermon and prayers. Dishes of water were ready for those who fainted. More was once quoted as exclaiming, 'Lord, dung us with Jesus Christ', while one or two individuals insisted they had seen Christ in bodily form.[65]

There was, no doubt, also considerable jealousy on the part of the Seceders, given the striking popularity of Whitefield in Scotland, and the remarkable success that accompanied his preaching within church groups they considered heretical. The Seceders even appointed a day of fasting and humiliation on account of the reception accorded elsewhere to Whitefield and 'the present awful work upon the bodies and spirits of men going on at Cambuslang'. Adam Gib, an eminent Secession minister in Edinburgh, was so appalled at the Cambuslang spectacle that he was 'like to freeze with horror, impotent of speech'.[66] He wrote a pamphlet, the lengthy title of which alone gave clear revelation of his thoughts:

A Warning Against Countenancing the Ministrations of Mr George Whitefield, published June 6th, 1742 ... Wherein are shewn that Mr Whitefield is no Minister of Jesus Christ; that his Call and Coming to Scotland are Scandalous; that his Practice is Disorderly and Fertile of Disorder; that his Whole Doctrine is, and his Success must be, Diabolical; so that People ought to Avoid Him from Duty to God, to the Church, to Themselves, to Fellow-men, to Posterity, and to Him! [67]

---

64. Westerkamp, *Triumph of the Laity*, p. 131.

65. ibid.

66. William L. Mathieson, *Church and Reform in Scotland*, Glasgow 1916, p. 45.

67. George Macaulay, *Times of Revival, or The Nature, Desirableness and Means of Revival in Religion*, Edinburgh 1858, pp. 17-18. Gib later wrote of his regret at penning this 'warm-blooded' outburst (Fawcett, *The Cambuslang Revival*, p. 189). James Fisher and Ralph Erskine also made vehement attacks on Whitefield and the Cambuslang/Kilsyth revivals (see Richard Owen Roberts, *Whitefield in Print: A Bibliographic Record*

In a bitter *Declaration, Protestation and Testimony,* the Cameronians decried their opponents' unfaithfulness to Scotland's covenanted religion, and described Whitefield as 'a limb of Antichrist' and the revival as 'a delusion of Satan'.[68] But it was the persistent outcries of the Seceders that attracted most attention throughout the land. They found it impossible to believe that the Holy Spirit could be the author of a work that so obviously began and was carried on in Established congregations, which, they believed, had become an apostate Church.[69]

The response from the revivalists was quick and strong. Robe penned four different pamphlets to James Fisher, one of the most vocal of the opposing Seceders. In one he stated that bodily manifestations weren't the direct work of the Holy Spirit but rather, the result of the work of the Spirit. How dare the Seceders presume to limit the activity of God's own Spirit, he challenged. Further, he noted, the Seceders' own sermons were clearly designed to play

---

of Works by, for, and against George Whitefield, Wheaton 1988, pp. 290-2, 308, 339. This substantial and impressive volume provides a comprehensive literary history of the 18th century revival in Britain and America).

68. *Declaration, Protestation and Testimony … against Mr George Whitefield and His Encouragers, and Against the Work at Cambuslang and Other Places,* quoted in Couper, *Scottish Revivals,* pp. 73-4.

69. The Secession Church's own historian, John McKerrow wrote: 'Truth and candour require me to state that the part which the leaders (of the Secession Church) acted on this occasion was by no means creditable to their cause' (Couper, *Scottish Revivals,* p. 77). While some later Secessionists, such as George Cowie (1749–1806), stated their approval of both Whitefield and the Cambuslang work, anti-revival rhetoric continued into the following century, when eminent historian, J. Hill Burton wrote that 'in a southern parish church called Cambuslang, there had arisen one of those strange and melancholy exhibitions called religious revivals, with which, fortunately, Scotland has been but rarely and but casually visited. The "Cambuslang Wark" … exhibited the usual phenomena of such orgies – the profuse fits of weeping and trembling, the endemic epilepsies and faintings, the contortions and howls, with terrible symptoms of contrition emitted by old obdurate sinners awakened with a sudden lightning-flash to all the horrors of their condition. But another and more potent spirit was invoked when Whitefield joined the reverend local leader and his cluster of zealous country divines. The spiritual tempest was worked up to its wildest climax, when, in an encampment of tents on the hillside, Whitefield, at the head of a band of clergy, held, day after day, a festival, which might be called awful, but scarcely solemn' (J. Hill Burton, *The History of Scotland,* vol. VIII, pp. 413-14, quoted in Fawcett, *The Cambuslang Revival,* p. 4). One notes Burton's apparent ignorance of the 'tents', which, rather than constituting an 'encampment', would have consisted of one or two sentry-box type structures, used for sheltering the preachers when out of doors.

on the emotions of their hearers, many of them being replete with frightful references to the devil and to hell. Not only so, but Robe had observed one follower of the Seceders being clearly caught up in religious enthusiasm, emitting with great outcries a string of denunciations of the Cambuslang wark in the guise of divine inspiration. A yet more scathing response, published anonymously by 'a soldier', accused the Seceders of 'envy and malice, because great numbers are drawn from your Communion'.[70]

Opposition came from other sources too. As was to become a common objection to religious revivals, some businessmen complained that devotion to revival meetings, which often ran late into the evening, resulted in absenteeism from work. McCulloch knew there was at times truth in this charge, observing 'numbers of idle boys in Glasgow, apprentices and others, who … came often out to Cambuslang … and they brought much reproach on the work here, by so often leaving their masters work, and strolling idly through the fields'. One who lost her job made no secret of her delight, 'thinking I would have greater liberty to come to the preachings at Cambuslang'. Sir John Clerk of Penicuik wrote to his brother-in-law, blaming Whitefield for inducing men to idleness by 'a gading after conventicles', and estimating the national loss of one day's work in the week at 'eight million of sixpences'.[71] John Napier, aged twenty-one, said that his laird called upon him and a friend, insisting they went to Cambuslang no more, on threat of arresting their crop and turning them out of the land. Whitefield he called 'a Damn'd Rascal who was putting all the people mad, that he put on his black gown to fright people out of their wits'. The two men defied their landlord, and were duly evicted.[72]

Some church leaders were initially sceptical of the revival but later changed their opinions on gaining additional insight. One such was eminent Edinburgh clergyman, Alexander Webster, who, after attending meetings in Cambuslang, jotted in his journal: 'Talk of a precious Christ – ALL seem to breathe after him. Describe his glory, how ravished do many appear! How captivated with his loveliness! – Open the wonders of his grace, and the silent tears drop almost from every eye …

---

70. Westerkamp, *Triumph of the Laity*, pp. 132-3.

71. Fawcett, *The Cambuslang Revival*, pp. 144-5.

72. T. C. Smout, 'Born Again at Cambuslang: New Evidence on Popular Religion and Literacy in Eighteenth-Century Scotland', in *Past and Present*, vol. 97, 1982, pp. 117-18.

These are the visible effects of this extraordinary work.'[73] Webster forth-with became an ardent supporter of the revival.

Results and Analyses

Despite the opposition from all sides, McCulloch focused his attention on the harvest at hand, spending long nights counselling converts and praying with them. He also compiled two large volumes containing the spiritual testimonies of over one hundred individuals,[74] while his colleague James Robe wrote a detailed history of the wider movement. In addition, more than a dozen other ministers wrote shorter accounts of the revival, while scores of pamphlets by clerical and lay participants were published, as well as two religious periodicals, including a weekly paper edited by McCulloch, which ran for a year. All this has led to the Cambuslang revival becoming one of the best-documented of any eighteenth-century awakening and a number of analyses have been provided during the twentieth century of the information presented.

T. C. Smout has undertaken a fascinating analysis of McCulloch's 110 testimonies.[75] He discovered that 75 were women and 35 men. All could read but only a few could write (typical of Scots people of this period). Forty cases, i.e., two-thirds of all those where the occupation was specified, came from the background of small tenants or low status craftsmen, 13 were from more humble backgrounds, and approximately one-ninth were from the 'middle class'. All of the 110 without exception were already in the habit of attending church with some regularity. Seventy had been taught to pray 'in secret' when they were children and many were already seeking after a more rewarding religious life at the time of the revival, some having recently joined a local praying society. A fifth of the cases were aged between thirteen and nineteen, and nearly three quarters were less than thirty years of age. The average age of the converts was 24.9 for women and 27.9 for men. The marital status of most male converts is unknown. Where it is known, half were unmar-ried, while three quarters of females were also unmarried.[76]

---

73. Stout, *George Whitefield in Three Countries*, p. 66.

74. A number of these are included in Macfarlan's *The Revivals of the Eighteenth Century.*

75. Many of these observations were first made by Ian A. Muirhead, 'The Revival as a Dimension of Scottish Church History', in *SCHSR*, vol. 20, 1980.

76. Smout, 'Born Again at Cambuslang', pp. 114-21.

Meanwhile, Ned Landsman's studies uncover a number of interesting findings. He ascertained that while most who fell under spiritual concern did so in response to the preaching of McCulloch or another minister, the majority accorded the clergy little influence thereafter. Influenced by Galbraith, a layman in the congregation who played a far bigger role in subsequent conversions than did McCulloch, they were instead guided by external signs such as inner voices, visions and premonitions. Such providences were not new to Scottish Presbyterians. What was new was their application to the question of individual salvation rather than to national and clerical causes. This aspect in fact became a focal point of the Seceders' attack on the awakening.[77]

Though McCulloch spent many months preaching the terrors of hell to his congregation, the Cambuslang converts declared with near unanimity that the fear of damnation played little part in their conversions. (Yet in the margins of testimonies denying influence by a dread of hell, we find the surprising spectacle of clerical editors arguing just as strenuously that there was indeed such influence!). There were, however, a few contrasting cases, where the fear of hell led to such personal torment that the anxious actually contemplated suicide.[78]

Ministers emphasised the dishonour done to God by lives of sin. Converts, however, seemed more concerned with matters of status – the loss of honour before men and women. More important still was the feeling of unworthiness – a word that appears repeatedly in the narratives. Additionally, they were less concerned with the fate of the revival than with their own responsibility for causing it harm.[79]

According to Landsman, converts hardly ever referred in their accounts either to doctrinal matters or to meetings with the minister. They focused instead on their subjective feelings. As an example of converts' quest for experience, Landsman stated that while ministers emphasised that full assurance could only be achieved in the afterlife, their converts invariably sought such certainty in the here and now.[80]

Landsman observed that artisanal groups, most notably weavers, had a very marked effect on the popular culture of western Scotland. 'They

---

77. Landsman, *Evangelists and their Hearers*, pp. 130-6.

78. ibid., pp. 137-8.

79. ibid., pp. 139-41.

80. ibid., pp. 142-3.

helped develop a greater awareness of the existence and affairs of allied religious parties throughout the transatlantic world ... only after Ingram More and his associates organised lay prayer groups (in Cambuslang) and began their instructional program, offering the prospects of certainty, emotional release and religious community in this world did the revival begin to take hold'. This latter aspect, and the tradition of the Psalms, had been important also to the Seceders, and it is interesting to note that the Seceders retained the support of some of the most influential of the long-standing Presbyterian families in the Cambuslang district.[81]

Landsman also found that the Psalms featured prominently in many conversion accounts. A number of converts testified that they came under the Spirit's conviction during the singing of these biblical songs. Such Scriptures 'provided at once an identification with the Presbyterian traditions of their ancestors and with the new and more selective religiosity developing within the artisanal community ... Among the most vivid images provided in the Cambuslang narrative is that of young servant girls who dominated the revival, the lone spinners singing their psalms as they spun at their wheels'.[82]

The Cambuslang 'wark' continued for six months, though few conversions were recorded after August 1742. However, the results were felt for a long time, and in 1751 McCulloch claimed that around 400 converts from the movement were either still steadfast in their faith or had remained so until death.[83] It may be added that Dr Robertson, who was inducted as minister of Cambuslang towards the close of the century, when some of the converts of the revival were still alive, confirmed from his own knowledge the favourable impression of the 1751 attestation.[84] Dr John Erskine attested in the year the revival took place that notwithstanding the thousands of people who may have

---

81. ibid., pp. 144-7.

82. ibid., p. 148.

83. Sinclair, *Reminiscences of the Life and Labours of Dugald Buchanan*, pp. 25-6. cf. Gillies, *Historical Collections*, pp. 433-5. An elder's attestation, also of 1751, stated that the number would have been greater than 400 had they included figures from Ayrshire and Renfrewshire, 'where we know very many of the subjects of the late awakening live, and of whom doubtless many are walking in the fear of the Lord' (Mechie, *The Psychology of the Cambuslang Revival*, p. 172).

84. Mechie, *The Psychology of the Cambuslang Revival*, pp. 172-3. Indeed, it has been claimed that a new church (Congregational) formed in Cambuslang as late as 1800

attended meetings at Cambuslang, yet among whom no visible effects were perceived ('though many good effects might have been produced which were neither observed nor related at the time'), there existed 'four hundred individuals who to the conviction of those who knew them, became better men, men more useful in their practical duties than they ever were before, and who preserve this character while they live; thus exhibiting a view of the religion of Cambuslang and Kilsyth which a wise man will not easily bring himself to reprobate, and which no good man, if he candidly examines the facts, and believes them, will allow himself to despise'.[85]

Cambuslang Environs

The Rev. John Hamilton testified that in less than two months after the commencement of the work there were few parishes within twelve miles of Cambuslang where some were not awakened 'to a deep, piercing sense of sin'. Indeed, including many from a greater distance still, the number awakened by that time was thought to have been over 2,000. The ministers of East Kilbride, Blantyre, Bothwell and Cathcart – each parish, like Cambuslang itself, being located in the Presbytery of Hamilton – all helped in the work directly. In these places, as well as in Old Monkland – where there was no settled minister, but where two elders in particular took an interest in the work – numbers showed deep concern about their salvation, many also paying a visit to Cambuslang to obtain spiritual nourishment for their hungry souls.[86]

The Rev. William Hamilton of Bothwell wrote of the work of grace which extended to his parish, occasioned by the visit of many young

---

was an indirect result of the revival sixty years previously (McNaughton, *Early Congregational Independency in Lowland Scotland*, vol. 2, Glasgow 2007, p. 125).

85. Quoted by Robert Buchan, in 'Introductory Essay' to Rev. James Robe, *Where the Wind Blows*, Belfast 1985, p. 28. So remarkable did a youthful John Erskine consider the revival to be that he concluded that Scotland was on the verge of the 'latter day Millennial glory' (quoted in Roxburgh, 'The Scottish Evangelical Awakening of 1742 and the Religious Societies', p. 272). Yet it has to be said that despite the huge popularity of the revivals of this period, the movement failed to garner support within the General Assembly of the National Church, which included many Moderate clergymen. Thus revivalism in both parish and non-conformist churches in mid-eighteenth century Scotland took place predominantly outside of the establishment.

86. Bill Niven, *East Kilbride Old Parish Church: A History of the Christian Faith in East Kilbride*, East Kilbride 2002, p. 25; Couper, *Scottish Revivals*, p. 62.

folk making the journey to Cambuslang, where they were awakened to their souls' dark condition. These were solicitous in bringing friends and neighbours to an acquaintance with Christ, and so was begun, noted Hamilton, 'a more than ordinary seriousness among a goodly number in several corners of this congregation; more conscience is made of family worship in several families ... as likewise there are some new societies for prayer and Christian conference set up ... wherein several persons, besides those awakened at Cambuslang, have joined'. [87]

Kilsyth

A similar movement commenced in Kilsyth three months after that in Cambuslang, under the attentive ministry of the scholarly James Robe (1688–1753). Kilsyth was the birthplace of John Livingstone, famed for his association with the Kirk o' Shotts revival in 1630. It was in this parish also that, on 15th August 1645, Montrose inflicted the heaviest defeat ever sustained by the Covenanters, when 6,000 were killed in pitiless pursuit. A local historian pertinently noted that, given that Kilsyth was of all the parishes in Scotland most heavily drenched with Covenanting blood, there is a certain spiritual propriety that it should also have been the scene of the 'richest outpouring of the heavenly Grace'.[88]

Robe had laboured in the district for almost thirty years, and praying societies were set up in early 1722. Since that time, however, a series of calamities had hit the parish, including a marked increase in theft and other immoralities, such as fornication, and 'a severe fever' in 1732, which led to over sixty burials in three weeks, including, to Robe's despair, 'the most religious and judicious Christians' in his fellowship. This was followed shortly after, in the summer of 1733, by a major storm, which caused great loss; then, in 1740 there was a famine. The minister noted anxiously that each visitation, rather than startling his parishioners into wakefulness, left them further removed from religious interests, while even 'the return of plenty had no better influence upon us – we were going on frowardly in the way of our own hearts'.[89] The praying societies had long ceased to exist.

---

87. Macfarlan, *The Revivals of the Eighteenth Century*, pp. 218-19.

88. P. Anton, *Kilsyth – A Parish History*, quoted in Fawcett, *The Cambuslang Revival*, pp. 125-6.

89. Couper, *Scottish Revivals*, p. 52.

Deeply disappointed, but never without hope, Robe delivered a series of discourses on regeneration to his congregation during 1740–41. He saw little direct fruit from this, nor did many from Kilsyth journey to Cambuslang when reports of the revival there came through. By April 1742, however, there were premonitory signs of awakening in his church following a sermon preached by the Rev. John Willison of Dundee on his way home from Cambuslang. Praying societies were re-instated; among them being a spontaneous meeting of young girls aged between ten and sixteen who met in an out-house.[90]

Then, on Sunday, 16th May, shortly after Robe returned from one of his numerous visits to Cambuslang, 'an extraordinary power of the Spirit from on high accompanied the Word preached. There was a great mourning in the congregation as for an only son ... above 27 were under visible concern for their salvation', including members of Robe's own family. The anxious were sent to Robe's barn for counselling, but this proved too small, so they returned to the church, where Robe interviewed them 'in my closet, one by one'.[91] The Kilsyth revival had truly begun.

The work grew rapidly and neighbouring ministers gladly came to Robe's assistance, while in June, George Whitefield preached twice in Kilsyth to a crowd numbering around 10,000. Soon Robe estimated that 200 of his parishioners plus a further hundred visitors had been awakened – all within a month of the work commencing. Throughout the summer months the track between Kilsyth and Cambuslang became well worn by the comings and goings of awakened souls. During the busy harvest season, Robe made enquiries with some farmers in the parish, asking whether the many revival meetings being held or the spiritual distress among some had resulted in work being neglected or poorly done. They replied in the negative, saying also they had heard the poorest folk say that their work went better on than ordinary, and they had not found any lack. They claimed also that their hay crops, a mainstay to many in the parish, was harvested in two-thirds of the usual time, and this they attributed to the singular goodness of God.[92]

---

90. Brian Edwards suggests, incorrectly it seems, that the children began meeting to pray two years prior to the start of the revival (Edwards, *Revival: A People Saturated With God*, p. 166).

91. Fawcett, *The Cambuslang Revival*, p. 129.

92. Couper, *Scottish Revivals*, pp. 54-5.

A communion was held in July and a further sacrament in October, when open-air services on the Lord's Day lasted from half-past eight in the morning till the same time at night. Robe invited eleven ministers from all over the wider region to assist him; others came to help of their own accord. Together they conducted twenty-two separate communion services, each consisting of about seventy people. Sunday evening, all day Monday, and Tuesday morning were all filled with preaching. While numbers awakened and publicity attracted by the Kilsyth revival may have been less than in the Lanarkshire movement, the work continued considerably longer. The communion in July 1743 was considered to be to such 'extraordinary satisfaction' of those that attended that another was arranged for the very next month, when 'there was a rekindling of the old flame'. There appeared again a discernible concern among the people, and numbers were awakened, including, as on previous communion sacraments held in Kilsyth, some from parishes many miles distant. Over 1,600 received communion, more than that of the corresponding celebration of the preceding year. Clearly the work was being wonderfully kept up; indeed by the end of the year Robe could still note that 'the Lord is yet remarkably among us'.[93]

After a period of around eight years, in 1751, Robe was able to offer a mixed report. The general community had again fallen into ways of dissipation and irreligion to such an extent that certain sins abounded 'more than ever I knew in this place, unless it was at the time of my first coming to it'.[94] Despite this, a list of over a hundred persons brought mainly under spiritual concern between 1742 and '43 showed that they all lived consistently righteous lives: as had the four or five on the list who had since passed away. Forty years later, in 1793, the parish minister of the day declared, 'There are persons yet alive who have proved by the uniform tenor of their lives' that they had been true to the profession they made half a century earlier.[95]

---

93. ibid., pp. 157-8; see also Robe, *Where the Wind Blows*, pp. 38-49; Fawcett, *The Cambuslang Revival*, pp. 124-32; MacMillan, *Restoration in the Church*, pp. 23-34.

94. Couper, *Scottish Revivals*, p. 59.

95. ibid. Fawcett provides evidence of considerable connection between the Cambuslang and Kilsyth 'warks' and revival in various parts of Holland a year or two later. For example, James Robe's account of the Scottish revival was quickly translated into Dutch, and went through six editions (Fawcett, *The Cambuslang Revival*, pp. 138-42). For discussion of the effect of the Evangelical Revival in Scotland on the '*Reveil*' in the

Kilsyth environs

Calder

Other than in Denny and Larbert, where a good work was done, the revival was little felt in the parishes to the east of Kilsyth. Instead, the movement quickly took a westward direction. Revival broke out unexpectedly in Calder, stretching alongside the north side of Barony parish, on 11th May 1742 when neither people nor preacher were prepared for it. The minister, the Rev. Warden (a relation, probably a cousin, of the minister of neighbouring Campsie) was accustomed to give an occasional lecture in Auchenloch, a small village in a distant part of the parish, but attendance had dwindled away to the point that he was almost on the point of discontinuing it. Intimating one week that it was hardly worth giving notice of the meeting as so few people seemed to care about it, the people, pricked to the heart, turned out in numbers the following week! Warden, arriving with low expectations, was amazed to see so many, and admitted to feeling somewhat dismayed, as, for the first time, he had not prepared a message! Retiring to a wood to pray, he was given the words, *'Unto you, O men, I call; and my voice is to the sons of men'* (Proverbs 8:4). From this text he opened up the fullness, the freeness, the grace of the gospel proclamation. The audience was melted under the word spoken as the Holy Spirit accompanied it with power. There was much outcrying, and around fourteen were on that day brought under great concern about the state of their soul. Thus began a deep movement in the parish, which in time saw over one hundred awakened to the truths of the gospel, and numbers hopefully converted.[96]

Baldernock

Although Baldernock had been without a regular pastor for some years, by July 1742 about ninety had been 'brought under the quickening influence of the Spirit of Promise' there.[97] This came about primarily

---

Netherlands during the following century see Professor Johannes Van Den Berg, 'The Evangelical Revival in Scotland and the Nineteenth-Century "Reveil" in the Netherlands', in *SCHSR* vol. 25 (1995), pp. 309-37. On a yet wider scale Arnold Dallimore spoke of 1742 as being 'indeed the year of jubilee; a time ... of pentecostal refreshment which was to carry the Church (of Scotland) forward with a strength which was to touch the ends of the earth' (Dallimore, *Whitefield and the Evangelical Revival in Scotland*, p. 20).

96. Macfarlan, *The Revivals of the Eighteenth Century*, pp. 230-1.
97. ibid., p. 36.

through the diligent ministrations of the parochial school-master, James Forsyth. From as early as February 1742 he had frequently exhorted the children under his charge, explaining to them the first principles of the Christian faith, the urgency of the need to turn from sin, imploring them to put their faith in Christ. This he did on an almost daily basis, and after a time an impression began to make itself felt on their young hearts. One lad went to Cambuslang and on his return began to meet with a few others for prayer and psalm-singing in the school-room. Within fourteen days around ten boys – between eight and twelve years old – had been awakened. They met as often as three times a day, morning, noon and evening, and were known to their school companions by their walk and conversation, and even by their general appearance. Other children were influenced, and 'they became remarkable for tenderness of conscience. A word of terror occurring in their lessons would sometimes make them cry out and weep bitterly'.[98] The children in turn made an impression on the adult population. Some went to Cambuslang and returned with the grace of God in their hearts. Others were converted at Calder and Kirkintilloch, but the greater number, Forsyth stated, were awakened at the private (twice-weekly) meetings for prayer held in the parish.[99]

Campsie

Minister of Campsie parish, to the north of Kirkintilloch, since 1732, the Rev. John Warden was a relative (probably a cousin) of the minister of Calder and a son of the minister of Gargunnock.[100] Robe spoke of him as a man of 'singular dexterity in instructing and dealing with the consciences of the people under his charge'.[101] Being adjacent to Kilsyth, some of the first awakened there belonged to Campsie, and the work went on to a greater or less extent in both parishes simultaneously. There were around a hundred anxious souls in Campsie before the end of August 1742. Attendance at the annual communion that year was double the usual number. At one of the services, an evening lecture was delivered by the Rev. Burnside of Kirkintilloch, on whom, in his opening prayer, and unusually for him, tears were seen running down his cheeks. Soon after he began to preach,

---

98. ibid., p. 38.

99. Gillies, *Historical Collections*, p. 446.

100. He later became minister of the Canongate in Edinburgh and is known as being the able and judicious author of a work entitled *The System of Revealed Religion*.

101. Macfarlan, *The Revivals of the Eighteenth Century*, p. 241.

'The Spirit of the Lord, like a mighty, rushing wind, filled the house in such a manner that almost the whole congregation was melted into a flood of tears, accompanied with bitter outcries on the part of some newly awakened'. The minister was obliged to stop; and, after a few exhortations, ended the lecture and left behind him a multitude of distressed souls, 'thirsting for a soul-satisfying discovery of the dear Redeemer'.[102]

John McLaurin spoke of the memorable service in this way:

> Of all the days of power, I never saw the like, considering the size of the meeting. The dear Redeemer, by the influence of the Holy Spirit, went from corner to corner, which was evidenced not so much in outcries, as in a sweet mourning and low motion. The last was truly the great day of feast. When the bulk of the meeting was dispersed, they came out of the churchyard like a company or two of soldiers, in three and four abreast, supporting the distressed men and women. The state of the parish before the Communion was eighty under soul distress, who had by this time found relief; but now the numbers are far advanced.[103]

A few more were converted over the following year, and there remained 'a fond desire after ordinances and a singular attention in hearing'.[104] When the minister left the parish in 1747, he knew of only four who had been false to their profession. Of the many others, the parish minister said, 'I could not but entertain the highest opinion and the greatest hopes … In a word, their devotion is exemplary'.[105]

Kirkintilloch

The first sign of spiritual reviving in the parish of Kirkintilloch was among the children. In April 1742, about sixteen of them began to meet in a barn for prayer, unknown for a time to their minister, the Rev. James Burnside. When he got wind of it he met with them a number of times, and they continued to improve. This becoming more widely known, the concern for spiritual things spread. Definite quickening was evident from as early as May 1742. The Reverends McLaurin of Glasgow and Robe of Kilsyth

---

102. ibid., p. 235.

103. H. N. Johnson, *Stories of Great Revivals*, London 1906, p. 156.

104. Couper, *Scottish Revivals*, p. 64.

105. Fawcett, *The Cambuslang Revival*, p. 171.

preached in Kirkintilloch on the Fast Day previous to the dispensation of the Lord's Supper. Burnside, minister of the parish, preached in the evening. The work of conviction that day was general and powerful. In the words of Robe, 'There we saw Zion's mighty King appearing in His glory and majesty, and His arrows were sharp in the heart of His enemies'.[106] Many were awakened and brought under spiritual distress. Shortly after, 120 were reported to have been under a 'more than ordinary' concern about their salvation, including many 'praying young'.[107] Burnside died in the autumn of 1743, but two months prior to this the elders attested in a statement that a goodly number of those awakened persevered in seeking God, and generally met once a week in praying societies. Dr Erskine, who succeeded Burnside as minister of Kirkintilloch in May 1744, further testified at some length to the lasting work procured by the revival in his parish.[108]

Cumbernauld

Further east, the parish of Cumbernauld also shared in the blessing that came to Kilsyth. Here, around fourteen were awakened under the preaching of Whitefield. Soon came news that the concern among the people there 'hath continued public and discernible' all the winter of 1742–3; there being people newly awakened from time to time. However, 'great opposition' was said to have arisen against the Lord's work in that congregation by the Seceders, including 'persecution, as far as mocking and the tongue can go', as there existed also in the east end of Kilsyth parish. The first time the Seceders preached at Cumbernauld, which was in February 1742, there was 'a greater stir and more sensible outcry' in the congregation of the parish church than had been for some considerable time before. The next Sabbath day, when the Seceders again preached in the district, there was a lad who went into the place of their meeting, cast his eye towards the parish kirk, and was immediately impressed with the thought, What reason can I give for forsaking the minister and following these folk? He was so troubled by this thought that he left the Seceders' meeting and went straight to the Established Church, where he was awakened and brought to a deep concern about his sinful and lost state. When later brought before the

---

106. Macfarlan, *The Revivals of the Eighteenth Century*, pp. 233-4.

107. Couper, *Scottish Revivals*, p. 65.

108. Macfarlan, *The Revivals of the Eighteenth Century*, p. 234.

seceding preacher, he was advised 'to mind and apply himself to his work'. A judicious Christian in the district noted that this was also the direction Cain took, by going to build cities rather than attending to more urgent matters – thus bringing the wrath of the Seceders upon him for imbibing such a thought. In the spring of 1743 Robe noted that spiritual concern was still in evidence among the Cumbernauld congregation, and new cases of awakening were occurring from time to time.[109]

Glasgow

That the movement was not solely restricted to country parishes and small towns is evidenced by the effect the revival had on Scotland's largest city, as well as in other principal centres, such as Dundee.[110] Whitefield first visited Glasgow in 1741 and returned there on nearly all his subsequent travels to the northern country. Being close to Cambuslang, the city came early under the influence of the awakening in that community. The Reverends John McLaurin of Ramshorn,[111] John Gillies of College Kirk (only inducted in 1742) and John Hamilton of the Barony Church (inducted 1737) all sought to extend the revival throughout the city. (Two other keen supporters, though less prominently, were John Anderson of the Tron Church and Michael Potter, Professor of Divinity at Glasgow University.) These men 'energetically fostered the influence produced by Whitefield's preaching', and in the city and neighbourhood many hundreds of people passed from death unto life, giving evidence of genuine conversion. Some had been awakened at Cambuslang, and these became revivalists in their

---

109. Robe, *Where the Wind Blows*, pp. 194-5.

110. Callum Brown suggests that prior to the 1859–61 awakening urban revivals on the scale of rural movements were unknown. Although Whitefield enjoyed considerable success in his Glasgow meetings, there was no organisational structure in place to promote them. On the contrary, his preference for rural missions is observable by the abandonment of his Glasgow preaching in 1742 to assist in the Cambuslang revival (Brown, *Religion and the Development of an Urban Society*, vol. 1, 1981, p. 419).

111. John McLaurin was the son of an Argyllshire minister who was distinguished in his day for being one of the translators of the Psalms into Gaelic. While his brother, Colin, became an eminent mathematician, John excelled as a preacher, pastor and theologian. Like William McCulloch and John Gillies (McLaurin's son-in-law), McLaurin's interest in revival extended to frequent and direct correspondence with leading revivalists in the American colonies (such as Jonathan Edwards), as well as in other parts of Scotland. Thus he was kept informed, and he was even in the habit of meeting weekly with interested parties in Glasgow to receive and communicate revival intelligence.

homes and among their friends. A schoolboy took the glad tidings to his heart at Cambuslang, and returning to the city, got his teacher to allow him to hold daily prayer meetings with some of his classmates, and in a week or two about twelve lads, from eight to thirteen years old, gave themselves to Christ.[112] Another story relates to 'two cynical and headstrong young women' who 'went to Cambuslang and returned to the city (Glasgow) unaffected, laughing at the idea of any one weeping at a revival meeting. Curiosity led them to attend another service; they were entirely broken down and in deep distress until they found relief at the Cross'.[113]

The Barony parish, of which John Hamilton was minister, covered a vast area north of the River Clyde, most of which is now contained within the city of Glasgow, but in the mid 1700s was predominantly rural, studded with a number of villages. In September 1742 Hamilton wrote: 'My parish has had some share in this good work. There have been above a hundred new communicants among us this summer who never did partake of the blessed sacrament before, which is five times as many as ever I admitted in any former year; most of them were awakened at Cambuslang, some of them in their own church.' This accession to church membership appears to have been general over the city – for an overall total of eighteen more communion tables were required at an October 1743 sacrament held in Glasgow (an increase of 1,200 communicants).[114] Indeed, in this city, with a population of 17,034 in 1740, the number of communicants admitted to the Lord's Table after careful presbyterial examination, rose from 3,600 to 4,800 as a result of the revival.[115] In addition, noted Macfarlane, given the population of Glasgow at the time, and the number of communicants in the Established Church alone (4,800), 'there could scarcely be fewer than one communicant for every three of the population, including persons of all ages'.[116]

Though very aware of the good done in Glasgow in the preceding decade, John Gillies remarked in 1751, 'There was but little revival here, comparatively speaking, when the Lord was watering His vineyard round about us'. But in this same year (1751), the interest usually excited on

112. Johnson, *Stories of Great Revivals*, p. 155.

113. ibid.

114. Couper, *Scottish Revivals*, pp. 61-2.

115. Dallimore, *Whitefield and the Evangelical Revival in Scotland*, p. 14.

116. Macfarlan, *The Revivals of the Eighteenth Century*, p. 229.

Whitefield's arrival had by no means abated on his return, and the evangelist wrote that he preached to 'nearly ten thousand souls every day. The parting at Glasgow was very sorrowful indeed. Numbers set out from the country to hear the word by three or four in the morning'.[117] In 1751, also, a statement was drawn up and signed by twenty-five members of the general session which testified that the fruits of the revival in Glasgow had continued over ensuing years, with the number of backsliders 'comparatively small'. McLaurin, one of the twenty-five, stated additionally that even if estimates of conversions had been exaggerated, the movement still surpassed anything he had known in twenty-eight years as a minister in Glasgow; the period of revival appearing to him 'the most extraordinary I ever saw as to evidences of the success of the gospel'.[118]

Ayrshire and the South

Several parishes in the extensive Presbytery of Paisley, which covered most of Renfrewshire, from the Presbytery of Irvine to the River Clyde, shared to a greater or lesser extent in the labours of Whitefield and the revival at Cambuslang. In Ayrshire itself, it was estimated that around 200 people journeyed from Kilmarnock, and one hundred from each of Irvine and Stewarton, to the second communion at Cambuslang. These parishes were

---

117. Butler, *John Wesley and George Whitefield in Scotland*, p. 49.

118. Macfarlan, *The Revivals of the Eighteenth Century*, pp. 228-9. McLaurin was acknowledged by his friends as being 'the chief contriver and promoter' of the Prayer Union. In January 1743 a number of prayer societies published their intention of holding a day of thanksgiving for the 'Outpourings of the Spirit from on high on several Corners of this wither'd Church', with petitions to God 'that he would carry on this good and unexpected Work ... that all Opposers ... may be at last obliged to own that it is the Doing of the Lord'. Twenty months later, in October 1744, McLaurin and other evangelical ministers in Scotland formed a union of prayer for the purpose of 'united extraordinary supplications to the God of all grace ... earnestly praying to him that he would appear in his glory, and favour Zion, and manifest his compassion to the world of mankind, by an abundant effusion of his Holy Spirit on all the churches and the whole habitable earth ...'. Part of Saturday evening, Sunday morning and the first Tuesday of every quarter were to be given over to this pursuit. The concert of prayer was endorsed by church leaders throughout Britain and North America, and in 1746 it was renewed for another seven years. Jonathan Edwards's church took the prayer call very much to heart, and in 1747 the American pastor wrote at length on the topic in book form. This *Humble Attempt to Promote Explicit Agreement and Visible Union of God's People in Extraordinary Prayer* was itself revived by Scottish Church leaders several decades later, prior to the Second Evangelical Awakening – see page 170 (Davies, *'I Will Pour Out My Spirit'*, p. 124; Iain H. Murray *Jonathan Edwards: A New Biography*, Edinburgh 1987, pp. 292-5).

in turn affected by the revival, and Whitefield preached repeatedly in all three places in August 1742. Prior to this, in June of the same year, the parish minister of Irvine, the Rev. William McKnight (a native of Lisburn, Ulster) had written to Whitefield, informing him of the 'awakenings among us at Irvine, not only of those who have been at Cambuslang, but several others are lately brought into great concern about their eternal state, and among them several children'.[119] Such promising tokens were probably what induced the English evangelist to include the town in his Ayrshire itinerary. Over the course of just five days, Whitefield preached five times in Irvine, four times in each of Kilbride, Kilmarnock and Stewarton and once in Stevenston (to which small town revival also spread[120]). He wrote: 'I never preached with so much apparent success before. The work seems to spread more and more … At Irvine, Kilbride, Kilmarnock, and Stewarton the concern was great; at the last three, very extraordinary.'[121] Revival appears to have been evidenced to some extent in Kilmarnock as a result of these efforts, while other places in the neighbourhood, such as Dreghorn also shared in the movement. In October 1743, when communion was dispensed in Irvine, the number of communicants then, and on the preceding occasion, was from 200 to 300 more than in former years, which 'was reckoned from a fourth to a fifth part of the whole'.[122] Elsewhere in Ayrshire, in the parish of Long Dreghorn, and other parishes near it, several were reported to have been awakened owing to the influence of the revival.[123]

The influence of this spirit of awakening was even felt in the south-east of Scotland. In the Borders' parish of Coldingham, near Berwick-on-Tweed, 'promising evidences of the outpouring of the Holy Spirit' were apparent, 'so that some of the elder Christians say that they never had such comfort and satisfaction as they have now'.[124] Johnson wrote:

> There is clear evidence, with regard to most places in Scotland where the revival flame reached, that the awakening was preceded by an unusual spirit of prayer appearing amongst the people and a

119. Macfarlan, *The Revivals of the Eighteenth Century*, p. 220.

120. Macpherson, *A History of the Church in Scotland*, p. 325.

121. Macfarlan, *The Revivals of the Eighteenth Century*, p. 220.

122. ibid., p. 221.

123. Gillies, *Historical Collections*, p. 447.

124. Gillies, *Historical Collections*, p. 453.

desire, gradually becoming intense, that God would manifest Himself as at Cambuslang. The praying mood grew contagious; private prayer was generally followed by public meetings for entreating God to pour out His Spirit upon all classes of the community.[125]

The Scottish Heartland

Stirlingshire

St Ninians

In Stirlingshire several parishes participated in the revival work. At the sacrament of the Lord's Supper at St Ninians, less than a mile south of Stirling, in August 1742, several were awakened by means of the Saturday sermons, many more on the Sabbath, and a far greater number still on the Monday, which was, according to James Robe, 'one of the greatest days of the Mediator's power ever beheld'. A few days later, at the regular Thursday lecture, a considerable number more were awakened. In a letter to James Robe in the early spring of 1743 parish minister the Rev. James Mackie stated, 'Impressions upon our people are far from wearing off: their behaviour is such that their enemies themselves cannot quarrel, and hitherto they behave very well – it would give you great pleasure to hear them pray and converse. Our audience is most attentive to the preaching of the word'.[126] The district of Dundaff, along the River Carron, is partly situated in Kilsyth parish, partly in St Ninians (separated from the former by a range of hills, from the latter by a distance of five miles). Here the awakening power of the Spirit was also at work during 1742, with attestations of its continuance even into the following year.[127]

Gargunnock

Minister of Gargunnock parish, seven miles west of Stirling, was John Warden, a native of Falkirk. His father had been a merchant in that town and had sided against the Covenanters during the troubled times of persecution. His son, deeply regretting this, committed himself wholly to the work of God and became minister of Gargunnock soon after the revolution. He was father of the minister of the same name in Campsie, and regarded as a 'faithful gospel minister, well seen in the doctrines of

---

125. Johnson, *Stories of Great Revivals*, p. 156.

126. Robe, *Where the Wind Blows*, p. 195.

127. Macfarlan, *The Revivals of the Eighteenth Century*, p. 240.

free grace'.[128] Far advanced in years in 1742, he yet greatly rejoiced in the revival that sprang up all around him. Prior to its appearance in his own parish, some of his parishioners were aroused to a sense of their spiritual need when attending sacraments of the Lord's Supper in Kilsyth, Campsie and St Ninians, during July and August 1742. A further eighteen were awakened under a sermon given by Warden one Thursday in August.

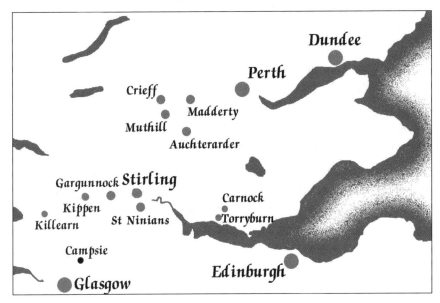

The following week Warden's son arrived from Campsie, and under both his and his father's preaching the awakening became general, deep and powerful, those coming under deep soul concern being reckoned at nearly one hundred, a considerable proportion of parishioners. By March the following year Warden could note; 'The concern in a great measure continues; fellowship meetings increase; and even the children's meetings for prayer continue; their outward concern continues even in the public; a diligent attendance upon ordinances, love of our God and Redeemer remains, and to all the children of our Lord's family, and especially crying to Christ and rejoicing in him with a sober and blameless conversation.'[129]

Killearn

From elsewhere in Stirlingshire it was reported that, 'a few are under spiritual concern in the parish of Kippen', while at the western extremity of the same county the influence of the revival was felt in the parishes of

---

128. ibid., p. 234.

129. Robe, *Where the Wind Blows*, p. 195.

Fintry and Killearn.[130] In the latter parish, located about seven miles north of Campsie, the minister, the Rev. James Bain, became enthused about the revival as soon as he heard about it, and went to assist in the work at Cambuslang on several occasions. A notable movement became apparent in his own district at the Communion service on the third weekend of July 1742, especially on the Monday, when both Mr Potter, professor of divinity at Glasgow University, and the Rev. Mackie of St Ninians, preached. In 1751 Bain wrote of his regret that the movement had been so limited in his parish, but gave thanks to God that almost a decade later some of the most eminent Christians he had ever met were among the fruits of that revival. They were, he said, 'poor in spirit, they attained to high measures of communion with God, and cherished fervent love for the whole human race, even their enemies'.[131] Meanwhile, in districts located in the region of south-eastern Stirlingshire, a number of people were awakened in Denny and in the united parishes of Dunipace and Larbert, some as a result of making the journey to Cambuslang and other revival centres, some in their own churches. Further south still, a work went noiselessly on in Falkirk, while in the parish of Torphichen, south of Linlithgow, seven were reputedly awakened when the Lord's Supper was distributed to them on the first Sabbath of August, 1742.[132]

Perthshire

Muthill

As early as January 1742, 'an unusual stirring' commenced in Muthill, Perthshire, pastored by sixty-five-year-old William Halley, who was finally beginning to see significant fruit from his longstanding labours (he had been inducted thirty-eight years previously, in 1704, having had to be ordained in the churchyard because most of the parishioners were devoted to episcopacy and resisted with swords and staves, also stoning the presbytery). And while chosen to be minister more for his physical strength than his spiritual graces, Halley soon developed into 'an able and sufficient minister and one who is known to be laborious and faithful'.[133] By July 1742 around fifty had been awakened, but it was at the sacrament a few

---

130. Couper, *Scottish Revivals*, p. 65.

131. Macfarlan, *The Revivals of the Eighteenth Century*, p. 240.

132. Gillies, *Historical Collections*, p. 447.

133. Robe, *Where the Wind Blows*, p. 185.

weeks later that the floodgates were opened. 'God was in the place', said the minister, and 'many were brought to the Conqueror's feet'.[134]

From then on, observed Halley, 'an unusual power hath attended the Word preached every Sabbath-day', especially one Sabbath day in September, which was 'a day of the Son of man in this place', when, apart from the general concern in the congregation, around eighteen people were 'pricked to the heart, and deeply wounded with the arrows of the Almighty'. Of this work of conviction among so many in his church, Halley commented:

> The work of the law has been severe, and outwardly noticeable upon all that I have conversed with; their convictions have been deep, cutting and abiding, not (as we have formerly seen), 'like a morning cloud and early dew, that soon passeth away'. And yet I have not observed in any that I have spoken with the least tendency to despair; but giving, so far as I can judge, satisfying evidences of a kindly work of the Spirit, and the law acting the part of a school-master, leading them to Christ, in whom, I hope, a great many of them are safely landed … some have received such a measure of the joys of heaven that the narrow crazy vessel could hold no more.[135]

A special 'down-pouring of his Spirit' was occasioned on the Sunday evening exercises which Halley began immediately after the evening service. A large crowd would flock into the manse for such occasion, filling both the house and the close before the doors, and evidencing such a thirst for the word that, noted the minister, 'their mourning cries frequently drown my voice, so that I am obliged frequently to stop till they compose themselves … I am taken up in dealing with them for some hours after the meeting is dismissed'.[136] Latterly, owing to the numbers attending, Halley held these exercises in the church itself, to which virtually the whole congregation stayed to attend, even though many had to walk through a long moor in the dark to get home. Others, after hearing a lecture and two sermons, as well as the evening exercise, went to retire for the night in the school-house, where they would spend some further hours in prayer, often to the conviction of bystanders outside.

---

134. Fawcett, *The Cambuslang Revival*, p. 133.

135. Robe, *Where the Wind Blows*, pp. 186-7.

136. Gillies, *Historical Collections*, p. 447.

So real a saving work was done, remarked the minister, that to doubt it would call into question the experience of long-established believers and even the saints recorded in Scripture. And so intense and widespread was the movement that at least once Robe of Kilsyth compared it with the revivals in Cambuslang and his own parish. The number of prayer societies rose from two to eighteen in one year, and twenty-seven walked the thirty miles from Muthill to Kilsyth in 1742 for the second Communion there.[137] As they walked home together, many of them were in such distress of soul that their bodies were weakened to the extent that they were barely able to journey further. Fortunately, several ministers, including the Rev. Porteous of Monivaird, who had been helping at the same Kilsyth sacrament, overtook the pilgrims on their homeward journey, and at once stopped to offer them counsel. By October, Halley remarked, 'The arrows of the Almighty King are still flying thick amongst us, and wounding the hearts of his enemies, and laying them down groaning at the feet of the Conqueror, crying under a sense of guilt and the frightful apprehensions of wrath, and thirsting after a Saviour'.[138]

A boys' and girls' prayer meeting quickly increased to twenty members. Halley offered them a room in the manse, where they met every night, 'and oh how pleasant it is', he wrote, 'to hear the poor young lambs addressing themselves to God in prayer, with what fervour, with what proper expressions do I hear them pouring out their souls to a prayer-hearing God, so that standing at the back of the door, I am often melted into tears to hear them'.[139] Soon another such meeting was set up in a different part of the parish, to which a further twenty attended twice a week; even though many had some distance to walk home at night; then another was commenced, which as many as forty were known to attend.

By January 1744 Halley could still report large congregations, while, as late as February 1751, he testified to the good work done and to the perseverance of many saints. 'I am fully persuaded', he said, 'that the gracious fruits of that glorious work will abide with many in the congregation to eternal ages.'[140]

---

137. Not the August 1743 sacrament as stated by Fawcett, *The Cambuslang Revival*, p. 134.

138. Robe, *Where the Wind Blows*, p. 189.

139. ibid., p. 191.

140. Couper, *Scottish Revivals*, p. 66.

Madderty and Monivaird

Regarding the ancient community of Madderty, in which a former church dedicated to St Ethernan dates back to the year 1200, William Halley of Muthill wrote: 'Soon after the sacrament at Foulis, a neighbouring parish, some few boys met in the fields for prayer, and when observed, were brought to a house, to whom many others, both young and old, resorted since, and are now, according to my information, in a very flourishing condition.'[141] From the parish of Monivaird, situated in the very heart of Perthshire, around a dozen miles west of Perth, the Rev. Porteous reported 'some stirring in his parish' around the same time. In the spring of the following year he communicated to Robe, 'several hopeful appearances', such as an unusual attention to the word, setting up the worship of God in many families where it was formerly neglected, the setting-up and increase of praying societies, and a noticeable concern among many young ones, who had started up two society meetings.[142]

Still in Perthshire, the community of Crieff was also touched by the awakening. This parish came under the lengthy ministry of the Rev. John Drummond (inducted 1699, continuing till 1755). During the revival there were discernible awakenings among his people and some brought into distress. No fewer than eight prayer meetings were set up around this time. Further south, in Auchterarder, manifestations of the same spirit appeared in the formation of six prayer meetings.[143]

Dundee, Fife and the North East

Whitefield preached in Lundie, just north of Dundee, in October 1741. His fellow-labourer, Thomas Davidson recalled, 'Scarcely had he begun, when the presence of divine power was very discernible. Never did I see such melting in any congregation'.[144] In other places, such as the parish of Strathmartin, to the north of Dundee, the revival was spread by ministers 'proposing to keep parochial thanksgiving days for the good news' received of revival elsewhere.[145] In Dundee itself, 'great numbers' were awakened, largely through the ministry of the Rev. John Willison,

---

141. Robe, *Where the Wind Blows*, p. 191.

142. ibid., pp. 193, 195.

143. Macfarlan, *The Revivals of the Eighteenth Century*, p. 248.

144. ibid., p. 249.

145. Couper, *Scottish Revivals*, p. 61.

who had visited revival scenes in Cambuslang and who helped spark the movement in Kilsyth.[146] Prayer meetings were set up so fast in the town and in such numbers, wrote Willison, 'that our difficulty is to get houses to accommodate them'.[147] By March 1743 there were over twenty such meetings, and in several of them between twenty and thirty in attendance.

While parts of Fife, such as Torryburn and Carnock, both situated to the west of Dunfermline in the south-west of the county, were 'more or less visited with the revival',[148] the country north of Dundee appears to have been little touched,[149] although Robe spoke of receiving a letter from 'some of the Lord's people from Angus ... expressing the most earnest desires and longing for such a reviving in the corners where they dwell'.[150] Whitefield

---

146. John McIntosh suggests that Willison was 'probably the most commonly read religious writer in eighteenth century Scotland', as well as 'the earliest and possibly the most fundamental opponent of Moderatism ... '. Willison, it seems, viewed the presence of evangelical revivals (e.g. at Cambuslang, Kilsyth and elsewhere in Scotland, as well as in New England) as clear evidence of God's blessing and also as a sign of the approaching millennium. This helps explain, says McIntosh, why he put increasing emphasis on preaching salvation through Christ, instead of, for example., making specific proposals 'to counteract Moderate influence in the General Assembly'. (John McIntosh, *Church and Theology in Enlightenment Scotland: The Popular Party 1740–1800*, East Linton 1998, pp. 32, 64-5).

147. Macfarlan, *The Revivals of the Eighteenth Century*, p. 250. In the aftermath of such blessing there arose an unusual commotion in Willison's church, following the rebellion under Young Pretender, Charles Edward. Wrote Willison: 'We had a good number of fierce lion-like men quartered in this town, who threatened us very much with plundering and killing if we complied not with their measures, travelling still up and down our streets with guns, swords and pistols in their hands and bosoms. Hundreds of them came sometimes into our churches, having their pistols loaded with ball, and threatening in private to let them fly at us if we prayed for King George ... One day five of their officers advanced towards the pulpit, and three of them coming up close to me, discharged me from praying for King George. I began to reason with them, but the women cried so much that, after attempting in vain to calm them, I had to dismiss the congregation. The officers afterwards sent to my house forbidding me to preach unless I complied with their terms. It was thought best to leave the churches, and we betook ourselves to private houses in different parts of the town.' (Johnson, *Stories of Great Revivals*, p. 157).

148. Fawcett, *The Cambuslang Revival*, p. 125. Regarding Torryburn, John Erskine wrote that 'something of the same kind seems to be happening' there in October 1742 (quoted in Roxburgh, 'The Scottish Evangelical Awakening of 1742 and the Religious Societies', p. 272).

149. Couper, *Scottish Revivals*, p. 248.

150. Robe, *When the Wind Blows*, pp. 196-7.

paid a brief visit to Aberdeen on his 1741 trip to Scotland, when he was still unknown north of the border. The city's magistrates refused him permission to preach in the kirkyard, and when he attended St Nicholas Parish (East) Church by invite, he had to sit and endure the approbations of John Bissett, the co-pastor, who, knowing Whitefield was present, referred to him by name, quoting from his printed sermons as evidence of his gross Arminianism! Whitefield then rose and preached from God's word, to a large and 'deeply impressed' congregation. The next day the city's magistrates apologised to Whitefield for the unseemly welcome given him, and awarded him freedom of the city. Couper suggested that in subsequent months Aberdeen was affected by the revival movement that so moved other parts of Scotland, but that 'particulars are wanting'.[151] Fawcett states that some ministers from 'a corner about a hundred miles north from Aberdeen' visited revival scenes in Muthill, Kilsyth and Cambuslang, and while they were surprised with what they saw of bodily agitations – a new experience to them – they were impressed with other aspects of the movement.[152] A praying society was established in this unnamed north-east locality in 1741.[153]

The Far North [154]

Sutherland

Rogart

In the northern Highlands the Sutherland community of Rogart saw a work of grace begin as early as 1740, when fifteen were awakened. These new converts, and a few other believers, found themselves, in the years 1741–2, 'fallen under sad decays of soul' while others in the parish 'were remaining under their former stupidity'. A prayer society was formed, where believers mourned such a situation. Prayer brought its reward, for in 1743 and 1744, especially the former year, there was a distinct revival

---

151. Couper, *Scottish Revivals*, pp. 68-9.

152. Fawcett, *The Cambuslang Revival*, p. 125.

153. James Hutchison, *Miners, Weavers and the Open Book: A History of Kilsyth*, Cumbernauld 1986, p. 29.

154. Alexander Auld was of the opinion that spiritual darkness in the Scottish Highlands deepened as the 18th century advanced, and oddly, given the wave of blessing that descended on some areas in the early 1740s, felt that such darkness 'may perhaps be said to have reached its greatest intensity about the year 1749, or the years corresponding to those of greatest spiritual prosperity in the century preceding' (Alexander Auld, *Life of John Kennedy*, London 1887, p. 84).

of religion, whereby about fifty more of the people were awakened, who were reported to be in a hopeful way.[155]

Golspie

In nearby Golspie the minister, John S. Sutherland, shared accounts of the revival in America and other parts of Scotland, and in 1743 was able to tell with great joy of his personal visits to Cambuslang, Kilsyth and Muthill. Later that year, on recommendation from John Balfour of Nigg, Sutherland instituted three district praying societies, which began to meet each Saturday evening. 'Silence and calmness' with 'abundance of tears' accompanied the deep work which ensued, until November 1744, from which time the

blessing became more public. Many spoke of long nights without sleep, loss of appetite and impaired strength while under conviction. So remarkable was the change in many in the congregation that, enthused Sutherland, 'we saw good cause to set a day apart for thanksgiving to God for what of His work appeared to us'.[156] A subsequent catechist in Golspie, John Cuthbert, could recall in his youth that a number of years after the revival there were sixty men in the small parish who could be called on to pray in public. These were thought to have been the fruit of the stated awakening.[157]

Lairg

It was probably around this time of widespread awakening that the inland parish of Lairg, too, was refreshed with a shower of spiritual blessing. John Mackay was a healthy man with a gigantic frame, who, as a young convert, came into contact with Thomas Hogg of Kiltearn, whose singularly holy

155. Gillies, *Historical Collections*, p. 457.

156. ibid., pp. 456-7.

157. Rev. Donald Munro, *Records of Grace in Sutherland*, Edinburgh 1953, p. 55.

life and fatherly counsels made a lasting impression on him. After training for the ministry, Mackay was inducted to Durness before being translated to Lairg in 1714. There was a certain laxity in the life of the community at that time; the Sabbath was profaned and there was a general lack of discipline. Through his arduous labours and earnest piety the minister earned respect and gained an authority which few cared to dispute. He kept the best interests of his people at heart and ever strove to persuade them to abstain from all appearance of evil and to follow that which is good. He was also a faithful preacher of the gospel and in time a pleasing change was to be seen in the ways and life of the community, while the house of God became thronged for public services. In addition to these, diets of catechising were well attended and family-worship became general.[158]

Easter Ross-shire

From the days of the Reformation Easter Ross was blessed by a succession of able and evangelical ministers. The first was Donald Munro who came in 1564 as the Assembly's Commissioner to Ross-shire. Munro served for eight or nine years in the county and his labours were abundantly blessed. As a result, the Reformed Church was firmly established in Ross-shire and quickly became a centre of major influence.[159] During the eighteenth century no other equal area of Scotland contained so many ministers of distinction. Their labours were manifestly acknowledged. The district became 'a garden of the Lord where blood-red roses grew', wrote one observer poetically. So gracious was the type of Christian life there developed that the district came to be known as '*Nead na smeorach*', i.e. 'the nest of the thrushes'.[160] Gustavus Aird, well familiar with this northern district, wrote: 'Upwards of a generation after the Revolution, in 1740 and thereafter, a real and extensive revival of true religion occurred throughout a very extensive part of the country, and continued until near the close of the century.'[161] During this revival, the

---

158. Times of refreshing were also known under the ministry of John's son, the Rev. Thomas Mackay, who succeeded his father in 1753. As with the father, so also the people thronged from miles around to hear the son preach, (ibid., pp. 100-106).

159. Donald MacLeod, *The Gospel in the Highlands*, a lecture given to mark the Centenary of Knockbain Free Church in the Black Isle in 1989, (www.freechurch.org – accessed 08/06/11).

160. MacRae, *The Life of Gustavus Aird*, p. 1.

161. ibid., p. 258.

tradition of pious laymen known simply as 'The Men', which dated back to the mid 1600s, came especially to prominence, in the form of their contributions to prayer and fellowship meetings.

'The Men' consisted of a group of often self-appointed lay churchmen (sometimes they were called forward by the minister), usually elders, catechists, schoolmasters or missionaries, found in many parishes in the Highlands, who became almost a spiritual elite within their districts and carried enormous sway over parishioners. They were, says Michael Lynch, 'charismatic … lay catechists … who combined the roles of modern evangelist and traditional seer. The legacy of "The Men" … was long-lasting; they left a tradition of strict Sabbatarianism, handed to the new parish ministers a role as prophets and leaders of their flocks.' [162] One writer said of 'The Men' of the Highlands: 'Like other people of cold climate and nature, they love the excitement of long and vehement preaching, and are capable of being roused by it to a dangerous frenzy, venting itself in scenes only short of the dreadful American revivals.' [163] 'The Men' were in some areas even known for their distinctive dress, letting their hair grow long, donning coloured handkerchiefs on their heads, and wearing long blue cloaks. Due to their general popularity, they would sometimes hold alternative services which might be better attended than those in the parish church. McGillivray wrote of them that 'they were keen-sighted; they abhorred hypocrisy, and when they detected the effectuation of piety, they gave it no quarter'. Yet, he continued, 'the real men of the north, instead of despising the ministry, were its strength and support … I have known one of them, when eighty years of age, spend nights in prayer for a young minister, whom he knew to be at the time in a state of darkness and discouragement.' [164]

Nigg

The good work accomplished by John Balfour from his settlement in the parish of Nigg in 1729 (see page 94) resulted in a significant revival, which reached a peak around 1739. One particular week in that year became known as 'The Great Week', as people visited the minister all

---

162. Michael Lynch, *Scotland: A New History*, London 1991, pp. 364-5.

163. Anon., 'Puritanism in the Highlands', p. 315, quoted in Roderick Macleod, *The Progress of Evangelicalism in the Western Isles, 1800–1850*, Unpublished Ph.D. Thesis, University of Edinburgh 1977, p. 215.

164. McGillivray, *Sketches of Religion and Revivals of Religion*, p. 22.

day and every day seeking spiritual direction and instruction in the faith.[165] The work came about without any special organisation or the use of unusual methods, but was largely the result of Balfour's regular work as parish minister. In addition, noted the pastor, 'the people here were much refreshed with the several accounts they had had of the glorious work of God elsewhere, and particularly in these parts of our native country where the same appears with such blessed and shining evidences of the divine power and presence'.[166] Writing to James Robe in 1739, Balfour said:

> The Lord's Day is very solemnly observed. After public worship is over, there are meetings in all parts where neighbouring families join in prayer, reading and repetition of sermons ... the ordinary diets of worship are punctually attended ... diets of catechising are much crowded with people from other parts ... The civil magistrate has had no crimes here to animadvert on for many years and the Kirk Session has little to do but to inform and consult about the religious concerns of the parish ... the people are more forward in the business of their husbandry than their neighbours in other parts of the country.[167]

As late as 1743, fourteen young communicants were admitted to the church. Writing in 1744, Balfour reported that for the past three years the general prayer meeting had been divided into two, each of which had since significantly increased. Besides these, he noted, 'Ten societies meet in several places of the parish every Saturday for prayer and other religious exercises', conducted by elders, while 'worship is kept up in all the families except three or four'.[168]

Thousands assembled for one open-air communion service, which, although of short duration, required so many tables that before the last one was served, night was at hand and the immense gathering had to be dismissed promptly afterwards. Balfour stood up and said, 'There is no time for an address – let us pray ... "O Lord, we have not done what Thou has commanded us; do Thou all that Thou hast promised, for the

---

165. John R. Martin, *The Church Chronicles of Nigg*, Nigg 1967, pp. 20-1.

166. Gillies, *Historical Collections*, pp. 453-4.

167. ibid., p. 454.

168. Gillies, *Historical Collections*, pp. 453-4.

Lord Jesus Christ's sake, Amen"'. Aged Christians were wont to say that they had never heard any prayer which so thrilled their hearts as this brief but comprehensive appeal to God. As late as January 1745, Balfour could record 'to the praise of sovereign grace that matters proceed still in my parish as formerly. New awakenings continue, and those formerly awakened persevere'. Even during the troubled times of the Jacobite rebellion all remained quiet in the parish, but the good work was largely ended with the death of Balfour in 1752 and the subsequent forced placement of an unsuitable successor to him. However, the resulting secession which occurred in the church was a strong testimonial to the work and character of Balfour's ministry.[169]

Kiltearn and Alness

Andrew Robertson had ministered in the Sutherland district of Farr from 1727 before settling in Kiltearn, Ross-shire four years later. He was, for some time, disheartened owing to there being no noticeable fruit following his labours and he regretted the removal from his former charge. At length, however, some tokens of good began to appear, and as time went on these increased. In 1742–3 both Kiltearn and Alness were affected by revival. Prayer meetings were set up in suitable centres throughout the parish. The day of the week chosen for these gatherings was Saturday, and there were no less than seven such meetings, which were largely attended. Saturday was chosen both to prepare people's minds and hearts for the sanctity of the Lord's Day and to plead for the blessing of God upon the services of the sanctuary.[170]

In Alness the ministry of James Fraser, who laboured there from 1726 to 1769, 'yielded a rich spiritual harvest', as did his father's earlier ministry in the same parish in the fifteen years up to his death in 1711.

---

169. Martin, *The Church Chronicles of Nigg*, pp. 21-2; Roberts, *Scotland Saw His Glory*, pp. 180-1. Patrick Grant was presented to the parish shortly after Balfour's death. Due to strong opposition from the congregation, it wasn't until July 1756, four years after Balfour's demise, that Grant was finally inducted. The people of the district refused to enter the parish church but continued the praying societies under their elders, attending neighbouring churches and receiving baptism for their children from John Fraser of Alness. They built a somewhat primitive heather-thatched meeting-house around 1763, which lasted for forty years, until the lease lapsed. John Balfour's son, George, also entered the ministry and was ordained to the parish of Tarbat after a disputed election in which his father's influence was considered by the other party as excessive.

170. John Noble, *Religious Life In Ross*, Inverness 1909, pp. 82-3.

The work of Fraser Jnr extended far beyond his own parish; he inherited from his father the estate of Pitcalzean, in the parish of Nigg, which Fraser often visited, and where, after the intrusion, he often preached and baptised, to the edification of many.[171]

Rosskeen

Rosskeen, a neighbouring parish to Nigg, was served by Daniel Bethune, one of the best known and most highly respected men of his day. 'From the harvest of 1742 to Martinmass 1743 or thereby, there came a remarkable revival and stir among the people ... about six and thirty men and women fell under a concern about their salvation during that period'. Three texts in particular were blest most for their awakening power; Hosea 13:13, Galatians 4:19 and John 3:3; 'especially the first of these subjects was the principal means of the first stir'. A striking feature of the work was the spontaneous movement which occurred among boys and girls aged between nine and fifteen. They conducted meetings among themselves on Sabbath evenings, and met again for prayer in a good widow's house every Monday night, to which some adults were also drawn. During these occasions each gave some note from the minister's sermon that Sabbath morning. The children kept strict discipline among themselves and allowed none to join them except such as would undertake to pray with them. Many of those who attended these meetings lived long as bright witnesses to the saving and keeping power of grace in Easter Ross.[172]

Kilmuir

The ministry of the gracious John Porteous of Kilmuir was signally owned in conversions, and he became so popular that people flocked to hear him from all sides.[173] It was not surprising that the people of Nigg went to him

---

171. MacRae, *The Life of Gustavus Aird*, pp. 1-3, 5.

172. ibid., p. 4; Alexander MacRae, *Revivals in the Highlands and Islands in the 19th Century*, Stirling, 1906, [reprinted 1998], p. 158; Gillies, *Historical Collections*, pp. 454-5.

173. A form of religious reformation had taken place in the parish under Porteous's predecessor, Rev. Walter Ross, who was licensed to preach in 1714. He found Kilmuir to be in a 'rude and unruly state', the people having relapsed, during the reign of Episcopacy, into 'approximate barbarism'. Methods 'suited to the times had to be adopted', the minister resorting to acts of physical force to change the ways of his people. In one village, watch was kept to see if the greatly feared minister should visit the place. One day the alarm was raised, and the inhabitants left at once for their boats, in which they sailed some distance from shore, knowing the minister would not be able to get near

after John Balfour's death, but many who were awakened under James Fraser of Alness also made occasional visits to Kilmuir. Some believers in Kilmuir became concerned that this might create some friction between Porteous and Fraser, both of whom they venerated so much and loved so dearly. When the Kilmuir minister went to speak to Fraser about the matter, the latter's reply was characteristic of the worthy man. He assured his colleague that the situation would never produce any alienation between them. 'It is entirely of the Lord', he said. 'He has given me a quiver-full of arrows, and it is not yet exhausted, and these arrows are piercing their consciences; hence their pain and cry for relief. But the Lord has given to you a breastful of oil, and they run to you for relief. The whole is from the Lord, and no coolness shall arise between us'.[174]

Rosemarkie

The work in Rosemarkie can be dated to a communion held in July 1743, led by parish minister, the Rev. John Wood. During the next nine months over thirty people waited on their pastor 'under convictions and awakenings of conscience through the Word ... I observe the steadfast eyes', he wrote, 'the piercing looks, the seemingly serious and greedy desires of many in the congregation at times of hearing of the Word who as yet have discovered their concern of soul in no other way, with some having been under conviction for two years'.[175] Though the movement was not large, Wood felt that 'the least gracious revival is the more remarkable to me as I had been groaning under the burden of labouring

---

them. Outraged at finding the homes empty, Ross took from some houses a number of cooking implements and locked them away in a safe place. On their return home, the villagers were unable to cook without their missing accoutrements, but were prepared to go without food rather than approach the formidable minister. Eventually sheer hunger forced them to meet with Ross, who, to their surprise, did not act in his customary manner of physical aggression. The villagers repented of their sins and promised henceforth to attend church ordinances and live in accordance with God's word. A decided change soon became noticeable in the morality and Sabbath-keeping of the community at large and some showed evidence of saving impressions (Noble, *Religious Life in Ross*, pp. 121-4).

174. MacRae, *The Life of Gustavus Aird*, pp. 11-12. As feelings ran high in the country in 1745, Porteous, an anti-Jacobite, was obliged to flee for refuge to Halmadary, at the head of Strathnaver, Sutherland. Here he lived in seclusion, preaching the gospel to those who resorted to him, till the final overthrow of Prince Charlie at Culloden in April 1746, when he returned to Kilmuir to the work which he loved.

175. Gillies, *Historical Collections*, pp. 455-6.

in vain'.[176] Hopeful appearances also showed themselves in Logie, Avoch and Kirkmichael, as well as in the town of Cromarty.[177] The Rev. William Taylor suggests that the 'divine influences' of this movement were also made manifest in the counties of Inverness and Nairn.[178]

Wester Ross-shire

The extensive parish of Lochbroom stands alone in the western Highlands as having partaken of the showers of revival blessing that fell on parts of the Scottish mainland during this period. On 10th February 1744 two eminent booksellers in Edinburgh, Thomas Lumisden and Joseph Robertson, wrote to an acquaintance in New England, sharing with him news of the spread of spiritual awakening in this remote district in Wester Ross. They wrote that, although no minister served the parish,

> their School-master, who is a pious Man, has travl'd amongst them and instructed them ... They have formed Societies in sundry places ... There they pray, sing Psalms and instruct one another. Their School-master goes round them; so that through the Year he is not a Sabbath of ten at his own House. His Presbytery ... allows him to explain the Scripture he reads ... he calls also on the People to give their own Thoughts on sundry Passages of Scripture ... The Name of the School-master is Mr Hugh Cameron.[179]

Subsequent ministries of Whitefield and Wesley in Scotland

George Whitefield

Following his first visit in 1741, George Whitefield made no fewer than thirteen journeys to Scotland over a period of twenty-seven years, and considerable stir was created on each occasion.[180] 'Never before

---

176. Couper, *Scottish Revivals*, p. 67.

177. Gillies, *Historical Collections*, p. 456.

178. Taylor, *Memorials of Rev. C. C. Macintosh*, pp. 11-13; Ian A. Muirhead, 'The Revival as a Dimension of Scottish Church History', in *SCHSR* vol. 20, 1980, p. 182.

179. Prince's 'Church History', quoted in Fawcett, *The Cambuslang Revival*, p. 205.

180. Just before the turn of the 19th century, Butler wrote: 'Whitefield affected Scottish towns by his preaching as Savonarola affected Florence; but Whitefield's preaching was more intensely spiritual than that of the great Florentine, and took a loftier flight ... That Whitefield taught the spiritual life of the whole Scottish Church to beat for

or since', wrote W. H. Fitchett, 'were such oratorical triumphs won by any single voice over Scottish audiences'.[181] During his fifth visit in July 1751, Whitefield preached twice a day in Glasgow. He wrote: 'Thousands attend every morning and evening. Though I preached near eighty times in Ireland, and God was pleased to bless his Word, yet Scotland seems to be a new world to me. To see the people bring so many bibles, and turn to every passage when I am expounding, is very encouraging.'[182] The following year Whitefield preached for twenty-eight days to audiences in Edinburgh and Glasgow of 'not less than ten thousand each day'. His ministry during this and subsequent visits had a powerful influence over the divinity students. Of his ninth journey north of the border, in 1757, he noted: 'Thousands and thousands, among whom were a great many of the best rank, daily attended on the word preached; and the longer I stayed, the more the congregations and divine influence increased.'[183] On his 1759 visit Whitefield preached a remarkable one hundred times in just seven weeks. On his last visit, in June 1768, his popularity was greater than ever. He met in Edinburgh friends of twenty-seven years' standing. 'I am here only in danger of being hugged to death', he wrote. Preaching with great persuasion to the waiting thousands, Whitefield was as a king among men, and all classes hung upon his lips. 'Could I preach

---

the moment with quicker pulse cannot be doubted.' However he felt that Whitefield 'left no permanent mark on Scottish religion. Edinburgh today no more bears his signature than does Florence that of Savonarola', he stated (Butler, *Wesley and Whitefield in Scotland*, p. 36).

181. Fitchett, *Wesley and his Century*, p. 242.

182. Butler, *John Wesley and George Whitefield in Scotland*, p. 48. The Scottish people's love for and familiarity with the Word of God has been remarked upon by many visiting preachers from south of the border. Daniel Defoe spoke favourably of the 'little rustling noise ... made by turning the leaves of the Bible ... when the minister names any text of Scripture' (Roberts, *Scotland Saw His Glory*, p. 22) William Haslam, the Cornish pastor famously converted through his own preaching, was invited to Aberdeenshire by the Earl of Kintore in 1862. He spoke from the Free Church pulpit at Keith, and during his sermon made reference to a particular Bible verse. 'In an instant hundreds of hands were stretched out to take up their Bibles. The rustling of leaves was so great that I had to wait till the text was found. This made a break in my speaking which I did not care for, so I gave no more Bible references!' (Chris Wright, *Haslam's Journey: 'From Death to Life' and 'Yet Not I'* (Abridged and Annotated), Godalming 2005, pp. 189-90).

183. Butler, *John Wesley and George Whitefield in Scotland*, pp. 49, 53.

ten times a-day', he predicted, 'thousands and thousands would attend'.[184]

One Edinburgh student deeply influenced by the revival in central Scotland was John Erskine, great-grandson of Lord Cardross. Erskine changed his studies from law to divinity and his subsequent ministry in the capital city from 1758 until his death in 1803 was fraught with rich consequences for the cause of the gospel. On one of Whitefield's later visits to Scotland, the evangelist heard of a dozen young men that were awakened under Erskine's ministry 'ten years ago', and were now eminently useful preachers.[185]

John Wesley

John Wesley also made regular journeys to Scotland during this period (indeed he met up with Whitefield in Edinburgh towards the close of the latter's ministry), first visiting the country in 1751. This was followed by a remarkable twenty-one further journeys to the northern land spanning thirty-nine years. No definite outbreak of revival resulted from his preaching in the Calvinist north, however, and he was often directly opposed for his Arminian beliefs.[186] Nevertheless, the Scots generally listened to him with great interest, and more than one city presented him with its honorary freedom.[187] His enduring triumph was undoubtedly the setting up of Methodist 'societies' after the pattern of his English work. Wesley's Scottish audiences astonished him by their order, gravity and absence of emotion. But he clearly loved his northern sphere, and last paid a visit to Scotland in 1790, when in his eighty-ninth year. Certainly Wesley had more success in some places than in others. He preached on a communion Sabbath evening on Calton Hill, Edinburgh in 1764 to a congregation which, he said, was by 'far the largest I have seen in the kingdom; and the most deeply affected. Many

---

184. ibid., p. 57.

185. Dallimore, 'Whitefield and the Evangelical Revival in Scotland', in *Banner of Truth*, vol. 79, p. 23.

186. Wesley F. Swift, *Methodism in Scotland: The First Hundred Years*, London 1947, p. 64.

187. Henry Johnson, too, noted that there was scarcely any opposition displayed towards the Wesleys, such as took place in England and Wales. Such exemption from 'mob violence and the animosity of individuals' Johnson put down to the fact that most of the meetings north of the border were held in churches and other buildings (Johnson, *Stories of Great Revivals*, p. 157). In fact, however, both Whitefield and Wesley, even during their Scottish visits, often preached outdoors.

were in tears; more seemed cut to the heart. Surely this time will not soon be forgotten. Will it not appear in the annals of eternity?' [188]

Of Arbroath, which Wesley first visited in May 1770, he said, 'The whole town seems moved; the congregation was the largest I have seen since we left Inverness, and the society, though but of nine months' standing, is the largest in the kingdom, next to that of Aberdeen'. Preaching in Arbroath exactly two years later he observed, 'In this town there is a change indeed! It was wicked to a proverb; remarkable for Sabbath-breaking, cursing, swearing, drunkeness, and a general contempt of religion. But it is not so now: no drunkeness seen in the streets: and many, not only ceased from evil and learned to do well, but are witnesses of the inward Kingdom of God, righteousness, peace, and joy in the Holy Ghost'. Again, in May 1774 Wesley reported, 'I know no people in England who are more loving, and more simple of heart, than these'.[189]

Wesley also had success in the North East, and over a period of time a number of Methodist chapels were established along the Banffshire coast. In 1782 we find the evangelist saying, 'The flame begins to kindle even at poor, dull Keith,[190] but much more at a little town near Fraserburgh; and most of all at Newburgh … where the society swiftly increases, and where not only men and women, but a considerable number of children are either rejoicing in God, or panting after him'.[191] The English evangelist preached here again two years later, when he described the Newburgh society as, 'according to its bigness, the liveliest society in the Kingdom. I preached in a kind of square to a multitude of people, and the whole congregation appeared to be moved, and ready prepared for the Lord'.[192]

The picture elsewhere proved less promising, and the Edinburgh society dwindled in just two years (1768–70) from 160 to around 50.[193]

---

188. John Wesley, *Wesley's Journal*, London 1902, p. 312.

189. John Wesley, *The Works of the Rev. John Wesley*, London 1827, pp. 391, 397, 462.

190. Such was Wesley's anxiety to establish his Methodist prayer societies that, in 1776, when the owner of the building being used by the Methodists in Keith decided to sell it, Wesley actually bought an estate there so that the society might have ground for a chapel (George Booth Robertson, *Spiritual Awakening in the North-East of Scotland and the Description of the Church in 1843*, Ph.D. Thesis, University of Aberdeen 1970, p. 55; Wesley, *Wesley's Journal*, p. 409).

191. John Wesley, *The Works of the Rev. John Wesley*, vol. 4, London 1829, p. 229.

192. Robertson, *Spiritual Awakening in the North-East of Scotland*, p. 51.

193. Mathieson, *Church and Reform in Scotland*, p. 48.

Indeed, despite Wesley's arduous and unrelenting labours throughout Scotland the Wesleyan Connexion had just over 1,000 members in this vast northerly circuit after Wesley's death in 1791, compared to 14,000 in Ireland and 57,000 in England and Wales.[194] However, the Scottish figure rose to 3,786 by 1819 before dropping to 2,143 by 1856.[195]

Later Eighteenth Century Revivals 1751–99

Evangelical church historians of a century ago are in general agreement that the second half of the eighteenth century comprised the most spiritually lifeless section of Scottish post-Reformation history hitherto. The fairly widespread revival movement that began with Cambuslang in 1742 seems to have had little overall impact on the reign of 'Moderate' church influence that marked much of the rest of the century. This makes all the more remarkable a string of seemingly independent revival movements that arose during these fifty years, almost totally confined to the north of the country, especially the far north. We will examine each localised revival in turn.

North and Central Scotland

Dugald Buchanan of Rannoch

Best known as a composer of fine Gaelic verse, Dugald Buchanan became a noted evangelist in his native Perthshire some years following his prolonged period of spiritual awakening, during which time he attended services connected with the Cambuslang revival of 1742 (see page 110). For many years a schoolmaster at Drumcastle near Fortingal, Buchanan was appointed a teacher with the SSPCK in 1753. Prosecuting unofficial evangelistic labours with the same care and zeal to which he continued to oversee his school, Buchanan earnestly sought to inculcate godly standards among the spiritually impoverished inhabitants of Rannoch. Within a year Sabbath pastimes such as football and drinking were entirely abandoned, and such an interest awakened in divine things that the schoolhouse of Drumcastle could not contain all who came to hear the word of God. In good weather hundreds met on the banks of the rivers Tummel or Rannoch to hear Buchanan preach. His services were attended by remarkable power and a deep and widespread revival resulted, characterised by the conversion of souls, numbers of whom traversed considerable distances to attend his meetings. Noting such desired outcome, the Dunkeld Presbytery of the

194. Kent, *Wesley and the Wesleyans*, p. 99.

195. Swift, *Methodism in Scotland*, pp. 64, 70.

Church of Scotland formally invested Buchanan with the functions of catechist and evangelist in 1755.

Jealous of his success and alarmed by his assuming ministerial authority (he did more of the work of a pastor there than the ministers appointed to the parish), some clergymen complained that Buchanan's public teachings were of a wild inflammatory character, fitted to fanaticise rather than to edify. Still the good work went on, lives being transformed by the catechist's earnest and generally tender appeals. The power attending his preaching is evidenced by a memorable service held at the head of Loch Rannoch. A bitter feud had arisen between the people of two adjacent townships of this district, who normally refused to come anywhere near each other. Both groups, however, agreed to hear Buchanan preach, albeit from different sides of a stream, in the middle of which, perched on a large stone, the evangelist addressed his audience. So powerful was the message that both parties were deeply and visibly affected. Confessing their faults mutually, these former enemies parted that day as friends.[196]

George Muir of Paisley

One of the many people who visited Cambuslang out of curiosity in 1742 and was converted as a result was nineteen-year-old George Muir from Haddington (1723–71), then serving in the office of writer to the signet in Edinburgh. Following his experience at Cambuslang, Muir studied for the ministry and was ordained to Old Cumnock, Ayrshire in 1752. Here there were drops of blessing on his ministry, as attested to in a letter to the Rev. McCulloch of Cambuslang.[197] Muir transferred to the High Church, Paisley in 1766, succeeding the Rev. James Baine, 'a minister of highly popular talent'. With 'an ample fund of divine knowledge' and being 'a powerful and impressive preacher', Muir

> became highly esteemed by his numerous congregation and from the surrounding countryside … He found it necessary with the voice of thunder sometimes to address his audience in powerful appeals to the careless and ungodly. In leading the prayers of his congregation, he poured out his whole soul; and a peculiar unction

---

196. Sinclair, *Reminiscences of the Life and Labours of Dugald Buchanan*, pp. 51–4. See also *The Diary of Dugald Buchanan, with a Memoir of his Life*, (Edinburgh 1836), which is more of a devotional than a historical aid.

197. *Edinburgh Christian Instructor*, May 1838, p. 186.

and enlargement with a fullness of rich and suitable expressions particularly distinguished his public devotional exercises.[198]

In consequence, his five-year ministry in Paisley was attended with 'a remarkable outpouring of the Spirit of God', and his preaching was accompanied with power to the conversion of many souls. One young lad who used to sit occasionally under Muir's ministry in Paisley when between the ages of nine and fourteen, was John Love (later distinguished theologian and minister at Anderston). Seven years after Muir's death Love 'feelingly recollected and deplored his misimprovement' of such evangelical teaching.[199] Unfortunately, Muir developed a cancerous growth in his foot, and for some time was carried about in a chair, which was set on a platform so he could preach to his parishioners. Shortly after, however, the foot had to be amputated, and Muir died through loss of blood at the age of 49.

The Barclayites

Born in the parish of Muthill, Perthshire, John Barclay (1734–98) was licensed to preach at the age of twenty-four, in which year (1759) he became assistant minister in Errol, Angus. Here he proved a faithful and acceptable preacher. His attention, not least to the young, the aged and the afflicted was unremitting in that extensive parish. Thus he won the hearts of many, old and young. In 1763 Barclay moved north to Fettercairn, to act as assistant to the ageing Anthony Dow. Here his ministry met with unprecedented popularity. Increasingly greater numbers came to hear him from within and outwith the bounds of the parish, and 'a sober, small-scale revival' took place.[200] The crowds were

---

198. ibid., April 1838, pp. 153-9.

199. John Love, *Memorials of the Rev. John Love*, vol. 1, Glasgow 1857, pp. 14-15. By that later date, however (1778), Love had developed a strong sense of spirituality, and he made detailed expressions of his feelings and thoughts in his diary. In this he makes repeated reference to times of personal spiritual revival. For example, while attending communion services at Carmunnock in May 1778, he writes of sensing 'the remarkable presence of the Lord with me … while it lasted my soul was so entirely carried out in direct spiritual actings concerning God and Christ that I had little leisure for the reflex consideration of what I was then feeling. My soul was taken up in wondering what a wonderful God, and what a wonderful Christ, I then saw, and with the infinite evil of sin. I thought not of the happiness of my state in having such manifestations; I somehow forgot this, I was so taken up with the objects I saw … my soul chiefly rested in God and His glory' (vol. 2, p. 298).

200. *DSCHT*, p. 62.

so large that the cramped church could not contain them. Wherever a seat could be found it was promptly occupied – on the window-sills, on the rafters, and on the seats placed outside for those who were unable to endure the heat.

Suspicions over his teachings only increased his popularity, and when Dow died in 1772, almost all the parish wished Barclay to become his successor. The Presbytery, however, refused this, due to conflict over aspects of his doctrine.[201] An appeal to the General Assembly also being turned down, Barclay and most of his congregation left the Church of Scotland and an independent church was built in nearby Sauchieburn. Membership quickly rose to an astonishing 1,000, by which time Barclay had moved to minister to another group of sympathisers in Edinburgh. His followers became known as 'Bereans', and before his death, further assemblies had been formed in Glasgow, Laurencekirk, Stirling, Kirkcaldy, Crieff, Dundee, Arbroath, Montrose and Brechin, and Barclay was wont to visit these places on foot. Several Berean groups were also formed in London, one in Bristol, and some even in America.[202]

Kilbrandon and Kilchattan

An awakening took place in the united parish of Kilbrandon and Kilchattan (the islands of Seil and Luing) in Argyll around 1784,[203] through the reading from the pulpit over many weeks of the entire contents of a Gaelic printing of Alleine's *Alarm to the Unconverted*, recently translated by Dr John Smith, assistant pastor of the congregation.[204] This

---

201. Among other things, Barclay applied most of the Old Testament prophecies, particularly the Psalms, to Christ, and not to Christian believers. Barclay also composed many hymns, which were used in public worship, in stark contrast to the standard Scottish Presbyterian practice of exclusive psalmody. Additionally, Barclayites were against the consecration of bread and wine in the Communion and held that assurance was essential to saving faith. In most other matters, however, this group maintained an orthodox Reformed theology.

202. *DSCHT*, p. 62. Only four pastored assemblies survived into the 1840s, however, and the movement apparently died out soon afterwards.

203. ibid., p. 255. The year 1786 according to Gavin Struthers (*History of the Rise, Progress and Principles of the Relief Church*, Glasgow 1843, p. 395); late 1790s according to Callum Brown (*The Social History of Religion in Scotland since 1730*, London 1987, p. 122).

204. Smith accepted a call to Campbeltown as early as 1781, the year his Gaelic book was printed in Edinburgh. The awakening clearly took place in his absence.

practice was introduced as a means of keeping the attention of those who gathered early in church each Sabbath morning while they waited on the rest of the congregation, whose arrival was irregular owing to having to be ferried from either of the other two islands that made up the parish. The effect of these public readings soon became visible among the people, and when the translation was finished, every family procured a copy. A surprising concern about religious matters was rapidly and extensively diffused among the people, and a great many were brought under serious impressions. They began fellowship meetings for prayer, conversation and reading of the Scriptures. As a result their proficiency in biblical knowledge became remarkable. They loathed seeing the Sabbath being profaned and they were cut to the heart to hear teaching which they considered 'another gospel'. Such was their regard for pure doctrine that they were known to publicly rebuke clergymen whose lives revealed any degree of hypocrisy.

It appears to have been because of these puritanical standards, to which they insisted every citizen should comply, that there arose a great furore against the movement. A presbytery was called. Smith's translation of *Alarm* was tried and condemned as containing twenty-two dangerous errors. Precentors were charged not to read it from their desks. Private families were forbidden to own a copy of it on pain of excommunication. The place where the people gathered for prayer was surrounded, and 'alarming threats were vented that it would be torn down about their heads. They were called in derision, "The people of the great faith". They were declared to be mad. When the communion was dispensed, railings and invectives against them constituted the main topics of the pulpit harangues. All were commanded to shun them'.[205]

Lady Glenorchy, a sympathiser with their cause, applied to the Relief Presbytery of Glasgow, who sent deputies to the spot. These were Niel Douglas (*c.* 1750–1823) and Daniel McNaught, both of whom were sponsored by Relief congregations in Glasgow. They attracted large audiences among the prosperous quarry workers of Easdale, among whom revivalist symptoms of crying, wailing and self-remonstration all appeared. However, amidst unrelenting opposition the promising mission was aborted and the awakening came to a premature close. Lady Glenorchy arranged for a new Gaelic minister to be sent to the district in an attempt to seek reconciliation, but he, too, was shunned, and those who received him were turned out of

205. Struthers, *Relief Church*, pp. 395-6.

their dwellings. As John MacInnes put it: 'What appeared at first to be a promising movement, degenerated into a fanatical sectarianism.' [206] 'Their enemies became exceedingly fierce', remarked Struthers. 'They maligned their new minister, and stirred up the proprietor not to grant them an inch of ground on which to build a chapel'. In such a rugged climate, open-air preaching could not be continued for any length of time. Amid the tokens of God's gracious presence, and the frowns of earthly greatness, the mission was unavoidably brought to a close.[207]

The Far North [208]

James Calder of Croy

The Rev. James Calder (1712–75), in his deeply devotional (though much-edited) *Diary*, gives us glimpses of a steady, gradual movement in his Inverness-shire parish of Croy from June 1763. Calder set aside two days that month 'for personal humiliation and prayer' with reference to his felt 'coldness' and to the state of his people.[209] Tokens of divine blessing multiplied at the parish communion shortly after, while, at a communion in neighbouring Inverness sometime later, as many as 200 attendants from Croy were among the partakers. One day in September Calder visited 'five distressed families', while a work of grace was also evident among his own three beloved sons, each of whom went on to become a respected minister in the north.[210] At the year-end Calder could look back and say:

---

206. John MacInnes, *The Evangelical Movement in the Highlands of Scotland*, Aberdeen 1951, p. 162.

207. Struthers, *Relief Church*, p. 396; cf. Brown, *The Social History of Religion in Scotland since 1730*, p. 122. Many adherents of the movement soon after placed themselves under the authority of the Reformed Presbytery, which since 1787 came under the inspection of the Rev. Thomas Henderson, whose jurisprudence extended as far south as the Vale of Leven and North Ayrshire (W. J. Couper, *Kilbirnie West: A History of Kilbirnie West United Free, Formerly Reformed Presbyterian Church, 1824–1924*, Kilbirnie 1923, pp. 12-13).

208. Apart from that which arose in the Shetland parish of Dunrossness, the distinct local movements that comprise this eclectic batch of later eighteenth-century revivals in the far north of Scotland tend to have been located to the near west, south or north of Inverness (Croy, Ardclach to the west; Moy to the south, and Creich to the north), or in the northern extreme of Sutherland (Tongue, Strathnaver, Eriboll).

209. William Taylor (Ed.), *The Diary of James Calder*, Stirling 1875, pp. 26-7.

210. Eldest son John became minister of Rosskeen; Hughie succeeded his father as minister of Croy, while Charles ('my dear little Benjamin') became the venerated minister of Ferintosh. John MacDonald, Charles' successor there, described his predecessor as

This by-past year has been happier than usual with respect to my flock, there having been some more remarkable instances of conversion-work than usual, and more confirmation and consolation, and spiritual prosperity and vivacity, among the Lord's people in this place and this neighbourhood, so that this has been a jubilee year to some – a year that will be remembered and celebrated to the praise of free grace through all the years and ages, if I may so phrase it, of a never-ending eternity.[211]

The following year – the twenty-fifth in Calder's ministry – was even busier and more successful, though not without personal weakness and woe.[212] Much of his work was extended to 'a poor, despised people in two neighbouring parishes' which had not been blessed with worthy evangelical pastors.[213] In 1766 the tide of blessing reached its height, and Calder called it 'the happiest year of my ministry' regarding the depth and solidity of the work, if not the number of conversions.[214] Individual cases noted in Calder's diary are interesting and moving. 'Jan. 3rd. In a little hut which I visited today, I met with a precious young jewel deeply exercised, and longing and crying out for Christ, and who seemed to be really in the very crisis of the new birth; brought this young pleasant person along with me for a mile or two, who weeped incessantly all the way, and from whom I expect a pleasant visit soon. This was another New Year gift which gave me unspeakable joy!' The process of 'depth, solidity and lustre' continued until 1771, though conversions during this period were not so plentiful, during which time Calder's health was also failing. However, as late as 1774, while administering the Lord's Supper in Kilmuir Easter, Calder

---

'the holiest man I ever met on earth', although some complained that, dwelling largely on the love of Christ in his preaching, he was the *piobaire an aon phuirt* (piper of one tune) [Beaton, *Some Noted Ministers of the Northern Highlands*, p. 111].

211. Taylor, *The Diary of James Calder*, p. 36.

212. His only daughter, Annie, died in 1764, while his own frequent bodily ailments and weakness were another trial (ibid., p. 37).

213. ibid., p. 51. This could not have been the neighbouring parish of Petty, for here Calder's saintly contemporary, John Morrison, ministered. Collins says that both Petty and Croy 'shared in the showers of blessing with which God was pleased to honour the work of His faithful servants – a work that did far more to pacify the turbulent Highlands than any of the rigorous and ruthless measures resorted to by George II and his government' (G. N. M. Collins, *Men of the Burning Heart*, Edinburgh 1983, p. 91).

214. Taylor, *Diary of James Calder*, p. 69.

wrote: 'The dear communicants, the virgin lovers of Jesus, I observed flocking with ardour to the sacred table, singing and weeping as they came along. For many years back I have not seen such tokens.' [215]

William Mackenzie of Tongue

William Mackenzie (1738–1834) was the first of a remarkable dynasty of evangelical ministers – father, son and grandson – who served the parish of Tongue (or Kintail as it was locally called) in Sutherland from 1769 to 1845. Converted through the ministry of James Calder of Croy, the young William Mackenzie resolved to devote himself to the ministry. For four years following his transfer from the Achness Mission in Strathnaver in 1769, Mackenzie's preaching made little impression, and carelessness had begun to increase. One Sabbath day in 1773 a horse was bought and sold at the church door. Next Lord's Day, therefore, when the usual rush took place (to get out after the sermon!), Mackenzie addressed his congregation in a voice of sombre authority, and told all who had Gaelic to resume their seats, as he had something to say to them. All obeyed at once. They were for the moment awed, and amid breathless silence, he addressed them as follows:

> I came to this parish four years ago, on your unanimous call, and I had then the impression that I had God's call to. But I fear I have been mistaken. I am doing no good among you; the Gospel is making no impression on you. What is worse, you are hardening under it. Instead of receiving it, you flee from it, and leave God's house on His own day to buy and sell in the churchyard. I trust the Lord will remove me to some other place, where I shall not be utterly useless, as I am here. 'Woe is me that I sojourn in Mesech, that I dwell in the tents of Kedar!' [216]

Mackenzie then burst into tears and sat down in the pulpit, and for the next five minutes wept and sobbed, his feelings too strong for utterance. When he at last rose again to preach, a new power was apparent. So deep was the impression made and so great the power of God in their midst that it was said that no fewer than thirty souls dated their conversion from that exhortation. Indeed, from that day forward, 'there was a fresh

---

215. ibid., p. 83; see also William Taylor, 'The Diary of James Calder' in *Banner of Truth*, July/August 1974, vol. 130; Iain H. Murray, *Puritan Hope*, Edinburgh 1971 (reprinted 1991), pp. 163-4.

216. MacGillivray, *Sketches of Religion and Revivals of Religion*, p. 17.

outpouring of the Spirit of God', the main arresting truth of which was the dying love of Christ. For years afterwards, Mackenzie never preached on the Lord's Day but some of his people, on the ensuing week, at times as many as six or eight, came to him under conviction of sin asking the way to Christ. 'The work was an extensive and permanent one, and what he found a desolate wilderness became as the garden of the Lord ... It was the sin of despising and rejecting that love that made them restless and wretched and self-condemned till they found in the love itself the appointed remedy'.[217] Mackenzie became well known in Sutherland as 'The Great Minister', and it was said of his ministry that there was scarcely any part of Scotland more saturated with Gospel teaching and godly living than the remote parish in which his lot was cast.[218]

One popular local, William Mackay never failed to trudge the sixteen miles across roadless ground to the church in Tongue each Sabbath. Asked why he did so, even in deep snow, he replied that not only was it his duty, but he wanted always to be there lest 'the Spirit of God should be moving in the church that day'.[219] Other parishioners included Lord Reay of Tongue House and his family, all of whom were devout evangelicals, as well as their servant, Mr Clark, who became an elder in the church.

Mackenzie was still preaching with vigour in Tongue at the advanced age of ninety-three,[220] by which time even the more elderly people of the parish were mostly those that he had himself baptised in his early ministry! Mackenzie was quoted as saying, in the twilight of his life,

217. ibid., p. 18.

218. John Macleod, *Memories of the Far North*, Caithness 1919, pp. 1-2.

219. Thomson, *Tales of the Far North West*, p. 39.

220. ibid.

'My heart is in my work; there is nothing on earth I care for but my work. I know that Christ sent me to the work; I know that He gave me success in the work, and I know that when I get to heaven, many a soul from the parish of Tongue will meet me and welcome me as the humble instrument of getting them to heaven'.[221]

Mackenzie's son, Hugh Mackay Mackenzie, along with *his* son and successor, William Mackenzie, both left the Church of Scotland at the Disruption, whereupon they were forced to leave the manse and move into a single room in the parish school-master's house, which they rented for four shillings a week. Hugh was then in his mid-seventies and very asthmatic, while his son was ill of a bilious fever. Partly as a result of the hardships they then endured, both ministers died within a month of each other in the summer of 1845.

John Mill of Dunrossness
In 1743 the Rev. John Mill was transferred from Cullen Church of Scotland to that of Dunrossness, Shetland, in which parish he found the people 'generally rude and ignorant'. In time his diligent catechising and direct gospel preaching had the effect of bringing 'both young men and maids to such a degree of knowledge that they could scarce be put out upon any practical question of Divinity in whatever shape it was proposed'. By 1753 Mill could testify regarding his parishioners, 'The Spirit of God had been at work with them', and that some lived 'in an habitual practice of (gospel) truths'. In particular, during times of communion, which Mill had deferred for his first six years in the district,[222] 'there seems to be an unusual stir among the people'. He mentions one young girl in particular who came under deep distress, then appeared to grow in grace and soon became engaged to a young local man who shared her faith.[223]

By 1770 Mill could report: 'There seems to be a common work of the Spirit of God on many, convincing them of the necessity of a supernatural

---

221. MacGillivray, *Sketches of Religion and Revivals of Religion*, p. 17.

222. This was due to the ignorance with which many in Shetland then regarded this sacrament. For example, in Lerwick many looked on Communion as 'a charm which confers some good thing, and puts away old scores of their sins'. Those who were most deeply engrossed in sinful living were the most eager to partake (John Mill, *The Diary of the Reverend John Mill, Minister of the Parishes of Dunrossness, Sandwick and Cunningsburgh in Shetland, 1740–1803*, Edinburgh 1889, p. 31).

223. ibid., pp. 12-14.

work of grace in order to their eternal salvation, that engage in severals on sick beds, yet seem to rest there mostly; but a woman I saw lately in these circumstances, upon hinting the absolute necessity of being renewed and sanctified, cried out, "Lord, take me not off this earth till I know it to experience".' In particular, Mill refers to another young man and woman 'whom the Spirit of the Lord seemed to have wrought upon; they were lately joined in marriage together' and both became partakers of the Lord's Supper.[224] As late as 1799, at the age of eighty-eight, this veritable minister was still in active service, then having the joy and honour of welcoming into his pulpit James Haldane, on that itinerant evangelist's extensive Scottish preaching tour.

From further north in Shetland, Catharine Cleveland records a period of dramatic revivalism in the parish of Northmaven in 1774, during which 'swoons and convulsions became common … fifty or sixty would sometimes be carried struggling or roaring into the yard, and they would rise perfectly unconscious of what had happened'.[225] Cleveland compared the phenomena to that experienced during the Kentucky revival of 1800.[226]

John Graham of Clyne

'The rain of heavenly influences' descended on Ardclach, Nairnshire, between 1776 and '78, during the relatively brief ministry of the youthful John Graham of Clyne, Sutherland (c. 1751–80). Many hundreds flocked to hear this assistant minister preach, including people from more than a dozen nearby parishes, some of whom would make a return journey on foot of forty or even fifty miles to be present at his vast open-air services by the River Findhorn.[227] Graham's ministry was also greatly

---

224. ibid., pp. 35-6.

225. Catharine C. Cleveland, *The Great Revival in the West 1797–1805*, Massachusetts 1959, pp. 107-8. Unfortunately, Cleveland gives no more details of this unusual movement.

226. A religious gathering at Cane Ridge in Kentucky in early August 1801, where, over a number of days, an estimated 10,000 people converged upon a Presbyterian log meeting-house in Bourbon County, and where occurred unrestrained outbursts of emotional feelings, and such physical manifestations as scores being struck down as if dead.

227. Principal J. Macleod, *Donald Munro of Ferintosh and Rogart, with Sketch of Rev. John Graham*, Inverness 1939, pp. 64-6. Macleod believed that one reason separatism took such a strong hold in the parishes south of Inverness was the folk-memory of the

blessed in Strathspey, which showed notable signs of revived life at this time. People travelled from far and near to Rothiemurchus where 'A' Bhan-tighearn bhan' (the Laird's fair lady) had secured Graham's services for a time. Memories of early trophies of redeeming grace under his ministry remained fragrant for generations, as in the case of three young women, all with the name Eliza, who sat together in the Rothiemurchus churchyard to hear Graham preach from the text, 'My son, give me thine heart'. All three were there and then converted and became exemplary Christians, excelling most others in Christian graces and influencing their descendants in matters of faith.[228] One memorable communion season in Duthil at which Graham assisted was also especially anointed.[229]

'Perhaps as blessed a congregation as ever assembled in Scotland' gathered for a similarly marked communion season in Kiltearn around 1785.[230] Hundreds of God's people from the surrounding district were there to hear Dr Fraser of Kirkhill preach in the open-air on the Monday, when, from the beginning of the service and during its whole duration, there appeared to be 'an extraordinary manifestation of the Lord's gracious presence in the congregation ... Many of the Lord's people from their ecstasy of soul and joy of spirit did not know whether they were in the body or out of the body'. 'This', said one, 'is heaven on earth'.[231] The occasion was regarded as being the culminating point of the spiritual prosperity of Ross-shire. Reflected Dr Aird, 'The pious people in the country – and there were many at that time – noted the following, viz., that the gospel was as faithfully and purely preached in that part of Ross-shire after that date as it was before that date, but it was not followed with the same power as it had been before then'. [232]

---

persecution and slander meted out to Graham, partly at the hands of church authorities (Campbell, One of Heaven's Jewels, p. 143).

228. Rev. Donald MacLean, Duthil Past and Present, Inverness 1910, pp. 16-7.

229. Prof. J. MacLeod in 'Bean Torra Dhaamh' (Hymns of Mrs Clark), p. 24, quoted in John McInnes, Evangelical Movements in the Highlands of Scotland, Aberdeen 1951, pp. 162-3.

230. John Kennedy suggests the date was 1782 (Kennedy, Days of the Fathers in Ross-shire, p. 26).

231. Noble, Religious Life in Ross, p. 87. It is not noted, however, whether the service had a saving effect on any non-believers in attendance.

232. Kennedy, Days of the Fathers in Ross-Shire, pp. 26-7. This may partly explain why John Campbell, on passing through Easter Ross on his evangelistic tour of the

George Wishart
(Reformer).

Robert Bruce
of Kinnaird.

John Welsh
of Ayr.

John Livingstone
(Covenanter).

Richard Cameron
(Covenanter).

Ebenezer Erskine
of Portmoak.

William Mackenzie
of Tongue.

James Haldane
of Airthrey.

John Macdonald
of Ferintosh.

Statue of John Knox, New College, Edinburgh.

The secluded Annick Valley, marking the flow of the Stewarton revival, 1625.

Shotts Kirkyard, scene of the famed Kirk o' Shotts revival, 1630.

Overshadowed by Edinburgh Castle, Greyfriars Kirk, where the
National Covenant was signed, 1638. *(Kim Traynor)*

Bible of Covenanter, William Hannay of Tundergarth, Dumfries-shire.
The bible was damaged by a sword-thrust during a raid by government troops. *(Kim Traynor)*

14,000 gathered to hear John Welsh preach at
Irongrey, Dumfries-shire in 1678.

One of numerous Covenanter grave-stones
in Fenwick Kirkyard, Ayrshire.

Extraordinary showers of blessing rained on William Guthrie's parish of Fenwick, early 1660's, resulting in lasting spiritual reform.

Strath Brora, in east Sutherland's Clyne parish, was once renowned for its high proportion of eminently pious inhabitants.

Preaching Braes, Cambuslang, where George Whitefield preached to
c 25,000 people in July 1742.

Very rare example of the public
commemoration of a Scottish revival.

Muthill Old Church, which operated as the Parish
Church during the Muthill revival, 1742.

Baldernock Kirk, East Dunbartonshire, which parish also experienced revival in 1742.

Lush meadows in Croy parish, Inverness-shire, where James Calder ministered 1763-75.

The Sutherland parish of Tongue, served by three generations of
the Mackenzie family 1769–1845.

Kilbrandon (Isle of Seil) experienced awakening c1784 through the reading of
Joseph Alleine's *Alarm to the Unconverted.* *(J. Denham)*

The fiery preaching of James Haldane and associates in Thurso, Wick (above) and rural Caithness c 1799, created an immense sensation, leading to deep spiritual reform.

The influence of the zealous and indefatigable George Cowie on the extensive region circling Huntly continued for generations through his innumerable 'spiritual children'.

Forrest-rich slopes of Loch Eck, Cowal – vast parish of Donald MacArthur of Strachur around the turn of the nineteenth century.

Located high on the banks of the Tummel valley, Moulin witnessed revival under the ministry of Alexander Stewart c 1799.

Like other parts of Orkney, Westray was deeply affected by the Haldane revival of c 1800, a Baptist cause being established that has experienced revival repeatedly.

Before its inhabitants were crudely ejected during the Highland Clearances, the well-populated Strathnaver in Sutherland's Reay country experienced waves of spiritual life from the 1720s.

Natural amphitheatre by the Burn of Ferintosh, Easter Ross, where John Macdonald preached to crowds of up to 10,000.

The Paps of Jura mountain range, as seen from the western shores of Kintyre.

A work of grace was wrought in remote Glenelg through a young John MacRae
(later of Knockbain and Lewis).

The magnificent Cuillin mountains overshadowed a mighty move of the Spirit in Skye, 1812–14.

Lochranza, Arran, where Angus McMillan ministered during the great revival of 1812-13.

Ardeonaig, on the south shores of Loch Tay, came under revival influences via the devoted John Farquharson in1802, blossoming again under Robert Findlater's ministry, 1816–17.

The sequestered Glen Lyon, scene of great awakening under James Kennedy 1816-17.

George Rainy of Creich

George Rainy, a native of Aberdeenshire, moved to Ross-shire as tutor to a family in Kilmuir-Easter in the mid-1700s. Parish minister, the Rev. John Porteous, took a genuine interest in him and urged him to study the Gaelic language, which he did, with remarkable success. Greatly encouraged by the preaching and pastoral work of Porteous, Rainy became the ordained missionary in Rosehall in 1766, and the parish minister of Creich, east Sutherland, in 1771, where he laboured for thirty-nine years. He was much loved and esteemed by his people and his simple, believing and prayerful personal dealing with them, especially the young, was blessed to the salvation of many. Many of the converts of Rainy's ministry became 'The men' of later days. In 1809 a fatal fever broke out through the parish, east and west, and almost all who died of it were eminent Christians. Few elders were left. Nevertheless, it was said that on Rainy's death a year later there were still more than a hundred men in the parish who could openly testify to a personal work of grace in their lives, and as many women. Such was the striking result of Rainy's faithful and blessed ministry. [233]

The strength of the work and the deep root it took in many households may be judged by the fact that when, in 1811, Murdo Cameron was inducted as minister of the parish against the wishes of the congregation, almost all the people left in a body and began to meet, first in the open-air at Spinningdale, then under the shelter of a giant rock on the north side of Loch Migdale near Badbea. These meetings continued for two years, summer and winter, presided over by Hugh Mackenzie,

---

north with James Haldane in 1803, regretted that he 'could not hear of one who preached the gospel' in that region (Robert Philip, *The Life, Times, and Missionary Enterprises, of the Rev. John Campbell*, London 1841, p. 337). Yet when Alexander Stewart transferred from Moulin to Ross-shire in 1805 he found 'numerous devout congregations, many lively Christians and a great door of utterance'. Unfortunately, the situation in Stewart's new charge of Dingwall was not so encouraging, yet within two months of his induction he noted how 'our serious people already remark an evident shaking among the dry bones. There is, in various instances, a melting under the word'. The house of D. M., an experienced believer, in which a few used to meet on Sabbath evenings to pray and read the Scriptures, was now crowded, with a 'precious select party' also meeting there each Friday evening for prayer and conversation (Alexander Stewart, *Memoirs of the Late Rev. Alexander Stewart, D.D.: One of the Ministers of Canongate, Edinburgh*, Edinburgh 1822, p. 231).

233. MacRae, *The Life of Gustavus Aird*, pp. 72-4, 132-4. Robert Rainy, famous Principal of the Free Church College in Edinburgh from 1874 and Moderator of the first General Assembly of the United Free Church in 1900, was a grandson of George Rainy.

catechist of the parish, and three other godly elders. Thereafter, for the convenience of the people (in a parish thirty-five miles long), two separate meeting places – in the form of long cottages – were erected. When visiting ministers preached in the parish the congregation would again assemble in the church, but they steadfastly refused to hear their own minister. They persisted in this till what was seen as 'the blessed Disruption' gave them as their minister the godly Gustavus Aird. There were 280 signatures to the call. It was thus that Aird found a band of eminent men in the parish who supported him by their private and social prayer and regular church attendance. Indeed, the minister often confessed to a sense of want of fitness to preside over such a session as he had. [234]

Hugh Mackay of Moy

Badenoch and neighbourhood, in the richly evangelised parish of Moy, to the south of Inverness, experienced 'the stirrings of revived life' during the ministry of Hugh Mackay (1761–1804) between 1793 and 1804 – the years of his induction and death – whom earnest evangelicals used to go long distances to wait on. Indeed, from as far away as Grantown-on-Spey, [235] 'many trudged summer and winter, through wild slochd-muie' to attend his ministry. Meanwhile, for the convenience of the people of Duthil, this zealous and faithful servant of God held open-air services near the old Findhorn Bridge, Tomatin, which were attended by 'many tokens of divine favour'. [236] Mackay had a great love for souls. On one occasion Lachlan Mackenzie was assisting him at a Communion. After the service on the Monday Lachlan found his host rolling on the ground weeping because no one had been converted. Great was Mackay's delight, however, when Mackenzie assured him that five people had indeed been hopefully converted as a result of the service. Aiding Mackay in his work until an early breakdown in health in 1798 was fellow clansman and catechist William

---

234. ibid., pp. 74-5; P. Carnegie Simpson, *The Life of Principal Rainy*, London 1909, pp. 3-12. For more on Hugh Mackenzie see MacGillivray, *Sketches of Religion and Revivals of Religion*, pp. 29-33.

235. Donald Maclean states that among those travelling from Grantown to hear Mackay preach were a number of disaffected Baptists, motivated by the 'burlesquing of sacred things' by the Grantown Baptist minister, which resulted in 'a rapid decay of Baptist influence in that quarter' (MacLean, *Duthil Past and Present*, pp. 23-4). This cannot be right, as Grantown Baptist Church was only established in 1805, a year after Mackay's death.

236. ibid., pp. 23-4.

MacKay (also catechist of neighbouring Croy), who, like his minister, belonged to the Reay country and was remembered as 'one of the ablest, as he was one of the most highly esteemed, laymen in the Far North'. [237]

Wester Ross – Lochcarron

Lachlan Mackenzie (1754–1819) was said to have been 'a key figure' in the spiritual revival which came to parts of the Scottish Highlands in the late eighteenth century. [238] Following University education he became school-master in Lochcarron in 1776, and despite initial opposition from a Moderate Presbytery (which opposition continued throughout his ministry in the Lochcarron district), Mackenzie was settled as minister there in 1782, a charge he held till his death thirty-seven years later. A man keenly devoted to God – much of his time was spent on his knees, and many a sleepless night he thus passed – so was he also to his congregation. At all hours of the day and even at night he was often to be found counselling, visiting or walking to the distant corners of his parish. His niece wrote that 'Lachlan lived singularly above the world while he lived in it', and referred to him as the '*Elijah*' of Lochcarron. Like Elijah – and indeed, like numerous other Highland saints – Mackenzie was known as something of a prophet. Indeed, according to John Kennedy of Dingwall,[239] remarkably, never did a sudden death occur in the parish during his ministry, without some intimation of it being given from the pulpit on the previous Sabbath.[240]

---

237. John Macleod, *By-Paths of Highland Church History*, Edinburgh 1965, pp. 86-90; MacInnes, *Evangelical Movements in the Highlands*, pp. 162-3.

238. Iain H. Murray (Ed.), *The Happy Man: The Abiding Witness of Lachlan Mackenzie*, Edinburgh 1971, flyleaf.

239. Kennedy's own father, also called John (see page 202), was raised up under Lachlan's ministry, and was ordained by him in 1795 (ibid., p. 31). Lachlan had a particularly sensitive disposition, and early one stormy Communion Sabbath, 'in a fit of unbelief', shut himself in his room, feeling 'it would be presumption to go out in the face of a frowning providence'. His friend, John Kennedy, suspecting Mackenzie's state of mind, forced his way into his locked bedroom and respectfully but firmly urged him to take up his duty and not give in to the Tempter. Lachlan yielded to such reason and as he made his way to the meeting place, the rain ceased and the sun began to shine. 'During the service of that day the Lord's servants and people enjoyed a "time of refreshing" that left its mark on their memories forever' (Kennedy, *Days of the Fathers in Ross-shire*, p. 130).

240. Kennedy, *Days of Fathers in Ross-shire*, p. 64. He also predicted, among many things, that his successor in Lochcarron would be a 'dumb dog that would not bark', and so, apparently, it proved (Murray, *The Happy Man*, p. 31).

A predecessor of Mackenzie, the godly Rev. Eneas Sage – and like him, a native of Easter Ross – had helped prepare the ground in this formerly dark parish, and on his death in 1774 at the age of eighty-seven, many of those who mourned his passing had become true and vital Christians through his ministry, and were themselves 'the primitive fathers of the spiritual generation that followed them'.[241] But what took place through Mackenzie was described as a spiritual and moral reformation. In 1792, for example, Mackenzie encouraged many parishioners to sign a document pledging themselves against evil habits previously common in the parish (such as drinking alcohol after a funeral or even a communion, and 'conversing on idle or worldly topics' after a church service).[242] There were also immense numbers who came from all over the north of Scotland to partake of the Lord's Supper at Lochcarron. In an account of one communion, an almost incidental reference is made to 'thousands' being present, while some 'two hundred were awakened to a sense of their lost state' – this in a parish with a population of less than 900.[243] Mackenzie himself referred to times of 'general reviving and outpouring of the Spirit' upon the district, when men and women came under the power of the gospel not simply in ones and twos but sometimes in large numbers together.[244]

During the height of his fame as a Highland evangelist, Lachlan Mackenzie was invited to preach in the old parish Church of St Nicholas in Aberdeen. At the evening service the church was packed to its utmost capacity and there was eager anticipation on the part of the worshippers. A titter went through the congregation on beholding a man ascend the pulpit dressed in rough homespun suit, with long shaggy hair – most unlike the usual clergymen of that time. But the moment Mackenzie gave out his opening psalm a solemn stillness began to pervade the audience, which deepened further with his opening prayer. The sermon was on Revelation 3:20, *'Behold, I stand at the door and knock'*. Mackenzie

---

241. Donald Sage, *Memorabilia Domestica*, Wick 1889 (reprinted 1975), p. 22.

242. Murray, *The Happy Man*, pp. 18-19.

243. One who joined the Church on this occasion and whose moving story has often been told, was 'Muckle Kate', a blind woman in her eighties, supposed to have been guilty of 'every forbidden crime in the Law of God except murder' (ibid., pp. 242-6). One of Mackenzie's first converts was his assistant; 'and a truly valuable coadjutor he found in big Rory' thereafter (Kennedy, *Days of the Fathers in Ross-shire*, p. 60).

244. Murray, *The Happy Man*, p. 20.

proceeded to preach, illustrating with a lengthy imaginative parable based on Highland tradition. Everyone listened with rapt attention, and when, in closing, the preacher twice asked, 'Who is standing at your heart's door and knocking tonight?', almost the entire congregation was deeply moved. It was said that 'there were six hundred seeking souls in the church that night'.[245]

The latter years of Lachlan's ministry were not marked with the same degree of blessing as the early part. When John Macdonald visited the area in 1816,[246] he referred to 'Lochcarron sinners' and how there were 'not many of a contrary description' to be found. But Mackenzie had accomplished much good and a century later his memory was still largely cherished by the elderly people of the parish. By this time, too, Lochcarron had sent no less than thirty men into the Christian ministry. According to Norman Macfarlane, 'Lachlan Mackenzie's gift of soul-winning underwent processes of multiplication'.[247]

Eriboll

In the parish of Eriboll, in north-west Sutherland, the labours of both the Rev. John Robertson, afterwards of Rothesay and of Kingussie, and, from 1800 to 1802, the Rev. Neil MacBride, later of Arran, were much blessed around the turn of the nineteenth century. Thus, when a young John Kennedy (later of Killearnan) was appointed missionary there between 1802 and 1806, the fruit of these men 'appeared in a goodly remnant of living souls, who were the "light" and the "salt" of the district, and in the respect for the means of grace entertained by the whole body of the people'. One 'excellent and truly eminent man' who resided in Eriboll at this time was John McIntyre, a 'Society schoolmaster', who came originally from Glenlyon, Perthshire.[248]

---

245. ibid., pp. 238-41.

246. Macdonald had come to Lochcarron on invitation from Mackenzie, who wrote to him: 'I hear that you keep a large store of powder which you use in blasting. I wish you to come and try your skill in breaking the hard rocks of Lochcarron'! (Steve Taylor 'Skye Revival' CD ROM 2003, Chapter 12, *Wild Man of Ferintosh*).

247. Murray, *The Happy Man*, p. 31.

248. He dwelt in Eriboll for 12 years, before emigrating, with several other families, to Prince Edward Island, Canada, in 1815. There they formed a small colony and called the place 'New Eriboll'. 'Such was the moral weight of his (McIntyre's) character that he was employed in conducting worship morning and evening with his expatriated countrymen, on board the vessel, in which there was a number of truly

There was reported to have been in the remote preaching station of Camus an Duin, on the shores of Loch Eriboll around the time of the Clearances, twenty-four male communicants who could be asked to participate in the monthly prayer meeting, suggesting also that attendance at services in this outpost was very significantly higher.[249] In one glen was a hamlet, built around the sides of an amphitheatre. Here resided about thirty families, in each of which could be found at least one who feared the Lord. 'On a quiet summer evening', remarked John Kennedy, 'one could hear the songs of praise from all these houses mingling together … One did feel … as if the place were none other than the house of God and the very gate of heaven'. [250]

---

pious persons. He was in the habit of paying an annual visit to his friends in Glenlyon' (William Findlater, *Memoir of Rev. Robert Findlater, Together with a Narrative of the Revival of Religion During his Ministry at Lochtayside, Perthshire 1816–1819*, Glasgow 1840, p. 177).

249. Campbell, *One of Heaven's Jewels*, p. 118.

250. Kennedy, *Days of the Fathers in Ross-Shire*, pp. 139-40.

CHAPTER 3

Highland Awakening 1797–1809

Introduction

With regard to the Highlands of Scotland towards the close of the eighteenth century, there existed a general dearth of evangelical witness among ordinary people, gentry and ministers alike, and even fewer instances of anything approaching intense religious feeling or commitment. In his *Revivals in the Highlands and Islands*, Alexander MacRae writes that, with the exception of the counties of Moray, Easter Ross and Sutherland, in some districts of which there could be found a lively evangelical spirit (as testified to in the accounts of *Later Eighteenth Century Revivals in the Far North* in the preceding chapter of this book – see page 154) 'the land was held in the deadening grip of the black frost of moderatism'. He continues: 'With two or three conspicuous exceptions every pulpit, from Mull of Kintyre to Cape Wrath along the western shores, and every pulpit in the islands, without exception, was without the light of the living gospel of the grace of God ...'[1]

An increased concern by believers in the south of Scotland regarding this shocking situation in northern districts, aided by an increasing degree of mobility across Britain generally, led to the advance of itinerant evangelism throughout this northern expanse from the close of the eighteenth century, especially by non-conformists such as Relief Church

---

1. Alexander MacRae, *Revivals in the Highlands and Islands*, p. 10. See also Donald Sage, *Memorabilia Domestica*, Wick 1889.

missionaries and the 'Haldane preachers'.[2] Also of huge influence was the completion of the translation of the Gaelic Bible around this time and the strong evangelistic thrust of the Gaelic School Societies, the first of which was established in 1811 by Edinburgh Baptist pastor, Christopher Anderson, and which became instrumental in spreading the gospel message over many years in numerous remote communities.[3] These organisations built on the foundations of experimental Christianity laid by the influential SSPCK throughout the eighteenth century, particularly in southern and eastern parts of the Highlands.[4]

Edinburgh seems to have been the centre of this fresh season of spiritual stirring in Scotland (occasioned, some historians believe, by the French Revolution and the public anxiety aroused by the possibility of similar unrest in Britain), in which Christians were being drawn together to engage in combined efforts to reach the unchurched masses with the good news of salvation in Christ. Meetings for united prayer with a specific view to the 'present alarming aspect of affairs' in the land generally were begun in the city and arrangements for similar meetings made for many other districts. Sabbath schools were extensively organised and zealously taught, while tracts were also numerously circulated. As a result, wrote Professor W. L. Alexander: 'the aggressive spirit of Christian zeal was firmly roused, and was distancing all competition by the rapidity of its movements, the energy of its efforts and the extent of its operations.'[5]

One historian speaks of spiritual awakening coming all of a sudden to Scotland towards the close of the eighteenth century, whereby

---

2. Allan MacInnes believes that the increased pace of revivalism (in Scotland) from the 1790s can be attributed primarily 'to the influence of itinerant preachers' and more so to 'the identification and inspiration of religious restlessness' than to institutional developments, such as Congregationalism and Baptism (Allan I. MacInnes, 'Evangelical Protestantism', in Graham Walker & Tom Gallacher, *Sermons and Battle Hymns: Protestant Popular Culture in Modern Scotland*, Edinburgh 1990, pp. 53-4).

3. Just three years earlier Anderson had set up the Baptist Itinerant Society, which was boosted in 1827 by the creation of the Baptist Home Missionary Society for Scotland (BHMSS).

4. See Alexander MacRae, *The Fire of God Among the Heather; or The Spiritual Awakening of the Highland People*, Tongue 1930, for a glowing testimony of the work of the Societies.

5. W. Lindsay Alexander, *Memoir of the Rev. John Watson, Late Pastor of the Congregational Church in Musselburgh, and Secretary of the Congregational Union for Scotland*, Edinburgh 1845, p. 13.

men, roused out of their long repose … felt that hunger of the soul for suitable spiritual food which naturally follows a long period of spiritual destitution or inadequate supply. And as the existing ecclesiastical bodies were not sufficiently elastic to meet the new and enlarged capacities and wants of the people – the latter impetuously rushed forth to find elsewhere what was denied them at home. Hence the crowds that followed Messrs. Haldane and Aikman in their first tours of preaching through Scotland. Hence the thousands upon thousands that covered the slopes of the Calton Hill to listen to the preachers from England. And hence the almost instantaneous rise into considerable strength of a new religious body hitherto nearly unknown in Scotland (Congregationalism). The new wine could not be stayed in the old bottles, and so when it burst forth it was caught and kept by those who alone at the time were prepared to receive it.[6]

The revival movements that arose in the north of Scotland in this period, as well as in subsequent years, took place during an era of great social change, when the notorious Highland Clearances were in operation. It is quite probable that the anxiety and insecurity that this upheaval caused had an effect on the attachment that many found in Christian fellowship and the soul comforts of the gospel message. D. E. Meek sees Highland awakenings as giving the people 'a beatific vision' in the midst of crushing poverty and social breakdown.[7] Allan MacInnes opines that there is no definite casual connection between revival and economic privation, as local revivals rarely coincided with famines or population removal and relocation. He feels that revival movements, however, 'cannot be dissociated from the social restlessness occasioned by Clearance and by rural congestion and deprivation within crofting communities'.[8]

Highland awakenings may also have been a substitute for political action, and poet Sorley MacLean controversially claims that the Highland revivals of the early nineteenth century actually dampened

6. William Lindsay Alexander, *Memoirs of the Life and Writings of Ralph Wardlaw*, Edinburgh 1856, p. 44.

7. D. E. Meek, 'Gaelic Bible, Revival and Mission: The Spiritual Rebirth of the Nineteenth-Century Highlands', in James Kirk (Ed.), *The Church in the Highlands*, Edinburgh 1998, p. 116.

8. MacInnes, *Evangelical Protestantism*, p. 54.

initial resistance to the Clearances, as resistance in a temporal world was seen as futile. For example he suggested that the fact that there were many more examples of resistance to the Highland Clearances in the period between 1780 and 1820 than in the period between 1820 and 1870 is partly accounted for by the spreading and deepening of religious revival after 1820.[9] This, however, has been disputed by others. As Roderick Macleod points out, resistance to evictions in Harris took place during the very period when that island was affected by revival. In the summer of 1839, for example, five arrests were made by the Sheriff and military during disturbances at Borve, Harris. Macleod additionally points to considerable resistance to house eviction occurring a few years after significant revival in North Uist.[10] Macleod's argument is weakened, however, by his failure to give evidence of revival in Harris in the year specified, 1839, which year, certainly, witnessed revivals in many other parts of Scotland, including several Western Isles. Nor has my own research uncovered spiritual awakening in Harris at this time.

It is also noteworthy that awakening in the Highlands during this period occurred within the international context of the 'Second Evangelical Awakening', when widespread revivals also occurred in Wales, England, America and Scandinavia from the 1790s.[11] Interestingly, an important precursor of the Second Evangelical Awakening was the revival of the Concert of Prayer, pioneered by Scottish evangelical ministers during the Great Awakening of the 1740s, and revived in the last decade of the century when John Erskine, one of Jonathan Edwards's numerous Scottish correspondents, re-published Edwards's 'Humble Attempt ...' (see page 128). Soon the prayer call was taken up by evangelical groups from various denominations, not only in Britain, but also in America and other countries.

We conclude the introduction to this chapter with the observation of Alexander MacRae that, 'The awakenings that took place throughout the north (of Scotland), almost simultaneously, in districts far removed from one another, during the first two decades of the century, did more for the moral and intellectual development of the people than it is possible now to compute'.[12]

---

9. D. E. Meek, 'Gaelic Bible, Revival and Mission', p. 116.

10. Roderick Macleod, *The Progress of Evangelicalism*, pp. 223-4.

11. See Davies, *'I Will Pour Out My Spirit'*, pp. 112-49.

12. MacRae, *Revivals in the Highlands and Islands*, p. 10.

Work of the Haldane Brothers

The tireless pioneering labours of aristocrat brothers, James (1768–1851) and Robert Haldane (1764–1842), and their missionaries throughout Scotland, but especially in the Highlands and Islands around the turn of the nineteenth century, added a massive impetus to evangelicalism in the country. While both men became preachers and theological writers, James's main contribution to the Church in Scotland was as an itinerant evangelist, while Robert's was as a philanthropist. The Haldanes founded the Society for Propagating the Gospel at Home (SPGH) and established a series of seminary classes under the teaching of evangelical ministers in Glasgow, Dundee and Edinburgh. These classes, which functioned between 1799 and 1808 and consisted of a two-year course, provided a cadre of home missionary preachers nearly three hundred strong, equipped with basic biblical and literary skills. In ten years the Haldanites had established more than a hundred independent churches, providing also for the training of many ministers.

The Haldanes were regarded by the Government as subversive, while opposition from the Established Church was even more intense; the General Assembly in 1799 passing an Act which attacked them and their itinerants as 'notoriously disaffecting to the civil constitution of the country'.[13] Ministers were not permitted to employ these untrained or unqualified preachers in their services. In his introduction to the Journal of their 1797 tour, James Haldane defended the practice of lay preaching: 'We consider every Christian is bound, whenever he has opportunity, to warn sinners to flee from the wrath to come, and to point out Jesus as the way, the truth and the life. Whether a man declares those important truths to two, or two hundred, he is, in our opinion, a preacher of the Gospel, or one who declares the glad tidings of salvation, which is the precise meaning of the word "preach".'[14]

Early Work in Edinburgh

James Haldane preached his first sermon in May 1797 at the collier village of Gilmerton, two or three miles south of Edinburgh. This was attended with a blessing, but the school-house where they had hitherto preached,

---

13. Angus Macdonald, *An Enduring Testimony*, p. 3. It was in this year also that the Haldanes turned away from Presbyterianism to embrace Congregationalism.

14. Alexander Haldane, *The Lives of Robert and James Haldane*, London 1852 (reprinted 1990), p. 155.

and which had been filled to overflowing, was now being deprived them by the Moderate minister, who had at first been quiescent but 'now burned with an indignation quite inconsistent with his professed Moderation'.[15] So they resorted to a large barn, which continued to be filled to excess by the people, who flocked from the neighbourhood and listened with great interest to the evangelists' earnest and affectionate appeals.

Haldane was not the only evangelist to have marked success in central Scotland at the turn of the nineteenth century. John Campbell, a native of Edinburgh, one of the dozen founders of the Religious Tract Society in Edinburgh in 1793, also engaged in fruitful exploits in Gilmerton and other townships to the south and east of Edinburgh at this time.[16] Meanwhile, the Rev. Charles Simeon travelled north from Cambridge for a holiday in 1796 and ended up conducting a successful preaching tour (the most noted outcome of which occurred in Moulin; see page 187). Similarly, English evangelist, Rowland Hill visited Scotland in 1798. His preaching was said to have been a complete novelty except to those who had heard Whitefield many years previously. During this visit Hill was invited to preach the first sermon in the Edinburgh Circus, which had been taken over by the Haldanes 'for the conversion of sinners and a genuine revival of religion'.[17]

Hill returned north of the border two years later, when, accompanied variously by Robert or James Haldane, he attracted massive crowds in

---

15. ibid., pp. 151-2.

16. In 1797 he also formed the Magdalene Asylum and co-founded the Society for Propagating the Gospel at Home (SPGH).

17. Kinniburgh, *Fathers of Independency in Scotland, or, Biographical Sketches of Early Scottish Congregational Ministers, A.D. 1798–1851*, Edinburgh 1851, p. 239. Other congregations (especially Secession churches) in metropolitan Scotland were also flourishing at the turn of the century. For example, the Original Burgher Associate Congregation in East Campbell Street, Glasgow was opened in 1799 to seat 1,600, and for over a considerable period every seat was occupied, with people filling the pulpit stairs as well as the elders' bench. 1,400 tokens were prepared for the 1802 communion (D. Robertson, *Blackfriars United Free Church, Glasgow: Being an Historical Sketch of the Church which was Originally 'The Original Burgher Associate Congregation', and Afterwards 'East Campbell Street Free'*, Glasgow 1901, pp. 12-13). Similarly, the chapel-of-ease in Clyde Street, Anderston, situated in the Barony parish, was at the beginning of 1800 one of the most popular and best-filled places of worship in Glasgow, the main drawing power being the ministry of the Rev. Dr John Love.

Glasgow, Paisley, Dundee, Aberdeen and especially Edinburgh. The Circus deemed far too small, Hill preached several times on Calton Hill to crowds which grew to an estimated 20,000, equal to a quarter of the city's population. These were undoubtedly the largest Scottish congregations since the high days of Whitefield, and the most solemn that Hill had seen for many years. John Aikman, the evangelist who travelled with Haldane on his north Scotland tour (see below), often preached at the Circus, and also, when this church outgrew its premises, at the spacious Tabernacle on Leith Walk, which opened in July 1801 and which, for a number of years thereafter, was nearly filled every Sabbath, and often crowded in all parts.[18]

First Haldane Tour

Later in the summer of 1797 James Haldane embarked on a major evangelistic tour, the first of a series of successive itinerancies over a period of nine years, during which he preached in almost every town or populous village in Scotland – from Berwick-upon-Tweed and the Solway Firth to John O'Groats and the northern isles of Orkney and Shetland.[19] He was accompanied initially by James Aikman, then by William Innes, or John Campbell. 'Upon the tour to the North in 1797', remarked Alexander Haldane, 'there was poured out a blessing which never can be mistaken'.[20] Indeed, it led to the formation of nine Congregational churches. Then, in the summer of 1898 Haldane traversed the west and south of Scotland; and, after his return, he again visited Dunkeld and other places in Perthshire, everywhere his preaching being greatly blessed. Then again, the following year (1799), another tour of the North was embarked upon, which took the evangelists as far north as to the Shetland isle of Unst, the most northerly inhabited island in Britain.

Orkney

The *Missionary Magazine* for 1797 reported that 'a revival of religion begins to appear' in Orkney, which gave evidence of being 'one of

---

18. Aikman cordially left to begin another new church, totally self-funded, in North College Street. This opened in May 1802. Here he preached gratuitously for the rest of his life (he died in 1834). Indeed, the Circus/Tabernacle became the mother church to various congregations which sprang up in and around Edinburgh such as one in Musselburgh, formed in 1801.

19. Haldane, *Robert and James Haldane*, p. 153.

20. ibid.

the most desolate places, in respect of Christianity, in all Scotland'.[21] James Haldane and co-worker John Aikman attracted huge attention in August 1797 when they preached throughout the islands. In Stronsay they spoke to 800 people, 'or about three-fourths of the whole population'. In Kirkwall, where the annual Fair was in progress, their sermons from day to day were 'an object of attraction', and were frequented by congregations amounting to an estimated three or four thousand people, and, on the Lord's day, even to upwards of 6,000. Haldane noted that as a result, 'the fair was, in a measure, emptied every evening' and that 'many of the people appeared much affected and in tears'. The missionaries stayed sixteen days in Orkney, and preached no less than fifty-five times over the course of ten days, so that each evangelist must have preached an average of three times a day, although, with the chief labour falling upon Haldane, the average of his sermons must have exceeded that number. [22]

Spiritual awakening in Orkney in fact began in the years immediately prior to Haldane's visit, through a prayer meeting established in Kirkwall in 1790 by John Rusland, a tailor who had returned from a holiday in Newcastle fired with the evangelical preaching he had heard in the Secession church there. [23] It was soon observed that 'numbers of people in various parts of the country meet regularly every Sabbath, when they have no sermon in the parish, to join in praise and prayer, to read the Scriptures, evangelical sermons and other religious books'.[24]

---

21. 'Missionary Magazine', 1797, quoted in McNaughton, *Early Congregational Independency in Orkney*, Cambridge 2006, p. 1. Thomas McCrie said that at that time Orkney was 'deplorably destitute of religious instruction, the great masses living in ignorance of the doctrines of salvation' (Thomas McCrie, *Life of Thomas McCrie, D.D.*, Edinburgh 1840, p. 27). Of Kirkwall Haldane wrote that only 'two or three individuals' were familiar with the doctrine of justification by faith. Orkney historian B. H. Hossack, outraged at such a claim, stated that on the contrary, 'there were within the Cathedral so many earnest people as to form, with their families ... an enthusiastic congregation of 700 souls' (B. H. Hossack, *Kirkwall in the Orkneys*, Kirkwall, 1900, p. 450).

22. James Haldane, *Journal of a Tour Through the Northern Counties of Scotland and the Orkney Isles, in Autumn 1797*, Edinburgh 1798, pp. 52-65; Haldane, *Lives of Robert and James Haldane*, pp. 167-75.

23. McCrie says the prayer meeting 'was held by a few individuals in a remote corner of one of the islands' (Thomas McCrie, *Life of Thomas McCrie*, Edinburgh 1840, p. 27).

24. McNaughton, *Early Congregational Independency in Orkney*, p. 1.

An 800-seater church was built in 1796 and William Broadfoot was appointed as its first minister the following year to an estimated congregation of over 500. [25]

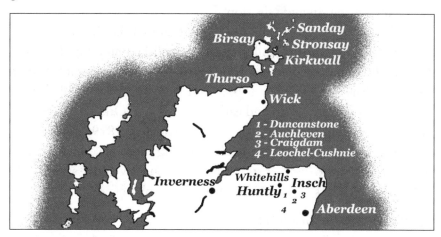

The revival led to an appeal for the supply of sermon from the Anti-Burgher Synod. When the Rev. Thomas McCrie (1772–1835) [26] came to preside at the ordination of Broadfoot in August 1798, he found that 'the excitement was very strong, being exhibited in the arresting attention and visible impression produced in the crowds which assembled Sabbath-day and week-day, to hear the gospel, and in the eagerness with which they sought the instruments and counsels of the ministers in private'. McCrie later recalled how one only needed to open one's mouth to speak of Christ and folk would listen; and when you had finished, they would follow you to your house and beseech you to teach them more. He said there was not one preacher from whom they would not receive the Word gladly, and not one sermon which did not bring

25. Frank D. Bardgett, *Two Millennia of Church and Community in Orkney*, Edinburgh 2000, p. 105. This church was packed to capacity when Haldane preached here in 1797 (Hossack, *Kirkwall in the Orkneys*, p. 446).

26. Such scenes left a 'very strong' impression on the mind of McCrie, and on his return to Edinburgh in September he gave an account of his mission. In his address he contrasted every one of the remarkable features he had witnessed in Kirkwall to the apathy and carelessness too often manifested in 'more favoured' parts of the land. The revival in Orkney led to a notable change in McCrie's preaching, and where previously his sermons had been too abstract and intellectual for ordinary hearers, he soon became one of the most respected preachers of his day, and later an eminent Church historian (*DSCHT*, p. 506).

tears from the eyes of some. Indeed, he said, it was 'no uncommon thing to see hundreds in tears, not from the relation of a pathetic story, nor by an address to the passions, but by the simple declaration of a few plain facts representing sin and salvation'.[27]

Such was the success of the newly-built church that just a few years after its construction the building was demolished and rebuilt to seat 1,200.[28] Four more Secession congregations had been established in various parishes of Orkney by 1803,[29] and there was considerable further expansion in the late 1820s and early '30s.[30] When Orkney native John Hercus paid a sixth return visit to the islands in 1819, he was sure the novelty of itinerating and field-preaching must have considerably subsided, but was delighted to be able to frequently address '600, 700 or 800 on weekdays, and 1,000 or 1,500 on Sabbaths'.[31]

Caithness: Thurso and Wick

Crossing the Pentland Firth from Orkney to Thurso, Wick and outlying districts, Haldane and Aikman witnessed even more noteworthy events. Everyone seemed to take great interest in both the evangelists and their message, and the two men regularly preached to crowds of several thousands in all weathers and at various times of day. They also aroused considerable opposition. One morning in Wick the parish minister preached a sermon. That evening Haldane preached in a yard, where it was thought there were 4,000 people assembled. He took occasion to show the fallacy of the doctrine preached in the forenoon. 'Some genteel people, but not religious people, called out "Stone him!" others,

---

27. McCrie, *Life of Thomas McCrie*, pp. 27-9.

28. For some time after its opening it was said, 'The audience seldom falls short of 1,000' (Hossack, *Kirkwall in the Orkneys*, p. 446).

29. These were in Sanday (1800), Stronsay (1800), Birsay (1801) and Stromness (1803). The first Secession minister in Stronsay was the young and energetic James Sinclair, who quickly attracted a large congregation; as many as 255 people partaking of communion in his new kirk one Sunday in June 1801 (W. M. Gibson, *Auld Peedie Kirks*, Kirkwall 1991, p. 85).

30. South Ronaldsay (1826), Eday (1828), Rousay (1829), Sandwick (1829), Shapinsay (1831) and Firth (1835). See also Brown, *Religion and Society in Scotland*, p. 89.

31. 'Christian Herald' 1819, quoted in McNaughton, *Early Congregational Independency in Lowland Scotland*, vol. 2, Glasgow 2007, p. 230. This was in great contrast to other places Hercus visited, such as Ayrshire, where the interest was considerably less.

"Stop him!" However, no one obeyed their commands and Haldane proceeded with his subject'.[32]

A Journal entry following the evangelists' return visit two years later records 'many pleasing fruits' of their labours on that former tour. It also stated, 'The desire of hearing is rather increased than diminished in Caithness; at the country places where they preached they always found large congregations. Those who have been already gathered in seem only to be a kind of first fruits of a more abundant harvest of souls in Caithness'. The preachers were greatly appreciative of a few godly ministers in the county, who not only preached faithfully in their churches, but also ventured out 'to the highways and hedges to compel sinners to come in'.[33] In William Ballantyne's meeting place in Thurso, were 180 communicants, including upwards of eighty from Wick, most of whom were brought to a knowledge of the truth since the itinerants first visited Caithness. Here the people obliged the evangelists to preach both within and outwith the building, and again at eight the next morning. Haldane then left for the south, while Aikman and Innes remained in the county two or three weeks longer. They later had occasion to give testimony 'to the remarkable work of grace evidently begun in Caithness, and give the pleasing intelligence that at least thirty young people in Inverness appear to have been brought to the knowledge of the truth by attending the Sabbath-schools and itinerant preaching in that place'.[34]

John Cleghorn, like Ballantyne, had studied in Haldane's seminary classes and was later sent to Wick, where he settled as pastor over the congregation he had gathered. He later wrote that through Haldane's visits (1797, 1799) 120 persons in his town had given evidence of saving change, and perhaps even a greater number in Thurso.[35] As a result, Congregational churches were erected in both locations. 'Many have spoken to me', he testified, 'of the effects of the word on this occasion, but they have always wanted words to express their views of them … Some have told me there was an astonishing authority and a sort of indescribable evidence attending the word, which they could not resist … So generally was the attention of people drawn to it that you could

32. Haldane, *Lives of Robert and James Haldane*, p. 182.

33. ibid., p. 271.

34. ibid., p. 272.

35. ibid., pp. 317-18.

hardly find two conversing together but religion was the subject'.[36] When James Haldane and John Campbell returned to Wick in 1803 they were pleased to find 'the voice of melody in almost every dwelling'.[37]

Huntly

On his way south Haldane stopped in Huntly, where he was welcomed by George Cowie (1749–1806), long-serving pastor of the Anti-Burgher (Secession) Church in that town.[38] Although Haldane's journal says little about this visit, it in fact sparked a controversy that had

---

36. Beaton, 'Ecclesiastical History of Caithness', p. 158, quoted in MacInnes, *The Evangelical Movement in the Highlands of Scotland*, p. 164. Blessed as the Haldane movement was, according to Alexander Auld, 'undoubtedly, the means most owned of the Lord for the creation and maintenance of spiritual life in Caithness during this generally dreary period was the mission charge of Achreny, in the parish of Halkirk'. Here, 'godly and gifted men, who were carefully excluded from parochial charges under the control of patrons, found refuge…. The names of … Hugh McKay, afterwards of Moy; John Robertson of Kingussie; John Macdonald of Ferintosh; John Munro of Halkirk; Finlay Cook of Reay – all successively occupied this sphere' (Alexander Auld, *Ministers and Men of the Far North*, Wick 1868, pp. 26-7). As late as the time of the Disruption, the Achreny Mission was referred to as 'a garden of the Lord' ('Free Presbyterian Magazine', vol. 19, p. 233, quoted in Rev. D. W. B. Somerset, *The Achreny Mission*, Part 3 – [www.fpchurch.org.uk]).

37. Philip, *Life, Times, and Missionary Enterprises, of John Campbell*, p. 337. The missionaries also came across an 'old Baptist church' (with twenty mainly elderly members), of which Sir William Sinclair had been the pastor. This humble saint used to regularly wash the feet of every member before eating the Lord's Supper.

38. Cowie's settlement in Huntly was largely influenced by William Brown, inducted to the parish of Craigdam in 1752. Through Brown's indefatigable labours (he was known as the 'rinnin' minister' because he was so active!), the Secession took firm root in north-east Scotland. He itinerated throughout the wider region, establishing congregations in Huntly, Keith and Shiels as well as numerous outstations, which extended as far north-east as Knoggan Hill, two miles south of Rosehearty, where he was especially popular with local fishermen. It was said of Brown that he added more churches to the Secession than some had added members. Later, contemporaneous with Cowie's period of ministry, under the thirty-nine-year ministry of the hugely popular Patrick Robertson, Craigdam continued to be a Secession stronghold, with a dozen prayer meetings and several large Sabbath schools being in operation at one time (George Walker, *Craigdam and its Ministers, the Rev. William Brown and the Rev. Patrick Robertson*, Aberdeen 1885, pp. 8-28). To Whitehill in the same period, crowds flocked to hear William Balass from every quarter, and membership of his church stood at nearly 700 towards the close of his ministry (James T. Finlay, *The Secession in the North: The Story of an Old Seceder Presbytery [i.e. Buchan], 1768–1897*, Aberdeen 1898, pp. 29-44, 135).

enormous implications for many inhabitants of both the town and the wider region. Though aware of the risks associated with allowing a lay preacher into his pulpit, Cowie nevertheless invited Haldane to preach in his church, while he himself remained at the door to listen. At the close of the service the minister, convinced that God was with the lay-preacher, rushed into the sanctuary and invited the people to return in the evening to hear the stranger another time. Cowie claimed that of all the 'many excellent preachers' he had heard in thirty years as a minister, 'I have very seldom heard anything so much to my satisfaction, and nothing that could exceed Mr Haldane's discourses'.[39]

A few months later, in early 1798, another unordained itinerant, William Ballantyne, preached here to 'a crowded audience ... who were very attentive. Religion seems flourishing here', he said. The following day Ballantyne spoke before 'upwards of a thousand people ... the hearts of the godly (and there are many here) seemed to be lifted up in prayer and praise ... truly God is present'.[40] Then again the following year, eccentric English evangelist Rowland Hill arrived in Huntly and preached to around 2,000 in the open-air, the next day speaking from Cowie's pulpit.[41] The influence of Haldane and his evangelist-friends on Cowie's congregation was considerable. When the first class in Haldane's theological seminary commenced its studies in January 1799, four of Cowie's 'spiritual children' were among the students.[42]

As a result of his association with (often lay) preachers from outside his own denomination, along with a number of additional 'offenses',[43]

---

39. Robertson, *Spiritual Awakening in the North East of Scotland*, p. 67.

40. ibid.

41. Harry Escott, *Beacons in Independency: Religion and Life in Strathbogie and Upper Garioch in the Nineteenth Century*, Huntly 1940, p. 22.

42. James Haldane later settled as a pastor in Edinburgh, where he remained for fifty years. His brother, Robert, who used his considerable wealth and influence for the furthering of the gospel abroad as well as at home, moved to Geneva, Switzerland, in 1816, where his doctrinal lectures resulted in a revival of evangelical religion, as they did, too, a year later in south-west France, though without the excitement or persecution that occurred in Switzerland. In the latter country, Haldane had great influence on a number of the nation's future Free Church leaders, through whom '*Reveil*' also arose in Holland. (Cairns, *An Endless Line of Splendor*, pp. 114-6; Davies, '*I Will Pour Out My Spirit*', pp. 128-9).

43. These included raising funds for the London Missionary Society (which had been chosen because it was non-sectarian); beginning prayer meetings for missions;

all of which had brought upon Cowie repeated censure from some of his Anti-Burgher brethren over many years, the Huntly minister was eventually deposed by his Synod in 1800. Undaunted, Cowie continued his ministry as an Independent and the work spread. Indeed, 'considerable revival was experienced'.[44] Cowie's preaching became famous and people, hungry to hear the words of life that had been deprived them all their lives, flocked from miles around to the Independent chapel at Huntly. Dr John Morrison, who knew Cowie well, later wrote of him: 'Mr Cowie was a person in all respects original ... He had no competition, no equal in the north of Scotland. He was a man of genius, bold and fearless in all his movements. In the pulpit Mr Cowie was truly great ... The power he had over an audience was great beyond description. He could make them smile or weep. His appeal to the conscience was unceremonious and direct ... I have seen hundreds dissolve in tears under his ministry.'[45] Services in Cowie's church were not short, however. His sermons were often two or three hours long, he could pray for up to an hour, and although in summer there was an hour's interval between the morning and afternoon Sabbath services, in the winter there was one continuous service lasting five or six hours!

A number of notable men of God rose up under Cowie's ministry. One such was Donald Morrison, who later began a church in Duncanstone with around forty members. Hundreds flocked to hear this influential preacher, who faithfully served his parish for around forty years, till his death in 1846. Another prominent of Cowie's converts was Alexander Wilson, who along with a number of other awakened souls used to make the pilgrimage from Insch to Huntly every Sabbath – and soon many found peace in believing. Ignoring the sneers and taunts of the ungodly

---

appointing monthly meetings for the spread of the gospel, at which laymen engaged in prayer, and establishing Sabbath schools taught by laymen.

44. Robertson, *Spiritual Awakening in the North East of Scotland*, p. 67.

45. Escott, *Beacons in Independency*, pp. 24-5. Said James Stark, 'Cowie's was a name that for many years carried with it an electric energy in the North. There was a Knox-like decision and force in the man, a keen vision for reality, a fearless abandonment to the sovereign principles and ends of life, that marked him out as a born leader of men ... Cowie was naturally of the stuff out of which martyrs are made. In other circumstances, and in another age, he would have been a marked man among the confessors of apostolic times, a pilgrim father, or one who bled for Scotia's Covenant' (James Stark, *Rev. John Murker: A Picture of Religious Life and Character in the North*, London 1887, p. 176).

– much of which came from within the converts' own homes – these faithful pilgrims began to meet in Wilson's brother's workshop, which became to them a veritable '*Bethel*', and many received the baptism of the Spirit during that 'pentecostal epoch'. Sabbath schools were set up all over the wider region; Wilson alone established such centres in places like Insch, Upper Boddam, Leochel-Cushnie and Auchleven.[46] Directly or indirectly, many hundreds were converted through Cowie's powerful preaching in the Huntly district, as well as through Aberdeenshire and in neighbouring counties.[47] Among the many other fruits of his ministry were James Skinner, later a missionary with the London Missionary Society, John Leslie, a notable pioneer of Sabbath schools in the north of Scotland, Dr Milne, a missionary to China, and several who became ordained ministers (such as Robert Philip and George Legge).[48]

The Highlands

Rothiemurchus

Small independent churches were formed in several Highland locations in the first few years of the nineteenth century (e.g. Grantown-on-Spey and Knockando), largely through the influence of travelling preachers like Haldane and Campbell and converts of the Perthshire movement. Due to the itinerant labours of men such as John Farquharson of Breadalbane and James Reid, a revival occurred in the Highland village of Rothiemurchus, at the foot of the Cairngorm mountains, just after the turn of the nineteenth century. Out of this, a few godly persons formed themselves into a Congregational church in 1804, which quickly attracted

---

46. Thomas Brisbane, *The Life of Alexander Wilson, Insch*, Aberdeen 1867, pp. 22-49.

47. In Aberdeen a Congregational chapel was opened a year after a group of like-minded believers began meeting together in 1797. In a short time, 1,500 were packing into the building, which was constructed to accommodate no more than 1,000. An early convert here was John Watson, later minister of Musselburgh Congregational Church and a successful itinerant evangelist in the south (Alexander, *Memoir of the Rev. John Watson*, p. 14).

48. Brisbane, *The Life of Alexander Wilson*, pp. 38-9; James Stark, *Memoir of Rev. James Troup, M.A., Minister of Helensburgh Congregational Church*, Helensburgh 1897, p. 71; D. P. Thomson, *David Inglis Cowan*, Edinburgh 1961, pp. 92-3; R. Carruthers, *Biographies of Highland Clergymen*, Inverness 1889, p. 78. Indirectly influenced by Cowie was his grand-nephew, Duncan Matheson, who became an intrepid evangelist with fearless qualities very similar to that of his forebear (John Macpherson, *Life and Labours of Duncan Matheson, The Scottish Evangelist*, London 1871, pp. 9-10).

a membership of around thirty. Most meetings were held in houses or barns. That same year, Peter McLaren, a young Perthshire student from Haldane's Theological Seminary, was sent to supply the little fellowship. He stayed for a year and a half, before moving on to Easdale, where not a few were converted through his ministry over five months.[49]

Dunkeld and Dowally

In the central Highlands at the same time, similar blessing was being experienced. A small company of believers formed an Independent church in Dunkeld and neighbourhood in 1800, James Campbell being ordained to the charge a year later. Campbell listed the continuing effects of a former Wesleyan Methodist meeting in Dunkeld as being among the factors at work prior to his arrival. Agents of Haldane's Society for Propagating the Gospel at Home had also occasionally laboured among the people with much success. Campbell wrote in 1803: 'As to the work of conversion here (in Dunkeld) I have been as accurate as I could, and find ... there have been 145 who have experienced the power of divine grace upon their souls ... since Mr Bogue[50] preached here (prior to August 1798). I only speak of those who either have been, or now are members with us ... I also observe that very few of those included are old, they are either lately married, or still are unmarried.'[51]

A young Ralph Wardlaw wrote in August 1801 of 'for some time past a considerable stir about religion' in Dowally, a village to the north of Dunkeld. The excitement existed almost entirely among the young folk and had produced 'a good deal of division in different houses'.

---

49. Kinniburgh, *Fathers of Independency in Scotland*, p. 436. Little more is heard of the Rothiemurchus church, which may have disintegrated after a short time. When in his early twenties, Robert Findlater was appointed Church of Scotland missionary in Rothiemurchus in the autumn of 1808, he regretted the low state of religious knowledge and feeling around him. He noted that 'With the exception of one or two Baptists', he found hardly anyone with whom he could hold Christian converse or fellowship (Findlater, *Memoir of the Rev. Robert Findlater*, p. 119).

50. David Bogue was one of the founders of modern Congregationalism in Scotland, as well as being an architect of the modern missionary movement, being instrumental in the formation of the British and Foreign Bible Society and the Religious Tract Society (*DSCHT*, p. 83).

51. SPGH Report 1802–3, quoted in William D. McNaughton, 'Revival and Reality: Congregationalists and Religious Revival in Nineteenth-Century Scotland', in *SCHSR*, vol. 33, 2003, p. 177.

The parish minister, Wardlaw noted, had done nothing whatsoever to diffuse the tension, but was rather disposed to encourage parents in opposing their children's enthusiasm. As a result, Wardlaw was sure the young converts of Dowally were in much need of 'encouragement and caution'.[52] Promising signs were still in evidence two years later, when John Campbell found his way to Dowally. He wrote of his visit: 'There were a few when I went who had been benefited by our brethren. I advised them to begin a prayer-meeting, which, I think, was the chief means of awakening the attention of that careless people. For some time there were some impressed at every meeting; for the people crowded in upon them, and as soon as they were impressed they immediately attended with us ...'[53] Meanwhile, in Aberfeldy around sixty attributed their salvation to the ministry of James Haldane's missionaries.[54]

Perth

East Lothian-born the Rev. James Garie had known several special occasions of divine influence in his independent St Paul's Chapel in Perth since his transfer there from Ireland in 1794. An eminently pious minister, Garie was known to 'declare the whole counsel of God, preaching from the heart to the heart, in demonstration of the Spirit and of power'. A beautiful work of grace followed visits from James Haldane and his missionaries towards the close of 1800. 'I have not seen, since I have been in Perth', wrote Garie in a letter, 'such evidences of a work of the Spirit of God upon the minds of the people as of late, both from solid joys in the Lord Jesus and deep convictions of the dreadful evils of the heart'. Over twenty applied for church membership during December 1800, seventeen of whom were received into church fellowship one sweet Sabbath the following month. The majority of these were young folk who had recently come under awakening influences. Garie referred to one young man whose first impression came on hearing Haldane preach at the mill in Inver, while a young woman was similarly awakened hearing the same evangelist speak in St Paul's.

Counselling those under conviction began to occupy a considerable portion of Garie's time; suitable helpers among his congregation he was

52. Alexander, *Memoirs of the Life and Writings of Ralph Wardlaw*, pp. 55-6.

53. SPGH Report 1802–3, quoted in McNaughton, 'Revival and Reality', p. 177.

54. Haldane, *The Lives of Robert and James Haldane*, p. 318.

reluctant to call on, for times were particularly tough and such men were dutifully employed providing for their families. 'I have seldom enjoyed greater delight in the Lord's work', Garie concluded, also admitting that while he was generally willing to leave the world whenever the Lord called him, on Saturday evenings of late he had found himself praying that that would not occur till the approaching Sabbath was over, so happy was he in the midst of the present move of the Spirit. Yet just eleven days after penning these words Garie received his home-call, passing away on the 24th January 1801, aged just 39.[55]

The West Highlands – Argyll

Cowal

Donald MacArthur, a shoemaker and fisherman from Strachur in Argyll (died *c.* 1840), was converted through the witness of his sister, Isabella, in the last decade of the eighteenth century. Abandoning his previous life as 'leader of the song and the dance', MacArthur immediately set up worship in his home. He lived with two brothers on the farm of Bailie Mor (modern Ballimore), and many of their cousins who came to worship and hear the expounding of Scripture also became deeply affected, so that there was scarcely a time when MacArthur opened his bible but there were some awakened and led to seek after salvation. Thus the movement increased and spread, producing culturally indigenised, Gaelic-speaking lay preachers with no previous theological training, who began to itinerate throughout Strachur and beyond. By this time MacArthur himself had abandoned his trades so that he could itinerate throughout Cowal (south-east Argyll) and as far away as the nearer parts of Dumbartonshire, Perthshire and the Lowlands. At Garelochhead he had many hearers, two of whom – Peter McFarlane and Donald Whyte – became eminent preachers.[56]

Baptised by immersion in 1801, MacArthur settled as a pastor in Bute a few years later, but continued his itinerating ministry, albeit in the face of increasing opposition from landlords – for example, a relative, John

---

55. James Garie, *Memoirs of the late Rev. James Garie, Minister of the Gospel in Perth*, Edinburgh 1801, pp. 42-3.

56. McFarlane later trained for the Baptist ministry at Bradford Baptist Academy; Whyte immigrated to North Carolina about 1807, where he organised Spring Hill Baptist Church near Wagram.

MacArthur, lost his farm in Strachur for 'harbouring' Donald – and also from church authorities, who despised what were termed 'Strolling Preachers', such as himself. Many were so affected under his preaching as to fall down and cry out. He made many converts throughout these places.[57] In 1805 MacArthur was attacked and taken prisoner by men acting for the local landowner. Handed over to the press gang in Greenock, he was released after five weeks and later won damages in court. Opposition continued, however, and MacArthur emigrated to America around 1810, where he became associated with the Seventh Day Baptists.[58] Regarded as isolationist, somewhat hyper-Calvinistic and very exclusive, his converts in Scotland were known for many years after his departure from the area as 'MacArthur Baptists' or 'MacArthurites'.

Kintyre

Great success followed the labours of Niel Douglas and Daniel McNaught as they pursued a missionary endeavour through Kintyre in 1797, this despite continuing opposition from clergymen of the district (though accusations were returned by Douglas with equal acerbity).[59] Audiences of from 500 to 1,000 regularly heard them, often following them from place to place. In Killean, around 1,500 assembled under a severely leaking tent on a stormy morning to hear the gospel. 'The tears of many visibly flowed, notwithstanding their efforts to conceal them, and their sighs and moans might be easily heard …They stood like statues under the heavy rain, while deep concern seemed painted in

---

57. See D. E. Meek, 'The Preacher, the Press-gang and the Landlord: The Impressment and Vindication of the Rev. Donald MacArthur', in *SCHSR* vol. 25 (1995), pp. 256-75; D. W. Bebbington *The Baptists in Scotland*, Glasgow 1988, p. 281.

58. G. N. M. Collins, *Principal John Macleod D.D.*, Edinburgh 1951, pp. 241-5; *DSCHT*, pp. 502-3. MacArthur has been likened to Dugald Sinclair (see page 232), who also did much to evangelise south Argyllshire and attract many of those unhappy with the Established Church into the Baptist fold. Interestingly, Sinclair also emigrated to the New World, settling in Ontario where he joined the Disciples of Christ group. Yet another branch of south Argyllshire Baptists who moved from Scotland to the Americas (like Sinclair, to Ontario), was a group who formed a High Calvinist church known as the Particular Covenanted Baptist Church of Christ in Canada (Campbell, *One of Heaven's Jewels*, p. 253).

59. See Niel Douglas, *Journey to a Mission to Part of the Highlands of Scotland, in the Summer and Harvest, 1797*, Edinburgh 1799. Rev. John Campbell, who itinerated in the area a few years later, said of it that 'for 70 miles, except in the town of Campbeltown, there was not a minister that preached the gospel' (Struthers, *Relief Church*, p. 399).

every look, and every eye was fixed on the speaker. At the close numbers were overheard to say, "The Lord pity us; we have been all our days in ignorance"'. On the return of the missionaries, deep interest was excited in Paisley and Glasgow, and listening crowds were collected night after night in Campbell Street Relief Church to hear the accounts of their labours brought back from the fields. The mission died a death soon after, however, following controversy over Douglas's political views.[60]

Following his visit to Kintyre in 1800 James Haldane prevailed on Mr Macallum, 'a worthy preacher' from that district, to return and labour in his native land. After a few months Macallum's work was 'crowned with signal success',[61] and where only two or three had come to hear Haldane preach two years previously, now over 400 flocked to hear the gospel message. Said Macallum, 'On leaving them, about a dozen of the people walked on each side of my horse, telling what miserable creatures they were when I first visited their country'.[62] One had acted as a fiddler at weddings but had now given that up. An 'aged, grey-haired man' had been chairman of a whisky-toddy meeting, but after hearing Macallum preach on his last visit, one after another had ceased to attend till he alone was left in the chair. Wondering what on earth could be a better attraction than good Highland whisky, he too went to hear the gospel being expounded, and was soon soundly converted! Being 'a heathen part of Scotland', Macallum found conversions in the country districts of Kintyre to be as numerous among the aged as among the young, 'which is seldom the case where the gospel has long been preached'.[63]

When John Aikman, who had accompanied Haldane on his Kintyre visit in 1800, returned to the peninsula in April 1803, he found it 'the most gratifying and the most reviving to my soul of any journey I ever made. Had I not been an eye-witness of the change which has taken place upon that most dark and dismal region since my former visit about three years ago, I could hardly have conceived such an alteration possible'.[64] It transpired in 1805 that the minister of one Kintyre parish had recently demitted his charge on account of the fact that so many of his people were

---

60. ibid., p. 398.

61. Haldane, *The Lives of Robert and James Haldane*, p. 289.

62. ibid., p. 290.

63. ibid., p. 291.

64. Robert Kinniburgh, *Fathers of Independency in Scotland*, pp. 240-1.

getting converted by the Haldane missionaries. The infuriated minister began to prevail on the laird to throw these converts out of their crofts. The landowner acquiesced, but within a short time his new tenants became Christians also! This time the laird felt it was in his interest not to expel them, not least because one of his former tenants had accidentally drowned on the forced eviction from his home. Thus it was that the disenchanted minister promptly decided to leave Scotland to start a new life in America.[65]

Central Highlands

Moulin

Ground Prepared

Alexander Stewart (1764–1821) was inducted to the parish of Moulin, near Pitlochry in Perthshire, in 1786 at the age of twenty-two. Yet though 'not a despiser of what was sacred', he felt nothing of the power of religion on his soul. He was delighted when his catechising class was poorly attended as it gave him more time to follow his fonder pursuits – playing cards and reading sentimental novels! Stewart preached vain and empty sermons to his congregation for ten long years, though at some stage during this period he was afforded his 'first perceptions of divine truth and redeeming love' [66] through the longstanding patience and wisdom of friend and colleague, the Rev. David Black of nearby St Madoes.[67] Black introduced him to the Rev. Charles Simeon of Cambridge (under whose devoted ministry that University town became 'a centre of evangelicalism and Calvinistic theology' [68]), and Stewart subsequently found salvation through a sermon preached by Simeon in 1796 when the latter was invited to speak from Stewart's own pulpit.[69] Such conversion was to prove highly fortuitous for many in the quiet Perthshire parish.

---

65. Robert Philip, *The Life, Times, and Missionary Enterprises, of the Rev. John Campbell*, London 1841.

66. James Stewart, *Memoirs of the late Rev. Alexander Stewart, D.D: One of the Ministers of Canongate, Edinburgh*, Edinburgh 1822, p. 41.

67. Alexander Haldane complained that the part played by his father, James Haldane, in the process of Stewart's awakening was not sufficiently recognised (Couper, *Scottish Revivals*, p. 81).

68. E. E. Cairns, *An Endless Line of Splendour*, Wheaton 1986, p. 107.

69. Nearly 1,000 attended the Moulin church when Simeon visited. The editor of the English preacher's memoirs speaks of this visit – the second of five he made north

Stewart attested that previous to the revival his people 'were not … addicted to open vice if we except lying and swearing. They were rather distinguished for sobriety, industry and peaceable behaviour'. But although they attended church and rested from work on the Sabbath, it was evident that this was a formality; they knew little of vital religion but trusted rather in their own works. Thus the now enlightened minister at once instituted a number of spiritual reforms. These included exhortations and warnings concerning abuse of the sacraments of Communion and Baptism. As a result there were only a dozen applications to the Lord's Supper in summer 1798, where previously there were regularly between thirty and fifty.[70] Likewise, the remarkable custom of parents choosing to carry their children a hundred miles to be baptised by a Catholic priest, rather than be refused Baptism at their demand, was abandoned.

The number of people being awakened to their spiritual condition gradually increased, and Stewart sought to encourage them. 'One might now observe at church, after divine service, two or three small groups forming themselves round our few more advanced believers, and with-drawing from the crowd into adjacent fields, to exchange Christian salutations, and hold Christian converse together while a little cousin, or other young relative, followed as a silent attendant on the party and listened earnestly to their religious discourse'.[71] Of additional encouragement was a meeting for prayer, meditation and fellowship held in the 'little smoky hovel' of a pious old woman until her death in 1799, when it was transferred to the manse, 'either in his (the minister's) kitchen, or at the door if the weather permitted'.[72]

Revival in Full Flow

The movement, however, did not become marked or general until after March 1799, in which month Stewart began a fifteen-month long series of discourses on regeneration. Cases of conviction were now evident almost every week. In September, Stewart wrote to Black: 'Oh, my dear brother, had you but been here with us for a week past, how your heart would have

---

of the border – as one of the most 'important episodes of Simeon's life' (Rev. William Carus [Ed.], *Memoirs of the Life of the Rev. Charles Simeon*, London 1847, p. 150).

70. Stewart, *Memoirs of the Late Rev. Alexander Stewart*, p. 140.

71. ibid., pp. 140-1.

72. Couper, *Scottish Revivals*, pp. 82-3.

rejoiced! Such hungering and thirsting after communion with God! Such genuine humility and contrition for sin! Such devotedness to the Saviour! Old converts quickened and new ones added to the Lord! Yesterday was, I trust, a great day of the Son of Man.'[73] Previous to the awakening, parishioners spent Sunday evening 'sauntering about the fields and woods in gossiping parties, or visiting their acquaintances at a distance'. Now hardly a lounger was to be seen, only people going to some house or meeting to hear the Scriptures read.[74] The house of one experienced believer was a chief resort of many anxious souls and new converts, keen to learn from the wisdom of their host. Other practices almost wholly discontinued as a result of the revival were the long-cherished ritual of excessive drinking, late night carousing and noisy sports on the occasion of a wake.

Stewart insisted that the awakening progressed without any excitement other than silent tears. Indeed, when a woman dissolved into a flood of tears at one meeting friends were quick to convey her out of church so as not to disrupt the service. What did accompany the revival, as is the norm during such seasons, was a degree of opposition. This came chiefly from well-educated people who knew their Bibles to an extent and who argued that there could be nothing substantial or necessary in an experimental knowledge which illiterate people might claim to have obtained.[75] New converts came in for considerable 'gross misrepresentation', especially in neighbouring parishes where facts were not so easy to establish.

Stewart could not single out cases of conversion as there was little 'diversity of operation'; awakening coming to most people in a quiet, gradual manner. There were no truly dramatic manifestations, such as an awakened person being struck down, and nothing was known of people trusting in 'dreams and visions, impulses or impression ... or external signs or tokens'.[76] 'The change', noted Stewart, 'has been from ignorance and indifference and disrelish of divine things, to knowledge and concern and spiritual enjoyment'.[77] Even among those who experienced no discernible change of heart there was evidenced a general concern about religious things.

---

73. Stewart, *Memoirs of the Late Rev. Alexander Stewart*, pp. 155-6.

74. ibid., p. 151.

75. Dudley Reeves, 'Charles Simeon in Scotland', in *Banner of Truth*, January 1973, vol. 112, pp. 15-32.

76. Stewart, *Memoirs of the Late Rev. Alexander Stewart*, p. 149.

77. ibid., p. 152.

Results

The minister reluctantly numbered the converts in his parish to around seventy, most 'people under 25 or 30',[78] though a number were older (e.g. in remote Glenbriarachan, which, through a Sabbath class conducted by a recent convert, and occasional visits from James Kennedy of Aberfeldy, was soon 'blossoming as a rose', and at a later date was 'still a favoured spot').[79] A good many children under the age of fourteen also appeared to 'have a liking to religion', but their condition could not be confirmed. Overall numbers would have been much larger, declared Stewart, if those from outside the parish were included, for the gracious awakening spread to many other parts of Perthshire during its progress from 1798 to 1802, including Stewart's native parish of Blair.[80] After that time, while the revived church continued in a flourishing and progressive state, there were no more accessions to membership or cases of awakening. 'The heavens appeared to be shut up and the showers were withheld'.[81]

Among the teenage converts of this revival were James Duff and Jean Rattray, who subsequently married and became the parents of Alexander Duff, renowned missionary and educator in India from 1830 to 1864.[82] Another young convert was twenty-four-year-old flax-merchant, Alexander Stewart from Logierait, a few miles from Moulin (four years his senior, Stewart's wife, whom he married a year after his conversion in the spring of 1799, was also a fruit of the revival). Stewart became a student at the Haldane Theological Seminary before serving as a Haldane missionary for several years in Kingussie, Avoch and Elgin.[83]

After David Black visited Moulin in the summer of 1800, he wrote: 'Such a revival I never witnessed before – it is truly the doing of the Lord,

---

78. ibid., p. 140. Later in his narrative, however, Stewart suggests that most of those awakened were 'about thirty years of age' (ibid., p. 152).

79. ibid., pp. 156-7.

80. Couper, *Scottish Revivals*, p. 84.

81. Stewart, *Memoirs of the Late Rev. Alexander Stewart*, pp. 247-8.

82. A. A. Millar, *Alexander Duff of India*, Edinburgh 1992.

83. Shortly after James Haldane's switch to the Baptist cause around 1807, Stewart also felt the call to receive full baptismal immersion. After labouring in and around Perth for some years he and his family emigrated to Upper Canada, settling in Toronto and establishing the first Baptist cause there, also engaging in arduous evangelism and church planting in surrounding townships (Glenn Tomlinson, *From Scotland to Canada: The Life of Pioneer Missionary, Alexander Stewart*, Guelph, Ontario 2008).

and marvellous in our eyes.' He noted how the converts had 'a keen appetite for the Word of God, and an evident love for the Saviour … A deep sense of unworthiness, and a strong affection for one another'. He noted finally that 'Dear Mr Stewart himself is mercifully preserved humble amidst all the honour that God is conferring upon him'.[84] As news of the revival spread, Stewart became a sought-after preacher in other places, and made, for example, the journey to Ross-shire in 1802 at the invitation of several ministers there. It was to Dingwall in that county that Stewart was transferred in September 1805, to the great disappointment of his former parishioners, for, to the deep regret also of Stewart, his successor did not hold evangelical views.[85] When the Rev. William Burns of Kilsyth visited Moulin in 1811, he was told that some believers had walked all the way to Ross-shire to wait on the preaching of their former pastor. At the same time Burns could observe 'unquestionable evidence in my short visit to Moulin of the reality of the far-famed revival in that district'.[86] As late as 1839 the then minister of the Perthshire parish could refer to the few converts of the 1799 revival who were still alive, as having lived consistently godly lives.[87]

Breadalbane

Arrival of John Farquharson

John Farquharson belonged to Glen Tilt in the parish of Blair Atholl.[88] It is known that he came under Haldane influence and trained for a brief

---

84. ibid., pp. 162-3.

85. As a result, Stewart, who made repeated visits to his former charge, noted that a 'great change' soon developed in the parish. Within three years, he lamented, 'all things about our place are growing worse and worse – iniquity abounding, and practised without restraint, the Sabbath much profaned and things turning to their old course – only the few who love the Saviour are still holding on, like Gideon, faint but pursuing'. These saints, he noted, were both 'sorrowful and rejoicing' (ibid., pp. 232, 248).

86. Couper, *Scottish Revivals*, p. 86.

87. Douglas MacMillan (Ed.), *Restoration in the Church*, pp. 67-78. Donald Meek has attested that the Moulin awakening was 'a defining moment in the spiritual history of Perthshire and the entire Grampian area' (Tomlinson, *From Scotland to Canada*, p. 9).

88. Next to nothing is known about Farquharson's early life or about his coming to faith. Given the proximity of Glen Tilt to Moulin, he may have been influenced by the revival in the latter place in the late 1790s. This might explain his subsequent commitment to revivalist preaching as well as his connection with the Haldanes (D. E. Meek, 'Evangelical Missionaries in the Early Nineteenth Century Highlands', quoted in *Transactions of the Gaelic Society of Inverness*, vol. 56 (1989), p. 278).

period at a Haldane class in Dundee. His academic performance was so
poor, however, that after six months he was dispatched to that mountainous
region of the southern Scottish Highlands known as Breadalbane (see
map, page 208) under auspices of the SPGH (Society for Propagating the
Gospel at Home). Farquharson rode from farm to farm on his black pony
carrying the message of Christ to the spiritually destitute people.[89] He faced
relentless and bitter opposition from both the Established Church and
landowners, and in a circle of thirty-two miles around Loch Tay it was said
there were only three homes that offered him hospitality. Undaunted, the
single-minded preacher helped inaugurate a dramatic revival in 1802 on the
south side of Loch Tay, around Gardenia, Acharn and Cartlechan. One of
the first to come under saving impressions by the missionary's labours was
twenty-year-old John Campbell from Ardeonaig.[90] Campbell developed a
close friendship with James Dewar, a man of the same age from the north
side of Loch Tay. They began to hold meetings in a barn, through which,
during 1801, several more friends were converted. At first those awakened
sought to keep their state concealed from Farquharson, but once he found
out, an increase in spiritual interest emerged among the people.

Some came under conviction in a dramatic manner, who being
'suddenly struck during the time of prayer; they fell to the ground, and
many of them, both young and old, continued speechless for twenty
minutes or half an hour'. From Ardeonaig the revival spread to places
like Acharn and Ardtalnaig. Converts flocked together and went from
house to house, with two hours or less sleep each morning for around
nine days on end, speaking to those under conviction. According to one
witness, 'It was at meetings for social prayer that the most considerable
awakening took place in April 1802. At one of them, at Cartlechan, a
most extraordinary influence was felt. Fourteen persons fell down to the

---

89. Alexander Haldane wrote that the district was spiritually impoverished to the
extent that, 'There were actually no Bibles, scarcely any Testaments, and the people
lived without prayer' (Couper, *Scottish Revivals*, p. 100).

90. Campbell's father, a farmer, was one of the few believers resident in the region
before Farquharson's arrival. He held prayer meetings in his home. These were disrupted by local authorities, who declared them illegal and ordered them to be stopped.
But while many were scared away the gatherings continued, to the blessing of all who
attended. Kinniburgh regarded this 'lion-hearted farmer' as the one who 'unfurled
… the standard of Independency … in Glenlyon' (Philip, *Life, Times, and Missionary
Enterprises of John Campbell*, p. 380).

ground crying for mercy. Worldly business was wholly neglected and whole nights spent in prayer and exhorting one another'.[91] Believers from a wide area assembled for worship at a tent in a wood at Ardtalnaig, a large boat being used to ferry those from the north across the Loch.[92]

Farquharson remained unpopular with many in the region – his nick-name was '*Black Farquharson*' – until those converted through him came to love and respect him. By such he was known as a man of great compassion, one who spent a lot of time in secret prayer, and one 'almost silent on every subject but the great concerns of eternity'.[93] But from others in the community fierce opposition rose against the movement Farquharson helped ignite, including 'violent means to deprive people of their farms and houses',[94] and in some instances the very lives of converts were threatened. Child converts were often castigated by their parents as heretics who were bringing indelible disgrace upon their families. Wives were at times cruelly treated by their husbands – one being so severely punished merely on account of her profession of faith that she was confined for some weeks to her bed, and deprived of one eye.

Ministerial Assistance

After a period of itinerant ministry and a couple of years spent at Haldane's seminary in Edinburgh, the youthful John Campbell spent eight months of 1804 evangelising in his native Breadalbane, where he preached with great success, and although subject to menaces, sneers and obloquy, his zeal was not dampened. Indeed, he later spoke of these months as the happiest in his life. His itinerary took him to such distant places as Glenlyon, Glenquoich, Glendochart, Glenlochy, Aberfeldy, Comrie, Callander and Fortingall. 'It was a time of shaking among the dry bones in most of the places I visited', he remarked. Campbell also took the controversial action of standing near the burial ground of the Established Church on the Monday of the Kenmore communion and conducting an open-air service. The young evangelist also took advantage of market day in Fortingall by

---

91. Couper, *Scottish Revivals*, p. 101.

92. W. D. McNaughton, *Journal of William McKillican*, Glasgow 1994, p. 3.

93. John Campbell, *Missionary and Ministerial Life in the Highlands, Being a Memoir of the Rev. John Campbell, Late Pastor of the Congregational Church, Oban*, Edinburgh 1853, p. 22. Principal Daniel Dewar of Aberdeen long afterwards described him as 'the most wonderful man he had ever known' (Couper, *Scottish Revivals*, p. 100).

94. Campbell, *Missionary and Ministerial Life in the Highlands*, p. 16.

intimating that he would preach in a nearby farm-house that evening, in direct competition to the annual market day ball being held that night in the local inn, the social highlight of the year for the youth of the village. Some would-be partiers felt at the last minute compelled to go and hear Campbell, where a deep impression was made on them. Several from that night dated their conversion and never after attended a ball.

The Rev. John Cleghorn spent four days in Breadalbane during the progress of the movement, where he devoted some time to conversing with recent converts. He was pleased to see no symptoms of over-enthusiasm either in their conversation or their behaviour, and all manifested a considerable knowledge of the truths of God's word. 'These are so glorious in their view', he wrote, 'that they occupy their minds when alone, and are the subjects on which they converse in company with great delight'. This vastly contrasted with their state when first awakened, when many came under 'awful apprehensions of the just discipline of God'.[95]

Several new churches were established and the Acharn congregation rapidly grew to one hundred. Surprisingly, however, some even within his own fellowship came against Farquharson – apparently over dissatisfaction with his preaching – forcing him to resign his charge as pastor in 1804, although he continued to itinerate throughout the area.[96] James Haldane visited the region in 1803 and again in 1805. He was accompanied on both visits by John Campbell (of Kingsland, not to be confused with the afore-mentioned John Campbell, later of Oban), who had close family links with Killin. Campbell wrote about preaching in a tent erected on the side of a mountain in the middle of a wood about two miles above Acharn to about 300 people, around half of whom were members of the Independent Acharn fellowship, having been 'converted to God within the last four years'. In Glenlyon Campbell met with over fifty people who had 'lately been converted to the faith there, and are united together as a church'. He also describes meetings at Glendochart ('two hundred were assembled') and Glenlochay ('several pleasant friends of the Lord Jesus live in this pleasant sequestrate Glen').[97] When Haldane and Campbell

---

95. ibid.

96. He ministered in Killin for a short stint before emigrating to Halifax, Canada, where he is believed to have died a few years later, in 1810.

97. Philip, *Life, Times and Missionary Enterprises of the Rev. John Campbell*, pp. 379-81. Campbell later became famous for his missionary travels in Africa.

reached Killin, birthplace of Campbell's father, they had to wait till 10 p.m. to preach, as all the locals were up in the hills cutting peats. Only when it got too dark did they come down, whence, despite being fatigued after a full day and evening's hard labour, they willingly filed into the meeting-house, which became full. Farquharson arrived from a trip to Edinburgh just in time to conclude the service with a prayer in Gaelic.[98]

Degeneration

By this time, however, a number of seemingly petty disputes over points of ritual and church government were beginning to surface in the Breadalbane churches. These concerned matters such as whether the congregation should sit or stand during prayer and praise, whether the minister should wear a black coat or one of a different colour, and the efficacy of public collections in support of gospel ordinances. John Campbell (of Kingsland) on a short supply visit to Killin around this time, noticed that everyone sat down for prayer, and more bizarrely – and to him highly inappropriately – at one point everyone turned with military precision and kissed the person on their one side, then on the other, squeezing their hand at the same time. Then came the debate, initiated by Haldane, over Baptism.[99] With the new doctrines being taught by some of the missionaries, sadly, many of those who had been called into spiritual life by means of the revival became the fiercest of sectarians. Wrote William Findlater: 'The clergy and the Church of Scotland were anathematized; her doctrines and institutions stigmatized, and her observance of duties ridiculed. The consequence was that duties were gladly discontinued by many; catechisms and other formularies of the church were despised, and almost the whole of her ministers rejected as unsound. These views were very extensively maintained and propagated throughout the country.'[100] Quickly the promising churches at Acharn and Killin were diminished in number and weakened in influence, and before long the people were as sheep without a shepherd. Four Baptist churches subsequently emerged in their stead.[101]

---

98. ibid., p. 380.

99. James and Robert Haldane adopted Baptist views around 1808.

100. William Findlater, *Memoir of Rev. Robert Findlater, Together with a Narrative of the Revival of Religion During his Ministry at Lochtayside, Perthshire 1816–1819*, Glasgow 1840, p. 134.

101. The one in Lawers was led by William Tulloch, a former Congregationalist, who was baptised in 1808. Yuille tells us that for some years Tulloch sought to maintain the

Stirrings on the Islands

Arran

A localised awakening occurred in the north of Arran in 1804–05, especially about the farms of Sannox and their neighbourhood. In December 1804 Archibald McCallum, an agent of the SPGH, reported: 'I wrote to you formerly concerning the appearance of a revival … Some of those with whom I conversed the last time I was (here) are now walking in the ways of the Lord.' [102] Angus McMillan, a native of the glen, seems to have been the means of initiating the movement.[103] He had laboured in the district for some time without any apparent success, but found out on the eve of his leaving that a few locals were anxious for their souls. Greatly heartened, the missionary decided to continue his efforts for a while, and his ministry became greatly blessed. The influence of the awakening that resulted gradually extended to other parts of the hitherto spiritually dark island. McCallum said that one memorable day 'after sermon we formed a small church, consisting of about fourteen members; six of whom were formerly members of the church in Kintyre who went there.[104] … There are also three fellowship meetings set up among them. Between this and the time before, it appears that there are about sixty persons awakened, eight of whom are received members into the above church'.[105] A generation later, and this godly valley became a ghost-glen, for the whole of its population, 500 persons in all, were obliged, due to economic hardships, to leave the island for New Brunswick, Canada.[106]

---

revival spirit that had enveloped the district, but that 'pressure of circumstances' forced him to move to Renfrew. Soon after, he moved back to the central Highlands, where he spent much time itinerating through the region. A visiting minister of another denomination described him as 'a modest, pious, intelligent man, and extremely well fitted for the important and honourable service to which he has devoted himself' (Rev. George Yullie, *History of the Baptists in Scotland*, Glasgow 1926, pp. 71-2).

102. *Missionary Magazine* 1805, quoted in McNaughton 'Revival and Reality', pp. 177-8.

103. Another tradition holds that McMillan, who was appointed to the mission at Lochranza in 1812 and who later succeeded Rev. McBride at Kilmorie, was converted in this early revival in Arran.

104. These were believers from three families from Carradale (Kintyre), who were dispossessed of their farms by the landlord, through the influence, it was supposed, of the parochial clergy, and who gratefully received the offer of a farm on Arran.

105. *Missionary Magazine* 1805, quoted in McNaughton, 'Revival and Reality', p. 178.

106. John K. Cameron, *The Church in Arran*, Edinburgh 1912, p. 109.

Still in Arran, further south in Kilmorie from 1803, the preaching of the recently-inducted Neil McBride (1764–1814) was also being signally blessed. His nephew wrote that, 'So eager were his parishioners to wait on his ministry that he was seldom able to conduct divine worship in the church, and even in winter crowds were obliged to stand outside the doors'.[107] Many people passed their own places of worship and resorted Sabbath after Sabbath to Kilmorie, or to the church at Clachan, where McBride preached every third Sabbath. In his sermons, which were frequently close and searching, the minister dwelt more on the consolations of the Gospel than on the terrors of the law, and it was notable that expressions of excitement were more common during these messages of God's love and grace than they were when the judgement of God was expounded. The revival movement does not appear to have come suddenly. Instead, from the beginning of the work at Sannox, 'a remarkable change began gradually to come over the people' regarding both their religious sentiments and their conduct. 'The slumber that previously prevailed was broken, and a distinction began to be drawn between truth and error'.[108]

The number of those who at first publicly professed conversion was comparatively small, while not a few assumed the form of godliness but denied the power of it in their lives. But many also remained unaffected, and resented the restraint being laid upon their lives by the general reformation taking place around them. The result was that some broke out into 'bolder ungodliness and became more abandoned to wickedness' than ever.[109] McBride and the God-fearing portion of his flock, grieved at this state of affairs, were driven to the throne of grace, where much spiritual wrestling took place. From this spirit of prayer came the conviction upon many that a time of richer blessing was at hand. Indeed, a much more extensive awakening was to spread across the island within the next couple of years (see page 227), at which time the embers of this early awakening were still glowing. For in 1810 the Kilmorie church, long and narrow as it was, was enlarged to seat more people, and when Dugald Sinclair preached on the island 'to a great number of people' in 'Mr Mackay's

---

107. Couper, *Scottish Revivals*, p. 89.

108. Cameron, *The Church in Arran*, p. 110.

109. McMillan wrote that as late as 1810-11, 'many were lower and more abandoned in wickedness than they had been at any former period' (Thorbjorn Campbell, *Arran: A History*, Edinburgh 2007, p. 124).

house' in the same year, his audience was 'very much affected. These good people', wrote Sinclair, 'seem very lively and affectionate'.[110]

Skye

Glimmerings of light began to dawn on the spiritually dark island of Skye from the early years of the nineteenth century, when a series of providential events occurred. In October 1805 John Shaw, a native of Moulin and one who was influenced by the revival there a few years earlier, was settled in the western parish of Duirinish. In that same year, and also from Perthshire, John Farquharson moved from Lochtayside to Skye,[111] various reasons being suggested for his translation there.[112] During his short time on Skye, Farquharson itinerated in parishes in the north and west of the island. He immigrated to Nova Scotia some months later, but not before sowing seeds which were to bear enormous fruit in the months and years ahead. As one example, it is believed to have been through Farquharson's influence that Donald Martin, who since 1785 had been minister of Kilmuir, 'heard to the saving of his soul'.[113]

Donald Munro, rendered blind by smallpox in his teens and now in his thirties, also turned to Christ through hearing Farquharson preach.[114] A man of extraordinary zeal and wisdom, Munro was enormously influential, initially in the north of the island, where, for

---

110. Dugald Sinclair, *Journal of Itinerating Exertions in Some of the More Destitute Parts of Scotland*, Edinburgh 1810–13, vol. 1, 1810, p. 16.

111. A member of the Established Church wrote that, through Farquharson, 'the doctrine of salvation by Christ alone was preached in Skye for the first time in 1805'; though there is some evidence to suggest that he preached on the island as early as 1801 (McNaughton, 'Revival and Reality', p. 186).

112. The reason proffered by McCowan in his book, *Men of Skye*, is that he landed on the island by chance, because the ship on which he was sailing to America had to seek shelter in the harbour of Uig. Couper thinks, however, that McCowan's version is 'in conflict with tradition and with what direct testimony is available' (Couper, *Scottish Revivals*, p. 96).

113. Donald MacKinnon, *Clerical Men of Skye*, Dingwall 1930, p. 60. Martin is believed to have been the first native Skye parish minister to preach Christ.

114. Steve Taylor has it that both Martin and Munro were converted on hearing Farquharson preach to a large open-air audience in Uig on John 10:9, 'I am the Door' (*The Skye Revivals*, Chichester 2003, pp. 23, 25). As there are differing records of some events of these early days, it is possible that these two men's testimonies have become mixed up and that they were not in fact both converted on that one occasion.

example, he established in Snizort a prayer meeting through which numbers were converted. A temporary check came to the movement in 1808 when Martin accepted a call to Inverness and his successor did not carry evangelical sympathies. The people refused to wait on the new incumbent's ministry and unofficially set Munro over them as their spiritual leader. The catechist continued to conduct meetings, which drew multitudes. Outraged, the new minister appealed to the Scottish Society for Promoting Christian Knowledge (SSPCK), whose strict rules prohibited their agents from preaching. Munro was dismissed from office, but the effect was to greatly aid his work, for the people flocked to hear him more than ever! Munro was careful not to conduct formal services, nor to directly preach. Rather, he 'lectured', 'and the burden of his doctrine consisted in exhortations'.[115] He moved from house to house and from farm to farm, gathering as large an audience as was possible. He taught from the Shorter Catechism, and also commented on sections of Gaelic translations of well-known spiritual classics, which were read aloud to his congregations. Regarding the Scriptures, it was said that blind Munro required no reader, for his memory was stored with Scripture and he had become, literally, a living concordance. Bible verses he recited with great animation. Being also a skilled fiddle player, the joyful singing of the Psalms made his meetings glad. 'In many instances he conducted that part of solemn praise with great unction, specially on winter nights when candles or oil were scarce'.[116] Munro's popularity increased further with the outbreak of full-scale revival in 1812 (see page 224).

The Far North – Sutherland

Strathnaver

Strathnaver lies in the valley of the River Naver, which flows northwards in west Sutherlandshire until it reaches the north coast at Bettyhill. Right up to the year 1814 the valley was occupied by about forty small settlements, each comprising a group of dwellings that were home to between three and fifteen tenant families as well as many untenanted cottars, who lived in hovels. The district had known rich spiritual blessing from as early as the 1720s onwards (see page 94). According to the Rev. Donald

115. Couper, *Scottish Revivals*, p. 97.

116. ibid.

Munro of Ferintosh, a fresh wave of spiritual life began to pass through the Strath about the end of the eighteenth century and beginning of the nineteenth.[117] Children and youth, impressed on seeing their seniors repair to Saturday noon prayer meetings – which were common in parts of the North at that time – eagerly began their own prayer groups.[118]

Some in Strathnaver and the wider parish of Farr were said to have been among 'the most outstanding of the men of the Highlands'.[119] One man could count seventy men in Strathnaver alone who could be called on a Friday to 'speak to the Question' (a public response to a given Bible text which gives evidence that the respondent is a true believer); and there were three times as many women as that who were believed to be God-fearing.[120] According to Munro, 'There is a well-founded tradition of a communion in Golspie when 31 men from the parish of Farr alone "spoke to the Question", and from the many other parishes that were represented from the County, and from Caithness and Ross-shire, more than another thirty-one men could have been called'. Munro obtained this information in his student days 'from a fine woman whose pious mother was present, more than 120 years ago'.[121]

A minister who commenced his ministry in Farr said, 'I knew the state of religion in the Highlands, in Inverness-shire, Ross-shire, and Sutherland; but whether, as regards the number of decidedly converted people, or the character of their religion, I never knew any place where the religion of Christ so shone, and flourished, and pervaded the community, as it did in Strathnaver'.[122] The district was served by the Achness Mission, which covered a vast territory of Sutherland, extending as far as the parishes of

---

117. Munro continues, confusedly, ' ... which left its mark in a very noticeable way during the great revival there under the ministry of Mr John Balfour about the middle of the 18th century' (Munro, *Records of Grace*, p. 228).

118. MacGillivray, *Sketches of Religion and Revivals of Religion*, pp. 15-16. This is despite the fact that the Established Church minister of Farr from the year 1780, James Dingwall, was known as 'a purely secular character' for much of his ministry (although some believe that he may have come into a knowledge of the truth towards the close of his period of service there) [Thomson, *Tales of the Far North West*, p. 21].

119. Munro, *Records of Grace*, p. 225.

120. ibid., p. 232.

121. Robinson, *The Rev. Alexander McIntyre*, pp. 30-1.

122. MacGillivray, *Sketches of Religion and Revivals of Religion*, pp. 15-6, 28; Kennedy, *Days of the Fathers in Ross-Shire*, p. 140.

Farr in the north and Kildonnan in the south. The object of the Mission was to supply the almost total lack of Established ministerial service in the region, being funded by the SSPCK and the Royal Bounty.

When the Rev. David Mackenzie settled as minister at the Mission in 1813, he found a congregation of between 600 and 700, among whom were many men and women – some of high military rank and some well-educated – who were 'eminent for piety, and their names still savoury among the churches of the north' in the late 1870s.[123] Over the next few years, during the period known as the Highland Clearances, every one of the Strath's 1,600 inhabitants was ruthlessly evicted from the area. The Rev. Donald Sage, the last of seven missionaries who served in succession at the mission, later wrote of the last Sabbath in the Strath before the Clearances, which also forced the Mission to close in 1819. It was an unusually fine morning so the service was held 'on a beautiful green sward' by the River Naver. After a sermon and the singing of a psalm, 'At last all restraints were compelled to give way. The preacher ceased to speak, the people to listen. All lifted up their voices and wept, mingling their tears together. It was indeed the place of parting, and the hour. The greater number parted never again to behold each other in the land of the living'.[124] One distressed witness of the evictions wrote of the sufferers: 'The truly pious noted the mighty hand of God in the matter. In their prayers and religious conferences not a solitary expression could be heard of anger or vindictiveness.'[125] Many found no resting place till they reached the backwoods of Canada.

Some decades later, a Sutherland newspaper reminisced about this 'noble band of godly men born and brought up in Strath Naver, parish of Farr, a district eminent for years, during the latter part of the last century (eighteenth) and the beginning of the present, as the residence of a number of pious, well-educated and intelligent Christians'. It was

---

123. Various Contributors, *Disruption Worthies of the Highlands: Another Memorial of 1843*, Edinburgh 1877, pp. 89-90.

124. www.chebucto.ns.ca (accessed 04/11/11).

125. Sage, *Memorabilia Domestica*, p. 215. During one violent clearing of Strathnaver residents, Donald Macleod, a young apprentice stonemason, witnessed '250 blazing houses. Many of the owners were', he stated, 'my relatives and all of whom I personally knew; but whose present condition, whether in or out of the flames, I could not tell. The fire lasted six days, till the whole of the dwellings were reduced to ashes or smoking ruins' (www.helmsdale.org [accessed 04/11/11]).

also reported that 'the common people of the Mackays (who lived in the Strath) are the most religious of all the tribes that dwell among the mountains north or south'.[126] The last survivor of this team of eminent believers was William Mackay, son of Robert Mackay, Rhifal, who served as elder and catechist in the Height of Farr. William became one of the first of six elders in the newly-formed Strathy Parliamentary Church within Farr parish in 1833.[127] He died in 1861.[128]

Assynt

Further south and west in Sutherland, awakening occurred in the district of Assynt during John Kennedy's assistantship (1806–12) to William Mackenzie, a godless man, addicted to drink, who avoided pastoral work and was often absent from his charge for many weeks on end without good cause. Left to his own devices, Kennedy set up preaching stations in numerous parts of his large and populous parish. His work was early blessed, and it was said that very seldom was so much done in so short a time in conversion and edification as during this period. Assynt became 'a nursery of Gaelic schoolmasters and catechists' who did enormous good throughout the north and west, and of these and other converts 'there was a peculiarity of feeling and of sentiment about them all that made them marked as a class … To these days of power in Assynt were bound the sweetest memories of those who then enjoyed the presence of the Lord … and from many a broken heart … wrung the cry, "Oh, that I were as in months past … when His candle shined upon mine head"'.[129]

---

126. Frank Bardgett, *North Coast Parish: Strathy and Halladale: A Historical Guide To A Post-Clearance Parish and Its Church*, Strathy 1990, pp. 16-17.

127. A Parliamentary Kirk was one built by a grant provided for by an Act of Parliament in 1823 for the building of up to forty churches and manses in communities without any church buildings.

128. The deep spiritual influences in Strathy continued for many years, under the ministry of successive worthy preachers, such as Malcolm MacRitchie, who, 'from the time of his first visit to Strathy (Free Church in 1862), the power of the Lord accompanied his services, and many received saving benefit through his ministrations'. When Walter Calder was inducted to the same church in 1886 he found 'a kirk session second to none in the county' (Walter Calder, *Strathy: An Account of the Parish*, Wick 1897, pp. 10, 14).

129. Kennedy, *Days of the Fathers in Ross-shire*, pp. 149-53.

CHAPTER 4

The Awakening Spreads 1810–29

The Awakening of the National Church

The spiritual tide was turning, not just in the Highlands, but throughout Scotland. Andrew Bonar, speaking of the year 1813, wrote: 'About that time, it is now evident to us who can look back in the past, the Great head had a purpose of blessing for the Church of Scotland. Eminent men of God appeared to plead the cause of Christ. The Cross was lifted up boldly in the midst of Church Courts which had long been ashamed of the gospel of Christ.' [1] Two striking men, in particular, appeared, who, in the whole range of Scottish Church history stood out as eminent gospel preachers, viz. Andrew Thomson (1779–1831) and Thomas Chalmers (1780–1847). 'Their thunder was genuine', wrote John Macpherson, 'Its effects were beneficent. The showers which fell from heaven, ere the reverberations of their mighty voices had died away, have made our country green.' [2] Thomson became minister of the newly-opened St George's Church, Edinburgh in 1814, in which charge his reputation as a preacher flourished. 'In many families of the congregation and in Edinburgh society generally', continues Macpherson, 'a work of reformation began, and was carried forward with great success. The ballroom and the theatre were forsaken. Many individuals and families in the upper circles exchanged the frivolities of fashionable

---

1. Andrew Bonar, *Memoir and Remains of the Rev. Robert Murray McCheyne, Minister of St Peter's Church, Dundee*, Dundee 1844 (reprinted Edinburgh 1886), p. 13.

2. John Macpherson, *Revival and Revival Work: A Record of the Labours of D. L. Moody and Ira D. Sankey, and Other Evangelists*, London 1875, p. 16.

life for the sober pleasures of religion – family worship and godly living with their peaceful train of blessings took the place of worldliness and sin.'[3]

Thomas Chalmers became minister of Kilmany, Fife in 1803, and remained there until 1815, when he was presented to the prestigious charge of the Tron Church, Glasgow, before moving to the nearby parish of St John's four years later. Chalmers achieved fame as one of the greatest pulpit orators Scotland had ever known. From the time of his settlement in Glasgow he never left the centre of the national stage.[4] Like Thomson, Chalmers 'preached, and taught a multitude of earnest men to preach, the full, glorious meaning of the atoning sacrifice of the Son of God'.[5] As a result, not only was a deep change wrought in the lives of many ministers up and down the country, but the principles of evangelical religion began to permeate congregations across the land. Systematic preaching, visiting, catechising, the formation of local prayer meetings, Presbyterial and parochial associations for the diffusion of knowledge, particularly missionary news, such were the methods used.[6] In a short time, the General Assembly of the Church of Scotland was no longer a Moderate stronghold.

We have already noted that numerous other churches in Edinburgh and Glasgow were in a flourishing condition in the early years of the nineteenth century, such as the Edinburgh Circus, established by James and Robert Haldane, the Anderston Church of Scotland in Barony parish, Glasgow, pastored by the energetic Dr John Love, and, in the same city, the Original Burgher Associate Congregation located in East Campbell Street (see page 172 fn 17). Evangelicalism continued to thrive in many city congregations over the years following, and writer and editor, John Gibson Lockhart, visiting both Edinburgh and Glasgow in the second decade of the nineteenth century, was amazed at the 'wonderfully strict observance of the Sabbath' to be witnessed, especially in the latter city. Here, not a sound was to be heard from one end of town to the other in the hour prior to Sabbath worship. 'But then what a throng and bustle while the bell is ringing – one would think every house had emptied

---

3. ibid., p. 17.

4. Nigel M. de S. Cameron (Ed.), *Dictionary of Scottish Church History and Theology*, Edinburgh 1993, pp. 158-9.

5. MacPherson, *Revival and Revival Work*, p. 18.

6. Robertson, *Spiritual Awakening in the North-East of Scotland*, p. 92.

itself from garret to cellar – such is the endless stream that pours along, gathering as it goes, towards every place from which that all-attractive solemn sermon is heard'. Then, when the service in any given church is over, and worshippers begin pouring out on to the street, for anyone walking in the other direction there was, continued Lockhart, 'nothing for it but facing about, and allowing yourself to be borne along, submissive and resigned, with the furious and conglomerated roll of this human tide. I never saw anything out of Scotland that bore the least resemblance to this' – even the emptying of a London theatre was a joke in comparison, he stated.

> For the most part the whole of the pious mass moves in perfect silence, and if you catch a few low words from some group that advances by your side, you are sure to find them the vehicles of nothing but some criticism on what has just been said by the preacher. Altogether, the effect of the thing is prodigious, and would, in one moment, knock down the whole prejudices of the *Quarterly Reviewer* or any other English High Churchman, who thinks the Scotch a nation of sheer infidels.[7]

Given these encouraging signs, it is intriguing to note that the massive surge of community-based evangelical revivals that breezed across the land in this period was confined almost exclusively to the northern half of the country.[8] Further south, revivals were notable by their absence, although in one or two places, within and without the National Church, small but interesting movements did occasionally arise. One such scenario appeared in the Borders' village of Denholm, which seems to have been early influenced by the preaching of evangelists holding to Congregational principles. As early as 1804, 'the people in this village had their

---

7. John Gibson Lockhart, *Peter's Letters to his Kinsfolk*, Edinburgh 1819, pp. 264-5.

8. D. E. Meek speaks of a 'revival impulse route' at this time, running broadly in an arc from the southern borders of the Highlands to the Inner Hebrides, and outwards to Lewis and Harris, with another route running west from Easter Ross to Skye and the Outer Hebrides (Donald Meek, 'Gaelic Bible, Revival and Mission', p. 119). Scottish historian Michael Lynch writes: 'In the Highlands the lack of an established ministry contributed to a pattern of spiritual rebirth, recession and reawakening some years later.' He suggests that this was 'perhaps the inevitable result of a faith which was forced to live on its nerves, nurtured by the charismatic presence of lay catechists like the "Men"' (for more on 'The Men' see page 140) [Michael Lynch, *Scotland: A New History*, p. 364].

attention much excited by the gospel', when Mr Paton, working under the auspices of Haldane's Society for Propagating the Gospel at Home (SPGH), 'laboured some months in it, and the neighbourhood'.[9]

Then, in the summer of 1810, John Watson, minister of Mussel-burgh Congregational Church, embarked on an extensive seven-week preaching tour of Scotland's southern counties. The highlight of this tour was Denholm, where on 25th August he preached on the green to over 200 people, a decidedly 'astonishing congregation in a place of its size'. The following morning was the Sabbath and Watson wrote: 'Never did I preach to a people who showed a greater readiness with even an equal one to hear.' On his last meeting two days later he preached in a crowded barn, with as many gathered without as within – the greatest number on a weekday Watson had seen.

> 'Never did I address a people more generally solemn and affected', he wrote. 'Many were weeping much; others were to appearance eagerly receiving the word. Indeed, it was a most refreshing meeting to me and an affectionate parting ... Some of them shook hands with me who could scarcely speak to me. Here the fields are just now whitened (literally) to the harvest ... I never was in a place where this seems to be more the case in a spiritual point of view.' [10]

Francis Dick later reaped considerable fruit in the region when he stationed himself in Denholm, on the estate of Douglas of Cavers, over the course of nine or ten successive summers from 1823. A Congregational Church was established in 1826, and Robert Wilson became its first established pastor in 1835. Denholm later became famed in Congregational history when, in March 1839 the first 'protracted meetings' to be held in Scotland were held in the village (see page 382).

Revival in the Central Highlands

Following the revival surge that stirred the Highlands around the turn of the nineteenth century (as outlined in Chapter 3), further periods of

---

9. Alexander, *Memoir of the Rev. John Watson*, p. 79.

10. ibid., pp. 79-80. Watson again visited Denholm the following June, during a similarly extensive tour of Galloway and adjoining counties. On this occasion, how-ever, while the meeting place was full, he was disappointed to find that there was 'not the anxiety evinced which was observed when I left them last year' (pp. 80-1).

intense local awakening continued to rise up throughout the North over the next few decades, as the gospel message penetrated more deeply and extensively through this vast landmass.

Breadalbane / Glenlyon

Arrival of Robert Findlater

Robert Findlater was a native of Kiltearn in Ross-shire and was licensed to preach in 1807 at the age of twenty-one. He came to Breadalbane in 1810 and began catechising his people by systematic house-to-house visitation (he personally taught and examined 1,600 people in one twelve-month period). After one year he settled into the manse at Ardeonaig, which church – originally built under the generosity of Lady Glenorchy – was in a state of disrepair, so he was forced to preach in the open-air in all weathers. He had another preaching station on the north side of the loch. In summer he preached on one side of the water in the morning, then crossed to the other side in the afternoon. In winter, he preached on each side alternately.

Visit from Macdonald of Ferintosh

Spiritual concern increased during 1814 and '15, when a small but growing band of devoted people from the secluded Glenlyon valley regularly trudged miles over hills to attend services by Loch Tay. The communion at Killin in August 1816 – noted as a year of great physical scarcity in the region – had a deep influence on many, and helped instil a prayerful and solemnising expectation for the proposed sacrament in the remote hamlet of Ardeonaig the following month. John Macdonald's services were secured for the event and he preached in various places in the district in the lead up to his action sermon on the Sabbath. Intimation of the service had spread far and wide and a striking number, estimated at between four and five thousand, gathered on the green braes of the Ardeonaig hillside in anticipation.

Findlater wrote to his brother, William, a minister in Dundee:

> He (Macdonald) preached two hours and twenty minutes from Isaiah 54.5. '*For thy maker is thine husband*'. During the whole sermon there was hardly a dry eye. Eagerness to attend to the word preached was depicted on every countenance, while tears were flowing very copiously, and literally watering the very ground. The most hardened in the congregation seemed to bend as one man, and

I believe, if ever the Holy Ghost was present in a solemn assembly, it was there. Mr Macdonald himself seemed in rapture. There were several people who cried aloud, but the general impression seemed to be a universal melting under the word. The people of God themselves were as deeply affected as others; and many have confessed they never witnessed such a scene.[11]

Findlater could compare it to nothing but the day of Pentecost, and similar scenes continued throughout the weekend, which became known as 'The Great Sacrament', during which many were converted. A teacher said he knew of fifty people who were awakened by the Sabbath sermon alone, he personally being among that number. Wrote William McGlashan, who visited the district in 1817: 'The impression of that day was carried in many a bosom to distant parts of the country, and into remote glens, in which, perhaps, the sound of salvation had never before been heard.'[12] Thus began a work of revival in the Breadalbane district, which continued for three years with more or less intensity and fruitfulness.

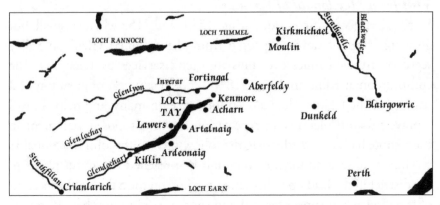

Large numbers could now be seen flocking from all over the wider region to attend services at Lawers or Ardeonaig, on the north and south shores of Loch Tay, respectively. The people from the Glenlyon

11. William Findlater, *Memoir of Rev. Robert Findlater, Together with a Narrative of the Revival of Religion During his Ministry at Lochtayside, Perthshire 1816–1819*, Glasgow 1840, p. 182.

12. William McGlashlan, *Letters on the State of Religion in the Highlands of Scotland*, Glasgow 1818, quoted in Meek, 'Evangelical Missionaries in the Early Nineteenth-Century Highlands', in *Journal of the School of Scottish Studies*, vol. 28, Edinburgh 1987, p. 295.

valley were especially influenced. During September and October of 1816, few remained at home who could face the arduous road between them and Loch Tay. 'One hundred persons might be seen in one company, climbing the hill separating these two districts of country, having to travel a distance of from nine to fifteen miles, and some even further'.[13]

Itinerating Ministry of James Kennedy

Hearing of the Glenlyon residents' continued longing to hear nothing but the life-changing truths of the gospel, James Kennedy of Aberfeldy came to the district for a three-day visit in October 1816, and 'found the valley aflame'.[14] Such was the interest excited by his arrival and such the manifest outpouring of divine power upon the people in connection with his preaching that his stay was protracted for three weeks. Known to some as 'The Whitefield of the Highlands',[15] Kennedy re-visited the Glen many times, and 'day after day, and night after night' he preached the truths these people were so solicitous to hear, sometimes in a house, sometimes by the roadside and sometimes on the rugged slope of a hill, with large rocks as pews. Just as commonly, 'crowds assembled in barns and under the shelter of the woods to listen to those strange things which had been brought to their ears. Sometimes amid bleak winds and drifting snows, with their lamps suspended, fairy like, from the fir trees which sheltered them, preacher and people were so overcome that the service was interrupted by the strength of their emotions'. Another hearer likened 'the moaning and sobbing' to 'a fold of lambs when separated from their dams'.[16] The great theme on these occasions was the love of Christ.[17] For weeks together the Aberfeldy pastor was compelled to neglect his own flock, or leave them to feed themselves.

---

13. Findlater, *Memoir of Rev. Robert Findlater*, p. 194.

14. Couper, *Scottish Revivals*, p. 105.

15. An epithet, which, in variance with 'The Apostle of the North', was also accorded to John Macdonald of Ferintosh (See *DSCHT*, p. 511). Though short in stature, the Aberfeldy preacher also earned the soubriquet, '*An Ceanadach Mor*' ('Great Kennedy').

16. Howard A. Kennedy, *Old Highland Days: The Reminiscences of Dr John Kennedy*, London 1901, p. 42.

17. *SCM* 1856, quoted in McNaughton, 'Revival and Reality', p. 189; cf. Couper, *Scottish Revivals*, p. 106.

The Rev. David Campbell of Lawers, a native of Glenlyon and a fruit of the revival, recalled the first time he heard Kennedy, towards the end of the autumn of 1816.

> I was but a laddie then, but the appearance, voice, manner and awfully solemn piercing appeals of the preacher I can never forget. He laboured with a most passionate ardour and marked success … he continued in Glenlyon preaching every Sabbath and week day – sometimes three sermons a day … and scarcely a sermon was preached but some new case of awakening occurred … However busy at their lawful avocations the people might have been, when … Kennedy's fixed hour to begin the sermon was come all work was thrown aside, and a rush to the barn, hamlet, or hillside might be seen from every corner of the glen.

Campbell noted further that he had seen Kennedy 'stand almost knee-deep in a wreath of snow, while at the same time it was snowing and drifting in his face all the time he was preaching, and the people gathered round him patiently and eagerly listening to the fervent truths that proceeded from his lips … "Ach gu bhi a-comhdhunnadh". "But to conclude"!, – when he came to that, his voice faltered, his eye brightened, and you would think he was as it were rushing between men and death, or plucking them out of the fire'.[18]

Not content with the frequency of these visits from their itinerant 'pastor', many in the glen would make the journey to Aberfeldy to hear him again – on one occasion over sixty of them together, returning at night. Kennedy's son later recalled seeing (c. 1817–18) 'the little Bethel (Aberfeldy Congregational Church) crowded with warm-hearted Highlanders, or on a summer's day adjourning to the village square for want of room, to listen to the words of eternal life'.[19] Many came

> every Sunday, fifteen or twenty miles, to sit under him in Aberfeldy, though they had to start at four in the morning to do it. The sight of these pilgrims travelling in carts, on horseback, and even on foot – the old men clad in homespun and often wearing the Highland bonnet, the old women wearing the snow-white

---

18. *SCM* 1864, quoted in ibid., p. 190.
19. *SCM* 1856, quoted in ibid., p. 188.

'mutch', and carrying sprigs of sweet-scented 'southernwood' as well as white handkerchiefs and the beloved Psalm-book in their hands – was by no means lacking in picturesqueness. Reaching Aberfeldy long before the hour of service, they were hospitably entertained at breakfast by the villagers. Then they streamed into the plain little chapel, and the worship began … As soon as the church was emptied the manse was crowded … .Many of them did not get home till midnight; but the way, though long, was made cheerful with 'songs of Zion' and with talk of what they had heard in the morning.[20]

Kennedy's son wrote that when John Macdonald was denied permission by the parish minister to preach in the town, he 'evaded an evil law by conducting worship seated on his chair in my father's parlour, with all the doors of the house thrown open, and every room in the house crowded'.[21]

By autumn 1817 Kennedy believed there to be around 200 in a hopeful way since the start of the revival, half of whom were now rejoicing in the truth (including some as young as between nine and fourteen years old), while the remainder were under deep conviction.[22] When the revival fervour had to some extent passed away, it was reckoned that only five or six families in the whole of Glenlyon had been left untouched. These families were looked upon as objects of pity.[23] However, a difficulty arose when the local parish minister complained that Findlater and other evangelists were intruding on his position as religious overseer of the glen. Couper insists that the rift proved of short duration, because soon afterwards Findlater was found assisting the minister at his sacrament.[24]

Return of Macdonald

John Macdonald returned to Loch Tay in April 1817, when huge crowds followed to hear so eminent a preacher speak in Kenmore, Lawers, Strathfillan and Glenlyon over the course of just a few days. Indeed, throughout the spring and summer of 1817 there existed a strong spirit

---

20. Kennedy, *Old Highland Days*, p. 44.

21. *SCM* 1856, quoted in McNaughton, 'Revival and Reality', p189.

22. Alexander, *Memoir of the Rev. John Watson*, p. 139.

23. It was said that scarcely one of Kennedy's converts afterwards fell away (Kennedy, *Old Highland Days*, p. 43).

24. Couper, *Scottish Revivals*, p. 106.

of concern throughout the region, few families were to be found in which no member was under conviction. Macdonald helped at a further sacrament in Breadalbane that September when his Monday sermon at Hog's Park in Lawers is on record as being one of the most powerful and effective sermons he ever preached in Breadalbane.[25] The weeping towards the end reminded one man of 'the bleating when lambs are being weaned – loud, general, as if the whole hillside were bleating'.[26] Macdonald was due to return to the area on 23rd November, and an immense crowd gathered to hear him. He failed to turn up however, and Findlater was almost overwhelmed at the prospect of leading the meeting himself. He cried out to God, and despite his feelings of inadequacy, was given strength to preach. Indeed, such was the power of his message that 'the greater part of the congregation seemed to be melted into tears, a gentle sweet mourning in every corner'. One witness wrote: 'Such was the holy unction with which he spoke, and the deep interest manifested by the congregation, to the solemn truths delivered, and his truly pathetic address to the different classes of his hearers, that I never witnessed a more affecting scene.' [27] Surprised and humbled, Findlater himself wrote: 'I never witnessed such a scene under my own poor preaching.' [28]

A crowd gathered to hear an unnamed visiting preacher who came to Glenlyon in October 1817,[29] and as it was dark, they asked for the use of a large flour mill in Invervar. The preacher recalled the event: 'Though busy at work, it was instantly stopped to give place to the bread of immortal life. When the broad two-leafed door was thrown open by the eagerness of the people to gain admittance, the press was so violent that we feared what might be the consequences; a vast number for want of room stood contentedly before the door, beaten by the high wind and pierced by the cold'. Remarked the visiting evangelist, 'I was so wedged

---

25. Findlater, *Memoir of Rev. Robert Findlater*, p. 196.

26. Couper, *Scottish Revivals*, p. 106.

27. Findlater, *Memoir of Rev. Robert Findlater*, p. 198.

28. Couper, *Scottish Revivals*, p. 107.

29. The awakening attracted considerable interest throughout Scotland and a number of ministers visited the Breadalbane area during or shortly after the time of the revival, including Rev. Gilfillan of Comrie, Rev. Young of Logiealmond and William McGavin, 'the well known champion of Protestantism'. As a result of such interest, evangelical libraries were set up in Glenlyon, Killin, Lochtayside and Fortingall (Couper, *Scottish Revivals*, pp. 107-8).

in where I stood that some of those behind had their chins almost on my shoulders'.[30]

Results and Obstacles

Throughout most of two years since the revival commenced, few Sundays passed without one or more brought under concern, although at a couple of points 'the interference of Dissenters' was said to have slowed down the work considerably. Findlater described the moral influences of the revival on the people as 'as much as I have ever seen. They all live in love and union with one another'. Even the ungodly, he observed incredulously, appeared favourably inclined to it. 'Masters who would grudge their time on other occasions, would allow their servants to embrace every opportunity of reading or hearing the Scriptures, and would often accompany them, and in several instances their hearts were opened to receive the truth'. A further mercy to Findlater was that 'nothing appeared like delusion or enthusiastic, fanatical feelings'.[31]

Findlater expressed his disapproval of a number of accounts of the revival which were published at the time – in magazines or pamphlets – as being not only partial and exaggerated, but also calculated to do more harm than good, in that many of the subjects were under strong mental excitement and therefore their judgement and experience were not yet sufficiently enlightened. They also had a tendency to convey a false impression to others – whose affections were merely excited – that they were the subjects of true conversion if they felt alarming terror, or joyous feelings. Besides, he thought a holy jealousy and watchfulness should be cherished, lest self-congratulation or attributing to human instruments the glory due to God alone might mix with the zeal excited and the efforts of all involved in the work.

Without elaborating, one local resident, Duncan Campbell, expressed his strong opinion that a great many revival converts who remained in the Church of Scotland showed gross insensitivity to the ways of God's Spirit. Nevertheless, his overall conclusion was that the revival 'was a genuine force which had far-reaching consequences'. It made the Church of Scotland 'strong, and more zealous in good works than had ever, in the Highlands at least, been the case before'.[32]

---

30. ibid., p. 106.

31. Findlater, *Memoir of Rev. Robert Findlater*, pp. 210, 218.

32. ibid.

One notable fruit of the movement was the change in character of a notorious fighter known as the 'Lion of Glenlyon'. He became as quiet as a lamb and was seen driving along in his peat cart reading the Bible. In addition, at least one minister was first aroused to his spiritual concern on hearing one of Findlater's sermons. Also as a result of the revival, several who were dissenters formerly, 'returned again to the bosom of the Church'. Conversely, some of those awakened were persuaded to join the glen's small Baptist congregation. This appears to have been part of the 'sectarianism and embittered controversy on ecclesiastical and doctrinal questions' which, Campbell felt, 'helped to bring the movement to a close'.[33] Other factors included the short-lived attraction of a fanatical preacher to Glenlyon and opposition from a member of the Presbytery, the Rev. Dr Alexander Irvine, who had been minister of Fortingall from February 1805 to May 1806 and who wrote a 'savage and unrestrained attack' against the Breadalbane revivals of both 1804 and 1816 (see Appendix, page 252).[34]

As a result of reports of some irregularities in connection with the revival, the Presbytery of Dunkeld inaugurated an inquiry into the role of Church of Scotland ministers and missionaries in the movement. This took place in March 1819. Among the allegations were that many individuals convulsed under the ministry of certain preachers, that John Macdonald had preached in parishes without the request or consent of the minister, that services were conducted in English instead of Gaelic, and that communion tokens were given to several strangers, without lines of character, and to people who did not choose to communicate in their own parish churches. Findlater and others were called to answer questions, but despite the strength of attack from the anti-revivalists, managed to convince the Presbytery that all the main charges were groundless. Nevertheless, considerable hurt had been caused to the accused, and it is noteworthy that the awakening, which was still in progress in early 1819, began to die down around this time.[35]

---

33. The emergence of Baptist and Congregational churches in the area, he felt, served only to stimulate further 'the activity and increase and power of the national Church between 1810 and 1843' (ibid.).

34. *Substance of a Speech Delivered Before the Commission of the General Assembly of the Church of Scotland*, Dunkeld 1819.

35. The Church of Scotland enquiry does not appear to have been initiated by Irvine's bitter allegations, which was published in that same year, 1819.

Lasting Influences

Thereafter, 'the dying fire did occasionally show expiring flickerings', but 1820 apparently saw the end of this special dispensation of grace.[36] Among the early fruits of the Breadalbane revival were John Ferguson, John Campbell and James Dewar, all of whom, along with Dewar's brother, Alexander, entered the Congregational ministry. A notable trio of brothers was also among the considerable band of converts from Glenlyon; Patrick Campbell, who became a schoolmaster and voluntary evangelist in his native glen; Duncan, subsequently minister of Lawers, Glenlyon and Kiltearn; and David, who succeeded Duncan as minister at Lawers.

John Macalister, a convert of another great Highland revival – in Arran, earlier in the century – was licensed to preach in 1824, in which year he also accepted a call to the newly-built Parliamentary Church in Glenlyon. 'Here the Lord mightily honoured and prospered his servant in his work – great multitudes flocking long distances, Sabbath after Sabbath, to attend his ministry'. The effects of his teaching and pastoral superintendence in the district were in evidence many decades later, in a variety of ways. 'It is impossible', said Macalister's biographer in the 1870s, 'for any discerning Christian, to pass through that wonderful glen without discovering what a sweet savour of Christ John Macalister was to many'. One who spoke with holy enthusiasm of these early years of Macalister's ministry was the above-mentioned David Campbell, later minister in the same parish.[37]

Elsewhere in Perthshire

Muthill

One of John Macdonald's biographers writes of him that while serving as minister of the Gaelic Chapel in Edinburgh (from 1807 to 1813)[38] 'he took a deep and active interest in the great revival at Muthill, under the ministry of the Rev. Mr Russel'. It would appear that the revival

---

36. Couper, *Scottish Revivals*, p. 109.

37. Various Contributors, *Disruption Worthies of the Highlands*, pp. 170-1.

38. It was in Edinburgh that Macdonald experienced 'a fresh baptism of the Spirit', whereby, among other blessings, 'his preaching now became instinct with life ... His statements of gospel truth were now the warm utterances of one who deeply felt its power. The Lord's people could now testify that he spoke from his own heart to theirs' (Rev. John Kennedy, *The Apostle of the North: The Life and Labours of the Rev. John Macdonald, D.D., of Ferintosh*, London 1866 [reprinted Glasgow 1979], p. 53).

referred to is that which in fact occurred a few years after Macdonald moved to Ferintosh in 1813. John Russel, a native of Kilmarnock, was inducted at Muthill in 1809, and served there until his death in 1826, when aged 41.[39] Deeply devoted to his parishioners, Russel visited every family once every second year and examined them throughout the following year. Robert Findlater, who had known Russel since their college days, regarded him as 'always the same firm and kind friend ... a most worthy and zealous man – a John Knox, making great reformation in a place which stood much in need'.[40] A popular preacher, 'his most striking and forceful appeals were often the effusions of the moment, and coming from the heart, had frequently a melting and overpowering effect upon his audience'.[41]

Both Russel and John Macdonald preached on the Thursday of the August 1816 Sacrament of the Lord's Supper at Killin during the Breadalbane revival. In return, both Macdonald and Findlater preached in Muthill and Russel noted in December 1817 that since his last sacrament, 'I have observed a new edge put upon the attention of my people to divine things'.[42] It seems to have been especially around this time that Russel became 'the instrument of turning many from sin to righteousness, and numerous are the attestations which his parish affords to the moralising effects of a gospel ministry'.[43]

Strathardle and Blackwater

On his brown pony named 'Tommy', James Kennedy journeyed to east Perthshire in 1820, when he visited the Strathardle and Blackwater valleys. A 'pious and devoted man of God' converted under Stewart

---

39. Russel's father, the Rev. John Russel, served as a schoolmaster in Ross-shire, where he became infamous for his severe discipline. Ordained to Kilmarnock in 1774, this reputation was enhanced by, for example, his strict Sabbatarian principles, being accustomed on Sundays to go out, staff in hand, and – being strong in physique as well as voice – forcibly turn back any of his parishioners about to indulge in the sin of Sunday walking. He has gained immortality through the satire of Ayrshire bard, Robbie Burns, cropping up in numerous of his poems, including *The Holy Fair*.

40. Findlater, *Memoir of Rev. Robert Findlater*, pp. 224, 159.

41. Thomas Chalmers (Ed.), *Sermons of John Russel of Muthill*, Glasgow 1826, pp. xxii-xxv.

42. ibid., pp. 81, 193.

43. ibid., pp. xxii-xxv. This Muthill revival came some seventy years after a similar powerful shower of divine blessing on this Perthshire community (see page 132).

of Moulin began a Sabbath-school for adults in the area. Through these, and Kennedy's visits, a time of revival commenced in both glens, producing 'the most remarkable change in the life and character of many'. People often travelled great distances through snow to hear Kennedy's sermons, which would be followed by meetings for the anxious after the congregation was dismissed. Those attending these 'little sermons' became objects of ridicule and mockery at the hands of the heathen.[44] Kennedy said that the 'men of Strathardle' were mostly moved by the terrors of the law, in contrast to the people he preached to in Breadalbane, who 'showed themselves most accessible to the sweeter influences of the gospel – the love of Jesus Christ'.[45] One convert of this awakening was Archibald Farquharson, later Congregational minister in Tiree. John McLaren, another fruit of the movement, said that he, along with many others who received benefit to their souls under Kennedy's ministry, 'came all the way from Strathardle to Aberfeldy (twenty miles) to attend Divine ordinances and enjoy Christian intercourse ... bands of us followed him to every place where he preached between Moulin and the head of Glenisla, Glenshee, Blackwater, Blairgowrie, Kirkmichael and Glenbriarachan'.[46]

Around the same time but further west in Perthshire, along the Strathfillan valley, Donald McGillivray, 'quaint and homely, but endowed with rare genius ... preached the gospel with great power and abundant tokens of blessing'. A close colleague of Robert Findlater, and highly esteemed by him, McGillivray preached at several communion services in Killin and Glenlyon during the time of the Breadalbane revival. His sermons were still remembered a generation later.[47]

Ross-shire

Ferintosh

Within a year of the young John Macdonald (1779–1849) coming as minister to Ferintosh, Ross-shire in 1813, his much-loved wife became seriously ill and died. While many expected him to postpone his first

---

44. *SCM* 1864, quoted in McNaughton, *Early Congregational Independency in the Highlands and Islands and the North-East of Scotland*, Glasgow 2003, pp. 80-1.

45. Couper, *Scottish Revivals*, p. 108.

46. *SCM* 1878, quoted in McNaughton, 'Revival and Reality', pp. 190-1.

47. Duncan Macgregor, *Campbell of Kiltearn*, Edinburgh 1874, p. 36.

Communion the following weekend, 10,000 people gathered at 'the Burn' for the services, when Macdonald's text was '*I will betrothe thee unto Me*' (Hosea 2:19). The preacher's self-denial and sorrow touched the vast crowd, and he was pressed to preach again in the evening. When Macdonald several times asked the question from his text '*Wilt thou go with this man?*', a middle-aged woman in the centre of the crowd stood up, threw her arms in the air, and exclaimed, '*Theid, Theid, O, Theid*' ('I will, I will, Oh, I will'). With this, 'the great congregation broke down. It was a scene never to be forgotten. The burn of Ferintosh was a Bochim indeed that day. Such was the weeping, the crying, the commotion among the people, that the preacher's voice was drowned'. Thus began a season of awakening among the people, and over the next few years scores were converted from within the parish and from many surrounding districts.[48]

In January 1816 Macdonald wrote in his diary of some fifty-eight persons 'awakened under my ministry, known to myself, besides others unknown to me'. Towards the close of his ministry, having preached over 10,000 sermons, Macdonald was said to have testified that from the day he entered a pulpit until then, he was unconscious of having ever left it without a free, unfettered call to every sinner in his audience to accept Christ freely as offered in the Gospel, on the warrant of God's call.[49]

However, not all evangelicals approved of Macdonald's ministry in revival. He came under strong criticism from Separatist, John Groat of Strathy, in regard to a preaching tour Macdonald made of Caithness, Sutherland and Ross in 1817, during which some of his listeners were known to cry out and display bodily agitations, yet were not converted. In a letter, Grant wrote: 'The trouble began in their heels and wrought up to their heads, and then they began to cry and to make an excessive motion with their hands and feet, and at evening many of them went home as sound as before.'[50]

A sermon preached between the parishes of Dornoch and Creich in the autumn of 1816 was said to have been 'one of the very greatest that

---

48. Kennedy, *The Apostle of the North*, pp. 46-52; Various Contributors, *Disruption Worthies of the Highlands*, p. 23.

49. MacRae, *The Life of Gustavus Aird*, pp. 269-70.

50. 'Letters of the Eminently Pious John Grant, Joseph McKay and Alexander Gair', quoted in Campbell, *One of Heaven's Jewels*, p. 141. John Kennedy of Dingwall, a great admirer of Macdonald, expressed very similar concerns in regards to a later revival movement that arose under the Apostle's preaching at a later date (see page 435).

had ever been delivered by the Apostle of the North'.[51] The service was initially arranged to be held at Clashmore, but at the appointed hour it was announced that Dr Bethune, the minister of Dornoch, would not allow Macdonald to preach within the bounds of his parish. The Rev. Murdo Cameron of Creich had come to hear the sermon, and at once proposed that Macdonald preach from Riaveg, Creich, just across the border from Dornoch, while his audience, who were not interdicted, could sit on the Dornoch side of the boundary. This was acted upon and proved most suitable. An immense concourse assembled from a number of parishes on both sides of the Dornoch Firth. 'Above all', noted Donald Munro of John Macdonald, 'The rich unction from the Holy One resting upon him gave him special unfitting for the work of the day'. Knowing that many of his hearers hailed from parishes which were not blessed with an earnest gospel ministry, Macdonald realised that he was now favoured with a precious opportunity of setting life and death before them. His heart was so fired with love to Christ and intense yearning for the salvation of souls that his words fell on the congregation like burning shot. The sermon was one of extraordinary power. Such was the preacher's energy in the delivery that it was claimed that the mark of his feet in the ground where he stood could be seen for some years afterwards. Even more permanent were the impressions which his fervent appeals had left on many hearts. It is said that individuals from all the parishes represented had been awakened, and at least one person was so overcome that he had to be carried out of the vast assembly.[52]

Avoch

Aware of the low state of religion in Avoch in the late 1820s, the Rev. Alexander Dewar called members of his Congregational Church to set aside days for prayer and fasting. This was dutifully carried out by some, and as a result, records Dewar:

> The church revived and the Lord began to bless the preaching of the Gospel so that seldom a Sabbath passed without good being

---

51. Macdonald had also become known as '*Ministear Mor na Toisidheachd*' ('The Great Minister of Ferintosh').

52. Munro, *Records of Grace in Sutherland*, pp. 94-5. This was seventeen-year-old Alexander Murray of Rogart, who later became a church elder and a man of eminent piety in his community.

done, and this was not only the case when at home, but in answer to the prayers of an enlivened people, wherever I went to preach, souls were converted. As an illustration I may mention that during that season (1829) I went as usual to Caithness, and six members were added to the Church in Wick shortly after, who ascribed their conversion to that visit.

Of the work in Avoch, Dewar reported, 'the greater number were young persons (but there were two among the converts above sixty years of age) and of that class which to all human appearance were the most hopeless characters. Very few of that class which might be characterised as hopeful were affected. The impressions were general, so that almost all subjects of conversation gave place to the enquiry, "How does it fare with your soul?"'[53]

Portmahomack

The Rev. William Forbes had laboured in the Ross-shire parish of Tarbat since 1800. One who often heard him preach wrote of

> the mighty mingled multitude who assembled to hear him, and whom the church of Tarbat could but ill contain ... we have felt as if breathing in the atmosphere of heaven whilst hearing petitions admirably adapted to every variety of case and of circumstances ...We have seen him labour under emotions too big for utterance, as his clear and comprehensive mind seemed pressed and overwhelmed under the grandeur and magnificence of things unseen and eternal; we have seen him sit down in his pulpit, unable to proceed further with the exposition of a subject which was felt to be intensely interesting ... He laboured as one who had to give an account ...[54]

---

53. The 1843 'Questionnaire', quoted in McNaughton, *Early Congregational Independency in the Highlands and Islands*, pp. 247-9.

54. Rev. Malcolm MacGregor, 'Prefatory Memoir', in Rev. William Forbes, *Communion and Other Sermons* (partly edited by the late Rev. John Kennedy), London 1867, pp. xxv-xxvi. Alexander MacRae records of Forbes: 'He gave himself entirely to his Master's work among the people', but then incorrectly states that 'though there were many striking cases of conversion during the years of his faithful ministry, there was not a general revival till he had gone to his reward in 1838' (Alexander MacRae, *Revivals in the Highlands and Islands*, p. 84).

Within this parish, a movement of 'heavenly power' was apparent among the fisherfolk of Portmahomack from about 1829,[55] at which time the village was a busy port, home to around one hundred boats. As a result of the awakening a significant number were brought under saving change. It appears that the Portmahomack converts had a reputation for not easily obtaining assurance of their salvation, for John Kennedy makes reference to their disposition to question their own conversion.[56] Yet at the Dornoch Communion a couple of years later (1831) the fourth table, which held sixty communicants, was wholly filled by young converts from Portmahomack, who had crossed the Dornoch Firth by boat to attend the sacrament.[57] When the service was over the linen cloth was wet with their tears, 'as though it had been taken out of the sea'.[58] Tragically, the lives of nearly all these young communicants were to be snatched away within around twelve months when the deadly cholera swept through the community (see page 268).[59]

Caithness

Watten

Spiritual awakening gradually spread through the Caithness parish of Watten some time after the induction of native Alexander Gunn (1773–1836) in 1805. Gunn was regarded as being 'possessed of much of the public spirit that animated the Scottish reformers'. By 1815, his ministry, which from its commencement was remarkable, had now ripened into commanding power. An interest in spiritual things was stirred, and truths were dropped into many minds that were little conversant with such formality. The result was that many besides professing Christians began to betake themselves to Watten on the Sabbath. Indeed, streams of people

---

55. Although writing much nearer the time of occurrence, Kennedy – mistakenly it seems – dates this episode about 1839 when there spread, indeed, a later flow of revival blessing throughout Easter Ross, not least in the parish of Tarbat; see page 429. (Kennedy, *The Apostle of the North*, pp. 290-1).

56. ibid., pp. 290-1.

57. It is possible that the awakening that occurred in Avoch and that in Portmahomack had some connection with each other, as both occurred in the same county around the same time, and both primarily within fishing communities.

58. Campbell, *Gleanings of Highland Harvest*, pp. 97-8.

59. Interestingly, this awakening preceded the cholera outbreak (1832), rather than being prompted by it.

gathered along the roads leading to the church, so that 'one wondered how the building could contain them; and it only did so by every pew and passage being filled'. The many converted and nurtured through Gunn's ministry became, almost all of them 'as the "sons of a king"; their Christianity of a living, solid and scriptural stamp; so that they have been the religious leaders or "men" of the communities where their lot has been cast'.[60]

Communion seasons drew believers from all over the county and beyond, and some were easily recalled decades later. Such was the thirst for biblical teaching that communion Sabbaths in Caithness sometimes saw four separate services being conducted with eight or nine ministers visiting to assist. Records one: 'An esteemed father, then young in his ministry, has told us that one of the seasons of greatest spiritual enjoyment he ever experienced was on the Monday of a communion at Watten.'[61] Another such occasion was at Olrig in 1816, when Gunn delivered 'a discourse of extraordinary power. The congregation seemed spell-bound as he unfolded to them and enforced ... the authority of the Divine lawgiver ... During the discourse the wind took the top off the tent, and the heavy hand of the impassioned speaker sent the book-board before him into fragments; but these incidents ... seemed but fitting adjuncts of this impressive scene'.[62] Many would cross the hill between Watten and Bower at the close of each day's exercises to the house of the eminent David Steven, 'where hospitality was extended on no limited scale'. Asked how he could accommodate so many people (some slept on straw in the barn), Steven replied, 'Love makes room'. Evening meetings were held in Steven's stackyard. Largely attended, they often went on till the sma' hours of the morning, and were the origin of the Sabbath night prayer-meetings which became popular on similar occasions throughout the county. Wrote Alexander Auld: 'Such tokens of the Lord's presence would be manifest in the spiritual liberty and enlargement of the speakers, and in the soul-refreshment of the hearers.' Steven was the most celebrated of Gunn's numerous converts and a warm life-long friendship followed.[63]

---

60. Auld, *Ministers and Men of the Far North*, pp. 32-4; 170.

61. ibid., p. 173.

62. ibid., pp. 34-5.

63. ibid., pp. 39-41; 173-4. Gunn found Steven 'a wise counsellor in various emergencies, and a zealous coadjutor in schemes of usefulness. On the other hand, David,

Western Highlands

Angus McIver in Ardnamurchan

Uig native, Angus McIver went to Ardnamurchan as a teacher with the Gaelic School Society in the late 1820s. Here people flocked to his classes and with much zeal and enthusiasm begged to learn to read the Word of God. The school and meeting-house became repeatedly crowded as McIver witnessed God's Spirit working in a marked manner. Indeed, said his biographer, 'The community was moved as perhaps it was never moved before or since, for God's Spirit was very manifestly present at the gatherings … the place was a well-watered garden at this time and the spiritual enthusiasm was immense'. Both old and young came under the power of the truth, and a number continued eminent Christians till the end of life; 'in ripe old age bearing all the marks of ripening for heaven'.[64]

McIver lodged during these years at a crofter's house, and spent a great deal of time praying at night by the seashore. By this means he contracted asthma, an illness which dogged him for the rest of his life. McIver also faced trials of a different kind during his time in Ardnamurchan. Although his district was far from the parish church, two moderate ministers complained to the GSS hierarchy that he and other teachers were 'holding services at canonical hours and preaching'. Summoned to Edinburgh, where he was told that he might be deprived of his salary, McIver replied that they might withhold his salary, 'but they would not be able to shut his mouth for the Lord had once opened it to show forth his praises … ' The accused was dismissed and his salary was not reduced.[65]

After two or three years McIver was called to leave Ardnamurchan. Old men, who had been notoriously careless in life were now writhing their hands and weeping as they parted with their catechist on the seashore, which became 'a very Bochim'. On McIver's transfer to Kenmore, Lochfyneside, a few miles south of Inverary, here, too, both

---

who was steadfastly attached to Mr Gunn's ministry till its close, held him in the highest esteem', not least because Gunn's 'personal and ministerial character was peculiarly intense' (ibid., p. 172).

64. 'Story of a Lewis Catechist: The Life of Angus McIver', serialised in *The Stornoway Gazette*, 22/01/1972, p. 5.

65. ibid.

old and young quickly became deeply interested in his incessant labours among them, day and night. Indeed, many of his male scholars, years after, while at the herring fishing in Lewis, to which island McIver had returned, travelled many miles to hear him preach.

John Macrae in Glenelg

It was through a sermon delivered by Dr Macdonald of Ferintosh at Port-na-cloiche in Wester Ross that a young John ('Big') Macrae (later Free Church minister in Knockbain, Greenock, Lochs and Carloway) had his first serious spiritual impressions. Shortly after, at a communion weekend on the other side of the county, Macrae came to a living knowledge of saving grace. The convert was zealous in his new-found faith and during his early studies gave part-time teaching service at Arnisdale, Glenelg, in the north-west Highlands. He exhorted people on the Sabbath and conducted prayer meetings through the week, and almost from the beginning his word was 'in demonstration of the Spirit and of power'. For, wrote his biographer, Nicol Nicolson, 'a work of grace began in the district as striking and as satisfactory as he at all saw in his after career'.[66]

Work in the Islands

Skye

A deep spiritual movement had begun on Skye from around 1805 (see page 198). However, it wasn't until 1812 that full-scale revival began; in Kilmuir parish – which acted as a centre of light for the whole island – and then spread to neighbouring parishes (Snizort, then Bracadale, then Duirinish), also breaking out spontaneously in other districts.[67] Blind catechist

---

66. Nicol Nicolson, *Reverend John Macrae ('Mac-Rath Mor' – 'Big Macrae') of Knockbain, Greenock and Lewis: A Short Account of his Life and Fragments of his Preaching*, Inverness 1924, pp. 12-4.

67. Doctoral student, Roderick Macleod, suggests that one factor influencing the subsequent revival in Skye was the uncertainty and unrest caused by affairs on continental Europe. A remarkable number of men from the Western Isles served in the British forces during the Napoleonic wars. The minister of Snizort claimed in 1863 that his native island had sent over 10,000 foot-soldiers to fight for their country over a forty-year span, commencing at the end of the 18th century. 'The first two Skye revivals – in 1805 and 1812–14', he writes, 'occurred at a time when the tranquillity of the island was disturbed by so many of the young men being involved in a foreign war' (Macleod, *Progress of Evangelicalism in the Western Isles*, pp. 209-10).

Donald Munro was the central figure in the movement. One who was well acquainted with the state of religion in the island in those days declared:

> Such was the influence of the Gospel on the people in general in the districts where Munro laboured, that if a stranger came to the place he would be disposed to think that the majority of the people were under its influence. Not that he believed that such was really the case, but that the decided change in the lives of those who were turned to the Lord awed outwardly those who were not, seeing the habits of those who were savingly enlightened so different from what they were before.[68]

Munro was hugely popular with the people and sometimes such was their respect for him that they were wont to carry him from place to place on their backs.

A 'lay member' of the Established Church wrote of 'offences' occurring during the revival, in that 'there were some among those who were awakened, particularly females, who became fanatical in the proper sense of the word'.[69] These may have been part of the 'large body' of people formed during the movement, as claimed by the Rev. Alexander Beith, whose religion, 'instead of being a reflection of the image of Christ, was no more than a reflection of that of his people – the work in whom was not of God, but of man; shortcomings in whom gave a handle in a few instances to enemies, who were but too ready, as has always occurred in such cases, to use it to decry the genuine work which had been produced in so many. They were the tares which the enemy had sown'.[70]

Despite strong opposition on this and other grounds,[71] the movement continued for two-and-a-half years. With both John Farquharson

---

68. James Ross, *Donald McQueen: Catechist in Bracadale*, London 1891, p. 4.

69. Anon., 'An Account of the Present State of Religion in the Highlands of Scotland', quoted in Macleod, *The Progress of Evangelicalism*, p. 214.

70. Alexander Beith, *A Highland Tour*, Edinburgh 1874, pp. 146-7.

71. One influence discouraging the movement emanated from no less eminent a preacher than Lachlan Mackenzie (1754–1819), considered something of a prophet in the Highlands, who was of the (erroneous) opinion that it was futile to send missionaries to 'Popish, Pagan and Mohamadean countries' because he felt from his study of biblical prophecy that spiritual declension would only increase up to the time of Christ's second coming. For a hundred years after his death, a number of believers in Skye did not consider revival a real possibility in their day because they unwaveringly

and Donald Martin (of Kilmuir) having left Skye for fresh pastures, John Shaw was thought to be the only minister on the island whom the converts 'esteemed or were inclined to hear'. Shaw had moved to Bracadale in 1814, and was seen as a godly man but not a strong leader. Evangelicals who lived too far from Shaw's church to be able to attend his services built meeting places of their own.[72] It is for this reason that Alexander Beith gave as one of the results of the revival an 'abandonment of ordinances as administered by the parochial clergy', the people flocking instead to meetings held by Munro, Shaw and others of like mind, turning en masse from previous practices associated with the Communion, when drunkenness, gossip and a complete lack of reverence were commonplace.[73] Indeed, over time, it came to be counted an evidence of seriousness not to apply to the clergy for the administration of ordinances. Still, this large body of believers, distinguished for the fervency of their piety and the purity of their lives, refused to detach themselves from the National Church, to whose constitution they continued to be warmly devoted; turning aside only from its ordinances.[74]

At one location at least, meetings were held three times every Sunday, when 'great meltings' would come upon the hearers.

> The silent tear might be seen stealing down the rugged, but expressive countenances turned upon the reader – the convulsive and half-suppressed sigh might next be heard – female sobbings followed – and, after a little, every breast was heaving under the unaccountable agitation which moved the spirits of the assembled multitudes ... Sometimes those affected cried aloud; but this

---

followed Lachlan's view of unfulfilled prophecy and expected no more revivals until the millennium (Murray, *The Happy Man*, p. 27, fn.).

72. Shaw had never been a well man and died in 1823 aged thirty-eight.

73. Beith, *A Highland Tour*, pp. 147-8.

74. This practice became something of a tradition in Skye, and became the central focus of a Committee appointed by the Assembly of the Church of Scotland two decades later, in 1835, and headed by Sir Reginald Macdonald Seton of Staffin, to tour the Highlands and Islands in order to assess the conditions of its people and the Church. An enquiry was set up in the parish of Bracadale, where Roderick Macleod was minister. Interestingly, the Commission found that it wasn't in Bracadale but in other parishes that the greatest number of unbaptised people were to be found, as well as those who were not fully in membership of the Church.

was not common: at other times they threw themselves upon the grass, in the utmost distress, and wept bitterly.[75]

When the service was concluded, the people were to be seen in all directions calling upon the name of the Lord. Such was the thirst for the Word of God that it was difficult to get the people to go to their homes for necessary nourishment and to attend to household duties.

Many of those converted during the revival through the exertions of Munro went on to exercise considerable influence in various parts of Skye or on other islands. For instance, Malcolm Nicolson became parish teacher in Barvas, Lewis; Donald Macdonald served as catechist in Kilmuir and Duirinish; Angus Munro was Gaelic teacher in Snizort; Neil Stewart went as catechist to North Uist, and John MacSween taught in Islay.[76] Perhaps the most longstanding example was set by Donald McQueen, who served for many years as an English teacher in Snizort, then, after the Disruption, acted as a Free Church catechist in Snizort, Stein, Duirinish and Bracadale.[77] In all, it was claimed that 'several hundreds were brought from darkness to light' as a result of the movement.[78]

Arran

Neil McBride in Kilmorie

Just as a spiritual awakening on Skye in the first years of the 1800s was followed by a deeper and more widespread revival around seven years later (see page 198 and 224), such was the case, too, with that revival movement which first showed itself in the more southerly island of Arran in 1804 (see page 196). In 1811 a 'little flock of tender-hearted Christians, scattered throughout' Neil McBride's Arran parish of Kilmorie set aside whole days for prayer and fasting, in the earnest seeking of a greater outpouring of God's Spirit in converting power upon their neighbourhood. In these devotional exercises some believers enjoyed 'uncommon nearness to God and great freedom at his throne of grace'.[79] Ten months later, in March

75. Couper, *Scottish Revivals*, p. 97.

76. Macleod, *Progress of Evangelicalism in the Western Isles*, p. 196.

77. Ross, *Donald McQueen*, pp. 13-14.

78. Douglas McMillan (Ed.), *Restoration in the Church*, p. 125.

79. Quoted in an 'old tract' re-quoted by Horatius Bonar in Kennedy/Bonar, *'Evangelism'*, p. 74. It is possible that the flames of the earlier movement in the Kilmorie district were still aglow at this date.

1812, a fresh wave of revival broke out in the district, the first sign of which, and coming as a great surprise to all, was the crying out of various individuals, initially at private cottage meetings, but afterwards extending to public meetings under McBride's guidance. Those first affected were the most tender, humble, and spiritually-minded among them, who later testified that no-one was more surprised at their outbursts than themselves, and that they could hardly have refrained from such outcry even had they been threatened with instant death. The first man who was thus affected gave a 'cry so powerful that he alarmed the whole meeting so that a portion of the people went out'.[80] Yet these believers avowed that their outcryings arose entirely from the state of their minds when powerfully impressed and affected with a sense of divine truth.

Such influence – now accompanied by bodily agitations such as 'panting, trembling, and other convulsive appearances'[81] – was soon extended to those who had previously been under serious spiritual impressions, and after that to those who were thoughtless and openly wicked. Indeed, while people of all description and age were affected, from children to the over-sixties, such impressions were most common among the young. McBride was said to have discouraged such manifestations 'with all tenderness and love'.[82] Conversely, Angus MacMillan, a leader in both this and the earlier movement on the island, at first encouraged these expressions, but later changed his mind. When he did so, his tone of disapproval was more severe than some experienced Christians considered prudent. He went on to examine several non-converted people who exhibited bodily manifestations and found to his approval that such were often accompanied by deep conviction of sin and an earnest desire to be united with Christ. For many others, however, who were deeply affected externally, conviction of sin failed to take root in their hearts and so any sense of awakening soon passed away. These outward manifestations, still generally disapproved of by McBride, sometimes caused services to become longer and longer, as well as more disorganised, while at the same time they did much to spread the revival over the island.

McMillan refers to one of several instances in his own ministry of an established believer who was blessed by refreshing influences of the

---

80. Couper, *Scottish Revivals*, p. 90.

81. McMillan (Ed.), *Restoration in the Church*, p. 62.

82. Couper, *Scottish Revivals*, p. 90.

Spirit to the extent that, even during public worship he or she would suddenly burst forth in an ecstasy of joy. Others, under awakening of conscience, would cry out with words like, 'O, what shall we do? Wash us from sin; let us not deceive ourselves, for we cannot deceive Thee'. In either case, stressed McMillan, these individuals were not puffed up, but bowed to the dust in humility, and genuinely afraid of self-deception. Andrew Bonar knew of 'a plain lad, whose heart was filled with joy in believing', who, being deeply aware of the average believer's many untapped riches in Christ, was heard praying at one meeting, 'Lord, pity the people in Kilmory who are content with tatties and sour milk, when they might have their soul satisfied with fatness'.[83]

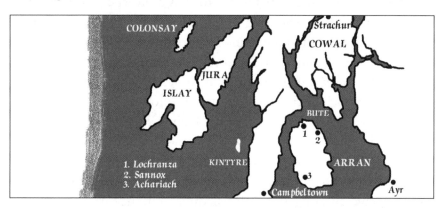

During the progress of the revival, which soon spread beyond Kilmorie,[84] no effort was needed to bring the people to the house of God. The recurrence of the Sabbath was longed for, and people wended their way from all parts of the island to wait upon the preaching of McBride, some having to set out before dawn in order to do so. For his preaching was distinguished by seriousness, fervour, and great zeal for the salvation of sinners. To travel ten or fifteen miles to a service was considered no big thing. When the sun rose, they hid their lanterns among the heather or left them at some convenient farm house and recovered them on their way home. After sermon, believers frequently

83. Campbell, *Arran: A History*, p. 124.

84. In the north the movement was invigorated by the preaching of Alexander MacKay of the Congregational Church at Sannox, thus ensuring that the fruit of the revival was shared by the Established Church and the Congregational Church (D. E. Meek, 'Dugald Sinclair. The Life and Work of a Highland Itinerant Missionary: Dugald Sinclair', in *Scottish Studies*, vol. 30, 1991, p. 74; *DSCHT*, p. 518).

congregated in one another's homes or in barns, to spend several more hours in religious exercises, and some even spent whole nights in this manner. The revival influenced the work-place too. Crofters in the harvest field, instead of jesting, would join in prayer and praise; while a lasting custom developed among fishermen to engage in family worship with regularity and reverence while at sea.

Angus McMillan in Lochranza

The movement came in the form of two principal three-month bursts, the first from January to March 1812, the second from December 1812 to February 1813. The latter phase came with the settlement of Angus McMillan at Lochranza. Highly regarded as a preacher, McMillan was also known 'to spend whole nights in a favourite and retired spot at the foot of one of the lofty mountains ... wrestling with God on behalf of sinners'.[85] This second period also saw the revival spread throughout much of the thirty-mile long parish of Kilmorie, which constituted the entire western half of the island, as well as into some parts of Kilbride, which formed the eastern side of Arran. Psalms alone were sung in public worship, the music known as 'Colehill' being almost the only tune used. Barns were frequently employed both for public and private prayer, and in every farm – a hamlet of eight to twelve families – there was a weekly evening prayer meeting, to which folk came from the surrounding areas. Effects of the revival extended beyond Arran; Bute and other western isles also shared in the blessing received.

The best known converts of the revival were brothers, Archibald and Finlay Cook from Achariach, just north of Kilmorie, both of whom became greatly revered and respected preachers throughout the Highlands. Finlay, in particular, had been one of the most thoughtless young men on the island. While in the act of jibing and mocking the Rev. McBride in his pew at church one Sabbath, the arrows of Divine truth smote him, and from that momentous hour he ceased to mock and began to pray, quickly growing in grace and understanding. Finlay used to say of his minister in Arran that he opened the people's mouths, and with his own hand put the Bread of God in.[86] While little has been recorded of the brothers' role in the revival on their native island, we are told they were regularly

---

85. Couper, *Scottish Revivals*, p. 91.

86. Rev. Norman C. Macfarlane, *Apostles of the North: Sketches of Some Highland Ministers*, Stornoway 1989, p. 54.

woken up at four o'clock on Sabbath mornings that they might make the long walk to listen to pure evangelical preaching (perhaps from Angus McMillan in Lochranza). Born in 1788 Archibald Cook later reminisced on the love converts had for each other; 'Christ's children wouldn't see a fault in one of their own without telling that person, but Oh! How they would remain loyal in your time of need!'[87] Finlay later served as minister in Cross, Lewis and in the Caithness parish of Reay; while Archibald took up charges in Latheron, Inverness and Daviot.

Demise and Effects of the Revival

The revival appears to have started to diminish before the death of McBride in July 1814. Its influence was further dampened thereafter, when his successor – a man who did not hesitate to deny the doctrine of regeneration – spoke vehemently against it.[88] There were about 250 professed conversions, but sadly, a good number of these showed a propensity to backslide. McMillan regretted that 'Like the stony-ground hearers, the religious impressions of many were slight and transitory … coldness, deadness, and formality in religion are now too prevalent among us'.[89] Nevertheless, for many years afterwards Communion seasons were notable in the parish and throughout the island as being times of great refreshing to God's people. Much blessing accompanied such occasions, not least when the Reverends Dr John Love of Glasgow, Kenneth Bain of Greenock, and other ministers came to preach and give wise counsel in Kilmorie during and following the time of the awakening.[90]

Not only so, but the effects of Arran's 'Great Revival' in scores of permanently changed lives continued for decades and led to several calls to the ministry. As well as the Cook brothers, these included John Macalister, later minister of Glenlyon, Nigg and Brodick (see page 215), Peter Davidson, who later became minister in Stoer before returning to

---

87. Campbell, *One of Heaven's Jewels*, p. 28.

88. This was Dugald Crawford, who was inducted to the parish against the wishes of nearly all parishioners, who, after his arrival, deserted the parish church in droves, setting up their own unofficial place of worship in '*The Preaching Cave*' near Kilpatrick, under the leadership of an ex-farmer called William MacKinnon. But in 1821 Crawford was drowned while crossing the Firth of Clyde and Angus McMillan was at last inducted as minister of Kilmory.

89. Campbell, *Arran: A History*, p. 124.

90. Various Contributors, *Disruption Worthies of the Highlands*, p. 159.

Arran to serve in Shiskine and afterwards Kilbride; and Archibald Nicol, the last surviving convert-turned-minister of the Arran movement. He served on Coll before also finishing his career on his native island. Then there was Alexander Cook, who became a lay preacher after his conversion around 1814. Cook became a highly respected catechist in Arran as well as co-superintendent of the Sunday school there. He was later given oversight of the Free Gaelic congregation in Saltcoats, where he died in 1865. Meanwhile, Peter McBride (later of Rothesay, see page 465), who resided chiefly with his uncle, Rev. Neil McBride, in Kilmorie in his early youth, seems to have received his first serious religious impressions about the time of the revival, at the age of fifteen or sixteen. Notably, all of the aforementioned men (including the Cook brothers) translated their loyalties to the Free Church at the time of the Disruption in 1843.

Ministry of Dugald Sinclair on Islay, Jura and Colonsay

Dugald Sinclair was born near Bellanoch, Argyllshire in 1777. Though brought up a Presbyterian, he became a Baptist in 1801 and spent three years at Horton Bible College in Bradford. After graduating, Sinclair was appointed missionary by 'English' Baptists, Christopher Anderson and George Barclay, who had recently formed a society to promote missions in the Highlands. His sphere of labour being Argyllshire and the Western Isles, Sinclair quickly proved himself a winsome evangelist, earning himself the title 'The Apostle of the West' by way of his frequent journeys through the Highlands and Islands at the end of the summer season and into the autumn.[91] In Islay, Sinclair preached from 'the face of a beautiful, green ascent at the west end' of Bowmore as well as in people's houses, in the autumn of 1812. 'The greater part of the inhabitants of the village, with many from the vicinity, attended on all the occasions', he wrote in his journal.[92] His audiences in June 1813 continued to be large and 'very attentive, and much affected … An awakening of some kind, and to some degree, appears prevalent all over the island, except in a few places', he added.[93]

Donald Meek states that in times past, 'when harvesters left their labour to attend a religious service, it was usually indicative of deep

---

91. Yullie, *History of the Baptists in Scotland*, p. 116.

92. Sinclair, *Journal of Itinerating Exertions*, vol. 3, 1812, p. 23.

93. ibid., 1813, p. 9.

spiritual interest of the kind associated with revivals or awakenings'.[94]
Dugald Sinclair records that when with a colleague in Jura in 1812, on

> reaching a field where the inhabitants of the farm were reaping
> close by the public road, we asked, 'Can you spare an hour for
> the gospel and your souls, though your harvest is necessary?'
> They frankly and without hesitation, said, 'Indeed we can, and
> are glad to have it in our power to do so'. They gathered into a
> corner of the field, close by the road, and patiently and attentively
> heard the word. The inhabitants of the farm which we had left
> behind, on seeing these waiting to hear the word, dropped their
> sickles all to a man, and with post-haste came to hear, except one
> individual, who made not his appearance among his neighbours.
> After brother Mck(ay), who preached, had done, we distributed
> a few tracts among them, and the people were dismissed with
> apparent satisfaction.

Sinclair met with a similar response in other parts of Jura at this time,
and, proposes Meek, 'this almost certainly indicates that a spiritual
awakening was in progress throughout the island'.[95]

On Colonsay, as in other islands that Dugald Sinclair visited on his
evangelistic sojourns, the people were quite astonished that a minister
should trouble himself to preach on a week day; it being entirely new to
them. The folk here were starved of regular ministerial provision as the
island was linked with Jura, where the parish minister resided, and his
visits to Colonsay were very infrequent. Sinclair found that the response
to his preaching here was more enthusiastic than in virtually any other
district he entered.

He first visited the island for a few days in August 1814, but after three
failed attempts to leave due to high winds, he deduced that the Lord must
have further need for him in Colonsay. The locals embraced his ministry
with 'joyful gratitude' and audiences gradually increased to 400 (out of a
total population of about 800), with a number of conversions occurring.
On his return to the island a year later, congregations were of a similar
size, and the islanders pleaded with him to come to them as frequently
as possible. One of his sermons, based on Acts 23:22, was on Baptism

---

94. Meek, *Dugald Sinclair*, p. 74.

95. ibid,, p. 75.

by immersion, a teaching utterly new to their minds. Such ordinance so impressed the people that it got passed down from generation to generation. As on his previous visit, storms again delayed Sinclair's departure, allowing spiritual interest to deepen noticeably, with all the signs of an awakening emerging in the community. The foundation of Colonsay Baptist Church was the direct outcome, and Sinclair returned to the island annually until his emigration to Canada in 1831.[96]

Shetland

Sinclair Thomson

Joining a whaling vessel at the age of seventeen, on which he made at least three voyages to Greenland, Shetlander Sinclair Thomson (1784–1864) later became a crofter, augmenting his meagre income by smuggling and selling gin. Twice he almost drowned, once he was tried for smuggling, and twice he narrowly escaped the press gang. Following a dramatic conversion to Christ in 1809 his subsequent lifestyle proved to be every bit as colourful as it had hitherto been.

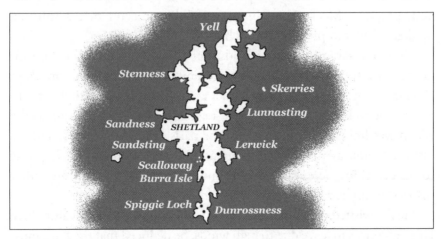

Indeed, for some years prior to his becoming the first Shetland Baptist by his immersion in Spiggie Loch in August 1815, Thomson had been winning many converts through his relentless efforts. As early

---

96. Sinclair, *Journal of Itinerating Exertions*, 1814, pp. 19-21; 1815, pp. 7-11; John McNeill, *The Baptist Church in Colonsay*, Edinburgh 1914. Sinclair laboured as a missionary in the Highlands and Islands for a decade, before serving with the Bible Society in England for a time, then relocating to Canada. He settled in Lobo, and the western part of that province became his mission field, and there his zeal and ability were long engaged. He died in 1870, aged 93.

as 1810 people were flocking from far and near to hear Thomson preach in an old especially renovated store near his Dunrossness home. On the Sabbath following the memorable day when that humble sanctuary was set apart for God and His worship, so great a number assembled in the absence of the parish minister that the service had to be adjourned to the open air. His biographer wrote:

> Mr Thomson, in preaching, felt all the inspiration of the occasion. At least five hundred persons were present, and as he held forth to them the precious truth, hearts were touched, consciences aroused, and the Word was proved to be 'in demonstration of the Spirit and with power'. It afterwards appeared that several were effectually awakened on that day, and induced to seek till they found a sure and saving hope in Christ. Like seasons were enjoyed on subsequent occasions, the regular, stated attendance at the chapel increasing, while there were not a few whose hearts the Lord touched.[97]

During the following half-century as pastor of the Baptist Chapel at Dunrossness, 'The Shetland Apostle', as Thomson became known, repeatedly travelled the length of the island on foot, on pony or by boat, preaching (6,000 sermons!), baptising converts and raising funds to build churches; all the while ministering to his own people as well as maintaining his family by working his croft and by fishing. He worked on his sermons as he travelled, usually on foot, though he rose early for prayer and study, and he said that for fully sixteen years, 'I do not remember being in bed, when at home and in health, after 3 o'clock in each morning'.[98]

Hundreds were awakened to eternal realities through his pioneering labours. He founded further churches at Sandsting on the west and Lunnasting on the east, as well as on Burra Isle, Scalloway and Lerwick. He even visited the lonely isles of the Skerries, ten miles east of the Shetland mainland (sixty miles from Dunrossness), where he not only founded a church, but began a day-school and became responsible for the teacher's salary. Thomson appointed ministers from among his own converts and established a preaching circuit in which he took his place

---

97. Rev. J. A. Smith, *Sinclair Thomson: The Shetland Apostle*, Lerwick 1969, p. 29.

98. ibid., p. 31.

with the humblest member.[99] His ministry was greatly blessed and he wrote that, 'Often have we had times of refreshing from the presence of the Lord'.[100] In 1837 Thomson could note, 'A spirit of grace has been poured out of late' upon the Dunrossness congregation – 'a little cloud'. During that year, he travelled 629 miles (exclusive of his home parish) and preached no fewer than 152 times (exclusive of Tuesday and Friday meetings) for exhortation, conversational meetings and Sabbath evening schools.[101]

John Nicolson and Samuel Dunn

Methodism also flourished in Shetland around this time,[102] following the return from the European continent in 1819 of John Nicolson from service in the Napoleonic wars, during which time he had come to a personal Christian faith. In 1822 Nicolson received help from Samuel Dunn, son of a Cornish sea captain and erstwhile smuggler, who preached extensively throughout the county for over three years. One day in July 1823, Dunn admitted twenty people to the Methodist 'Class' in Sandness. He reported, 'I think I have not seen a more glorious work since the great revival in Cornwall in the year 1814[103] than there is at present in this little parish, in which there are only about seventy families, and we have now no less than eighty persons who meet in class. Under almost every sermon some appeared to be awakened, old and young, moral and abandoned characters. I trust ere long that

---

99. Yullie, *The Baptists in Scotland*, p. 109; Smith, *Sinclair Thomson*, pp. 50-8.

100. Baptist Home Missionary Society (hereafter BHMS) Report 1862, p. 11.

101. ibid., 1837, p. 21. Further blessing was bestowed upon this locality in 1858–59.

102. A Moravian influence had long preceded Methodism in these northerly isles, and may well have paved the way for it. Two Moravian evangelists visited Lerwick at some point during the 18th century to try and locate descendants of a colony of Moravian Waldenses who, fleeing from their native land in search of liberty of conscience, had settled in the Shetland town. As it turned out, all traces of the colony had disappeared by the time of the evangelists' visit, though its memory still remained (E. R. Hasse, *The Moravians*, London 1912, p. 70).

103. Beginning in Redruth, this movement spread throughout Cornwall and in a period of only a few weeks an estimated 5,000 people were added to the Methodist churches. In just one week, 2,000 made profession of faith at Tuckingmill during a meeting that lasted from Sunday 27th February through to the following Friday, with people coming and going all the time. (Peter Isaac, *A History of Evangelical Christianity in Cornwall*, Gerrards Cross 2000, pp. 113-4; Edwards, *Revival: A People Saturated with God*, p. 179).

all will catch the flame …' [104] Dunn also records preaching to around 250 fishermen in Stenness, 'who all sat on the beach, in their fishing habiliments and paid the greatest attention. At eight I spoke in the same place to a still greater number. It was a most interesting sight. I was never more delighted. It forcibly reminded me of the Great Master, who spent so much of his time on the sea coast, preaching to the inhabitants of Zabulon and Naphtalim'. [105] By the time of Nicolson's death in 1828 there were four Methodist circuits in Shetland and 1,000 members.

Outer Hebrides

Introduction

The Isle of Lewis slowly began to emerge from deep spiritual darkness shortly after the start of the nineteenth century. Several factors contributed to this. Of prime importance were the Gaelic Schools, which were started in 1811. These quickly spread and there were eight by 1815 and fifteen by 1833; the sole textbook used being the Bible. The translation and circulation of the Gaelic Bible was a further major influence in spreading scriptural knowledge. [106] Said Robert Finlayson of Lochs, 'The Gaelic Bible found its way to Lewis as the cake of barley fell into the camp of Midian, which smote their tents and overturned the camp'. [107] The schools brought inestimable benefits to the Outer

---

104. H. R. Bowes (Ed.), *Samuel Dunn's Shetland and Orkney Journal 1822–1825*, Sheffield 1976, p. 43.

105. ibid., p. 47.

106. As evidence of the powerful spiritual influence of the Gaelic schools stands the testimony of Norman Macleod of Uig, Skye, who left the island to serve in the army, during which time he was blinded. 'At length I found myself in my native land', he recalled. 'Here I found things not as I left them. I found the Bible of God, of which I was totally ignorant, among my friends; and schools among them for teaching the knowledge of that blessed Book. I found such a work among them, with Bibles and schools as was altogether new to me. Nay, the very children would correct and reprove me, though an old man. In one of these schools the Bible caught my ear; it sunk into my heart; it there opened an eye that sin had ever kept sealed; it read to me my deeds; it led me to trace my former ways; yea, times, places, and deeds, that were quite banished from my memory were recalled into full view; it recorded a blank catalogue against me; and seemed to fix my portion among the damned. I thought my case altogether a hopeless one. But the same Bible brought to my ears tidings of unutterable worth – salvation through a Crucified Saviour' (*Highland News*, 28/03/1896, p. 2).

107. 'Gaelic School Society Report' 1834, quoted in Macleod, *The Progress of Evangelicalism*, p. 206. Another Lewis resident wrote that the effect produced by the

Hebrides, as to other parts of the Highlands and Islands, and played a great part in preparing the islanders for the blessings which were soon to shower on them from above. As literacy in the islands increased through the work of the Gaelic Schools, Gaelic translations of popular evangelical literature also began to circulate.[108]

Barvas

Revival began in a township in Barvas in 1822,[109] when a young girl who attended the Gaelic school read out the lessons she had been learning to her sick mother, whom the girl had stayed home from school that day to look after. The story she read was that of the crucifixion of Christ, which account had a deep impact on her mother, who started to weep. Thinking she had taken a turn for the worse, the girl ran to get help from a neighbour. Hearing by what means the sick woman had been agitated, the neighbour asked for the story to be read to her, too, upon which she was similarly affected. Woman after woman was called upon, and all displayed similar emotions on hearing the story. Soon the sick woman's husband returned home from a day's work in the peats, and, discovering the cause of the commotion, requested the story also be read to him. He, too, was touched in like manner, and so the work quickly spread from hamlet to hamlet within Barvas, and also to other districts, such as Gress and Callanish,[110] until 'a great number' had been converted.[111]

Gaelic Bible on those reading it for the first time in their own language was, 'in many instances a frantic consternation, similar to that felt by a person discovering himself on the brink of destruction. But the frantic fever soon subsided; and in that infallible mirror in which they discovered the disease, they also discovered the consolatory efficacy of the Divine Physician's prescription' (Lundie Duncan, *History of Revivals of Religion in the British Isles*, p. 356).

108. Murdo Macdonald, one of the leaders among the *'Men'* in Lewis' early evangelical days, was converted while listening to the translation of Thomas Boston's, *The Fourfold State* being read at a meeting in Stornoway. During Alexander Macleod's time in Uig, that same book was read to 'groups of weeping and wondering hearers' (Macleod, *The Progress of Evangelicalism*, p. 207).

109. K. M. Macleod suggests that from as early as 1820, 'there were signs of revival in various parts of the island' (K. M. Macleod, *A Brief Record of the Church in Uig (Lewis) Up To the Union of 1929*, Stornoway 1994, p. 6).

110. Appendix to *FCRSRM* 1874, pp. 10-11; John Macleod, *Banner in the West: A Spiritual History of Lewis and Harris*, Edinburgh 2008, p. 134.

111. Macaulay, *Aspects of the Religious History of Lewis Up to the Disruption of 1843*, Inverness nd, p. 153.

One Barvas convert was thought to have been Catriona Mackay, 'tall and handsome in her bearing ... with a face that radiated beauty'. Catriona became known for her simple trusting faith and her prophetic gifting.[112]

A result of these developments was that meetings for prayer and exhortation were begun in various places. A strong degree of fanaticism attended the movement, with the occurrence of spasms, screaming and trances (some lasting over twenty-four hours).[113] Some converts, while in such state of physical prostration, claimed to be favoured with visions of heaven and hell.[114] Others, also in a trance, could, with their eyes closed (and unable to read in any case), turn to and put their fingers on chapter and verse in the Bible, which they then proclaimed as the passage to be read aloud to enable them to recover from their trance. One noted visionary, Mary Macleod of Melbost, said she was guided to the correct scripture verse by a 'person' standing beside her who told her when to stop turning pages of the Scriptures, and when to stop moving her finger on the appropriate page. Yet it is noteworthy that this woman, and indeed perhaps even the majority of those who experienced trances and the like, showed no sign of saving change either at the time of the revival or in later life. In some cases, it is reported, the reverse was evident.

---

112. Annie Morrison, *Christian Women*, Lewis nd, pp. 5-9.

113. John Macleod even speaks of women swooning 'by the dozens, in excited gatherings' (*Banner in the West*, p. 135).

114. A woman from Barvas related, among many visions personally received and shared, one of her minister, the Rev. William Macrae on his white horse (which he was very fond of), and both falling headlong into hell. When Macrae heard the story he immediately rejected it, remarking that whatever was to come of himself he was quite certain his white mare would never end up in hell! (Rev. Calum I. Macleod (Ed.), *Pronnagan: Gospel Advent in Barvas Parish*, Barvas 2008, p. 31.)

On one occasion, a person at Bayhead, Stornoway was directed while in a trance to send for someone at Ness, over twenty miles away. Stranger still, the person sent for had been mysteriously summoned while in a trance to rise and go to Bayhead to relieve the person there who was in the same state. The woman in Bayhead could tell when her expected visitor left their home, and the different stages of the journey until his or her arrival. In the prescribed manner, the Bayhead resident was recalled from her extraordinary state.[115] Some men were also known to fall into trances, such as John Macleod of Shawbost, who never, even in later life, made any profession of faith, seeming to be a careless, easy-going man, who was said to have became slightly conceited in later years on account of his gifting as a 'medium'. Another example was John Macleod of Bragar, who was so highly regarded that he was called the Bragar Angel, and was often carried shoulder-high from one place to another – once as far as Bernera. However, when a ship's captain, dubious of his character, offered him some money on account of his prophetic abilities, which the 'Angel' at once accepted, his high repute promptly faded! Macaulay writes that 'this man, although quiet and decent, gave no evidence in after life that he was either a saint or an angel'.[116] As a result of all these types of phenomena, 1822 became known as 'Bliadhna an Fhaomaidh' – 'The year of the swoonings' – and it was said that for upwards of forty years thereafter events in some parts of the island were dated from this year of incredible happenings.

Itinerant Preachers

A few Gaelic teachers, such as John Macleod of Galson,[117] in their enthusiasm to win souls, broke the Society's rules by holding their own

---

115. John Macleod believes these bizarre phenomena can be explained by natural means. Most of those present were probably illiterate and so would have had no idea whether the Bible verses the visionary was 'supernaturally' led to were the ones spoken out. Further, amidst such excited and awed atmosphere, and long before the days of modern telecommunications, it would have been very difficult to confirm departure times and journey details. In such a setting exaggerated or fanciful stories could easily emerge (*Banner in the West*, p. 137).

116. Macaulay, *Aspects of the Religious History of Lewis*, p. 150.

117. Natives of Kilmaluag, Skye, Macleod and his wife were products of the Skye revival of 1814–16. MacAulay said MacLeod might be termed the 'Star of the Lewis Reformation' in that it was he who brought the gospel to the Ness and the Barvas areas, though this wasn't true of the east side of the island. Dismissed by the Gaelic School Society, Macleod continued his itinerant preaching on the island, as, similarly, did Neil Murray in Ness (ibid., pp. 143, 145).

services, often in the open-air. They, along with even less cautious 'satellites',[118] spread throughout the island, and drew considerable crowds as they roused sinners from their indifference, preaching 'hell-fire' sermons and issuing prophetic denouncements, often resulting in emotional frenzy among their hearers. Parish ministers such as Macrae of Barvas, Simson of Lochs and both Simon Fraser and his successor John Cameron of Stornoway, alarmed and outraged by the activities of these 'blind daring fanatics', wrote of the insanity, convulsive fits, mental derangement, suicide, domestic violence and despair which they claimed were outcomes of the religious mania. Macrae further claimed that 'idleness, theft and disorderly conduct' resulted from the revivals.[119]

Sometimes church services were disrupted by outcries from over-enthusiastic individuals. Such was the case in Back and also in Lochs, which 'experienced great upheaval and unrest. Vast enthusiasms through the revival had spread over the whole people ... the revival had taken a firm hold of the minds of the people, many being yet in the first fervour of conversion'. One Communion Sabbath in Lochs, five men (three young converts from Harris, and a resident from each of Back and Shawbost) stood up among the congregation and called the (Moderate) minister 'a murderer of souls'. This sudden and un-looked for interruption caused no small stir in the congregation. They proceeded from the calmness of a sacred feast to the most admired disorder. Most of the congregation sided with Simson. Violent hands were laid on the disturbers of the peace, who were nearly torn to pieces as a result. The men were shortly afterwards imprisoned in Dingwall for violating law and order.[120] Simson wrote a letter to Lady Seaforth's factor claiming: 'Already has one deluded woman done away with her own life, another breathed her last in a fit of despair, several are in a state of insanity, the peace of many a family is destroyed, the most dreadful doctrines are inculcated, and the most impious rites are performed.'[121] Meanwhile, in Ness an estate factor was concerned that the fishing in 1823 had

---

118. The term used by Rev. Macrae of Barvas to describe other itinerants such as Murdo MacDonald from Callanish, who 'thinks that he is a prophet that can tell anything' (ibid., pp. 145, 147).

119. ibid., pp. 144-5.

120. ibid., p. 91.

121. Macleod, *The Progress of Evangelicalism*, p. 215.

been neglected partly on account of the 'fanatic mania which has seized the people'.[122]

In addition to the fruit of John Macleod's labours, many of the first crop of evangelical witnesses in Lewis during this period were fruits of the preaching of Finlay Munro (see page 251), a colourful itinerant lay preacher who had an implicit trust in God to provide for his every need.[123] Munro travelled extensively through the island on at least two occasions; once before 1822[124] and again shortly after Alexander Macleod became the island's first evangelical minister in 1824. Observed Munro, '*Uibhist fhuar, na Hearadh nas fhearr, ach Leodhas mo ghraidh air an do dh'eirich a' ghrian*' ('Uist is cold, Harris better, but my beloved Lewis – on it the sun rose').[125] A grace which Munro offered when given hospitality at a house in Ness was said to have led to the conversion of Marion MacRitchie, later to be known *as 'Mor Bheag an t-Schisgeil*' ('Little Marion of the Gospel'). Two other well-known Lewis converts of Munro were the MacIvers of Rawnish, who each became gifted lay leaders on the island.[126] Donald Duff, a noted catechist in Inverness-shire, said that Finlay's work was more fruitful than any evangelist he had ever heard, his converts being deeply exercised and steadfast, godly Christians.[127]

Malcolm MacRitchie in Aline

Another evangelist winning converts in Lewis before Macleod's Uig settlement was Malcolm MacRitchie from Uig, who was converted in 1818 at the age of fourteen through reading the New Testament and two Puritan classics which were loaned to him. At that time there were known to be only two Bibles in the entire parish, but when John Macleod arrived in Lewis in 1820 MacRitchie was advised that the Gaelic School Society, whom Macleod served, sold Gaelic Bibles, so he walked the twenty miles to Stornoway to buy the book, only to have to walk home

---

122. Douglas Andsell, 'The 1843 Disruption of the Church of Scotland in the Isle of Lewis', in *RHSCS*, Edinburgh 1992, p. 188.

123. For inspiring testimonies of this, see Macaulay, *Aspects of the Religious History of Lewis*, pp. 130-41.

124. Tradition has it that Munro first came to Lewis by landing unexpectedly on the shores of Ness on a London lobster smack.

125. Macleod, *The Progress of Evangelicalism*, p. 284.

126. Norman C. Macfarlane, *The "Men" of the Lews*, Stornoway 1924, p. 97.

127. ibid., p. 52.

again without it, for he didn't have the necessary five shillings to procure it. Providentially obtaining the required money, Malcolm repeated his forty-mile journey and secured his Bible. Soon neighbours were crowding into the MacRitchie home, eager to hear Malcolm read the Scriptures to them. Such conduct greatly offended the local minister, who saw such spiritual enthusiasm as a sign of delusion!

Malcolm became teacher at Aline (Ath Linne), on the marsh between Lewis and Harris, in 1823, at the tender age of twenty. A work of grace ensued, and children, parents and grandparents would all crowd into the schoolhouse to hear him speak, both by day and by night. As a result there were many conversions. The ardent evangelist won many more Hebridean souls to the Lord in his itinerant travels across Lewis, Harris and Skye as teacher under the auspices of the Gaelic School Society and afterwards the SSPCK. Normally sent to places with no gospel ministry, he had to serve as both teacher and pastor to his people, and much blessing accompanied his work. MacRitchie later became a minister, being ordained by the Free Church in Knapdale at the relatively late age of fifty-one, and he went on to serve in Strathy (Sutherland) and in Knock on his native island from 1869. But despite a long and faithful ministry in these districts, he remarked in later years that he would have been very happy if he had seen as much fruit from his labours in his three respective charges as he had seen many years previously in that small township of Aline alone.[128]

Alexander Macleod in Uig

With the arrival of Alexander Macleod (1786–1869)[129] in Uig, the revival movement was no longer an unchecked phenomenon existing solely outside the Establishment. For soon after settling in his new charge a deep movement of spiritual awakening spread through the entire parish.

---

128. Macaulay, *Aspects of the Religious History of Lewis*, pp. 170-1; Macleod, *Banner In The West*, p. 144. Most inhabitants of Aline later emigrated to America, from where, in the 1850s they sent MacRitchie a numerously-signed call to become their pastor, thus testifying to the longstanding benefits they had derived from his labours among them.

129. A native of Stoer in Sutherland, Macleod, for a short time in his youth, came under the influence of the colourful and controversial Separatist, Norman Macleod, who, though unlicensed, preached to separatist congregations which he established at Assynt and Ullapool (where he was employed as schoolmaster). Amidst strong feeling and his salary being stopped, Macleod emigrated to Nova Scotia with several hundred followers. He later set up a base in Cape Breton, before sailing, with nine hundred

But unlike that which preceded his arrival on the island, the revival which developed under Macleod's guidance was applauded for its freedom from excesses.[130] Its beginnings were worked out amidst a mountain of difficulties, each of which Macleod turned to with determination and diligence. Illiteracy and superstition abounded in Uig at the time. Virtually no one – not even the church elders – understood elemental Christian truths and no one anywhere in the parish (including, up to that point, the manse) was known to conduct family worship. The Sabbath was universally desecrated, and people would sell whisky and tobacco outside church on both the Lord's Day and weekdays alike. Yet the custom was that as soon as anyone came of age they joined the church. Consequently, there were between 800 and 1,000 names on the Communicants Roll. Horrified, MacLeod took some drastic measures. He cancelled communion for three consecutive years, causing his name to be maligned throughout the island, not least among his ministerial colleagues. He commenced prayer meetings, set up teaching meetings, and inaugurated a pattern of systematic pastoral visitation.

These measures proved highly effective. For, remarkably, and despite further obstacles,[131] just fourteen months after his induction, people were flocking to Macleod's services from all over Lewis, and he could write: 'Many, young and old, seem to be under serious impressions. They now give close attention to what is spoken. Many young and old are in tears every Lord's Day, and several are so affected as not to be able to contain themselves or to retire'.[132] Such impressions deepened with time, and by December 1825 Macleod was offering heartfelt praise to the Lord 'for his goodness to my people since I came among them, especially of late! They now come to me from every corner, crying, "What shall we do to be saved?" It is manifest that many of them are the subjects of deep

---

'Normanites' to New Zealand, where the group settled in Waipu (Beaton, *Some Noted Ministers of the Northern Highlands*, pp. 129-31; *DSCHT*, pp. 531-2).

130. Macleod knew that a balance was required, and felt that there was a danger of underrating revivals on the one hand, and of exaggerating them on the other (Donald Sage, *Memorabilia Domestica*, Wick 1889 (reprinted 1975), p. 297).

131. These were mainly of a practical nature; e.g., Macleod had to lobby for a new church; the existing shack being unfit for use and the minister having to preach in the open-air from a preaching box erected behind the manse.

132. Alexander Macleod, *Diary and Sermons, With Brief Memoir by the Rev. D. Beaton, Wick*, Gizborne, N.Z. 1961, p. 11.

conviction and others enjoy some of the consolations of the gospel by faith. In April 1824 I could get none in the parish that I could call upon to pray at our prayer meeting; but now I have more than twelve that I can call upon, with liberty and pleasure, to that duty in public'.[133] He added further, ' ... there is plainly a revival exhibiting itself under the preaching of the gospel, and a marked and almost incredible change in the morals of the people'.[134]

Macleod was a man of commanding presence and a beautiful silvery voice, which, it was said, could be heard a mile away.[135] Remarkably, although he wasn't known as a talented preacher, conversions were again and again traced to what friends called very weak sermons.[136] Although he often spoke on the love of God, according to Evander MacIver, a former army Sergeant and subsequently receiver of wrecks in Uig, his preaching to his Uig congregation often contained 'violent denunciations as to their future' and 'wild descriptions of hell and its punishments'. Even when he preached on Christmas Day 1825 on the words '*Fear not*' in Matthew 28:5, MacIver said that Macleod pronounced that these seemingly encouraging words were 'turned vice versa to all unbelievers, and that their fears and terrors, terrors unspeakable, would never terminate through the rounds of eternal ages'. It was precisely this type of preaching that hit its target, however, for, claimed the minister, it seemed as if 'every heart was pierced, and general distress spread through the whole congregation'.[137] Such depth of conviction during the awakening produced the occasional highly unexpected beneficial outcome. One commentator noted that 'the number of sheep annually lost has wonderfully diminished since the commencement of the revival'![138]

The movement gradually spread throughout much of Lewis, although Uig remained its centre. Macleod held his first communion in June 1827. No more than twenty communicants came forward (many recent converts holding back). MacLeod records that,

---

133. ibid., p. 12.

134. Couper, *Scottish Revivals*, p. 116.

135. *The Stornoway Gazette*, 15/01/1972, p. 5.

136. Macfarlane, *Apostles of the North*, p. 85.

137. Macleod, *Diary and Sermons*, pp. 12, 15.

138. Steve Taylor, *The Skye Revivals*, p. 111.

When the elements were presented there appeared as a shower of revival from the presence of the Lord through the whole congregation, and in serving the ... tables, the heavenly dew of gracious influences was evidently falling down on the people in so conspicuous a manner that, not only the friends of Christ, but also the enemies of the Lord cannot forget an occasion and a scene so singularly remarkable, in which all acknowledge that God was of a truth among us. But all this might be called the commencement of what happened afterwards, for when our young converts saw the uncommon liberty that was granted to the pastors in addressing those who sat at the table, they were still more impressed and filled, as it were, with new wine and holy solemnity. Much disappointment now appeared among several of them that they had not taken out tokens, and so were not prepared to come forward. Pungent conviction, towards the evening, took hold of some of them for not obeying Christ's command. It was a night ever to be remembered in this place, in which the whole of it was spent in religious exercises, whether in private or together with others in cases mingled with unusual instances of joy and sorrow. While these things were carried on, the ungodly themselves were in tears, and iniquity for a time dwindled into nothing, covered her brazen face and was greatly ashamed.[139]

John Macdonald of Ferintosh – en route to St Kilda – had tramped with his son over the hills from Harris to Uig to participate in this communion. On the second day of the event, 'The Apostle' rose and 'preached with the Holy Ghost sent down from heaven. The great congregation was smitten as by a mighty wind and the people were laid prostrate on the earth. There were loud outcries. The precentors ... sang, but the congregation was overcome with silence. Dr Macdonald stood behind them singing, and it is said that in the congregation of many thousands these were the only voices to be heard'.[140] A minister-acting, officiating at that occasion, said that 'when he removed the Communion cloths from the tables, they were as wet with the tears of the communicants as though they had been dipped in water'.[141]

---

139. MacAulay, *Aspects of the Religious History of Lewis*, pp. 177-8.

140. Kennedy, *Days of the Fathers in Ross-shire*, pp. 281-2.

141. *The Oban Times*, 24/09/1898, p. 3.

The revival continued to intensify and seemed to be at its strongest between 1828 and 1830. It has become legendary in Lewis church lore that an estimated nine thousand people from all over the island assembled for Communion at Uig in 1828,[142] a staggering number given the remoteness of the location, and more so given the population of Lewis at the time (around 12,000, that of Harris being no more than 3,500).[143] It was surely of such occasions that 'widow Mackenzie' later spoke of when 'she frequently told of seeing days in Uig in which the hillsides and moors were literally covered with people pleading for mercy on their own souls and the souls of their neighbours. She has told that it was no uncommon thing to have to travel miles of the moor before one could find an unoccupied nook in which to bend the knee, so as neither to be disturbed by nor to disturb others similarly employed'.[144]

In 1830 a deputation from the SSPCK visited Lewis and noted that the people were 'so much alive … to the necessity of religion and personal piety that a person who does not long possess personal piety and great devotion of character, will not be esteemed as a Teacher in the island'.[145] In 1833 Macleod was able to claim that attendance on the public ordinances was probably as punctual and full as in any parish in Scotland.[146] A year later he rejoiced that, 'Ten winters have I passed here, all wonderfully short, pleasant, and delightful'.[147]

---

142. John Macleod believes the year to have been 1833 (*Banner in the West*, p. 148).

143. When it was suggested that 9,000 might be an overestimate, Rev. William Macleod, then Church of Scotland minister in Uig, replied that he had never in his life heard the number doubted, and he had no difficulty accepting it as being true (personal communication, 21/09/2001). It is certainly an oft-quoted figure, and at least one contemporary Lewis historian seems happy accepting it as factual (Macleod, *Banner in the West*, p. 148). Estimating the size of a crowd is always a matter of personal judgement, however, and is often highly debatable. For example, a local newspaper claimed the number attending the June 1845 Free Church communion at Ferintosh, Ross-shire was 3,000; while another correspondent set the figure almost five times higher, at 14,000 (Campbell, *One of Heaven's Jewels*, p. 201).

144. Ms Mackenzie recounted this information in person to Rev. P. Macdonald, Stornoway, who later put it in writing (being published in *The Highland News*, 28/03/1896, p. 2).

145. Macleod, *The Progress of Evangelicalism*, p. 221.

146. 'New Statistical Account' 1833, quoted in ibid., p. 218.

147. MacMillan, *Restoration in the Church*, pp. 101-2.

Such season of spiritual revival and reformation, having taken deep and enduring root upon the island, spread into districts previously untouched or little affected throughout the following decade (see page 283 for accounts of movements in Knock, Back, Bernera and Lochs in the 1830s). Meanwhile, a fresh wave of awakening arose in Uig parish as late as November 1835, melting many new hearts, and with 'silent tears, in general, pervading the whole congregation'.[148]

Angus MacIver, who was converted during the Uig revival, and witnessed its longstanding effects, said of the movement that it was 'one of the most genuine and remarkable that was ever in Scotland'. He said that he

> saw much of the blessed fruit (that the revival) bore in after years, and they were undoubtedly fat and full of sap and aye flourishing. I have seen many Christians in my day in home and foreign lands, but I have never seen – taking them all over – finer or more intelligent Christians than the first generation of Christians in the parish of Uig. All the beautiful graces of the spirit were visited upon them. They were wonderfully free from excesses of any kind and grew up symmetrical and beautiful as the cedars of Lebanon, and spread out as the palm trees.[149]

Similarly, Professor George Smeaton said the Uig movement was the purest revival that he knew of in the history of the Church in Scotland, unless the awakening in Arran surpassed it in freedom from wildfire and fanaticism.[150]

John Morrison in Harris

Harris was also deeply influenced by revival at this time, especially via the ministrations of the remarkable John Morrison (1790–1852), a local blacksmith and poet, converted in 1822 through the preaching of John Macdonald. At once Morrison began to share the good news with those with whom he came into contact. Renowned for his intellectual powers,[151] some now looked on Morrison with pity; others hoped

---

148. ibid.; *DSCHT*, p. 530.

149. *The Stornoway Gazette*, 15/01/1972, p. 5.

150. Macaulay, *Aspects of the Religious History of Lewis*, p. 179. John MacLeod calls it 'the biggest parochial revival the Long Island has ever seen' (*Banner in the West*, p. 141).

151. With unusual skill in engineering matters, Morrison was said to have been familiar with the principles and construction of the steam engine before he had ever seen

time would cure him! Undaunted, Morrison began to read publicly the Scriptures in his house in Rodel; some came to scoff; others to debate with him on spiritual matters. Morrison answered with great wisdom and prudence and in this way critics were silenced, and esteem for the blacksmith grew. Morrison waxed bolder and ventured to neighbouring villages, where he again shared the gospel with clarity and power. Thus, convictions quietly gained ground.

By this time, the meetings in Morrison's house were crowded at time of evening worship. At one meeting the blacksmith was assisted by Murdoch Macleod, a catechist from an area which was experiencing revival – presumably Uig. At the start of the meeting, Morrison was 'so overwhelmingly melted' that he could not address the gathering. Many others present were, during the reading of the Scriptures, likewise silently melted and overcome. Thus Macleod was constrained to exhort the people, during which time some cried out in distress. Morrison, partly recovered, also spoke, so that impressions were heightened and rendered more general, and there was 'a mighty shaking among the dry bones'. This service was seen by some as marking the beginning of the general religious movement that spread through Harris.[152] Soon Morrison could write: 'Appearances throughout the island furnish very cheering evidences that there is plainly a revival, exhibiting itself under the preaching of the gospel in religious impressions, in a general thirst after instruction, and in a marked and almost incredible change in the morals of the people.'[153]

Meetings were held in Morrison's home in Rodel on weekday nights and thrice on Sabbath, and the people were extremely eager to attend. The first Sunday service commenced at seven in the morning, continuing till ten; the next from eleven o'clock till five in the afternoon, and the last from six in the evening till between nine and ten o'clock at night. From Rodel, awakening spread as Morrison exhorted and catechised throughout the rugged parish. At the close of meetings those awakened,

---

one! He also made artistic spinning wheels of a unique design and locks on the Chubb principle which no one was able to open. He was even known to possess an incisive understanding of veterinary surgery (Taylor, *The Skye Revivals*, CD-ROM, Chapter 14, *Iain Gobha*).

152. Roderick MacCowan, *The Men of Skye*, Glasgow 1902, pp. 42-3; 'Free Church Home and Missionary Record', May 1847, quoted in Macleod, *The Progress of Evangelicalism*, p. 196.

153. Sage, *Memorabilia Domestica*, p. 297.

... with every appearance of a desire to conceal themselves, would each quietly escape to the rocks or caverns in the shore, there to pour out their souls before the God of mercy. Even a stranger could now see the seriousness depicted on almost every countenance ... The vain voice now gave place to the songs of Zion; jollity and merry-making to mourning for sin, prayer and serious conversation; backbiting and abuse to the provoking to love and good works, and to mutual injuries frankly confessed. The Bible, covered with dust, lying in some bye corner, was now brought forth from its seclusion, and its leaves opened and perused with trembling hands and profound reverence. On the Sabbath morning, which used to be passed in lounging on the bed, might now be seen one going to this retired corner, another to that retired corner among the rocks, and another returning from the creeks of the shore – all thoughtful, serious, or going heavily. Even the children laid aside their youthful amusements, and might now be seen here and there, in furrows of the field, on their little knees, lisping their supplications to the Father of mercies.[154]

As those awakened began to grow in knowledge and experience, prayer meetings were arranged wherein three or four Gaelic teachers in the island assisted Morrison. His first open-air prayer meeting in Tarbert around 1830 attracted over two thousand people.[155] Family worship was set up in each home, 'and all, old and young, that could lisp were given to frequent private devotion'.[156] Morrison, himself a bard, was impressed with hymns written by Dugald Buchanan. He gave a copy of Buchanan's spiritual songs to Norman Paterson of Berneray and this resulted in the latter's conversion (Paterson became one of the 'Men' of mainland Harris when he went to live there). Morrison's friend, Alexander Macleod of Uig, said of the Harris blacksmith that he 'had as much realised the meaning of the Good News as all the ministers he knew put together'.[157] John MacIver, not remembered in tradition as an evangelical, made reference to the

---

154. MacCowan, *The Men of Skye*, p. 43.

155. MacAulay, *Aspects of the Religious History of Lewis*, pp. 164-8.

156. MacCowan, *The Men of Skye*, p. 42.

157. Taylor, *The Skye Revivals*, CD ROM, Chapter 14, *Iain Gobha*.

'powerful revival' in Harris in the *New Statistical Account*, stating that 'in consequence, the Sabbath is strictly observed'.[158]

Finlay Munro in North Uist

Evangelist Finlay Munro – a man known to have had 'extraordinary powers of insight'[159] – met with great success in North Uist in the 1820s.[160] Crowds of people gathered from time to time to hear him (e.g. on a hillock in the Tigharry area still known as '*Cnoc Fhionnlaigh*' – 'Finlay's hillock'[161]), and 'the Holy Spirit accompanied the Word preached with saving efficacy'. According to Ewan MacRury, 'A religious revival followed which completely altered the outlook of many people who hitherto had been indifferent to the Gospel, and as in Antioch of old, "the grace of God was seen".' The school-masters in the employment of the Gaelic Societies contributed largely to the progress of the revival by conducting meetings on the Lord's Day, and prayer meetings during the week.[162] North Uist now assumed quite a different aspect from that which it bore so long under a 'dead ministry'. As the result of Munro's labours many excellent Christians were raised up in the parish. The people in general came to see that there was more in religion than they had long been accustomed to learn from the pulpit. They therefore, with few exceptions, turned their back on the parish church (though not on the Church of Scotland),[163] and followed the means of grace at the meetings conducted by godly local men (such as John Macdonald and John Maclean, both of whom were, after the Disruption, catechists in connection with the Free Church).[164]

---

158. Macleod, *The Progress of Evangelicalism*, p. 219.

159. Macfarlane, *Men of the Lews*, p. 51; Macleod, *The Progress of Evangelicalism*, p. 216.

160. This despite the fact that Munro was also said to have called Uist 'cold' in contrast to Harris and, especially Lewis (see page 242).

161. John Ferguson, *When God Came Down: An Account of the North Uist Revival 1957–58*, Inverness 2000, p. 31.

162. Ewan MacRury, *A Hebridean Parish*, Inverness 1950, pp. 32-3.

163. This in essence constituted a local disruption long before the general Disruption event of 1843. Wrote MacRury: 'While these Separatists were advocating purity in doctrine and practice, they did not exhibit a censorious spirit, but the tendency of their dealings was to discourage a public profession of religion, while trying to shun the evils of what was termed Moderatism' (ibid., p. 33).

164. Rev. D. Macfarlane, *Memoir and Remains of Rev. D. Macdonald, Shieldaig*, Glasgow 1903, pp. 3-5.

APPENDIX (TO CHAPTER 4)

Opposition to the Breadalbane Revivals 1802–4, 1816–18

Even some who supported the Breadalbane revivals of the early nineteenth century, and who took an active part in their progress, expressed surprise at and dissatisfaction with several of the irregular and somewhat bizarre practices that became popular among small groups of believers from an early stage in its progress (see page 214). Robert Findlater observed that the energetic Independent missionaries who were responsible for encouraging these practices were 'zealous active, and ... some of them useful also; but their instilling into their tender minds their own peculiarities, when they stood in need of the Gospel being declared to them, was certainly unseasonable'. Further, he said, they 'both publicly and privately endeavoured to unhinge the minds of his inquiring flock'.[165] Additionally, Findlater's biographer, among others, expressed dismay at the fierce and unchristian sectarian rivalry that resulted when, he said, the Established Church and virtually all its ministers and remaining members became rejected, stigmatised and ridiculed, and believers en masse exchanged the Presbyterian beliefs which they had at first so heartily imbued for the more exciting teachings of numerous itinerant missionaries that made their presence felt in the region.

Writing as an old man, Duncan Campbell, a native of Breadalbane, said he had observed that many revival converts from the district in the first two decades of the nineteenth century remained within the Established Church, but that they quickly took on a spirit of gross insensitivity towards older believers who didn't quite share the focused zeal they had. These converts, Campbell stated, 'introduced a hotter and more intolerant spirit' than even the best evangelical minister could approve of.

> Hypocrites who made loud professions imposed upon them until they were found out. They looked upon men with life-long, blameless records, including elders of the old stamp, as being devoid of the unction of grace, and little better than heathens. Hysterical revivalist spouters called the old people who had only a good record of morality and humble practical faith, 'Gray Egyptians'

---

165. Findlater, *Memoir of Rev. Robert Findlater*, p. 222.

and later on 'Black Moderates' … They (the more experienced believers) gave the revivalists credit for good intentions, but said they were doing evil unconsciously in denouncing innocent enjoyments such as dancing and singing of songs, practised by the preceding generations. They unfavourably compared the morality of the revival period with that of the last 25 years of Mr Macara's spiritual superintendence during which they said there had been only two illegal children born in Glenlyon. They regretted that there were no resident landlords in the Glen to modify, by their influence, the new religious tyranny which, with all the good it was doing, or intended to do, was being pushed to a height of intolerance which would only end in evil.[166]

Discontent was also expressed by another native of Breadalbane, Major-General Stewart of Garth, Glenlyon, but for very different reasons. Stewart was probably making particular reference to his native Perthshire district when, in his history of the Highlanders, he vented his anger by saying that the people's

character and habits have undergone a considerable alteration since they began to be visited by itinerant missionaries and since the gloom spread over their minds has tended to depress their spirit. The missionaries, indeed, after having ventured within the barrier of the Grampians, found a harvest which they little expected and, amongst the ignorant and unhappy, made numerous proselytes to their opinions. These converts, losing by their recent civilisation – as the changes which have taken place in their opinions are called – a great portion of their belief in fairies, ghosts and second-sight, though retaining their appetite for strong impressions, have readily supplied the void with the visions and inspirations of the 'new light', and in this mystic lore have shown themselves such adepts as even to astonish their new instructors … Thus have been extirpated the innocent, attractive, and often sublime superstitions of the Highlanders.[167]

---

166. Duncan Campbell, *Reminiscences and Reflections of an Octogenarian Highlander*, Inverness 1910, p. 78.

167. Couper, *Scottish Revivals*, p. 109.

The most bitter and sustained attack on the revivalist spirit inculcated by Independent preachers in the early years of the nineteenth century, however, came from a Highland clergyman. The Rev. Alexander Irvine, latterly Church of Scotland minister in Little Dunkeld, had, around the turn of the nineteenth century, served as a missionary in Breadalbane, being based in Fortingall. In 1819 he published a 73-page document, sharing his strong views on the 'Independent invasion' of the Highlands and the considerable harm it had done. Owing to the mass of interesting (albeit strongly prejudiced) detail contained in this little-known report, and its bearing on the rise of the Independent movement in the Highlands, and in particular on more extreme aspects of the revival that spread through the Breadalbane region in 1802–04 and again from 1816–18, some of Irvine's concerns are here considered.

Irvine was well aware that the state of religion in the vast Highland region was very inadequate. Many parishioners never saw a minister's face, and until missions were established some never had the opportunity of hearing a sermon by a Protestant minister more than twice in their entire lives. For decades, groups like the SSPCK and the Royal Bounty had done much good and in particular rapid progress had been made since around 1780. But there were still whole swathes of the Highland population who never were confronted with the challenges or the blessings of the gospel of Jesus Christ.

It was for this sad reason, Irvine lamented, that missionaries from Independent groups such as Congregationalists and Baptists (Irvine called them 'Freemen', a term he claimed they also used of themselves) began to spring up throughout the land.[168] Irvine based his observations on what he had witnessed personally as well as on 'a most impartial and careful investigation' carried out by others some years previously.[169] But he insisted the situation was the same throughout the country.

The first independent missionary to the district of the Highlands where Irvine served was, he said, incapable of teaching almost anything but error (and was, it seemed, chosen only because he could speak

168. Included among those he denounced were a number within his own Church of Scotland denomination, whom he saw as restless ministers who left their charge for several weeks on end, roaming the country as itinerant evangelists.

169. Rev. Alexander Irvine, *Substance of a Speech, Delivered Before the Commission of the General Assembly of the Church of Scotland … on the State of Religion and the Necessity of Erecting New Parishes in the Highlands and Islands of Scotland*, Edinburgh 1819, p. 31.

Gaelic). His fellow missionaries, with a few exceptions, were men of similar character, 'full of intolerant zeal, without a particle of scriptural knowledge, talking of divine graces, without knowing anything about it'. These 'ignorant though zealous men', who couldn't even read or write, spoke 'as if they were among the Tartars'. With these 'messengers of damnation' Irvine often sought to converse, but never found a single one of them possessed of gospel knowledge. 'They could, by the mere exercise of memory, quote passages of Scripture, which they did not understand, and which they almost uniformly misapplied'.[170] Irvine wrote of their

> nightly meetings, their groanings, and howlings, and roarings, and fightings with the Devil, and triumphs over him, when their missionaries were in reality sapping the foundation of all true religion, and substituting in the room of it, a gloomy, senseless, murderous superstition, almost the grossest that ever graced human nature. Whole families and neighbourhoods became scenes of confusion, recrimination, and discord. You would meet on the road men, women, and even children, running about perfectly frantic, and all this for the good of their souls, roaring and howling in the most wretched state which human imagination can conceive.

Irvine said he often conversed with them, and pitied them.[171]

The disgruntled minister claimed that the 'votaries of these ignorant and fanatical teachers', as they gathered in numbers, at once proclaimed war against every other denomination of Christians. 'Some of them, indeed this moment, seldom if ever attend religious worship in any form', Irvine remarked. 'Some of them fell from their high pretensions, and were expelled from the congregation ... Here is the quintessence of popery. Auricular confession, absolution, purity, or no salvation beyond the pale of the Missionary Church. Every missionary became a Pope or priest, and could exalt to heaven, or sink to hell, just as he pleased, or rather as he was paid or obeyed. The whole fabric is Popish', he insisted.[172] Irvine referred to 'the presumptuous and intolerant spirit' of the Independents. Like the papists, too, no difference of opinion could be allowed for a moment.

---

170. ibid., p. 17.

171. ibid.

172. ibid., p. 19.

Irvine said he corresponded with those in power and out of power, with colleagues in the ministry – indeed, with everyone he could think of, to urge the necessity of immediate action. But his voice had been 'but the faint sound of the bending heath'. He claimed that such scenes as he drew notice to occurred on a daily basis even in Edinburgh, and every other city in Scotland, yet he aroused little attention. 'The city was besieged, and the defenders were asleep ... They fortified themselves behind the Forth, and left the battle to their videttes'.[173]

Irvine's longstanding desire, nay longing, was to get more Church of Scotland ministers established within smaller, more manageable parishes throughout the Highlands. This, he felt, would eradicate the need for these free-range preachers to continue their malevolent roaming around the country, preying on the naivety of locals. Many Highlanders, though not able to read or write, Irvine was sure were well informed, indeed better acquainted with the contents of the Bible than many of those who could do both. They had a remarkably retentive memory, and despite their illiteracy, could give an account of a sermon almost verbatim; could repeat many of the psalms and their own sacred songs, as well as many passages of the Bible, with wonderful propriety and accuracy. Irvine considered a great many, if not most, of the Highland population to be decent, quiet-living, albeit unlearned and simple Christians.

One consequence of the itinerant preachers' unbalanced teaching, Irvine observed with horror, was that some of their devoted followers, who hung on their every word, began to view the affairs of this world as being 'unworthy of notice', and they 'expected that miracles would be wrought to provide for their indolence. Why, they said, care for the body? Mortify the flesh. God provideth for the ravens and the young lions, He will provide for us'. Irvine did not go as far as saying that the teachers, ignorant as they were, directly encouraged such absurdities. 'But their harangues, unstudied, incoherent, unguarded, and often fantastic, led to consequences which their education or ignorance could not enable them to contemplate'.[174]

What concerned Irvine deeply was that the sole desire of these teachers was to gather recruits, 'to make proselytes by means of terror. Their frantic gestures, their bold assertions, their dreadful howlings or

173. ibid., p. 20.
174. ibid., pp. 24-5.

bawlings, astonished the hearers, frightened hysterical women, and, from a momentary conviction of change, soothed the fears of the hypocrite and ungodly, that they were now regenerated. Many of the converts became emaciated and unsocial. The duties of life were abandoned. Sullen, morose, and discontented, some of them began to talk of their high privileges, and their right, as the elect few, to possess the earth'.[175]

It was certainly lamentable in Irvine's eyes to see poor children starving and roaring for bread, when their parents were perhaps twenty miles away attending a conventicle. The business of the farm was neglected. The rent fell behind. The landlord was pronounced unchristian because he insisted on his dues, and because, upon their refusing to pay them, he declined having such tenants.

To add to the mischief, Irvine observed, families became scenes of discord and disorder, which only an eyewitness could comprehend. The children were taught to disobey unbelieving parents, as were servants their masters. 'In short all mutual obligations were made to depend upon this conversion. No faith was to be kept with heretics; another beautiful trait of popery'.[176] Such insistence on the necessity of forsaking the world and breaking off every former connection led to 'the most monstrous cruelties' being committed. The children would not even dress the parents' victuals, or hold any converse with them, for fear of contagion. One man in Rannoch took it in his head not to speak to any of his neighbours, even when they asked him how he was doing, as if to say, 'I cannot look at a man perishing in his sins'. On one occasion this resulted in the offended party dealing a blow to the offender's head, and telling him in no uncertain terms that he was not his judge! [177]

The people also quickly developed, according to the Dunkeld minister, a contempt for reason and education. They even boasted of their want of human learning, maintaining that study and preparation were altogether unnecessary; as they knew they would be told at the proper time what to say. Their gifts, they proudly claimed, were in the heart and thus were inspired; and in order to bring out these gifts they would beat their breasts and foreheads, till at length they elicited a torrent of confusion and nonsense.

---

175. ibid.
176. ibid., p. 26.
177. ibid., p. 47.

Additionally, Irvine said he often met men, 'chiefly young men, running about like bedlamites, unable to attend to any work, but roaring hideously, and denouncing woe against themselves and the human race'. To Irvine's relief, this tempest soon subsided, but he said he never found the moral atmosphere to be purified by it. Instances of females especially, from 'terror, sympathy, watching, long fasting, and other causes' being thrown into convulsions or hysterical fits, Irvine claimed, were not uncommon and were often regarded as expected accompaniments of true conversion. He recalled one instance when he managed to seize the knife in the hands of an aged woman who was about to cut her own throat in a fit of despair.[178]

The effects of such false religion Irvine observed in the majority of cases as being utterly dismal. Family affairs were neglected. Poverty and wretchedness followed. The rhetoric emanating from the preachers had the perhaps undesired yet desperate effect of 'interrupting the occupations from which they derive subsistence, and reducing many of them to beggary, and driving them to discontent'.[179] 'I have known', said Irvine, 'women leave their sucking infants whole days and nights, and follow these teachers; and they were defended for so doing upon scripture authority; poor afflicted widows, especially, became a prey to the rapacity and machinations of these men'.[180]

Love of money Irvine saw as another ruinous intent of these false shepherds. 'They actually reduced to beggary many families, by entertainments, and by taking money as gifts of love, to which they were moved by the spirit ... However much these teachers condemned the world and the flesh, they took good care of both ... Indeed', continued Irvine, 'their private and public teaching was uniformly at variance, which was the first thing that awakened my attention'.[181]

Believers often met together at night for fellowship and instruction, in woods, hollows and retired places. The missionary would select one or more young females, and retire with them one by one to hold a secret conference. Irvine told of one teacher, formerly a piper, who came from the north – 'a stout good looking young man, of ready utterance, great

---

178. ibid., pp. 49-50.

179. ibid., p. 24.

180. ibid., pp. 51-2.

181. ibid., p. 52.

boldness and greater ignorance. Many of the young and handsomest women flocked to his nightly meetings. I often saw him on an evening attended by seven at a time. The number seven was held sacred. I saw clearly that the man would do mischief. Every one of the seven strove for his favours, that is, for the look of love. A young girl, remarkably handsome, after some unfavourable surmises, married him, and then he left the country'. Irvine, however, insisted he was not accusing the piper of gross immoralities, only that he did not abstain from every appearance of evil.[182]

During the early days of their operations, the first thing the 'freemen' found it necessary to subdue was the devil. One young boy would pray himself into a frenzy, then fall into a trance and see visions and share them publicly, to the no small terror of the neighbourhood. Battling with the devil, he and his mother 'danced him down, and trampled on the ground to keep him down'. The neighbours often assembled to see the scene. Some believed and some not. The victory, however, was soon after disputed, and Satan remained master of the field.[183]

One fine Saturday evening in July 1804, a large group of revival enthusiasts assembled on a shelf under a covering rock in Glenlyon to worship God and communicate their experiences. Irvine was out walking in the district with a friend when they heard a shriek as if from a thousand throats. 'The rocks re-echoed. We thought somebody had fallen over the precipice', exclaimed Irvine. 'We shuddered. It was as if a house were falling on its tenants' heads ... We saw men, women, and children running and roaring for life, tumbling heels over head, to the great risk of their necks'. Asked the cause, an old man said he had just been attacked by the devil, whom he had seen in shape of a huge black bull with white horns. It transpired that two bulls of like description were kept in fields nearby. From behind the rock, one would often challenge the other to fight. It was apparent that 'the height of the rock, the dimness of the light and the instantaneous alarm magnified his size into that of the turf stack'. When the reality of events were told to the old man, he, being unconvinced, replied, 'The bull is better than a dozen of preachings'. The people later said that the cause of their dispersion was a sudden impulse of heavenly power, by which some

---

182. ibid., p. 54.
183. ibid., pp. 54-5.

of them expected, owing to the strength of their faith, to be wrapped in the whirlwind, though there was no wind at all, and carried into heaven.[184]

Irvine claimed that the most preposterous expectations were formed from the Independents' ideas of the efficacy of faith. They supposed that it would do everything, that it would remove mountains, and hurl them into Loch Tay, and if strong enough, carry them to heaven without tasting death, any time they chose. He quickly discovered that there was no point in seeking to reason with these people – they simply informed him that he had no light in him. 'They expected a miraculous supply of food in the wilderness, and I knew of several instances of long fasting in this expectation ... They declared that Benlawers and Craigmore bowed their heads and became plains, and that like Peter they could walk on the sea of Tiberias, meaning Loch Tay'. By 'they' he meant some extraordinary characters, 'considered as saints of the first class, perfect in everything'.[185]

After hearing a sermon on faith one Sabbath, one decent, worthy man went home, took dinner with wife and children, attired himself in his best tartans, blessed his family, and with great composure, told them he was leaving them for heaven. He was sure that his faith, greatly strengthened by the sermon he had heard, was strong enough to get him there. He mounted the top of his hut, spread forth his hands, and with the sun having burst through a cloud which rested on top of Benlawers, he cried, 'The hour is come, the clouds are opening, and I shall soon see you no more, till we meet in our father's house'. Wife and kids in tears, some neighbours gathered, perplexed at seeing John on top of his house for such a long time! After many hours, the poor man was obliged to desist, and return to his earthly surroundings, with many tears and groans of disappointment.[186]

The doctrine that the new converts were free from sin Irvine believed led to most deplorable consequences. 'They exulted with joy in the possession of immaculate purity, and exemption from all sin, and all liability to, or possibility of sinning. Every passion, every propensity might be flattered or indulged. Every action was indifferent'. A certain

---

184. ibid., p. 56.

185. ibid., p. 57.

186. ibid., pp. 57-8.

married man with whom a woman was serving, convinced her that she was with child by him, but he then denied it, and said it could not be, for he could do no sin. That man gave up preaching. Another man applied for permission to marry his niece, his wife's sister's daughter. Numerous other instances of fornication, adultery and incest were said to have come to light. Some who committed them were thrown out of the group (and thus became 'freemen' indeed), or were found not to have been in any real sense associated with them in the first place, being lone rangers, under no human authority.[187]

Very occasionally, Irvine surprises his readers by making a complimentary remark on those he otherwise denounces so bitterly. At one point he says of Independents, 'I esteem many of them for their good qualities'. He is at his most optimistic when observing that the fanaticism of the first years of the century had subsided to a good extent by the time of writing. 'The present race', he notes, 'is more sober and peaceful than any of its predecessors', though he puts this down to their finding that 'the citadel could not be taken by storm ...' [188]

In conclusion, Irvine claimed that the revivalists had rendered thousands miserable by what they called the gospel. Not least in his list of offences was that, 'they entice young children of parents, who are members of other churches, to come among them. The Sunday evening schools, which they are very fond of teaching, give them fine scope for proselytising the young'.[189] In addition, noted Irvine, the itinerants were often hostile to one another, yet they were remarkably united in seeking to overthrow the establishment. 'There is a kind of crusadic phrenzy got amongst almost all our sectaries', he claimed, as to 'who shall be first in the work of disorder, quite forgetting that they are in a Christian country'.[190]

It is curious to note that when the Rev. John Brown of Whitburn Secession Church (grandson of John Brown of Haddington) made a tour of the Central Highlands on behalf of his Synod in 1818 after hearing the anti-revivalist charges made by Irvine prior to his publication of 1819, he made specific enquiries about those enthusiasts known as 'Freemen',

---

187. ibid., pp. 58-9.

188. ibid., p. 60.

189. ibid., p. 71.

190. ibid., p. 68.

only to find that nobody he spoke to knew anything about their existence. Brown noted with approval the lasting effects of the revival throughout the Breadalbane area, saying of Glenlyon: 'Everything about it wore the impress of divine influence, and its consequences have been of the most satisfactory kind. As one of them, it may be mentioned that an intimation of sermon, which a few years ago would with difficulty have drawn together a dozen or two, will now collect the inhabitants by hundreds.' [191] Other visitors to the region also spoke most approvingly of the revival that had taken place.

It is apparent that there were two very different strains of intense religious influence in operation in the wider Breadalbane region during the revival period – that balanced and orderly movement that came under the direction and guidance of Robert Findlater, and on a smaller scale, the more chaotic proceedings of various independent parties as graphically depicted by Irvine above. It is important to realise that these two strains operated largely independently of each other, having very little or no inter-connection. Findlater deplored fanaticism and any appearance of it that arose in gatherings he attended he immediately sought to eradicate. Such fringe and deeply disturbing fringe movements notwithstanding, we can state with some confidence that the revival in Breadalbane in the second decade of the nineteenth century – as documented from page 207 to page 215 of this book – progressed in a largely very satisfactory manner.

---

191. John Brown, *A Brief Account of a Tour in the Highlands of Perthshire, July 1818,* Edinburgh 1818.

CHAPTER 5

Thirties Revivals 1830–7

'The Cholera Revival' 1832 [1]

Introduction

The cholera epidemic began on the Indian sub-continent and spread by trade routes (land and sea) to Russia, thence to Western Europe. The first case of the water-borne disease in Scotland became apparent in December 1831. Typically, it spread with frightening rapidity. Haddington, Musselburgh and other towns and villages in East Lothian were affected by the first days of 1832, from whence the plague soon extended to Edinburgh and Glasgow, in which latter city 3,000 people died of the disease. Before the end of the year the epidemic had spread throughout most of the country.

March 21st 1832 was appointed by the government as a day of prayer and fasting on account of the cholera that was spreading so swiftly and causing such great distress throughout Britain. The day was observed with remarkable reverence and solemnity all across the land. 'On that day', noted a correspondent at the time, 'there were more people than ordinary, of all ranks and ages, in every place of worship through the whole country; a great fervency of prayer was manifested, and it is thought that the Lord has poured his Spirit on the churches, from the

---

1. This term, at least in its Scottish context, was coined by Donald Meek in 'Gaelic Bible, Revival and Mission', p. 122.

results; as many, many are now crying out for mercy, especially among the young people of Sunday Schools'.[2]

The connection between the cholera epidemic of 1832 and a marked increase in spiritual earnestness is observable in numerous western nations where its ravages were felt. Religious revivals occurred in many parts of the British Isles as a direct result of the epidemic. For example, during the preaching of John Elias in North Wales, 'the new epidemic of cholera now heaped the fire' (of revival).[3]

In England, the twelve months up to March 1833 saw the largest membership increase ever recorded in Wesleyan history.[4] Revival was strongest among the Methodists according to R. J. Morris, for that group appealed to people of lower status, who were most at risk during the epidemic, and they also had a living tradition of recruiting large numbers by revival preaching. Revivals were particularly observable along the Tyne, in the Black Country and in the declining lead-mining district of Chewton Mendip in Somerset.[5] In the West Midlands, the chapels of the Wednesbury circuit were full as cholera spread through Tipton, Dudley, Bilston and Sedgely.[6] Further north, in Manchester, a strategic street mission scheme was adopted by the Primitive Methodists

---

2. Quoted in D. Geraint Jones, *Favoured With Frequent Revivals: Revivals in Wales 1762–1862*, Cardiff 2001, pp. 36-7.

3. G. Penrhyn Jones, 'Cholera in Wales', in *National Library of Wales Journal*, vol. 10/3, Summer,1958.

4. D. W. Bebbington, *Evangelicalism in Modern Britain: A History From the 1730s To the 1980s*, London 1989, p. 115; see also Kenneth J. Jeffrey, *When the Lord Walked the Land: The 1858–62 Revival in the North East of Scotland*, Carlisle 2002, p. 33.

5. For example, after the explosive outbreak of cholera at Gateshead in late 1831, the chapels were filled and 300 new members admitted. At Walbottle a prayer meeting in a widow's house drew people from a riotous dance and began a revival which brought sixty probationers into the local congregation.

6. In the latter town, more shops closed on Sundays as the epidemic approached, and marriages increased as fear stimulated by the cholera roused the consciences of many who had long lived together out of wedlock (R. J. Morris, *Cholera 1832: The Social Response to an Epidemic*, London 1976, pp. 144-5). In the same area, in and around Darlaston, there was, through the preaching of Primitive Methodist Hugh Bourne, 'a great turning to religion … since the cholera began its ravages' (John T. Wilkinson, *Hugh Bourne 1772–1852*, London 1952, p. 142). Still in the Black Country, 'some tried to protect themselves (from cholera) by liberal doses of brandy, but others crowded into the (Methodist) chapels, and those who had baited bulls and fought their dogs a few days previously now sought forgiveness for their sins' (R. B. Walker,

'on account of the cholera epidemic in 1832, when there seemed to be a deepened spiritual need and new sensitiveness to appeal'.[7]

Cholera also swept through London in 1832 and in the city's East End, the Rev. Andrew Reed arranged special services after seeing clear evidence of 'God being at work in the midst of the tragedy unfolding all around them'. Many professions of faith were recorded.[8] In several Cornish villages, such as Redruth and Camborne, 'The dread name of cholera seemed to awake the people like the trumpet of doom. Anxiety became deep and general. In many places such numbers flocked at all hours to the chapels, that their doors could not be closed for days together'.[9] Communities such as St Just, Sowah, Sennen and Mousehole (all in Cornwall) also saw dramatic revivals in 1832.[10]

The first Methodist preacher arrived on the Channel Islands of Jersey and Guernsey in May 1832. As a result of the simultaneous 'invasion' of the islands by cholera, a considerable awakening followed. In Jersey alone, where there were 790 cholera cases and 344 deaths, the local newspaper estimated at the end of the year that, 'not less than three hundred persons have embraced the doctrine of the Wesleyan Methodists'. However, as R. D. Moore noted, the members enrolled during this period were not all faithful and many names had afterwards to be removed – the invariable sequel to this type of revival.[11] Across the Atlantic in America, where the ravages of cholera were first felt nearer the close of 1832, 500 lives were lost in Lexington, Kentucky alone. Yet in the midst of such suffering many turned to God and churches were well filled. One church saw 500 professions of faith after four days of special services.[12] In New

---

'The Growth of Wesleyan Methodism in Victorian England and Wales', in *Journal of Ecclesiastical History*, vol. 24, 1973, p. 271).

7. Wilkinson, *Hugh Bourne*, p. 145.

8. Ian J. Shaw, *The Greatest Is Charity: The Life of Andrew Reed, Preacher and Philanthropist*, Darlington 2005, pp. 214-15.

9. Samuel Coley, *The Life of Rev. Thomas Collins*, London 1876, pp. 302-3.

10. Isaac, *A History of Evangelical Christianity in Cornwall*, pp. 115-17. Isaac, however, makes no mention of a connection between revival in these villages and the spread of cholera.

11. R. D. Moore, *Methodism in the Channel Islands*, London 1952, p. 90. A similar experience accompanied the later epidemic of 1849.

12. Shaw, *The Greatest is Charity*, pp. 144-5.

York in September 1832, revivalist preacher Charles Finney personally caught the cholera disease, only returning to full strength many months later.[13]

As regards Britain, factors other than the cholera outbreak may also have been conducive to the turning of many to God at this time. In 1832 the country was in the throes of a political agitation threatening revolution. The first Reform Bill had just passed amid intense excitement – parts of society were in a state of ferment.

A further major outbreak of cholera overtook much of the British Isles in 1848–9. Luker relates the Cornish revivalism of 1849 to the second British cholera outbreak.[14] Evans makes similar correlation in regard to dramatic growth of congregations in Welsh churches in this latter year and the next,[15] although during the 1849 cholera epidemic in the East End of London, Andrew Reed did not witness 'the spiritual upturn there had been in the cholera outbreak of 1832'.[16]

Interestingly, there appears little in the way of revival occurrence in Scotland in 1849. In Dumfries, where over 300 people fell victim to the cholera epidemic which spread through the town in late 1848 and early 1849, the newly-inducted minister of the Free Church, James Wood, met with his office-bearers to 'bow with submission to the will of Almighty God', and to pray that God would send a revival to quicken His own people. Local church historian Audrey Millar sees an answer to this prayer in the 'glorious events such as had never been seen before' during the revival that swept the town over a decade later, in 1860.[17] The same is true for the period of the 1853–4 lesser cholera outbreak, an exception being evidenced in the awakening in Jordanhill and Hillhead, near Glasgow (see page 477). This serves to rule out any strong, regular cause-and-effect connection between the two phenomena. Similarly, I

---

13. Garth M. Rosell & Richard A. G. Dupuis (Eds), *The Memoirs of Charles G. Finney*, Grand Rapids, 1989, pp. 356-82.

14. David Luker, 'Revivalism in Theory and Practice: The Case of Cornish Methodism', in *Journal of Ecclesiastical History*, vol. 37, no. 4, October 1986, p. 618.

15. Eifion Evans, *When He is Come: An Account of the 1858–60 Revival in Wales*, Denbigh, 1959, p. 19; Jones, *Favoured With Frequent Revivals*, pp. 101-6.

16. Shaw, *The Greatest is Charity*, p. 215.

17. Audrey Millar, *St George's, Dumfries, 1843–1993: The Life of our Church*, Dumfries 1994, p. 30.

have come across no reports of spiritual revival anywhere in Scotland being influenced by the spread of influenza throughout the land in the winter of 1836–7, which led to many hundreds of deaths.[18]

Cholera was still lingering in Caithness in 1859, with cases being reported from Thurso, Wick and some country districts, where three members of one family died from the disease. This may have had some effect on the revival which occurred in the area around the same time.[19] However, Scottish historian T. M. Devine believes that by the time of the third cholera epidemic of 1853, which so closely followed the devastating outbreak of 1848–9, the minds of the wealthier classes were mainly terrified lest the dreaded disease should escape from the poorer areas and cause widespread carnage in the more affluent districts. 'In this crisis cholera was seen not so much as an act of God but as compelling proof that the slums had to be cleared' he writes.[20] Robert Morris similarly put the much more muted religious response to later outbreaks of cholera down to the fact that people were no longer so ready to connect natural epidemics to the judgement of God. 'God the Avenger was not dead but in retreat'.[21]

Returning our attention to the 1830s, by all accounts, the religious community of the time saw the 1832 cholera outbreak as a direct result of the will of Providence. God was an interventionist, a God who directed 'natural' disasters with justice and purpose. Thus the epidemic which raged through the country could only be seen as a form of punishment.[22]

---

18. Some districts were particularly affected. At the start of one week in 1837, the whole Fife parish of Arbirlot, in which Thomas Guthrie was minister, was in its usual state of health and activity; but before the end of the week, almost every house was smitten. In literally every home one or more was ill with the disease. Of the eleven parish churches in the Presbytery of Arbroath, more than half were shut the following Sunday (David K. & Charles J. Guthrie, *Autobiography of Thomas Guthrie, and Memoir*, vol. 1, London 1874, pp. 147-8).

19. *The Inverness Advertiser*, 1/11/1859.

20. T. M. Devine, *The Scottish Nation*, London 1999, p. 337.

21. Morris, *Cholera 1832*, pp. 202-3. For comments on spiritual awakening in Scotland and the fourth national cholera epidemic (1866), see the author's forthcoming book on revivals covering that period.

22. For example, in Dundee, where 750 were afflicted with the disease and 500 died, Rev. John Bowes of the Christian Mission Church lost no time in publishing a twelve-page tract entitled, *Sin, The Cause of the Pestilence, or Cholera Morbus, Reformation the Cure*, (John Bowes, *Autobiography or History of the Life of John Bowes*, Glasgow 1872, p. 113).

Therefore, for some, pain and death became more explicable, legitimate and bearable. There was considerable evidence that God's purpose in sending cholera was being fulfilled and people were recalled to religion. To put the matter more sociologically, 'religious revival thrived in conditions of social instability and physical danger, as men needed to reassert their values and seek security in the promises and community of faith'.[23]

The Far North

The Black Isle

The cholera was thought to have been brought to the far north of Scotland in the summer of 1832 by fishermen from East Lothian ports who docked at Wick and Helmsdale in July of that year. Avoch, Dingwall, Urquhart, Rosemarkie, Cromarty, Nigg and many other localities were hit. Indeed, perhaps nowhere in Scotland was more affected by the cholera than Easter Ross. Entire villages were wiped out. In particular, Portmahomack, Inver and other villages in the Tarbat district of Ross-shire were almost decimated. Such was the terror among the people, especially the fishermen, that the fishing was almost brought to a standstill, no one daring to venture from home. From Helmsdale the disease spread to communities in Easter Ross in August 1832.

We previously noted a wave of intense revival in Portmahomack about the year 1829 and the fact that converts remained steadfast and committed two years later (see page 221). Tragedy struck the community soon afterwards, however, when 'a deadly plague of cholera broke out' in the district, one report speaking of 'the population of Portmahomack dying like flies'. One consequence of the fast-moving epidemic was that it made almost a clean sweep of this crop of young converts.[24] Angus Murray, a much respected believer from Dornoch, said of them that 'the Lord took them away with Him to heaven soft and warm as they were'.[25] The bodies of the young people of Portmahomack were buried two miles outside the village on the beach towards Inver, it being normal for cholera victims to be buried some distance from the local community.

The population of Inver was just over a hundred, but in one day eleven bodies were committed to the earth, without shroud or coffin. Two days

---

23. Morris, *Cholera, 1832*, p. 144.

24. Campbell, *Gleanings of Highland Harvest*, pp. 97-8.

25. Morris, *Cholera, 1832*, p. 144. See also Kennedy, *The Apostle of the North*, pp. 290-1.

later, nineteen more had been buried, while more died later.[26] Many of the survivors fled from the village and took shelter, some in the woods, some among the hollows of an extensive tract of sand-hills. But the pestilence followed them to their hiding-places and they expired in the open air. Whole families were found lying dead on their cottage floors. Rows of cottages, entirely divested of their inhabitants, were set on fire and burned to the ground.[27] The poverty of the people was such that in some instances not a bit of candle was to be found in any house in an entire village, and when the disease seized the inmates in the night-time, they had to grapple in darkness with its fierce pains and mortal terrors, and their friends, in the vain attempt to assist them, had to grope around their beds. Before morning they were, in most instances, beyond the reach of medicine.[28]

The people of neighbouring parishes were startled and terrified. Regular guard was appointed in every village and district. Men of all ages took their turn at watching lest anyone from the infected area should come within their borders. When they came to Tain or other centres to buy provisions, their goods were faithfully executed by the guard, and their parcels placed at a point from which they could be taken away by their owners without fear of infection. The continuance of the scourge drove the people to prayer. The churches and meeting houses became crowded. In most villages in Ross-shire meetings for prayer were held regularly twice a week. 'The ploughman left his plough in the furrow and went to pray at the appointed hour', noted Alexander MacRae. This continued after the scourge had ceased. Many went to church meetings who were never known to have been there before. The fear of God fell upon the community, and the religious life was quickened.[29] 'The alarming and affecting state of the

26. It was reported on September 10th that there had been forty-one deaths as a result of the cholera in Portmahomack, fifty-three in Hilton, over sixty in Balintore, and sixty to sixty-five in Inver, where only fifty-two were left alive (Alexander Fraser, *Tarbat, Easter Ross: A Historical Sketch*, Evanton Ross & Cromarty Heritage Society, 1988, p. 183).

27. Although it caused huge devastation, the cholera in Inver died down fairly quickly. One reason for this is attributed to the courage of two men who apparently saw it as a cloud, caught it in a sheet and buried it between a hillock and the sea. The same thing is said to have happened in Nigg, where the cholera was buried in the churchyard and the 'Cholera Stone' covering it may still be seen.

28. Hugh Miller, *Scenes and Legends of the North of Scotland; or, The Traditional History of Cromarty*, Edinburgh 1869, pp. 246-9.

29. MacRae, *The Life of Gustavus Aird*, pp. 29-30.

Country under Visitation of the Lord of Pestilence' was also noted in a Minute of the meeting of the Presbytery of Tain held in September 1832, when all members were enjoined to hold public meetings for prayer and humiliation, and it was recorded in November that prayer meetings had been regularly held in respective parishes 'during the prevalence of cholera in the country'.[30]

It was also during this terrible cholera year that nineteen-year-old Ross-shire student Gustavus Aird rapidly developed his gifts as a comforter of hearts and winner of souls.[31] Aird shared in the general revival and found vent for his enthusiasm in many ways. In particular he made a point of visiting all the non-churchgoing people in his neighbourhood. He knocked on the doors of some people early on Sabbath and led them out to church. As a means of warning the people of their spiritual condition and the claims of Christ, Aird often related the case of a person whom he used to visit at this time, who always promised to go to church but never went. He suddenly lost the power of his limbs and became unable to go. It was then that he was awakened to see his lost condition and he deplored his negligence with tears, claiming that he would crawl to go and hear the gospel if he now could, but felt he had left it too late.[32]

Wick and Thurso

The cholera was said to have been transmitted to Wick by fishermen from other parts of the UK or mainland Europe, several thousands of whom had congregated in the Caithness town for the summer-herring fishing season. Scare stories added greatly to people's already heightened anxiety. Some fishermen from East Lothian ports caused great alarm when they spoke of the effects the epidemic had induced in their home county, further alleging that Dr Allison, an Edinburgh doctor who had come to Wick to administer aid, was deliberately poisoning people so that he could bring their corpses back to the capital for research. A mob of over 1,500, mainly visiting fishermen, gathered around the quarantine hospital, threatening the Edinburgh doctor and causing some vandalism. Allison was forced to resign his position and promptly return south on the train.

---

30. Fraser, *Tarbat, Easter Ross*, p. 184.

31. Aird was probably a student in Aberdeen at this time, where he studied for the ministry, receiving a license to preach in 1839.

32. Macrae, *The Life of Gustavus Aird*, pp. 30-1.

Amidst all the distress, many in Wick and nearby Thurso looked to the Church for relief. Many in Wick, among them numerous Protestants, attended services led by Walter Lovi, a Catholic priest who, while nurses and doctors were fleeing the 'awful pestilence', sought to distribute medicines and personally attended to the very fever-stricken people who had at first accused him of bringing cholera to the town. Out of over 300 cholera cases, there were, miraculously, only 66 deaths. In Thurso, the Rev. Edward Mackay said that of thirty years' ministry in Caithness he had never seen such an intense desire to hear the gospel as in 1832, when the cholera outbreak caused so much sickness and death in both the towns. The cholera visitation, he declared, had made 'a great impression on the public mind'.[33]

Inverness

During August and September 1832, 'The cholera outbreak … struck terror to the heart of the citizens' of Inverness.[34] Many feared that the illness came from impoverished Highlanders evicted from their homes during the Clearances, and who were now to be found begging on the streets. Although there was no evidence to support such claims, strict laws were enacted to persecute these itinerants. Well over 400 were victims of the cholera's ravages in the Highland capital and almost one hundred deaths resulted. Among such cases was that of Robert Findlater of Breadalbane, who had been minister at Inverness Chapel of Ease for the past eleven years.[35] Findlater had predicted that Inverness would be affected by the epidemic and was paying his annual preaching visit to Breadalbane when the first case of cholera was confirmed in the Highland capital. On the Sabbath following his return home, he preached on Psalm 106:29: '*Thus they provoked him to anger with their doings; And the plague brake in upon them*', and in the afternoon from Joel 2:14: '*Who knows whether He will not turn and relent And leave a blessing behind Him*'. Such passages were seen as peculiarly appropriate to many.[36]

---

33. *BHMS Report*,1832, p. 12.

34. Alexander MacRae, *Revivals in the Highlands and Islands*, p. 83.

35. Free Presbyterian Publications, *Sidelights on Two Notable Ministries*, Inverness 1970, p. 134.

36. William Findlater, *Memoir of the Rev. Robert Findlater, Together with a Narrative of the Revival of Religion During his Ministry at Lochtayside, Perthshire 1816–1819*, Glasgow 1840, p. 307.

Everyone wondered if they were going to be the next victim. The feelings excited in the minds of the inhabitants and depicted in their countenances none could adequately describe but those who were eyewitnesses. Whole families were found dead on the rotten straw of their beds. Several families fled to the country to escape the disease. Findlater, though somewhat 'timid and sensitive', felt his duty to stay among his people, and united with them at a prayer meeting on the Tuesday evening, one of numerous such prayer gatherings held every evening in various quarters of the town. The following day the pastor took ill and was confined to bed. Owing to the stupor and spasms that were symptoms of the disease, he often could hardly reflect or connect a thought, but at intervals. His untimely death at the age of forty-four led to huge sorrow and a feeling of utter desolation among his congregation. It also provoked a loud warning to all to 'watch and pray', for hitherto deaths had mainly been confined to those from humbler walks of life.[37] Now, however, there was alarm among every class.

Highlands and Islands

Lochgilphead

The heightened spiritual interest evident around this time also showed itself in Lochgilphead, where the Baptist minister rejoiced at what God had wrought. 'The appearance of cholera amongst us has excited more than common attention', he wrote. More than fifteen were baptised and added to the church from between Lochgilphead and Oban, and the congregation was said to be 'walking in the fear of the Lord'.[38]

Mull

In December 1830, a Baptist church was established in Tobermory, Mull, being served by Alexander Grant, who was ordained in the summer of 1832, during which year also the cholera epidemic made its mark

---

37. ibid., pp. 309, 311. The epitaph on his tomb read: 'He was by the mysterious visitation of providence cut off by cholera during the time it visited this place, in the course of its desolating career over a rueful world. He died in the midst of his usefulness' (ibid., p. 314). When Findlater's successor, Finlay Cook, was inducted to the East Church in late 1833, Sabbath attendance was low. It was said, however, that 'he ... was not six weeks in the church when there was not a seat unlet', for many locals, as well as virtually every Separatist from many miles around, flocked to hear Cook preach, 'and these crowds continued for nearly three years' (Campbell, *One of Heaven's Jewels*, p. 109).

38. *BHMS Report*, 1832, p. 13.

on the island. In the last six months of that year, fifteen were added to the church roll as 'the clouds distilled a few drops of heavenly rain on the barren mountains'.[39] Some of the growth came from the Ross district, where a baptism in a small lake attracted 300–400 mainly young witnesses, who listened attentively to a two-and-a-half hour sermon before being deeply impressed with the solemn and affecting scene of seeing four young men and two young women go down into the water. Afterwards thirty members, consisting of 'all the friends in Ross, and a few from Tiree', met in a house to share the Lord's Supper. 'We were abundantly satisfied with the fatness of His house' said one, 'and He made us to drink of the rivers of His pleasures'. Another communion was celebrated some months later, 'on a beautiful green near the sea', which again drew a large crowd, many showing deep concern of soul and several applying to join the church.[40]

Grantown-on-Spey

The cholera outbreak spread throughout the Highlands and Islands. When it reached Grantown-on-Spey in 1832, a number of church-going folk in the community interpreted it in the way believers across the nation did – as a judgement from God on moral and spiritual laxity – and many set apart half an hour daily for secret prayer, 'particularly for our families, and the revival of the Lord's people'.[41] When the Rev. Peter Grant (1783–1867)[42] returned from his annual preaching tour of other remote Scottish districts the following summer, the church began to be greatly revived, the people manifesting an unusual desire to hear the word of God. The meeting-house was enlarged to seat a hundred more people – almost at

---

39. Donald Meek, *Sunshine and Shadow: The Story of the Baptists of Mull*, Edinburgh 1991, p. 7; Donald E. Meek, 'The Baptists of the Ross of Mull', in *Northern Studies*, vol. 26, 1989, p. 32.

40. *BHMS Report*,1832, pp. 12-13. Professor Donald Meek sees this revival movement as that 'which was experienced in two phases by both ends of Mull during the 1830s and early 1840s' (Meek, *Sunshine and Shadow*, p. 5*)*. For the 1840s revival in Mull, see page 426.

41. *BHMS Report*,1832, p. 7.

42. Also a noted precentor and composer of many Gaelic hymns. At the time of writing a renewed interest is being shown in the ministry of this remarkable man. A book of his sermons has been recently published (Terry L. Wilder, *The Lost Sermons of Scottish Baptist Peter Grant, the Highland Herald*, Arkansas 2010) as well as a biography (George Mitchell, *Highland Harvester: Peter Grant's Life, Times and Legacy*, Kilsyth 2013).

once it became full in every corner.[43] For many months the work was solely that of conviction. This most welcome stirring of God's Spirit in the locality served as a precursor of a deeper and more widespread revival in and around Grantown-on-Spey just a year or two later (see page 279).

Central Scotland

The cholera scare, while not always leading to outright revival, led not infrequently to an increased sense of spiritual awakening in various places. From Fife, the Rev. Alexander Gregory of Anstruther referred to the overpowering emotions vented by the fishing community of Cellardyke during meetings held 'at the time of the (undated) cholera'.[44]

Further west, Kirkintilloch was greatly affected by the epidemic, and the town was forced into isolation. Horses were stopped one mile either side of the canal, their barges towed through by paddle wheel boats. Altogether, there were ninety-six recorded cases of cholera and thirty-six deaths. News of the outbreak caused much alarm in nearby Kilsyth, of which Islay Burns wrote: 'The near approach of the cholera ... while sounding its own terrible peal, at the same time summoned the pastor to lift up his voice in another earnest call to repentance and newness of life'.[45] That pastor was Dr William H. Burns, who later wrote that 'a weekly meeting was commenced in the year of the cholera, 1832, with us, as it had been in many places. It was often thinly attended, but never given up. Not a few have obtained saving impressions when they dropped in to these meetings ... Besides, there were weekly meetings held in two rural districts'.[46] As it turned out the cholera outbreak never in fact touched Kilsyth.

Musselburgh

The first case of cholera appeared in Musselburgh on 18th January 1832. From the announcement of that first case, thirty instances and

---

43. *BHMS Report*,1833, p. 7.

44. William Reid, *Authentic Records of Revival*, London 1860 [reprinted 1980], pp. 463-4. Not far from Fife, Thomas Guthrie noted that in his Angus parish of Arbirlot, 'cholera, raged like a fire around us, but never crossed the boundary of the parish', due to great precautions taken, such as the appointment of a committee and a constable to watch over the safety of the community, and not allowing any tramp or beggar to enter (David K. & Charles J. Guthrie, *Autobiography of Thomas Guthrie*, vol. 1, pp. 143-4).

45. Islay Burns, *The Pastor of Kilsyth, or, Memorials of the Life and Times of the Rev. W. H. Burns, D.D.*, London 1860, p. 128.

46. ibid.

ten deaths were reported within forty-eight hours. In little over a month there were as many as 780 cases in the parish, and 256 deaths. John Watson, minister of the Congregational Church, immediately arranged for prayer meetings to be held in his chapel. He wrote in regard to the first of these: 'Such a meeting never was held for prayer, I apprehend, in the parish of Inveresk. That large house, so far as I saw or learned, was completely packed, and below, many standing the whole time.' For many years prior to 1832 Watson had bemoaned the low attendance and lack of conversions in his church. Despite the severity of the dreaded disease, he could clearly see the Lord's hand in the situation. 'Oh with what effect God can speak to people!', he wrote. 'I have sometimes said the Apostle Paul would not *draw* people out here for religious exercises; but the scourge of the Almighty can *drive* them out!' [47]

A week later, on the 6th February, Watson wrote in a letter: 'Last week was an awful week in this place. It was a week of terrible judgements and destruction; and it was a week of much prayer.' [48] Two days of humiliation and prayer were held by the town's three dissenting churches on the 2nd and 9th February. The whole town seemed to rally to the appeal, for not a shop remained open, and attendance at the prayer meetings was 'astonishing'. A day or two later, noted Watson, 'we had a larger meeting than usual in the afternoon'. At the evening meeting, however, no sermon was delivered – such was the sense of solemnity, awe and emotion that the minister confessed, 'I do not think I could have preached'. [49] So remarkable was the turnout at the meetings that Watson could candidly declare that the Lord had effected much more in the previous two weeks than he had been able to do even with His own word in twenty-six years. The Congregational pastor was hopeful that lasting good had been done. Many, he was sure, had been crying out, 'What must I do to be saved?' leading to much joy in heaven over repenting sinners. As well as the prayer meetings, Watson began a weekly sermon every Thursday evening from the 23rd February.

Watson suffered from a degree of 'nervous weakness' as a result of the stress related to the outbreak of cholera in the town; on top of this he developed a heavy cold which he felt made him more susceptible

---

47. Alexander, *Memoir of the Rev. John Watson*, p. 161.

48. ibid., p. 162.

49. ibid., p. 163.

to contagion. He worried also about the advisability of so many folk gathering together, night after night, in church when the town was in the throes of this onslaught from 'angels of darkness'. He was, however, able to testify that he did 'sometimes enjoy much serenity of mind from the blessed word of God' and that he could 'look at the worst with sympathy like a sacred smile'. And throughout all these months of death and sickness, Watson marvelled that all his family were 'in wondrous mercy spared', as too, remarkably, was every member of his congregation.[50]

By early summer attendance at both the prayer meeting and the Thursday sermon had fallen off considerably, although the average attendance was still far greater than before the cholera outbreak began. Indeed, as late as the 10th October, meetings were still being kept up, with an average of one hundred attending the Thursday sermon and about a third more the weekly prayer meeting. Watson thanked God that 'wonderful was the attendance manifested by the members to every meeting during the violence of the disease', and he had hope 'that a revival was effected in many minds'. As the epidemic subsided, however, the discerning Congregational minister came more and more to fear that 'much of the goodness is but as the morning cloud and the early rain'.[51] At the same time, it should be noted that Watson was known for his inclination to despondency and for taking an unduly gloomy view of things.[52] His biographer was of the opinion that considerably more spiritual good amongst his congregation was brought about by the cholera than the pastor himself recognised. Nevertheless, it is sad to note Watson's belief sometime after the epidemic had passed, that, 'as a church we are very low; never were more so, but the Lord is able to revive the work'.[53] In December, a day of thanksgiving for both the removal of the cholera and the recent abundant harvest was held in the town. Once again scarcely a shop was open that day, and the meetings in church were largely attended. Watson continued to labour faithfully and incessantly among his flock for many more years, and altogether

---

50. ibid., p. 164.

51. ibid., p. 165.

52. At several points before the cholera outbreak he had even considered leaving the ministry altogether, and in 1837 he did just that; only to retract his letter of resignation shortly after on the strong request of denominational authorities.

53. Alexander, *Memoir of the Rev. John Watson*, p. 177.

preached four thousand sermons during his thirty-eight years' ministry in Musselburgh.

Southern Scotland

Hawick

Congregationalists in Hawick had held a well-attended week-night meeting for many years, but, noted one of their number at length:

> As the memorable year of 1832 approached, the salutary appre-hensions and anxiety awakened in the minds of the people by the death-dealing arm of the cholera contributed greatly to the increase of our audiences, so much so that our meeting place became too strait for us. We then rented a schoolroom, which contained two hundred … We continued in this order through-out the winter, greatly to our own comfort and the benefit of not a few. The fearful pestilence that had now appeared frightened many into a temporary seriousness, who, for the time, wished to be religious and sought the company of those who were so. Our meetings from this cause became crowded. They were held every night for weeks. God gave us power in the eyes of the people, and our place became crowded to suffocation. We then applied to Mr Douglas (of Cavers) for a large room which he rented, and which was most readily granted, but this place also proved insufficient to hold the people that crowded for admission.[54]

Throughout this trying time, William Munro, who became pastor of Hawick's Congregational Church from its establishment in 1832 – the year of the cholera outbreak – was known to have shown a most 'noble spirit'. Decades later, many of the older people still spoke highly of how 'at that time he contributed a courage which rose superior to all fear'. Without any hesitation he visited the sick and dying all through the town. His house was thrown open, and his neighbours during the prevalence of the pestilence came in considerable numbers every morning to have the privilege of uniting with him in family worship.[55]

---

54. *General Account of Congregationalism in Scotland from 1798 to 1848*, quoted in McNaughton, 'Revival and Reality', pp. 193-4.

55. 'Scottish Congregationalist' 1883, quoted in William McNaughton, *Early Con-gregational Independency in Lowland Scotland*, vol. 1, p. 451.

Congregational Movements of the '30s

Greenock

James Haldane paid several preaching visits to Greenock, on the south bank of the River Clyde, the last recorded being in September 1803, when he spoke in the Burgher Meetinghouse to a great crowd. That same year, 21-year-old John Hercus, a native of Orkney, began a three-year period of study in Haldane's theology school before being ordained and inducted to the newly-established Greenock Congregational Church in 1806.[56] Hercus quickly proved himself an earnest and able minister, also undertaking itinerancy tours for a month or two each summer and taking a keen interest in the welfare of local seamen, many of whom were active churchgoers. He suffered a stroke in 1827, depriving him the use of his left side and partially affecting his speech and memory. But despite living 'under the daily sentence of death', Hercus was soon back at work with an energy that surprised everyone.

'Very depressed' at the coldness and indifference prevailing among his congregation, and by the fact that there were more deaths than additions to membership, Hercus proposed an additional weekly prayer meeting throughout 1829, at the close of which, adding to his list of woes, his wife also died. Little changed until an unexpected two-month visit at the start of 1830 from 'Mr Fraser of New York', who preached in almost every pulpit in town and from house to house. At last Hercus's unwearied zeal and unreserved consecration were rewarded. Most of those who were now being brought under deep impression belonged to his congregation, where 'an interesting revival' ensued, to such an extent that many from other denominations were so attracted by the spirituality of the Congregationalists that they applied for membership.[57] A church officer noted that from March 1830, 'We have had 34 additions to the church – on the Lord's day, August 22nd, eight young persons, and two old persons, joined the church, two of these were only thirteen and one female above eighty'.[58] Hercus went to his eternal reward in

---

56. Another Orcadian evangelist with Haldanite views, David Ramsay of Kirkwall, had also been evangelising in Greenock prior to the formation of the church.

57. 'Nelson Street Evangelical Union Congregational Church, Greenock, Centenary Anniversary 1846–1946', quoted in McNaughton, *Early Congregational Independency in Lowland Scotland*, vol. 2, pp. 195, 201.

58. *Congregational Magazine*, 1830, p. 516.

May of that same year – at the age of forty-eight – but the revival continued, and just over a year later church membership had increased from about 75 to 160.[59]

Forfar

A Congregational chapel was opened in Forfar in 1835. Said its minister, the Rev. William Lowe; 'In connection with the stated ministry of the Gospel we have had special meetings for prayer and the results under the Divine blessing have been the rapid increase of the church, so that in two years from our commencement we had added about 150 members and not a few of these were persons reclaimed from open infidelity and total indifference to the outward forms of religion, some of whom have died rejoicing in the Lord and others are still spared adorning the Gospel by their walk and consecration'.[60]

Highland Revivals

Grantown-on-Spey

Towards the close of 1834, according to Peter Grant, Baptist pastor at Grantown-on-Spey, 'the Lord visited us in mercy, poured down His Spirit, and some were awakened'. At this point the church received a propitious visit from Duncan Dunbar, a native of the village, then a minister in New York. Known to virtually everyone in the community as a former ring-leader of notorious laddish behaviour and a dare-devil almost devoid of fear, the lively preaching of this now fervent evangelist with a popular parish ministry on the other side of the Atlantic made a deep and dramatic impact on those who flocked to hear him.

The result was a powerful revival of religion, marked by a surge of conversions, and a flow of baptisms almost every month for no less than four years, the great majority of them previously careless about matters of eternity. 'The movement', Grant insisted, 'was not produced by any extraordinary means, but by the Lord blessing His own word, teaching sinners by His Spirit to sit down and count the cost and to attend to

---

59. Hercus's two sons, Hugh and Peter, became active members of the Greenock church after their father's departure.

60. This was a reply to a part of a questionnaire compiled by the Congregational Union of Scotland in 1843, quoted in McNaughton, *Early Congregational Independency in Lowland Scotland*, vol.1, pp. 214-5.

the one thing needful'.[61] Most converts were aged between seventeen and thirty, and included four young men from one family. In addition, four members of Grant's own family were brought within the fold at this time, to the pastor's great delight. Fourteen young men, 'all in the ranks of the enemy a few months ago', commenced a prayer meeting on Sunday mornings. 'It would have made you weep for joy to see them go to the house of God in company', noted Grant. Gradually the awakening spread to the country areas, where meetings in outlying stations were well attended. Nine Sabbath schools in total were in operation, averaging from twenty to forty scholars each, 'and generally the house full of hearers'.[62] Explained Grant, 'It was *our* way to awaken professors of religion and that *they* should awaken the careless; but the Lord's way was, that *He* should awaken the careless, and *they* have awakened us'.[63]

Much opposition attended the revival, such as from those who said the church was receiving converts too soon. The counter argument was that most new believers were growing up quickly and were in a flourishing state. Influenza also afflicted a number in the church, including Grant and his family – 'our strath was like a great infirmary', he noted – while he also suffered the death of his wife around this time. On top of these and other set-backs, food shortages caused considerable hardships.

Amidst all these difficulties, the movement continued unabated, and was still in full flow in 1837, when it was estimated that eight were being baptised every quarter (and a further sixteen in 1838–9), making a total of over sixty additions to church membership in all, besides some who, lamented Grant, 'were not spared to enjoy that privilege, although it was their hearts' desire'.[64]

---

61. *BHMS* Report 1836, p. 6.

62. ibid., 1836, pp. 7, 9.

63. ibid., 1836, p. 6.

64. ibid., 1837, pp. 16-17. See also D. E. Meek, 'Gaelic Bible, Revival and Mission', pp. 122-3; A. B. Thomson, *Sketches of Some Baptist Pioneers in Scotland*, Glasgow 1903, pp. 28-9. A considerable degree of tension was experienced in many Congregational churches in the early nineteenth century, as a result of disagreement between paedobaptists and Baptists, and many schisms ensued. On at least one such occasion, revival was a contributory factor. Peter Grant and John Munro of Knockando often itinerated together prior to a dispute which arose from Munro's fear that some of his own people were 'inclining to be baptised' as a result of the recent revival being experienced by the Grantown-on-Spey Baptists (McNaughton, 'Revival and Reality', pp.

Badenoch

Meanwhile, in a neighbouring Baptist community to the west of Grantown-on-Spey in 1835 'the Lord was pleased to grant a little revival in Badenoch', a sprawling sparsely-populated area to the south-west of the Grampians. Where formerly the district was 'a proverb on account of its barrenness', and, in the opinion of one minister, 'the most backward place I knew in the Highlands', it became, in 1835, 'a wonder on account of the grace of God'. The movement occurred under the preaching and pastoral supervision of the Rev. William Hutchison, who served as minister of Kingussie Baptist Church from its inception in 1808 to 1850. Hutchison was a close colleague of Peter Grant, and several times the two men engaged in arduous summer preaching tours throughout the Highland and Grampian regions. Already in the throes of exciting revival in his own church, Grant was nevertheless quick to come and aid Hutchison in the extra workload entailed by the Badenoch movement. Further assistance came from Alexander Grant of Tobermory and the Rev. Souter of Aberdeen, both of whom wrote encouraging words about the movement's progress. Over a year later, new instances of awakening were still being reported 'here and there' and around eighteen had been added to the Kingussie fellowship.[65]

Breadalbane

The parish of Lawers was blessed with spiritual awakening following the induction of Duncan Campbell in 1834.[66] Duncan and younger brother, David, minister in neighbouring Glenlyon, were seen as 'burning and shining lights and the people, almost to a man, were willing to rejoice in their light'. Duncan also had a special tie to Strathtay, in that he assisted the minister of Grandtully on sacramental occasions and also passed through the area to visit his brother after his appointment in 1832 as an agent of Perth City Mission. A sermon Duncan preached

---

184-5). It is unclear, however, exactly what specific period of revival is being referred to here.

65. *BHMS Report* 1836, pp. 10-12; 1837, p. 18.

66. Thomas Brown, *Annals of the Disruption*, Edinburgh 1893, p. 9; Macgregor suggests that at Lawers Campbell resumed the work begun by Findlater more than twenty years previously (see page 207). 'Findlater laid the foundation and began to build; Mr Campbell entered into his labours and carried the walls up higher' (Macgregor, *Campbell of Kiltearn*, pp. 43-4).

in the schoolhouse of Balnaguard at an early period of his ministry was blessed for the conversion of souls.[67] As he passed through the valley on a subsequent date, the people in the cornfields from Logierait and onwards, thinking that he would likely rest to bait his horse at Balnaguard Inn, threw down their sickles and followed him, and before he had been half-an-hour at the Inn, a congregation of some hundreds gathered and requested him to preach to them. He at once joyfully agreed, and preached one of his rousing gospel sermons, with all the energy and freshness of his youth. 'The presence of the Lord was manifestly there, and the impression made was deep and permanent'.[68] Refreshed and joyous, the people then returned to their crofts and reaped their fields by moonlight. Many Christians in Strathtay traced the beginning of their new life to that sermon. In later days, Campbell often referred 'to these great days of the Son of man'.[69]

Over the course of two weeks in September 1835 John Macdonald of Ferintosh preached on a daily basis throughout the Breadalbane district, attracting large crowds who were frequently moved to tears. Macdonald noted in regard to his 'action sermon' at the Lawers communion, 'the Lord undoubtedly was present, for His word had a melting effect'.[70] Repeatedly did the evangelist note in his journal his longing that the blessings that fell on this 'spot once highly favoured to me by various considerations' (in the years 1816–17) would be seen again, and so he was happy to note the effect of his preaching in Glenlyon: ' … very crowded house. Many of the hearers were in tears. The scene reminded me in some measure of the days of other years in this place'.[71] Shearers who had gone to work for some days in Perth and Dunkeld, a considerable distance away, returned immediately on hearing that Macdonald was in the area, their employers graciously giving them the liberty to do so.

Exactly a year later Macdonald was back in Breadalbane, preaching in Ardeonaig to a crowd of seven thousand. He wrote of the occasion:

---

67. Macgregor, *Campbell of Kiltearn*, p. 51. In that same school-house, some time later, William Chalmers Burns preached the gospel 'with the Holy Ghost sent down from heaven' (see Chapter 6, page 351).

68. ibid., pp. 87-8.

69. Brown, *Annals of the Disruption*, p. 9.

70. Kennedy, *The Apostle of the North*, p. 130.

71. ibid., p. 131.

'The attention (was) deep and fixed. Every face among the vast multitude gave indications of earnestness and solemnity in hearing the word, and not a few were in tears almost the whole time.' The following day, Macdonald preached at the tent to a smaller congregation, but larger than any that had been seen on the Monday of a communion since September 1817 – 'a Monday of great awakening, and indeed a day of Messiah's power. This day reminded us of it in some measure', he rejoiced.[72] Around four thousand assembled a week later in Lawers for Macdonald's last discourse before heading north. As he spoke, 'Not a few were all the time in tears, while the eyes of others glistened with joy. The word had truly a melting effect'. After a further service held in the church, a nearby house immediately filled with people seeking to attend family worship. 'We were almost all in tears', Macdonald wrote, 'and parted in that state'.[73]

Revival in Lewis

Angus McIver in Back and Bernera

Angus McIver moved to the Lewis district of Back in the early 1830s, where a member of the influential Seaforth family, who owned Lewis, built him a house. Here he taught young and old during the week-days and lectured to the people on the Sabbaths. All except one churchgoer stopped walking the six miles to the parish church in Stornoway on Sundays, preferring to hear 'the layman who spoke to them nearer their homes'. A deep and lasting impression was made in this large and populous community by McIver's residence among them for some years, and the effect of his ministry was evident for a long time afterwards. Indeed, it was said that, 'A spiritual revolution took place which changed the whole aspect of things in that part of Lewis'. Sometimes McIver would cross the Broad Bay on the Sabbath to hear the (evangelical) minister in the quoad sacra church,[74] and the people of Back used to accompany

---

72. ibid., p 135.

73. ibid., pp. 137-8.

74. A parish constituted for practical ecclesiastical purposes solely, without any civil responsibilities. Such charges might be formed in situations where the existing parish church had become outgrown, or because its location was considered too far distant from where most parishioners dwelt. The creation of quoad sacra charges and the rights of ownership of the buildings became particularly hotly debated topics at the time of the Disruption.

him. John Cameron, parish minister in Stornoway, was outraged at such offence, and soon McIver was called before the Lewis Presbytery. He was moved to Bernera shortly after, but the attachment of the people of Back to him was 'unbounded and their devotion and love for him deep and lasting'. Thus, when he returned to Back after an absence of eighteen years,[75] he was again welcomed with open arms by the community.

In Bernera, as well as teaching the people English and Gaelic, McIver preached to them on Sabbath at noon when they were unable to get to church, and again in the evening. People thronged to hear him from every township of the remote island and numbers even crossed on boats from south-westerly parts of mainland Lewis. They listened with 'rapt but subdued attention', and so much did they revere McIver that the rostrum he preached from was valued by the islanders ever after. On Thursdays the meeting-house was as filled for the mid-day meeting as it was on Sabbaths. No work was done in any part of the island at that hour, nor did the fishermen go out to sea, though it was remarked on that they 'never lost by it'.[76] Some of the godly men wept as they prayed, tears streaming down their cheeks. Some could never pray without being thus affected, despite all being 'retiring, modest men who engaged in anything of that kind with much reluctance'.[77] The meeting-house was located in a hollow, surrounded by cragged, broken hills all around. On dark nights, folk came to the meetings from all quarters with peats fixed to iron spits or held in tongs. These were lit and used as torches while traversing the rugged terrain, there being no roads of any description on the island, while additional peats were carried under folks' arms in case of need. By the time McIver left Bernera, the majority of young men on the island could read and write as well as perform basic arithmetic functions. Perhaps more importantly, virtually every family was known to conduct worship in its home, to the extent that any which didn't was marked out as singular and godless. Additionally, all, both young

---

75. McIver also served as catechist in Back from July to November 1843 (Neil Murray, *Chum Fios A Bhi Aig An Al Ri Teachd* ['*Back Free Church*'], Back nd, p. 2).

76. As further evidence of the Lord's protection and provision, McIver's son remembered only one fisherman being lost at sea during his father's eighteen-year ministry on Bernera.

77. 'Story of a Lewis Catechist: The Life of Angus McIver', serialised in *The Stornoway Gazette*, 29/01/1972, p. 5.

and old, could repeat the Shorter Catechism and many understood the doctrines contained therein.

Robert Finlayson in Knock and Lochs

The season of spiritual reform that commenced with outbreaks of dramatic revival in parts of Lewis in the 1820s (see page 237) continued to extend its deep-rooted influence across the island into and throughout the following decade. This generally took the form of more gradual localised awakenings rather than the bursts of intense revival that were witnessed in the 1820s. When Robert Finlayson came to the east Lewis parish of Knock in 1829, it was for the district, 'a leap into the light'. His first sermon dwelt on the theme, '*Behold the Lamb of God*', and this became the pursuit of his entire ministry while he remained in the district. 'He was all for Christ', noted Norman Macfarlane; 'there was no ego in his world'. People in the Point district crowded to him, and many also walked all the way from Stornoway. Some begged admittance of evenings to the manse for family worship. Soon the house (little parlour, lobby and stair, and every available inch of space) became packed, upstairs and down, with eager listeners. 'His comments on psalm and chapters were', remarked Macfarlane, 'spearlights that stung the memory. His soft, deep sonorous voice was the carrier of many a sparkling word. For long years after, men and women spoke of those evenings at the manse as moments at Heaven's gate, and his comments as gems of amethystine beauty ... He was lighted from inward fires'. Finlayson remained in Knock only two years, being replaced by the equally influential Duncan Matheson in September 1831.[78]

Although revival had been underway in (predominantly western) Lewis for a number of years prior to Robert Finlayson moving to Lochs in 1831, he found that parish 'a moral wilderness. The people sat in darkness and in the shadow of death'. There was an almost entire lack of public roads in the district, which was described as being 'deeply indented with arms of the sea ... no parish in the Highlands presents

---

78. Macfarlane, *Apostles of the North*, pp. 22-3; MacAulay, *Aspects of the Religious History of Lewis*, p. 85; *The Stornoway Gazette*, 10/08/1861. As Finlayson was to Knock, so was Finlay Cook to Cross in the north-west of Lewis, being the means of considerable spiritual reform throughout that parish during his time of ministry there from 1829 to 1833, when he was succeeded by John ('Big') Macrae (see Macaulay, *Aspects of the Religious History of Lewis*, pp. 75-8; Macfarlane, *Apostles of the North*, pp. 55-8).

such obstacles to pastoral oversight except Lochbroom'.[79] Yet Finlayson enjoyed an outstanding twenty-five year ministry in the extensive district. His earnest preaching and prayers – frequent tears fell from his cheeks as he pled with sinners – and his diligent catechising of the whole parish once a year, from which 'a great harvest of souls was reaped', led to a transformation of the district, 'like the reviving breath of spring on the frost-bound earth'.[80]

Known as 'Finlayson of prayer' in his youth, it was said of him that 'he lived in heaven'. A cave near the manse at Crossbost became his oratory. There he spent hours and hours daily in prayer on his knees. Once when asking a blessing at the dinner table, the minister quickly became oblivious to his surroundings and poured out his soul in prayer for over half-an-hour! Finlayson was a passionate winner of souls, and when often his wife remonstrated with him regarding his intent to cross the seas in stormy weather, he would say, 'Souls at Gravir are calling me today and I cannot stay. It's easier to battle with the elements than to silence the cries that ring through me'.[81]

Of one village which was seen formerly as a hard, careless spot, Finlayson spouted, 'O Balallan, you are the Devil's kitchen where he cooks his meals. He may dine elsewhere, at Keose, or Cromore or Crossbost, but it is here he cooks. O Balallan, throw water on those cooking fires'. Some time later, amidst a season of revival which swept over the community of Balallan,[82] Finlayson could remark, 'O Balallan, the Devil's quondam kitchen, you are now become a very Bethel, a House of God'.[83] Indeed, in April 1836, Finlayson noted in the Kirk Session minutes that because of the recent revival in his parish, prayer meetings had been established, not only in Balallan, but also in Laxay, Luerbost, Ranish, Gravir and Loch Shell.[84]

But Finlayson was not the only soul winner in the parish. Angus MacLeod, a native of Uig and a convert of the revival there,

---

79. *The Scottish Guardian*, 10/08/1861.

80. ibid.

81. Macfarlane, *Apostles of the North*, p. 27.

82. ibid., p. 25.

83. ibid., pp. 20-30; Macaulay, *Aspects of the Religious History of Lewis*, pp. 96-101. See also Donald Beaton, *Some Noted Ministers of the Northern Highlands*, pp. 212-23.

84. Macleod, *The Progress of Evangelicalism*, p. 218.

subsequently a resident in Lochs, enjoyed an extremely rare and profound communion with the Lord, and soon made his mark felt throughout the Lochs parish. Finlayson said that from careful inquiry he found that this poor witless man could claim more spiritual children in Lochs than all the ministers who had preached there in that generation.[85] Said a correspondent to *The Scottish Guardian* regarding the overall spiritual transformation of the parish, in a lengthy tribute to Finlayson on his death, 'the narrative of the steps by which a change so great was effected would form a most interesting chapter in the religious history of Scotland'.[86]

We have already noted the purity, depth and enduring effects of the famed Uig revival of the 1820s. Having spread throughout most of the island by 1840, Donald Sage was able to write in that year that a result of the awakening across Lewis was that 'in that land God is well known; the gospel is not only understood, but ardently sought after …(Lewis) has become one of the most enlightened parts of Christian Scotland'.[87] According to the Gaelic Society, by the time of the Disruption in 1843, there was scarcely a home in Lewis in which the family altar was not maintained.[88] Wonderfully, a further burst of revival blessing was experienced in one or two Lewis communities with the occurrence of that Disruption event in May 1843 (see page 455).

Methodist Revival

Thomas Collins in the Far North

Skarfskerry and Stronsay

Rousing revivalist scenes appeared at Skarfskerry, on the north Caithness coast, when visited by Donald Brotchie of Inverness in 1832. 'Under the Word many were so powerfully smitten that they fell to the earth, where, prostrate in prayer, they remained, refusing all comfort, until God's own witness of peace came into their souls'. One of their number, Edward Lyall, became the leader, regularly teaching on Sabbath

---

85. MacAulay, *Aspects of the Religious History of Lewis*, pp. 192, 195.

86. *Stornoway Gazette*, 10/08/1861.

87. Sage, *Memorabilia Domestica*, p. 297.

88. 'GSS Report' 1844, p. 23, quoted in Macleod, *The Progress of Evangelicalism*, p. 217.

evenings and midweek, and forming a Society which grew to around two dozen members. When Methodist preacher Thomas Collins, who had already witnessed considerable revival in Cornwall, visited this Caithness district in 1836, he was comforted to find 'the most part walking in the comfort of the Holy Ghost … As we finished by singing together of the heavenly meeting where we shall part no more, feeling grew into rapture. My soul was much blessed by the childlike faith and earnest gladness of these simple people', he said.[89] Thomas Collins also ministered with success at Skarfskerry in the summer of 1836, creating further stir as he spoke to small crowds in barns, huts, halls and smithies in various parts of the county.

His greatest success, however, was among the fisherfolk of Stronsay, one of Orkney's north isles. The people had written to him, pleading: 'We have no school, no teacher, no guide, no spiritual food, no ordinances. We are entirely neglected. These things being so, it will not surprise you to hear, though it would fill your eyes with tears to see, how the Sabbath is profaned, and the young people go astray.'[90] Such a touching plea prompted Collins to make the long journey north. On his arrival, he spent repeated seasons of fasting, intercession and other 'knee business' – sometimes for a whole day at a time – in a sheltered cave in the cliffs. He said that his 'heart was broken with desire for conversions. I wept much as I besought the Lord to give me souls. I felt unusual nearness, sweetness of intercourse, and strength of faith; and came away sure that my covenant God had engaged Himself to me to make bare His wonder-working arm'. Sure enough, 'drops of blessing' fell at a Sunday service, sinners cried aloud for mercy, and within a fortnight from that date, 'forty-two known, clear' cases of conversion had occurred, including one who later entered the ministry. Collins had to contend, however, with 'no small muttering in the Samaritan camp … the Secession minister, fearing loss if we gain, prattles against us. This finding pardon of sin stumbles him. He compares me to a Popish Priest, and slanderously insinuates that I profess to forgive'.[91]

---

89. Coley, *The Life of Rev. Thomas Collins*, pp. 107-8.

90. ibid., p. 86.

91. ibid., pp. 86-101. Sporadic visits were also made to Orkney by several Shetland Methodist preachers, and a few Societies were formed (with a maximum membership of 1,912), but in 1841 the dwindling causes were handed over to the Free Church

Alexander Patrick in Central Scotland

North Lanarkshire

Scottish Methodist preacher Alexander Patrick moved to the Airdrie circuit in 1830, where his initial attempts at temperance reform proved a great success. More especially, he engaged incessantly in establishing and participating in prayer meetings throughout the district. Meetings at Coatbridge, Lee End, Calder, Carnbroe, Bellshill and Holytown were frequently crowded, and many became so conscience-stricken that they cried out aloud in distress. Several hundred were 'enabled to venture by faith on a crucified Saviour', and so the Society grew, while many who were savingly blessed remained in, or now attached themselves to, other denominations in their area, in the hope of infusing new life into these fellowships. Some considerable commotion and occasionally seeming disorder attended the meetings, which led to much criticism from outsiders.[92] Patrick, too busy in the work of saving souls, rarely attempted to vindicate himself. Aware that there may have been a few cases of hypocrisy and deception, he nevertheless knew that the good greatly outweighed the bad. He was often 'exhausted so completely in the violent and energetic exercise of these occasions' that often no strength was left him.[93] He also contracted a disease in his eyes, which remained with him throughout his life and at times almost totally deprived him of sight. In time, the congregation outgrew their meeting room in Airdrie, so they removed to Lee End. Here fresh classes were formed from time to time and the society increased so much that a new building was soon deemed necessary. This opened in May 1841.

Kilsyth

A Methodist presence came to Kilsyth in 1827, but membership five years later had reached a mere fifteen. With the arrival of preacher Alexander Patrick attendance quickly increased and two classes were formed. During the winter of 1834–5 there occurred several cases of

---

of Scotland (H. R. Bowes (Ed.), *Samuel Dunn's Shetland and Orkney Journal*, p. 60; Coley, *The Life of Rev. Thomas Collins*, pp. 111-12).

92. Rev. John Drake, *The Wallacestone Reformer; or, A Sketch of the Life and Labours of Mr Alexander Patrick, Wesleyan Local Preacher*, Kirkintilloch 1848, p. 55.

93. ibid., p. 52.

deep awakening. Then on the last Sunday of February 1835,[94] while the teacher was addressing the children,

> it appeared as if an overpowering light broke in upon their minds; an unusual solemnity pervaded the school, and soon there were heard in all directions sighs and sobbings … The business of the school was stopped, and for a considerable time nothing could be heard but mingled lamentations and prayer for mercy. Meantime the hour arrived for the adult congregation to assemble for the public preaching, but the hall was pre-occupied by the young people, who could neither be removed nor restrained from crying aloud to God with groans and tears for the salvation of their souls. The congregation was therefore obliged to take their places in the midst of the agitated and agonising youths.

Patrick was called for – his sense of spiritual discernment showed him at once that 'the suddenness, the extent and the character of the excitement on the occasion, together with the inadequacy of the human means employed', meant that this was very much a direct work of God.[95]

The following Thursday was a fast day, and as Patrick preached in the evening a woman cried aloud. A prayer-meeting was set up on her behalf, and so evident was the presence of the Spirit that at the close of the meeting thirty-two people claimed to have found liberty in the Lord. Within a week about a hundred persons of all ages had found peace with God. Suspicion arose among some believers in town that the work was 'mere animal sympathy'. Patrick was careful to ensure, however, that the words, temper and conduct of the young converts were incessantly watched and the fruits of the Spirit searched for.[96] Still, in the midst of such revival, Patrick 'seemed almost to forget that he was in the body', such was his overwhelming joy at the work of the Lord all around him. At the same time, it was said that his own faith rose to a pitch of confidence that one must have witnessed in order to have conceived. One man who came to deride the work, 'suddenly was struck with a panic and fled from the window where he had placed himself, with all the symptoms of a ludicrous terror'.[97]

---

94. J. H. Hudson, T. W. Jarvie & J. Stein, 'Let the Fire Burn', Dundee 1978.

95. Drake, The Wallacestone Reformer, pp. 97, 99.

96. ibid., pp. 99, 103.

97. ibid., pp. 105, 109.

Prayer meetings were held in homes throughout Kilsyth, often being protracted to a great length. An invisible charm seemed to draw many to a particular cottage just outside the town, and here numbers of folk were awakened and saved, including the three daughters and son of a godly woman from Kilsyth. At one memorable house-meeting at which Patrick was present, 'about forty souls were converted to God before the closing of the evening exercises'.[98] Sometimes Patrick led whole households in prayers of submission to Christ; at other times a believing mother was the means of salvation for her family. At the end of a year, forty steady members were added to the Society and two new classes formed. For years afterwards, the 24th February was observed as a high day among the Methodists of Kilsyth.

The movement became known among Methodists as 'The Revival of 1835'. At intervals thereafter, converts continued to be made throughout the town among the various congregations.[99] For example, in 1836, William H. Burns presented an essay before the clerical society of Glasgow on the subject of revival and described the tokens of spiritual awakening that were taking place in his own parish. Prayer meetings – including those specifically for revival – were thronged; members of the congregation were visibly moved at communions and several remarkable conversions took place.[100] The way was being prepared for a more powerful outpouring of the Spirit, which occurred just a few years later (see page 318).

APPENDIX (TO CHAPTER 5)

West of Scotland 'Charismatic' Movement 1830–3

Introduction

In the early 1830s, more than seventy years before the influential Pentecostal movement began in the United States,[101] occurred a form of

---

98. ibid., pp. 107-8.

99. W. J. Couper, *Scottish Revivals*, p. 119. See also Islay Burns, *The Pastor of Kilsyth, or, Memorials of the Life and Times of the Rev. W. H. Burns, D.D.*, London 1860, pp. 128-30.

100. Hutchison, *Miners, Weavers and the Open Book*, p. 63.

101. The movement is traditionally seen as having its origins in cottage meetings held at Bonnie Brae Street, Los Angeles in the winter and early spring of 1906, and from April 14th of that year at the Apostolic Faith Mission at 312 Azusa Street, under the leadership of William J. Seymour. The mission here ran until 1913 and drew

charismatic revival to the west and north of Glasgow which both shocked
and fascinated the religious world of Britain.[102] The movement has been
consistently dismissed in studies of religious awakenings – including
even those that focus on charismatic revivals – owing largely to the controversial nature of the manifestations that attended it, and/or to the
fact that several of its leading players, though outstanding figures, came
to espouse doctrines that were long considered contrary to the teachings of the Reformed faith. When it *has* been offered attention, this
early charismatic movement is commonly either given overtly favourable treatment, ignoring the inconsistencies and controversies which
dogged certain aspects of it from its beginnings,[103] or is all too quickly
dismissed as a series of emotional extravagances whipped up by individuals who lacked grounding in basic biblical precepts; and in any case to be
rejected on grounds of the heretical teachings associated with it.[104] Such

---

thousands from all over the world to the long and largely spontaneous, racially mixed
meetings, which included singing, testimonies, prayer, preaching, altar calls for salvation, sanctification and baptism in the Holy Spirit, as well as specifically *Pentecostal*
manifestations such as speaking in tongues, prophecy and being 'slain in the Spirit'.
Pentecostalism soon became a worldwide movement.

102. Although David Pytches records that this was 'the first recorded manifestation
of the gifts in a reformed Church among cultured Christians in Britain since the Reformation' (David Pytches, *Prophecy in the Local Church*, London 1993, p. 217), there
had, in fact, been more than one previous outbreak of Pentecostal manifestations in
Scotland alone. Around the turn of the eighteenth century a group of 'prophets' in
Edinburgh and Glasgow, the most prominent of whom were women, claimed direct
inspiration from the Holy Spirit, and spoke in tongues, while one of their number,
Ann Topham, even claimed to have levitated (A. M. King et al, *Warnings of the Eternal
Spirit*, Edinburgh 1709, in Neill Dickson 'Modern Prophetesses', in *SCHSR*, vol. 25,
Edinburgh 1993, p. 93). A century earlier still, John Welsh, eminent minister of Ayr,
was overheard in prayer – the mainstay of his entire life – speaking 'strange words'
(considered to have been tongues) in regard to his spiritual joy (George Jeffreys, *Pentecostal Rays: The Baptism and Gifts of the Holy Spirit*, London 1923, p. 200).

103. Such as D. W. Dorries's otherwise most informative historical account (Stanley
Burgess (Ed.), The *New International Dictionary of Pentecostal and Charismatic Movements* (hereafter *NIDPCM*), Grand Rapids 2002, pp. 1189-92).

104. Such as the critical survey written by B. B. Warfield – considered by John Murray to be the 'master theologian' of the twentieth century (John Murray, *Collected
Writings of John Murray*, Edinburgh 1982, p. 3) – who devoted an entire chapter of his
popular *Counterfeit Miracles* (originally published 1913 [reprinted 1972]) to a (highly
unfavourable) examination of the Scottish movement, which he dismissed as 'a sordid
story' (p. 147). For a further considered argument against goings-on in London, and
west Scotland, see *The Edinburgh Review*, June 1831.

predisposed reporting, from either side of the fence, fails to allow events in the Rhu and Port Glasgow districts to be viewed through the wider kaleidoscope of hues in which they occurred. This unusual and colourful movement therefore deserves fresh examination, from as objective a standpoint as possible and relying on a wide range of primary source material. The following narrative seeks to set out the main facts pertaining to its progress, not shying away from any dubious extravagances and controversial doctrines that played a part in it, but neither overlooking its more laudable elements.

Ministries of John McLeod Campbell and Edward Irving

While laypersons were the chief actors for the duration of the movement, its initial inspiration and theological foundation were contributed by various ministers of the Established Church. The movement centred initially on the Gareloch region of Dunbartonshire, where John McLeod Campbell (1800–1872) served as Church of Scotland minister of Rhu (Row) parish. During his years in Rhu, Campbell began to declare, contentiously, that assurance of God's love could be founded only on a doctrine of 'universal pardon' – i.e. that Christ's death had secured forgiveness for all in this life (though ultimate salvation in the next could only be secured through genuine repentance). Under his deep earnestness, devoted piety and the fresh light he shed on divine truth, the parish began to awaken as new life stirred the souls of a peculiarly dead and irreligious population.[105]

Despite, or perhaps partly because of growing opposition to Campbell's new views, but more so as a result of the remarkable power of his fervent sermons and prayers, crowds were attracted to the Rhu church from far and near. 'Campbell's new light created no small stir around the Gareloch and all over the land', wrote a contemporary reviewer. 'There was an awakening of religious life there, which got its first impulse from the Row-kirk. Greenock, Glasgow, Edinburgh thrilled as with the gush of a fresh spring-tide'.[106] As an example, at the height of the controversy regarding his teaching (1832, the year after being deposed by the General Assembly

---

105. Drunkenness, immorality and smuggling were rampant in the district, and, remarkably, from a population of only around two thousand, were scattered as many as thirty public houses. Campbell tried all measures to reach the hearts of such a people.

106. Rowland A. Davenport, *Albury Apostles: The Story of the Body Known as the Catholic Apostolic Church*, Birdlip 1970, p. 40.

of the Church of Scotland, following violent controversy and lengthy
and complex proceedings), Campbell preached in the new churchyard at
Greenock to a congregation of around six thousand.[107] 'Whilst the wicked
were stirred up to wrath by the preaching of living facts, and not empty
doctrines', noted Catholic Apostolic author, C. W. Boase, 'thousands were
converted, and such a confidence in God awakened in them as they had
never before experienced'.[108]

The teaching of Campbell's young assistant, Alexander J. Scott,
with its emphasis on the restoration of the spiritual gifts, also played a
part in instigating the revival, as did the Rev. Robert Story's preaching
of doctrines similar to Campbell's in neighbouring Rosneath (which
doctrines he seemed to have arrived at independently of Campbell).[109]
Yet another influence were guest visits to the area from Edward Irving
(1792–1834), a young Church of Scotland minister from Dumfries-
shire who had previously served as assistant to Thomas Chalmers in
Glasgow. Irving moved to London in 1822 to pastor the Caledonian
Chapel in Covent Garden. Over a period of time Irving came to focus
on certain controversial doctrines; especially the imminence of Jesus'
second coming, the humanity of Christ,[110] and, due to the influence of
Campbell, universal atonement. And as with Campbell, such unorthodox
teaching led to growing opposition from other church leaders.

---

107. Henry Henderson, *The Religious Controversies of Scotland*, Edinburgh 1905,
p. 150.

108. C. W. Boase, quoted in Gordon Strachan, *The Pentecostal Theology of Edward
Irving*, London 1973, p. 216. From 1834 to 1859 Macleod Campbell pastored a Congregational church in Glasgow, during which time he also wrote his classic treatise, *The
Nature of the Atonement*, which was received with mixed response (*DSCHT*, pp. 129-
30; See also J. M. Macleod, *Reminiscences and Reflections, Referring to his Early Ministry
in the Parish of Row, 1825–31*, London 1873; Donald Campbell (Ed.), *Memorials of
John McLeod Campbell*, London 1877).

109. Story, despite never recanting his controversial views, managed to narrowly
escape trial. Interestingly, a local newspaper claimed that the revival in Row parish
originated in Story's labours, and that 'it was not as is frequently the case with revival
efforts, of a transitory character, but abiding in a life of fruitful usefulness and beauty
of character in many of its adherents' (Various Contributors, *Sketches of Churches and
Clergy in the parishes of Row, Rosneath, and Cardross*, Helensburgh 1889, p. 118).

110. N. R. Needham, in *DSCHT*, suggests that in regard to his teaching on Christ's
human nature at least, Irving's declamatory and passionately rhetoric language was
more at fault than his theology (p. 436).

But for the meantime his personal charisma and brilliant rhetorical powers ensured Irving's ongoing popularity. From London he made several trips to Scotland, the first in 1828. He created a stir in his native Dumfries-shire, where neighbouring ministers shut up their churches and went the long Sabbath-day's journey across the Annandale moors to hear him, along with their people. Irving purposely arrived in Edinburgh during the General Assembly week in May, where his early morning lectures – a series of discourses on the Apocalypse – were transferred from St Andrew's Church to the larger West Church (St Cuthbert's), the largest church in Edinburgh, which vast building became packed to capacity day after day. Out of curiosity Dr Chalmers went to hear him, but found his message 'quite woeful'. Still, he admitted, 'there must have been a marvellous power of attraction, that could turn a whole population out of their beds as early as five in the morning'. His biographer, too, exulted that the Edinburgh public, 'not over-excitable, crowded to the streets in the early dawn, thronging that point where the homely West Church with its three galleries, stands under the noble shadow of the Castle Hill, and his wonderful popularity was higher at the conclusion than at the beginning'.[111]

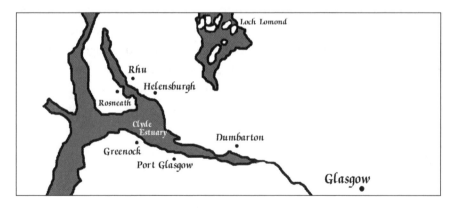

Irving moved on to Glasgow and thence to 'the little westland paradise of Rosneath', where, under the rich sycamores and blossomed laurel he preached from a tent (wooden outdoor pulpit), close by the little church, to a vast crowd. Next day little boats ferried people from all points to Rhu, on the opposite shore of the loch, where a similar scene was repeated. 'The whole district', writes his biographer, 'was stirred by

---

111. Mrs Oliphant, *The Life of Edward Irving*, London 1862, pp. 22-3.

his approach'.[112] Before heading back to London, Irving preached also in Perth and Kirkcaldy, in which latter place so large a crowd packed into the church to hear him before his arrival that the gallery gave way and in the panic that followed as many as thirty-five people were killed (only two or three from the actual fall of the gallery).

In the late spring of the following year (1829) Irving made another short but intensive preaching tour of lowland Scotland. Commencing again in his native Dumfries-shire, 'thousands went after him wherever he appeared, boldly preaching his assailed doctrine before the multitudes who wondered after him'.[113] Irving spent several days in this region. On the Sabbath his tent was pitched in the Annan churchyard, but so many came that they were forced to repair to a large field, where around ten thousand listened to the word, from noon till 5.30, with an hour's interval (a local surveyor went as far as measuring the ground to estimate the attendance, which he reckoned at thirteen thousand). At Dumfries he preached one morning for four hours in the Academy grounds, on the banks of the River Nith, to about ten thousand people. Later the same day he preached for a further three hours at Holywood to around six thousand. In Dunscore, a rural district to the north-west of Dumfries, two or three thousand of Irving's 'beloved brethren' assembled to hear the London preacher.[114] In the Gareloch region Irving was once again welcomed with great warmth and excitement, though in larger towns like Edinburgh and Glasgow, attitudes towards him had cooled notably since the preceding year, and he was repeatedly refused a pulpit in which to preach.[115]

---

112. ibid., pp. 27-8.

113. ibid., p. 83.

114. ibid., p. 85.

115. Partly influenced both by the deeply-held convictions of Scott, who he appointed his assistant in London, and by the movement in Rhu parish, Irving became convinced that the biblical gifts of the Spirit, including tongues and prophecy, should operate in the Church in the present day. But it was his belief in universal atonement that resulted in his ejection from the Church of Scotland in 1833. (Shortly after which, still in 1833, Irving is pictured 'addressing thousands of excited and sympathetic listeners at Cummertrees – on the sands of Dumfries – and on a hillside in Terregles' [A. L. Drummond, *Edward Irving and His Circle*, Cambridge 1934, p. 220]). Many in his congregation remained loyal to their pastor, however, and this led to the formation of the Catholic Apostolic Church, which grew into a worldwide movement after Irving's death in 1834 at the age of 42.

Outpouring of Charismatic Manifestations

It was in the Gareloch district, at the farmstead of Fernicarry, that Isabella Campbell, a frail twenty-year-old, had recently passed away. Her devoted Christian life was considered so beautiful that her pastor, Robert Story, wrote a short memorial of her, and her home became something of a shrine to which pilgrims resorted, gathering round her sister, Mary, on whom the mantle of the departed seemed to fall. Mary had recently become influenced by the teachings of Scott and Irving, with both of whom she was personally acquainted. One Sabbath evening towards the end of March 1830, Mary, who was now thought to be dying of an illness similar to that which had taken her sister, lay in weakness on the sofa while a group of friends around her were engaged in prayer, not least for the restoration of the spiritual gifts. Suddenly, as if possessed by superhuman strength, Mary broke forth in an unknown tongue, in loud ecstatic utterance, for over an hour.

Across the River Clyde in Port Glasgow lived twins, James and George Macdonald (born 1800), and their three sisters. Shipbuilders by trade, the brothers set up a local business shortly after their father's death. James came to knowledge of Christ in the spring of 1828; this having a major impact on George, who, after a few weeks also came into saving faith. To their joy, all three sisters were brought into the same blessed fold at various points soon after. The spirit of prayer poured out upon the brothers was extraordinary – James, especially, often praying for two or even three hours each evening. Although they regularly attended the local parish church, much of their doctrine was learned from the Bible alone, which they studied at every opportunity. Their biographer insists that up to around the turn of the 1830s at least, they had never read any of Irving's volumes, and while they had begun to cross the Clyde to hear the teaching of MacLeod Campbell (whom they disagreed with on some issues, as also Irving), this was because they had previously been taught of God the same truths, and were attracted to Row by love for two of their sisters who had also taken lodgings there.

Margaret, the youngest Macdonald sister, aged just fifteen, suffered from an illness for which the family doctor held little hope of recovery. One day in March 1830, just a few months after coming to faith, and not connected to events in Fernicarry, of which she had not yet heard, a power came upon her, through which she broke forth in mingled praise, prayer and exhortation for two or three hours, also prophesying that 'a mighty baptism of the Spirit' would come to their home that day. When James and George arrived home from work at lunchtime, Margaret addressed them at length, concluding with a prayer that James be endowed with the power of the Holy Ghost. Claiming almost instantly to have received this blessing, James boldly proceeded to command his sister to rise and walk in the name of Christ. She did so, instantly healed.

The next day James wrote to Mary Campbell, whom he knew to be ill, encouraging her to rise by faith from her sickbed and walk. Suggesting that if healed she come at once to Port Glasgow to share the glad tidings, James fully expected to meet Mary at the quayside the following day, and was not surprised when he did! Mary said that as she read his letter it was as if the voice of Christ was speaking to her. 'A mighty power was instantaneously exerted upon me', she said. 'I first felt as if I had been lifted up from the earth, and all my disease taken off me'.[116] She rose and dressed, and though still pale and emaciated, began to take her place in the family circle again.

News travelled fast around the Gareloch region and beyond, and daily meetings continued in both the Macdonald and Campbell homes, where several conversions took place (at one meeting, which continued till six in the morning, four people were converted).[117] In Gareloch, thousands lined the streets and riverbank after Mary announced she was going to pray for the miraculous recovery of a lame boy. The boy was healed, to the delight and applause of the crowd, and was able to walk the several miles home without assistance, albeit with a limp.

It was this combination of factors – the effect of Macleod Campbell's preaching, along with, occasionally that of Irving or Scott, the influence of Isabella Campbell's piety and the impact of Story's '*Memoir*' of her, along with the more recent charismatic influences such as the healing of the lame boy – that gave way to what Margaret Oliphant called

> the singular condition of mind into which the entire (Gareloch) district seems to have been rapt at this special period ... religion had at this crisis taken a hold upon the entire mind of the population,

---

116. Thomas Erskine, *Letters of Thomas Erskine of Linlathen, from 1800 till 1840*, Edinburgh 1877, pp. 179.

117. 'Almost every notable Christian man of the time took the matter into devout and anxious consideration', notes Irving's biographer (Oliphant, *The Life of Edward Irving*, p. 134).

which it very seldom possesses. It was not only the inspiration of their hearts, but the subject of their thoughts, discussions and conversations. They were not only to have been stimulated in personal piety, but occupied to an almost unprecedented degree with those spiritual concerns which are so generally kept altogether apart from the common tide of life. [118]

Mary Campbell's renown spread and people continued to flock to her temporary home in Helensburgh, to which larger premises she moved in the summer of 1830. Other meetings started up in Edinburgh, Glasgow, Musselburgh, Greenock, Rhu and Rosneath. Visitors from different parts of Scotland, England and Ireland flocked also to Port Glasgow, where both the Macdonald brothers had now also received the gift of tongues, accompanied by prophecy and interpretation (both of which commonly centred on Jesus' imminent return).

Controversy Ensues

Not unexpectedly, in a predominantly Calvinist country, events in the west of Scotland came in for some strong criticism. At the 1830 General Assembly of the Church of Scotland the movement was 'treated with jeering and scoffing'.[119] The Rev. Arthur Robertson of Greenock, alarmed by activities in nearby Port Glasgow, made persistent attacks on the movement, claiming that 'the extravagances of the Gareloch Enthusiasts may be traced to constitutional temperament, circumstances under which they have been placed, and the peculiar doctrines which they have gradually imbibed'. The beliefs of those involved, he claimed, were a 'heresy', and the so-called healings which occurred were easily explicable by natural means; e.g. Mary Campbell was already in a convalescent state when the letter arrived commanding her to rise and walk.[120]

---

118. ibid., p. 107.

119. Robert Norton, *Memoirs of James and George Macdonald, of Port-Glasgow*, London 1840, p. 113. Interestingly, while influential Scottish church leader, Andrew Thomson made his opposition to the Row heresy very clear, the Rev. Dr Thomas Chalmers remained curiously detached from the case, and apparently regarded McLeod Campbell's deviation from orthodoxy as microscopic (J. H. S. Burleigh, *Church History of Scotland*, London 1960, pp. 333-4).

120. Rev. A. Robertson, *A Vindication of the Religion of the Land from Misrepresentation and an Exposure of the Absurd Pretensions of the Gareloch Enthusiasts, in a Letter to Thomas Erskine, Esq., Advocate*, Edinburgh 1830, p. 248.

In like manner, an article in *The Helensburgh and Gareloch Times* claimed that: 'The healings were probably the result of strong religious excitement which raised persons more or less hysterical above the nervous disorders by which they suffered.'[121] Rowland A. Davenport's observations are equally significant. He points out that both Isabella and Mary Campbell, as well as Margaret Macdonald, all suffered from the same lung disease. He says this is worthy of note, not because it offers a complete explanation of what happened, but because 'this physical condition does quite often give rise to a heightened psychical sensitivity – as witness John Keats and many another poet and artist who died young'.[122] Meanwhile, John Darby and Benjamin Newton journeyed north as representatives of the Brethren group to investigate goings on, and came to the conclusion that the displays were demonic.

Not wishing to get too involved in these unusual developments, both J. M. Campbell and A. J. Scott distanced themselves from the movement they had helped instigate. Edward Irving, however, was greatly excited by regular reports of goings on in Scotland and doubly encouraged by Mary Campbell's revelation that Irving's own teaching had been the key to her receiving supernatural gifting. Wasting no time, a small team of independent enquirers from London decided, in the autumn of 1830, to travel to the scene to investigate developments first-hand. As a result of the delegates' very positive findings over three weeks, Irving focused on preparing his London church for a revival of the Spirit's empowerment.[123] A contemporary of Irving, William Nixon, spoke of 'events of stirring power in Glasgow and down the Clyde' causing 'a widespread excitement for the time. Refined and educated ladies like one with whom I was personally acquainted, residing near Greenock, ladies who had been remarkable for their retiring character and habits, caught the rising spirit, and might be seen vehemently

---

121. Various Contributors, *Sketches of Churches and Clergy*, p. 103.

122. Davenport, *Albury Apostles*, p. 44.

123. When the manifestations of tongues and prophecy spread to the main meetings in his 2,000-member church, and he did not censure their operation, Irving was ejected from the pastorate of the church he had built. He and hundreds of his followers moved to a church in Newman Street, where the charismatic expressions continued, albeit under an ecclesiastical framework equally opposed to the more organic developments occurring in Scotland.

holding forth at meetings and even, at least one case known to myself, on the public streets'.[124]

Very quickly from their genesis, the two main strains of the movement, one in Ferincarry, the other centred on Port Glasgow, were received by those who became familiar with them in quite contrasting manners. Initially Robert Story of Rosneath was fully convinced of the genuineness of the movement in his locality. He wrote to Dr Chalmers of his conviction 'that these things are of God, and not of men. If a delusion, it is one of the most cunning Satan ever devised'.[125] It didn't take long, however, for the pastor to imbibe deep reservations about all that he had heard or seen regarding events in the Fernicarry district. He was particularly disturbed by the change in Mary Campbell's character.[126] In 1831, having married William R. Caird, a businessman from Edinburgh who had shown interest in the movement, Mary moved with him to London to supervise the Catholic Apostolic Church, founded by Irving's followers. Now a respectable 'lady' of high society in London, Mary occasionally returned to her native parish, accompanied by friends of similar station, and a servant with them. Elegantly draped in expensive silk attire, she now seemed indifferent to the humble surroundings of her mother and siblings. Not only so, but she seemed to have forgotten the prophetic word given her just a year or two previously, that having risen from her sick-bed, she would at once go forth to evangelise the heathen, otherwise she and her father's house would be destroyed, and that speedily.

Story had also been deeply disturbed by the attitude of Mary and her companions in the Campbell home around the time of her healing. By prophetic 'confirmation', two young men were encouraged to idle themselves for days or weeks on end in the house, while Mrs Campbell worked herself into a state of exhaustion in order to provide for them. More so, Samuel Campbell, a brother of Mary and the head of the

---

124. William Nixon, *Autobiographical Notes*, Perth 1929, p. 23. While Nixon believed that 'a portion of the many' who were awakened at that time 'became serious on good grounds, and to their own permanent well-being', he felt that for others the interest awakened was not lasting (ibid.).

125. Robert H. Story, *Memoir of the Life of the Rev. Robert Story, Late Minister of Rosneath*, Cambridge 1862, p. 209.

126. Robert Norton, who later chronicled the Scottish movement, also felt that Mary's healing became 'much tarnished by subsequent extravagances' ((Norton, *Memoirs of James and George Macdonald*, p. 109).

family, was at the time dying a painful death, and, his room being
directly below Mary's, had to endure the shouting and leaping which
night after night disturbed his rest. One night, as if by a desperate effort
of his decaying energies, he laboured to ascend the stairs in order to
entreat the inspirited revellers to be quiet. He was promptly rebuked,
'Get thee behind me, Satan'. The poor boy was apparently not even left
in peace on his death, when there ensued a vain and unseemly attempt
to raise him back to life.[127]

There was controversy, too, over the 'tongues' spoken, which Robertson of Greenock dismissed as pure 'gibberish'. For a while Mary was
convinced that her main 'tongue' was the language of the North Pacific
Pelew Islanders, although she made no claim to ever having heard or read
that language.[128] To her spoken tongues Mary added automatic writing,
feeling occasionally compelled, under divine guidance, to transcribe her
heavenly communications at great rapidity on to paper. Being keen to
see these jottings, samples were sent to Dr Chalmers, who in turn passed
them on to two linguistic experts. The scholars concurred that the combination of letters formed did not fit any regular phonetic style nor did it
resemble any language of which they were remotely acquainted. It soon
became settled among the believers, therefore, that the 'tongues' uttered
were no earthly dialect but some type of ecstatic otherworldly speech.

Before she moved to London, but 'only after a schism had occurred
among the "gifted" people', the Rev. Story managed after some time to
induce Ms Campbell to leave 'those tumultuous meetings in Helensburgh', and stay with him and his wife in their country cottage at

---

127. Other concerns Story had with Fernicarry events were the 'blasphemous appeal-
ing to God to decide by lot, that which was no sooner decided than set aside ... the
ramblings of two persons, each inspired as they said by the spirit of the Lord, directly
contradicting each other' in Story's own presence, and the prophecies which the minister heard and which were written to him, that never came to pass (Story, *Memoir of
the Life of the Rev. Robert Story*, pp. 222-3).

128. She also claimed she could speak both Turkish and Chinese and that God had
given her these 'tongues' so that she could serve as a missionary abroad, an ambition
she never truly fulfilled. Believing 'tongues' to be natural languages was also common
during the early stages of the Azusa Street awakening, when many who had received
that gift went to countries where they believed their 'tongues' would be understood
by natives. Invariably this turned out not to be the case, although, often – as with A.
G. Garr, who went to India under the impression that his 'tongue' was Bengali – they
remained as successful evangelists in the countries they moved to.

Mamore. Here, writes Story, 'away from those blasphemous scenes, where such gross familiarity was dared with the name of the Eternal, she came to herself, and confessed that she had spoken and prophesied in the name of the Lord God Almighty when only giving vent to her own fancies'. Lest it be thought this confession was drawn out of her under pressure, it was at an earlier period that Mary, in a similar spirit of remarkable humility, wrote to Story to say she had 'come to the resolution to … confess my sin and error for calling my own impressions the voice of God. Oh, it is no light thing to use the holy name irreverently, as I have been made to feel'.[129]

The Macdonalds in Port Glasgow

By all accounts events in Port Glasgow proceeded along more balanced and consistent lines, and were accorded highly favourable praise from many (often distinguished) visitors, some of whom spent several weeks in the district. One learned man who met the Macdonald twins just prior to the unusual manifestations that arose among them, wrote: 'I was conscious that I had met with no Christians, anywhere, less likely to be themselves deceived or more incapable of attempting to deceive others. I know none more simple in their views of divine truth, or more entirely devoted to Jesus in their lives than they.'[130] Robert Norton states that both men were naturally very cautious towards any form of supernatural manifestation and had no thoughts of the spiritual gifts until 'the very eve of His miraculous manifestations in them'. Unlike Mary Campbell's group in Fernicarry, the twins stated their belief that tongues were not naturally-spoken languages and repeatedly did they exhort believers to trust, not in any supernatural gifting, but in the Rock of their salvation.[131]

J. Thompson, a doctor from London, curious of goings on in the north, paid a visit to Port Glasgow in early 1831. Having been told that an extraordinary degree of excitement prevailed among this little band of the Lord's followers, occasioning a suspension of their daily occupations, Thompson found the opposite to be true; 'They were walking orderly, and instead of being lifted up with pride, were humble', he

---

129. Story, *Memoir of the Life of the Rev. Robert Story*, pp. 231-2.

130. Quoted in Norton, *Memoirs of James and George Macdonald*, pp. 99-100.

131. ibid., pp. 78, 109, 118, 191.

observed. 'A godly sobriety of mind, the most remote from any feverish excitement of a heated imagination, chastens and regulates their conduct, a sobriety that would ill assort with the visions of a superstitious enthusiasm, as with that indulgence of the flesh which is ever hunting after signs'.[132] For over three weeks Thompson enjoyed an almost uninterrupted intercourse with these disciples, meeting with them every evening, and often for prayer in the morning and at noon.

At some, but not all, of the meetings Thompson attended, tongues were spoken, sometimes accompanied by a message 'from the Lord' directed to him personally. In each instance the word gave specific guidance concerning an issue of which no one but Thompson had any knowledge and which would have made no sense to anyone else. Regarding the tongues spoken, the English visitor stated, 'to have any adequate perception of their power they must be both seen and felt'. In Thompson's lodgings worked a young Christian servant – 'in conversation slow and incapable of putting together two sentences with any regard to arrangement'. Yet this girl could speak in tongues, and would then give an exhortation 'in a manner and with a power such as must irresistibly lead any witness of it to the conclusion that ... the finger of the Lord was manifested therein'. Thompson was not alone in referring to an individual whose natural singing voice was inharmonious and who had no ear for keeping time. Yet, singing in the Spirit, this person 'could pour forth a rich strain of melody of which each note was musical, and uttered with a sweetness and power of expression that was truly astonishing'.[133]

Significantly, and generally overlooked by historians of this intriguing movement, the gift of tongues was the only one the believers acknowledged to have received, in the sense of an abiding talent resident within them. For this reason they did not recognise as gifts, interpretation, prophecy and revelation, which they occasionally exercised. Thomson concluded that the movement was indeed, 'a fresh instance of the mercy of God ... a sprinkling of the latter rain, a fruit of the Pentecostal effusion of the Spirit'.[134] Equally open to misinterpretation, any instance of

---

132. J. Thompson, *A Brief Account of a Visit to Some of the Brethren in the West of Scotland*, London 1831, pp. 14-5. 17.

133. ibid., pp. 27-30.

134. ibid., p. 14.

prophecy uttered was not in the form of predicting future events, but by way of offering edification, exhortation and spiritual comfort based on the infallible word of God.

Notable also is the response of Thomas Erskine of Linlathen, a Christian and prominent advocate. Fascinated by news of events in Port Glasgow, he at once repaired to the Macdonalds' home, where he stayed for no less than six weeks and often witnessed the famed manifestations. Thoroughly impressed by what he saw, Erskine at once published a tract, followed by a more sizeable volume in strong defence of the charismata. He concluded: 'Whilst I see nothing in Scripture against the reappearance or rather continuance of miraculous gifts in the Church, but a great deal for it, I must further say that I see a great deal of internal evidence in the West Country to prove their genuine miraculous character, especially in the speaking with tongues.'[135]

The London delegates, who spent three weeks in the Port Glasgow area investigating the movement, were also highly impressed with what they witnessed. On their return to London, leader of the group, John B. Cardale, a solicitor, issued a lengthy and most favourable report. He concluded enthusiastically:

> ... the individuals thus gifted are persons living in close communion with God, and in love towards Him, and towards all men; abounding in faith and joy and peace; having an abhorrence of sin, and a thirst for holiness, with an abasement of self and yet with a hope full of immortality, such as I never witnessed elsewhere, and which I find nowhere recorded but in the history of the early church: and just as they are fervent in spirit, so are they

---

135. Erskine, *Letters of Thomas Erskine*, p. 182. Erskine found that two of the Macdonalds' prophetic deliverances appeared to be based on reports contained in the local newspaper. When this was brought to the attention of the brother in question, he immediately acknowledged his error, insisting, to Erskine's total satisfaction, that it was done subconsciously, and at once dismissing those particular utterances as not being supernaturally received. However, it was most notably as he closely followed developments in London rather than with what he personally witnessed in Port Glasgow, that a complete overturn took place in Erskine's judgement. Before the end of 1833 he required to write, 'My mind has undergone a considerable change ... I have seen reason to disbelieve that it is the Spirit of God which is in M__ , and I do not feel that I have stronger reason to believe that it is in others' (ibid., p. 145). He became ever more strongly convinced that the manifestations he had witnessed were delusive and that the entire movement had originated and been maintained through a dreadful mistake.

diligent in the performance of all the relative duties of life. They are totally devoid of anything like fanaticism or enthusiasm; but, on the contrary, are persons of great simplicity of character, and of sound common sense. They have no fanciful theology of their own: they make no pretensions to deep knowledge: they are the very opposite of sectarians, both in conduct and principle: they do not assume to be teachers: they are not deeply read; but they seek to be taught of God, in the perusal of, and meditation on, his revealed word, and to 'live quiet and peaceful lives in all godliness and honesty'.[136]

Robert Norton, a doctor and one of Irving's six-member delegation, went on to marry Margaret Macdonald, who moved with him to reside in London. Becoming well acquainted with the Macdonald brothers (who, like him, came to distance themselves from aspects of the London movement, though always believing that its origins were divinely inspired),[137] Norton became familiar with how the Macdonalds

attached a sacredness to the Bible which many other Christians would have considered almost superstitious, and most jealous were they for its infallible completeness, its supremacy, and even exclusiveness as the only and all-sufficient rule of faith and practise ... There was about them both, at times, when the power of the Spirit was most upon them, such heavenliness and awe-inspiring solemnity in their whole appearance and manner; such deep-toned inimitable music in their voices; such ecstatic rapture in their eye; such a supernatural brightness upon their countenances, as stamped upon their utterances a seal of heavenly authority, the impression of which is quite incommunicable.[138]

While almost to the last, noted Norton, the brothers' domestic circle was broken in upon by an almost continual succession of visitors, their private lives of deep devotion and their outward characters of piety

---

136. 'The Morning Watch', December 1830, quoted in Strachan, *The Pentecostal Theology of Edward Irving*, pp. 71-2.

137. They disagreed, for example, as did Norton, with the rising up of members in Irving's church of men assuming apostleship, who made the voice of the prophets subordinate to their superior office, gradually suppressing it.

138. Norton, *Memoirs of James and George Macdonald*, pp. 158, 160.

underwent no deterioration. In fact, their regard for Sabbath observance became even stronger, and they maintained to the end a routine of regular fasting. They continued to attend their parish church, 'although continually alluded to and attacked in a very painful manner, and made the gaze of the whole congregation'.[139] The deposition of J. M. Campbell from the Church of Scotland they saw as their own expulsion, and only then did they resign their membership.

The Macdonalds continued to feel a strong urge to preach the gospel to sinners, opening both their own house and a hired small chapel in neighbouring Greenock for that purpose, to which both places great crowds attended for a while. Often their home and stairs, and even the street, were crowded, and at least one evening, James stood on a chair under a lamp and preached in the driving rain to a crowd estimated at upwards of 1,000 people; yet they stood there all the time. Emphasis on the charismata continued to distinguish their teaching, while conversions at their meetings continued to occur (one convert was a boy of five, whose transformation in terms of change in morals and depth of spirituality astonished all who knew him).

All the ministers in the district spoke vehemently against the two brothers, yet it was noticeable that during the cholera epidemic of 1832, nearly all of them fled the area, leaving the multitude of perishing souls to die around them unvisited. In Port Glasgow almost the only individuals who would enter the houses of the sick were the Macdonalds; and to the infirm these brothers devoted themselves day and night, not merely going wherever they were sent for, but seeking out neglected cases, and ministering to both the body and the soul. Not satisfied with this, James felt constrained to walk each week to the hospital in Greenock, and there minister from ward to ward to the neglected dying. Wrote their biographer: 'Their Christian devotedness at this period, and its contrast with the very opposite conduct of others, did not pass unnoticed, and almost universally secured for them, ever afterwards, at least a silent respect.'[140]

---

139. ibid., p. 179.

140. ibid., p. 198. Another facet of the Macdonalds' lives was their repeated decline of invitations – on the grounds that they did not feel it to be God's will – to go to London made by some of the affluent and influential members of Irving's congregation; commendable given the honourable provision that undoubtedly would have been made for them and the inadequate maintenance of their business, which through various losses and misfortunes, had never been successful, and was then, as always, a most anxious, laborious toil.

Decline of the Movement

After three years the revival intensity began to decline, shortly after which time the brothers' health began to deteriorate, and in 1835 both died of tuberculosis.[141] Accounts of their last days on earth are sublimely poignant. In the days prior to James' death on 2nd February, he often said, 'Jesus smiles on me' – 'Twas almost a vision', observed his sister; 'the veil was almost rent; he was so near the upper sanctuary … The whole of his illness was peace; his rest was so perfect in his God, and his will so lost in the will of the Father'.[142] George passed away seven months later, 'his eyes fixed upwards with a rapturous gaze, and his countenance shining with the radiance of that glory which God hath prepared for them that love him'.[143]

As suggested previously, this early charismatic movement is often dismissed in its entirety as a woeful mixture of erroneous teaching and purely fleshly manifestations; thus ignoring, for example, the numerous reports of the orderly manner in which the Port Glasgow meetings were conducted, or the consistent walk of manifest godliness in which both James and George Macdonald lived to their very last breath. Exceptions do exist, such as the studious research of Dave MacPherson, who nevertheless holds strong views on the issues concerned, seeking to prove that a seemingly small error made by an otherwise godly family (the Macdonalds) in a remote Scottish community nearly two centuries ago is the true genesis of all the errors, false prophecies, and end-times hype prevalent among dispensationalists (those who believe in a pre-tribulational rapture), whose views are rampant throughout the world today.[144]

---

141. It is a tragic irony that both of the recipients of the physical healings that sparked off the movement (Mary Campbell and Margaret Macdonald), along with the man who played such an active part in both healings, James Macdonald, as well as his confidant and brother, George, along with the leader of the movement in London, Edward Irving, were all to meet their deaths within around a decade of these initial events (Mary died while ministering with her husband in Austria in 1839 and Margaret passed away about a year later, aged around thirty).

142. Norton, *Memoirs of James and George Macdonald*, p. 238.

143. ibid., p. 246.

144. Dave MacPherson, *Incredible Cover Up*, Plainfield, N.J. 1975. See also Arnold Dallimore, *The Life of Edward Irving: The Forerunner of the Charismatic Movement*, Edinburgh 1983).

There was one further major, lasting influence of this oft-overlooked Scottish movement. While the influence of events in west Scotland on the ministry of Irving have been clearly noted, it is becoming increasingly recognised that Irving's own teaching on the gifts of the Spirit may have played a role in the origins of American Pentecostalism. For example, leading Pentecostal pioneer, Charles Parham mentions Irving in a sermon preached in Kansas City just three weeks after his students first received the gift of glossolalia in 1900. Other pre-Pentecostal pioneers such as Alexander Dowie – himself a native of Scotland – Kelso Carter and Horace Bushnell, also wrote of Irving and his teachings prior to 1901.[145] Further, a revived interest in Irving and his movement has been observable from the second half of the twentieth century.

Did this movement constitute a genuine evangelical revival, as identified in the Introduction to this book (see page 21)? Some will answer with a definite 'No', not least given the occurrence of tongues and other unusual manifestations during its progress; which they claim have no biblical warranty in the Church today; neither owing to the clearly heretical doctrine openly taught by the likes of Campbell and Irving. Others will point to the use and encouragement of the use of spiritual gifts – including tongues and prophecy – in the New Testament Church as clear evidence of their ongoing validity, and will regard errors made by believers in the Rhu and Port Glasgow areas (such as wrongly assuming their tongues to be an existing language) as being natural mistakes among those exercising gifts that were new to both them and the wider Church of the time. And some of the new views espoused by the likes of Campbell and Irving, though truly

---

145. In regard to this area of research, Dorries remarks that the scope of the influence of this 'three-year revival … has yet to be measured fully'. (Burgess (Ed.), *NIDPCM*, p. 1192). Yet it does appear that direct links between the two movements – while not non-existent, as most historians have hitherto assumed – were few. Yet similarities between the two groups are striking. Both saw tongues as a) the first and foremost gift of the Spirit; b) evidence of Spirit-baptism; c) of the same nature as the tongues in Acts 2, and therefore; d) as being a naturally-spoken language which e) God was giving them to use in missionary endeavours overseas. In addition, both groups viewed the charismata as a permanent possession of the Church, which gifts had been previously withheld because of believers' lack of faith. Other similarities are that both groups were essentially Arminian, each was rooted in strong expectations of the second advent, and both were initially regarded by the mainstream Church as unorthodox cults.

radical in their day, are now quite widely held by millions of believers across the globe.[146]

Ultimately these spiritual stirrings to the west and north of Glasgow in the early 1830s – like all evangelical movements, to a greater or lesser degree – can be viewed as a mixture of the divine and the human, the genuine and the counterfeit. Certainly the human element is more discernible at various distinct points, particularly in regard to the practice of the spiritual gifts; whether this is true of the movement overall, and if so, to what extent, church historians and theologians may, naturally, continue to debate for many years to come. Whatever the case, and not least given growing recognition of Irving as the true 'Forerunner of the Charismatic Movement',[147] it can hardly be disputed that the worldwide impact of this fascinating, controversial movement in one or two west Scotland parishes has been considerable.

---

146. It is interesting to note that as esteemed a church leader as Robert Murray McCheyne regarded the likes of Irving, notwithstanding his deposition from the Church of Scotland, as an eminent man of God. 'I look back upon him with awe', he wrote after Irving's death, 'as on the saints and martyrs of old. A holy man in spite of all his delusions and errors. He is now with his God and Saviour, whom he wronged so much, yet, I am persuaded, loved so sincerely' (A. A. Bonar, *Memoirs and Remains of the Rev. Robert Murray McCheyne*, Edinburgh 1892, p. 27).

147. See Dallimore, *The Life of Edward Irving*, p. 175.

CHAPTER 6

The 1839–42 Revival

Introduction

The years 1838 to 1842 saw a powerful revival movement spread throughout much of Scotland. Fascinatingly, what distinguishes this remarkable movement from other widespread Scottish revivals of both an earlier era, such as the Evangelical Revival of the eighteenth century, or a later period, such as the even more extensive 1858–61 movement is that it was largely exclusive to Scotland. It's not that other parts of the British Isles experienced nothing in the way of spiritual awakening in the years 1838–42. They did. But these were generally confined to specific localities. For example, in Wales 'a wonderful revival' descended on the parish of Llanuwchllyn, six miles from Bala, in Merionethshire, during the closing weeks of 1839, although other parts of Wales were unaffected.[1]

Neither was there any corresponding general awakening in England between 1838 and 1842. Or was there? Certainly several quite significant revivals did occur in different parts of England within these few years, albeit again mainly of a localised nature. A remarkable revival broke out in Wycliffe Chapel, Stepney, in the East End of London in early

---

1. In one or two localities (e.g. Henllan) it has been considered that they showed more the work of man than of God, having been influenced by a Welsh translation of Finney's *Lectures on Revival*, which appeared in 1839 (Jones, *Favoured With Frequent Revivals*, pp. 39-41).

1839. Minister of this Church of England parish was philanthropist, pastor and founder of numerous children's charities, the Rev. Andrew Reed. During the course of the year, over 300 people under conviction spontaneously and separately conversed with the minister, and 200 professed Christ as Saviour and joined the church. The awakening, Reed emphasised, occurred not in a large district but within a single congregation – which had previously just over one half of its number in communion – and without making one addition to itself from any neighbouring community.

As it turns out, this revival wasn't totally confined to one particular locality. Fascinatingly, when a Congregational minister in Tewkesbury in Gloucestershire – over a hundred miles west of London – read Reed's account of the Wycliffe movement to his congregation, the church set itself to pray and a religious awakening followed, through which fifty-eight people were added to the church. In like manner, a Baptist minister near London reported fifty-seven additions to his membership roll following a public reading of Reed's 'Narrative', and a Wesleyan minister reported 1,600 new members to his circuit as a result of the stimulus given to his ministry by reading 'Revival of Religion'.[2] Elsewhere, among the Wesleyans, in 1841–2 there occurred an emotive revival among the Methodists in Jersey,[3] while a degree of awakening was also reported from southern Ireland during this period.

Perhaps the most fascinating revival to have occurred in England during this period, or indeed, anytime during the nineteenth century, was that which overcame the small rural parish of Charlinch, in north Somerset, at the close of 1841. The revival centred around the ministry of the colourful and controversial Rev. Henry James Prince (1811– 1899), and continued for several months, with many people of all ages undergoing deep spiritual awakening.[4]

It is possible that there was a common theme linking many or all of the above movements together – along with others not mentioned

---

2. Shaw, *The Greatest Is Charity*, pp. 226-234.

3. Moore, *Methodism in the Channel Islands*, p. 98.

4. Murray McCheyne was aware of the Charlinch revival and refers to it in a letter dated August 18th 1842 (Andrew A. Bonar, *Memoir and Remains of the Rev. Robert Murray McCheyne*, p. 272).

here – though no historian has ever suggested this. Clearly, further research is required in this area. But at the least it is apparent that no deep spiritual awakening spread across England or the British Isles as a whole in the period under review. Nor, indeed, was there any widespread revival in America in the late 1830s and, notwithstanding Finneyite influences, it is incorrect to claim, as Fergus Ferguson of the Evangelical Union Church did, that the British movement of 1839–42 'came across the Atlantic from America as it subsequently did in 1859 and 1873'.[5] It is fair to assume, then, that Scotland was alone in its experience of extensive evangelical revival during the years 1838–42.

When we look for the specific dynamics within Scotland that prepared the way for the revival movement that gripped many parts of the land in the late 1830s we find a number of contributory streams – these of an ecclesiastical, political, spiritual or economic nature. Regarding economic factors, in the years following 1836, crop failures, especially of the potato, caused enormous hardship and misery. Richard Carwardine argues that for the industrial belt of the Lowlands, the economic depression of the late 1830s and early 1840s created conditions in which revivals could flourish. Colliers in Lanarkshire, jute-mill workers in Dundee, factory workers in Perth, Shotts ironworkers, and servants, quarrymen, colliers and carpet-factory workers in Kilmarnock were all drawn into the revival. But, argued Carwardine, it was the group hardest hit by depression, the handloom weavers of e.g. Kilsyth, who made the biggest contribution to 'an evangelical explosion that helped set the tone of the whole revival movement'. For these and others living marginal existences, he suggested, 'the revival perhaps offered spiritual succour and support'.[6]

The 1830s was also a decade of social and political change, in which developed an increased suspicion of both government and Church. Within the Church the challenges of radical leaders such as Edward Irving, John McLeod Campbell, James Morison and John Kirk forced a renewed consideration of Calvinist orthodoxy. In conjunction with these new views, the commotion created by the release in Britain of

5. Fergus Ferguson, *A History of the Evangelical Union from its Origin to the Present Time*, Glasgow 1876, p. 7.

6. Carwardine, *Transatlantic Revivalism*, p. 96.

Charles Finney's *Lectures on Revivals of Religion* in 1839 (four years after it was published in America), led to a novel outlook by many in regard to the promotion of revivals and the work of the Holy Spirit. Finney's 'new methods' were a primary impetus for the wave of revivalism that affected many Congregational churches in Scotland in the period under consideration and also for the inauguration of the Evangelical Union, an association of Arminian Congregational churches, in 1843 (see page 372).[7]

Another factor which contributed to the spread of revival during this period was the massive Church Extension scheme, launched by Thomas Chalmers in 1834. Necessitated by the enormous growth in population during preceding decades, the project constituted a great campaign for the multiplication of churches and the subdivision of parishes, so that, predicted Chalmers, 'there will not one poor family be found in our land who might not, if they will, have entry and accommodation in a place of worship and religious instruction'.[8] Within four years, Chalmers had raised over £200,000 for the scheme and had added 187 congregations to the Established Church.

Within the Church of Scotland the single most significant factor that pre-empted the showers of blessing that fell on many parts of Scotland in this period was the conflict between Church and State over issues relating to church governance. In actual fact the contention that eventually resulted in the Disruption (see page 441) had been simmering since the passing of the Patronage Act of 1712, whereby landowners gained the right to choose their local parish minister. Such policy was strongly contended by the Evangelical party within the national Church, who, in the 1830s, had assumed a majority in the General Assembly for the first time in approximately 100 years. The Evangelicals passed a Veto Act within Established Church statutes, allowing parishioners a right to regulate patronage. Following a lengthy, complicated and embittered ecclesiastical and judicial process, which became known as the 'Ten Years Conflict',

---

7. The opening of minds to new expressions of Christianity may also be observed in the growth of Brethrenism, the Church of Christ, Primitive Methodism, the Catholic Apostolic Church and Mormonism, as well as in a renewed Millennialism, all around this time.

8. *DSCHT*, p. 160.

during which the Veto Act was annulled, over 450 ministers and 60 per cent of church members left the Established Church to form the Free Church of Scotland.

The issues being debated led to a re-examination by many church leaders and lay believers in Scotland as to their true values, as well as to a deeper unity and passion among non-intrusionists regarding spiritual matters. As the 1830s wore on, the debate became more and more heated. Scotland was in a flame of doctrinal discussion and argument. Families became divided; and even boys at school ranged themselves into hostile camps of moderates and non-intrusionists. The polemical literature was incredible in quantity – Thomas Guthrie knew of '782 distinct pamphlets on this one subject, printed during these years, circulated by thousands and falling like snow-flakes all over the land'.[9] Newspapers teemed with adverts and reports of meetings from all sides – in towns, villages and hamlets. All of these factors helped lead to the development of a powerful and widespread spiritual awakening across the land.

The South

Initiatory Awakenings

James Blair in Beith and Girvan

The son of a Secession minister from Fife, James Blair trained in the Baptist ministry before taking up his first charge at Saltcoats, Ayrshire from 1836. He was a zealous evangelist who laboured throughout the county with untiring diligence,[10] and a good work commenced in his second year of service in the town of Beith. Gatherings were large and Blair found impressions 'increasingly great'. He said of his work there that he was 'gratified above all other scenes almost; although Bridge of Weir and Ayr have been exceedingly interesting. Surely the

---

9. David K. & Charles J. Guthrie, *Autobiography of Thomas Guthrie, and Memoir*, vol. 2, London 1874, p. 27.

10. From March 1838 to March '39, Blair preached 'in all 429 times; 272 of these missionary; 157 to church meetings; 59 out of doors and about 24 in different towns and villages; baptised 14'. This was in addition to prayer meetings, private conversations and a class for boys and girls on Friday evenings (Rev. James Blair, *The Scottish Evangelist. The Life and Labours of the Rev. James Blair, of the Bridge of Allan*, Glasgow 1860, pp. 41-2).

Lord was with us this week. Many seem impressed. A general serious feeling exists'.[11]

A more blessed work still accompanied Blair's labours further south, in Girvan, two years later, which coastal town was 'in great ferment about Socinianism' (Unitarianism). On his four-day visit in March 1838, Blair's evening congregations rose daily, increasing from 240 to 270, then to 300 and finally to 350, by which point the meeting place became totally crammed, with others standing round the windows outside. A further visit in June saw equally large congregations and numerous cases of personal conversion. Out of these, Blair formed a meeting of thirty-seven for religious instruction. So deep was the impression made that about twenty persons agreed to aid their neighbours by holding meetings in their homes for reading and conversing on the Scriptures. 'Indeed, there seemed to be', wrote Blair, 'an extensive awakening about the things of God, and to all appearance, numbers of souls were, through the blessing of the Most High, brought to know and love the Saviour'.[12]

On a further visit to Girvan in August, Blair preached for four days with still greater encouragement and excitement than ever. His diary reads: 'Monday, Methodist chapel, 200; Tuesday, back of the old kirk, 500; Wednesday, Down corner, 700 or 800; Thursday, Methodist chapel, ten minutes past nine in the morning, a meeting for serious enquirers, about fifty … Baptised three persons about six in the morning, and another about one p.m.; in all two men and two women.' Blair returned to Girvan several times that year, but never again achieved the impressive numbers he had earlier attracted.[13]

Horatius Bonar in Kelso

Horatius Bonar (1808–1889) was ordained at Kelso Church of Scotland in November 1837.[14] His brother Andrew, who officiated at the event, records: 'At the moment of laying on of hands I felt a strange thrill of

---

11. ibid.

12. ibid., pp. 55-7.

13. ibid., p. 58. Blair went on to serve as an evangelist with the Scottish Baptist Union (1844–48), before becoming pastor at Bridge of Allan (1853–59).

14. Horatius was the brother of Andrew and John Bonar, both also notable ministers in the Church of Scotland (until the Disruption, when all three went over to the Free Church).

solemnity and love towards him. The prayer was most excellent; I think the Lord was there.'[15] God's presence continued to be felt, thanks largely to Horatius's faithful and earnest ministry. His first sermon in Kelso was a call to prayer for revival.[16] Indeed, he incessantly exhorted his congregation to pray – 'prayer for myself, their minister – prayer for the conversion of sinners – prayer for the outpouring of the Spirit ... I lay much weight on this'.[17] Following a return visit to the Borders town less than two months later, Andrew records (24th January 1838) that he 'heard at Kelso of a work beginning; two or three have already come to Horace in deep anxiety, chiefly people that seemed to know the truth'. When he again preached there twelve months later, Andrew Bonar stated, 'Horace's people seem very much solemnised'.[18] The work grew steadily and impressively over ensuing months (see page 377).

Congregational work in Alexandria

Robert Simpson was a young man from Saltcoats who had established a drapery business in Glasgow by the age of twenty. A keen church-goer, he soon developed the desire to become a minister and was thus admitted to the Glasgow Congregational Academy. He used to relate how tough it was for him to get up and be at Woodside Place for his Hebrew class at 7 a.m.; then back in town for the opening of his shop at Candleriggs; and to run from hall to business, from business to college, from college back to business, and then again to hall in the afternoon, closing with business in the evening! A band of students used to gather in his home for food, fellowship, prayer and earnest discussion. A death of a friend caused them to consider more seriously their witness for Christ and they agreed to venture to some outlying villages of Glasgow on their next vacation. When the spring recess of 1838 arrived, only six proved true to their word (including Simpson, John Kirk and Fergus Ferguson), and these journeyed to the Vale of Leven, where, in Alexandria, there appeared a providential opening.

15. Bonar, *Andrew A. Bonar: Diary and Life*, Edinburgh 1893 (reprinted 1961), p. 57.

16. A. W. Medley, 'Horatius Bonar D.D.: A Brief Sketch to Commemorate the Centenary of his Death', in *The Evangelical Library Bulletin*, Spring 1989, pp. 2-6.

17. Presbytery of Aberdeen, *Evidence on the Subject of Revivals Taken Before the Presbytery of Aberdeen*, Aberdeen 1841, p. 62.

18. ibid., pp. 58, 76.

The nightly gatherings – led from the start by Kirk and on the basis of protracted meetings known to be successful elsewhere – were crowded, especially on the closing Sunday, when a prolonged evening meeting was followed by another service, then an inquiry meeting. When at last the evangelists plucked up the courage to ask anxious enquirers to remain behind, they were so surprised when sixteen people did so that they barely knew how to deal with them! All sixteen professed to find Christ. A general awakening ensued and soon a Congregational church was formed with over fifty new members. By the time a chapel had been constructed six months later that number had doubled.[19] Until this church was established, it was seen as 'a memorable day among the Congregationalists of Glasgow when a large contingent of the converts came up, after due examination, to partake of the ordinance of the Lord's supper in Mr Pullar's church in North Albion Street'.[20] Out of this first batch of converts emerged several ministers of the gospel, including two Hutcheson brothers and two MacAuslane brothers.[21]

Kilsyth

Beginnings

Prayer meetings had been carried on in Kilsyth since the revival days of 1742, but by the turn of the century these had become largely neglected and the state of the parish on the induction of the Rev. William H. Burns to the Church of Scotland in 1821 was 'deplorable', leading to

---

19. W. D. McNaughton, *Helensburgh and Alexandria: A Tale of Two Congregational Churches*, Glasgow 1996, pp. 12-14. Some Congregational records place emphasis on the fact that this movement occurred some nine months prior to the mighty nation-wide movement assumed to have been sparked by the Kilsyth revival in the summer of 1839; apparently suggesting that events in Alexandria marked the real beginning of the larger awakening. Fergus Ferguson believed the two movements were independent of each other, though he does singularly compare John Morison to William Chalmers Burns, both being young unordained licentiates embarked on zealous itinerant evangelism in Scotland at the same time (but he insists that Morison was more scholarly) [Ferguson, *A History of the Evangelical Union*, pp. 12, 277].

20. 'Scottish Congregationalist Magazine' 1887, quoted in McNaughton, *Early Congregational Independency in Lowland Scotland*, vol. 2, p. 82.

21. Simpson also began to conduct Sabbath evening services in a hall at Bridgeton, where 'great good was done', and where soon a church was formed on the site of a garden donated by a godly believer. Simpson became, for a time, the pastor of this congregation – known as Muslin Street Congregational Church.

his comparing it 'in its spiritual and moral aspect' to Sodom.[22] More meetings were started in 1832, the year of the cholera outbreak, and again in 1836, following a specific prayer meeting for, and address on, revival. Burns's attention had been drawn increasingly to the need for a fresh outpouring of the Spirit, and on a Sabbath afternoon in August 1838, standing on the grave of his reverent predecessor, Mr Robe, on the anniversary of his death, and taking as his text the words inscribed in Hebrew letters on his tomb, Isaiah 26:19, he pled before a vast assembly the necessity of new birth unto eternal life, in tones of unaccustomed earnestness, which stirred the hearts of many in a manner never to be forgotten.[23]

One of the most significant factors to pave the way for the revival which was soon to descend in power was the continued blessing being experienced by the town's Methodists. This fact is entirely overlooked in most accounts of the Kilsyth revival.[24] In the autumn of 1837 a considerable number were brought to the Lord, chiefly through the instrumentality – as had been many previous cases of conversion in the locality – of Methodist preacher Alexander Patrick (see page 289). A sermon of his around this time was especially remembered for years thereafter. One man who formerly considered Patrick a fanatic became his friend, and many meetings were later held in this man's house.

The most memorable of these occurred in April 1838 when his room was crowded almost to suffocation, and, through Patrick's heart-wrenching prayers, six people professed faith, four of whose conversions proved lasting. One religious woman was offended by Patrick's discourses and went to speak with him at some length. She soon came under

---

22. W. J. Couper, *Scottish Revivals*, Dundee 1918, p. 118.

23. Growth of interest in foreign missions during 1838, leading to the formation of a regular 'missionary meeting', was another factor which Burns believed helped stimulate spiritual earnestness in his parish.

24. As John Drake, Methodist preacher and biographer of Alexander Patrick, noted, Islay Burns made no reference whatever to the influence of the Wesleyans on the subsequent revival in Kilsyth in his biography of his father, the Rev. W. H. Burns. However, he corrects this omission in his account of the life of W. Burns Jnr, when he notes the early stirrings of revival among the Wesleyan Methodists, whose distinctive teaching on the 'new birth' and their 'unwearied activity and zeal for the gathering in of souls, spread by a happy infection to the hearts of others' (Islay Burns, *Memoir of the Rev. Wm. C. Burns, Missionary to China from the English Presbyterian Church*, London 1870, p. 86).

conviction and found peace with Christ. At once she began praying
for her husband. He also cast away his confidence in formality and put
his trust in Jesus. The husband's concern for his mother led that aged
woman to come also and converse with Patrick. She too was converted,
as were two others of her sons as well as her two daughters. All continued
in their new-found faith. By now a new class consisting of forty converts
could be instituted, although Drake makes it clear that not even half of
those who benefited from the revival joined the Wesleyan Society due to
the very strong anti-Methodist prejudice prevalent in the town.[25]

On one occasion Patrick made particular prayer for all the other
congregations in Kilsyth as well as those in Falkirk, Denny, Stirling,
Doune and Fintry. It was to be observed that 'a literal answer was soon
given to almost all this mighty prayer', as virtually all these churches and
places shared in the showers of revival blessing that followed. Some of
the converts of the revival among the Kilsyth Methodists being members of other churches in town, these remained within their denominations, and sought to bring back to them something of the zeal and
joy which they had now attained.[26] Thus, as Islay Burns acknowledged,
conversions 'of a more than usually striking kind' were becoming more
frequent in the parish church and in other congregations in Kilsyth.[27]
Gradually, prejudice against the Methodists began to subside.

'The Spirit Descends' July 1839

Of those praying societies that were begun in Kilsyth at the time of the
famed awakening of 1742, it is recorded that at least one had continued
uninterruptedly until the period of W. H. Burns's ministry in the parish
from 1821. Burns had an absorbing interest in revivals, and regularly
encouraged his congregation to pray earnestly for an outpouring of the
Spirit on their town. In the summer of 1839, Burns's son, twenty-four-
year-old probationary minister, William Chalmers Burns (1815–1868),
stopped at Kilsyth on his way back to his temporary charge in Dundee
after attending a family funeral in Paisley.[28] He decided to stay for the

---

25. Rev. John Drake, *The Wallacestone Reformer*, p. 115.

26. ibid., pp. 113-17.

27. Burns, *Memoir of the Rev. Wm. C. Burns*, p. 86.

28. Since beginning his public ministry at the age of twenty, Burns lived in the constant expectation of a coming revival to his much beloved Scotland. He spent much
time on his knees praying for so much spiritual blessing that there would not be

Alexander Macleod
of Uig.

Peter Grant
of Grantown-on-Spey.

Robert Finlayson
of Lochs.

Robert Murray McCheyne
of Dundee.

John Milne
of Perth.

A. N. Somerville
of Anderston.

Charles C. Mackintosh
of Tain.

Roderick MacLeod
of Snizort.

Peter McBride
of Knapdale.

Viewed from St Ninian's Isle – Dunrossness, home parish of Sinclair Thomson 1815-64. *(Lowlihjeng)*

Crowlista, Uig, in which remote Lewis parish revival dramatically began through the preaching of Alexander Macleod in the mid-1820s. *(John Blair)*

The fishing village of Portmahomack, Tarbat parish, Easter Ross, saw a movement of 'heavenly power' in 1829, ushering scores of young folk into the Church.

The longstanding devotion of Orkney-born John Hercus's Congregational ministry in Greenock was rewarded with marked blessing in 1830, two months before the pastor's death.

Inverness, one of many Scottish townships devastated by cholera in 1832, yet also blessed by the rich tokens of spiritual renewal that emerged from it.

The splendid River Spey, near Grantown, scene of repeated revival under the Baptist ministry of Peter Grant from 1832.

Parish Kirk of Rhu, Dunbartonshire, where a 'charismatic' revival broke out in 1832.

Obelisk of R. M. McCheyne, St Peter's, Dundee, where he ministered 1836-43.

Several districts of Glasgow were visited with revival in 1742 and again in 1839–40. *(M. Sruber)*

Burngreen, Kilsyth, home town to dramatic revivals in the 18th, 19th and 20th centuries.

The Borders' village of Ancrum, scene of Congregational revival, 1839.

William Chalmers Burns preached with remarkable success in Perthshire 1840–2,
not least in the village of Balnaguard.

Plentiful revival showers were felt in Horatius Bonar's Kelso parish, 1838–41. *(Georgesixth)*

Baptist minister, Duncan Cameron of Lawers found a 'wonderful movement' in progress in the Rannoch district of Perthshire, 1842.

Fishing village of Avoch, Black Isle, recurrent scene of revival during 19th and early 20th centuries.

Collace Kirk, Angus, where Andrew Bonar ministered amid revival 1839–40 and 1843.

Row of cottages on St Kilda, dramatically visited with revival in 1841. *(J. Gough)*

Bracadale, western Skye, scene of open-air preaching during the 1842-3 revival.

The fertile Strathbogie, visited by R. M. McCheyne, Andrew Bonar and John Macdonald 1840–43.

The 1839–42 revival even reached out-of-the-way places like Croick, ten miles up Strathcarron, on the Sutherland/Ross-shire border.

Tobermory, Mull saw revival c 1840 ad again in '43, thanks in part to the labours of the Rev. Peter Maclean. *(Colin/Wiki)*

Revival came to several North Uist communities in 1843, such as Paible, Trumisgarry and Heisker.

From country areas like Glen Lonan people flocked to revival meetings in Oban 1840–41.

Kilmaurs, one of the Ayrshire locations
moved by James Morison's
'simple gospel', 1840s.

Rejuvenated Leith, former scene of repeated
revival activity, notably through
W. C. Burns, 1842.

Kenmore, Perthshire, keen participant in the Breadalbane revival 1816–18, was blessed afresh with heavenly showers during 1846.

One highly favoured revival 'hot-spot', the fishing village of Ferryden, Angus, felt revival touches in 1846, and repeatedly right up to 1913, most notably in 1859–60.

weekend to assist his father with the imminent Communion. While it is generally assumed that this stream of the Kilsyth revival had its dramatic beginnings with Burns Jnr's sermon on the last day of the Communion, some claim it began on the Sabbath, with a remarkable message by Alexander Somerville of Anderston (who had also preached on the Fast Day [Thursday]) from the words, '*Behold I stand at the door and knock*'. Somerville's sermon was marked by 'a peculiar unction and power', and imprinted itself on many hearts, afterwards being referred to as marking a new era in the religious history of the parish.[29]

As W. C. Burns preached on Sunday evening, he 'felt such a yearning of heart over the poor people among whom I had spent so many of my youthful years in sin, that I intimated I would again address them before bidding them farewell'. He announced that he would speak at an open-air meeting in the public square on Tuesday morning, before returning to his locum charge in Dundee. Due to unfavourable weather that day, 23rd July, the service had to be held in the church, which was crowded in every part, with 'an immense multitude from the town and neighbourhood filling the seats, stairs, passages and porches, all in their ordinary clothes, and including many of the most abandoned of our population'.[30]

Burns preached on Psalm 110:3, '*Thy people shall be willing in the day of Thy power*', also relating the mighty outpouring of the Spirit on the day of Pentecost, followed by the story of the Shotts revival of 1630. He later wrote that his soul became deeply moved 'in a manner so remarkable that I was led, like Mr Livingstone, to plead with the unconverted before me *instantly* to close with God's offers of mercy, and continued to do so until the power of the Lord's Spirit became so mighty upon their souls as to carry all before it, like the rushing mighty wind of Pentecost'. Up to then, the people had listened with the most

---

enough room to receive it. One morning his mother, calling him to breakfast, found him lying on his bedroom floor, where he had been detained all night in mighty pleadings. He greeted her with the words, 'Mother, God has given me Scotland today'! (James A. Stewart, *Opened Windows: The Church and Revival*, Asheville, N.C. 1958, pp. 100, 138).

29. George Smith, *A Modern Apostle: Alexander N. Somerville, D.D. 1813–1889*, London 1890, p. 41; Thomas Adamson, *Free Anderston Church, Glasgow. A Centenary Sketch*, Glasgow 1900, pp. 23-4.

30. Burns, *Memoir of the Rev. Wm. C. Burns*, pp. 91, 93.

riveted and solemn attention, but as Burns reached the height of his appeal, with the words 'No cross, no crown', at last they could restrain their emotions no longer, and many broke forth simultaneously in weeping and wailing, tears and groans, intermingled with shouts of joy and praise from some of the believers present. Continued Burns, 'The appearance of a great part of the people from the pulpit gave me an awfully vivid picture of the state of the ungodly in the day of Christ's coming to judgement. Some were screaming out in agony; others, and among these strong men, fell to the ground as if they had been dead'. For a time the preacher's voice was quite inaudible; a psalm was sung tremulously by the precentor and a portion of the audience, most of whom were in tears. The meeting concluded at 3 p.m., having lasted five hours. A mighty revival had begun.[31]

From that time, daily services were held in the church and the churchyard, while in the Market Square it was not uncommon to see several hundred gather very early in the morning for a prayer meeting, led by visiting speakers such as Dr Heugh, who then rushed to Auchinstarry to catch the half-past-seven boat for Glasgow. Ministers would visit places of employment, where all work would be stopped and a time of prayer would ensue. Indeed, such was the commotion caused by the influx of people upon Kilsyth that the roads became thronged with vehicles, people had to sleep under hayricks and hedges, and provisions were difficult to obtain. A second Communion was held on 22nd September, for which an estimated 12,000–15,000 people flocked to the town from many parts of Scotland. Communicants partaking of the sacrament numbered 1,300, with at least eight ministers presiding. Thursday night 'was a remarkable night of prayer, secret and social; probably there was not an hour or watch of the night altogether silent'. Services continued till 5 o'clock on Monday

---

31. ibid., pp. 95-6. Congregational records provide a somewhat different slant. A small congregation, originating in nearby Banton in late 1838, thereafter moved to Kilsyth. 'They were for some time supplied with sermon by the students of the Glasgow Theological Academy. The audience increased, and a few were added to the Church. The Church and preachers were honoured to be instrumental in beginning and helping forward the revival of Religion, with which the town and parish were then favoured, and which progressed satisfactorily until it was made a party glorification and public spectacle' ('General Account of Congregationalism in Scotland from 1798 to 1848 ... ', quoted in McNaughton, *Early Congregational Independency in Lowland Scotland*, vol. 1, pp. 279-80).

morning, after which a number retired to the session-house where they remained till 9 a.m.[32]

On one occasion amid Methodist ranks, under the influence of the word preached, 'forty or fifty stout able bodied persons fell to the ground as if dead. On being removed to a house, and recovering themselves, they all cried aloud to God for mercy'.[33] After the evening addresses, which were often held in the open-air, prayer meetings were begun, which not infrequently continued till well after midnight. One person returning home at two o'clock in the morning reported hearing 'the sounds of prayer and praise, weeping and rejoicing, on every hand in various parts of the valley. I suppose we passed by twenty or thirty prayer meetings on our way home, chiefly composed of young persons who had retired in small companies for a more private devotion'.[34]

Two or three church leaders visiting Kilsyth in the first few days of the revival gave a vivid impression of the excitement prevailing in the town. They came across some young girls, from thirteen to sixteen years of age, who had been in church all night, but still felt no desire to go home. The ministers listened to an impressive address given by an Independent preacher in the Market Square early on the Monday morning. Turning a corner, they came across a group receiving sound instructions from another preacher. A little further on they found 'a disputatious person' inviting the large crowd gathered around him to debate the issue of adult versus child baptism. Whenever they entered a house, or walked on the street, they invariably encountered 'an atmosphere of religion'.[35]

That same Monday, W. C. Burns preached both in the afternoon and evening, after which he made the 'extraordinary intimation' that those who were unconverted come and occupy the front six pews so that he and the rest of the congregation might pray for them. After 'some pressing' by a visiting minister, 'many young and old betook themselves to these seats'. Burns wrote:

---

32. Couper, *Scottish Revivals*, p. 123.

33. Drake, *The Wallacestone Reformer*, p. 119.

34. ibid., p. 120.

35. Anon., *A Narrative of the Surprising Work of God in the Conversion of Souls in Kilsyth, Finnieston, and Cumbernauld, and the Revival of Religion in Anderston and Paisley; with an Account of the Remarkable Occurrences which took Place at the Dispensation of the Sacrament at Kilsyth, on 22nd September, 1839*, Glasgow 1839, pp. 6-7.

In this work I was assisted, I think, as much as ever before in my life, having a degree of tenderness and affection which my hard, hard heart is rarely privileged to feel, and in prayer I was favoured with peculiar nearness to God, inasmuch that one time I felt as if really in contact with the Divine presence, and could hardly go on, while at the same blessed season there seemed to be a general and sweet melting of heart among the audience, and many of the unconverted were weeping bitterly aloud, though I spoke throughout with perfect calmness and solemnity.[36]

The 'most appalling cries' came mainly from young lasses aged from fourteen to eighteen, and six or eight of these were removed to the session-house, where, on their knees and still crying most piteously, they were 'frequently pressed to give some reason for their violent grief', in order to determine whether it was of the Spirit or of the flesh. One girl, on ceasing to cry, broke out into song, 'with a very sweet voice and a joyful countenance'. Meanwhile, amidst all the turbulence that was around, yet another girl was carried in a swoon into the session-house.[37]

Ministerial Helpers

Among the many ministerial helpers in the revival, John (Rabbi) Duncan was one of the first to visit the scene, for his heart and mind became absorbed in the work as soon as it commenced. At Kilsyth he preached with great power from the words, 'Deliver from going down to the pit: I have found ransom'. He also gently encouraged Burns to bring out more broadly the sovereignty of God in his preaching, saying to him, 'To leave out election is to leave out the keystone of the arch'. On the occasion when Burns invited inquirers to remain to take seats set apart for them, Duncan went forward. When reminded by other ministers present that the seats were for those spiritually anxious, Duncan replied, 'But I'm anxious'![38] Though regarded by others as a man of obvious piety, the intensity of the Spirit's convicting power led Duncan at that moment (as on other occasions) to doubt his own salvation.

---

36. Michael McMullen, *God's Polished Arrow: W. C. Burns: Revival Preacher*, Fearn 2000, pp. 161-2.

37. Anon., *Narrative of the Surprising Work of God*, pp. 7-10.

38. A. Moody Stuart, *The Life of John Duncan*, Edinburgh 1872 (reprinted 1991), pp. 53-5.

Another visitor was Thomas Guthrie, the 36-year-old minister of Old Greyfriars Church in Edinburgh, whose wife was a niece of the Rev. W. H. Burns. As he journeyed along the canal to Kilsyth, Guthrie observed 'more religious conversation in these boats for last six weeks than for six years before'.[39] One man, a native of Kilsyth but not a believer, said he, like many in the town, knew not what to make of the revival, but that a great change and reformation had taken place was beyond doubt. Kilsyth was formerly full of rudeness and discord, but this was no longer true. The man mentioned the case of a local farmer whose turnip fields were formerly often pillaged and destroyed. But this year was different – religion had guarded them better than an armed force! While the man stated his disapproval of meetings going on late, another man remarked that when on one occasion a speaker was exhorting the people to go home and get sleep so that they would be refreshed to work for their masters, an employer stood up and said they had never wrought so well as they were doing now.

Guthrie met with ninety new communicants of the past two months, aged from twelve to seventy, and almost all of them 'under the most solemn and serious impressions'. A precious work, Guthrie noted, was accomplished among the children of Kilsyth. One woman, walking alongside a field, heard from a nearby wood, the gorgeous melodious tones of a familiar psalm followed by 'a shrill voice ... in accents of solemn prayer'. Curious, she drew nearer, to find a band of young boys, who had retired to the wood to pray. To the charge that the revival was a gross delusion, Guthrie responded, 'It had saved many a mother a broken heart had the son who has been a curse to her, been under such a "delusion"!' He also spoke of the marvellous sight of seeing men and women, in their working clothes, assembled in the house of God at meal times, instead of loitering in groups on the street engaged in idle chatter.[40]

Results

The immediate change in the spiritual and moral condition of the town was enormous. Noted one eyewitness: 'The web became nothing to the weaver, nor the forge to the blacksmith, nor his bench to the carpenter, nor his furrow to the ploughman.' They forsook all to crowd the

---

39. David K. & Charles J. Guthrie, *Autobiography of Thomas Guthrie, and Memoir,* vol. 1, p. 393.

40. ibid., pp. 395-6.

churches and the prayer meetings. There were nightly sermons in every church, household meetings for prayer in every street, twos and threes in earnest conversation on every road, and 'single wrestlers with God in the solitary places of the field and glen'.[41] Recalled Burns Snr, 'Politics are quite over with us. Religion is the only topic of conversation … the influence is so generally diffused, that a stranger going at hazard into any house would find himself in the midst of it'.[42]

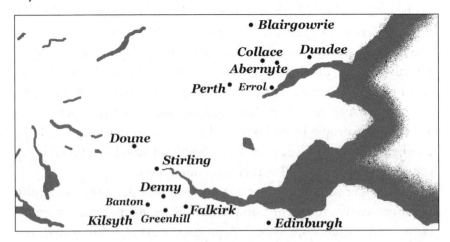

At the height of the movement as many as twenty prayer meetings were operating within Kilsyth's Church of Scotland congregation, as well as eighteen among the Methodists, ten in the Relief Church and nine among the Congregationalists – all this within just one parish. Indeed, for a period of time all these churches co-operated together in a wonderful spirit of unity. The Relief Church, like others in the town, was at times crowded to capacity. The Rev. Anderson, minister of that congregation, went to exhort members of a dancing club which had been formed in Kilsyth eighteen months previously, and was made up of nine couples. One person was led to reflect on her spiritual state and was soon converted. This had a ripple effect on her comrades and in a fortnight the dancing club had been turned into a prayer group![43] Meantime, the ongoing work among the Methodists had in no way abated. By December 1839 their chapel could boast 166 members, besides those 'kept on trial'. The Masonic Lodge which had thereunto been used for

41. Couper, *Scottish Revivals*, p. 122.

42. MacMillan (Ed.), *Restoration in the Church*, p. 136.

43. Anon., *Narrative of the Surprising Work of God*, pp. 29-30.

Methodist meetings was now far too small for the numbers attending, and a new plain building, seating 400–500, was constructed. This was opened in May 1840.[44]

Kilsyth environs

Banton

In nearby Banton an enthusiastic congregation had been built up through the energetic ministry of the Rev. John Lyon, working under his mentor, the Rev. W. H. Burns. A church had been opened in 1837 as a 'chapel of ease' and Lyon was ordained there in 1840 (where he remained until 1843 when he left to become Free Church minister at Broughty Ferry). William Chalmers Burns had preached in Banton 'with considerable assistance' on the Saturday of the legendary Communion weekend in Kilsyth, when revival broke out so dramatically in that town.[45] With Burns being detained in Kilsyth, Lyon went to Dundee to fill his place for a time. Shortly, however, revival spread from Kilsyth to Banton, where it was suddenly ignited. At a prayer meeting in the school there, virtually everyone present – well over one hundred men and women, not a few of them hardened miners and colliers – were 'melted'.[46] Lyon's labours were greatly blessed and for a short time meetings continued nightly. Things continued here 'in a manner fully as surprising' as in Kilsyth and a number of ministers came to assist in the work.[47]

Cumbernauld

In regard to 'abounding iniquity', Cumbernauld was deemed 'considerably worse than any other country village in the whole county of Dumbarton'.[48] However, with news of recent dramatic events in Kilsyth, just four miles distant, revival had become a prominent topic of conversation within the community. On the last Saturday of August 1839, the bell went round the village, intimating that a sermon would be preached the following evening at 6 p.m. This created quite a sensation, and almost the whole village turned out in their working clothes. At the

44. Drake, *The Wallacestone Reformer*, pp. 118-23.

45. McMullen, *God's Polished Arrow*, p. 147.

46. Burns, *Memoir of the Rev. Wm. C. Burns*, pp. 99-100.

47. Anon., *Narrative of the Surprising Work of God*, pp. 26, 28.

48. ibid., p. 18.

close of the service, when those who desired conversion were asked to retire to the United Secession Church, the whole audience, amounting to between 800 and 1,000 people, did so.

The next evening the church was again packed. Many were moved by the sudden death of a young collier who had heard the previous evening's sermon, gone to his bed in good health, then uttered a scream at two in the morning, before instantly expiring. Next evening, for a service that lasted two-and-a-half hours, the church was 'excessively crowded', with some having to sit down on the floor in the passages. Such interest continued unabated for the rest of the week, after which meetings were held each Wednesday night, as it was found difficult procuring ministerial assistance. Prayer meetings took place each Sabbath at 8 a.m., to which 150 might attend, as well as on Friday evenings. Regarding early results it was said that 'hundreds of people have been placed in new circumstances and many of them have heard and seen what they never can forget'.[49]

Greenhill

The youthful James Robertson, recently inducted minister at Greenhill, near Falkirk, went repeatedly to Kilsyth, less than ten miles distant, to assist W. H. Burns in the revival work. Though decidedly sympathetic to the movement, he was yet most anxious to distinguish between the true and the false. He endeavoured to guide and keep converts 'in such channels as were in accordance with wisdom and Scripture'. It was said of him that 'no one shrank more from extravagances of every sort, or was more concerned to keep the balance of truth'.[50] During this period Robertson also made numerous preaching excursions to places as distant as Dunfermline, Bathgate and, particularly, Alloa. On visiting one revival scene he said he wished 'there could be less morbid excitation, but more fervent affectation; less bustle, but more work; less feverish agitation, more wholesome fervour. It cannot be denied', he continued, 'that there are excesses and extravagances. Like spots on the sun's disc, they appear more conspicuous from the pure and holy scenes with which they are connected'.[51]

---

49. ibid., pp. 18-21.

50. M. H. M., *James Robertson of Newington: A Memorial of his Life and Work*, Edinburgh 1887, p. 73.

51. ibid., p. 74.

Dundee and Neighbourhood

Dundee

Outbreak of Revival

After his memorable labours in Kilsyth, William Chalmers Burns returned to St Peter's Church, Dundee, where he was standing in for the equally youthful Robert Murray McCheyne (1813–1843), widely regarded as one of the most saintly ministers of his day – or, indeed, any day (see Appendix to Chapter 6, *Influence of Robert Murray McCheyne*). The reason for McCheyne's absence at this time was his undertaking on behalf of the Church of Scotland, along with his friend Andrew Bonar and two others, to conduct a six month fact-finding tour of Palestine and a mission to the Jews therein.[52]

A work of conviction and expectation had been in progress in St Peter's Church ever since McCheyne's settlement there. On transferring there as locum minister, Burns quickly discovered, 'such evidences of the Lord's work, in convincing and converting sinners, as was truly refreshing to my soul'.[53] McCheyne had a strong personal interest in revivals and would read accounts of their historic progress to his congregation. In July 1838, preaching on Isaiah 44:3-4, he had said, 'These words describe a time of refreshing. There are no words in the whole Bible that have been oftener in my heart and oftener on my tongue than these'.[54] This was no fallow ground that required to be broken and prepared. On the contrary, Burns found himself in a field sown and watered, where the green blade was already springing up.[55]

Thus it was that almost immediately on Burns's return to Dundee from Kilsyth, while recounting from the pulpit recent events in the latter town, 'suddenly the power of God seemed to descend, and all were bathed in tears'. The next evening, as soon as the vestry door was opened to admit the anxious, 'a vast number pressed in with awful eagerness. It

---

52. McCheyne was of the firm opinion that the revival at St Peter's that swiftly followed his mission to Palestine came as a result of his congregation's interest in God's chosen people, a connection that had previously been proposed by the likes of Samuel Rutherford, Thomas Boston and Richard Cameron.

53. Smellie, *Robert Murray McCheyne*, p. 104.

54. Derek Prime, *Travel with Robert Murray McCheyne: In the Footsteps of a Godly Scottish Pastor*, Leominster 2007, p. 93.

55. Smellie, *Robert Murray McCheyne*, p. 103.

was like a pent-up flood breaking forth; tears were streaming from the eyes of many, and some fell on the ground, groaning and weeping, and crying for mercy'.[56] Revival had begun and from then on, night after night, St Peter's became packed to capacity; many having to stand in the aisles or sit on the pulpit steps, while scores outside were unable to gain entry. As a result, services were often held in the open air.

It was on his way home from Palestine to Scotland, while stopped in Hamburg, that news came to McCheyne that revival had broken out in his church, causing him to overflow with thankfulness. In fact, even though separated from his flock McCheyne had been holding his people before the Lord in prayer for their conversion and sanctification. It might have been natural for him to have held a degree of jealousy that the revival which he had so longed for was being reaped so manifestly by Burns. But there was never a single trace of such; his constant desire was that Burns's ministry be 'a thousandfold more blessed' to the people of St Peters than ever his own had been.[57] Indeed, he and Burns continued as the very best of friends, holding each other in great esteem and affection, and labouring earnestly together in their Father's vineyard.

Progress of the Movement

Meetings in St Peter's continued on an almost nightly basis for nearly four months. The Rev. Alexander Cumming of Dunbarney went to Dundee for one week in November 1839, to assist Burns. One afternoon he had been out of town and arrived back at St Peter's a little late. Burns beckoned him up to the pulpit while the congregation was singing, and told him he would have to preach, as he was so overwhelmed with fatigue as to be unable to discharge his ministerial functions. Taken by surprise, Cumming protested that he was completely unprepared, to which Burns replied, 'Stand up and say something in the strength of God, and if you are not supported, sit down!' Cummings spoke for over an hour on Zechariah 3, during which, he noted, 'a greater solemnity was diffused over the audience than I had yet seen; the stillness became more and more breathless'. He then suggested seven minutes' silence, that 'every sinner may flee to the waters of the well of Bethlehem, and break through all opposition in his way'. The silence was intense, many feeling that evening that they must be saved then or never.

---

56. L. J. Van Valen, *Constrained By His Love: A New Biography on Robert Murray McCheyne*, Fearn 2002, p. 310.

57. Bonar, *Life of Robert Murray McCheyne*, p. 239.

Burns said afterwards that he had come into contact with fifteen people who on that night appeared to have passed from death to life.[58]

Into the meeting each evening, arriving a little late, poured great numbers of workers straight from the mills. Cumming noticed that of all who came, 'a vast and striking proportion' were men. He was also impressed with the number of boys in their early teens who crowded the pulpit stairs, listening with riveted attention, and who remained clinging to their places after the blessing was pronounced, anxious that some word should be addressed to them by the officiating ministers.[59]

From the start, some spoke against the movement, criticising Burns for 'putting all the people mad, for they were crying out in the church'.[60] Even many believers doubted whether the work was genuine. In August a large open-air meeting was arranged in the Meadows, but was prohibited by the city authorities, so it was held instead in St Peter's graveyard. Meanwhile, the local press published a lively correspondence for and against revival. One newspaper, the *Dundee Warder*, reported positively on the movement, while another, the *Courier*, mocked the meetings being held, stating that those who attended them fell under one of six categories;

1) People of small brains, little or no judgement, and perhaps too much nervous susceptibility

2) People who had a craving for excitement

3) Idlers

4) The curious … who go for novelty

5) Indiscriminate church-goers, who go from a sort of mania

6) A few (such as journalists), who go to see what is the matter[61]

---

58. Smellie, *Robert Murray McCheyne*, pp. 238-9. Cumming compared the work of revival in Dundee to that in Perth, in which he later assisted. While the movements were similar, he found that that in Dundee did not proceed in so quiet a manner. 'The cries of those impressed were louder, their convictions more thrilling, and the whole aspect of those assembled in church such as to excite the notice of the surrounding community more strongly than in the case of Perth' (ibid., p. 234).

59. ibid., p. 236.

60. David Robertson, *Awakening: The Life and Ministry of Robert Murray McCheyne*, Carlisle 2004, p. 113.

61. 'Courier', 17/09/1839, quoted in Prime, *Travel with Robert Murray McCheyne*, pp. 99-100. These criticisms were repeated in *The Scotsman* in the days that followed.

As the work grew, many other ministers came to help Burns, including Horatius Bonar, John Macdonald (of Ferintosh), Cesar Malan, and seventy-six-year-old Robert Haldane, who travelled from Geneva. In October, a huge Communion was held in St David's, to which larger church some meetings had now been transferred. According to Van Valen, 'the revival reached a climax' at this point. Many of the 'hungry souls' seated at the Lord's table 'seemed burning with desire after near-ness to Jesus'. Three congregations were present, one gathered in the church and two in the adjoining school classrooms.[62] Meanwhile, con-siderable sensation was caused in the town by the event of a Miss Miller making her way to the lodgings of Burns to converse about her spiritual condition. As Burns spoke with her, the young woman fell down and was found to be dead. Rather than being disturbed by this occasion, both Burns and the girl's two sisters found cause to rejoice, as they claimed that the girl was in a state of spiritual peace when she died, and had now gone to heaven.[63]

Return of McCheyne

Immediately on his return home in November,[64] McCheyne threw himself into the work, both preaching and counselling, setting aside an evening a week to speak with those under soul concern. He would often converse with twenty or more in one evening. One notebook records 400 visits made to McCheyne by inquiring souls during the course of the revival. Altogether, over 700 came to converse with ministers about their hearts' concerns. Much of Dundee society was affected, and men as much as women, though the affluent were least moved. The revival was truly ecumenical, as McCheyne was happy to work alongside members of the Methodist, Relief and Independent Churches, as well as with other Church of Scotland leaders, with whom McCheyne met weekly to pray for the city. Other Established churches noticeably affected were

---

62. Van Valen, *Constrained by His Love*, p. 332.

63. Anon., *Narrative of the Surprising Work of God*, pp. 30-1.

64. McCheyne came in for criticism from a disaffected group in St Peter's who bemoaned the fact that their pastor made no mention whatever of his trip to Palestine in his first sermon on return to Dundee. In his absence some had become particularly attracted to the ministry of W. C. Burns, whom they considered a more powerful preacher than McCheyne, and to whom they now transferred their allegiance (John S. Ross, *Time for Favour: Scottish Missions to the Jews 1838–1852*, Stoke-on-Trent 2012, pp. 164-5).

St David's and the Hilltown Church. It would be a mistake, however, to suggest that the whole of the city was moved by the revival. A contemporary minister, the Rev. William B. Borwick, stated that prayer meetings were numerous 'over a portion of the town' only, in contrast to the 1859–61 revival, when the whole town was affected.[65]

Thirty-nine prayer meetings were in progress in the town by November 1839, including some held in factories and five conducted entirely by children. Such was the Spirit's work among these young ones, that many, from the age of ten upwards, were admitted as members, giving 'full evidence of their being born again'.[66] In addition no fewer than sixteen converts from St Peter's Church went into the ministry, several of whom went on to become the 'spiritual fathers of hundreds'.[67] Breaking from normal practice, four communions were held in 1840, three more than usual, and the first, held on 19th January, was, to McCheyne, 'the happiest and holiest that I was ever present at'. Wrote Van Valen: 'The Lord was in this place; it was a Beth-El, a house of God. The ladder was lowered down from heaven and the blessings flowed into many hearts … A new awakening had begun in the congregation.'[68]

Even during the course of the revival, McCheyne did not decline invitations to preach elsewhere in Scotland. In the summer of 1840 he and Alexander Cumming were appointed to travel north and speak in Strathbogie. Following this, McCheyne made for Edinburgh, to attend a meeting of ministers and elders wishing to sign the 'Solemn Engagement' in defence of the freedom of the Church from State interference. Cumming conducted services in St Peter's the following week, and noticed how 'the blessing was increased rather than diminished' in spite of McCheyne's attention to the affairs of the national Church.[69] Even at this stage in the

---

65. Reid, *Authentic Records of Revival*, p. 178. This contradicts the claim of Van Valen who states: 'The entire city of Dundee was moved; it seemed as if it was being transformed' (*Constrained By His Love*, p. 310).

66. Bonar, *Life of Robert Murray McCheyne*, p. 495.

67. John Macpherson, *Revival and Revival Work: A Record of the Labours of D. L. Moody and Ira D. Sankey, and Other Evangelists*, London 1875, p. 20.

68. Van Valen, *Constrained By His Love*, pp. 331-2.

69. Smellie, *Robert Murray McCheyne*, p. 246. 'I cannot describe how his bosom laboured with the guilt this country was incurring in permitting its civil courts to encroach on the prerogatives of Christ', said Cumming of McCheyne's passion for the Scottish Church (ibid.).

revival, McCheyne could still note that a few in his church were 'crying out in extreme agony'. But such expressions became less and less, and life in St Peter's revealed a stream 'flowing gently; for the heavy showers had fallen, and the overflowing of the waters had passed by'.[70]

At that time McCheyne told his congregation that some months previously, 'I could number more than sixty souls who I trusted had visibly passed from death unto life during the time I had been among you. Now I do trust I would number many more – aye twice as many more – I trust there is not a family in this church who have not some friend or relative really born again'.[71] At a later date McCheyne wrote: 'The half is not told … no words can describe the scenes that have taken place in this place, when God the Spirit moved on the face of our assemblies. The glory is greatly departed, but the number of saved souls is far beyond my knowledge.'[72]

There were of course backslidings, However, observing that some people were influenced more by feelings of strong attachment to their pastor personally than by the power of the truths he preached, McCheyne became more reserved in his dealings with them. The opinion of both he and his colleagues was that the vast majority of those who turned back were those who had never really believed.

Further Burst of Blessing

Though not widely known and little reported, a further season of spiritual awakening arose in Dundee during 1842. In September of that year, James B. Hay – an assistant to Horatius Bonar in Kelso, and one who threw himself heart and soul into the revival movement underway in that Borders town (see page 378)[73] – paid a visit to Dundee and wrote to a friend regarding, 'much to tell you of what the Lord has done and is doing in this town'. Three weekly meetings were being held in the house

---

70. Bonar, *Life of Robert Murray McCheyne*, p. 129.

71. Robertson, *Awakening*, p. 115.

72. Horatius Bonar, *Life of the Rev. John Milne of Perth*, London 1869, p. 66.

73. Hay served as a Sunday school teacher in Kelso, and Bonar wrote of him that he laboured with great zeal, often rising at four o'clock on Sabbath mornings and continuing to pray for his class for hours together. 'He met with them, visited them, prayed with them, wrote to them' and did everything humanly possible to win them for Christ (I. Walker, *Memoir of the Rev. James Ballantyne Hay, Late Minister of the Free Church of Scotland at North Berwick*, Edinburgh 1870, pp. 16-17).

in which he was staying, at which Hay was often asked to officiate, 'and never did I witness such interesting scenes', he said. 'The number on Sabbath nights, within the last two months has increased from sixty or seventy to nearly two hundred. Most of them are mill girls, and many of them have truly become members of the family of God'.[74]

Carse of Gowrie

Errol and Abernyte

Revival also diffused rapidly from Dundee to nearby districts. The well evangelised valley known as the Carse of Gowrie – the fertile region that stretches between Dundee and Perth – became as 'an electric spot' during the years 1838 to 1843, in which time, 'the Rose of Sharon shone especially when the table was prepared and the cup of Christ's love overflowed in many hearts'.[75] Numerous villages along this valley were affected, including Errol, where the Rev. James Grierson had served as pastor since 1819, with much blessing among his people, especially during the year 1820; and Abernyte, one of the smallest parishes in the country. The minister here was the aged James Wilson,[76] and his assistant was James Hamilton, a close friend of McCheyne who later became the celebrated Dr James Hamilton of Regent Square, London. In Abernyte, even before 1839, 'the moving of God's Spirit was certainly noticeable'.[77] The parish in fact seems to have been the centre of a significant move of the Spirit at this time. It is singled out in one report alongside the popular revival centres of Dundee and Perth, viz, 'The spiritual movement appeared at Dundee, Perth, Abernyte and wherever Somerville and Burns went',[78] which suggests that either or both of these eminent evangelists preached in the Angus village around this time, as, it is believed, did McCheyne.

---

74. ibid., pp. 17-18.

75. Van Valen, *Constrained By His Love*, p. 235.

76. Thomas Guthrie described Wilson as a 'devout, good man', yet also a 'curious specimen of humanity' in that, for example, he openly and resolutely denied basic scientifically proven theories such as the theory of gravity (ibid., pp. 228-9). Having been minister in Abernyte for forty-two years, Wilson passed away in 1850, aged eighty-five.

77. ibid., p. 238.

78. Adamson, *Free Anderston Church*, p. 41.

Collace

Especially blessed in the Carse of Gowrie was Collace, a small district with a population of less than 800 and no large village. On his arrival as minister of the parish in the autumn of 1838, Andrew Bonar (1810–1892) found 'not much open or gross vice among the people, but there had been a silent and perpetual flow of worldliness'. The season of Handsel Monday was a day of unchecked and open transgression, and many really believed that drunkenness, riot and folly at that time were no way sinful. However, during Bonar's first eight months in the area, the people began to manifest a great relish for ordinances, and a great anxiety to be visited and catechised. To the weekly prayer meeting which Bonar instituted, the people flocked in crowds, even during the severest nights of winter.

It was a time of awakening, though of few conversions. One elderly woman commented, 'If Mr Bonar goes away now, he will leave us worse than he found us, for we are halting between two opinions'.[79] In fact her minister did go away – on that famed mission trip with McCheyne to the Jews in Palestine (see page 330) – and no one was available to fill his place during his absence. Bonar returned in November 1839 to find the parish largely as he left it, but with an increased hope, held by himself and his people, of a blessing, given news of revivals in various nearby localities. Soon, attendance at the weekly meetings was noted as being 'remarkable', and several people came to Bonar in distress of soul.[80]

Then one night in April, on the fast day appointed by the General Assembly 'in prospect of the solemn crisis of the Disruption', when Horatius Bonar and Alexander Cumming spoke, many people burst into tears, old and young, and among the rest, several boys of twelve to fourteen years of age. A deep and awful solemnity spread over the whole meeting, and, after the blessing was pronounced, fifty or sixty people remained in their seats, most of them in tears. Two or three elderly people came along the passage to speak with the ministers, their faces wet with weeping, a deeply affecting sight to Bonar.

This was the start of 'a shower of the Spirit ... not very extensive'[81] which descended on the parish, during which 'the hearts of anxious

---

79. Bonar, *Life of the Rev. John Milne of Perth*, p. 61.

80. Bonar, *Andrew Bonar: Diary and Life*, pp. 79-80.

81. Bonar, *Andrew A. Bonar D.D. Diary and Letters*, London 1894, p. 86.

people ... burst open' as they would freely tell their feelings and ask counsel. Unfortunately, the impressions of a number, both young and old, who were initially 'very deeply awakened ... completely faded away'. However, of the 400–500 who had been attending the weekly parish prayer meeting, Bonar said he could detail the circumstances of at least thirty persons in whom he believed a decided change had taken place. He continued, 'In all these cases, without exception, the individuals became most decided in their views regarding the headship and Crown-rights of the Redeemer; and neither in this nor any of the neighbouring parishes did any of these awakened persons remain in the Establishment when the crisis came [in 1843]'.[82]

Bonar also stated, 'I never, to this day, have known any case of irregularity arising from our meetings'.[83] and 'For months there was talk of a work of conviction and deliverance of lost souls',[84] while 'the change on the aspect of the parish at large is one of the most striking effects'. Bonar further remarked that the revival he had witnessed in his neighbourhood corresponded 'exactly to what I, from my youth, had been led to pray for and expect as the results of prayerful and faithful preaching of Christ crucified for sinners'.[85] Bonar concluded: 'We have seen the steps of our God and King in His sanctuary, and we expect Him again.'[86]

Blairgowrie

Another area in the proximity of Dundee where 'a prolonged and concerted spiritual revival'[87] occurred was Blairgowrie, where many of those converted were previously utterly careless about their souls; 'despising and disliking all who seemed in any degree serious about eternal things; prayerless, living in the neglect of family worship, scoffers, swearers, Sabbath-breakers, drunkards, unfeeling and rude'.[88] The Rev. Robert

82. Brown, *Annals of the Disruption*, pp. 10-11.

83. Gillies, *Historical Collections of Accounts of Revival*, p. 559.

84. Van Valen, *Constrained By His Love*, p. 339.

85. Presbytery of Aberdeen, *Evidence on the Subject of Revivals*, p. 63-4; Bonar, *Andrew Bonar: Diary and Life*, p. x.

86. Bonar, *Life of the Rev. John Milne of Perth*, p. 66. Indeed, in Bonar's own parish there was a further period of awakening coinciding with the Disruption (see page 451).

87. Robertson, *Awakening*, p. 96.

88. Gillies, *Historical Collections*, p. 559.

Macdonald was a close friend of McCheyne, and members of St Peter's at times journeyed to Blairgowrie to support the work there. Macdonald also worked heartily alongside Francis Gillies of adjoining Rattray, holding special evening services twice-a-week during the winter of 1839. One girl who appeared to be savingly converted was just eight years of age. Soon it could be stated that 'many evil practises to which she was addicted, especially that of telling lies, she has entirely forsaken'.[89]

When Macdonald first came to the parish he knew of not a single meeting for social prayer, but, he noted, 'previous to what may be called the revival, I observed a spirit of growing prayerfulness among my people, which encouraged me to expect that God was about to bless us with such a season of refreshing as we actually experienced'.[90] As a direct result of the revival the number of prayer meetings in the parish rose to around thirty. In addition, the minister observed 'a growing interest in the cause of missions, and a very striking and abundant increase in liberality'.[91]

Ministry of William Chalmers Burns
in the Scottish Heartland

With reports of spiritual blessing pouring in from various quarters, Robert Murray McCheyne opined that never before was there a time 'when the Spirit of God was more present in Scotland'.[92] Greatly used in spreading the revival during this period was William Chalmers Burns, who, with the return of McCheyne to his Dundee parish, was free to itinerate extensively. In the early part of December 1839 we find Burns detailing a whole list of places where he went to preach. These include Greenock, Dundee, Port Glasgow, Paisley, Bo'ness, Kilsyth, Dunfermline and Perth. Burns arrived in the latter town on Christmas Day 1839 to assist with just one service – but as it turned out his visit extended to over three months!

---

89. Presbytery of Aberdeen, *Evidence on the Subject of Revivals*, p. 65.

90. ibid., p. 65-6.

91. ibid., p. 66. Two years later, in 1841, in Blairgowrie's Independent Chapel, the Rev. John Tait began a series of protracted meetings each morning, followed by public evening meetings. As the days progressed the chapel became packed, many being 'aroused to serious consideration respecting their souls' (*SCM*, 1841, quoted in McNaughton, *Early Congregational Independency in the Highlands and Islands and the North-East of Scotland*, p. 204).

92. Van Valen, *Constrained By His Love*, p. 336.

Perth

Introduction

The good work in Perth originated with the settlement of the Rev. John Milne (1807–1868) to St Leonard's Church of Scotland in the late autumn of 1838, soon after which several cases of conversion occurred. The new minister also became aware, among his congregation, of 'a kind of godly and humbling jealousy that the Lord should visit other places (e.g. Kilsyth and Dundee), and yet pass them(selves) by'.[93] While W.C. Burns clearly played a significant part in the progress of the spiritual movement that ensued here, its direction and balance were due largely to the guidance of Milne, a pious man held in esteem by all who knew him.

Striking Beginnings

The last night of 1839 proved to be 'the most remarkable night of all in the beginning of that revival'. A considerable number of people assembled spontaneously at the church for counsel. Alexander Cumming of Dunbarney, who came to assist, said that people's hearts were unusually fallow. He felt that the 'plough could pierce the soil with ease and turn up clods to expose them to the pulverising influences of heaven'.[94] Each individual seemed to tremble on reflecting that another year was waning to a close and they had still not embraced the gospel. Wrote Milne of the occasion: 'There was deep solemnity, which gradually almost awfully increased; many began to shed tears, and to throw themselves on their knees at prayer, in the seats and passages.'[95] Burns delivered a plain, simple address, yet it was felt that perhaps at no time during the whole

---

93. Bonar, *Life of the Rev. John Milne of Perth*, p. 57.

94. Alexander Cumming, *Memorials of the Ministry of the Rev. Alexander Cumming*, Edinburgh 1881, p. 138.

95. *Report for the Synod of Merse and Teviotdale*, quoted in ibid., pp. 57-8. Ms Margaret Stewart of Bonskeid arrived home from abroad on the last day of 1839 and witnessed the revival in Perth from its beginnings. She later described the preaching of Burns by stating that 'the first part of his discourse always embodied a mass of telling doctrine, holding up the Divine law right in face of the conscience. The appeals in the latter part were irresistibly winning, brimming over with the freely offered love of Jesus. The Spirit was glorified. He arrested many before the preacher had time to enter his subject ... His theology was unbiased, and swung like a pendulum across the truth of God, avoiding all limited, classified, partial and one-sided expressions of it' (Margaret F. Barbour, *Memoir of Mrs Stewart Sandeman of Bonskeid and Springland*, London 1883, pp. 137-8).

season of revival was there more of the effectual presence and power of the Lord than on that night. Many felt that the wings of the Saviour were overshadowing Perth so that His feathers seemed touching them. Almost everyone present was either quickened or lastingly impressed. Hour after hour passed, and still they would not or could not go away. A policeman on duty outside later remarked that one meeting had a marked effect in repressing wickedness in the town and of 'so overawing the minds of profligate desperados that they were unable to plunge into the usual excesses of depravity'.[96] It was two or three in the morning before they all retired. The following morning over 200 anxious souls sought out Burns for personal counsel. A great many who had closed one year in God's fear began the next in His favour.

This was the beginning of great things. Milne said, 'Next day it was the same, and the next, and the next'; and thus for nearly three months these daily double meetings continued without interruption, the evening ones always densely crowded and continuing usually for three or more hours – the passages within and without being completely filled with people standing. Milne compared events to the work of God that accompanied the Apostles' preaching – the multitude was divided, so were families, the people of God were knit together, and, filled with zeal, joy and heavenly-mindedness; they continued steadfast, growing in doctrine and faith; and numbers were constantly turning to the Lord. Thus it was that the minister could testify, 'I have been busy, very busy, almost unceasingly, night and day for the last three weeks, and the result is, I trust, one of the most hopeful and widest revivals that has as yet taken place in Scotland'.[97]

---

96. Cumming, *Memorials of the Ministry of the Rev. Alexander Cumming*, p. 139.

97. Bonar, *Life of the Rev. John Milne of Perth*, p. 60. Milne became 'intimately acquainted' with Burns during the latter's three to four months' stay in Perth. He said of him, 'I never knew any one who so fully and unfalteringly obeyed the apostolic precept, "Meditate upon these things, give thyself *wholly* to them". I was struck with his close walk with God, his much and earnest prayer, his habitual seriousness, the solemnising effect which his presence seemed to have wherever he went, and his almost unwearied success in leading those with whom he conversed to anxious, practical, heart-searching concern about their state in God's sight'. (Gillies, *Historical Collections*, p. 558). In a similar way one of Milne's elders praised his pastor, for 'the grace of humility was so wonderful in him that he stood aside and gave place to this stranger (Burns) in his own pulpit, rejoic-ing in the work of the Lord, whoever was the instrument. He entertained Burns at his own expense, and alone, and unaided, took on himself the great responsibility of having such large meetings' (Presbytery of Aberdeen, *Evidence on the Subject of Revivals*, p. 71).

Revival Scenarios

In a general sense the revival in Perth ran along similar lines to that in both Kilsyth and Dundee, although in Perth more of the affluent in society were reached (and for their benefit public meetings every forenoon were kept up for several months), and, according to Cumming, Perth proved exempt from ministers and helpers 'flocking from all quarters to speak with those awakened and marring the work of the Lord by ministering to their self-complacency and pride'. While people were awakened by many means, the four most popular were the regular preaching of the word, occasional remarks dropped in the pulpit, remarks made on the psalms sung, and public reading of the Scriptures.[98]

Even on the evening of Queen Victoria's marriage (10th February 1840), which was celebrated throughout Britain and the occasion in Perth to be marked by a grand fireworks display on the Inch, the church was nevertheless quite full, and after a time not a few were forced to stand. So many gathered for another meeting that it was supposed there were more collected in the street an hour before the time than would have several times filled the church. Indeed, the press was so great when the doors were opened that several people were injured.

Both Milne and Burns were known to be great favourites with children and the young – 'they flocked round them – the pulpit stair was planted with them'. One twelve-year-old boy, Jamie Thomson, almost totally blind, was one whose life was greatly changed, after thinking, during a Communion service, 'what a happy thing it was to be among the people of Jesus, and to be clothed with the white robes'.[99] A thirteen-year-old who came under serious impressions during this period was David Sandeman who came from an aristocratic family in Bonskied, Perth. The ministry of Milne and that of his predecessor, the Rev. Millar – who left his charge during 1839 – produced a considerable impression on Sandeman's mind, which was deepened by attending the services conducted by W. C. Burns, and later through attending A. N. Somerville's church in Glasgow.[100]

---

98. Cumming, *Memorials of the Ministry of the Rev. Alexander Cumming*, p. 187.

99. Bonar, *Life of the Rev. John Milne of Perth*, p. 71.

100. Andrew Bonar, *David Sandeman, Missionary to China*, London 1861, Chapter 1. Sandeman went on to become an influential missionary in China (for more on him see page 477).

'Great good' was accomplished among young men in particular, as in one baker's shop, where each worker was awakened, 'one after another, till the whole four were impressed'. In addition it was said that, 'household servants have been benefited to a great extent'.[101] Milne said he was proud to have 'a peculiar people growing up among us, who are separate from the world, know and love one another, watch over, exhort, and aid one another; they seem to grow in humility and zeal, and entertain frequent and endearing intercourse, both by letter and mutual visits, with the good people of Dundee, Aberdeen and other places'.[102]

Revival Setbacks

But the work was not without its share of opposition, which included scrawls of chalk-graffiti on the walls of St Leonard's Church 'with figures and sentences, some ridiculous, some abusive and vile'.[103] Andrew Bonar wrote after one of several visits he made to Perth: 'The whole town is stirred; everybody is talking of the movement; worldly men are outrageous in their opposition; newspapers also misrepresenting and vilifying those concerned in it, ministers and people.'[104] Perhaps even more seriously, Milne wrote that opposition from elders in his church and from other ministers in the town became 'more violent as the work goes on ... Mr Gray is the only town minister who stands by us'.[105] Burns preached a number of times in Andrew Gray's West Church, which 'partially experienced' the benefit of the revival. In February 1840 sixteen young people applied to Gray for admission to the Lord's Table, most of whom had been impressed on hearing Burns preach.[106]

---

101. Presbytery of Aberdeen, *Evidence on the Subject of Revivals*, p. 71.

102. Bonar, *Life of the Rev. John Milne of Perth*, pp. 58-9.

103. Stephen S. Blakey, *The Man in the Manse*, Edinburgh 1978, p. 55.

104. Bonar, *Life of the Rev. John Milne of Perth*, p. 23.

105. Couper, *Scottish Revivals*, p. 125. This seems odd, as Burns was invited to preach before several congregations in the town other than Milne's and Gray's, e.g., repeatedly at the Rev. Turnbull's church in Kinnoul Street, where the evangelist said he had 'more melting of heart under a sense of the love of God than ever I remember to have had in the pulpit, and I think shed more tears than ever before in preaching' (McMullen, *God's Polished Arrow*, p. 175). 'Dr Finlay's immense church' was also open to Burns on more than one occasion, as was Dr Easdale's East Church. A Mr Maclagan also spoke of blessing among his people as a result of Burns's meetings in Perth (ibid., pp. 169-76).

106. Presbytery of Aberdeen, *Evidence on the Subject of Revivals*, p. 57.

Sadly, there occurred during the revival the death of a young woman, which was attributed to a cold caught in attending the meetings at the beginning of the season.[107] More unusually, the 'Thirteenth Annual Report of the Directors and Physicians of James Murray's Royal Asylum for Lunatics, Perth' recorded that 'at least the more immediately exciting cause of the derangement of three patients brought to the Asylum was some forcible and alarming appeals to which they had listened under the ministry of a certain preacher'. The three patients alluded to were all melancholic, all deeply impressed with the enormity of their sins, and two of them suicidal. By careful attention and judicious management, all three gradually improved and ultimately recovered. They were advised not to attend any more revival services, and, in so doing, two of them were noted as having 'hitherto continued well'. The third, however, did not heed the doctor's advice. 'His health became disordered', the report stated. 'He has imbibed frightful and delusive impressions, and has had a complete relapse. As usual, the second attack is more obstinate than the first; and the Physician entertains faint hopes of being able to do him much good.'[108]

No Let-Up

Yet for the vast majority of those caught up in it, the revival was good news in every sense of the term. In this way, 'the sacred spring-tide flowed on with unabated force to the last', as Burns neared the close of his first year as a preacher, and the twenty-fifth year of his life. During one of his last meetings in Perth, on 22nd March 1840, 'an extraordinary measure of the Holy Ghost' accompanied his preaching. One man cried aloud; then the great mass of the congregation gave audible expression to their emotion in a universal wailing. 'To me', said Burns, 'looking from the pulpit, the whole body of the people seemed bathed in tears, old as well as young, men equally with women'. The benediction was eventually given, but even after all the lights in the church but two had been extinguished one by one, a few hundreds still remained in the church, who 'would not, and in some cases could not, retire'. Those in distress were led away and spoken to for an hour, this being followed by singing, which was continued for some time longer. Burns reflected:

107. ibid., p. 60.

108. ibid., Appendix, p. xii.

This glorious night seemed to me at the time and appears from all I have since heard to have been perhaps the most wonderful that I have ever seen, with the exception perhaps of the first Tuesday at Kilsyth. There was this difference chiefly between the two occasions, that a great many of those affected at this time had been convinced or converted during the previous weeks, while at Kilsyth almost all but the established children of God were awakened for the first time.[109]

Milne felt as if the presence of God were resting on the whole town; 'and the country round was shaken for many miles ... People who were worldly then, and who are worldly now, were drawn and kept, as by a charm, night after night, in the house of God, instead of straggling about the streets, or haunting places of amusement and dissipation'.[110] Indeed, 'the watchmen at night often remarked that they had little now comparatively to do, the streets were so quiet'.[111] It appeared as if the greater part of the town had come under spiritual influences, and such was the want of judicious, experienced believers to lead prayer meetings that they had to be necessarily entrusted to young men. In St Leonard's Church alone at the Communion in April 1840, no fewer than 140 were admitted to membership for the first time. Shortly after, Milne could testify to having admitted 'more than two hundred young persons' to Communion.[112]

For some years after the revival great warmth and life exhibited themselves in St Leonard's congregation. A weekly prayer meeting was begun, which was still being continued decades later. The Perth Young Men's Tract Society was also formed at this time. The church became noted as a centre of blessing in the community and more than once the response was given, 'You'll be from St Leonard's' to an individual who was found reaching out in love and respect to a fellow citizen.

---

109. 'Journal' of W. C. Burns, quoted in McMullen, *God's Polished Arrow*, pp. 177-8.

110. Bonar, *Life of the Rev. John Milne of Perth*, p. 60.

111. Presbytery of Aberdeen, *Evidence on the Subject of Revivals*, p. 59.

112. Bonar, *Life of the Rev. John Milne of Perth*, p. 59. Such was 'that extraordinary work which affected the whole town of Perth and its neighbourhood', that Bonar wrote in regard to it: 'Having seen a good deal of it at the time, and heard of it from those directly concerned, I would only add that the half has not been told, nor indeed can be' (ibid., p. 66).

Perthshire and Fife

Amidst Burns's heavy schedule in Perth, he still managed to make evangelistic journeys to numerous other places within Perthshire and neighbouring Fife. These included Auchtermuchty, Strathmiglo, Dunfermline, Muthill, Stanley, Auchtergarven, Caputh and Kinfauns. By this and other means, wrote Horatius Bonar: 'the surrounding districts were also moved, and many came in to Perth to attend the services, returning home during the night.'[113] Selected entries from Burns's diary of several excursions from Perth provide fascinating insight into his labours during this period.

> Feb 18th 1840: Forenoon: Drove out to Stanley in gig ... Evening: immense crowd in the spacious church ... .subject Luke 24:47; more aided than ever on the same subject. A very solemn season; many met me deeply affected as I retired. Walked home to Perth seven miles ... .Feb 25th: I drove out to Balbiggie to preach in the Secession Church. The man who drove me ... told me that of late, especially since our meetings began here, there had been an astonishing change on the face of the country round in point of morality and anxiety about religion ... The hour of meeting was six; the people were many of them assembled at two o'clock, and at half-past four, when I went, the church was full... . March 19th (returning from Auchtergaven): We made up on the way to the Stanley people, a great crowd, and I knelt down with them at the roadside under the bright moon and prayed. Their love and deep solemnity put me much in mind of the first Christians ... March 22nd (in Kinfauns Church): I saw the tears streaming from the eyes of some men advanced in years, and felt that the Lord was indeed present. The meeting lasted three hours and a half ... [114]

Of nearby Dunbarney, near Bridge of Earn, the Rev. Alexander Cumming wrote: 'Revivals have taken place in my parish' but 'what has happened of this nature has been on a small scale.'[115] In time, Burns's unrelenting itinerary paid its toll; the evangelist became increasingly weak, and for a brief period went to stay at the Collessie manse to rest. In less than a fortnight, however, he was preaching again with renewed vigour. During

---

113. ibid., p. 60.

114. Burns, *Memoir of the Rev. Wm. C. Burns*, pp. 148-9.

115. ibid., p. 60.

mid-summer he made visits to Strathmiglo, Milnathort, Cleish, Kinross, Dunfermline, Stirling, Gargunnock, Kippen, Kilsyth, Glasgow, Loch Lomond, Glen Falloch, Moulin, Logierait and Kirkmichael.

On his first visit to the county, Burns spoke of 'poor parched Fife, the Valley of the Shadow of Death'. In places like Anstruther and Largo, however, there were heartening signs, and he said that in the latter place, 'the meetings are deeply solemn as well as crowded, and I hear of not a few who are under some anxiety about their state'.[116] Burns wrote that in Dunfermline he saw:

> the clearest tokens of His mighty working, and last night the work was so glorious that hardly one out of about 150 seemed free from deep impressions of the Word and Spirit of Jesus, and many were evidently pricked in their hearts, whilst some heavy-laden souls emerged into the glorious liberty of the children of God. This forenoon again, from 200–300 came to the church between one o'clock to three o'clock, to converse about their state, with whom we had a united meeting of the most blessed kind.[117]

Elsewhere in Fife, Burns was to pay at least one further visit to Milna-thort, in which town a genuine awakening occurred; R. M. McCheyne also made a subsequent preaching visit here,[118] as did John Milne, who, as late as 5th June 1841, could report 'many openings', and that he and the people enjoyed 'a great day here in the fields. The Lord was with us of a truth'. A year previously Milne had evidenced 'good signs' in other Fife locations, including Strathmiglo, where he witnessed 'unequivocal marks of the Lord's power'.[119]

St Andrews

Two Congregational evangelists, Henry Wright and Ebenezer Cornwall, held two weeks' protracted meetings in St Andrews from 18th November 1839. This was followed later in the month by a transient visit from the inexhaustible W. C. Burns. Burns spoke in the Secession Church and elsewhere in town. After one evening service he wrote that 'not a few of

---

116. Alexander Smellie, *Robert Murray McCheyne*, London 1913 (reprinted 1995), pp. 145, 152.

117. Letter dated 30/12/1839, quoted in McMullen, *God's Polished Arrow*, p. 266.

118. Bonar, *Life of Robert Murray McCheyne*, pp. 137-9.

119. Bonar, *Life of the Rev. John Milne of Perth*, p. 31.

the people as well as myself appeared to be in a very tender frame'. As they stopped to converse with him at the close of the meeting, many were weeping profusely, and Burns expressed hope that 'the Holy Spirit was sealing some souls to the day of redemption'.[120]

The labours of these evangelists heralded a time of spiritual awakening in the town. Many among 'the highest classes of society', as well as those utterly opposed to the meetings became striking exhibits of the grace of God. Remarked one Christian, 'I have seen the strong minded and the intelligent – the vigorous, the prejudiced, the persons, of all others, furthest removed from hypocrisy, or the mere sentimental display of religious feeling – weeping on account of their guilt and danger in view of eternity; and I am constrained to believe this is no other than the finger of God'.[121] On one Sabbath 'the work was carried on (with little interval) from eight in the morning till eleven at night. In the evening, besides five public services on the former parts of the day, two chapels were crowded at the same time'.[122] By 1840, well over 100 had given evidence of having 'turned to the Lord', most of them joining either the Congregational Church or the Church of Scotland (subsequently moving to the Free Church).[123]

Breadalbane

Great Beginnings at Lawers

William Chalmers Burns preached in numerous locations in the expansive Breadalbane district during this period and it was throughout this vast region, from mid-August 1840, that his focus now rested. Revival had been so prominent here twenty years earlier, and tokens of divine blessing were also wonderfully displayed as recently as three years previously (see page 281). But now, once again, many in Dugald Campbell's Lawers congregation were 'longing for such a change'. Prayer meetings

---

120. Burns, *Memoir of the Rev. Wm. C. Burns*, pp. 133-4.

121. *SCM* 1840, quoted in McNaughton, *Early Congregational Independency in Lowland Scotland*, vol. 1, pp. 126-7.

122. *SCM* 1840, pp. 27-9, quoted in ibid., p. 128.

123. *SCM* April 1874, quoted in W. D. McNaughton, *The Congregational Church in Kirkcaldy and Other Congregational Churches in Fife (From their Beginnings to 1850)*, Ventura 1989, p. 322. Elsewhere in Fife, Robert Aikenhead added nine young folk to his Kirkcaldy Congregational Church in 1843 as a result of spiritual stirring evident in the district in preceding months (Robert Kinniburgh, *Fathers of Independency in Scotland*, p. 428).

were kept up and reports of revival elsewhere in the world were 'regularly laid before the people', greatly stirring them to seek the Lord. Revival began visibly with Burns's visit. One resident said:

> The whole country was ringing with the wonderful movement in Kilsyth, Perth and Dundee … A great multitude assembled, not only with the ordinary feelings of curiosity, but with feelings of wonder and solemnity deepening almost into fear. I can remember the misty day, and the eager crowds that flocked from all directions across hill and lake. The service was of course in the open air, and when the preacher appeared many actually felt as if it were an angel of God. There was an indescribable awe over the assembly. Mr Burns's look, voice, tone; the opening psalm, the comment, the prayer, the chapter, the text (it was the parable of the Great Supper in Luke 14), the lines of thought, even the minutest; the preacher's incandescent earnestness; the stifled sobs of the hearers on this side, the faces lit up with joy on that; the death-like silence of the crowd, as they reluctantly dispersed in the gold-red evening – the whole scene is ineffaceably daguerreotyped on my memory. It was the birthplace of many for eternity.[124]

Campbell said that Burns 'dwelt continually upon the love of Emmanuel, in laying down his life for sinners, but it was chiefly during prayers that the results which fell under our observation took place'.[125] After one meeting, from 150 to 200 waited about the door, and with these Burns engaged in prayer while also giving 'a series of miscellaneous remarks tending to bring them immediately to surrender to Jesus'. Burns added to his journal entry: 'Many I saw in tears and among these a number of fine stout young Highlanders.' Some of the anxious came to converse privately with the evangelist the next day.[126] Burns's first week in the district, claimed Campbell, was 'like a resurrection, the work of the Spirit was so intended, powerful and evidently independent of the means employed'.[127] As a

---

124. Burns, *Memoir of the Rev. Wm. C. Burns*, pp. 188-9.

125. Presbytery of Aberdeen, *Evidence on the Subject of Revivals*, p. 560.

126. Journal of W. C. Burns, quoted in McMullen, *God's Polished Arrow*, p. 184. He gives details of eight of these. One was aged 'above twenty', three were about twenty or twenty-one, one was eighteen, one seventeen, one fifteen and one fourteen.

127. Letter dated 21/09/1840, quoted in McMullen, *God's Polished Arrow*, p. 275.

mark of thankfulness, 'four fat lambs' were sent to Campbell and Burns as presents, with many other articles, such as butter.[128]

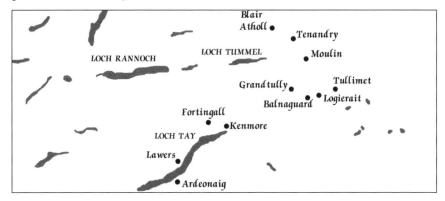

Burns felt peculiarly at home in Breadalbane. Wrote his brother; 'The solemn forms of the everlasting hills and the great shadow of the supernatural which they seemed to cast even over the spirit of the people were congenial to him ... Never probably at any period of his life was he more happy in the best sense than during this interval of quiet thoughtfulness and restful labour'.[129] One night, after an especially solemn service, Burns pressed on the people to retire directly home to the throne of grace. He was later informed that for a quarter of a mile from the church, 'every covered retreat was occupied by awakened men and women, pouring out their hearts to God'.[130]

Looking back on the work towards the end of August, it seemed clear to Burns that this was more

> the fruit of the sovereign operations of God's Spirit than almost any other that I have seen. We have never needed to have any of those after-meetings which I have found so necessary and useful in other places, the people were so deeply moved under the ordinary services. I never saw so many of the old affected as in this case. The number of those affected are greater in proportion to the population than I have ever seen, and there has been far less appearance of mere animal excitement than in most of the cases that I have been acquainted with.

---

128. 'Journal' of W. C. Burns, quoted in ibid., p. 186.

129. Burns, *Memoir of the Rev. Wm. C. Burns*, p. 189.

130. ibid., p. 54.

Burns attributed such features in part to Campbell's excellent ministry and to his flock's universal acquaintance with conversion as a necessary change. It was said that most of the congregations of the district received 'the divine showers' connected with Burns's visit.[131] After he left Lawers, the church devoted a whole Wednesday to public thanksgiving for the Lord's mercy towards them.[132]

Ardeonaig and Moulin

Elsewhere in Breadalbane, Burns preached in the 'dead parish' of Fortingall, whose Moderate minister had, surprisingly, welcomed him. One Sabbath Burns crossed Loch Tay from Lawers, accompanied by hundreds of people, to preach at the missionary station of Ardeonaig. 'There was', he said, 'an immense assembly, collected from a circuit of from twelve to twenty miles, which could not amount to less than three thousand'.[133] Climbing Ben Lawers one beautiful evening, Burns reflected on the Lord's wonderful works during the week 'among the poor inhabitants of this splendid theatre of the Lord's creation. The events that had passed before me were so remarkable and so rapid in succession. It has been indeed a resurrection of the dead, sudden and momentous as the resurrection of the last day ... '[134] A month later it was reported that the market at Kenmore, which used to be a resort of all the 'thoughtless and giddy among the young', passed over without a single individual of this description attending it.[135]

---

131. ibid., p. 189.

132. Before he left, Burns went to pray with a young man on his sickbed, a son of the local Baptist minister. There seemed less of an ecumenical spirit some time later, however. Rev. Campbell, keen to guard the work of the Lord, which was 'still going on' in March 1841, was 'much annoyed by a few Baptists, who seem more anxious to press their own peculiar tenets upon the minds of the converts in my congregation, than the grand doctrine of Christ and Him crucified' (Presbytery of Aberdeen, *Evidence on the Subject of Revivals*, p. 75).

133. 'Journal' of W. C. Burns, quoted in McMullen, *God's Polished Arrow*, p. 188.

134. ibid., p. 187.

135. Letter dated 21/09/1840, quoted in ibid., p. 276. Agents from the Angus, Mearns and Perthshire Itinerant Society reported in 1842 that following the revival that arose in Breadalbane, as well as in Glenbriarachan, following Burns's labours, 'Succeeding labourers have found much better meetings since his visits, and more deep anxiety to profit by the word of life' (*SCM* 1842, quoted in McNaughton, 'Revival and Reality', p. 204).

Then on to Moulin, another favoured spot, where Burns preached to an audience of about 500 in the open air, though with little liberty. Pronouncing the benediction, he intimated that he felt there must be some cause, either in himself or in some of them, for the withdrawal of the Spirit; nevertheless he made it clear that he would remain to talk with any in distress. No one left. Burns prayed and the congregation seemed more solemnised. He said he then spoke 'for a long time with such assistance that I felt as if I could have shaken the globe to pieces through the views I got of the glory of the divine person of Christ … ' As a result, 'the people were bent down beneath the Word like corn under the breeze, and many a stout sinner wept bitterly'.[136] Impressive gatherings also took place on the green braes of Grandtully and at Logierait.

Balnaguard and Tenandry

Burns passed through the village of Balnaguard while the people were out working in the harvest. At once two young men ran over to him and begged him to hold a meeting in the nearby schoolhouse. In the course of not more than seven minutes the room was crowded to the door by people of all ages, 'from the child of seven to the grandfather of seventy'. Noted Burns, 'There could not be fewer than 120 present, and among these I hardly saw one that was not shedding tears'. Again, when he spoke to a packed house in the village a few days later, 'so remarkably was the presence of God granted that all were in tears, and some cried aloud'.[137] Dugald Campbell said that when he on one occasion preached in nearby Grandtully, 'there was not one word of terror in my sermon, and yet I saw three fainting; and I can never forget the feelings of my soul on that evening, when, owing to the voice of lamentation that filled the church, I was obliged to stand for some time without saying a word in the pulpit'.[138]

Burns also spoke in the church at Tenandry, near the pass of Killiecrankie, just north of Pitlochry. At first he found little liberty in his preaching, but after earnest prayer was given much assistance. 'The people were so much affected that all were riveted in their looks and some were weeping audibly', he noted. Although, for the benefit of those who had long distances to walk home, the meeting had started at five in

---

136. McMullen, *God's Polished Arrow*, p. 55.

137. 'Journal' of W. C. Burns, quoted in ibid., pp. 197-8.

138. Presbytery of Aberdeen, *Evidence on the Subject of Revivals*, p. 75.

the afternoon, it didn't finish until nine, the hearers hanging upon the preacher's words 'until the sun had set and the full moon had arisen. It was a memorable night in the history of many'.[139]

Blair Atholl

Burns preached in the churchyard at Blair Atholl in August 1842 for five hours before four thousand people, to the great impression of many. It was, said one, 'a most imposing sight. Most of them were men, and the ground being a dead level, and inconvenient for sitting, most of them stood. The thirst to hear was so intense, and the blessing which had crowned his previous visits so widespread, that almost the whole population, not only from the vale of Athole, but from Straloch, Strathardle, Kirkmichael, Glenerochy, Dalnacardoch, Foss, Glenfincastle, Strathtay and Strathtummel, flocked to hear the great preacher'. Burns's words 'cut deep into many a heart that day'. One white-haired old man was seen weeping at the gate and saying 'Oh, it's his prayers; I canna stand his prayers!'[140] Burns preached again in the evening in the church for three hours to an audience that would have remained till daybreak. There was one old woman who could speak no English, yet always sat on the pulpit stairs when Burns preached. Asked why she did so, when the message was delivered in English, she replied in Gaelic, 'Oh, I can understand the Holy Ghost's English!'[141] Macdonald of Ferintosh also preached during the deep awakening that occurred in Blair Atholl at this time.[142]

Repeated requests were made to suppress the movement that had spread across the Breadalbane district, and to exclude both Macdonald and Burns from the pulpit. When the Rev. Atholl Stuart refused these appeals, one embittered person petitioned the Sheriff to call the infirm and dying minister, the Rev. Stuart (Snr), and to 'inhibit, indict and discharge' him from ever allowing any such meetings again in the church. Sadly, Stuart died the following month, but the harassment continued, for the aggrieved party again petitioned the Sheriff, this time to try and have the walls of the deceased minister's grave moved, or, failing that, the corpse dug up and reburied elsewhere. The petition

---

139. Burns, *Memoir of the Rev. Wm. C. Burns*, pp. 208-9.

140. McMullen, *God's Polished Arrow*, pp. 74-5.

141. Burns, *Memoir of the Rev. Wm. C. Burns*, pp. 240-1.

142. *Free Church Monthly Record*, 1895, p. 247.

was later revoked, but only after considerable grief had been borne by the Stuart family. [143]

Back in Dundee

For four months from December 1840, just over a year after revival had initially broken out in Dundee's St Peter's Church, Burns was invited to take temporary charge of a new church in the Dudhope area of the city. As always, the untiring evangelist made full use of his time. He preached at three services each Sunday at Dudhope and other churches in the town (including St Peter's for much of March when Robert Murray McCheyne was sick). During the week, he led meetings at schools in nearby districts, and also in the Barracks. In addition, Burns could be found preaching on the streets during lunch hour and at work places where permitted, as well as visiting the sick and a host of other activities. [144]

His own estimate for the first month or two was that there was comparatively little obvious spiritual fruit. 'Still he laboured and prayed, and then blessing came' – to such an extent that one man said that young people would run after him on the street professing anxiety and seeking direction. [145] Long lists appeared in Burns's notes of the names and addresses of enquirers and converts, and often the mill or factory in which they worked. Several decades later, in the 1880s, the Rev. Andrew Inglis, minister of the Dudhope (Free) Church – who heard Burns preach numerous times in later years and was privy to several personal conversations with him [146] – went over the lists with any who could give information on them. 'Of many I could get no account', he wrote, 'of a few, a bad record is all I have heard, of many, that they lived devoted lives … Some still remember this short ministry as the most blessed time of their lives'. [147]

---

143. The harassment continued well after May 1843, at which point many parishioners left the Established Church to join the new Free Church (Rev. Atholl Stuart, *Blair Atholl as it Was and Is*, Edinburgh 1857, pp. 1-3).

144. Rev. Andrew Inglis, *Notes of the History of Dudhope Free Church, Lochee Road, Dundee*, Dundee, 1890, pp. 11-13. Burns's official biographer, Islay Burns, (as well as, consequently, Michael McMullen) make no reference to the evangelist's four months' ministry in Dundee from 5th December 1840 to 1st April 1841.

145. ibid., p. 14.

146. Inglis had the highest regard for Burns, and recalled that the evangelist never rode if he could walk and never allowed anyone to carry for him if he could carry it himself.

147. Inglis, *Notes of the History of Dudhope Free Church*, pp. 14-15.

Baptist Revival in Central Highlands

It is interesting to note that while the general awakening of this period, 1839–42, arose in part out of evangelical dissatisfaction within the Church of Scotland, this was clearly not the only cause, for congregations of other denominations also experienced a spiritual reviving around this time. For example, a number of Baptist churches gained significantly in membership in this period. This said, Baptist preachers sometimes found that the Free Church debate temporarily curtailed their evangelistic endeavours. When visiting Strathmore in 1843–4, Daniel Grant said he found 'so much strife among the people, respecting the late Disruption that I returned sooner than I intended'.[148] In other places, however, much good was accomplished within this denominational group.

Tullimet

Sometime in 1839 two sisters from a Perthshire glen – one 'under great concern', the other 'careless' – came over the hill to hear the Rev. John McEwan preach in Tullimet. The former obtained peace and her sister was awakened – thus both returned home in a different state from which they came, and both were subsequently added to the Baptist Church.[149] It marked the beginning of a prolonged awakening in the parish, continuing, after McEwan's departure to Canada in 1840, under the supervision of Donald Grant from Grantown-on-Spey. Grant could soon speak of many becoming 'subjects of divine teaching – of course we may be deceived, but are determined not to be … hitherto the conduct of those who have joined us is truly becoming'. While many were in great distress, there were 'no groanings nor swoonings', nor were protracted meetings held. Rather, the work was advanced by 'simply speaking the truth in love on the Lord's day, and from house to house'.[150]

By 1842 four prayer meetings were being held on Sabbath mornings plus two or three in the evening. So engaged was Grant in travelling throughout the parish and in dealing with the anxious that he wrote: 'It is often very late before I get to bed, and I am unable to attend in one-fourth of the places where I am invited to preach.'[151] Conversions continued unabated until

---

148. *BHMS Report* 1844, pp. 22-3.

149. ibid. 1840, p. 4.

150. ibid., p. 5.

151. ibid.

1844, when Grant could testify: 'The Lord has graciously kept from falling, with the exception of three, all the 86 who have joined the church since I came here ... The greater part are poor in this world but they are rich, some of them making such progress in the knowledge of the Scriptures that I find it difficult to keep before them.'[152] A new, bigger church was deemed necessary a few years later and opened in 1847. Grant's name was long honoured in the parish, where he served for no less than forty-five years.[153]

Ministry of Duncan Cameron of Lawers

Duncan Cameron of Lawers found the spiritual condition of his parish most favourable from 1839, when it was 'not a rare thing to see 300 hearing on the side of a hill upon Sabbath evening'. Over the next few years, the church continued to be 'lively and prosperous', and eight were added to the congregation between March and June 1842.[154] Even in quieter periods, Cameron trusted that God was converting some during that time. By March 1844, five more applicants were under consideration and a number more appeared to be impressed. So busy was the minister in the work and in demands from other districts that he was led to proclaim, 'Although I had the wings of an eagle, I could not supply all the places which are calling for a visit'.[155]

For all along the shores of Loch Tummel and Loch Rannoch a wonderful movement was also in progress. When Cameron preached from two passages of the Bible at Loch Tummelside in 1842, the whole congregation seemed affected. He said that in Foss the next day, 'the house was crowded ... I could hardly get away from the people'. Such a 'stir' continued over following months and when Cameron returned to the area in July 1843, 'the silent tear profusely stole down their cheeks' as he preached to them. The minister was aware it would take but little effort from him or anyone present to effect audible groaning or crying out from those most emotive. Cameron disapproved of such outward manifestations and he was glad to note that none occurred.[156]

---

152. ibid. 1844, p. 23.

153. He was fondly remembered not only as a good pastor and preacher (he itinerated widely throughout the Highlands), but also as an expert bone-setter (chiropractor).

154. *BHMS Report* 1839, p. 16; 1842, p. 7.

155. ibid. 1843, p. 17; 1841, p. 17; 1843, p. 18.

156. ibid. 1843, p. 17.

Of Rannoch Cameron wrote that 'the Lord is taking out a people for himself'. For the occasion of baptising a man who had been awakened under his preaching there a year previously, the people assembled in crowds, some from the distance of twelve or fourteen miles; and though the glen was thinly peopled, upwards of 200 were present. The minister preached twice to the gathering, who did not seem disposed to go away; then again in the early evening to a very attentive congregation, at a place four miles distant. On a further trip to the Rannoch shores in December 1843, not satisfied with a long sermon every night, so eager were the people to hear that Cameron had to sit up till two in the morning conversing and praying with enquirers, to the point that he was utterly exhausted. On yet another occasion Cameron arrived in the district after dark. He was, he noted, 'excessively fatigued', but the news of his arrival soon spread to the distance of three or four miles, and they flocked to hear. 'Although the Sabbath was both rainy and windy, the largest congregation I ever saw there, assembled', he wrote. At this latter 'time of refreshing, both to myself and others', Cameron said he offered the right hand of fellowship to four persons, two of whom were baptised in the loch.[157]

Awakening Throughout Central Scotland

Edinburgh and Leith

Following his appearance before the Committee in Aberdeen (see page 398), William Chalmers Burns immediately continued his itinerant preaching. After labouring successfully in the north of England, in the winter of 1841, he went to Edinburgh to temporarily take the place of the Rev. Moody Stuart at St Luke's Church while the latter was recuperating from a serious throat infection in Madeira. Since opening in 1837 as a Church Extension Charge, the congregation of St Luke's had rapidly increased to around 800 people under the dedicated ministry of Moody Stuart. Burns, likewise, threw himself into the work. He attended the College Missionary Association; took a special care for, and interest in, the students who were attracted to his ministry; visited the military barracks to speak to the soldiers and hand out tracts; and frequently visited and preached at the shelter, the jail, the asylum, the orphan hospital and many other institutions. Soon the church was being filled to the door 'with a strange medley of ever-varying countenances – Newhaven fishwives, sneering young men,

---

157. ibid.

etc.' By the end of December, forty-eight people were seeking admission to the Lord's Table, thirty-seven of whom were admitted.

In addition to his labours in Edinburgh, from January to March 1842 Burns could regularly be found preaching in nearby Leith.[158] Here he spoke to densely crowded and what Burns termed 'hungry' audiences. Even though the weather during those months remained severe, the numbers attending his meetings continued to grow so much that even on the Wednesday evenings the meetings were overflowing. So deep was the impression on them, says Burns, that the people would not go away, even after the parting blessing. So he held an after-service for prayer and counselling and such was the distress of those who remained that they were removed to the vestry for further help. Robert Murray McCheyne helped in one of these services and to all intents and purposes it looked 'as if the ever-memorable scenes of Kilsyth, Dundee and Perth were to be repeated in Leith'.[159] So widespread was the movement of God that individuals said that the residents of the district 'were all going mad'. So many were converted to Christ that Burns could write that 'the Lord gave me spring, summer and harvest that winter in Leith'.[160]

Back in St Luke's, the culminating point of Burns's ministry in the capital was his protest against the running of Sabbath trains between Edinburgh and Glasgow. For the next three months, Burns's usual Sabbath duties consisted of four services; two at St Luke's and two at the railway station. In addition he resolved to hold prayer meetings every Monday, Wednesday and Friday at noon to pray about this issue. He supplemented these with open-air preaching and turned his female class into an evangelistic service in the church. At this time, 'the church was overflowing, The word was sharper than a two-edged sword. There was a Bethel-like fear over the congregation. Every head was bowed. It

158. In spite of such a pressing schedule, Burns also managed to make four evangelistic tours away from the capital city. In April 1842 he preached in Milnathort, Bridge of Earn, Perth, Burrelton, Collace, Abernyte and Dundee. In June, he was to be found back in Dundee, but also in Kilspindie, Anstruther, Logie, Cupar and Falkland. In August and September he made two tours to the Highlands of Perthshire (McMullen, *God's Polished Arrow*, p. 74).

159. Two or three years previously, in 1839, McCheyne preached at a school in Edinburgh's St George's parish, to 'many weeping children' (quoted in Blakey, *The Man in the Manse*, p. 55).

160. McMullen, *God's Polished Arrow*, p. 73.

was felt that the living God was in the place'. At the close of a Monday prayer meeting some remained behind who seemed to be under 'a divine convincing work', and as they went away an elder said with eyes sparkling, 'That's the Lord's work beginning'.[161]

So it was. Much fruit appeared over that winter and spring. On not a few Sabbaths, on Burns's preaching, 'the people fell into a state of calm weeping'. In his young communicants' classes Burns met continually with many who had been recently awakened, and heard of similar cases. At the springtime, remarkably, 200 people joined the church – though the large majority of these were from other congregations.[162] Decades later, David Maclagan, a native of Edinburgh, well remembered the distinct 'work of revival' in St Luke's at this time. Although a member of St George's Church of Scotland, Maclagan lived in George Street, immediately behind St Luke's. 'I can recollect the crowded meetings, the open windows of the church in the long summer evenings, and the singing of Psalms till nearly midnight', he wrote.[163] Mentioning several evangelistic tours which Burns made in the midst of his Edinburgh work, one tribute to the evangelist concludes: 'One recalls it with amazement. Here was a man who crowded the work of years into months – of months into weeks – of weeks into days. The work of many a lifetime was compressed into this single winter in Edinburgh.' [164]

Apart from Burns's ministry, a separate movement developed in Leith in 1841 as a result of revival meetings held by James Douglas of Cavers in the 'Tower' by the shore.[165] Interest and attendance increased,

---

161. Burns, *Memoir of the Rev. Wm. C. Burns*, pp. 235-6.

162. ibid., p. 236.

163. David Maclagan, *St George's, Edinburgh. A History of St George's 1814 to 1843 and of St George's Free Church 1843 to 1873*, London 1876, p. 60.

164. R. Strang Miller, 'Greatheart of China: A Brief Life of William Chalmers Burns, MA, Scottish Evangelist and Revival Leader, and Early Missionary to China', in Various, *Five Pioneer Missionaries*, Edinburgh 1965, pp. 121-2.

165. During this time in Edinburgh Douglas also held nineteen noon and evening meetings at 16 Charlotte Square, in the city centre. Conducted over ten days, these were led by Robert Machray, Congregational minister in Dumfries. 'The rooms were always full', said Douglas, 'and generally there were some on the stairs trying to hear … I cannot recall the number of those who conversed with him (Machray), but, considerable as it was, I am convinced there were several profited by the meetings who were never known of' (*SCM* 1873, quoted in McNaughton, *Early Congregational Independency in Lowland Scotland*, vol. 1, p. 422).

necessitating a move in 1843 to larger premises in the Kirkgate, where the cause took deeper root still. A further move was required, this time to the 'Old Seaman's Academy' on Dock Street. The work progressed, with frequent visits and powerful preaching from such fervent Congregational evangelists as James Morison, Fergus Ferguson (Snr) and John Kirk, whose labours were 'productive of great good, attracting much attention from the people of the town'. Leith's Second Congregational Church was established in the Dock St premises in 1844, before removing to larger premises in St Andrew Street where revival services were now organised anew, and carried on with vigour.[166]

Glasgow

A. N. Somerville in Anderston

The first Glasgow church to be affected by revival during this period was Anderston Church of Scotland. Alexander Neil Somerville (1813–1889) was inducted here in 1837, and quickly proved to be a popular young preacher. From the beginning of September 1839 the Anderston church was open every night except Saturday, for three months,[167] the earnest pastor also setting apart a portion of every forenoon to converse with penitents in the session-house.[168] Such was the crush throughout these months and the demand for seats that mothers set their children on the front of the balcony and held them there by their clothes so they wouldn't fall over.

William Chalmers Burns came to Anderston on 26th September, for which meeting the building was packed in every part two hours before the appointed time. Indeed it was said that more were turned away from the church than gained admittance. As it happened, Burns arrived half an hour late, having been redirected to the larger Hope Street Church,

---

166. John Laurie, *Chronicles of the Evangelical Union Church of Leith*, Edinburgh 1871, pp. 87-8, 98.

167. W. F. Somerville (Ed.), *Precious Seed Sown in Many Lands*, London 1890, p. xiv. Like the vast majority of ministers in the Established Church who were involved in the revival movement of 1839–42, Somerville (along with his congregation, with scarcely an exception) walked out of his denomination and joined the newly formed Free Church; his new church in Cadogan Street, Glasgow, being opened in February 1844.

168. Somerville's sermon on the Church of Laodicea, which had recently been published, was at that time a great favourite both of his own and of his hearers, and was much blessed.

which was simultaneously filled in expectation of Burns preaching there instead. Somerville, therefore, stood up on the wall outside the church and intimated to the crowd that he himself would preach in Hope Street, where he would be joined by Burns after the services at Anderston were concluded. The meeting in Hope Street was believed to have continued till around two o'clock the following morning.[169]

A host of church activities sprang up during and in the aftermath of the revival in Anderston. The central prayer meeting multiplied into five other local ones and the Sabbath school increased by the addition of ten kitchen classes. A Sabbath school library was added to the one already in existence. The Sabbath school was followed by a teachers' prayer meeting. Tract distribution sprang up and kitchen meetings and open-air preaching became common. Additionally, a mothers' meeting, a young men's fellowship association, a literary society, a temperance society, a ladies' auxiliary Bible society, a ladies' clothing society and a number of other associations gradually came into existence. So useful were all these groups deemed to be that not only was every one of them continuing in even greater strength by the time Somerville's active ministry ceased in 1877, but others had also been added over the years.[170] The most remarkable branch to emerge within this energetic church, however, was the ministers' Bible class, to which young men from all over the city flocked. These carefully disciplined gatherings proved of enormous benefit to hundreds, including many who later became church leaders themselves (such as Malcolm White of Blairgowrie and Archibald Black of Dundee).

Jonathan Ranken Anderson in the Gorbals

Ostensibly independent of the work elsewhere (but quite probably influenced by news of the movements in Kilsyth and Dundee),[171] there commenced a significant movement in Kirkfield Chapel in the Gorbals area of Glasgow between 24th November 1839 and 5th January 1840, under the ministry of the Rev. Jonathan Ranken Anderson (1803–1859). Born in Paisley, Anderson was converted at the age of sixteen

---

169. Anon., *Narrative of the Surprising Work of God*, p. 22.

170. Adamson, *Free Anderston Church*, p. 25.

171. In a letter to Horatius Bonar, Robert Murray McCheyne links the Kirkfield revival with other prominent movements of the Holy Spirit in Scotland around the same time (letter of 25/12/1839, in Horatius Bonar, *Life of the Rev. John Milne of Perth*, p. 33).

while working away from home. Even at this tender age – both naturally and spiritually – he held family worship in his lodgings, to which a number of neighbours would come along. Shortly afterwards he entered Glasgow University to study for the ministry.

Inducted in Kirkfield (Church of Scotland) in 1834, Anderson's sermons were noted for containing a 'special unction from above' and, 'multitudes were pricked to the heart; some were constrained to cry out under soul trouble with audible voice, and good evidences were given that many were brought under a work of conviction, which issued in the saving conversion to God and His Christ'.[172] Anderson's biographer wrote: 'This was the day of the power of the Lord's right hand among them', and as a result the congregation 'became very lively in all the exercises of religion. Many a poor sinner looked back to these days of Divine power with thankfulness to the Lord for the change they had experienced then'.[173] It was not in Kirkfield only that Anderson's labours were eminently blessed at that time, but in many other congregations where he was invited to preach. 'It will not be fully known till the last day how fruitful his ministry was in those days', noted Neil Cameron. 'It will then be seen that "he who went forth weeping, bearing precious seed, shall come again with rejoicing, bringing his heavy sheaves with him"'.[174]

Finnieston

The considerable poverty evident in the Glasgow suburb of Finnieston was thought to have been alcohol-related, as the area was largely

---

172. Jonathan Ranken Anderson, *Days in Kirkfield: Being Discourses on a Revival Occasion in Kirkfield Chapel, Gorbals of Glasgow, From 24th November 1839 to 5th January 1840*, Glasgow 1872, p. vi.

173. Neil Cameron, *Sketch of the Life of Rev. Jonathan Ranken Anderson*, Glasgow 1914, p. vi.

174. ibid. Anderson sided with the Free Church in 1843, but was suspended nine years later for professing views that 'in certain ways, were held to be contrary to the Westminster Confession of Faith' (Various Contributors, *'The Revival of Religion': Addresses by Scottish Evangelical Leaders delivered in Glasgow in 1840*, Edinburgh 1840, p. 445). The essence of the charges against him centred on 'slanderous and injurious' accusations Ranken was purported to have made about John Milne of Perth and against his own office-bearers (Campbell, *One of Heaven's Jewels*, pp. 191-2). Ranken continued to exercise his ministry in an independent congregation in the Gorbals – the John Knox Kirk of Scotland Tabernacle – and also continued to distance himself further from former Free Church colleagues. To date only a small volume of extracts has been published from his eight-volume diary, which covers the years 1851–8.

inhabited by 'potters, bottle-blowers, engineers and steam-loom weavers' – all well-paid professions. Robert Kidston, proprietor of Finnieston Glass and Pottery Works, appointed Mr Buchan, a missionary from Aberdeen, to come and start a school in the district, as well as a library. Buchan also held Sabbath meetings in Kidston's home. These became popular and in time, 'some individuals of a rough and ungainly exterior' came to him in distress of soul. Then, on Sunday 1st September 1839, as Buchan preached in church, 'many began weeping … and all were deeply affected'.[175] Almost everyone stayed for the after-meeting, and Buchan counselled the anxious until after midnight, while two Sabbath-school teachers remained to converse with others till some hours later. Many who had been exhorted to go home returned from their beds, unable to find any rest in sleep.

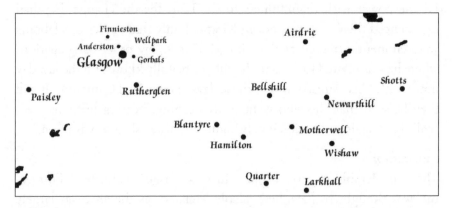

Critics claimed Buchan was driving the people mad, but the enthusiasm continued. On Monday, a prayer meeting was held at five in the morning, and others were held during the day at mealtimes. At one Monday evening's meeting, over 300 were unable to gain entry to the church, so were addressed by Buchan from the top of an outside stair while three ministers from neighbouring churches addressed the packed services inside. Such was the emotion felt that some had to be carried out of the church in a swoon, while others continued all night in prayer. An impressive meeting was also held in a neighbouring park. For several weeks, public and private meetings continued unabated, while many from Finnieston also attended packed meetings in the neighbouring Anderston church.

---

175. Anon., *Narrative of the Surprising Work of God*, p. 13.

A special class was formed for adults who, previous to being awakened, were unable to read. Converts also began their own prayer meetings. One was started by boys between the ages of ten and eighteen. A visitor who attended one of their meetings was struck by 'the remarkable earnestness and ease of expression in prayer' of the young lads, who had all previously lived 'very loose' lives. One, who had never before prayed or thought anything of his soul and eternity, and though he still had not obtained peace of heart, 'prayed in such a melting strain of supplication'; one could hear his 'muffled sob, and the droppings of the falling tear'.[176]

Great Hamilton Street

It was in March 1839 that the Rev. William Symington transferred from the Reformed Presbyterian (Cameronian) Church in Stranraer, where he had enjoyed nineteen years of thoroughly successful ministry, to Great Hamilton Street Church in Glasgow, having received an (honorary) degree from Edinburgh University a year previously. Very soon the church (which seated 1,000) was regularly crowded, and three services had to be conducted each Sabbath. As many as fifty or sixty people were received into church fellowship at one time; in this way membership grew rapidly, rising from 300 when Symington first arrived, to three times that figure at the time of his death in 1853. In particular a series of monthly evening lectures proved so popular that arrangements had to be made for the same discourse to be given to church members in the afternoon and to visitors in the evening.[177] In time two mission churches emanated from this thriving congregation, as well as a school system involving over 900 students and 50 teachers.[178]

Similarly, within a few months of the Rev. William Arnot transferring to Glasgow's St Peter's Church on Oswald Street in January 1839, he had gathered 'a large congregation, until the demands for sittings was

---

176. ibid., pp. 16-17.

177. James Gage, *Historical Sketch of the Congregation: Great Hamilton Street Free Church (formerly Reformed Presbyterian), Glasgow*, Glasgow 1890, p. 67. It should be noted that the Reformed Presbyterian Church, like later groups that seceded from the National Church (in the 18th century), was generally against displays of emotion and enthusiasm.

178. Thomas Binnie, *Sketch of the History of the First Reformed Presbyterian Congregation, now the Great Hamilton Street Free Church, Glasgow*, Paisley 1888, pp. 112-14; *DSCHT*, p. 808. Dr Symington was succeeded in the Hamilton Street Church by his son, also Dr William Symington.

more than could be met'.[179] Meanwhile, to the east of the city centre, the parish of Wellpark was 'decidedly quickened from on high' well before the close of 1839, according to correspondence from Robert Murray McCheyne in December of that year.[180]

Lanarkshire

Rutherglen and Paisley

The Rev. James Munro of Rutherglen testified that 'a very considerable number' from his parish – including himself – made the journey to Kilsyth to attend revival meetings, sometimes on a number of occasions. As a result of this, in Munro's congregation 'a very unusual solemnity and spiritual concern manifested themselves and continued for a period of many weeks, more or less generally … in connection with personal visits made to Kilsyth, and the loud-voiced rehearsal of the Lord's glorious doings there'. Several gave the impression of being savingly changed through these visits, 'and a greater number … were most sensibly quickened and revived'. One of these was a doctor, then in his seventies, who visited Kilsyth, the place of his birth, 'and returned rejoicing in God as he certainly had never done before'.[181]

The revival also extended itself to Paisley. In the Rev. John McNaughton's Established Church a large number of people under spiritual concern, from the age of twelve to seventy, applied to him for advice during one fortnight in September-October 1839. Prayer meetings were held in some of the churches during the week, and many less formal ones sprang up in homes throughout the town. These multiplied quickly.

John Kirk in Hamilton

After a year's attendance at the Glasgow Theological Academy, John Kirk was invited to be ordained at Hamilton Congregational Church. Accordingly, he moved there in September 1839, being finally ordained at the end of November. In those intervening weeks before his ordination it soon became clear that, under Kirk's leadership, a new era was beginning in the life of the Hamilton congregation. While the cause of this 'remarkable revival' was no doubt largely to be found in the fervent and powerful addresses of the preacher, it was inspired continually 'from

179. John Goodwin, *History of Free St Peter's Church, Glasgow*, Glasgow 1886.

180. Bonar, *Life of the Rev. John Milne of Perth*, p. 33.

181. Burns, *Pastor of Kilsyth*, pp. 165-6.

abroad and around'. For example, Finney's *Oberlin Evangelist* was regularly read by many of the leading workers, and was a major influence on their methods and aims. Kirk was at the time seen as 'a pupil of Finney'.[182]

Kirk's ministry almost immediately took the itinerating form which it continued ever after to bear. At first he was continually passing between Hamilton and Larkhall, which two places divided his congregation in fairly equal proportions. But soon his preaching attracted men from other neighbouring villages, and these in turn besought him to come and preach in their houses, or in the open air for the benefit of their fellow townsmen. Thus Kirk's influence rapidly widened. In Bellshill, Quarter, Blantyre, Wishaw, Strathaven, Motherwell, Stonehouse and Glasgow, 'he early won trophies for the Saviour', and a movement began which aroused the countryside.[183] Soon we find him writing to a friend that church membership had risen to one hundred and in two weeks to 112. Meetings were also held throughout the town on Sabbath evenings by the leading brethren in the church. So many became actively engaged that the evening service in the chapel suffered a little.[184] Nonetheless, the Blackswell church became so regularly filled that a new chapel was constructed in 1841–2.

Airdrie

A decided 'revival … which had a beneficial effect upon the surrounding neighbourhood' was evidenced in Airdrie in 1840. Mr Taylor of Blackburn began a month's labours in the Congregational Church in July of that year. He found the congregation to be 'in a very low state', and decided to take advantage of the immense crowd that turned up for a formal parade of the 78th Regiment one Sabbath afternoon, by conducting an open-air service immediately on the back of it. Around two thousand people heard his message, many adjourning to the chapel, which was filled to the door. This became a pattern for the following fortnight –

---

182. H. Kirk, *Memoirs of Rev. John Kirk D.D.*, Edinburgh 1888, pp. 154-5.

183. Kirk even travelled as far distant as the north Ayrshire towns of Saltcoats and Stevenston. He was especially well received in the latter place, and as many as 32 inquirers waited for counselling at one meeting. One Wednesday an early prayer meeting was held at half-past seven in the morning. More than 100 attended, many of whom, after it finished, spread all over the town to continue prayer meetings in private houses during the day. 'This day more than sixty inquirers rewarded their efforts' (ibid., p. 161).

184. ibid., p. 159.

open-air preaching followed by a chapel service. These meetings excited much attention and not a few were led to the Saviour.[185] Taylor accepted a call to pastor the church in October, but previous to this some brethren from outwith the district came to hold a series of 'revival meetings' in Taylor's church. These 'were productive of much good', and as a result both of Taylor's previous labours and these meetings, from July 1840 to 1st January 1841 one hundred members were added to the congregation. In the following fourteen months, additions were made 'almost every week', so that by March 1842 the church had a membership of 300, a congregation of 700 and a Sabbath school of over 650.[186]

Fergus Ferguson Snr in Bellshill

The Rev. Fergus Ferguson Snr – distinguished as the leader in whose Bible class in Hamilton's Black's Well meeting-house a very young David Livingstone [187] committed his life to the Lord – began meetings in a saw-pit by the highway-side in Bellshill around 1840.[188] These were transferred to a small schoolroom, which quickly became so packed that steps were taken to erect a building – which opened in 1842 as Bellshill Congregational Church. By the time the middle-aged Ferguson was ordained and inducted to the charge in March 1843 (with no formal theological training), the number of converts had grown to about 200. These additions consisted not only of Bellshill residents, but converts of an 'almost unbroken series of revival meetings' that Ferguson held in the mining villages around Bellshill, such as Motherwell, Newarthill, Carfin, Holytown, Chapelhall, Carnbroe and Coatbridge. Indeed as

---

185. 1845 'Questionnaire', quoted in McNaughton, *Early Congregational Independency in Lowland Scotland*, vol. 2, pp. 147, 145.

186. ibid., pp. 145-6. By October 1842 Taylor had embraced anti-paedobaptist views and resigned his charge, subsequently forming a Baptist church in the town and drawing scores of members from his previous charge to the new cause.

187. This is the same David Livingstone who became the world-famous missionary explorer in Africa, and one of the most popular national heroes of late nineteenth-century Britain. Virtually no biography of Livingstone, however, provides details of his Sunday School days.

188. Bellshill and surrounding district was formerly a stronghold of the Relief Church. After its founder, Thomas Gillespie, preached here in 1763 a church was built seating 700, and this was often filled on Sundays. By 1840 nine further Relief congregations had been added within a circle of nine miles (William Thomson, *The First Relief Church in the West: An Account of Bellshill West United Free Church*, Glasgow 1913).

a result of his powerful ministry and the 'great blessing attending his services ... a great awakening was experienced' among a number of mining communities in mid-Lanarkshire. Ferguson's method was to fix upon a village for a fortnight's protracted meetings, preaching night after night and conversing with anxious inquirers, before driving what had become known as his 'gospel chariot' back home around midnight.[189]

Fergus Ferguson Jnr in Shotts

A remarkable work was done as a result of Ferguson's exertions in Shotts Iron Works, which, as elsewhere, became the cause of great excitement. After his season of protracted labour here, around fifty people began to make the journey on foot or in carts to the chapel in Bellshill (most later joined the church), which was soon attracting up to 500 to its Sabbath services. Meanwhile, another series of revival meetings was conducted at Shotts Iron Works in 1843, this time by Fergus Ferguson Jnr – 'the boy preacher' – who was at that time only eighteen years old and at home from college on vacation. 'It was a time of deep spiritual interest among young and old', noted the Rev. David Hislop, who attended these meetings as a young boy. 'We felt as if a new world was beginning, and as if the way of salvation and the love of God had never been understood till then ... The "new views" ... were so fresh and unwonted in that country village, and spoken so vividly and powerfully, that quickening and spiritual openings were widespread and great'.[190] The mission resulted in the formation of a church in the district, the nucleus of which consisted of a worthy band of 'such men as make the backbone of the Evangelical Union churches'.[191]

Elsewhere in Central Scotland

Congregational work in Stirling and Beyond

In Stirling, a work of grace commenced among the Congregationalists in February 1840, apparently before Burns paid a visit to the town.[192]

---

189. Various Contributors, *The Worthies of the Evangelical Union: Being the Lives and Labours of Deceased Evangelical Union Ministers*, Glasgow 1883, p. 245.

190. William Adamson, *The Life of the Rev. Fergus Ferguson, M.A., D.D., Minister of Montrose Street Evangelical Union Church*, London 1900, pp. 30-1.

191. ibid., p. 32.

192. Couper, *Scottish Revivals*, p. 126; See also Anon., *Narrative of Revival Meetings at Stirling*, Stirling 1840.

Protracted meetings were conducted over a fortnight, commencing with a nine o'clock prayer meeting (which sometimes drew over 400 people), and including a short address from a minister present. A prayer meeting was also scheduled for noon and another in the evening following the public meeting; while at least half-a-dozen others took place in private homes. To these prayer meetings the ministers looked with peculiar interest, as being the power-house of the movement. They never were present at them, but left the people to conduct them as they felt led.[193]

The main meetings were so successful that on some evenings the John Street (Secession) Church was crowded with around two thousand people, after-meetings drawing in from 400 to 1,000, while over 300 persons were conversed with separately, many of them four or five times each. *The Stirling Observer*, which gave a full, fascinating report on the meetings, said: 'For our part we can see nothing to blame, except it be the over-working of the ministers.' The parish minister, however, complained that the Congregational preachers had succeeded in drawing off proselytes from both the Established Church and from the Seceders.

Still among Congregationalists, deep conviction was also observed in Dunkeld.[194] Further south, a system of cottage prayer meetings for an outpouring of God's Spirit was begun in Haddington in 1838. Two weeks' protracted services commenced in March 1840. On the second Sabbath evening, both of the Independent chapels were crowded to excess, although other places of worship in the small town were also open at that hour. The result was 'a season of sweet refreshing'. Over 600 remained to after-meetings, a third of whom sought private conversation with ministers.[195] It was particularly through the holding of 'protracted meetings' like these, that Independent congregations in Edinburgh, Glasgow, Dundee, Paisley, Dumfries, Kilsyth, Hawick, Anstruther and other locations reported considerable increase in membership. The planting of new churches within the Congregational fold was also more common during this period.[196]

---

193. *SCM* 1840, quoted in McNaughton, *Early Congregational Independency in Lowland Scotland*, vol. 1, pp. 267-8.

194. ibid., quoted in McNaughton, *Highlands and Islands*, pp. 154-5.

195. ibid., pp. 221-2, quoted in McNaughton, *Early Congregational Independency in Lowland Scotland*, vol. 1, pp. 373-4.

196. Harry Escott, *A History of Scottish Congregationalism*, Glasgow 1960, pp. 106-7.

Bathgate

James Morison's confidence as an evangelist grew following his successful probationary labours in Moray (see page 391), and on return to his home area of Bathgate in early 1840 – where his father served as a Secession minister – he was not afraid to preach before those who had known him since childhood. Local ministers, former school-mates and others in the neighbourhood were astounded at the intensity of his utterances and the manner in which he spoke. Morison arranged a series of meetings in May, which proved highly successful, and after they closed the work was carried on by converts of the mission, 'and a rich harvest was reaped'. Members of his own family were among those deeply affected by his witness,[197] including his own father, who although having been a Secession minister for twenty-eight years, freely admitted that, while previously he had preached Christ as an all-sufficient Saviour, he now was able to claim and proclaim Him as his *own* Saviour.[198]

Wallacestone

The Relief Church shared in the general awakening of this period, as too did the Methodist cause.[199] Methodist evangelist, Alexander Patrick arrived in Wallacestone, a few miles south east of Falkirk, in February 1842 and lodged with non-religious hosts. A woman visiting the home, who considered herself a Christian, was astonished by what she heard when she conversed with Patrick about spiritual matters. Thoroughly awakened, and now wondering whether she was previously guilty of sinning unpardonably, she anxiously sought forgiveness, and came through to a place of peace before the next day dawned. Her husband, amazed at the change in his wife, now also became awakened, and after conversing with Patrick and crying out to God, was also converted. All this so affected the host and his wife that they spent a whole day conversing with their godly guest about the claims of Christ, and they too were soon rejoicing in His name. The news of these events spread quickly, and many came to see what was going on and to talk with the visiting preacher. The local school-room was acquired and every evening for the next several weeks Patrick preached to large congregations,

---

197. William Adamson, *The Life of the Rev. James Morison*, London 1898, p. 71.

198. Fergus Ferguson, *A History of the Evangelical Union*, p. 175.

199. Swift, *Methodism in Scotland*, pp. 66-7.

from which a considerable number claimed to find 'the pearl of great price'. Many felt keenly 'the pangs of penitence' and 'could little restrain themselves in expressing their distress or joys'. However, amidst this 'boisterous revival', wise steps were taken to prevent the good work evaporating in mere excitement.[200]

After six weeks, forty-six people were capable of uniting in fellowship – most having obtained peace of soul – and two classes were instituted by the Rev. Williams of Glasgow. Following a powerful message from Williams, the people managed to restrain their deep feelings till after the benediction, when one young man cried out vehemently for prayer. The congregation, who were on their way out of the building, turned back and a prayer meeting commenced. Shortly, more than twenty penitents were crying at the same time for mercy, several receiving peace before they went home.[201]

By June, a church with seventy members had been formed, which increased in numbers and grace over subsequent months. Patrick preached in folks' houses and in the open air, with vast numbers attending, some coming from great distances. The outdoor meetings were held on the summit of one of the Ochil Hills, near the stone erected to commemorate William Wallace. At this vantage point, the preacher could be observed from all over the district, and crowds began to gather without any other summons. It was a sight to behold numerous parties of pilgrims, who a few weeks before were revelling in 'open and abandoned wickedness', now thronging from all directions towards this spot and toiling up the steep, to bow before their Maker, and listen to the tale of redeeming love. 'On some occasions', wrote John Drake, 'the word delivered on this spot has been accompanied by a power similar in its effects to that which attended the ministrations of Wesley and Whitefield. The hearers have literally fallen to the earth in companies, deploring their past ingratitude and rebellion against God, or rejoicing with an overpowering joy because they had now found his mercy.'[202]

At length a church was built for the thriving congregation, being formally opened in the autumn of 1843. Considerable opposition

---

200. Drake, *The Wallacestone Reformer*, pp. 132-7.

201. ibid., pp. 137-8.

202. ibid., pp. 138-41.

attended the movement. Some tried to convince believers that they had entered a 'soul-ruining course'. This proved unsuccessful, as did a short anti-revival publication, written 'with affection and distributed with zeal', which was viewed by most as so ridiculous that a response was deemed unnecessary.[203]

By this time, Patrick had taken up residence in the village, so he was better placed to help build up converts in their faith, as well as to preach in nearby localities. Despite many sneers and much obloquy, he made converts in Redding, Lauriston, Grangemouth, Borrowstouness, Avonbridge, Western Divities, Shieldhill, Rumford and Blackbraes. Soon eleven classes were in lively operation, attended by 150 members, along with a Sunday school of one hundred (and twenty teachers). It was true that several converts fell back, and some moved away from the area, but there remained a thriving church which quickly proved too large for their existing building.[204]

Ayrshire

Kilmarnock and Wallacetown

In the anniversary historical record of Henderson United Free Church in Kilmarnock, Robert Tulloch notes the previous ministry of the Rev. David Landsborough (also a well-respected botanist, author and artist) in the then Church of Scotland, going on to state that this minister had 'a vivid recollection of the great revival of 1839', and in this connection recalled an incident which left a very deep impression on his mind. An old soldier who lived by himself in a little garret was in the habit of walking in the woods near Stewarton, where Landsborough was born and where he spent his childhood. Landsborough, then a lad of twelve or thirteen, along with his schoolboy friends, was curious to know where the soldier was going, so they followed him. In the silence amid the trees, the old man knelt down to pray, and this quaint and humble scene left a profound impression on young David, and later played a part in forming his rich Christian character.[205]

---

203. ibid., p. 142.

204. ibid., pp. 142-9.

205. Robert Tulloch, *History of Henderson United Free Church, Kilmarnock 1773–1923*, Kilmarnock 1923, p. 32. Landsborough's son, William, born in 1825, became renowned as an Australian explorer.

In the same period, the Rev. James Stewart of Wallacetown Church of Scotland was delighted to have large, often crowded congregations during 1839, but was nevertheless aware of the great danger, 'lest outward success should be a covering to inward unproductiveness'. An entry in his diary in January 1840 notes him having 'a prayer meeting tonight in my church. The attendance was large and encouraging. I trust that the spirit of supplication is in some small measure poured out upon the people'.[206]

The Early Ministry of James Morison

Just three weeks after his ordination as minister of Kilmarnock's United Secession Church in Clerk's Lane in 1840 James Morison noted, 'These last two Sabbaths have been "days of power". There is also an omen of a "plenteous rain"'.[207] This proved prophetic, for his church quickly became a thriving centre of evangelistic influence, and 'an extensive religious awakening' developed in the town and neighbourhood.[208] Yet, less than a year after coming to Kilmarnock, Morison was ejected from that denomination for teaching the doctrine of the universal atonement of Christ. Almost his entire congregation left with him to form an Independent church in the Clerk's Lane Chapel, which was their own property. Morison's removal and his controversial teachings created a great stir, and as they became more widely known (e.g. by means of the publication of Morison's tract *The Nature of the Atonement* in 1841), so 'an extensive interest was excited, more particularly in the west of Scotland'.[209] The 'new views'[210] were welcomed by large numbers, who left churches where the doctrines of the Westminster Confession were preached, and formed themselves into groups for Bible study and the preaching of the gospel. (In time, an attempt was made to unite all such

---

206. William Baird, *Sixty Years of Church Life in Ayr: The History of Ayr Free Church from 1836 to 1896*, Ayr 1896, pp. 62-3.

207. Adamson, *The Life of the Rev. James Morison*, p. 98.

208. ibid. Prior to Morison's arrival in Kilmarnock, the Congregational cause was flourishing. By late 1836 the average attendance of John Ward's congregation was '700 and gradually increasing' (McNaughton, *Early Congregational Independency in Lowland Scotland*, vol. 2, p. 240).

209. ibid., p. 243.

210. The Morisonians, as they were termed, were aware that these weren't 'new' teachings at all, but claimed, 'The same doctrines had been preached by the Wesleys and their followers for a hundred years, and also by the independents of both England and Scotland', but, it was noted, 'few ever preached as James Morison did' (ibid., p. 241).

disaffected believers within a single body – thus the Evangelical Union was formed in May 1843.)

On Morison's return to his church after being suspended from his office by the Synod of the United Secession Church, he made the controversial decision to go ahead and conduct the Communion on the following Sabbath, when a remarkable 183 communicants were to be added to the church roll, all of whom had made professions of faith during the previous three months (regarding 1841 as a whole, an amazing 400 believers were enrolled as new members). In the lead-up to the Communion applicants had been interviewed several times by the minister and elders to test their suitability for membership – an immensely time-consuming duty in the midst of Morison's stressful, drawn-out judicial proceedings. While the majority of these new members were under thirty and some as young as sixteen, a number were of middle-age, and a few were over seventy. The utmost silence prevailed as the ejected minister proudly conducted this momentous and solemn sacrament, and so impressive was the whole scene that few in the crowded church could control their emotions, both Morison and his most experienced elders being among those visibly affected.[211]

As an independent, Morison ministered with renewed spiritual vigour. His eloquence, burning zeal and eminent expository power markedly affected those hungry for spiritual nourishment. 'A Pentecostal season was experienced in Clerk's Lane Church, and hundreds by the divine blessing were shaken out of their carelessness, and brought in contrition to the foot of the Cross'.[212] Morison was at heart an evangelist. He was said not only to have converted the worst of men – in addition he made them all preachers! Certainly scores were brought by him into a knowledge of 'the truth', and many of these immediately became zealous firebrands in and around Kilmarnock. One such was William Taylor, who was later a colleague of Morison's in the Evangelical Union Theological Hall. Meanwhile, kitchen meetings were held all over Kilmarnock, which was divided into districts.

Morison kept up a relentless schedule of Sabbath-day services, separate week-night Bible classes for young men and women, prayer meetings, visiting the sick, visiting church members, and itinerant

---

211. ibid., pp. 199-200.
212. Adamson, *The Life of the Rev. James Morison*, p. 98.

evangelism in nearby towns and villages in the summer months; while on certain nights of the week his manse was almost full of inquirers waiting for conversation. To cope with the workload, John Hart was employed as an evangelist around 1843. So many people flocked to services that it became a sight to behold several hundred people converging on Clerk's Lane to augment the crowds which were already in and around the church. As a result, overflow rooms often had to be engaged – the 'Crown Inn' for fore- and afternoon meetings, and the larger 'George Inn' for evening gatherings. Yet it was not sensational preaching with intent to excite emotions that drew such large numbers to hear Morison, for the minister was against such techniques, preferring instead the more methodical approach of expository preaching on Sabbath mornings. The Monday evening prayer meetings also drew large numbers – 600 regularly attending – and the galleries had to be opened to accommodate them. We're told that during the second as well as the first year of his ministry in Kilmarnock, 'spiritual blessing was received at every service'.[213]

The prosperity of the new cause came at the expense of not a little persecution. This appears to have been on account both of the 'new' doctrines being propounded as well as the numbers of people leaving (or being ejected from) existing churches in and around the town. The term 'Morisonian' was used as an expression of derision; children of families who attended Morison's church were taunted at school; servants, colliers, quarrymen and others were dismissed by their employers simply for being seen attending their place of worship, and as a consequence they had to leave the town and move up to Glasgow in search of new employment. Despite such exodus, Morison could say that 'still the chapel is full, and was yesterday crowded to the door. I am very happy'.[214]

The influence of Morison's teaching quickly spread well beyond Kilmarnock. Indeed we're told that from the beginning of his ministry he became 'the centre of a great spiritual movement which sent its influence over the whole of the West of Scotland, and gradually encircled the land'.[215] From the start, many people in North Ayrshire became deeply interested in the revival movement in Kilmarnock, and longed for him to

---

213. ibid., p. 227.

214. ibid., pp. 251-2.

215. Adamson, *The Life of the Rev. James Morison*, p. 97.

visit their communities. In one historic village near the town (thought to be Kilmaurs), Morison's preaching created great excitement. The inhabitants of that ancient village were ripe and ready for the 'simple gospel' which he preached. The Secession minister of that time, a good man, was yet a bitter enemy of the 'new gospel' and a determined Calvinist. Still we're told that Morison made a great many converts here.

In many places in Ayrshire that Morison visited by his own estimate many hundreds and often thousands gathered to hear him. In Fenwick and Riccarton he preached to 'immense crowds'. In Troon and Darvel the estimated figure was over four thousand. In the 'sheperdless' hamlets around the Water of Ayr, Morison preached before 700 people sitting or standing quite contentedly for nearly two hours under a heavy rain.[216] From Galston a deputation who regularly waited on Morison's ministrations in Kilmarnock pleaded with him to visit their town. He did so one Sabbath evening, preaching to between 4,000 and 5,000 people. The meeting was most uncommonly attentive, and Morison learned that 'great excitement has been the consequence of the sermon'. Alexander Forsyth, a lay missionary in Morison's church, became a devout follower of his pastor and laboured in Galston 'with much acceptance'.[217] Soon an Evangelical Union cause was established there, and at the ordination of Mr Drummond in September 1843, Morison had to preach from a cart in a large field as the people could not be accommodated otherwise than 'under the blue canopy of heaven'.[218] Like his mentor, Drummond became a tireless promoter of Morisonian teaching, holding three services on a Sunday, as well as evangelising throughout Ayrshire and beyond whenever he could.

When Morison was invited to address an anniversary open-air service to commemorate the battle of Drumclog in June 1843, the field next to the Martyrs' Monument where such meetings were traditionally held was denied him by the landowner, and only after considerable difficulty was another site secured. A witness observed that there gathered 'an immense multitude of people, and still numbers were to be seen flocking from all quarters to the scene. The evening was calm and beautiful while everything around was calculated to produce the deepest impression. It

216. ibid., pp. 209, 227.
217. ibid., p. 232.
218. ibid., p. 267.

was as wild a moorland scene as one could see'. Undoubtedly inspired by his surroundings, Morison preached passionately for over an hour. 'Never even from him', noted a companion, 'did I hear a more thrilling discourse and my impressions were shared by many', many who could vividly recall this remarkable occasion decades later.[219]

The Morisonian movement continued to flourish throughout the 1840s, though by the time of Morison's removal to Glasgow in 1851 the intense excitement which was manifested in the previous decade had to a considerable extent subsided. 'The flame of zeal on behalf of evangelism gave place to a deep religious fervour which permeated the people, and found vent in works of faith and labours of love', Morison's biographer wrote. While the meetings were not so crowded as during the first year of Morison's pastorate, they were yet sufficient to fill the chapel.[220]

The Borders

Jedburgh

In the Established Church of the Borders town of Jedburgh, which was pastored by John Purves, 'a more silent, but very solid work of conversion was advancing'.[221] Robert Murray McCheyne came to preach here on at least one occasion during this period, also visiting Kelso. Purves felt that the main means of awakening sinners to holy impressions and for bringing down 'a gracious influence' was the many prayer meetings that arose in the district in the winter of 1839. In addition to these the town hall was used on week-nights, where the meetings differed in almost no respect from the usual Sabbath services except that they were less formal.[222] Purves regarded himself as almost the only instrument, very seldom having help from without. 'I did not preach sermons', he wrote, 'but spoke to the people about their souls and the great truths of the gospel, as I would have done to them, face to face, about a piece of important business, not in a formal, but business way'.[223]

---

219. ibid., pp. 241-2.

220. ibid., p. 295.

221. Bonar, *Life of Robert Murray McCheyne*, pp. 140-1.

222. Gillies, *Historical Collections*, p. 560.

223. Purves said he preached a free salvation through the blood of Christ just as he would have done in a heathen land which had never before heard the gospel; persuaded as he was that the want throughout Scotland was not structural but foundational; 'that the elementary facts of the Gospel are not believed' (ibid.).

As a result, the church advanced more in one year than in the previous ten of his ministry there. As a result, also, Purves now felt, 'There is a true and living Church amongst us, however small, which I never did (have) before; a little band to co-operate with me in every way, and to lay themselves out for the spiritual welfare of their fellow-sinners'. They, 'after their working hours, go about visiting their former companions in wickedness, when ill, or any opening that presents itself for speaking to them about their souls'.[224]

Hawick

Three years after a Congregational church was established in Hawick in 1836, a series of protracted meetings was held in the Relief Chapel, conducted principally by Robert Wilson and Henry Wright. Held in June 1839, these services were instrumental in the conversion of William Bathgate, later a distinguished Evangelical Union minister, who wrote, 'There are at present interesting meetings taking place at Hawick, properly they may be termed Revival Meetings … We have had Mr Douglas, Cavers, addressing us several times, and oh, for a rich and fertile mind he is hardly to be surpassed'.[225] John Purves of Jedburgh compared the movement in Hawick to the blessed work of revival that sprang up in his own congregation.[226]

Kelso

Even before the widespread revivals of 1839 a remarkable though quiet work of the Spirit had begun in Horatius Bonar's parish of Kelso (see page 317). A notable preacher, it was said of Bonar by 'an intelligent mechanic in the Merse' that 'every separate sentence tells like strokes of a hammer, every stroke sends the nail further in and deeper down'.[227] Since his induction in 1837, Bonar had incessantly exhorted his congregation to pray, and he directly traced 'the good that has been done here to the earnest supplications of a praying people' – prayer for individuals as well as for the outpouring of the Spirit on His Church. What further

---

224. Presbytery of Aberdeen, *Evidence on the Subject of Revivals*, p. 73.

225. Various Contributors, *Worthies of the Evangelical Union*, p. 389.

226. Presbytery of Aberdeen, *Evidence on the Subject of Revivals*, p. 72.

227. Rev. James Wylie, *Disruption Worthies – A Memorial of 1843*, Edinburgh 1881, p. 43. Bonar was also a hymn-writer, composing over 600 hymns over the course of his life, and becoming one of the few Scottish hymn-writers to gain widespread acclaim outside Scotland (Faith Cook, *Hymn Writers and their Hymns*, Darlington 2005, pp. 289-308).

helped forward the work was the preaching of the word, prayer meetings, the efforts of visitors, the circulation of tracts and books, and the
zealous exertions of church workers in the parish.

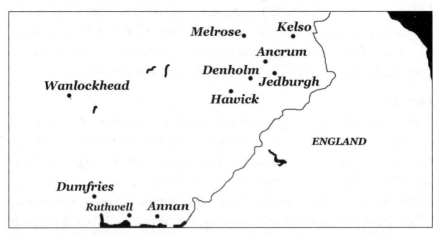

Sometime in 1839 Bonar paid visits to witness in person the revivals in progress in both Kilsyth and Dundee and gave enthusiastic public
accounts of them on his return to Kelso, stating that 'about four thousand
people (were) stirred up to seek the Lord'.[228] And seek they did. Prayer
meetings were begun as early as five or six in the morning and Bonar and
his assistant James Ballantyne Hay were called on an almost daily basis to
visit anxious souls. In one undated letter Hay could report: 'God seems
to be pouring out his Spirit in large abundance, many souls are being
gathered to Himself, before the millennium dawn.' Soon, not only was
Bonar kept busy from morning to night on a daily basis, but Hay, too,
was holding 'meetings, meetings, meetings, almost nightly' especially in
the outlying district stations. This led to increased bodily weariness for
the thirty-year-old worker, and to 'a good drilling from my mother, for
exerting myself so much'! The almost unmanageable workload continued
weekly for many months on end and Hay's diary was filled with a constant assignment of meetings. 'Yet what an honour', Hay noted, 'that
I, so unworthy, should be chosen by heaven to help in carrying (the
work) on'. Throughout, Hay often laboured alongside his minister, and
both men made sure they spent a good deal of time, both separately and
together, in prayer for the furtherance of God's will among them.[229]

228. Walker, *Memoir of the Rev. James Ballantyne Hay*, pp. 30-1.
229. ibid., pp. 42, 47.

In a letter to his sister, Hay issued a vivid, poetic picture of the work of God so apparent in their midst.

> What a blessed work is going on around, what a change! Many, many of the outcasts and wanderers, the sheep bleating on the mountains of Israel, have found their way to the fold, where green pastures are, and living streams appear; they, now clothed and in their right mind, eat the manna which falls around the tents of Israel, and drink the waters from the smitten rock. What a change! It is good to be here. Oh, how precious to hear such tell what the Lord has done for their souls, they scowl no more at a preached gospel, they frown no more at the saints of God, as they pass by, they are themselves become the precious ones of the earth; no longer tossed and exposed to the rage and fury of the billows, they float safely, on calm and deep tide, close to the shore. And while others around are still dashing against the cliffs, the breeze of heaven (the good Spirit of the Lord) from the east and the west, from the north and the south, is filling their wide spread sails, and carrying them onward to the haven of repose ... A sun has risen with healing under his wings, which to them goes not down; they stand in southern hills, warmed by his rays. Yes, the morning star has truly dawned to many, their fears and doubts are dispelled as the darkness of morning is chased away before the beams of the early sun; a smile now sits on their countenances, their faces are lighted up, their minds are no more confused, unsettled, and fluctuating; but calm, listening with child-like submission, to divine teaching. In a word, they feel as resting upon a rock, which cannot be moved by the billows beating around; Jesus in his fullness and freeness, is the admiration and all captivating theme of their souls.[230]

Altogether, by February 1841, Bonar could safely say there had been upwards of one hundred conversions. Of that number, less than a fifth had been openly profligate; the others having 'a name that they lived, but were dead'.[231] The minister noted that several conversions of 'persons the most careless', who attended no church, occurred without any human instrumentality at all – not by any sermon, nor by a minister

---

230. ibid., pp. 45-6.
231. Presbytery of Aberdeen, *Evidence on the Subject of Revivals*, p. 62.

or friend, nor even by the Bible. The Spirit of God seemed to work in them apart from all outward agency, and Bonar could not conceive 'a more incontestable proof of God's presence amongst us than such cases afford'.[232] He also noted 'nothing of what is called excitement amongst us; but a calm, deep, steadfast, solemn impression. Not that I condemn excitement, I simply state the fact, we have had none of it'.[233]

A minister from a neighbouring parish to Bonar's felt that it was,

> not perhaps so much the stir and excitement of one or more revivals, as the spiritual power, the still solemnity, the continuous life and action of a revived church, that made it the centre of life and refreshing to all the district round, through many a successive year. The Spirit came less as 'the rushing of a mighty wind' or 'as floods upon the dry ground', than as 'rain upon the mown grass, as showers that water the earth'. Meetings for prayer abounded, and 'they that feared the Lord spake often one to another', so that to some of us who had only begun our ministry, a visit to Kelso was felt to be a season of refreshing, whence we returned to our own work with new encouragement and hope. Classes for the young were greatly blessed. And none more so than (Bonar's) boarding-school classes drawn from all parts of the country, the fruits of which are still to be met with in many a family throughout the land.[234]

Looking back on those early years, Bonar wrote: 'I found plenty of work, plenty of workmen, and plenty of sympathy – zealous elders, zealous teachers, and zealous friends. The keynote which I struck was, "Ye must be born again", and that message found its way into many hearts. It repelled some, but it drew many together, in what I may call the bond of regeneration.'[235]

Ancrum

In mid-summer 1839, Robert Wilson, a Congregational preacher, came to Ancrum from nearby Denholm and spoke on nine successive evenings in a packed schoolroom, with much effect. Numerous 'auxiliary means of

---

232. ibid., p. 63; Gillies, *Historical Collections*, p. 559.

233. Presbytery of Aberdeen, *Evidence on the Subject of Revivals*, p. 63.

234. Wylie, *Disruption Worthies*, pp. 42-4.

235. Various Contributors, *Horatius Bonar, D.D. – A Memorial*, Edinburgh 1890, p. 10.

grace' were effective in promoting the work; viz. the distribution of *The Monthly Visitor* to every family; the use, on the part of many, of tracts and religious books of various kinds, by Sabbath schools; and especially, Sabbath-evening preaching in different parts of the parish. Wilson had to return again and again to Ancrum, as, he noted with delight,

> The work has broken out afresh, and there is a considerable stir in the village … the work seems to be gradually progressing … Last night the house was so crowded that they could scarcely get stirred together, and that fully an hour before the time of the meeting. Even on these cold nights, many stood around the door and windows, who could not gain admittance … On both evenings I spoke nearly three hours, and yet at the close, the greatest part seemed reluctant to separate. Last night, upwards of 150 remained as anxious inquirers.[236]

The work of revival was just as prominent within the Established Church. Andrew Bonar noted that 'The whole parish, but especially the men of the place', were awakened to the most solemn concern, as the breath of God's Spirit continued to stir across the land.[237] According to parish minister, the Rev. John Paton, there was an 'almost simultaneous reformation' in the behaviour of those previously addicted to outward immorality and an anxious inquiry concerning spiritual things within the community at large. So great did this feeling all at once become, and so rapidly did it extend, that week-night services were set up, which were attended by crowded and deeply interested audiences. There was 'a visible reformation from sin', but it could also now be said that 'the subject of politics, once the more heart-stirring in the village, has given way to the blessed solicitude about an interest in that deliverance which is eternal'.[238] Nine weekly prayer-meetings were operating in the village at the time – five of them conducted by females. One began at six on Sabbath morning and was more numerically attended than any of the

---

236. *SCM* 1840, quoted in McNaughton, *Early Congregational Independency in Lowland Scotland*, vol. 1, pp. 442-3. (Protracted) meetings were also held in numerous other places in the vicinity, including Haymount, where 'several gave pleasing evidence of being truly converted', some of whom went on to join the Congregational Church in Denholm.

237. Bonar, *Life of Robert Murray McCheyne*, pp. 140-1.

238. Presbytery of Aberdeen, *Evidence on the Subject of Revivals*, pp. 91-2.

others. The fruits of this 'season of refreshing' were still manifest twenty years later.[239]

Denholm and Melrose

Denholm is famed for being the location of Scotland's first protracted meetings, held in the spring of 1839. As a result of these gatherings fifty-four people had been received into the local fellowship under the leadership of Robert Wilson, with still others being conversed with in regard to admission. This number, it has to be said, included a number of converts from Wilson's labours in various neighbouring communities around this time.

In the following spring, 1840, Ebenezer Young, a member of Denholm Congregational Church, began meetings in his native Melrose, as well as in a number of adjoining villages, being accompanied in June by Douglas of Cavers. 'A few Christians in the place were soon greatly revived', he wrote. A series of eight protracted meetings was held in Melrose in September, followed by three further meetings near the start of October, which were 'crowded to overflowing, and the interest much increased'.[240] Young's time was now divided between giving public addresses and conversation with inquirers. In March 1842, a Congregational church was formed in the town.

When James Morison spent some days in Melrose in February 1843, he found the interest 'exceedingly great. The place was crowded in all its passages and porches', he observed, 'and this before the hour. Our anxious meetings were attended by hundreds … Every hour of the day was occupied in conversing with the young believers, or, as was generally the case, with awakened sinners. The higher classes became deeply interested, and I was sent for by many of them that I might converse with them … the brethren know of sixty persons who are hopefully brought to the knowledge of the truth'.[241]

Dumfries and Galloway

The expansive Lowland region of Dumfries and Galloway seems to have been among the districts least affected by the revival of 1839–42. Denominational records report that in the winter of 1839, 'a considerable awakening' took place in the Congregational Church at Dumfries,

239. Reid, *Authentic Records of Revival*, pp. 273-4.

240. *SCM* 1840, quoted in McNaughton, *Early Congregational Independency in Lowland Scotland*, vol. 1, p. 462.

241. ibid., p. 463.

then pastored by the Rev. Robert Machray, formerly of Perth. However, when James Morison came to Dumfries in December 1841 he found the town 'very cold and dead … and the chapel thinly attended'. Morison's preaching soon filled the church, however, 'and believers seemed to be considerably humbled for their sloth, and stirred up and provoked to love and good works'.[242]

Giving up his charge a couple of years later, Machray became an itinerant evangelist of some repute, preaching from place to place with support from 'that devoted servant of God', the influential James Douglas of Cavers.[243] On a personal note Douglas of Cavers testified that 'though for two or three years previous I had some understanding of the way of salvation, it seemed to come to me with new force and clearness in listening to Mr Machray'.[244]

Meanwhile, the labours of Robert Murray McCheyne in the busy last few years of his short but deeply influential life were also blessed in numerous places to awakening effect. The Rev. Thomas Hastings of Wanlockhead, nestled in the Lowther Hills in north Dumfries and Galloway, pointed to the changes that had taken place in his congregation since the Communion sacrament of July 1841, when, he said, 'the late Rev. Mr Murray McCheyne assisted me. Many, indeed, were melted under his preaching, and became obviously more serious in their demeanour, and the chapel afterwards more regularly crowded'.[245]

McCheyne's preaching was also greatly blessed in a number of locations even further south; for example, in the summer of 1842 in the parish of Ruthwell, situated between Dumfries and Annan (and the scene of many happy summer visits for McCheyne as a boy). Back in the parish of his youth, the Dundee pastor had an influence on the youthful Stephen Hislop (later renowned missionary in India) and under his

---

242. McNaughton, *Early Congregational Independency in Lowland Scotland*, vol. 1, p. 422.

243. Ferguson, *A History of the Evangelical Union*, p. 310. Douglas also assisted pastors of other denominations, through whom 'a good work was being done'. The aristocrat also wrote a booklet on revival which touched on the 1839 movement, entitled *The Revival of Religion*, (Edinburgh 1839) [See Richard Owen Roberts, *An Annotated Bibliography of Revival Literature*, Wheaton 1987, p. 134].

244. *SCM* 1873, quoted in McNaughton, *Early Congregational Independency in Lowland Scotland*, vol. 1, p. 422.

245. Brown, *Annals of the Disruption*, p. 12.

preaching two of Hislop's cousins were converted.[246] To McCheyne's even greater joy, three of his own cousins from Ruthwell district were also converted during this memorable visit. 'Gay and accomplished but destitute of vital godliness', these relatives at first jauntily dubbed their clerical friend 'Perfection'.[247] McCheyne's winsome manner and stealth of argument quickly broke their resistance, however, and soon they became deeply interested in all he had to say, and even became wont to attend his prayer meetings. During prayer one day, the most carefree of the sisters sobbed aloud, and soon all three were in tears on account of their sins. All became decided and earnest Christians, and in October 1842, all three were present in St Peter's, Dundee for a communion led by McCheyne. Long after McCheyne's death these women said it was their cousin's sympathetic spirit and pitiful look that initially struck them.

Further east in November 1842 the Rev. John McRobert of Cambuslang came to preach to the small group of believers in the town of Annan who held to Congregationalist views. He quickly found in them 'a very great and earnest desire ... to hear the gospel. The hall was filled, often crowded ... A considerable number professed to come to the knowledge of the truth as it is in Jesus'. While arrangements were being made to receive these new converts into formal church fellowship, they continued to be supplied by the ministry of visiting preachers. With this supply, 'the spirit of enquiry and awakening again prevailed in their meetings', and a number more were added to their group, out of which a new church was soon established.[248]

---

246. George Smith, *Stephen Hislop, Pioneer Missionary and Naturalist in Central India from 1844 to 1863*, London 1888, p. 19. However, the ministry of W. C. Burns played an even greater role in Hislop's conversion. Orr states that both Hislop and John Wilson, another Borders-born pioneering missionary to India, were products 'of the revival of the early 1800s in the Scottish border country' (J. Edwin Orr, *The Eager Feet: Evangelical Awakenings 1790–1830*, Chicago 1975, p. 175). In fact, Wilson was converted in Lauder at a considerably earlier date than Hislop, and not during a time of revival, He sailed for India in 1828 (George Smith, *The Life of John Wilson*, London 1878, pp. 7-11).

247. William Lamb, *McCheyne From the Pew, Being Extracts From the Diary of William Lamb*, London 1914, p. 81.

248. *SCM* 1844, quoted in McNaughton, *Early Congregational Independency in Lowland Scotland*, vol. 1, p. 432. J. Edwin Orr says that Annan 'was mightily moved' as a result of the revival of this period (*The Eager Feet*, p. 149).

Appendix (to Chapter 6)

Influence of Robert Murray McCheyne

The Free Church minister of St Peter's at time of writing relates his annoyance at the 'hagiography' that has been accorded McCheyne, turning his church into something of a Protestant shrine, given the hundreds who flock each year to the former charge of this most revered of ministers.[249] Such understandable irritation notwithstanding, one cannot help noticing that it was none other than Andrew Bonar, and others who knew McCheyne well, who bestowed on him the most lavish of praises, some of it uttered while McCheyne was still alive. Bonar perhaps knew the Dundee pastor better than anyone, the two having been close friends since university days, frequently corresponding with one another and preaching in each other's pulpits, and spending a whole six months travelling and living together on their mission to the Jews. If anyone knew McCheyne's faults and failings, Bonar did. Yet he was still able to say, at the very outset of his biography of him, written shortly after McCheyne's death, that for years he 'walked calmly in almost unbroken fellowship with the Father and the Son'. He writes further: 'Holiness in him was manifested … in a way so natural, that you recognized therein the easy outflowing of the indwelling Spirit … Some felt, not so much his words, as his presence and holy solemnity, as if one spoke to them who was standing in the presence of God … There is still some peculiar fragrance in the air round Robert McCheyne's tomb.'[250] Meanwhile, in his own diary Bonar remarked: 'How very unlike Robert am I!. O that his mantle would fall upon me! … He was so reverent toward God … His lamp was always burning, and his loins always girt. I never knew it otherwise, even when we were journeying in Palestine.'[251]

Others who knew him give equally flattering testimonies. Dr Baxter of Dundee's Hilltown Church wrote: 'He was one of the most complete ministers I ever met. He was a great preacher, an excellent visitor, a full-orbed saint.' Dr R. S. Candlish, who once said, 'I can't understand McCheyne; grace seems to be natural to him', also remarked, 'He had more of the mind of his Master than almost anyone

---

249. Robertson, *Awakening*, p. ix.

250. Bonar, *Life of Robert Murray McCheyne*, p. 147.

251. Bonar, *Andrew A. Bonar: Diary and Life*, p. 98.

I ever knew'.[252] James Hamilton of Abernyte said he questioned 'if the Church of Scotland has contained a more seraphic mind, one that was in such a constant flame of love and adoration toward "Him that liveth and was dead"'. Alexander Cumming of Bridge of Earn wrote of his close friend that his 'heart mirrored so brightly the Divine purity'. Another close friend, Robert Macdonald of Blairgowrie, remarked on McCheyne's holiness, which he said was noticeable even before he spoke a word; 'his appearance spoke for him'.[253] Thomas Guthrie wrote of the Dundee minister: 'He had in a rare and singular degree his "conversation in heaven" and the influence for good he left in every place he visited was quite extraordinary.' A minister from the north of Scotland stayed overnight with McCheyne and was 'marvellously struck' by the fact that every time McCheyne left the room, he burst into tears, saying to himself, 'Oh, that is the most Jesus-like man I ever saw!' [254] Similarly, Dr Anderson said that while he was minister of St Fergus, McCheyne had spent a day or two in his manse, and not only while he was there, but for a week or two after he had left, it seemed a heavenlier place than ever before. Associated with McCheyne's person, appearance and conversation, on the walls of the house and everything around seemed to be inscribed, 'Holiness unto the Lord'.[255]

Such unconditional praise is even more surprising given that all of the above praise came from ministerial colleagues, men who (from 1843) adhered to the Free Church, men of Calvinist stamp who knew well man's corrupt nature and the futility of flattery. A host of similarly praiseworthy comments are on record from non-clerical friends and parishioners. I can honestly say that of the probably hundreds of Christian biographies that I have read or seriously perused, I have never come across such strong and united testimony to the Christ-likeness of any individual, except perhaps the Indian mystic, Sadhu Sundar Singh, who was also removed from this world as a young man. It seems abundantly clear that McCheyne indeed enjoyed an unusually close walk with God, the very aroma of which oozed through his personality, being immediately apparent to virtually all who met him.

---

252. Prime, *Travel with Robert Murray McCheyne*, pp. 93, 27.

253. Smellie, *Robert Murray McCheyne*, pp. 245, 173-4.

254. ibid., p. 174.

255. David K. & Charles J. Guthrie, *Autobiography of Thomas Guthrie*, vol. 1, pp. 217-18.

CHAPTER 7

The 1839–42 Revival: The North

Introduction

The preceding chapter has clearly revealed that, with Kilsyth and Dundee as its two main centres, the pre-Disruption revival swiftly spread throughout central Scotland and the central Highlands, south-west Scotland and the Borders, thanks largely to the tireless labours of yielded evangelists utterly committed to being used as instruments of God's blessing – men like William Chalmers Burns, Robert Murray McCheyne and Andrew Bonar – as well as to the dedicated ministry of scores of faithful local ministers. Burns's indefatigable exertions, in particular, were especially influential in spreading the revival so dramatically sparked off by his own preaching in his father's parish in July 1839. In Scotland's two main cities the work was led by preachers of no less rank, men such as Alexander Somerville and Jonathan Ranken Anderson (in Glasgow) and Alexander Moody Stuart in Edinburgh. Centring on Kilmarnock, but extending throughout Ayrshire and beyond, the bold and innovative views propounded by James Morison attracted great multitudes and won many converts wherever he preached, while in the Borders, another Bonar brother, Horatius, in Kelso, and the itinerant labours of a number of evangelists of the Congregationalist stamp, but imbued with the 'new views' of Kirk and Morison, proved a means of vast ingathering throughout that expansive land.

The present chapter serves to show that the spiritual awakening of this period was not restricted to the Lowlands and central Highlands, or to districts where prominent figures like Burns, McCheyne, Bonar or Morison were a central attraction. For although, interestingly, each one of these men itinerated throughout the Strathbogie district of Aberdeen-shire during these months, none of them set foot in the widely disparate areas all over the north of mainland Scotland and the remote Highland and Island districts which became stirred by revival fires every bit as potent as those that occurred in the south.

Initiatory Awakening – Skye 1838–9

As a result of emigration and following various internal problems, Uig Baptist Church in Skye numbered only nineteen people in 1832. However, a year after Angus Ferguson of Mull settled as pastor there in 1836 the meeting house, which seated 300, was packed to capacity. Smallpox began to ravage the island in 1838, and a day was set aside 'for beseeching the Lord to pour out his Spirit upon ourselves and others'. Before the year end, Ferguson could report 'a great revival in Uig; the appearance is more promising than any I have ever yet seen … Sabbath last we had three additions of young but married men. After preaching to an audience of about 400, we went to the bank of a small river in the neighbourhood. The congregation stood silent and composed on both sides … There is a great reformation in this place'.[1]

The blessing continued, and by June 1839 Ferguson could say, 'Our congregation upon the Lord's day amounts generally to about four hun-dred. Our Sabbath School is also doing well. It has already been a means of a great moral change among the young. Many of them carry their bibles to the fields, and commit passages of it to memory'.[2] A year later it was claimed that at least twenty-five had been hopefully converted.[3] Ferguson could also report in March 1840 that from the 'eastern part of

---

1. *Baptist Home Mission Society Report* 1838, p. 17.

2. ibid., 1839, p. 11.

3. ibid., 1840, p. 11. Emigration, however, continued to have a detrimental effect on church membership and attendance. Ferguson estimated in 1842 that about 600 were to emigrate from his area. Both he and James MacQueen preached to packed ships about to leave from Uig. 'I never witnessed deeper impressions', remarked Ferguson. On the Sabbath MacQueen 'preached on shore in the morning, and in the evening one of us preached on each vessel to a great number of people. On Monday some of them came ashore, and insisted that we should preach to them again. We preached to them five or six times, and had a good opportunity of conversing with the poor people, and we trust our labour was not in vain' (Steve Taylor, *The Skye Revivals*, p. 82).

my station', too – the Kilmuir/Staffin district – 'large houses, containing 200–300, were crowded to excess'.[4]

At the other end of Skye, too, there began a considerable stirring. James MacQueen of Broadford Baptist Church reported in 1839: 'There is a desire to hear, almost in every part. For six weeks past, our congregation has increased greatly. On some Sabbaths our meeting-house could not contain above one half of the people, and last Lord's day, not more than one third of the hearers, so that we had to take to the field. The number of hearers was from 400 to 500; and in the evening, even after dark, many were about the doors and windows'.[5] Significant as the Uig and Broadford movements were, they were only initiatory tokens of a more powerful revival that was soon to spread through the island (see page 421). Meanwhile, when MacQueen visited Lochcarron and Gairloch in December 1838 he noted: 'The people attended better than for years past. On the Lord's Day many came from far to hear, and some appeared much impressed'. In June the following year, MacQueen reported of Lochcarron – amazingly, given that there was no Baptist cause anywhere in that area – '600–800 attended on the Lord's Day.' [6]

Angus and the Mearns

Forfar

The Central Highlands and Aberdeenshire excepted, Forfar was virtually the only location in the north of the country to share in William Chalmers Burns's devoted labours in the exciting days leading up to the Disruption. His efforts were not in vain. James Mitchell Robbie, just turned twenty, was one of many who got a blessing through his quickening appeals. During this period vital religion in the town was greatly quickened, and meetings for prayer and exhortation were numerous and well attended. Robbie played a principal part in instituting and conducting several

---

4. *BHMS Report* 1840, p. 13. Impressive as this scenario appears, Ferguson did not consider it to constitute revival, for he writes in December, after a similar mission in the same area: 'Our meetings were well attended and apparently deep impressions made … Although I have had grief and trouble here, yet, I have also comfort and happiness, and although there is no appearance of revival at present, yet we hope for better days' (ibid.).

5. *BHMS Report* 1839, p. 11.

6. ibid., p. 6.

of these meetings, also leading Sunday evening services in the nearby villages of Padanarum, Drumgley, Carsebank, etc.[7]

Inverbervie and Laurencekirk

From an unnamed village in Angus in 1839, many had journeyed upwards of six miles night after night to attend protracted meetings in a neighbouring town. When Mr Lowe of Forfar, a member of the Perth, Angus and Mearnshire Itinerant Society,[8] visited the place so great was the anxiety evinced that he spent nearly five hours one evening preaching, conversing with enquirers and 'exhorting the people of God, who sat with tears of joy for what the Lord appeared to be doing for the village'. Early next morning almost the whole community met to hear the word. Interest was unabated almost a year later when it was reported that there were two prayer meetings in the village, one of them composed of youths from twelve to sixteen years of age.[9]

Lowe met with more encouragement still at Bervie (now Inverbervie).[10] Where formerly not above thirty people could be collected to hear the word of God on a weekday evening, the chapel was on this visit crowded night after night by an audience who appeared not only deeply interested, but seriously awakened. On one occasion, after being nearly two hours-and-a-half assembled in a place crowded and heated to no ordinary degree, and after the blessing was pronounced, not one person appeared willing to leave. According to the Itinerant Society's Report for 1840: 'The congregation stood, many of them in tears. It was an indication that they wished the service to be prolonged. The preacher gladly complied. About one half remained after ten o'clock for prayer, and some, under great anxiety, continued to be conversed with after that service was over.'[11]

---

7. 'The Scottish Congregationalist', 1891, p. 318, quoted in McNaughton, *Early Congregational Independency in Lowland Scotland*, vol. 1, pp. 216-17. Robbie began studies at Aberdeen University in 1845 and went on to become Professor of Church History, Homiletics and Hebrew in the Theological Hall of Congregational Churches in Scotland.

8. The Perth, Angus and Mearnshire Itinerant Society was formed in 1825 with intent to augment and improve the Church's outreach to its fellow countrymen.

9. 'Perth, Angus and Mearnshires' Itinerant Society Report' 1840, quoted in McNaughton, *Early Congregational Independency in Lowland Scotland*, vol. 1, p. 228.

10. Once again, the precise location is not disclosed, but the town was stated as being 'in the east of Mearns-shire', has a Congregational chapel, and begins with the letter '*B*', which suggests it is most likely Bervie (ibid.).

11. ibid., pp. 228-9.

Six miles inland from Bervie, on a visit to his parents in his home village of Laurencekirk, a believer by name of David Moir was deeply concerned by the low state of religion in the area. He returned the following summer and preached in the Town Hall and often in the open air. By and by he found himself surrounded by a little band of believers – chiefly the converts of his own labours. By autumn 1842 a congregation of sixty-three members was in existence, plus a Sabbath-school of over one hundred. Besides visiting fully a dozen outlying preaching stations, which were 'marked with prosperity', Moir was also held 'revival meetings' in many other parts of the wider region.[12]

North-East Scotland

James Morison in Moray and Nairn

Cabrach and Knockando

Youthful graduate, James Morison, later founder of the Evangelical Union (see page 373), was sent as a ministerial probationer of the United Secession Church to rural Moray in the summer of 1839. In August he preached on the first two Sabbaths in Cabrach, and on the following two in Knockando, before returning to Cabrach by September. His first labours in this district had been much appreciated by both Independents and Seceeders, 'and a deep impression was produced on the whole community … I know not the cause of this change', wrote the young preacher at the time, 'for my discourses, being now entirely extemporaneous, are much more searching. I never preach without seeing many wistful looks and moistened eyes. The church was filled last Sabbath to overflowing – it has not been so full for many years (it holds comfortably about three hundred)'.[13]

His afternoon sermon being 'an exceedingly solemn occasion', Morison later rode to a farm-house three miles away for an evening meeting, where he preached in a barn crammed with one hundred listeners. The following evening in a nearby township a prayer meeting, long discontinued in the district, was held. 'We had a meeting the like of which has not been seen on a week day in the memory of the oldest residents', exuded the probationer. 'The large room in which we assembled was first filled almost to suffocation; then a long passage to the kitchen was filled, and many had

---

12. *Scottish Congregational Magazine*, 1842, pp. 94-5, quoted in ibid., pp. 241-3.

13. Adamson, *The Life of the Rev. James Morison*, pp. 59-60.

to stand in the kitchen and around the open window and door'. Bursts of 'uncommon emotion' were exhibited during the three-hour meeting, and Morison 'experienced uncommon enlargement'. On the Tuesday evening a meeting for young folk was held in Cabrach, and to the astonishment of all, the chapel was half-filled with young and old together. The interest of many was enhanced by Morison relating the story of the revival that had taken place in Kilsyth just a few months previously, accounts of which he had received from his father in several long letters.[14]

From Cabrach, Morison moved again to Knockando, only to find the religious commotion there even greater than in the former place, not a meeting being held without some souls, old and young, being blessed. The thatched meeting-house was crowded and the audiences hung on the lips of the speaker, in some instances for the space of three hours. From early morning till late at night he was engaged in conversations, prayer meetings or preaching. Some of the cases he had to deal with were remarkable on account of their peculiar experience, and Morison often walked four or even six miles to converse with these anxious souls.[15] George Smeaton also referred to the 'overwhelming outpouring of the Spirit upon the whole district' of Cabrach and Knockando, such that 'many souls were saved and a most blessed revival of religion commenced'.[16]

Nairn

Similar scenes were repeated in and around Nairn, which Morison visited on three separate occasions between October 1839 and May 1840. Much good was accomplished on each visit, but especially the third, when he remained for a fortnight, during which time there was hardly an hour of day or evening not spent preaching, praying or conversing with the anxious. His biographer records that around this time Morison 'frequently felt as if he were the subject of supernatural influences which strengthened his inner and outer man. When in the pulpit he seemed as if in a trance – having an open vision – and only with difficulty could he conclude his discourses'.[17]

---

14. ibid., pp. 60-1.

15. ibid., pp. 61-2.

16. George Smeaton, 'Principal James Morison', Edinburgh 1901, p. 58, quoted in Oscar Bussey, *The Religious Awakening of 1858–60 in Great Britain and Ireland*, Ph.D. Thesis, University of Edinburgh 1947, pp. 234-5.

17. Adamson, *The Life of the Rev. James Morison*, p. 73.

Greatly encouraged by these experiences, Morison continued his ministry with renewed vigour. A strong appeal was made to visit Edinkillie, six miles south-west of Forres, and here Morison preached twice in the late morning and early afternoon from a tent in the open-air to an immense assembly gathered from all around. On two Sabbaths he preached three times to huge congregations, dozens crowding around opened windows and doors. Indeed, so keen were many to wait on Morison's preaching that they remained in their pews from an hour before the morning meeting till the close of the third service at night. Many claimed that Nairn had seen nothing like it except in past days of the great northern communion.[18] Shortly after, a tract was published by a local man, Isaac Ketcher, entitled, *A Brief Account of the Recent Revival of Religion in Nairn*, in which he concluded that his district had received a definite 'time of refreshing from His own presence'.[19] The Church of Scotland also shared in the blessing. As early as Christmas 1838, church members had resolved to pray in their own homes each Saturday at 9 p.m. for an outpouring of the Holy Spirit. Some time later, an additional prayer hour was added and great expectations of revival developed. A considerable number turned to the Lord in the awakening that ensued.

Grantown-on-Spey
No sooner had one deep and influential season of awakening in Grantown-on-Spey drawn to a close (1834–8 – see page 279) than another burst into flames, once again coinciding with a visit from Grantown native, the Rev. Duncan Dunbar of New York. Once again also, no special efforts, such as 'revival meetings', were used to work up a move of the Spirit. Rather, it began when least expected, in the middle of the busy barley harvest season of 1840. Peter Grant, pastor of the Baptist chapel, said that when Dunbar 'saw the grace of God, he was glad, and preached among us for three weeks. He then left us but the Lord did not leave us … Multitudes come to hear the truth, and every week some take warning to flee from the wrath to come … '. Baptisms proved a great source of impression upon the public at large, and Grant was overjoyed to find three more of his own children among

---

18. ibid., pp. 74-5.

19. Isaac Ketcher, 'A Brief Account of the Recent Revival of Religion in Nairn, Especially in the Union Associate Congregation there by One of Themselves', Nairn 1840, quoted in Fergus Ferguson, *A History of the Evangelical Union*, pp. 12-13.

the candidates, making him, in his own words, 'now the happy father who has seen seven of my children putting on the Lord Jesus Christ'.[20]

Grant preached as doors were opened, 'through mountains and valleys, north, south, east and west', and noted that some of the converts hailed from as far away as Glenlivet and the parish of Edinkelly, fifteen miles to the east and north of Grantown respectively. Twenty-three names were added to the church roll in just one year – a number of these stemming from the seven Sabbath schools in operation in the area – but many more conversions followed.[21] In 1842, 'an interesting station' was opened up in a destitute place around twenty-five miles from Grantown. At first there was little evidence of anything hopeful, but soon 'a considerable awakening' commenced.[22]

The year 1842 proved difficult in Grantown itself, when a small group of believers left the Baptist church over a dispute regarding doctrine and discipline. They set up a separate meeting, which continued for several years before dwindling to nothing. The division proved a great stumbling block to the public in general, and over the following six years an average of only three baptisms a year took place. In the midst of this setback, small tokens of blessing were nonetheless apparent, for, in the summer of 1845, Grant happily reported the appearance of, 'something like the beginning of a time of refreshing from the presence of the Lord'.[23]

Aberdeenshire

William Chalmers Burns in Aberdeen

Revival meetings

W. C. Burns first journeyed to Aberdeen in April 1840, where deep impressions were made wherever he preached, not least among a group of soldiers in the barracks. Burns records that one late afternoon he preached 'at the foot of Barrack Hill to an immense audience ... with perhaps more of the divine assistance than I had done at any time before. Towards the end especially, many were screaming and in tears. I felt as if I could pull men out of the fire; indeed I never had more of this feeling

---

20. *BHMS Report* 1841, p. 9.

21. *BHMS Report* 1841, p. 10.

22. ibid., 1842, p. 13.

23. ibid., 1845, p. 14.

than this evening, and on Sabbath evening in Castle Street.[24] In order to escape the crowds I slipped into the barracks ... '[25] Reflecting on his visit before leaving the city, Burns opined, 'there seemed to be very hopeful symptoms of an extensive awakening'.[26]

Burns returned to Aberdeen in October and remained for two months, preaching daily and dealing with inquirers individually and in small groups. He observed some remarkable scenes. One night he preached in a packed Trinity Church from 7 p.m. They parted at ten but so many crowded around him that he had to return with them to the church. The place was filled in a few moments and almost all fell on their knees and began to pray. Burns was unable to close the meeting till after midnight, all the while 'feeling in my own soul that the Lord was indeed in the midst of us'. The next night he spoke to 350 mill-girls in a local school. 'Almost all were in tears and many cried aloud, and although I dismissed them 3 or 4 times, hardly any would go away, the greater part crying aloud at the very mention of dispersing ... It was indeed to all appearance a night of the Lord's power'. From then on, locals saw something they had never seen before; many mill workers walking to work with Bibles under their arms.[27]

As a result of each of Burns's visits to the city, a considerable number of small evening meetings were initiated for the purpose of instruction, prayer and catechising those who had been awakened. From one factory alone, around fifty girls were divided into four groups, while another

24. On that occasion, the audience consisted chiefly of men. One man remarked that once when he heard Burns preach in Castle Street, 'excluding those on the outskirts where there was a good deal of going and coming, the number of those who appeared to be really attentive was more than would have filled the largest church in the town twice over' (Presbytery of Aberdeen, *Evidence on the Subject of Revivals*, p. 30).

25. 'Journal' of W. C. Burns, quoted in McMullen, *God's Polished Arrow*, p. 180. Islay Burns says that W. C. Burns met some of these soldiers again five years later, when 'they rallied around him, and acted as his gallant body-guard amid the rude assaults of the ruffianly mob at Montreal' during the evangelist's Canadian visit (Burns, *Memoir of the Rev. Wm. C. Burns*, p. 163).

26. Letter dated 1/05/1840, quoted in McMullen, *God's Polished Arrow*, p. 181.

27. McMullen, *God's Polished Arrow*, pp. 55-6. It was observed that when the place of meeting became a veritable '*Bochim*' under Burns's preaching, as it generally did, the evangelist seemed to obtain as complete a control over a large section of the audience as a skilful player has over the instruments on which he performs – the result being that hundreds in Aberdeen professed to find peace in Christ through his ministry (William Robbie, *Bon-Accord United Free Church Aberdeen. A Retrospect of 100 Years, 1828–1928*, Aberdeen 1928, p. 18).

single group held the same number of people. One man, Alexander Laing, held two classes in his own house, averaging around seventeen inquirers each. The two groups combined, with one or two exceptions, also met with Mr Laing in an infant school on Sabbath mornings; this being immediately followed by a similar meeting, composed of a different set of people, in John Knox's Church, for the purpose of training young communicants. As if this was not enough, Laing held yet another class on Saturday evenings, attended by around thirty people, most of whom did not attend any of the other classes.[28]

Growing Opposition

Dissension arose in the city when a leading newspaper published a thoroughly negative report on the more enthusiastic aspects of Burns's meetings. The *Aberdeen Herald* reported in some detail on two meetings led by Burns, the first being on Saturday, 21st November in the Bon-Accord Church of Scotland. Most of the 'downstairs' church was filled, mainly with working class females, and there 'were not more than half a dozen of males present'. (The females were mainly girls from fifteen to eighteen, and women upwards of fifty.)[29] The journalist described Burns as 'rather a silly looking lad, with a sort of meaningless simper on his face', who repeatedly sought to work up his audience into a state of high emotion by his 'drawling, unearthly voice, his theatrical attitudes, his outré expressions of countenance' and his pithy remarks. There arose 'an increased howl from the "affected corner"' of the congregation, and when the preacher quoted the text, "*They looked upon him whom they had pierced and mourned*", the noise, which had been considerable before, now became perfectly appalling' and 'some of the females changed their drawling expressions into absolute shrieks'.[30] A number of girls were seen to be lying prostrate on the

---

28. Presbytery of Aberdeen, *Evidence on the Subject of Revivals*, pp. 24, 32, 36, 44. Laing gave a personal impression of Burns's preaching style: 'His illustrations are striking and natural, reaching often to sublimity, chaining the attention of his hearers, and speaking to their understanding in language that they can comprehend; yet never plain to vulgarity or irreverence; all accompanied with fervent and persevering wrestling with God in prayer for the message and upon the message' (ibid., Appendix, p. xv).

29. ibid., p. 17.

30. Other eyewitnesses compared the female noises to 'the caterwauling of an enormous quantity of cats' or to 'the noise of pigeons in a very large dovecote', while a third witness testified that he 'never heard any such sounds from a human being, except from a man who had been shot through the body' (ibid., pp. 8, 20, 41).

floor. The journalist summarised the meeting, which lasted from 6.30 till about 9.30 p.m., as 'little less than daring blasphemy'. He concluded: 'We do not believe that Mr Burns is inspired, and we cannot admit that the roaring or raving of a few ignorant females is an extraordinary outpouring of the Spirit.' He hoped that few more people would be 'smitten with the Revival mania', for which he felt certain 'there is no Scripture warrant'.[31]

Burns's sermon in the same venue two nights later was attended by many curious 'spectators' who had heard or read the reports of this charismatic and controversial preacher. Though seated mainly in the balcony, they were not unnoticed by Burns, who aimed his main address at them.[32] This was quoted almost verbatim in the *Herald*, which also denounced Burns's preaching as 'violent and denunciatory'. The paper also criticised the fact that this meeting went on till 11.30 p.m. It was about this time that one girl emotionally affected by Burns's 'wild and incoherent rhapsodies' was 'seized with a determination of blood to the head' and had to be carried to the session house. Here she continued in a most alarming state for a considerable time, causing concern to those around her. However, having cold water poured upon her temples and every other means applied that could tend to her recovery, she was able, with assistance, to walk home.[33]

Interestingly, the Rev. John Kennedy of Dingwall, then a young student in Aberdeen, also had concerns about Burns's revivalist methods and claims. 'I found myself there in the midst of the movement, in which William Burns was the leader.' Kennedy continued:

> For that man of God, with his rare talents, his rich attainments, his devotional spirit, and his burning zeal, those who knew him had such respect, as if in him an apostle of Jesus Christ had risen again from the dead. I was a witness to the marvellous effects of his addresses. I went to hear him with a fervent desire to be impressed, but, with all my reverence for the preacher, and my heart's hunger for benefit from his services, I was constrained even then, young and inexperienced as I was, to conclude that his method was not judicious. Five or six addresses he would sometimes deliver during the time of service, assured that what he said was given to him,

31. ibid., pp. ii-v.

32. Even Burns's supporters admitted that the evangelist also pointed a few people out as they left the meeting, and publicly termed them 'spies' (ibid., p. xi).

33. ibid., pp. vi-xi.

and that when he ceased to speak, it was because the Lord had ceased to supply. This impressed me, even then, as indicating far more zeal than discretion, and as what would, in the case of a less gifted and spiritual man, be very dangerous.

He went on:

> A year thereafter, I was present when Mr Burns asked those who were impressed, during his former visit, to meet in a certain place at an appointed hour. I resolved to be, and I was, present there and then. Eleven young women appeared, and no more; and their cases, if one might judge by their demeanour, were not very hopeful. I am far from saying that this was all the fruit of the wonderful move-ment in Aberdeen; and, even after this experience, my soul was fired with indignation at the conduct of the men who scoffingly decried it, and would brand the servant of the Lord, because of this earnestness in seeking to bring souls to Christ. Precious would the fruit have been, if but these eleven had been truly turned to God, for unspeakably great is the salvation of one soul. But how different this result from the sanguine estimate of the year before, when Mr Burns, as he pointed to hundreds before him, declared his persua-sion that they were all true converts! Mr Burns entered the place of meeting, looked down on the little group before him, crossed his arms on the book-board, bent his head on them, and wept. That most impressive scene I cannot forget. I learned a life-lesson then.[34]

So concerned was the Aberdeen Presbytery by the *Herald*'s reports that they appointed a Committee to investigate the situation.[35] Around fifteen individuals were personally interviewed, including the journalist who wrote the newspaper articles, a doctor, a procurator fiscal, an elder and a coach-smith, all of whom had heard Burns preach on at least one occasion.

---

34. John Kennedy/Horatius Bonar, *Evangelism: A Reformed Debate*, Port Dinorwic 1997, pp. 112-13.

35. One member of the Committee, the Rev. James Bryce of Gilcomston South Church in central Aberdeen, did not attend many of the examinations, and was not present at the final meeting which approved the revival. Willie Still, minister at Gilcomston South over a century later, said that 'from the accounts, Bryce (who left the Church of Scotland with most of his congregation to join the Free Church in 1843) does not seem to have been a real leader of men' (Francis Lyall & William Still, *History of Gilcomston South Church, Aberdeen, 1868–1968*, Aberdeen 1968, p. 9).

Some vouched for the truth of the newspaper's remarks; others strenuously denied many of the details. Even opponents of Burns accepted that many other meetings which he led in Aberdeen were completely free of excesses. Burns himself was also summoned for examination and gave his full co-operation. The Committee additionally received written statements from a number of clergymen in various other parts of Scotland where revival had been reported, giving testimony to the extent and genuineness of the movements in these locations.

After deliberation 'and a division', a resolution was adopted by a large majority of the Committee members. While accepting, with a note of concern, that the revival meetings under special examination had been 'protracted to a late hour, and much outward excitement prevailed', the Presbytery concluded that a genuine, 'extensive and delightful work of revival' was in progress in the land, and that 'a very considerable number of persons, chiefly in early life, have been strongly, and, it is hoped, savingly impressed, with the importance of eternal things, and are in the course of further instruction'. It was also accepted that many of all ages had been awakened and quickened to activity and well-doing, 'and that the labours of Mr W. C. Burns, preacher of the gospel, are peculiarly discernible in connection with these results'.[36]

Strathbogie

Considerable stir arose in Strathbogie – the fertile region running along the River Bogie which straddles north-west Aberdeenshire, Banffshire and Moray – in the years prior to the Disruption, over a vacancy in Marnoch Church of Scotland in the year 1837. The minister presented, John Edwards, was supported only by the innkeeper, while 261 heads of families exercised the veto, preferring instead their assistant minister, David Henry. A series of appeals followed, and on a bleak January day, amid scenes of considerable uproar and unhappiness, Edwards was admitted as minister of the parish. All bar one parishioner left the church and began to conduct independent services.

But for many months prior to Edwards' contentious settlement, the ecclesiastical stir caused by the Strathbogie case was felt throughout Scotland and led to an unusual interest in spreading the gospel message in this rural hinterland. What was described as 'the blessed fruit of the stirring times' leading up to the Disruption 'was the free running of the

---

36. Presbytery of Aberdeen, *Evidence on the Subject of Revivals*, pp. 96-7.

word of God in Strathbogie, such as that land had never known from the
beginning ... the doctrines of the gospel were in a great measure new to
the people, and salvation was welcomed with deep inquiry and intense
delight'.[37] Murray McCheyne, John Macdonald of Ferintosh,[38] Thomas
Chalmers and Andrew Bonar[39] all preached in this district during 1840
and beyond, despite itinerant evangelical preaching there being officially
prohibited by the Court of Session while the case was running. To this
interdict McCheyne replied, 'I can say with Paul that I have preached the
Gospel from Jerusalem round about unto Illyricum, and no power on
earth shall keep me from preaching it in the dead parishes of Scotland'.[40]

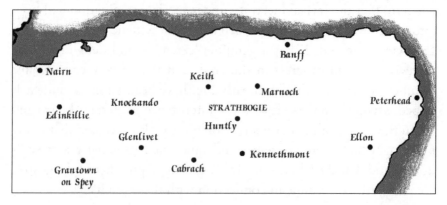

And preach he did, travelling with Alexander Cumming as a deputation of the Church of Scotland to administer the Lord's Supper in
Huntly in August 1841. His communion Sabbath sermon at 'the well' in
Huntly was easily remembered a quarter of a century later. 'McCheyne
was enabled to preach with remarkable power', one person recalled;
'the impression on the congregation was general, and the number of
inquirers large'. Indeed, about a hundred waited after the sermon for
prayer, many of them in deep anxiety. Expressed an old Highland elder

37. Rev. A. Moody Stuart, *Life and Letters of Elizabeth, Last Duchess of Gordon*, London 1865, p. 279.

38. For preaching in the same area without the consent of the parish minister many
years previously (1817), Dr John Macdonald was brought before the General Assembly, whereupon, although no special censure was passed upon him, his movements in
the district were severely censured (Various Contributors, *Disruption Worthies of the
Highlands*, p. 21).

39. Brown, *Annals of the Disruption*, p. 748; Bonar, *Andrew A. Bonar: Diary and Life*,
pp. 86, 158-9; Moody Stuart, *Duchess of Gordon*, pp. 287-92.

40. Brown, *Annals of the Disruption*, p. 748.

to McCheyne at the close of one service in the district, 'I saw you were feeding yourself on what you were giving to us; for the Lord will not have the ox muzzled when he is treading out the corn'.[41] Church politics formed no part of the deputation's sermons, only the gospel of the grace of God. 'They preached what they appeared to feel', observed Mr Robb of Keith, 'and it came home with power, so that many, young and old were led to the knowledge of the truth'.[42] The people, wrote Moody Stuart, were 'attracted, awakened, melted; and many who took no interest in the ecclesiastical testimony were riveted and converted by the word of salvation ... The convictions were intelligent, deep and abiding, and the fruits in many cases remain to this day (1865). Some have been blessed to the souls of others in teaching, in the eldership, and in the ministry'.[43] One young woman, driven away from home by her father because she wouldn't stop praying, was recalled after some months; 'and in due time saw her father and mother praying like herself, and living and dying in the Lord'.[44]

It was said that before the Disruption in Kennethmont, the talk on the Church road was nothing but 'country clutter', but now it centred around the sermons. Revival blessing had begun in the church previous to the momentous May 1843 event, and the Rev. Rose reported that many people told him after he led many of his flock into the Free Church that 'though they had only then come to decision, the first religious impressions made on them had been by sermons or sayings of mine many years before, even within what may properly be called Disruption times'.[45]

Also within this region, in the parish of Keith, an elder of the Established church who had long been praying for a blessing on that district and finding few in his church who were willing to join him in prayer, formed a united prayer meeting consisting of Independents and United Presbyterians. Around this time, one of the two Secession churches in Keith happened to be vacant, and this church was used

41. Moody Stuart, *Duchess of Gordon*, pp. 279-80.

42. Brown, *Annals of the Disruption*, pp. 748-9; Bonar, *Andrew A. Bonar: Diary and Life*, p. 159.

43. Moody Stuart, *Duchess of Gordon*, p. 280.

44. ibid.

45. Robertson, *Spiritual Awakening in the North-East of Scotland*, pp. 473-4.

by the congregation adhering to Free Church principles as a place of worship. That church became the birth-place of many saved souls. By 1842 seven prayer meetings were being held every week in various parts of the parish, in addition to the weekly prayer meeting held in the church and a Sabbath morning meeting attended by upwards of one hundred in the house occupied by the probationer. Some who later became 'honoured and faithful' ministers of the Free Church had attended the Sabbath school and Bible classes held during these years in Keith.[46]

Peterhead, Aberdeen and Ellon

It seems to have been due to the general atmosphere of awakening in Aberdeenshire during this period that Primitive Methodist evangelist John Bowes found himself preaching 'with great liberty' on a number of occasions in both Aberdeen and Peterhead in the summer of 1841. The latter town being inundated with visiting fisherfolk, hundreds listened to Bowes's open-air message at seven in the morning, while he could attract at least 1,500 listeners to his evening meetings at the Market Cross. At one, where he preached for nearly two hours, 'the truth seemed to bear down on them with great effect, and to carry all before it'.[47] A new church established in Aberdeen in 1841 had a membership of ninety-seven after twelve months, fifty-six of whom were added from 'the world'.[48]

In Aberdeen the ministry of the Rev. James Stewart at the South Church from his induction at the close of 1842 was marked by 'the wave of religious revival which followed his ministrations'. The church was crowded Sunday after Sunday and the audiences were most attentive. The people hung upon Stewart's lips with extraordinary earnestness. The prospect of such enormous gatherings was, noted the minister, 'quite oppressive. I can, however, do all things through Christ strengthening me'. As expected, Stewart demitted his charge with the Disruption and joined the Free Church. Sadly he died in the prime of life just three years later; and at his largely attended funeral some claimed they had never seen so many men in tears.[49]

---

46. Brown, *Annals of the Disruption*, pp. 753-4. A further decided work of grace also arose in Keith following the Disruption (see page 454).

47. John Bowes, *The Autobiography or History of the Life of John Bowes*, p. 285.

48. ibid., p. 291.

49. Baird, *Sixty Years of Church Life in Ayr*, pp. 64-5.

To the north of Aberdeen, many parishes in the district of Buchan were blessed with the preaching of Robert Murray McCheyne in the early part of 1843, and in Ellon, as elsewhere, he left precious fruits of his ministry. Accordingly, though a year before the Disruption there were not known to be half-a-dozen non-intrusionists in the whole parish of Ellon, when the event came, a congregation of above one hundred, with more than eighty communicants, was at once formed in this 'stronghold of Moderation' and over the next few years the congregation greatly increased.[50]

Inverness-shire

Inverness

As it continued to spread though the Highlands and Islands, many were in perplexity as to the true character of this revival movement which had taken hold of the mass of the people. While many had no problem attributing its source to divine sovereignty, others likened it to some form of mesmerism, or declared it to be mere excitement occasioned either by the violent preaching of terrorising doctrines or the ignorance and credulity of a certain class of the population. In Inverness, which Alexander MacRae says 'was not then wholly won for evangelism', Dr John Macdonald assisted at a communion in the East Church in 1841.[51] On the Monday, Thanksgiving Day, he preached from Acts 2:33: '*Having received of the Father the promise of the Holy Ghost, He hath shed forth this, which ye now see and hear*'. It was a complete and masterly defence of the revival he had both witnessed and taken part in in various parishes in the north (see page 429). He sounded unusually calm until towards the close of his discourse, when he shared the effects of the revival on Easter Ross, at which point he came alive with passion, and what was a warm glow burst into a blazing flame. Macdonald urged his hearers to resist not the Holy Ghost, but to yield themselves up to Him. 'The capital of the Highlands was won', noted Macrae. 'He won their head and heart by the one superb effort. Souls were won to

---

50. J. H. Hudson, T. W. Jarvie & J. Stein, '*Let the Fire Burn*', Dundee 1978.

51. MacRae, *Revivals in the Highlands and Islands*, p. 83. MacRae, incorrectly it seems, suggests that this event occurred 'about the year 1832'; In contrast, Leask more credibly posits the scenario amid the general awakening of 1839–42, i.e., eight or nine years later.

Christ, while many who had been opposed to revivals were completely won over'.[52]

The effects of that one sermon were great and far reaching. For one thing, it had a most remarkable effect on the mind of the young Thomas McLauchlan, a native of Moy where his father was minister, and whom he succeeded in 1838. Although initially somewhat sceptical of the true character of the pre-Disruption movement of which he had heard accounts from various parts of Scotland, the Rev. McLauchlan was soon won over and Macdonald's sermon ever afterwards practically determined his relationship to these movements of spiritual power. It was said that wherever McLauchlan preached in those days the congregations that gathered were always on the increase, and 'definite spiritual results followed his presentations of the truth and uplifting of Christ'.[53] Meanwhile, Inverness East Church became the centre of special work around this time, and for a number of years thereafter a service was held there each Thursday, where, once a month, John Macdonald was the preacher.

Still with the 'Apostle of the North', returning home to Ferintosh after preaching in Skye during the time of revival there (see page 421), Dr Macdonald sent word ahead that he would preach at Invermoriston, by Loch Ness, and on arrival he addressed the people at a sheltered spot in the open air. An eyewitness records of that occasion: 'He preached with great power, from the words of Paul to the Philippian jailer. The impression of that day was extraordinary. The place was like a battlefield

---

52. William K. Leask, *Dr Thomas M'Lauchlan*, Edinburgh 1905, pp. 134-5. Mac-Rae, *Revivals in the Highlands and Islands*, pp. 83-4. Dr Buchanan said of Macdonald that 'He was the Whitefield of Scotland ... The proudest and most powerful chieftain of the Gaelic race never possessed such mastery over the clans with "the fiery cross", or the wild pibroch, as belonged to this humble minister of Christ ... Ten thousands have often been swayed as one man, stirred into enthusiasm, or melted into sadness, by this mighty and faithful preacher's voice' (Robert Buchanan, *The Ten Years' Conflict: Being the History of the Disruption of the Church of Scotland*, Glasgow 1849, p. 537). Certainly, and as we have observed, Macdonald played a catalytic role in numerous awakenings around this time. Bussey is mistaken, however, in supposing that 'practically all the revival movements' which took place in the north of Scotland during the first half of the nineteenth century were the immediate results of the apostolic labours of Macdonald (Bussey, *The Religious Awakening of 1858–60 in Great Britain and Ireland*, p. 35).

53. Leask, *Dr Thomas M'Lauchlan*, p. 135.

strewed with the dead and dying. Not a few survived to testify that the Lord was of a truth present that day.' [54]

Argyll and The West Highlands

Kintyre and Cowal

Callum Brown refers to a revival movement in Kintyre around 1839–40, but provides no details.[55] Similarly, Douglas Ansdell speaks of a revival in the Cowal peninsula of Argyll around the same time, but fails to give further information, except to say that Archibald Crawford, an impressive poet in the region, was converted during its progress.[56] Crawford, born in 1815, had produced Gaelic verse from the age of eight. By his early twenties he had a volume of poetry ready for publication but he destroyed it along with his other compositions at the time of his conversion, believing, like most evangelicals of the day, that this art form like all others (such as playing the fiddle or bagpipes, dancing, and storytelling) were part of secular culture and therefore sinful.

Lochgilphead

First signs of awakening in Lochgilphead occurred as early as 1838, when Baptist sources claimed that 'in some places there is an unusual movement', and 'in one village a great reformation has taken place'.[57] By 1842 congregations in both town and country districts had increased significantly. A few months later, Baptist minister, John Macintosh, exhausted from his constant labours, could yet 'rejoice with trembling; we have never seen anything like this – sinners awakened or receiving peace at almost every sermon. We are as cautious as possible, yet there is danger of building with wood, hay and stubble'. In the country towards Lochgair, eight miles south, there was 'an uncommon movement and an insatiable desire to hear … the houses can hardly contain the hearers'; thus two meetings were often held in each place. Likewise a good work was being done still further north in Craignish, where some shepherds were among those seeking baptism. Wrote the minister, regarding 1843: 'This has been a singular year for us.

---

54. Various Contributors, *Disruption Worthies of the Highlands*, p. 23.

55. Brown, *The Social History of Religion in Scotland since 1730*, p. 125.

56. Douglas Ansdell, *The People of the Great Faith: The Highland Church 1690–1900*, Stornoway 1998, p. 150.

57. *BHMS Report* 1839, pp. 13, 15-16.

God has smiled upon us, and the tide of mercy flowed over our heads.' [58]
By 1844, the town congregation had more than doubled, with over fifty
having been added to the church. Great crowds attended the numerous
baptisms, with sometimes as many as a thousand spectators at the river
side. Despite such wonderful developments, Macintosh kept a level head,
aware that there were 'still many willing servants of sin' in the locality.[59]

Lochaber and Sunart

Further north in Argyll, the Lochaber and Sunart areas had what
was said to have been their first experience of revival shortly before
the Disruption, under the preaching of parish minister, Alexander
McIntyre (c. 1807–78).[60] His biographer described his manner as
being 'peculiarly his own. Faithfully and solemnly he warned the
wicked of his evil way. Few who heard him ever forgot him … So vivid
was he in describing the terrible woes of the hereafter, and warning
people of the wicked place, that some have been known to have been
so gripped and held by the picture, as to actually raise themselves
high above their seats in amazement without being aware of it'.[61] One
witness wrote of McIntyre:

> People flocked from all quarters to hear him and the effects were
> wonderful. In the parish of Kilmallie, especially – one of Scotland's
> largest parishes, being sixty miles long and thirty miles at its widest,
> and covering 400,000 acres – were his incessant labours, day and
> night, attended with extraordinary results. The earnestness of the
> preacher, his electrifying eloquence, and his awful description of
> perdition and the deplorable state of the unconverted, produced

---

58. ibid., 1843, pp. 12-13.

59. ibid., 1844, p. 12; Bebbington, *The Baptists in Scotland*, p. 291.

60. A native of Strontian, McIntyre, after beginning ministerial studies, was noted
for his zeal in preaching. Despite some opposition, even his 'unfriendly Presbytery'
could not keep him from holding family worship. This was attended by his neighbours
morning and evening, and they came in such numbers that the house could not contain them. They crowded about the door, at which opening he would sit and conduct
worship. This was kept up for about two years (Robinson, *The Rev. Alexander McIntyre*,
pp. 5-6). A contemporary of MacIntyre, John Campbell of Oban, also referred to the
'great awakening' taking place in Strontian under McIntyre's ministry (Campbell, *Missionary and Ministerial Life in the Highlands*, p. 135).

61. Robinson, *The Rev. Alexander McIntyre*, p. 25.

such effects upon the hearers as baffles my power of description
... The people fell under the power of the Word like the grass
before the mower.[62]

Another said, 'though the snow was up to the people's knees, such a
congregation gathered at Kilmallie that the church could not hold
them, and they met on the hillside near a clump of wood above the
church. There they stood for hours while the terrors of the law of God
were thundered in their ears'.[63] One who was present on that day, Flora
Matheson, told in her old age how a company of the young folk that
were awakened, including herself, set out on foot after they were ferried
to the Ardgour side and walked, in spite of the depth of snow, the nine
miles or so that lay between them and Corran Ferry, where Mr McIntyre
was to preach in the evening.[64] McIntyre often said it was a wonder the
feet of many did not perish with the cold.

A native of the district who, like McIntyre himself, emigrated to
Australia in the late 1840s on account of the hardships brought by the
potato famine (see page 414), and who knew him well, reminisced on
those early days of gospel blessing:

One night in particular ... in a crowded church in Fort William,
the weeping was so loud and continuous, the voice of the preacher
so completely drowned, that after repeated attempts to still the
people had been made, but in vain, the congregation had to be
dismissed without the intended sermon ... The effects of such times
of refreshing from God upon the whole district generally was truly
great, and never to be forgotten. The wilderness blossomed as the
rose. Open ungodliness under its various hideous forms hid its face
with shame. Old and young, far and near, flocked to the preaching
of the Word, whether in church or in the open field. Crowded prayer
meetings sprang up in abundance. Even children had their juvenile
meetings to make their requests known to Him who said, 'Suffer
little children to come unto me and forbid them not'. And for years
after, dancing halls, heathenish sports, and other kindred vanities

62. ibid., p. 25, pp. 7-8.

63. ibid., pp. 7-8.

64. Principal John Macleod, *By-Paths of Highland Church History*, Edinburgh 1965,
pp. 46-7. See also Collins, *Principal John Macleod D.D.*, p. 10.

which lead the soul away from the fountain of living waters were things of the past in the then highly favoured parish of Kilmallie.[65]

Plockton and Shieldaig

Ordained in 1823, Alexander Macdonald became the first minister of the Parliamentary charge of Plockton in 1827 (see map, page 422), officially part of the civil parish of Lochalsh, which was served by an incumbent said to be 'neither calculated to draw people to him nor to edify those who came'. The Rev. Colin Mackenzie, who settled in nearby Shieldaig in 1832, said that Macdonald quickly became the most popular preacher along the entire west coast of Ross-shire and Inverness-shire, people flocking to hear him from all quarters. Before long it was found necessary to get a gallery put up in the church. A special meeting was held one Sabbath per month to which, wrote the Rev. James Macdonald of Urray:

> many of the Lord's people, and always the best of them, came to the Plockton church, and remained for the fellowship meeting on Monday, which was a great help to them. The Sabbath and meeting day were high days both with preacher and hearers. His preaching was as a well of living water to the Lord's people. They came to it and drank, and went home rejoicing. They could not get the living water in the pulpits of the surrounding parishes. They got it in Plockton.

Communion seasons were also most precious occasions, when from 12,000 to 14,000 gathered from fourteen parishes. John Macdonald of Ferintosh was frequently there, as was John Kennedy of Redcastle.[66]

As a result of this most encouraging work over a number of years, there occurred, two or three years before the Disruption, 'a very decided revival movement in Plockton and the other parishes on the west coast'. Alexander Macdonald threw himself into the work, labouring heartily alongside Colin Macdonald of Shieldaig. The Rev. George Macdonald of Aberdeen, noting that there was much to disappoint in connection with the spiritual fruit of this movement, yet observed that 'such faithful labour yielded permanent results in both districts. The devotion of the people of Shieldaig to the gospel and to the principles of their church

---

65. Robinson, *The Rev. Alexander McIntyre*, p. 8.

66. Various Contributors, *Disruption Worthies of the Highlands*, p. 110.

has drawn to them the attention of other churches as well as their own. Tokens of beneficial results equally gratifying could be given with regard to the Plockton congregation'.[67]

But pre-Disruption blessing in the West Highlands was not confined to the evangelical wing of the National Church. In 1842, when the Rev. James MacQueen of the Baptist Church in Broadford, Skye, journeyed to Applecross, 'there was such a desire to hear that a house could not contain the people; they stood outside under wind and rain, and in the dark'.[68]

Oban

According to his biographer, John Campbell, pastor of the Congregational Church in Oban, experienced 'several revivals' during his ministry from 1811 to 1853. While greatly cheered by these, Campbell was frequently disheartened by the deadness and torpidity in his church during the periods between these awakenings. The most powerful revival took place in 1840–1, and was preceded by a season of special meetings on Sabbath mornings and at other times to pray specifically for that very outcome. In July 1840 a series of protracted meetings was also begun, though little outward good came from them, other than that the prayer meetings became better attended. In early September, the Rev. Farquharson of Tiree came to hold a week of evening meetings, following which the Rev. McLean arrived to continue the good work begun. Soon the chapel was almost full every night, and packed to overflowing on Sundays. These services were arranged just a day in advance, the intention being that they only continued as long as folk were evidently hungry for the things of God. In fact, they were kept going every night save Saturdays for ten weeks.

It was a quiet work, the only signs of emotion being the bowing of heads to conceal 'tears in large drops' rolling down folk's cheeks. Anxious souls were directed to the manse, where for several weeks a number came almost every night, some in such agony of spirit that they could not converse until their burst of feeling had abated. Many of these, on obtaining peace of heart, could barely settle to sleep for the joy within

---

67. ibid., p. 111. Following the Disruption, with which event he heartily concurred, Alexander Macdonald was transferred to Glen Urquhart, which vast parish had apparently not been favoured with a true gospel ministry since the Reformation.

68. *BHMS Report* 1842, p. 19.

them. Some, who came to town on business or who attended a meeting out of curiosity, left with arrows of deep conviction in their consciences. Others, hearing of the revival, flocked from miles around, and while many requests came for Campbell to visit these outlying districts, so full were his hands in Oban that for many weeks he was completely unable to comply. Soon, however, numbers of country folk were holding their own bi-weekly meetings on their farms and crofts.[69]

One interesting case involved two brothers, the younger of whom became greatly alarmed at his spiritual condition after attending a meeting. His brother, noting his sibling's dejection, inquired why he was so sad. On hearing his reply he cried out, 'If you, who are so young, are such a sinner, what must I be?!' Both men were soon rejoicing in Christ as Saviour. Meanwhile, a close friend of these two, unaware of their new-found freedom, came to spend a night of merriment with them, but was arrested on approaching their house by the voices of prayer from his friends within. Shocked by what he heard he turned away in a state of alarm, and, kneeling beside a stook of corn, made the first prayer of his life. Within a few days he, too, had found the pearl of great price.[70]

It is recorded that for some weeks in Oban, it seemed as if the fear of God had fallen on the inhabitants in general.[71] The revival and its effects became the main topic of conversation. A visiting comedian applied to the Mason's Lodge for a booking but was promptly turned down, being told that the people of Oban were at that time absorbed with matters of a very different kind! New Year's Day 1841, which was formerly a day of revelry and dancing, was kept as a day of humiliation, prayer and sermon – the streets remaining as quiet as if it had been the Sabbath. While every age group was moved, most converts were from the fifteen to twenty-five age bracket and almost totally confined to the working class. Campbell gave an overview of proceedings by saying that Farquharson had sowed the seed of truth, McLean had steered the plough and broken up fallow ground, while he personally was left to break up the clods and harrow the land as best he could. The outcome, he observed, continuing his farming metaphor, was 'a field that the Lord hath blessed'. Around fifty people were added to the church as a direct

69. Campbell, *Missionary and Ministerial Life in the Highlands*, pp. 124-31.

70. ibid., pp. 128-9.

71. ibid., p. 129.

result of the movement.[72] Meanwhile, Oban's Established Church also experienced a time of notable growth during the years 1839–42.[73]

Lismore and Easdale

Close to Oban, a movement began on the island of Lismore at the turn of the New Year of 1843.[74] It commenced by means of a young Gaelic-only speaking man who, just six months previously, seemed to be anxiously seeking after the truth himself. He held meetings both for prayer and for exhorting the people about the state of their souls. By this means were two of the most notorious characters on the island awakened. John Campbell of Oban spent a fortnight on Lismore, during which time the number of those newly rejoicing in their salvation rose from thirty to around fifty. Wrote Campbell, 'Some were awakened at every meeting. The farm houses were so crowded – peat lofts and every apartment – that we could scarcely move'.[75] Even the schoolhouses could not contain all who came. So constantly did Campbell preach and speak with individuals that his throat was affected and he could scarcely be heard. His last meeting was near Kilchiaren, when over 200 heard him, many more failing to gain admittance. It later transpired that ten men and six women were awakened that evening.

John Macintosh, Baptist minister of Lochgilphead, went to preach in Lismore in the early spring whilst in the midst of an awakening in his own parish, and was informed that by that time, 'from ninety to one hundred profess to have received the truth'.[76] In addition, the Rev. J. Millar of Oban crossed to the island a number of times. On a visit in the latter half of 1843 he made mention of the fact that many appeared to be awakened, noting some, too, however, who had relapsed into indifference.[77] Other parts of Argyllshire were also in very hopeful condition around this time, especially Easdale, of which it was said that

---

72. ibid., pp. 129-33.

73. John J. Murray, *The Church on the Hill: Oban Free High Church, A History and Guide,* Oban 1984, p. 11.

74. One account says it began 'a little before the New Year' (*BHMS Report* 1843, p. 13), another 'on the 12th of January' (Campbell, *Missionary and Ministerial Life in the Highlands*, p. 135).

75. Campbell, *Missionary and Ministerial Life in the Highlands*, p. 135.

76. *BHMS Report* 1843, p. 13.

77. ibid., 1844, p. 14.

'the houses cannot contain the people who meet to hear the prayers and exhortations of the brethren'.[78]

The Western Isles

Tiree

In Tiree, Congregational minister, Archibald Farquharson, had heard a great deal about revivals and protracted meetings all over Scotland throughout 1839. Towards the close of that year he decided to commence them in his own church, also telling his congregation he was reliant on their support. 'Some of the brethren were gifted with excellent gifts for prayer', he wrote. 'I tried one or two of them to engage in prayer, and they did so. In this way the work went on'.[79] Revival ensued and Farquharson was able to write in February 1840: 'We have been accustomed to hear of revivals, but I am happy to say that we have both seen and felt one.' [80] Unlike some places, 'there was no roaring and crying and fainting down in Tiree while the revivals were going on … The fact is' said Farquharson, 'we would not give any countenance to it'.[81] Around forty new communicants were added to the roll, raising membership to around one hundred. John Campbell, along with a number of other ministers, visited the island shortly after to attend a regional Congregational event, and a great number of meetings were held over the course of eight days. Campbell found them well attended, the people listening to and receiving the word with great avidity.[82]

The movement spread to the Baptist chapel, which, in the late 1830s, had, the pastor Duncan MacDougald lamented, 'sunk too much into

---

78. Campbell, *Missionary and Ministerial Life in the Highlands*, p. 131.

79. *SCM* 1848, quoted in McNaughton, 'Revival and Reality', p. 199.

80. ibid., p. 199.

81. McNaughton, *Highlands and Islands*, p. xxv. Farquharson had studied under Grenville Ewing and Ralph Wardlaw, who between them had helped train scores of Independent ministers for over half a century. Personal experience had taught them the dangers of uninformed and unrestrained enthusiasm, and showed them the importance of an educated ministry and recognition of Scripture as the sole authority in all church matters. 'There was no place in Scottish Independency for emotional fanaticism', observes McNaughton. 'Everything was subject to the reality check of Scripture and whether or not it contributed to spiritual well-being' (McNaughton, 'Revival and Reality', pp. 199-200).

82. Campbell, *Missionary and Ministerial Life in the Highlands*, pp. 133-4.

formality, and we almost despaired of prosperity'. Some began to 'seek the Lord with more fervency and earnestness', and a number of new prayer meetings arose. Just after Christmas 1840 MacDougald could exult, 'Our winter is past, the rain is over and gone, the time of the singing of birds is come, and the voice of the turtle is heard in our land'.[83]

A year later even more joy filled his heart: 'The whole church is revived and animated with more zeal and love than ever before, which adds not a little to my happiness'. The pastor immediately cancelled his winter tour, finding instead that 'my occupying four or five stations each night could not satisfy the desire to hear', especially in the east of the island. As he travelled on foot, MacDougald sometimes found himself 'up to the knees in bogs, with my staff in one hand and a lantern in the other … At some of the stations were pretty large barns and school-houses, but not in all; so that people had to sit without, and many were obliged to return home who could not bear the cold'.[84] The preacher knew of over forty 'under convictions' at the same time, 'mostly among grown up and old people'. Frequent baptismal services were arranged as a result of the revival. At one, in April 1840, from 300 to 400 assembled on the margin of a loch to hear MacDougald and the Rev. Grant of Mull read from Scripture and preach, before six candidates were baptised by immersion.[85] The movement continued for some years (see page 458).

Alexander Grant of Tobermory crossed to Tiree a number of times – 'to deliver lively and evangelical discourses' – as he had frequently done over the previous twenty years. Yet he could now say that he never saw such favourable prospects for the Tiree church.[86] As late as September 1845, as many as thirty-two were baptised and added to the island's Baptist fellowship, while in nearby Colonsay a work was also in progress

83. Using another metaphor, MacDougald wrote that 'though the natural sun removed further from us in winter, and almost hid himself from our view, the Sun of Righteousness drew nearer, on whose wings we found healing. We had a reviving and refreshing morning, our risen Lord drew nigh, and after our toilsome and unsuccessful efforts during the night he commanded us to cast our nets on the right side of the ship, and some fishes were caught' (*BHMS Report* 1840, p. 21).

84. ibid.

85. Donald E. Meek, *Island Harvest: A History of Tiree Baptist Church 1838–1988*, Tiree 1988, pp. 9-10.

86. *BHMS Report* 1842, p. 21.

with eight being baptised around the same time.[87] Meanwhile, while his own church was experiencing revival, Farquharson of Tiree delivered seventeen discourses in Islay during an itinerancy in 1841. He reported: 'The desire for hearing in Islay was good … I spoke to two men who were awakened at the time, and who appeared to have found peace in believing. The members of the church seemed to be in a lively state.' [88]

Tiree's Baptist chapel had grown to one hundred members by the close of 1846, around which time blessing seems to have come to a halt due to the arrival of the potato famine, which particularly affected the western mainland and the Hebrides in the autumn of 1846. In fact, around a third of the population of this region migrated permanently between the early 1840s and the later 1850s.[89] By 1851 membership of Tiree Baptist Church had dropped to thirty-two, with two-thirds of its former membership having sought new homes across the Atlantic.

St Kilda

Pioneering Labours of John Macdonald

In 1698, in the first written record of St Kilda – the most remote islands to be part of the British Isles, situated 200 kilometres west of the Scottish mainland – its population was stated as 180. Whilst some of the islanders' customs showed a possible early Christian influence, their beliefs were seen as being a mixture of 'popery and druidism', prompting the Church of Scotland to send out a series of missionaries from 1705 onwards. John Macdonald of Ferintosh, under auspices of the SSPCK, made at least four journeys to St Kilda between 1822 and 1830.[90] Appalled by the moral conditions of the islanders, Macdonald was unable to find even one 'decidedly religious person'. His education, literacy, and experience of the world, as well as his religious zest and knowledge, all appealed to the islanders, however, and they listened with rapt attention to his long sermons. In 1823 'every member of the

---

87. ibid., 1845, p. 21.

88. *SCM* 1841, quoted in McNaughton, 'Revival and Reality', p. 200.

89. This fits in with the observation of Donald Meek, that 'waves of spiritual revival tended to peak immediately prior to periods of more intense emigration' (Donald E. Meek, 'Religious Life in the Highlands Since the Reformation', in Michael Lynch (Ed.), *The Oxford Companion to Scottish History*, Oxford 2001, p. 519).

90. viz. 1822, 1823, 1827 and 1830.

community met at 7' on a Sabbath morning to hear Macdonald preach, and by 1827 they were pleading for a third daily sermon instead of the usual two! Many were affected by his preaching and at one time almost all were in tears. During one visit, the evangelist could even 'hear praise of God and prayer ascend from almost every family in the village' in the evenings. But Macdonald found that such impressions were of short duration,[91] although he did find at the close of his last visit that a few were under conviction and 'in a hopeful way. There are blossoms at least', he observed.[92] Thus, contrary to the opinion of some,[93] and despite his commitment to the islanders and their unquestionable attachment to him, Macdonald's labours did not directly result in a general awakening bearing lasting fruit.

Arrival of Neil Mackenzie

Thus, sadly, when ordained missionary Neil Mackenzie was installed on the island in 1830 he found the moral tone of the inhabitants every bit as bad as Macdonald had first described it. For example, he remarked that Macdonald preached 'several eloquent and powerful sermons, to which (the people) apparently paid great attention; but I soon found that they were only charmed by his eloquence and energy, and had not knowledge enough to follow or understand his arguments'. He found further that, 'Not only was every moral obligation disregarded, but they seemed to have no idea that they were doing anything wrong'.[94]

Mackenzie immediately threw himself into the work, beginning a vast range of reforms which resulted in an almost complete reformation of the community. He reorganised the island's farming methods and also persuaded the islanders to rebuild their village with greatly improved 'black houses' and better hygiene and living conditions. He also supervised and helped in the construction of a new church and manse, the funds having been raised by John Macdonald under auspices of the SSPCK. With regard to religious and educational instruction, he began Catechism classes, a Sabbath school and a day school to teach

---

91. Kennedy, *The Apostle of the North*, p. 76.

92. Neil Mackenzie, *Episode in the Life of the Rev. Neil Mackenzie at St Kilda*, Aberfeldy, privately published 1911, pp. 31-2.

93. e.g. Norman Macfarlane is among those who paint a picture of revival coming to St Kilda through Macdonald's efforts (Macfarlane, *Apostles of the North*, p. 5).

94. Mackenzie, *Life of the Rev. Neil Mackenzie*, pp. 31-2.

reading, writing and arithmetic. For several years, little obvious spiritual fruit was observable, but by 1838 a small church could be formed and the following year Dr Norman Macleod of Glasgow arrived to examine applicants, about sixteen of whom were admitted into fellowship. Macleod wrote of this communion service: 'It was one to be held in remembrance. I thank God I was there. I have not passed a sweeter day on earth.'[95] Wrote John Mackay many years later: 'The people of St Kilda have ever since maintained a record of morals and religion unexcelled – so far as I know – by any community of its size.'[96]

Outbreak of Revival

For some time after this, however, the people seemed to grow more cold and formal, and Mackenzie urged his small band of believers to unite with him in prayer for an outpouring of the Spirit, while he also preached weekly on what it means to know Christ. Then, one weekday evening in September 1841, 'the minds of his hearers melted into unusual tenderness, the tears gushing like a fountain'. One formerly careless woman cried out in agony of soul. One man present 'afterwards heard one of the men telling some who were arriving with the boats from their day's work, "I believe the Spirit of God was formed upon our congregation tonight". This was the beginning of the revival'.[97] In preparation for the forthcoming Communion, Mackenzie dwelt at considerable length on the sufferings of Christ, their multiplicity, intensity, and the ends they answered in the economy of salvation. The result was an increase in sobbings and excitement. 'Spiritual things seem to absorb their whole soul', observed the missionary pastor, 'their very language is altered, an awful solemnity pervading all their intercourse'.[98]

At the communion service held on Sabbath Day, 8th October, the whole congregation, including children, 'became strongly excited' and cried aloud, to the extent that the preacher's voice was drowned out. Mackenzie gave out a psalm to be sung, but the precentor, also overcome with emotion, could not sing and so the missionary had to lead

---

95. John Mackay, *The Church in the Highlands*, London 1914, p. 247.

96. ibid.

97. Quoted in Charles Maclean, *Island on the Edge of the World*, Edinburgh 1972, p. 125.

98. Mackenzie, *Life of the Rev. Neil Mackenzie*, pp. 34-5; 'SSPCK Report', quoted in Michael Robson, *St Kilda: Church, Visitors and 'Natives'*, Port of Ness 2005, p. 361.

the psalm himself, 'with only a few tremulous voices joining'. When Mackenzie went through the service of the first table, 'such a sense of unworthiness was experienced by the members that they could scarcely be induced to approach the table … '.[99]

At every meeting during the whole winter new cases occurred, or many of those who had already been awakened became more or less excited again. The more pious members of the little congregation were also enlivened and their souls greatly refreshed. 'Every night someone was pricked in the heart and constrained to cry out, and sometimes several whom we thought had been already saved were among the most distressed. Young and old felt the power of that influence which reached the hearts not only of the more tender-hearted, but also of the most hardened'.[100] Mackenzie noted that the people evinced 'great desire of solitude and retirement for the purposes of devotion', and that 'to steal away at night to get a retired spot to pray is deemed a luxury; scarcely a wall, old building, a large stone, that is not made a place of prayer. Great delight is also experienced in the means of grace; in short their own language is, "We are as if in a new world"'.[101] As a result, the community in St Kilda was in Robson's words, 'clearly of a sudden transformed'.[102]

Mackenzie wrote that the physical symptoms which attended this revival were in their general aspect the same, yet in every individual they varied in intensity and duration. 'At first one noticed a movement of the hands like that of one drowning, while the breathing got quicker and more laborious, and if they were women it often ended in their fainting … At times the scene was most distressing. Here there would be a strong man on a seat supported by two friends; there, others rolling in the dust on the floor, and perhaps one or two being carried out fainting'. At last 'with an almost superhuman voice', they would exclaim, 'I have found Him whom my soul loveth', or similar refrain.

99. Mackenzie, *Life of the Rev. Neil Mackenzie*, pp. 34-5.

100. ibid. See also D. E. Meek, 'Gaelic Bible, Revival and Mission', p. 132, which sees the St Kilda revival as part of the general awakening that spread out from mainland Scotland around this time, affecting the Inner and Outer Hebrides before moving out further to touch this lonely isle.

101. 'SSPCK Report' 1843, quoted in Robson, *St Kilda*, p. 367.

102. Robson, *St Kilda*, pp. 361-2. Robson put the transformation largely down to the St Kildans' 'reputation for credulity'.

Once or twice Mackenzie heard them petitioning the Almighty to take them at once to Himself rather than allow them to remain and sin again. 'To give any realistic or complete view of the scene is beyond my power', he wrote.[103] Mackenzie conversed with the anxious at great length and said that, 'often when perfectly exhausted I would go home, get something to eat, and after an earnest prayer for guidance, return and speak again till I could speak no more, and yet fail to satisfy their longing to hear the word'.[104]

Towards the end of spring the excitement attending the revival became much less intense, but things flared up again in the autumn of 1842. This time the pastor was assisted by his elders and some of the previous year's converts, who now conducted many of the evening meetings themselves, leaving Mackenzie to lead the Wednesday meeting, two services on Sunday and three weekday morning meetings to converse with the anxious.

Results

Looking back, Mackenzie could observe 'the happiest results' from the awakening. Perhaps the most striking change in the islanders was their confessing openly their former sins. Any injury or deception of their neighbours, even up to forty years before, was now immediately acknowledged, and they 'do not rest till they have made restitution', although the offence itself was not known or even suspected by the

---

103. Mackenzie, *Life of the Rev. Neil Mackenzie*, pp. 35. In a report to the SSPCK, Mackenzie gives a similar, typical description. 'First, the person affected seems to be labouring under an uncommon oppressive weight, the whole frame greatly excited. During this time the individual so affected seems to be powerfully restraining himself from crying; at last he bursts out with a violent outcry, which continues for a longer or shorter time, according to the effect of the discourse upon him. When it begins to subside, it is followed by great trembling, and if attempting to speak, chattering of teeth, accompanied with great weakness and absorption of mind'. One parishioner explained how, after going through this experience, 'he felt as if his joints had been powerless, accompanied with trembling. He remarked that when thus affected it was highly painful' ('SSPCK Report' 1842–3, quoted in Robson, *St Kilda*, p. 363).

104. Mackenzie, *Life of the Rev. Neil Mackenzie*, pp. 36. Charles Maclean, whose study of St Kilda won him high acclaim, clearly had a high estimation of Mackenzie and of his commitment to the islanders. He noted, however, that he 'used all the techniques of revivalism to whip up his audience and kindle a kind of hysterical fervour in their hearts'. Unhappy about blaming such emotionalism on Mackenzie, Maclean states, despite evidence to the contrary, that 'the revivals had in fact been started by the Apostle of the North' (Maclean, *Island on the Edge of the World*, pp. 125-6).

person against whom it was committed.[105] In addition, 'envy, cunning, theft, uncleanness, Sabbath-breaking, excessive talking and irritability of temper breaking out on every trifling occasion into violent rage' – all formerly highly common sins – had all disappeared. 'The everlasting talker has become comparatively taciturn. You would think that they were almost afraid to speak lest they should sin', and when they did talk, it was about 'the doctrines and precepts of our most holy religion, the state of the soul, and the experiences of holy men'.[106] Mackenzie also observed that 'the feelings – the morals – the habits and the manners of the people seem to have undergone a most complete and a happy change. Their sole delight is now in religious exercises and in secret communion with their God – they are more industrious in their habits, more quiet and orderly in their manner, and more kindly and affectionate towards each other'. An enthusiasm for the administration of the sacrament was also evident.[107]

In conclusion, Mackenzie said that in only a few instances was he doubtful 'whether there is any real work of the Spirit or only a mere wave of feeling … I feel sure that there has been a true work of grace in their souls'.[108] The SSPCK was also delighted with the movement and remarked that 'surely this is the doing of the Lord, and it is wondrous in our eyes'.[109] So pleased was Mackenzie with what was accomplished, yet so fatigued by 'the labours and anxieties of the past two years … both on my bodily health and mental vigour', that he decided to retire from the island – rather abruptly –in 1844.[110] Thus the people of St Kilda, recently awakened, were left once more to worship as they might see fit, it being many years before another minister was settled among them.

---

105. 'SSPCK Report' 1843, quoted in Robson, *St Kilda*, pp. 367-8.

106. Mackenzie, *Life of the Rev. Neil Mackenzie*, p. 37.

107. 'SSPCK Report' 1843, quoted in Robson, *St Kilda*, p. 367.

108. Mackenzie, *Life of the Rev. Neil Mackenzie*, p. 37.

109. 'SSPCK Report', quoted in Robson, *St Kilda*, p. 263. The Society suggests, incorrectly it seems, that St Columba visited St Kilda prior to his visit to Iona, and that this was the occasion when 'the light of the Christian religion first dawned upon Scotland' (ibid., p. 368).

110. Mackenzie, *Life of the Rev. Neil Mackenzie*, pp. 36-37. He settled in Duror in the Presbytery of Lorn, where a vacancy had been created with the Disruption.

Sad Aftermath

Before he left the island, Mackenzie had noted that the islanders became more seriously religious with each succeeding year. Naturally superstitious, they took easily to the missionaries' fundamentalist teachings. These visitors were the only people with education and experience of the outside world to come and dwell on the island, and they were regarded with considerable awe and respect by all in the community. Such unswerving obedience and implicit trust were exploited under the 'blinkered despotism' of the Rev. John Mackay's twenty-four-year ministry on St Kilda from 1865. With an 'alarming capacity for zeal … he established a vibrantly harsh rule over his parishioners'. Services on Sundays at eleven, two and six o'clock were made to last from two to three hours each, so that effectively the islanders spent the whole day in church. During the week a prayer meeting or period of religious instruction was held every day except Monday and Saturday.[111] Indeed, Maclean claimed that all labour was banned for twelve hours either side of any church service, meaning that little work could be done. Attendance at services was compulsory for everyone over the age of two, save the sick. Writes Tom Steel: 'For a people whose livelihood so depended upon the elements, such strict regulations and such time-consuming devotion was a danger to their survival.' The Church also banned the island's use of song and poetry, as well as, incredibly for an island people, swimming, which was viewed as a sport and therefore sinful. From Saturday night to Sunday morning no islander even dared to indulge in conversation. All but the recitation of the Bible was thought sinful. 'The Sabbath is indeed a day of intolerable gloom', wrote John Sands. 'At the clink of the bell the whole flock hurry to the Church with sorrowful looks, and eyes bent upon the ground. It is considered sinful to look to the right or the left. They do not appear like good people going to listen to glad tidings of great joy, but like a troop of the damned whom Satan is driving to the bottomless pit.'[112]

John Macleod is virtually alone in suggesting that the Presbyterian fundamentalism imposed on the St Kildans brought to their lives nothing

---

111. Maclean, *Island on the Edge of the World*, pp. 126-7.

112. John Sands, *Out of the World; or, Life in St Kilda*, Edinburgh 1876, p. 52; George Seton, *St Kilda*, Edinburgh 1878 (reprinted 1980), p. 271; Tom Steel, *The Life and Death of St Kilda*, Glasgow 1975, p. 99.

but good.[113] Secular historians are virtually unanimous in their scathing denunciation of the same, arguing that ultimately the Free Church must take the greatest blame for the breaking of St Kildan culture, helping doom the island to uninhabited status by the early 1900s. Michael Robson, however, points out that nearly all that is publicly known of issues regarding Mackay's incumbency on the island has come from one writer's 'facetious and demeaning tale' (that of Robert Connell, correspondent for *The Glasgow Herald*), which, he insists, should not be relied on to provide a faithful picture of events or personalities. Robson's exhaustive research leaves him believing there is 'no clear evidence for concluding, as popular belief still has it, that Mackay or his church had anything to do with the ultimate "death" of St Kilda's community'.[114] Indeed, other factors may have been just as, or even more, responsible; such as the natives' increasing dependence on mainland supplies. It is noteworthy, for example, that numerous other Scottish islands without the ecclesiastical structures existing on St Kilda also became uninhabited in the late 1800s and early 1900s. Whatever the truth, the events that followed Neil Makenzie's departure from the island mark a sad conclusion to the arduous and commendable reforms of a social, moral and spiritual nature brought about by the fervent, forward-thinking efforts of this devoted missionary.

Skye

Beginnings in Waternish
Awakening had been underway in both the Uig and Broadford districts of Skye from 1838 (see page 388). Apparently independent of the awakenings elsewhere, a movement began in the hamlet of Unish in Waternish, in 1842[115] through the labours of Norman Macleod of the

---

113. Macleod, *Banner in the West*, p. 165; see also Bill Lawson, *St Kilda and its Church*, Northton 1993, pp. 31-2.

114. Robson, *St Kilda*, p. 631.

115. Most authors set the start of the revival at April/May 1840 (Couper, *Scottish Revivals*, p. 127; Alexander MacRae, *Revivals in the Highlands and Islands*, p. 66; L. M. McKinnon, *The Skye Revivals*, printed privately, 1995, p. 12; Rev. William Macleod, 'The Beginning of Evangelical Religion in Skye', in *Banner of Truth*, Aug/Sept. 1995, vols 383-4, p. 18); D. E. Meek dates the revival at 1841-2 ('Falling Down as if Dead: Attitudes to Unusual Phenomena in the Skye Revival of 1841–1842', in *Scottish Bulletin of Evangelical Theology*, vol. 13/4, Autumn 1995, p. 117); while Rev. Taylor of Fiske places events at 'about the month of April 1843' (Brown, *Annals of the Disruption*, p.

Gaelic Schools Society. Macleod was a former soldier who had been present in Egypt in the Napoleonic war under Sir Ralph Abercrombie and was later converted through the ministry of John Macdonald of Ferintosh.[116] His three years' service in Unish was drawing to a close and during the last day of the school session there naturally existed much tenderness of feeling. At the evening meeting, when a number of fishermen from the nearby island of Isay were present, Macleod challenged his listeners regarding their spiritual condition. Remarked Roderick Macleod, 'The most extraordinary emotions appeared among the people; some wept and some cried aloud as if pricked in their hearts, while others fainted, and fell down as if struck dead'.

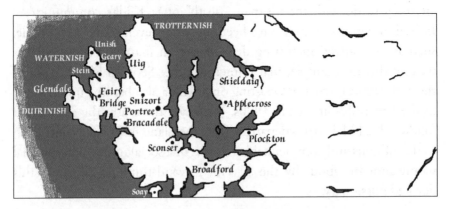

Another who thoroughly investigated the revival wrote: 'For two days they would not go to bed at all, and would give the old man no rest from speaking to them, praying with them and reading the Bible. Awakened to a sense of eternal realities, hearing the voice which called the fishermen of Galilee, they left their nets and followed him.'[117] This

---

203). Steve Taylor, however, provides good evidence to suggest that 1842 is the correct date (Taylor, *The Skye Revivals*, Chapter 7).

116. Macleod's grandson, also named Norman Macleod, was reared in the warm atmosphere of the revival days in which his grandfather had been so instrumental. Receiving Christ at a young age, he was appointed head of the Ladies' School in Soay before entering the ministry, becoming the popular and long-serving minister of Portree Free Church from 1894 (D. A. Macdonald, *In Memoriam: A Brief Sketch of the Life and Labours of the Rev. Norman M'Leod, M.A. United Free Church Portree*, Edinburgh 1913, pp. 8-10).

117. W. Dickson, Free Church Convenor of the Committee on Sabbath Schools, who made his enquiries on a trip to Skye in 1844, quoted in Brown, *Annals of the Disruption*, p. 204.

continued for sixteen days and nights, during which time Macleod got only two hours' sleep each morning. People started flocking to Unish from other parts of Skye, 'many of whom became similarly affected with the rest'.[118] Soon, awakening broke out at the Gaelic School in nearby Geary, as well as at Glendale, Duirinish.

Roderick MacLeod at Fairy Bridge

Meetings were transferred to the village of Stein in Waternish, then, due to adverse tidal conditions, which hampered the many boats that ferried eager souls to the scene, to Fairy Bridge, a convenient junction, which continued to be the scene of a weekly preaching to thousands for about two months. Roderick Macleod of Snizort (1795–1868) was the main preacher at the Fairy Bridge meetings. Oral tradition suggests that he would preach from his horse, circling the vast crowd as he did so. Indeed, all over north Skye during this period, Macleod played a highly prominent part in the work, and the power which on many occasions about this time attended the preaching of the evangelist was said to have been 'overwhelming … The word was quick and powerful, and many who seemed to feel little while under it were struck with convictions on their way home, and turned aside to pray'.[119]

On one occasion an eyewitness at Fairy Bridge saw 'the young and the old, male and female, pouring forth from all sides of the land, from hills, and valleys, villages, hamlets and the lonely hut. The surrounding waters too were covered with about fifty skiffs, like the multitudes which dotted the sea of Tiberias, in pursuit of the Lord himself when he was manifested in the flesh'.[120] One Wednesday Macleod preached from the words, *Behold I stand at the door and knock.* On this occasion the presence of the Spirit of God was manifested in great power. Mr Macleod

---

118. Taylor, *The Skye Revivals*, p. 46. MacIntosh Mackay stressed that revivals in Skye occurred at a time of transition in the island's religious history, and that such a period, in the popular mind, could scarcely happen without being accompanied by extreme views, and not infrequently with violent revulsions (M. Mackay, 'Sermon Preached in the Free Church, Snizort', quoted in Macleod, *The Progress of Evangelicalism*, p. 214).

119. Donald Gillies (Ed.), *The Life and Work of the Very Rev. Roderick MacLeod of Snizort*, Skeabost Bridge 1969, p. 61. MacIntosh Mackay refers to 'a moral and religious seething in Skye' in the years just prior to the Disruption, and attributes this spiritual excitement to the work of the Gaelic Schools and the preaching of Macleod (Macleod, *The Progress of Evangelicalism*, p. 196).

120. *GSS Report* 1843, p. 19.

was using the words, 'Oh! It is not my fear that Christ will not accept you, but my fear is that you will not accept of Christ', when the cries of the people were such that his voice was drowned, and he had to stop speaking. Some, after that solemn sermon, refused to remove from the place. When their friends offered to take them they would cry, 'Oh! Will I go away without Christ? Will I go home without Christ?'[121]

A report from the Rev. James MacQueen, pastor of the small Baptist church in Broadford, dated September 1842, spoke with some concern at 'what has happened in the other end of the island. They had the sacrament last week, and, I hear, that between 12,000 and 15,000 attended, and that hundreds fell down as if dead. This usually commences with violent shaking and crying out, and clapping of hands. Those affected were mostly women and children'.[122] After several months of vast audiences gathering at Fairy Bridge to hear Macleod preach – one was estimated to have attracted about 20,000 people, which seems unlikely given Skye's population at the time of around 25,000 – the advance of the harvest season rendered it expedient to discontinue them.

Spread Throughout the Island

The awakening, 'in a series of regular successive movements ... traversed the whole extent of the island, from north to south'[123] in subsequent months. Ministers from outside Skye (such as Alexander Fraser from Kirkhill and James MacDonald from Urray[124]) came to help in the revival work. A meeting was arranged at one remote village near Bracadale in the autumn of 1842. Hundreds made the long journey over the moors and

---

121. Brown, *Annals of the Disruption*, p. 204.

122. *Report of the Baptist Home Missionary Society for Scotland, chiefly for the Highlands and Islands*, 1843, pp. 8-9.

123. R. Macleod, quoted in *GSS Report* 1844, pp. 17-18. In 1883, aged 90, long-standing catechist to Skye, Donald MacQueen, spoke of the extent of evangelical revival he had witnessed on the island over the decades. 'I have seen a great deal of the power of the gospel', he reminisced. 'I first saw a revival begin at Trotternish and spreading through the island. I have seen again the Rev. Mr Shaw in Bracadale – it was he who brought me here – and then I saw the Rev. Mr MacLeod, and in his time the gospel had great power, and was spreading through the island district in Trotternish and MacLeod's country and Duirinish and over other places' (Allan MacColl, *Land, Faith and the Crofting Community: Christianity and Social Criticism in the Highlands of Scotland 1843–1893*, Edinburgh 2006, p. 54).

124. G. V. R. Grant, *Urray and Kilchrist Church of Scotland*, Ross-shire 1998, p. 53.

hills on a day of torrential rain. At one point everyone got thoroughly soaked on passing across a swollen river, which even the visiting clergy on horseback only managed to cross with difficulty. As the ministers preached, every head was bowed in silent weeping. On another occasion shortly afterwards in Sconser, the crowd sat on the wet shingle of the seashore to hear the same visiting preachers speak from a pulpit made of oars set on end with a sail thrown over them.[125] After the service, the people pleaded with the ministers not to leave, so a promise was made to preach the next day in Broadford. Crowded services were held here also and several times as they preached they had to stop to sing a few verses of a psalm in order to calm the feelings and emotions of the people.

In this year (1842) the Gaelic Society reported that 'with scarcely an exception, the fourteen schools in Skye all shared in the outpouring of the Holy Ghost'.[126] It was the opinion of Dr John Macdonald, who made a preaching tour of north Skye in 1842, that the revival on the island 'exceeded in intensity and extent anything of the kind in modern times'.[127] It was said that few families in the whole of Skye did not have at least one person seriously impressed. The work continued through 1843 and 1844.[128] Roderick Macleod reported from Snizort in 1843 that 'the whole parish is one Gaelic school this winter'.[129] The work in these later years was perhaps most notable among the Baptists, when crowds of nearly 1,000 were still attending open-air meetings. With the Disruption, some of the chief laymen in the Free Church on the island were 'the ripened fruits' of the Skye revival of 1812, while others were converts of the 1839–42 movement. After 1843, when many of the Free Church parishes in Skye and elsewhere in the Highlands and Islands were without a settled ministry for a long period, services were often conducted by these lay revival converts.[130]

---

125. Brown, *Annals of the Disruption*, pp. 658-60.

126. *GSS Report* 1844, pp. 15-16.

127. Quoted in Taylor, *The Skye Revivals*, p. 48.

128. *GSS Report* 1843, pp. 16-19; Gillies, *The Life and Work of the Very Rev. Roderick MacLeod of Snizort*, pp. 58-60. As in the case of Tiree and other areas of north-west Scotland, a significant number of those converted during the revival emigrated to Canada following the potato blight of 1846.

129. *GSS Report* 1843, p. 23.

130. Macleod, *The Progress of Evangelicalism*, p. 220.

Mull

Tobermory, on the isle of Mull, had been under a Moderate ministry prior to the Disruption and it was said that 'there were few among the people who truly feared the Lord'.[131] One old man, John McInnes, a weaver, spent whole nights wrestling in prayer in hope that the Lord would bless his island in the day of trial. One day he emerged from his closet, face shining with joy and with an assurance that his prayers would soon be answered. They were.[132] John Campbell of Oban was one who later referred to the 'great awakening' taking place in Tobermory.[133] The Rev. Duncan Campbell of Kiltearn was another who faithfully visited the island during the time of blessing that ensued between 1839 and 1842, as he did annually for nineteen years.[134]

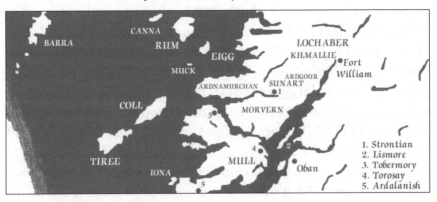

Success here was also thanks largely to the tireless labours of the Reverends Peter McBride of Rothesay and Peter Maclean of Storno-way. In the stirring days leading up to the Disruption, the labours of these two men throughout the Western Highlands and Islands – both individually and as they joined in hearty co-operation – 'seem to have been very abundant and remarkably owned and blessed'. Maclean had recently returned from America and had regained strength after a short

---

131. W. Dickson, quoted in Brown, *Annals of the Disruption*, p. 194.

132. Later, with the Disruption, 'the people seemed instinctively to turn to McInnes' house, round which, the first Sabbath, five hundred assembled for admission' (ibid.).

133. Campbell, *Missionary and Ministerial Life in the Highlands*, p. 135.

134. MacGregor, *Campbell of Kiltearn*, p. 101. Alexander MacRae's stance is that this was Mull's first 'special experience of the spirit of revival … Even then it was not moved so deeply as many other places in the Islands have been' (MacRae, *Revivals in the Highlands and Islands*, p. 57). In fact there had been a significant movement on Mull just seven or eight years earlier, in 1832 (see page 272).

period of rest.[135] Neil Dewar of Kingussie said of him, 'Wherever he went, immense crowds flocked over moors and seas to hear him. The effects were remarkable; oftentimes large assemblages seemed powerfully moved as one man, numbers being unable to refrain from giving audible expression to their feelings'. Considerable fruit resulted, which, when harvested, was a blessing to the Highland Church for decades to follow.[136] (see page 459 for post-Disruption blessing on Mull).

The Small Isles

The poor and nominally Protestant minority on the 'small isles' of Rum and Eigg was also deeply touched by this powerful pre-Disruption season of blessing. Writes the Rev. Alexander Cameron in regard to parish minister, John Swanson: 'The hardships of a Colonial or Indian missionary are not to be compared to those endured by Mr Swanson, even before the Disruption. Gradually, however, his labours of love began to tell, for the Lord was graciously pleased to visit these islands with an extensive revival of religion, which greatly refreshed the spirit of his servant'.[137] On Eigg Swanson reported that the reaction of his congregation to a sermon he preached in the course of his ordinary Sunday service was as if the words of Scripture were being literally fulfilled: *'They shall look upon me whom they have pierced and mourn'* (Zech. 12:10). His message that August day was on the sufferings of Christ, based on Acts 17:3. Contrition on account of sin affected the whole congregation, and the meeting house became 'a place of weeping', from which cries could apparently be distinctly heard at the distance of half a mile.[138]

Noted Swanson in his journal: 'It was an outburst of the whole, so that no mouth was silent, and no eye dry; old and young mourned together, and the blooming and withered cheeks were all wet with tears.

---

135. Born in Uig, Lewis, in 1800, Maclean was converted at the age of twenty-five during the island's first revival. Entering the ministry, he accepted a call to Cape Breton in 1837. After five years overseas, during which time there was a deep move of the Spirit among his congregation, Maclean moved back to Scotland in 1842, suffering from ill health as a result of the overwork, fatigue and strain experienced during that blessed period overseas (Macleod, *A Brief Record of the Church in Uig*, p. 15).

136. Various Contributors, *Disruption Worthies of the Highlands*, p. 216.

137. ibid., p. 133.

138. *GSS Report* 1843, p. 30.

The scene was indescribable, and I sat down mayhap to weep too'.[139]
The meeting place was 'a low dingy cottage of turf and stone … a pulpit
grotesquely rude, that had never employed the bred carpenter; and a few
ranges of seats of undressed deal'.[140] Yet from this lowly church arose
the living soul of a Christian community, convinced of the truth of the
gospel, and hearts softened and impressed by its power. While Swanson
admitted that at the beginning of the revival there had been 'a good deal
of physical excitement', he observed with obvious satisfaction that 'this
gradually subsided as the judgement is becoming more enlightened'.[141]
Most of the island's population, however, considered the revival as being
'of the devil' and viewed its physical manifestations as 'the braxy' – a
disease which affects sheep and results in them falling dead. On a lesser
scale, the movement also affected Canna and Muck.[142]

The Far North
Ross-shire

Avoch

Following the deep spiritual impression made upon two young folk in
Avoch in 1840, and 'awareness of the low state of religion among us,
and the great need we had of the outpouring of the Holy Spirit to revive
believers and convert sinners', prayer meetings were begun in the Congregational Chapel.[143] These continued nightly for nine weeks, being
attended by 200–300 and out of which thirteen cottage prayer meetings
arose. One of these was composed of a group of four girls who met in
the minister's house, and this grew steadily until around thirty between
the ages of eight and sixteen were attending nightly. Meanwhile, a band
of young boys met to pray in a nearby barn. It was said that the showers
of grace which fell on the village then took a westward direction, before
turning north and east; not ceasing until the whole district was affected.

139. Various Contributors, *Disruption Worthies of the Highlands*, p. 133.

140. Hugh Miller of Cromarty, on a visit to Eigg in April 1845, quoted in Taylor, *The Skye Revivals*, pp. 93-4.

141. *GSS Report* 1843, p. 21.

142. ibid., pp. 18, 20-1, 30-1.

143. Indeed, in regard to the issues which subsequently led to revival, Alexander Dewar was able to compare the 1840 awakening to that which had occurred in his parish in 1829 (see page 219).

While the effects of the revival were mighty in one spot, a nearby area would seem completely barren, until visited by the Lord afresh. The Congregational church more than doubled in size during this period.[144]

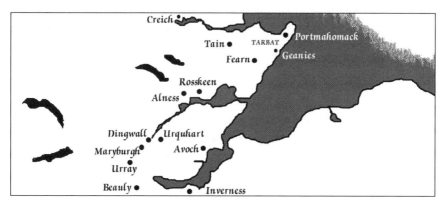

Tarbat

Meanwhile, 'a tide of revival passed over the greater part of the Synod of Ross' at the turn of the 1840s. In Tarbat, under the ministry of the Rev. David Campbell,[145] 'a considerable movement' began on Saturday 6th July 1840 when John Macdonald of Ferintosh preached in Gaelic at Communion services there.[146] He appealed forcibly to the consciences of the people with reference to the high privilege which they had enjoyed under the preaching of their late venerable pastor (the Rev. William Forbes, d. 1838), under whom the first symptoms of awakening occurred. Many were conscience-struck by the appeal and, 'convinced

---

144. 1843 'Questionnaire', quoted in McNaughton, *Highlands and Islands*, pp. 247-9.

145. Writing in 1864, Campbell said that he had 'witnessed three religious revivals – one in Breadalbane in the year 1816; one in Tarbat and other parishes in Ross-shire in the years 1840 and 1841'; and 'a third in Lawers in the year 1861. Let sovereign grace have all the glory', he exulted on reminiscing about these three blessed events (Brown, *Annals of the Disruption*, pp. 9-10).

146. Taylor, *Memorials of Rev. C. C. Macintosh*, p. 41. Alexander MacRae marvelled at how the gospel was so faithfully preached in many parts of the north of Scotland in the early nineteenth century, and made note of a host of contemporaries of John Macdonald, 'both seniors and juniors, a galaxy of men remarkable for their ministerial ability, faithfulness and spirituality of mind, and success in the work of the Lord'. These included Dr Bayne, Kiltarlity; Rev. McAdam, Nigg; Rev. Forbes, Tarbat; Rev. Donald Fraser, Kirkhill, and his son Rev. Alexander Fraser; Rev. Sage, Resolis; Dr Stewart, Dingwall and his son Rev. Stewart, Cromarty; Rev. Matthew, Kilmuir; Dr Ross, Lochbroom; Rev. Duncan Grant, Forres; Rev. Macdonald, Urray; Rev. Macdonald, Glen Urquhart; Rev. Shepherd, Kingussie; Rev. Macleod, Lochbroom (MacRae, *The Life of Gustavus Aird*, pp. 267-8).

of all, and judged of all, received the sentence of death in themselves and were constrained to cry out, "What must I do to be saved?" And thus', wrote the Rev. Malcolm MacGregor, 'the bread cast upon the waters by the late worthy minister of Tarbat has been found after many days – the seed sown by him, though long under the clod, has suddenly sprung into active vegetation'.[147] One person reported seeing 'multitudes weeping and multitudes rejoicing on Communion Sabbath'.[148]

John Kennedy relates that,

> when this movement was arousing attention Mr Campbell's friend, Mr Stewart of Cromarty, went to visit him to see for himself if it was only a time of sensational and emotional excitement or if it was a real awakening to spiritual conviction and concern. He saw some of the converts and questioned them. One of them vividly related that when he was awakened to concern he felt himself to be shut in by the justice of God as a mighty mountain to an ocean of everlasting destruction. So touching were his words that Stewart was ready to cry out himself, and as the outcome of his queries he was more disposed to question his own conversion than that of the Portmahomack fisher-folk! [149]

Kennedy shares another story from this season of blessing. One young woman who lived in a wood near Geanies with her father, was one of the awakened and in her excitement her mind was affected. Her father kept her at home tied in her bed, following the custom of the time. One day she asked her father to loose her, insisting it was quite safe to do so, for, she said, 'The Lord has spoken to my heart and said that He has blotted out my sins as a thick cloud, and I shall not be left long with you'. Once untied, the young woman arose and dressed with the light of reason restored and the hope of eternal life in her heart. In less than a week, as she had foretold, she passed away.[150]

Malcolm MacGregor, a later Free Church minister of Ferintosh, claimed that there was no parish within the county of Ross that was more moved and influenced by the revival than the parish of Tarbat.

---

147. Rev. Malcolm MacGregor, 'Prefatory Memoir', p. xxvii.

148. Fraser, *Tarbat, Easter Ross*, p. 56.

149. Kennedy, *The Apostle of the North*, pp. 290-1.

150. ibid., p. 291.

It was said to have 'acquired a degree of interest owing to late circumstances, which it never previously possessed'.[151]

Tain

A week after revival had broken out in Tarbat it 'assumed much greater proportions' in Tain, where the Rev. Charles C. Macintosh (1806–1868) was minister. During the previous year Macintosh became increasingly concerned at the apparent deadness of his people. He took counsel with his elders, as a result of which both his prayers and theirs for an outpouring of the Spirit on the parish became persistent and impassioned. General prayer-meetings became more numerous and more largely attended; and a deeper seriousness manifestly pervaded the congregation. It was during the communion season that 'the smouldering flame burst into a fire'. At a Gaelic service on the Monday evening, at which a large number of persons from many parishes were present, Dr Macdonald of Ferintosh preached on Luke 13:24 (*'Enter through the narrow door'*). Just after he had made one of the freest offers of salvation to sinners, and had uttered the words, 'Will you not close with Christ?', a heartrending cry arose from every part of the densely crowded church. There had been many silent weepers before; but now the preacher's voice was drowned, so that he was forced to pause, and announce a psalm to be sung. The movement quickly spread through a wide district.[152]

---

151. 'Inverness Herald', 24/7/1840, quoted in Forbes, *Communion and Other Sermons*, p. xxiv.

152. Taylor, *Memorials of Rev. C. C. Macintosh*, p. 43. This seems to be a different set of events from that related personally by Macintosh to Dr Rainy late in the former's life. One Saturday evening Macintosh was quietly preparing his heart for the services of the morrow. Mysteriously, he was led out in thought to review the years of his ministry in Tain. Its barrenness pained him deeply. He could find no comfort in the large congregation, nor in the loyalty and kindness of his people. Travail of soul set in. Alone with God, reality now dominated his surging thoughts. It was the hour of his distress. He resolved to resign, humbling though it would be. Another voice, another ministry might mean blessing to the people. Tomorrow he would tell them. Next day this resolve was stronger. When he preached that morning a brooding silence pervaded the church. Tenderly he told them of his previous night's experience and of the decision he had made. His yearning for their salvation had prompted it. Another voice might prevail with them where he had failed. But the Holy Spirit used these strange tidings, for a wail was heard throughout the entire church as men and women were convicted of the sin of unbelief. Their repentance meant a turning to the Lord, and numbers passed from death unto life in that memorable hour. It was indeed a day of harvest, which

Macintosh testified to 'the sovereignty of that God who works when and how he pleaseth ... sermons of equal power to those on which such an abundant blessing rested during the past year have been often listened to on former occasions, when no similar results followed'.[153] He referred to prayer meetings (including those formed and conducted by and for the young) which were more frequent than previously; as well as to the week-night sermons given in most of the parishes, to which the people flocked in crowds, the discontinuance of which would have been deeply regretted. Macintosh wrote of the movement:

> The excitement continued during the whole summer and autumn ... The experience which I had of the revival of religion, though limited and partial, is such as would lead me to long for its continuance and to pant for its return, as bringing with it the blessed results for which a minister of Christ would desire to live and die – the conversion of sinners and the increasing consolation and edification of saints. There is a peculiar amount of labour and anxiety which attends such a season, but there is also a peculiar pleasure and unwearied strength for the discharge of duty.[154]

At that time Macintosh, by himself or with assistance, was holding four Sabbath services, besides fulfilling all the other work which a revival season in so large a parish entailed. The revival was still in progress a year later.[155]

Alness, Creich and Beauly

In the course of a few weeks the revival which had so powerfully affected Tarbat and Tain appeared in a great measure and under similar circumstances in many other parishes within the bounds of the

---

continued to be reaped for many a Sabbath afterwards. The travail of that night of distress gave birth to a heaven-given joy. Day after day this minister lived among a people who knew the 'joy unspeakable and full of glory' (Andrew Stewart (Ed.), *The 'Albatross' Yacht Mission: A Story of Joyous Christian Adventure*, Edinburgh nd, pp. 9-10).

153. Presbytery of Aberdeen, *Evidence on the Subject of Revivals*, p. 95.

154. Taylor, *Memorials of Rev. C. C. Macintosh*, pp. 41-2. See also Noble, *Religious Life in Ross*, pp. 240-1.

155. By the time of the Disruption, 'the admiring fondness' with which Charles Macintosh had been regarded from the very first had already deepened into 'love, reverence and unbounded confidence'. (ibid., pp. 43-6).

Synod of Ross, particularly in Alness and Urquhart.[156] The Rev. Alexander Flyter of Alness remarked on the 'influences with which the Lord accompanied the preaching of the gospel. This influence', he observed, 'was striking and impressive in various parts of the country in 1840. About that time in every district of the parish of Alness there were some sin-stricken souls'.[157] As a result, 'many were added to the Lord'.[158]

The Rev. W. Taylor said that the awakening in Tain – 'a remarkable event' – was 'part of a very general movement in Ross-shire'.[159] Fearn and Creich were also touched by the revival, as was the remote inland district of Croick, in which parish Gustavus Aird had recently been settled. Aird had been 'in full sympathy with the movements (elsewhere in Ross-shire) and in the enjoyment of a high degree of spiritual fervour, life and power, whose influence was soon manifested in the religious life of the parish'.[160]

Effects of the movement, along with the impetus of the Ten Years' Conflict, were very apparent two years later, when an open-air service was held in the churchyard of Beauly Priory. Crowds assembled from the neighbouring parishes of Kirkhill, Kiltarlity, Urray and Killearnan. 'Everywhere was to be seen', noted Duncan Macgregor, 'the gathering people; the countryside seemed to be moving to one centre'. There was an eager desire to hear, as the Rev. Duncan Campbell (then minister of Kiltearn), himself deeply impressed with the scene, preached from Psalm 69:4, with a voice that was 'clear, full and musical, and rose and fell in thrilling cadence'.[161]

Rosskeen

Unlike most ministers who have the privilege of experiencing revival during their ministry, the Rev. David Carment (1772–1856) of Rosskeen was well advanced in years when a wave of the Spirit breezed through his parish. Nor had he recently moved to a new charge. He

---

156. Presbytery of Aberdeen, *Evidence on the Subject of Revivals*, p. 93.

157. Brown, *Annals of the Disruption*, p. 10.

158. Various Contributors, *Disruption Worthies of the Highlands*, p. 39.

159. Taylor, *Memorials of Rev. C. C. Macintosh*, p. 41.

160. MacRae, *The Life of Gustavus Aird*, pp. 42-3.

161. Macgregor, *Campbell of Kiltearn*, pp. 60-1.

had previously served as assistant minister to Hugh Calder of Croy (1803–10), then as minister of Duke Street Gaelic Chapel, Glasgow, before transferring to Rosskeen in 1822. Carment's preaching made a great impression in the parish from the outset, and he soon acquired an influence over the people such as is rarely attained.[162] His own impression, however, was that a considerable portion of his subsequent ministry in Rosskeen was less fruitful of spiritual results than those in his previous charges.[163]

This, however, seems a little odd considering the fact that in January 1841, sixty-eight-year-old Carment could offer the following testimony: 'The prospects of this parish are becoming increasingly bright and pleasing. There has been since 1840 a very remarkable awakening and religious revival in this parish and neighbourhood, especially among the young; and numbers, I have reason to believe, have been savingly changed … I have been enabled to preach frequently on week days to attentive, impressed, and weeping congregations, who flock by night and by day to hear the Word'. At the previous communion Carment had admitted more communicants than during the whole of the preceding eighteen years of his ministry. Like many of his ministerial colleagues, he saw the spread of revival in various parts of Scotland as 'a token for good that our present contendings as a church (the Ten Years' Conflict) are approved by God'.[164]

Maryburgh

A native of Latheron, George Macleod (1803–1871) was awakened at the age of twenty-eight, undergoing such deep conviction that for days and nights he could neither eat nor sleep. Following a dramatic conversion, he studied for the ministry, and was inducted to Maryburgh Church of Scotland in the Presbytery of Dingwall in November 1839. This was, of course, in the neighbourhood of John Macdonald of Ferintosh, whose fame was in all the churches. With no thought of any danger of

---

162. This despite the fact that open dissension arose between Carment, who was both straightforward and independent of spirit, and 'the Men'. In Carment's case, unusually, the people left 'the Men' and followed the minister. (see page 140 for more on 'the Men').

163. Various Contributors, *A Memorial of Disruption Worthies*, Dalkeith 1886, p. 150.

164. Brown, *Annals of the Disruption*, p. 11. Carment joined the Free Church in 1843. Out of a parish population of over 3,000, it is believed that fewer than fifty remained in the Established Church.

sinking into absolute obscurity under the shadow of such a renowned preacher, Macleod was not long settled when his power was felt in all the parishes around him. People flocked from all quarters to hear him, and the Maryburgh church was crowded from Sabbath to Sabbath with hundreds more than it could comfortably hold. The passages were literally crammed with people standing during services and every conceivable sitting-place was occupied. Decades later, some could still recall the rare and amusing spectacle of men and women sitting on book-boards and in front of the gallery. This state of things continued throughout Macleod's three-year ministry in the Ross-shire community.[165]

Contention over External Manifestations

Rev. John Kennedy of Killearnan did not waver in his staunch distrust of the awakening in the north and elsewhere at this time (a year or so before his self-prophesied death in 1841) due to the unnecessary excitement that he believed accompanied it. His son, John Kennedy of Dingwall, said, 'His anticipations were, alas, too fully realised. The rich flush of blossom that then appeared withered prematurely, and almost entirely away, and bitter disappointment awaited those who formed a more sanguine estimate than his of the fruit that might in the end be produced'.[166] A great admirer of John Macdonald of Ferintosh, who went on to write his biography, Kennedy said of the effect of his preaching, 'Hundreds have I seen deeply affected in one congregation'. Nevertheless, Kennedy generally found in regard to the movement that 'the greater the excitement, the less, to my consciousness, the power'. Indeed, Kennedy, while in no way criticising Macdonald, had strong reservations about the movement that arose in his parish:

> This was the season, too when the crisis of my own life had come. I went then to hear the gospel as one to whom the issue was to be life or death for ever. I craved with all my heart to share in the impression made on other hearts, if it verily resulted from the operation of the Spirit's power … I well remember, when, in the

---

165. ibid., pp. 188–9. Then, in the lead-up to the Disruption, Macleod acted as a deputy to many parts of the West Highlands, with a view to prepare them for that event. Macleod's subsequent ministries in Strathspey (six months) and in the vast expanse of Lochbroom parish were also significantly blessed.

166. Kennedy, *Days of the Fathers in Ross-shire*, pp. 193-4.

midst of hundreds of mourners, an old man, who had spent the two nights preceding on the hill-side in an agony of distress, arose, and, in a loud wail, exclaimed, '*tha mi caillte*' (I am lost). But not four days had passed before he was as callous and as worldly as before. Nor was his case, in its last phase, an exceptional one; for those who knew the district well could tell of scarce any abiding fruit as the result of that remarkable movement.[167]

A well-educated farmer from the region, Robert Walker, also spoke out strongly against the Ross-shire revivals. He wrote that preachers 'breathing out the terrors of hell' resulted in making folk lose the use of reason and stopped the circulation of blood, so that their bodies lose sense and feeling, and they fall into hysterics. Instead of expressing vehemence, he insisted, ministers should speak worlds of tenderness, having a Christ-like spirit of 'serenity, of self-possession of impassioned sweetness'. Walker referred to three young lads employed by him, aged from twelve to fourteen, who were especially wont to cry out during services. When questioned about their motives they apparently admitted to seeking attention – when attending meetings in other parishes they were often supplied with food and drink, and sometimes clothes. Walker made specific reference to the thanksgiving Monday of the Lord's Supper in Alness in August 1840, when what he termed 'the most popular minister in Ross-shire', prompted by someone in the congregation making a disturbance, got into a passion, and denounced those who did not cry out as being under the influence of Satanic delusion. In conclusion, Walker felt that the fruit from the revivals ably proved that they were in general the works of man rather than God.[168]

Dr Charles Macintosh of Tain accepted that in his parish 'there was a good deal of excitement on some occasions under the Word' but stated that 'this gradually diminished'.[169] Neither he nor any minister visiting his district actively encouraged the external manifestations; indeed it was said that these were sometimes greatest under sermons containing not a single word fitted to alarm. This said, neither Macintosh nor Macdonald

---

167. John Kennedy/Horatius Bonar, *Evangelism: A Reformed Debate*, p. 112.

168. R. Walker, '*Expostulatory Letters to Free Church Ministers, on their Secession from the Church of Scotland*', Dingwall 1846, pp. 45-8.

169. Taylor, *Memorials of Rev. C. C. Macintosh*, p. 43 (See also John Gillies, *Historical Collections*, p. 560).

of Ferintosh (who had more than once over the years come under criticism for the unrestrained excitement which accompanied his preaching – see page 218) thought it warrantable authoritatively to suppress the outward expressions of emotion or agitation, preferring to allow events to take their natural course while keeping an ever watchful eye on the progress of the movement. As a result, Macintosh was unaware of 'any effects other than beneficial which (the revival) has produced' within the area of his ministry. Sixteen years later, the preacher could still emphatically describe it as 'a real work of God',[170] a view with which a great many others in Ross-shire – ministers and laymen alike – could heartily concur regarding the movements that developed within their own districts.

Caithness and Sutherland

Wick and Thurso

A series of morning and evening meetings was organised by the pastors of the Congregational churches of Wick and Thurso in 1840, supported by the ministers of the three congregations in Orkney and a young man about to be ordained in Lerwick. Continuing daily for a fortnight, and supported by open-air preaching, 'which was found useful in collecting hearers', almost one thousand people packed into the Congregational chapel in Wick night after night, while the audiences in Thurso reached twice the usual Lord's Day attendance. 'The spirit of prayer seemed to be greatly excited among the members of the churches', wrote a reporter for the *Scottish Congregational Magazine*. Altogether, 160 came forward as anxious enquirers, with 'some very affecting cases'.[171]

Lairg and Tongue

John MacDonald of Lairg was appointed catechist of his native Sutherland parish in 1841. Old and young flocked in such numbers to his meetings that accommodation became a problem. On occasions the cattle had to be turned out from the byre-end of Macdonald's house (divided from living quarters by a wattled partition), so that their stalls might be used to seat those who could not get into the house proper, and there they sat on pieces of bog pine or windlings of straw. The unusually

---

170. ibid., p. 43.

171. *SCM* 1840, quoted in McNaughton, *Early Congregational Independency in the Highlands and Islands and the North-East of Scotland*, p. 238.

high attendances were attributed partly to the 'wave of spiritual life passing over many districts in the Highlands' at the time, and partly to 'the catechist's own warm, spiritual manner in the conducting of the duties of his office'.[172]

It was in this year, too, that the minister of Tongue, further north in Sutherland, reported, 'It is rare now to find one who cannot repeat the Shorter Catechism and the writer knows not that such a thing exists among the native peasantry as a family without the daily worship of God'. In yet another Sutherland parish, it was said that 'the people gather together on Sabbath evenings to repeat the Shorter Catechism and read the Scriptures'. Their meetings always began and ended with prayer, which in the words of the minister, 'spread a moral and religious influence over the hamlet'.[173]

The North Isles

Shetland

A Congregational report from Shetland in 1839 exulted in the news that their chapel in the south-west parish of Walls had been for the last two years 'much favoured of the Lord'. During that period about thirty individuals had been added to their fellowship. Indeed, the congregation had so much increased that it was found necessary in the summer of 1839 to enlarge the building, although constructed just two years previously. Additions to the chapel complete, the church began holding protracted meetings in an attempt to promote a revival of religion in the neighbourhood. Students from Glasgow Theological Academy came to help the local minister, and such was the success of these meetings that the chapel, even in its enlarged state, proved to be too small for the increased Sunday congregations, and during the services some had to stand outside the doors and windows.[174]

The following year, James Morison – a twenty-four-year-old United Secession probationer, later principal founder of the Evangelical Union

---

172. Munro, *Records of Grace in Sutherland*, pp. 122-3.

173. *New Statistical Account of Scotland* vol. 15, 1841, quoted in George Robb, 'Popular Religion and the Christianization of the Scottish Highlands', in *Journal of Religious History*, vol. 16 (1990), p. 30.

174. *SCM* 1840, quoted in W. D. McNaughton, *Early Congregational Independency in Shetland*, Lerwick 2005, p. 46.

and recognised as Scotland's most prominent Arminian preacher and theologian (for more see page 372) [175] – paid a brief visit to Lerwick, where he spoke on several occasions. As in other places he visited, Morison's force of personality and the passion of his preaching made a strong impact on all who heard him. Altogether, nearly one hundred, in anxiety concerning the state of their souls, were conversed with, not merely 'young and illiterate people' moved with the excitement that prevailed in the town, but including 'some of the best-educated ladies and gentlemen of the place'. [176]

Orkney

Congregational Church records make mention of the 'revivals of religion' which took place in different parts of Orkney in 1840, e.g. through the labours of Thomas S. McKean, recently-inducted minister in Kirkwall, who itinerated with other brethren 'through these remote and long neglected isles' during the summer of that year. [177] In Rousay an interest in Independency had been established in the hearts of some following a visit by one of Haldane's associates as early as 1797. Some of those influenced were drawn into fellowship with the Secession Church in Kirkwall, though the stretch of water that lay between (Eynhallow Sound) made communication at times inconvenient. Finally, in 1833–4 a building was erected on the island and a local congregation established. The Rev. John McLellan from Wigtown was ordained as minister in November 1837. Sabbath attendance improved considerably. It was reported that 'revival influences came in soon after to stir into blissful activity'. By 1843 this Rousay church, one of several congregations in a flourishing state on the small island around this time, had a membership of 170 and attendance of around 250. [178]

---

175. It was whilst in Lerwick that he wrote his maiden publication, *The Question, 'What Must I Do to be Saved?', Answered*. Published later that year (1840) under the pseudonym *Philanthropos*, the booklet was to play a significant part in the development of Scottish theology.

176. William Adamson, *The Life of the Rev. James Morison D.D.*, p. 75.

177. *SCM* 1862, 1866, quoted in McNaughton, *Early Congregational Independency in Orkney*, p. 43.

178. Robert Small, *History of the Congregations of the United Presbyterian Church From 1733 to 1900*, Edinburgh 1904, pp. 507-8.

Meanwhile, a Baptist minister who visited many parts of Orkney in 1840, and the north isles in particular, reported 'a little revival in some places'. A year later regret was expressed in that many who had been awakened were attending other churches, yet also consolation in the thought that, 'if they are saved in the Lord, all is well'.[179] However, it became apparent by 1845 that 'though there is much profession, and many gospel preachers, the power appears to be wanting'. When William Tulloch of Westray did a preaching tour through the isles in 1843, he noted the appearance of 'a stirring everywhere ... a little movement throughout the islands', some of which spiritual interest may have been occasioned by the recent Disruption event, which led to fourteen new places of worship being established by the Free Church.[180] In the early spring of 1844, six names were added to the Baptist cause in Eday.

During the winter and spring of 1842, a heavy responsibility for their fellow men came upon the leaders of Westray Baptist Church, who set out to preach earnestly in every district of the island. A similar course was pursued during the same seasons the following year, by which time 'a great shaking' and a 'deep work of grace' was apparent. Many struggled with their convictions until they could no longer endure the strain upon them, and naturally reserved though they were, many felt constrained to seek the direction of an undershepherd.[181] In February 1843, as a result of the movement, a hole was cut in the frozen loch, and eleven converts were baptised on confession of faith. At that time, the Rev. Tulloch could look back and state, 'This has been a year of high favour to us. The Lord has been graciously pleased to send us a revival and to add to us around 36, and twelve are seeking admission ... God is pleased to employ human instrumentality but He alone makes it effectual'.[182] The following year a further eighteen were baptised.

179. *BHMS Report* 1840, p. 11; 1842, p. 15.

180. ibid., 1843, p. 11; 1845, p. 15.

181. Henry Harcus, *The History of the Orkney Baptist Churches*, Ayr 1898, p. 82.

182. *BHMS Report* 1844, p. 26.

CHAPTER 8

The Disruption Era
1843–5

Introduction

Disruption as a Result of Revival

As previously noted (see page 314), throughout the 1830s and early '40s the Scottish Church was stirred over the controversy between the Church and the State, which came to a dramatic head with the emergence of the Free Church from the Church of Scotland – 'The Disruption' – in 1843, when over 450 ministers and 60 per cent of church members left the Established Church to form the Free Church of Scotland.[1]

The awakening that spread throughout much of Scotland prior to this date, the record of which was recorded in Chapters 6 and 7, can be seen partly as an effect of this ecclesiastical conflict, while in turn it also influenced it. George McGregor believed that the Disruption 'flowed from deep pools of an evangelical revival whose head-waters are to be found in the days of the Covenanters and the times of the Praying Societies'.[2] George Smeaton wrote: 'The whole (Disruption) movement sprang from a revival of religion.... Thousands were impressed and awakened to divine things who were indifferent before. The testimony to Christ as a real Prince and Head awoke many; the self-denial of the demitting pastors

---

1. Some evangelicals, however, remained within the Church of Scotland, believing it better to preserve the unity of the Church than provoke a schism.

2. George McGregor, *A Short Sketch of the History of Lochee Free Church, now Lochee East Church of Scotland 1846–1946*, Dundee 1946.

led others to enquiry; the new message that arrested and solemnized the congregations everywhere, and especially in long shut-up parishes where moderate doctrine had blinded the eyes of men, were all-important elements. But above all the Spirit of God accompanied the Word'.[3]

Some believe that it was the revival of spiritual life in the Church that eventually brought the tense, longstanding co-existence of evangelical Christianity and Moderatism to a head. Where for decades respect for parish boundaries had meant that many districts in Scotland had languished for lack of the life-bringing Gospel of Christ being preached to them, with the renewal of spiritual fervour evangelical ministers felt they could no longer leave neighbouring parishes' needs unmet by waiting for an invitation from local ministers. The conflict resulting from itinerant preaching in such areas was in itself sufficient to lead to a crisis. But, in the view of Iain H. Murray, the main reason so many ministers were willing to give up their homes and salaries, and walk by faith, with thousands of members of their congregations into an uncertain future was that the newly-formed Free Church was, in the words of one of its ministers, 'nursed in the bosom of religious revival'. 'Difficulties which would have alarmed another generation', Murray comments, 'were swept away by the new ardour of love to Christ and the joy which men had in the Holy Spirit. Accordingly, the very Disruption day, when all these hazards had now to be faced, was a time of thanksgiving and praise'. Murray concurs with the Rev. Samuel Miller of Glasgow, who asserted, 'If there had been no spiritual and increasing reviving in the Church, the event of 1843 had never taken place'.[4] Writing well after Miller, Michael Lynch described the Free Church as 'a child of the age of religious revivals .... Its Evangelicals drew inspiration from events like the "awakening" at Kilsyth in 1839 as well as feeding on a growing animus against the state'.[5]

Disruption as a Cause of Revival

But it is to the much overlooked reality that the crisis in the Church of Scotland itself led to a burst of renewed spiritual life throughout Scotland that we now turn. For as well as being in large part the product of the revival which

---

3. George Smeaton, *Memoir of Alexander Thomson of Banchory*, Edinburgh 1869, pp. 290-1; cf. John Keddie, *George Smeaton: Learned Theologian and Biblical Scholar*, Darlington 2007, pp. 49-50.

4. Iain H. Murray, *A Scottish Christian Heritage*, pp. 109-11.

5. Michael Lynch, *Scotland: A New History*, pp. 401-2.

preceded it, the Disruption event has been viewed by many historians and church leaders as a real spiritual movement in itself, not just an ecclesiastical struggle. As William Couper put it: 'The Revival of 1839 merged into the religious awakening that spread over the land in 1843.'[6] In the early days of the Free Church to which he belonged, Dr MacIntosh Mackay, who well knew the Highlands and its religious history, asserted, 'I feel the strongest conviction that never since the first light of the Reformation dawned on the land of our fathers has there been such a universal religious movement over the whole of the Highlands and Islands as there is at this day'.[7] George Smeaton wrote: 'A revival movement accompanied the Disruption as well as preceded it'.[8] Free Church Professor and one-time Principal, W. G. Blaikie concurred: 'The spirit roused by the Disruption was tremendously strong. There was both good and bad in it, the good greatly predominating'.[9]

It has been alleged that the triumphs of the Disruption and the spiritual blessings that followed in its train have been considerably exaggerated by the seceding group's ministers, theologians and supporters in order to show that such blessings proved beyond doubt that their actions carried the full approval of the Almighty.[10] However, attestations to the success of the Disruption appear, not only from those within the Free Church, but also from many outwith its ranks. Writing on the centenary of the Disruption, Professor G. D. Henderson, later Moderator of the Church of Scotland, wrote of those times: 'There was an uprush and outpouring of feeling and energy. Ministers, elders and congregations felt themselves able for anything, as after another Pentecost. Everyone had a cause, a call, a message, a duty'.[11] Dr Charles H. Waller, Principal of the London School of Divinity from 1893 to 1897 and a seemingly unbiased English

---

6. Couper, *Scottish Revivals*, p. 129.

7. Brown, *Annals of the Disruption*, p. 665.

8. Keddie, *George Smeaton*, p. 49.

9. Blaikie, *David Brown: Professor and Principal of the Free Church College*, London 1898, p. 73.

10. Such claims even came from a few within the Free Church's own ranks. Archibald Cook was reputed to have said shortly after the Disruption that the Lord would not honour the Free Church because they had too much pride in what they did (Campbell, *One of Heaven's Jewels*, p. 180). Donald Withrington's paper, 'The Disruption: A Century and a Half of Historical Interpretation' helpfully analyses the use made of history by the infant Free Church (*RSCHS* 1993 Vol. 25 pp. 118-53).

11. G. D. Henderson, *Heritage: A Study of the Disruption*, Edinburgh 1943, p. 147.

observer, is on record as having told students that 'the nearest approach that he knew of in the history of the Church universal to apostolic conditions of faith and living was what was to be seen in the Free Church of Scotland in its early days'.[12] As long as eight years after the Disruption, Dr J. W. Alexander of New York wrote that the Free Church of Scotland 'seems to me all in one great revival'. Following a visit to Britain in 1851, he said: 'These few days in Scotland have shown me a permanent revival of religion, such as proves to me that God has a favour to his covenanting people'.[13] Meanwhile, even *The Scottish Guardian* remarked that although 'the Disruption was never particularly characterised as revival, yet it was so radically'.[14]

The outworking of this movement within the fledgling Free Church could be witnessed in the fact that there was an amazing enthusiasm and such a general flocking to the hearing of the gospel as had not been seen in Scotland for many years prior to 1839. In the years 1843 to 1845, 163 new congregations were added to the original number which came out at the Disruption. By 1848, when the position over the refusal of sites had eased, some 700 churches had been constructed (In addition, by May 1845, 280 schools had been established by the Free Church and by 1847, 46,000 children were being taught in them).[15] Indeed, during the 'glow of the Disruption' scores of young men, a number of whom were of considerable academic distinction, entered the newly formed Free Church College, which started with a much larger number of students than were in the theological faculties of all the four Scottish Universities put together.

Overview
It should be noted that it wasn't just the allegiance of hundreds of Church of Scotland ministers and members that came into question in the late 1830s and early '40s. The formation of the Evangelical Union and the Churches of Christ in Scotland were two other events which caused considerable ecclesiastical stir within a twelve month period of

---

12. Quoted in Murray, *A Scottish Christian Heritage*, p. 78.

13. John Hall (Ed.), 'Forty Years' Familiar Letters of James W. Alexander', (Edinburgh 1974), p. 157, quoted in Murray, *A Scottish Christian Heritage*, p. 78.

14. *The Scottish Guardian*, 21/03/1860. Indeed, the report went as far as suggesting that the general revival of religion in Scotland in 1859–61 'had its initial movement in the Disruption'.

15. Angus Macdonald, *An Enduring Testimony*, p. 13.

the Disruption. Nevertheless, it is to be observed that nearly all the definite evidences of spiritual awakening occurring in Scotland in the three years subsequent to May 1843 took place among fledgling Free Church congregations. This is not to suggest that full-blown revival was experienced in each of the localities mentioned (clear evidences of localised revival were confined mainly to the Western Highlands and Islands), but rather that indications of revived spiritual life were to be found in various places all over the country – in cities, towns, villages, and country and island parishes – and these, taken together, give testimony to a definite, widespread movement of spiritual awakening across Scotland. And so it is that we turn to a region-by-region study of the spiritual movement occurring within the Free Church of Scotland following its secession from the Established Church.

Glasgow and The West

Glasgow
Glasgow was much stirred by the Disruption. The Rev. Dr John Lorimer of St David's Free Church said that shortly after May 1843, he became conscious of

> more lively attention on the part of the people to the Word preached. More than one has assured me that my entire services come home with much more power to the heart and conscience than they once did. From time to time I hear of cases of spiritual good. Among the believing members of my flock there is more activity and prayer, and greater zeal for the good of others. This is particularly apparent among the youth of both sexes …'.[16]

Bothwell and Luss
Dr Lorimer also testified that 'many of the young people who applied for admission to the Lord's table at Bothwell (Lanarkshire), in the summer of 1844, when I resided there for a short time, and took ecclesiastical charge … attributed their first serious thoughts of religion to that great event (the Disruption) and its immediate consequent widespread and warm gospel preaching'.[17] Meanwhile, of Luss, Dumbartonshire,

16. Brown, *Annals of the Disruption*, p. 199
17. ibid., p. 201.

Lady Colquhoun wrote: 'A great change since the (Disruption) event is manifest in the spiritual concern of many, and the conversion of some. The appearance of the congregation is also most encouraging from the apparent impression under the Word preached, frequently from a solemn silence'.[18]

Rothesay

Along with his congregation, Robert Craig, Free Church minister in Rothesay, Isle of Bute, was granted use of the town's Gaelic Church until a new building was opened two years later. The Church was packed for the first Sabbath service of the Free Church congregation in May 1843. Craig preached with 'remarkable unction and power' on this never to be forgotten day, in which was felt 'not a little of the Spirit's presence and the Spirit's power'.[19] The following month, on the occasion of their first Lord's Supper, a courtyard granted to his congregation was covered over with a makeshift roof and fitted with a thousand seats. Of the Thursday fast day it could be said, 'The Lord was felt to be in the midst of them of a truth; and the grace of God was visibly displayed'. Over the course of subsequent months, also, blessing was not withheld from this fellowship. Prayer meetings thrived, as did the zeal and liberality of the people.[20]

Ayrshire

Wallacetown and Monkton

From its beginnings, the Free Church congregation of Wallacetown, near Ayr, were wont to meet in the open-air or in a spacious woodshed offered them. Here the Rev. William Grant conducted his first Communion service before a large and expectant crowd. 'It recalled the days of the Covenanters', wrote William Baird, 'and it was long afterwards spoken of as a time of blessing'. During this fledgling period, twenty-nine-year-old Grant undertook to supply the religious ordinances in thirty-three charges in the county. He preached on average twenty-seven times a month. It was reported as 'a time of earnest sowing and rich harvest'.[21]

---

18. ibid.

19. Robert C. Craig, *Memorials of the Life and Labours of the Rev. Robert Craig, A.M., Free Church, Rothesay*, Glasgow 1862, pp. 220, 227.

20. ibid., pp. 227-9.

21. Baird, *Sixty Years of Church Life in Ayr*, p. 98.

Favoured as they were during the summer months with calm bright weather for open-air meetings, the people flocked in crowds to the gospel preaching. These summer evening meetings were generally held in the cattle market-place, and occasionally on the Fort Green, on the very spot of ground where formerly stood John Welsh's church. Many in after years acknowledged with thankful hearts how they had been touched at these meetings with the power of the gospel and brought into saving faith. One such meeting in July, when the Rev. Chalmers of Dailly preached for two hours, was described by a local newspaper as 'certainly the largest witnessed in Ayr for many years', the number present being estimated at fully three thousand. For some years previous to this, the deadness in regard to religion in Ayr was said to have been such that those who loved the gospel had to seek it elsewhere than in the parish churches of Ayr.[22]

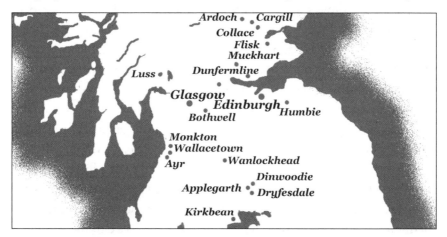

Years later, and shortly before his death, Grant could make the striking assertion that he had lived 'to see the revival of 1859 and the religious movement of 1874. I cannot speak of other localities', he admitted, 'but I may safely say that in Ayr the earnestness was deeper and the fruit more abundant in the summer and autumn of 1843 than during any part of my ministry. It was not merely nor mainly a time of ecclesiastical controversy about church government, but specially a time of deep, earnest and widespread spiritual awakening. As I gazed on the upturned countenances of the assembled people, they always seemed to me to say, "Sir, we would see Jesus"'.[23]

---

22. ibid., pp. 99-100.

23. ibid., p. 99; Brown, *Annals of the Disruption*, pp. 201-2.

Elsewhere in Ayrshire, the Rev. John Macfarlane of Monkton wrote that in his Free Church parish, 'many of the elders hold prayer-meetings, and preside at fellowship meetings, in their several districts', while 'there is a great increase in regularity of attendance on ordinances'.[24]

Dumfries and Galloway

Applegarth

Dozens of parishioners of Applegarth, near Lockerbie, were engaged in the immensely popular sport of curling on a frosty spring day in 1843 when the minister, the Rev. Dr William Dunbar, called them to a meeting in a huge barn at Dinwoodie Green in opposition to a non-intrusionist (anti-patronage) deputation who were holding meetings elsewhere in the area. As it turned out, both Dunbar and members of the visiting deputation gave impassioned addresses at the impromptu meeting, which was packed to the door – every inch of space, including rafters and window-sills, being occupied. As it progressed, one young man in particular, William Brockie, was overcome with a sense of sin as he had never before experienced, and later came to a place of spiritual peace. Brockie recalled, 'How many like myself were convinced of sin I never got to know; but of this I am certain, that there was a power greater and higher than the arguments of the deputation – a power moving on the hearts of that meeting'. Additionally, it is recorded that three ploughmen on the farm offered their adherence to the Free Church in consequence of what they heard and felt on that occasion – all three men showing evidence of having given their hearts to Christ.[25] Furthermore, multitudes are said to have flocked to a service in the church of the neighbouring parish of Dryfesdale on the following Sabbath. 'The truth was felt in much of its power over the district', observed Thomas Brown. The settlement of Hugh McBryde Brown at Lochmaben and Thomas Duncan at Lockerbie, contributed to deepen and extend the impression, serving to revive spiritual interest at both Sabbath and weekday meetings.[26]

Wanlockhead and Kirkbean

The Rev. Thomas Hastings, minister of the Free Church in Wanlockhead, the highest village in Scotland, wrote of his congregation's under-canvas Sabbath meetings following the Disruption: 'We enter the tent

24. Brown, *Annals of the Disruption*, p. 750.
25. ibid., pp. 757-8.; cf. pp. 70-1.
26. ibid., p. 758.

with more earnestness and seriousness in meditating upon our own responsibility; and the people seem to listen with a greater degree of attention and self-application.'[27] Further south in the same region, from the personal observation of the Rev. Gibson of Kirkbean, near Dumfries, the Disruption was 'in its own sphere instrumental in producing the conversion of many souls ... Many are under deep impression, and are asking the way to Zion', he noted.[28]

Lothian and Fife

Humbie

During the summer of 1843, while a church building was being constructed in the parish of Humbie, East Lothian, the sizeable Free Church congregation, along with its pastor, the Rev. James Dodds,

> met for worship on the Sabbaths in Humbie Dean – a sequestered retreat, one of the most beautiful and romantic spots in the country side. There the congregation gathered on the green sward, beneath the wide-spreading branches of the large, tall trees, with the pure stream murmuring below; and as the voices of the people united with the voices of nature, and rose up to heaven in the service of praise, the effect was thrilling in the extreme. Many a worshipper was reminded of the conventicles of covenanting times, when our forefathers met in similar circumstances to worship, according to their consciences, the God of their fathers. Impressions were produced at these services which will never be effaced. Many can look back to the spiritual good they received from the earnest and eloquent discourses that were there delivered.[29]

Dunfermline

The Rev. Henderson of Dunfermline wrote in 1860 that his first impressions of religion had been received at a revival meeting in 1843.[30] There was a time for the ordinary preaching of the word, he believed; a time for instruction, for meditation, and Christian action; but there were also seasons for

---

27. ibid., p. 749.

28. ibid., pp. 751-2.

29. James Dodds, *Personal Reminiscences and Biographical Sketches*, Edinburgh 1888, pp. 10-11.

30. Unfortunately he does not specify the location of this influential meeting.

arousing, elevating, and refreshing feeling. And his intellect convinced him that a genuine revival was such a time. Induced by the excitement caused by the meetings, Henderson attended one, and it was there that he was first awakened to a true sense of his condition as a lost sinner. To show that this was not a transient emotion, he could personally tell of thirty-seven other young men who, like him, had also been impressed, and who had begun to meet together for prayer and religious exercise. Henderson said he had since lost all contact with five of these, but of the remaining thirty-two he could report favourably. Not one of them had fallen away from their first hope. Some by 1860 had passed away, but all the others were, like himself, doing their best to live up to their profession.[31]

Flisk

Still in Fife, the Rev. James W. Taylor spoke of his labours among 'the farmers and ploughmen and villagers' of Flisk, near Newburgh. 'Amongst these God's saving grace was effectually put forth in the Disruption year, and in some of the years which immediately followed … The great scriptural principle was literally fulfilled – the kingdom of God cometh not with observation. There was a measure of hearty interest among the people, and hopefulness in connection with ordinances, which was encouraging. But it was years afterwards', continued Taylor, 'before I knew of cases of conversion which had really taken place at that time'. One case was that of 'a poor ploughman of simple mind and manner … He had been with us at the Disruption, and had worshipped with us in the barn. He was affected at parting and he said with much feeling, "Sir, the Word gripped me in the barn". One and another of the most decided of the people have spoken to that as the time when they were affected by spiritual things as they had never been before'.[32]

Stirlingshire and Clackmannanshire

Larbert

John Bonar's Free Church congregation in Larbert, Stirlingshire, was one of the many that met in a tent while a new church building was being constructed for them. Commented the Rev. B. F. Greig of Kinfauns,

---

31. 'The Dunfermline Press', 10/09/1860, quoted in Rev. P. C. Headley, *The Reaper and the Harvest: Or Scenes and Incidents in Connection with the Work of the Holy Spirit in the Life and Labours of Rev. Edward Hammond*, New York 1884, p. 87.

32. Brown, *Annals of the Disruption*, pp. 202-3.

Services were conducted with a fervour and earnestness that made that time the happiest to himself … of all John Bonar's ministry, as certainly it was, for quickening, to the people the most markedly blessed … the minister was cheered by seeing from his new pulpit all the godly whom he had been wont to address (in previous years), and by-and-by, of many more besides, in whom even he must have thankfully wondered at seeing spiritual life getting developed'.[33]

Muckhart

The Rev. James Thomson of Muckhart, Clackmannanshire, told of how, in consequence of the Disruption, 'a very great and decided change had taken place in the whole aspect of the congregation … There is much more of cordial and kindly interest in each other. I have got much better acquainted with them than I did for the ten preceding years … the people in general seem to listen to the Word with much more earnestness. Considerable emotion is from time to time manifested. They seem much more alive to the realities and importance of religion … Some, apparently, have been awakened for the first time, and more quickening and life imparted to those previously renewed'.[34]

Perthshire

Collace and Cargill

Especially blessed with showers of revival in the years immediately prior to the Disruption was the Perthshire district of Collace (see page 336). Virtually all of the congregation having followed their minister Andrew Bonar into the Free Church, 1843 proved another 'year of blessing' in the parish, at the end of which period Bonar noted in his diary: 'No year in my memory has been more remarkable for awakening of souls here … most of them were awakened in a way that quite proved the Lord's hand without my words'.[35] Bonar remarked on the 'most favourable circumstances in our congregation' since the Disruption, noting in particular 'the visiting of their districts by the elders in a spiritual manner, and the much purer exercise of discipline … three months after the Disruption one of the most intelligent, but most careless, lads in the place,

---

33. ibid., pp. 749-50.

34. ibid, pp. 199, 201.

35. Bonar, *Andrew A. Bonar: Diary and Life*, pp. 111, x.

but not very friendly to us, was the subject of so decided a change as to be remarked in the whole neighbourhood. He soon found joy and peace in believing, and has proved one of our steadiest and most efficient helps in the deaconship'.[36]

In neighbouring Cargill, for many months following the Disruption the Rev. Michael Stirling and his Free Church congregation met in a large barn. One June Sabbath he preached to around 800, many of whom 'cheerfully joined in the praise standing round the door'. After prayer Stirling delivered 'an impressive discourse with a fervency which caused deep emotion, and tears started to many an eye not accustomed to weep, on beholding their aged pastor (then in his early sixties) who had broken the Bread of Life amongst them for 34 years, forsaking all earthly benefits, that he might be at liberty to preach the Word of God in its purity'.[37]

Ardoch

After eventually being turned out of their church, the Rev. Samuel Grant of Ardoch in Perthshire met with his Free Church congregation for a number of wintry Sabbaths in an open field before shelter was obtained in the form of a wooden shed. Yet the people could still rejoice, their pastor stating, 'There has been a greater spiritual concern manifested, and much greater solemnity in hearing the Gospel than before the Disruption, especially on sacramental occasions, when the sufferings of our Lord brought nigh made His people forget their own. Indeed, I may say that never before did minister or people enjoy such seasons so much before ... there has also been exhibited much greater union of heart among the members of the congregation'.[38]

Angus and The North-East

Dunnichen and Arbirlot

The Rev. Donald Ferguson of Dunnichen, located between Forfar and Arbroath, laboured not only in his own parish but also among the other congregations in the Presbytery of Forfar. He testified, 'We had a busy time during that summer and autumn (1843), but I believe that the

---

36. Brown, *Annals of the Disruption*, p. 201.

37. Ian MacCraw in Various Contributors, *A Collace Miscellany*, Collace 1993, pp. 31-2.

38. Brown, *Annals of the Disruption*, pp. 749, 200.

Spirit of the Lord was honouring the means of grace as I have seldom, if ever, seen them honoured before or since'.[39]

We are told that after the Disruption, the Rev. John Kirk of Arbirlot, to the west of Arbroath, 'preached in the barn, which became his church; but the crowd was often so great that they had to remove to the field, which was no great hardship, the Sabbaths being fine that summer and the warm devotion of the hearers, and the deep impression made, caused thankfulness and joy. Often did the people speak of the good they got at that time; several have dated their new birth from that period'.[40]

Following just a few years on the heels of revival in the district in 1839 (see page 335), a movement in the village of Newtyle, further west in Angus, in 1844 showed promising signs of coming to blessed fruition, the Rev. John Milne of Perth believed, provided, he remarked, that men did not interfere with what was being wrought by God.[41] Interestingly, Milne, Robert Murray McCheyne and Andrew Bonar had each preached on separate occasions in this village in the months preceding the awakening.[42]

Dundee

Robert Murray McCheyne, never a well man, succumbed to an outbreak of typhus fever less than two months prior to the Disruption – in March 1843, aged just twenty-nine. Islay Burns, brother of William Chalmers Burns, succeeded him as minister at St Peter's, Dundee.[43] Although the powerful revival which began in 1839 had long since drawn to a close, drops of spiritual rain still occasionally fell on the much-blessed congregation. During a communion season late in 1843 or 1844, an hour-long address was given to around five hundred children, many of whom appeared notably arrested. Burns wrote that when he afterwards went into the vestry,

---

39. ibid., p. 752.

40. ibid., p. 200.

41. Bonar, *Life of the Rev. John Milne of Perth*, p. 85.

42. ibid.; Andrew Bonar, *Memoir and Remains of the Rev. Robert Murray M'Cheyne*, p. 282; Andrew Bonar, *Diary of Andrew Bonar*, p. 106.

43. Initially, Islay Burns tried to be a 'second McCheyne' to the St Peter's congregation, knowing how popular and successful his predecessor was. Once aware of the folly of such attitude, he sought simply to be himself. However, he never managed to connect with his people in the way that McCheyne had clearly done, and attendance at his services soon began to fall away.

whom did I find but Mr Milne from Perth, dropped as if from the clouds. What had brought him, or where he had been, I know not, for he set off again immediately after his own part of the meeting, but he was evidently sent of God, for a more divine, melting and powerful message I never heard, and just such as I had been longing and praying for during the whole communion. He spoke for an hour and a quarter, and from the strain of riveted and intense earnestness which rose as he went on, and towards the end became almost painful, he might have gone on much longer without any one feeling that he had unusually detained us.[44]

Strathbogie

In many districts of Aberdeenshire the spiritual awakening which had begun in the years leading up to the Disruption (see page 399) continued in the months after that event and the number of Free Church adherents grew markedly. This was particularly true of Kennothmont and Ellon. Meanwhile, in Keith, at the first communion following the Disruption, no fewer than sixty young people applied for admission to the Lord's Table, and, noted the Rev. Thomas Bain of Coupar-Angus, 'a great number of them gave most satisfactory evidence of having given their hearts to the Lord'. The Rev. Robert Macdonald of Blairgowrie (later of North Leith) was providentially used during this season, and by seven o'clock on Tuesday morning the Keith church was crowded to receive a parting word from their erstwhile minister before he left by coach at nine. Thus began a significant work of grace, the long lasting fruits of which were most apparent years later in the life and conversation of many who became office-bearers and members of the church.[45] Free Church records also refer to a 'time of special blessing' at Kirktown of Culsalmond in Strathbogie at the 'time of the Disruption'.[46] Meanwhile, in Aberdeen's East Church congregation it was said that 'there has been a large increase in the number of prayer-meetings since the Disruption'.[47]

---

44. W. G. Blaikie, 'Memoir of Islay Burns', in Islay Burns, *Select Remains of Islay Burns*, London 1874, p. xxi.

45. Brown, *Annals of the Disruption*, pp. 753-4.

46. *FCRSRM* 1890, p. 2.

47. Baikie, *Revivals in the Far North*, pp. 37-9.

The Western Isles

Lewis and Harris

Uig

In Lewis, in the lead-up to the Disruption, catechist Angus MacIver and Uig parish teacher Alexander MacColl travelled throughout the island, giving addresses on what they saw as the principles contended for in the Ten Years' Conflict. Both men were stationed in Uig, and it was this parish that 'felt the quickening breath of the Holy Spirit' in 1842–3.[48] All but two people in Uig left the Established Church at the Disruption. With the departure of the Rev. Alexander Macleod from Uig to Lochalsh very shortly after this decisive event, McIver and MacColl continued to labour in the Uig district.

This appears to have been the 'wide and populous parish' of which its 'excellent and honoured minister' said at that time that 'scarcely a family can be found, in which the worship of God is not regularly maintained', which blessing he largely ascribed to the labours and example of the Gaelic School Society.[49] It was recorded that, 'On the hillside or in the (Uig Free) church after it was built (as in many other places, by the people themselves) large congregations listened with rapt and unflagging attention to the thrilling and stirring discourses of these two men' (McIver and MacColl) who were thoroughly 'alive and earnest' in their faith. McIver's son, a child at the time, well remembered 'these animated scenes and the enthusiasm of the people' in those exciting days.[50] The Rev. G. L. Campbell of Glasgow wrote: 'Subsequent to the Disruption, the work of grace continued to bear fruit in Uig and Lewis generally. It was long noted by those interested in the extension of the Kingdom of Christ that no communion passed without traces of the divine presence in the rousing of careless sinners to soul concern.'[51]

---

48. Alexander MacRae, *Revivals in the Highlands and Islands*, p. 75. See also the *Report to the General Assembly* of 1901, which mentions 'the quickening breath of the Holy Ghost' felt in this parish in 1842 (*Free Church General Assembly Report* 1901, p. 11).

49. *GSS Report* 1843, p. 22.

50. *Stornoway Gazette*, March 1972.

51. Various Contributors, *Disruption Worthies of the Highlands*, p. 231.

Knock and Harris

Elsewhere in Lewis, Knock parish was said to have been 'aglow with Disruption enthusiasm'.[52] Donald Murray's Free Church ministry there from 1844 'began well, and steadily increased in spiritual power. It became extraordinarily influential'.[53] Likewise, 'in Harris, where also some drops of the spiritual shower had been experienced', the results were said to have been 'equally satisfactory in the confirmed and advancing piety of the converts'.[54] G. N. M. Collins records that 'the spiritual revival which had accompanied that historic event (the Disruption) had spread to many parts of the Western Isles' and even affected the tiny Harris island of Scalpay. He continues: '... once more, the re-vitalising power of the Spirit was in evidence. As at Pentecost, so now, the Lord was adding to the Church daily such as were being saved.'[55]

North Uist

Paible

Meanwhile, from the Paible area of North Uist a revival commenced in 1843, which quickly spread south.[56] Alexander McIntyre came here and preached repeatedly at Creag Hastain, where 'the men' had often conducted their meetings prior to the Disruption (having become part of a secession movement from the Established Church), and continued to do so following that event. One who heard McIntyre here was eighteen-year-old Donald MacDonald – a native of North Uist, subsequently joint founder of the Free Presbyterian Church – who sometimes became 'so much overwhelmed with a sense of his lost condition that he could

---

52. Macfarlane, *Apostles of the North*, p. 84.

53. ibid., p. 85.

54. *GSS Report* 1844, pp. 14-15; Brown, *The Social History of Religion in Scotland since 1730*, p. 125.

55. G. N. M. Collins, *Gleanings from the Diary and Ministry of James Morrison*, Edinburgh 1984, p. 1.

56. Duncan Campbell, who had connections to a revival movement in North Uist in the 1950s, wrote, 'It is a recognised fact that Uist had never known revival' previous to that time (*God's Answer*, Edinburgh 1960, p. 93). This assertion is repeated in a testimony by Mary Morrison, a convert of Campbell's (*Hearken O'Daughter*, Three Hills, Alberta 1966). Although such movements are not mentioned in standard works on Scottish revivals, such as MacRae's, *Revivals in the Highlands and Islands*, in fact the 1840s movement in North Uist was not the first season of spiritual awakening to occur on the island during the nineteenth century (see page 251).

not walk home from the place of worship. His friends had often to carry him. At other times he would, it is said, not only walk, but leap with joy after hearing Mr McIntyre'.[57] He was in this condition for two-and-a-half years, wading into even darker waters before finally passing into a 'happy transition' in 1849. Another who preached on the island during this period was John Macrae of Knockbain. When he spoke here in 1845 his services attracted between 500 and 600 worshippers on weekdays, with 'upwards of a thousand' on the Sabbath.[58]

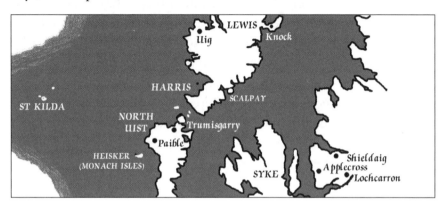

Trumisgarry

Those brought to the Lord flocked to attend the Gaelic Schools, earnestly desiring to be acquainted with the Word of God. As agent of the Schools, Norman MacLeod of Skye came to North Uist to preach, where, particularly in Trumisgarry, in the north of the island, many children (aged eight to fourteen) were awakened. The Report records that Macleod had scarcely set his hand to the work when several, especially among the young, became 'sensibly distressed at his meetings under conviction of sin and their lost condition'. It was, wrote Macleod, 'an affecting sight to see their parents, as I have more than once seen them, carrying them out of the meeting-house, apparently lifeless with exhaustion from overpowered feelings'. From Trumisgarry as a centre point, the revival spread south and north. Persons of all ages and sexes were affected; but the majority were in the period of early adulthood.[59] The

---

57. Robinson, *The Rev. Alexander McIntyre*, p. 12.

58. Rev. David MacInnes, *Kilmuir Church, North Uist 1894–1994*, Kilmuir 1994, p. 26

59. Rev. Norman Macleod of Trumisgarry, North Uist, quoted in *GSS Report* 1844, pp. 17-19; 1845, p. 14; cf. John Ferguson, *When God Came Down*, p. 32.

fifteen grandchildren of one poor man on the island were awakened through the work of the Gaelic School, and ten of them were thought to have undergone definite saving change, while all the other five came under deep spiritual concern.[60] The revival was marked by 'secret prayer and the attentive perusal of the Scriptures',[61] while the maintaining of the family altar was daily becoming more prevalent.[62]

Heisker

On Heisker, a tiny (long since uninhabited) island west of North Uist (also known as the Monach Islands), a revival was reported in 1844, among a spiritually neglected people who had only been visited once by the parish minister – and that was sixteen years previously! Now all the island's inhabitants attended a service in the schoolhouse on the Sabbath and initiated prayer and family worship times – all previously unheard of activities in the community. A collection was also made 'for the cause of the Redeemer' – the first ever on this island – and some gave all the little money they had. [63]

Tiree

In Tiree a revival had been in progress since 1839, particularly among the Baptist and Congregational fellowships (see page 412). Particularly among Presbyterians on the island, remarkable blessing attended the ministrations of the Rev. Macrae of Knockbain (1794–1876) and other Free Church deputies who preached over the whole of the island with much power and success shortly after the Disruption. Meanwhile, Independent congregations continued to expand during this period of blessing, which was unusually prolonged. Sixty-four names were added to the Congregational church alone. Scores of converts emigrated to Canada shortly afterwards.[64] W. D. McNaughton suggests that the movement

---

60. *GSS Report* 1846, p. 11.

61. Macleod, *The Progress of Evangelicalism*, p. 218.

62. ibid., p. 217.

63. *GSS Report* 1845, pp. 14-15; 1846, pp. 14-15; See also *GSS Report* 1844, p. 31; 1848, p. 14.

64. One of them, Neil McKinnon, who emigrated around the year 1846, ministered in Manilla, Ontario and surrounding districts, until c. 1875. He was unable to speak English but Rev. A. Farquharson could say of him in 1848, 'When he left, he carried out the fire and zeal lying within him, and the consequence is that a considerable

lasted from 1837 to 1846.[65] Donald Meek gives the time-span of revival within the Baptist Church as 1839–46, further reporting that Baptist membership reached one hundred in this latter year.[66]

Mull, Islay and Iona

The Rev. Peter Maclean was settled as Free Church miniser of Tobermory on the island of Mull in the autumn of 1843, and applied himself energetically to his new sphere (see page 426 for an account of the pre-Disruption blessing on Mull). Within a short time, there were about a thousand adherents to his church. Known pre-eminently as a thorough pastor who ever sought to edify, instruct and protect his flock, he could not help but extend his field of labour to all the surrounding regions that were but scantily supplied with gospel preaching. He made frequent evangelistic excursions to Ardnamurchan and Morvern, as well as to various places on the island of Mull. In this manner 'the Lord continued to countenance his labours; for years a manifest blessing accompanied him'.[67]

'Gracious tokens of the Lord's presence and of the mighty working of his Spirit' also seem to have been vouchsafed to Peter McBride of Rothesay after the Disruption, both in Mull and in other places he visited throughout the Highlands and Islands. A native of Mull wrote of McBride: 'The awful solemnity, the unction and tenderness of his labours during the communion services at Tobermory, a few days before his death (in September 1846), will never be effaced from the memory of many who were privileged to be there'.[68] The Rev. Duncan Campbell of Kiltearn was another preacher who faithfully visited the island at this time (as he did annually for nineteen years).[69] Still in Mull, a few years later (1847), a visiting evangelist reported that despite initial apathy among the people, 'instances could be specified where the whole congregation was bathed in tears, and the cry on the day of Pentecost seemed to be that of many'.[70]

---

number of individuals have been converted in that place' ('SCM' 1848, quoted in McNaughton, *Revival and Reality*, p. 201).

65. ibid., p. xxv, 95.

66. Meek, *Island Harvest*, pp. 10, 16.

67. Macleod, *The Progress of Evangelicalism*, p. 217.

68. Quoted in ibid., pp. 165-6.

69. MacGregor, *Campbell of Kiltearn*, p. 101.

70. *Report of the Gaelic Committee* 1848, p. 241.

Mull's Baptist churches also shared in the blessing of this period. The churches in Ardalanish in the south of the island and Tobermory in the north both grew substantially in the early 1840s, while Torosay, to the east, was also affected.[71] The Rev. Alexander Grant reported that in 1843 he had preached to the largest congregation he had ever seen on the island. 'The meeting house could not have contained more than one-third of the people, but the day was very favourable, and they sat in the field very comfortably, and listened with great attention'. The isles of Islay and Coll also experienced deep blessing at this time.[72] From the former place, the Rev. Donald McMaster of Kildalton remarked, 'It cannot be doubted but often in circumstances of great outward discomfort, much of the Lord's presence was felt, and a time of tribulation was turned into a time of rejoicing'.[73] The movement also spread to Iona, where there were several conversions.

Western Highlands

Argyll

During the Disruption period people travelled from great distances to hear the Word of God. The Gaelic Bible Society, formed around this time, provided a great service in the Highlands and Islands through its thorough system of colportage, whereby it sought to visit every single home throughout the vast region. As a sign of the hunger for the word of God in the Scottish Highlands at the time, one colporteur managed to sell in four years 7,944 copies of the Scriptures at a fixed cost of just over a shilling (a huge amount to the average Gael, being before the period of low-cost publishing), and gave away only around twenty. Knowing he was in their area, some people trudged many miles over hilly terrain to secure their copy.[74]

Kilmallie

Because a site had been refused in Lochaber, the people of Kilmallie erected a large canvas tent just above high-water mark on an exposed shore. Macdonald of Ferintosh stopped to preach here on his way south

---

71. Yuille, *History of the Baptists in Scotland*, p. 113.

72. Brown, *Annals of the Disruption*, p. 664.

73. Various Contributors, *Disruption Worthies of the Highlands*, p. 122.

74. George Smith, *A Modern Apostle: Alexander N. Somerville, D.D. 1813–1889*, p. 41.

in the spring of 1844. An unusually severe storm had arisen, but it failed to stop several hundred people from packing into the tent to hear the 'Apostle of the North'. Macdonald had to shout to make himself heard above the flapping of the canvas and creaking of ropes amidst the raging storm. He spoke to a deeply interested audience from Isaiah 32:1-2, on 'the Man who is a hiding-place from the wind and a covert from the tempest'. It proved a word in season to many, who that February evening 'sought refuge under the shelter of the Rock of Ages from a storm more dreadful than that which blew on them from the brow off Ben Nevis'. When the brief service came to an end, many were heard saying, 'we hoped he was but beginning when he brought the sermon to a conclusion'.[75]

Applecross and Shieldaig

The movement was also evident in the Free Church parishes of Applecross and Shieldaig, which were served with great diligence and untiring zeal by the Rev. Alexander MacColl.[76] The local catechist reported that there had been 'a revival of vital godliness in this district, especially among the young, and produced by the simple instrumentality of reading the Word of God. The whole aspect of the congregation bore evident marks of the power of the Spirit of God'.[77] In addition, a Gaelic School Society inspector said he was 'exceedingly refreshed with the conversations he had with the children. They evinced a lively concern about their spiritual interests'.[78] The Rev. Dr James Begg visited Applecross in 1845 and recalls,

> We were little prepared for the scene we were now to witness. The night was very chilly, and when we asked where the people were to meet, we were led along to a place on the very shore, amidst the stones and tangle of the sea-beach, and which could only be approached by clambering over a precipice. Here the tent (pulpit) was erected, and old and young assembled and sat without a murmur, singing the praises of God in these singularly wild and plaintive notes ... hearing the Gospel preached in the face of a biting

---

75. Various Contributors, *Disruption Worthies of the Highlands*, p. 123.

76. Carruthers, *Biographies of Highland Clergymen*, p. 115.

77. Brown, *Annals of the Disruption*, p. 661.

78. *GSS Report* 1844, p. 15.

wind, and with the waves of the Atlantic dashing at their feet. I question if the world, at this moment, can match such scenes as these … A more noble people I have never seen, and the eagerness with which they listened to the preaching of the Gospel was indeed remarkable. We were particularly struck with one woman, who told us that, from her youth, she had occasionally walked fifty miles to hear the Gospel. 'Death', she said, emphatically, 'has reigned in this place for many years'. She has still to walk fifteen miles to hear the Gospel; but (now) walks that distance most cheerfully'.[79]

The following day Begg, with many from Applecross, hiked the ten miles over a rough mountain (there being no pathway) to Shieldaig, where, amid the naked rocks on the sea-shore, similar scenes were witnessed.

Lochcarron

The Rev. Alexander MacColl also served the parish of Lochcarron, where an awakening had been making progress from the early months of 1843, following a visit to localities within Lochcarron Presbytery from the Reverends John Macrae of Knockbain ('Big Macrae') and James McDonald of Urray. Macrae later wrote:

The word spoken had such a remarkable effect on the minds of the people that none but an infidel would fail to see the finger of God in the work. Old and young were brought under the power of the truth. Unholy practices were at once given up. Errors, particularly those which keep careless sinners bound fast under a covenant of works, were clearly seen and scattered to the winds. It was felt almost universally that the way of justification freely by grace is the only way through which a guilty creature can escape from the wrath of the righteous Judge.[80]

Macrae made a number of further visits to Lochcarron over the following fourteen months, and found the work of the Spirit to be progressing among its inhabitants. Believers, he said, were growing in faith while awakened sinners were anxiously seeking an interest in Christ. 'Often

---

79. Brown, *Annals of the Disruption*, pp. 660-1.

80. ibid., p. 663; MacRae, *Revivals in Highlands and Islands*, p. 68.

have I commenced to address these people under a deep sense of exhaustion, and concluded much refreshed', he wrote.[81]

In April 1844 the Gaelic School Society reported from the area that 'scenes of deep emotion ensued whenever anyone addressed the children … Some boys built a small hut in a retired spot that they might hold regular meetings for prayer in it. They collected their scanty pence and expended them in the purchase of candles, to be used when the shades of evening darkened on their little meeting'.[82]

Blessing in the General Assembly

The 1844 General Assembly of the Free Church of Scotland was crowded with church leaders who had been 'solemnised and quickened' by the experience of the first year after the Disruption. In an impassioned opening speech, Dr Candlish stated that all over the country ministers had found the people 'waiting on their ministrations with a seriousness, attention and devotion as they never before observed, the young more open to instruction, the aged more anxious for consolation, the careless more ready to be awakened, the worldly more ready to be rebuked, the people of God expecting large advances in the Divine life'. Congregations everywhere, Candlish emphasised, had been labouring under the impression that something ought to come out of this great work of God. Ministers ought to ask themselves, 'How much of this has been counteracted by my unfaithfulness, by my want of an inadequate sense of the importance of this most important event'.[83]

During its deliberations, the best part of two days was set aside as a period of humiliation and prayer in which delegates were to consider the state of personal religion in the Church. In his sermon on Tuesday, 21st May, Dr Charles Brown chose as his text Habakkuk 2:1 and proceeded to show what reasons his listeners had to humble themselves in deep repentance before God. Records Dr William M. Hetherington: '… the whole vast multitude were bowed and shaken like a forest of trees beneath a mighty wind – melted and fused together like masses of golden ore in a seven-times heated furnace'.[84] A visiting minister from

---

81. MacRae, *Revivals in Highlands and Islands*, pp. 68-9.

82. *GSS Report* 1844, p. 15.

83. Brown, *Annals of the Disruption*, p. 627.

84. ibid., pp. 633-4.

Ireland reportedly stated that as a body, they confessed, 'in deep prostration, the plagues of their own hearts and the sins of their own lives, and in one universal cry that prayer arose – "God be merciful to us sinners". We never witnessed a scene more solemnly sublime', he claimed.[85]

This spirit of humility and profound solemnity continued to consume the meeting after the sermon had concluded, when a heavy silence pervaded the gathering. Hearts were too full for words, and the meeting had to be suspended until the evening. Ultimately, and unanimously, the General Assembly of 1844 issued a statement in which in its concluding lines it proposed: 'With profound humiliation, and in reliance on the great strength of Almighty God, solemnly to devote, dedicate, and consecrate anew themselves and their fellow labourers to the service of God, and His holy purpose of glorifying His great name, in saving souls through the preaching of the truth, and the operation of the Holy Ghost.' Horatius Bonar wrote afterwards: 'Revival had brought the Church back to her chief work. All other discussions and church arrangements had to take a lower place, and men gave themselves first to the real business of the Church of Christ.'[86]

The Assembly authorised deputations of two and two to preach in all the congregations of every Presbytery in the land, instructing them to say nothing about funds, nor about any controversy with the Established Church, 'but to preach the gospel pure and simple, and nothing else'.[87] As an example, the Rev. John Thomson of Paisley and Dr James Henderson of Glasgow were appointed to Ayrshire and Dumfries-shire, where they preached every weekday evening and twice or thrice on the Sabbath for a fortnight, visiting around twenty-five parishes in all. At Thornhill, they laid the foundation stone of the new Free Church and spoke to an audience of between 2,000 and 3,000. At Keir the following day Thomson preached to nearly as many in a picturesque glen, where his pulpit was a country cart.[88] In this way most of Scotland was pervaded by earnest evangelistic preaching from deputies of this young, burgeoning denomination.

---

85. ibid., pp. 634-5.

86. Bonar, *Life of the Rev. John Milne of Perth*, p. 108.

87. Blaikie, *David Brown*, p. 74.

88. Various Contributors, *Disruption Worthies of the Highlands*, p. 163.

Later Movement in Argyll: Knapdale

In connection with the Disruption movement there was awakened in many quarters a great desire to hear the preaching of the gospel, which was new to multitudes in the West Highlands. One of the gifted Gaelic-speaking ministers who was chosen and commissioned by the Free Church to itinerate throughout this vast area was the Rev. Peter McBride of Rothesay, nephew of the Rev. Neil McBride of Arran. Though he visited many places during his travels, his native parish of North Knapdale, which sits between Kintyre and the rest of Argyll, had a special place in McBride's heart. He had visited it frequently before the Disruption, but expressed grief at the want of apparent fruit. Returning from a preaching tour in the Hebrides in the winter of 1844–5, McBride spent a Sabbath in Knapdale. Though under the painful impression that no good was being done, he was pressed to preach again on the Monday. To his astonishment, many were awakened to deep concern and from that day the work rapidly increased. Well before service time, the church would be packed full, so that people were reluctantly pressed to take turns at staying home!

For a number of months, McBride returned to Knapdale almost every week, and on every visit one or more souls were awakened to the gospel. The total number awakened by May 1845 was between 200 and 300 – many having been brought to peace in Christ – and the work was still going on. One observer noted that many converts seemed to be 'emerging beautifully. There was a humbleness, a self-abasement, a sense of personal worthlessness, a love of the Saviour, and a devotedness to the glory of God, which it was delightful to witness'.[89]

While there were some outcries and bodily agitation, these were not leading features of the movement, though weeping did occur to an extent McBride had never before witnessed. He insisted he had used no means whatsoever, other than open preaching, in his work among the people.[90] He seldom spoke with them in private, and indeed took no 'notice of the particular circumstances of the work at all'. But in his preaching he did emphasise the need to be born again and not merely awakened. In 1846, a few months before his death, McBride rejoiced that 'the work does not appear to be done. The people are as eager to

---

89. Various Contributors, *Disruption Worthies of the Highlands*, p. 163.

90. Brown, *Annals of the Disruption*, pp. 663-4.

hear as ever. They as readily as at the first stop their work on the week days to hear sermon, and even little children cannot be kept at home'. Several decades later, a succeeding minister of Knapdale could still point to living 'memorials' of McBride's preaching who had 'found refuge in Christ', and were still 'holding fast the beginning of their confidence firm unto the end'.[91]

Post-Disruption Awakenings 1845–50

Introduction

Spiritual quickening in the immediate post-Disruption years began to broaden out from containment within Free Church parameters to embrace other denominations engaged in earnest evangelistic work at this time, such as the fledgling Evangelical Union Church, the Baptists, the Congregational Church and others. Meanwhile, several Free Church congregations continued to experience distinct tokens of spiritual blessing. Other than in the quickly expanding Evangelical Union Church, there appears to have been no noticeable general movement in operation during these years, either linking revivals within a particular denominational stream or connecting awakening in any one locality with that in any other. All that can possibly be discerned is the concentration of blessing in the first few years of this period in the southern half of the country, while those of the latter years of the decade were more predominant in the north. Interestingly, none of the following narratives gives any suggestion that spiritual awakening was directly precipitated by the potato blight – analogous to the great Irish potato famine of the same period – which caused widespread devastation in Scotland from the mid 1840s, particularly in the Highlands.[92]

Glasgow

Quite a stir was created by the trial of James Morison before the Kilmarnock Presbytery of the United Secession Church in March 1841, which, according to one Evangelical Union advocate, had the favour-

---

91. Various Contributors, *Disruption Worthies of the Highlands*, pp. 164-5.

92. Though not as ultimately catastrophic as the Irish famine, and certainly less well recorded, the potato blight resulted in widespread malnutrition, disease and crippling financial hardships to hundreds of Scottish communities. The trauma and disruption caused is evidenced in the fact that around 1.7 million people were forced to leave Scotland during the six-year period 1846–52.

able consequence of leading to 'a widespread awakening in the public mind in regard to religious matters … It was no uncommon thing for groups of people to be found asking, "What about Christ, are we to believe that we might be saved?"'[93] It was decided to hold a series of protracted meetings in the Trades Hall, in Glasgow's Glassford Street in the summer of 1844. From the start the meetings were a decided success. Large numbers attended on week nights, while on the Sabbath, especially at the evening service, the hall could not contain the crowds that assembled. All the leading figures of the 'Morisonian movement' came to speak, including John Kirk of Hamilton, Fergus Ferguson (Snr) of Bellshill, and the Rev. McRobert of Cambuslang, as well as Morison himself. The ministers themselves were surprised at the impression made and the numbers who remained for personal conversation. Wrote Adamson: 'The excitement, though not outwardly demonstrative, was deep, and the good done of the most encouraging nature. Christians were refreshed and advanced in the divine life, and those who had cared nothing for personal religion were led in scores to the foot of the Cross.'[94]

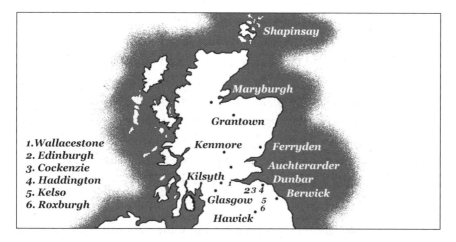

1. Wallacestone
2. Edinburgh
3. Cockenzie
4. Haddington
5. Kelso
6. Roxburgh

Shapinsay

Maryburgh

Grantown

Kenmore   Ferryden

Auchterarder
Kilsyth   Dunbar
23 4   Berwick
Glasgow 5
6
Hawick

Indeed, seventy or eighty people had put down their names in token of their willingness to be formed into a church in Glasgow 'on the basis of the unlimited love of Father, Son and Holy Ghost to the whole world'.[95] The church was formed in July 1844, and a few months later Fergus Ferguson

93. Adamson, *The Life of the Rev. Fergus Ferguson*, p. 54.

94. ibid. cf. Fergus Ferguson, *A History of the Evangelical Union*, pp. 349-51.

95. Adamson, *The Life of the Rev. Fergus Ferguson*, p. 59.

(Jnr), newly twenty, accepted the call to be its first pastor.[96] The people continued to meet in the Trades Hall until it became totally outgrown. A suitable church building was secured in Blackfriars Street (eventually purchased in 1859). This quickly became 'a centre of spiritual power in the city', becoming known as a place where a zealous young preacher just out of his teens was preaching to hundreds three times every Sunday, and the fact that not a few were being converted excited attention from many in the neighbourhood, who soon found themselves among the anxious. For several years, 'There was scarcely a Sabbath, or a sermon delivered, when there was not one or more who confessed they were brought to the knowledge of the truth, had found the Bible a new book, rejoiced in prayer, and had views of the relation God stood in to man which they had never thought of before … The fellowship roll increased in numbers, money came in freely, and in the early days it might be said regarding the members of Mr Ferguson's church, "Behold how the Christians love one another"'.[97]

Dunbar

Wallacestone, in which Falkirk district Methodist preacher Alexander Patrick had witnessed a powerful revival from 1842 (see page 369), was constituted a separate Circuit by Wesleyan authorities later in the decade. Patrick therefore felt it somewhat less necessary to confine himself to that locality and consequently made excursions to distant places, as he had formerly been accustomed to do. Consequently, on invitation, he visited Dunbar, Cockenzie and Edinburgh; and in each of these places was made the instrument of leading souls to Christ. The Rev. John Drake wrote: 'Particularly in Dunbar during his later visits the Spirit of God was poured out, and a pleasing revival took place, so that the number in the Society was nearly doubled.'[98]

Kilsyth

Around the same time (1845), within the same denomination, 'a good work' commenced among the young people of Kilsyth, being occasioned

---

96. Despite his tender years, Ferguson had in fact been drawn into the gospel ministry at least five years prior to this, by the wave of enthusiasm excited by the Kilsyth revival, during which time he could be found conducting meetings each Sunday evening for the Duke of Hamilton's miners in the village of Quarter, by the River Avon.

97. Adamson, *The Life of the Rev. Fergus Ferguson*, pp. 63-4. Membership continued to grow through the 1850s and '60s, and stood at 788 in 1872.

98. Rev. John Drake, *The Wallacestone Reformer*, p. 150.

by a tragic event which befell three young men who occasionally attended church services, and had been under a degree of spiritual conviction, 'but who trifled with the grace of God and their own souls'. They went swimming in the dam one hot Sabbath day; one was drowned, while one of his friends almost faced the same fate through trying to rescue him. The grief caused by this event among many who knew the lads was overruled to the spiritual good of a number of them, and the two survivors themselves turned to the Lord in penitence and prayer and came into a living faith. Methodist preacher Alexander Patrick was soon in the midst of the inquiring youths, aiding them by his advice and prayers, and it was reported that a number 'are now steadily walking in the ways of the Lord, and give promise of becoming ornaments of the Church'.[99]

Ferryden

In 1846, in the last year of his life and lengthy ministry in Ferryden, the Rev. Dr James Brewster of the Free Church[100] witnessed a movement among the fisherfolk of the village. Andrew Bonar, who came from Collace to assist, wrote: 'I spent three hours speaking with anxious souls in private, and preached to them twice. The scene one day reminded me of Dundee times. They were so easily moved to tears and sobs, though their faces were those of hard rough fisher-women. There are at least about thirty very deeply convinced of sin, and many more under the Spirit's strivings.'[101] Two months later, in November 1846, Bonar returned to assist the Ferryden minister in conducting a communion service, and noted that 'there is much of God's work to be seen'. Unfortunately, Brewster, in poor health, was only able to serve one table.[102] Bonar wrote in his diary: 'Ferryden is still very interesting. Some souls have found rest,

---

99. ibid., pp. 124-5.

100. Brother of Sir David Brewster, one of the foremost physicists of his age.

101. Brown, *Annals of the Disruption*, p. 773; See also Bonar, *Andrew A. Bonar: Diary and Life*, p. 123. This movement is also referred to in Mrs Gordon, *Hay MacDowall Grant of Arndilly: His Life, Labours and Teachings*, London 1876, pp. 134-5 and Couper, *Scottish Revivals*, pp. 14-15.

102. Bonar noted in his diary how often he had been called to help 'sick brethren' in the ministry, 'guided by God's ministry'. He mentions help offered to Robert Murray McCheyne, John Milne, Alexander Moody Stuart, James Hamilton and now Rev. Brewster in their times of sickness (Bonar, *Andrew A. Bonar: Diary and Life*, pp. 123-4).

though most are still tossed with tempests.'[103] One in this category who had been deeply swayed but not savingly changed by the events of 1846, a young girl, was later soundly converted, and was regarded by many as 'a spiritual mother' in the later, more powerful Ferryden revival of 1859. The texts and hymns she had learned in the earlier episode returned to her mind thirteen years on.[104] This appears to have been Brewster's infant-school teacher, Miss Petrie, who was 'remarkably useful' in the 1846 revival,[105] later serving as a counsellor to anxious souls in the powerful 1859–60 movement in the village, having also commenced a women's prayer meeting in the summer of 1859 to pray specifically for revival.[106]

Auchterarder

At the Disruption George Smeaton was instrumental in forming a Free Church congregation in Falkland, Fife, but later on in the year he accepted a call to Auchterarder, in south-west Perthshire, notorious in Free Church history as the place where the spark was lit that initiated the Ten Years' Conflict which led ultimately to major schism within the Church of Scotland. In Auchterarder, for ten years, Smeaton laboured, first in a large tent erected for field preaching, then in an imposing new tower church completed in 1845. During his period of labour in the parish a profound spiritual awakening occurred. His ministry in the district, noted one who had attended upon it in earlier days, 'was one of great spiritual fruitfulness. Many young men and women whom I know owned their souls' life to his instrumentality, and spoke of him as their father in Christ'.[107] Eminently a man of prayer, Smeaton was also a faithful gospel preacher. By 1848 membership of the church had risen to 770, while a mission work begun in nearby Aberuthven was success-ful enough for a church to be formed there in 1851.[108]

---

103. ibid., p. 124.

104. William Nixon, *An Account of the Work of God at Ferryden*, London 1860, p. 34.

105. Brown, *Annals of the Disruption*, p. 751.

106. D. W. Bebbington, 'Revival and the Clash of Cultures: Ferryden, Forfarshire, in 1859', in Dyfed Wyn Roberts (Ed.), *Revival, Renewal, and the Holy Spirit*, Milton Keynes 2009, p. 22.

107. Keddie, *George Smeaton*, pp. 51-2.

108. Smeaton was also a great scholar and theologian, and became professor of New Testament exegesis at Edinburgh's New College in 1857. He went on to author several books, including *The Doctrine of the Atonement as Taught by Christ Himself* and *The*

Kenmore

At Kenmore, on the shores of Loch Tay, a vacancy of nearly three years existed in the fledgling Free Church following the Disruption of 1843, but under the influence of the Marquis of Breadalbane, able ministers were brought to supply the pulpit, and the Rev. Allan Sinclair (who later translated McCheyne's *Memoir and Remains* into Gaelic), on beginning his labours in this Perthshire region in the spring of 1846, found 'abundant evidence' that the preaching had been blest to not a few of the people. The first communion in the summer of 1846 was a precious and refreshing season – a time of revival. Commented Sinclair: 'So was the next communion in the winter following. In particular, on the Sabbath, and during a powerful and affecting address in Gaelic by the late Mr McRae of Knockbain, there was an impression so deep and general that it has left its memories to this day (1877) in the hearts of the people.'[109]

Roxburgh and Berwickshire

Horatius Bonar of Kelso remarked that until the Disruption came he had no access to the neighbouring parishes, but after that event he found open doors and open ears in that populous district among all ranks of the people. 'Year after year the work grew, and the people flocked to hear', he wrote. Thus Bonar's name became 'fragrant in every little village, and at most of the farms'. He conducted many meetings in farm kitchens and village schoolrooms, and often preached in the open air.[110] It soon became necessary to procure assistance. Two zealous missionaries, whom Bonar styled 'The Evangelists of the Borders', were employed. Thus it could be said decades later that Mr Stoddart and Alexander Murray 'traversed the three counties of Roxburgh, Berwick and Northumberland with blessed success, and the fruit of their labours remains to this day all over the Borders … Whole villages were awakened, besides many stray souls, both young and old, gathered into the Church of God, from various quarters … Many rebuffs we got, many angry letters, many threats of ecclesiastical censure; … but in spite of all this, the work went on'.[111] Bonar wrote: 'The missionary

---

Doctrine of the Holy Spirit, which may have been influenced, to a degree, by the spiritual outpouring he experienced in Auchterarder.

109. Brown, *Annals of the Disruption*, p. 750.

110. Various Contributors, *Memories of Dr Horatius Bonar by Relatives and Public Men*, Edinburgh 1909, p. 99.

111. Various Contributors, *Horatius Bonar D.D.: A Memorial*, p. 11.

work which thus went on for ten or twelve years was of the most striking kind; and the journals of these two men of God, in that wide Border district, would furnish narratives which the Church would rejoice to read.'[112] Another occasional helper was the future Lord Polwarth, while the work also progressed through the distribution of a large number of evangelistic tracts written by Bonar, published in book form in 1846 as the *Kelso Tracts*.

Hawick

Even before the Rev. John Kirk (1813–1886) publicly asserted his adherence to the doctrine of universal atonement in 1842, he had adopted Charles Finney's revival and temperance ideals. He came to believe, with Finney, that 'a revival is not a miracle, nor dependent on a miracle, in any sense. It is a purely philosophical result of the right use of the constituted means'.[113] Kirk's compilation of thirteen lectures published as *The Way of Life Made Plain* in 1882 created a great stir, and as justification for his new views, Kirk claimed he knew of 'many hundreds' who had 'found peace and a total change of character and experience' through reading these sermons.[114] With like motive he also undertook Finneyite-style itinerant evangelism, which produced much sensation. He became pastor of a new Evangelical Union church in Edinburgh in 1845.

Soon after, William Munro, pastor of the second Hawick Congregational Church, became concerned at the low ebb of religion in the town, and invited J. H. Rutherford to conduct a course of meetings.[115] These began in March 1848. After the first week the crowds were such that alternative premises had to be found. John Kirk was called to assist. He and Rutherford held open-air services at breakfast (9.20 a.m.) and dinner hours (2.20 p.m.) for the benefit of working people. This was followed by

---

112. ibid., pp. 91-2.

113. Quoted in Brian Talbot, 'Reserved From Erroneous Views? The Contribution of Francis Johnston as a Baptist Voice in the Scottish Evangelical Debate, in the Mid-Nineteenth Century, on the Work of the Holy Spirit', in Roberts (Ed.), *Revival, Renewal and the Holy Spirit*, p. 97. Two other prominent purveyors of Finneyite doctrine in Scotland at this time were James Morison of the United Secession Church and Baptist leader, Francis Johnston.

114. John Kirk, *Way of Life Made Plain: Being Lectures on Important Propositions*, Kilmarnock 1842, pp. vi-viii.

115. Oddly, Munro seems not to have agreed with the 'new views' of the very evangelist he invited to his church (which one assumes he knew about beforehand), and he withdrew his support from the meetings after Kirk's arrival.

a general evening meeting, which attracted vast numbers. Even the Sub-scription Rooms, to which the meetings had made their third and last shift, were not big enough, and many had to be turned away. For seven weeks these two evangelists, occasionally relieved by other Evangelical Union leaders, laboured shoulder to shoulder, night after night 'in the great fight for free grace, preaching a full, free, complete and everlasting salvation for all men'. A new E.U. church was at once instituted with forty-five members, this being doubled after a week of further meetings the following month (June 1848).[116] Kirk's memoirs refer briefly to this season of 'revival', in which 'many were turned to the Lord, Christians were also enlightened, and a new church was formed'.[117]

Grantown-on-Spey

A revival, by no means the first to be experienced in the town, began in Grantown-on-Spey in August 1848, coming 'like a stream that has been accumulating for years, which has at last broken through the banks'. It began shortly after the Rev. Peter Grant's son, William, came to assist his father in the ministry, with the conversion of a woman whose reason was recently restored after being 'three years deranged'.[118] Several others found peace in believing after long struggles. As two of these were young girls who resided on the banks of the River Spey, it was deemed appropriate to hold a public baptism there. Over a thousand came to witness the spectacle, listening also with great solemnity to Peter Grant's message. After that day souls were awakened at almost every sermon and prayer meeting, inquirers were numerous and the church was revived. Over 1,200 came to witness the next baptism a month later, when in addition to the five appointed for immersion, a man of seventy, a believer of thirty-six years' standing, at the last minute requested the same ordinance. Such request was there and then granted.

There were further public baptisms in October, November, December (1848) and January (1849); fifty-four people in all, the vast majority being 'converts from the world', who, Grant observed, 'generally prove brighter Christians, and have less rubbish to be removed'. Many of these were

---

116. 'Hawick Congregational Church Centenary Commemoration 1848–1948', quoted in McNaughton, *Early Congregational Independency in Lowland Scotland*, vol. 1, p. 454.

117. H. Kirk, *Memoirs of Rev. John Kirk D.D.*, p. 234.

118. *BHMS Report* 1849, p. 7.

people of strong moral character. Candidates were thoroughly examined before being accepted, as the Grantown pastor knew that 'nothing can be more hurtful to the persons received, or to the church receiving, than the admission of such as are strangers to the grace of God'.[119]

'Under the mighty hand of God', said Grant, 'it is our prayer meetings that hold our souls in life'. Over one hundred, in addition to children, attended the twice-weekly meeting from the outset of the movement, and on occasion the attendance was nearly 300.[120] By March 1850 so many were being drawn to the Sabbath morning services that when the large congregation was dismissed the chapel was immediately refilled with eager souls who had been waiting outside. At some services every church member was engaged simultaneously in speaking with inquirers, while on many nights, seekers would gather at Grant's home, sometimes till after midnight, waiting to speak with the pastor.

The revival spread to outstations on every side of the town. At these Sabbath schools flourished, though the one in Grantown was particularly 'a wonder to every beholder', being attended by a hundred children under twelve years of age, and sometimes more. Grant's son conducted a packed Sabbath morning meeting for young men, and his father/pastor 'sometimes listened and shed tears of joy behind the door when they were not aware of it'. In April 1852 Grant could rejoice that he only had to exclude four 'of the one hundred added to us during our happy revival two years ago … and even some of these we yet hope that their spirit will be saved in the day of the Lord'.[121]

Shapinsay

What was described as 'a great religious awakening' occurred on the small fertile Orkney island of Shapinsay in 1850. A 'pious and consistent' stone-mason, working on the construction of the island's Balfour Castle, brought north with him some pamphlets on the controversy surrounding the Atonement. After circulating them around the island, 'such a hungering and thirsting after the word was excited' that William Crombie and Robert Wallace (then students of the Evangelical

---

119. ibid., pp. 7-8.

120. ibid., 1849, pp. 8-11.

121. ibid., 1850, pp. 6-9; 1852, p. 17. See also A. B. Thomson, *Sketches of Some Baptist Pioneers in Scotland*, pp. 28-9; D. E. Meek, 'Gaelic Bible, Revival and Mission', pp. 130-1.

Academy in Glasgow), were induced to visit Shapinsay, where they preached night after night to attentive audiences.[122] The meetings were first held in a barn, then in a joiner's shop, and subsequently at various other locations on the island. Several ministers of the Evangelical Union paid visits to the northerly isle and 'preached with acceptance', before one of them, Thomas G. Salmon – with family – moved from his charge in Duns to settle there as missioner in 1851. Mr Balfour, the island's proprietor, readily provided land for a new manse, glebe and church, which sanctuary, built in the centre of the island, was opened in 1853. At first the fledgling congregation was viewed with considerable suspicion by many of the island's one thousand populace, almost all of whom already belonged, at least nominally, to one of two other churches established in the small parish. Opposition gradually died away and in 1855 the church formally joined the Evangelical Union, with Salmon as its first pastor.[123]

Maryburgh

Angus McIver was transferred to Maryburgh, to the north of Inverness, around 1850, a 'cold and uninteresting' parish, 'without much appearance of vital godliness', and where the Sabbath sermons were 'wanting in animation' and 'apt to put folk to sleep'![124] Here he joined the half-dozen folk who gathered for the weekly prayer meeting, and also started Sabbath evening services in the school-house, the parish church being point-blank refused to him. These meetings steadily grew until there was no place to sit or stand, and in the summer months many were forced to linger outside near the door or windows to hear McIver preach, some coming from as far as Ferintosh or Strathconnon, sixteen miles distant. The change in Maryburgh was described as being, 'so remarkable and the people greatly stirred from former coldness and apathy … All classes of people from all quarters flocked there, as if by magic'.[125]

Outwith the place of meeting, too, McIver had much influence, going out at all hours to stop brawlings in the street, and often entering the pub

---

122. F. Ferguson, *A History of the Evangelical Union*, p. 373.

123. Various Contributors, *The Worthies of the Evangelical Union*, pp. 151-4; H. Escott, *A History of Scottish Congregationalism*, p. 265.

124. *The Stornoway Gazette*, 26/02/1972, p. 5.

125. ibid., 4/03/1972, p. 5.

across from where he stayed to remonstrate with patrons. The publican, outraged at such intervention, employed a solicitor who threatened proceedings against McIver. These were completely ignored, and custom at the pub dropped so low that the owner eventually had to shut-up shop.[126] Several drunkards – one an absolute 'terror to the people' – became changed men through McIver's witness and one paid a tearful visit to the teacher on his deathbed. McIver died in October 1856 and his funeral was said to have been the largest in that part of the country since that of Dr Macdonald of Ferintosh seven years previously.[127]

Later Movements 1851–7

Introduction

Isolated yet noteworthy occasions of spiritual quickening continued to arise in various disconnected localities of the country; north, south, east and west, throughout the first seven years of the 1850s. Stirrings among Baptist congregations were especially prominent in these years, as was continued extension of the Evangelical Union cause. Most significant of all, perhaps, was the emergence of young Methodist preacher, James Turner, who promptly developed into something of a firebrand evangelist in his own Peterhead neighbourhood. Although he could hardly have conceived it at the time, the work of this flaming gospel pedlar was to result in a titanic burst of emotional revival all along the north-east coast, from Inverness to Aberdeen and beyond, by the beginning of the following decade.

Strontian and Skye

The Rev. John MacQueen, a native of Uig, Skye, was ordained in the Argyllshire parish of Strontian in 1853, and he there experienced, in the first decade of his ministry, a season of blessing. In addition to the Highland ministry of MacQueen in this post-Disruption period, the ministries of Peter MacLean of Tobermory, John Macrae of Knockbain, and Francis MacBean of Fort Augustus were also blessed to an eminent degree.[128] It was among such a crop of noteworthy believers

---

126. ibid., 11/03/1972, p. 5.

127. ibid., 18/03/1972, p. 5.

128. Rev. Murdo Macaulay, *Hector Cameron of Lochs and Back*, Edinburgh 1982, pp. 5-6.

that Hector Cameron (later of Lochs and Back, in Lewis) began his Christian profession and later felt called to the ministry of God's Word. Meanwhile, in MacQueen's native Skye, in the vicinity of Stein in the northern district of Waternish, during the winter and spring of 1854–5, under the influence of Norman MacLeod, who was also instrumental in the revival in the same area in 1840 (see page 421), several cases occurred of persons, who were formerly pupils at the local Gaelic school, being 'secretly and silently brought to serious concern, and to seek the way of salvation'.[129]

Jordanhill and Hillhead

James Allan, a probationer of the Free Church from the Aberdeen-shire parish of Huntly, made 'fervent and impassioned' gospel appeals in the colliery villages of Jordanhill and Hillhead, on the outskirts of Glasgow, during 1854. After a visitation of cholera at the end of that year, 'a decided work of awakening' began among the miners and their families. Seven years later Andrew Bonar testified to being personally acquainted with very many of those who were then brought to Christ. 'Though it did not extend to great numbers', he said, 'those who were then taught of God took up their cross and have continued to follow their Lord through good and bad report, and the Lord has not forsaken them'.[130] In 1855 Allan was replaced through ill-health by Perthshire evangelist, David Sandeman, who also laboured here with considerable triumph for three months.[131] Elsewhere in Glasgow, services conducted by Gilbert McCallum in the Dovehill district in 1854–5 were 'crowned with success', and over thirty professions of faith were recorded – out of which came the Wardlaw Memorial Mission House in 1856.[132]

Elgin

Although over two thousand people had turned up to hear a series of 'Lectures on Popery' given by various Protestant ministers of Elgin and its vicinity during the winter of 1853–4, the Rev. William Tulloch

---

129. *Report of The Society for the Support of Gaelic Schools*, 1855, p. 4, quoted in Steve Taylor, *The Skye Revivals*, p. 116.

130. Bonar, *David Sandeman, Missionary to China*, p. 149.

131. ibid., pp. 151-2. For more on Sandeman, see page 341 fn 100.

132. McNaughton, *Early Congregational Independency in Lowland Scotland*, vol. 2, pp. 105-6.

considered the spiritual situation in the region to be 'dark and discouraging … so that we were in danger of giving way to despondency'. Nevertheless it was in his own Baptist church that 'a most precious and refreshing shower' of the Holy Spirit descended in the following springtime. Six people were accepted for baptism in the space of a month, including three of the most well-educated young men in the district. Two others were among the fruit of Tulloch's labours at two countryside preaching stations. By November, the Elgin pastor could boast, 'The little cloud which then appeared above the horizon, and distilled some precious drops, has since increased in size, and discharged itself in a more copious shower, reviving and enriching the garden of the Lord, and irrigating and reclaiming portions of the moral waste beyond'. It has been my privilege', said Tulloch with thanksgiving and a sense of awe, 'to witness more of the work of God in this respect within the last eight months than I ever witnessed in the same limited period since I became a preacher of the Gospel'.[133]

A sermon on Ezekiel's vision of the dry bones was a vital means in the awakening of some within the jurisdiction of the earnest Elgin minister, and the testimonies that issued forth were most striking. One man, a tailor to trade, had 'freely indulged in dissipation and vice', which only increased after both his wife and only child died within a short time of each other.[134] Soon after, he himself was suddenly struck with paralysis in his whole left side, and being told that nothing could be done for him, he tried to end his life by taking an overdose of pills. He was found just in time, and by the use of a stomach pump and other means his life was saved. Such drama seemed to have little effect on his lifestyle, however, for he returned to his previous habits. But for some reason he was induced to attend one of Tulloch's outstations, where 'the barbed arrow of conviction … pierced his heart' and he was savingly changed. Wrote Tulloch in conclusion: 'The Church is greatly revived, and an earnest spirit of prayer prevails.' This took the public form of numerous weekly meetings, a Sabbath morning prayer meeting, plus another in the evening to seek special blessing on that day's sermons. On top of all this a number gathered in the vestry first thing on Monday morning in

---

133. *BHMS Report* 1855, pp. 22-4.
134. ibid., p. 24.

order to pray, while a group of young men met privately twice-a-week for the same purpose.[135]

Tiree

Tiree's Baptist congregations grew significantly in the early 1850s after the induction of the island's first native-born pastor, John MacFarlane, whose Balemartin family had been touched powerfully by the Tiree revival of 1839–46. (Three of his brothers also became ministers). This growth led to the Balemartin meeting-house being extended in 1854 to seat 300 people. By 1856 another awakening had developed and in that year and the next, six and twelve people respectively were added to membership through immersion. In addition, believed MacFarlane, there were as many converts who had not joined the fellowship. Some had moved to the mainland, some had joined other churches, and some were struggling against opposition. This came largely, the pastor claimed, from Free Church ministers in their 'violent preaching against us'. They 'try everything in their power to make Christian immersion odious in the view of the people'.[136] So busy was MacFarlane in this mini-revival that he was unable to attend the Annual Meeting of the Baptist Home Missionary Society in Edinburgh in 1857, at which he would normally have made every effort to be present.[137]

Grantown-on-Spey and Tullimet

Having been repeatedly drenched by showers of divine blessing under Peter Grant's ministry over the previous twenty-five years (see pages 273-4, 279-80, 393-4, 473-4), the Baptist Chapel in Grantown-on-Spey was again to come under gracious influences of the Spirit in 1857, in which year the congregation 'enjoyed a year of the milk and honey of the land of Canaan'. Eleven were added to the church, with the additional occurrence of a few convincing deathbed conversions. Another case was that of a young girl who, on being awakened, wept night and day until

---

135. ibid., pp. 24-5.

136. Meek, *Island Harvest*, p. 13. Donald Meek makes the point that the Free Church's hostility to the Baptist Church in this case was probably not based solely on doctrine. 'When the Free Church came to Tiree, it was twenty years too late to capture the whole of the dissenting constituency. Many crofters and cottars had already put their weight behind the Baptist body' (ibid).

137. Interestingly, Tiree Baptist Church does not appear to have been noticeably affected by the national revival movement that broke out just two years later (1859–61).

she obtained peace. Membership of the church rose at this time to 203, while there were many attendants who were not members.[138] Similarly, further south, the same year, the long-serving Rev. Daniel Grant said of his Baptist congregation in Tullimet, near Pitlochry (which fellowship had also experienced revival blessing under that pastor's ministry fifteen years previously – see page 354), 'The Lord has been graciously pleased to revive his work amongst us and many have been, I believe, converted to God'.[139]

Leith

'Revival services'[140] were often conducted by fledgling Evangelical Union churches and in Leith's Second Congregational Church 'the spiritual zeal of the church was sustained, and many souls converted ... by frequent evangelistic efforts'. It was in one of these 'revivals' that James Strachan was roused to seek the Lord and brought to personal decision for Christ.[141] Strachan became the first member to join the Leith church under the pastorate of Joseph Boyle (who was inducted there in March 1853). He later entered the Evangelical Union ministry, as did several other young converts from the Leith congregation. A few years later, from 2nd to 16th August 1858, Boyle and an assistant conducted a further series of 'revival services' in the Leith church. These consisted of 'preliminary special prayer meetings, open air services, and special sermons thereafter in the chapel, and were continued daily with increasing success, and many members (were) added to the Church'.[142]

Peterhead and Collieston

James Turner (1818–1863) was born into a poor family in Peterhead, received scanty education and was of feeble physical constitution. He was

---

138. *BHMS Report* 1857, pp. 15-6. Since the time of Grant's settling in Grantown thirty years previously (1828), there had been 375 additions to membership. Of these fifty had died believing, while thirty-six (sixteen men and twenty women, including many longstanding members of the church) had been excommunicated. Others had withdrawn from membership or moved away from the area.

139. ibid., 1857, p. 18.

140. The term, 'revival services' was frequently used by Evangelical Union correspondents to denote a series of often protracted meetings held with the specific aim of obtaining 'decisions for the Lord'. There often existed an intentionally charged atmosphere in the aim of creating a genuine revival scenario.

141. Various Contributors, *The Worthies of the Evangelical Union*, p. 102.

142. ibid.

converted at the age of twenty-two following months of inner struggle. After a period of backsliding, he renewed his vows to the Lord and aligned himself to the local Wesleyan Chapel. On 6th March 1854, he received, through the prayers of 'two dear sisters', what he termed the experience of 'perfect love (baptism in the Spirit) … When the power of God came down on me, it sunk me to the floor speechless, and then I lay for some time full of the glory of God … '. Six days later, at the Sabbath afternoon Bible class, which he led, Turner said he

> felt the power of God so rest on my soul that I could not keep from weeping. Before we got through with our experience, every soul was broken down. 'The Lord is about to work a work amongst us', I said, and truly He did, for in a few minutes the power of God came down on A.M., then on my wife, and then on J.Y. and E.C. My brother George also and C.R.. Four of them fell to the floor insensible. Our dear sister, Mrs J. was afraid and cried, 'Lord, stay Thy hand'. But I said 'No Lord, we are all in Thy hand; do with us what you please'. What a house! God's power never was in such a manner in Peterhead before. They all got perfect love. Lord humble me and take the glory.[143]

Empowered with this fresh anointing, Turner burned with evangelistic zeal and preached whenever and wherever he could, his labours leading to a degree of spiritual awakening in and around Peterhead. At Collieston just a week after his dramatic spiritual encounter, he jotted in his diary: 'Preached three times in the open air … Many people attended, hungering for the bread of life … God was among the people. I could not get away from them. One dear young man, J.A., came running after me about his soul, and I pointed him to Jesus. What a feeling was among the people. My Jesus never gave me such power before'.[144] During each of the following three years (1854–7) in particular, Turner held around 150 prayer meetings in private homes, led a similar number of Bible classes and stood by the sick and dying more than five hundred times. During the same period many lost souls were led to the Saviour while numerous others received a fresh baptism

---

143. Elizabeth MacHardie, *James Turner: or, How to Reach the Masses*, Aberdeen 1875, p. 9.

144. ibid., p. 10.

of the Holy Spirit (again Turner uses the phrase 'entered into perfect love'). Those converted included, on three particular occasions, 'a father, a son and two daughters all in one house', three 'aged people' and three servants from the same household.[145] Remarkable as these experiences were, Turner's success as an evangelist was only just beginning. More intense flames of spiritual revival were to ignite through his ministry in many north-east communities just a few years later.[146]

---

145. ibid., pp. 12-20.

146. See Elizabeth MacHardie, *James Turner*, pp. 21-39.

Afterword

Land of Many Revivals is first and foremost a historical narrative, and virtually all its space is taken up with chronicling that history, although a degree of analysis is included within the text, particularly the footnotes. In fact, an entire further book could be written analysing the observations made in *LMR*, examining a host of relevant factors, such as natural facilitators of revival, the types of human agencies used and in what manner, the main characteristics of the movements narrated, the geography of revivals, as well as denominational variances, opposition to revivals, and so on.

In regard to natural facilitators, while many regard revivals as manifest works of God, requiring no further explanation, clearly there are a number of 'natural' factors that help inaugurate them. These include issues such as political and social instability within a nation or region, ecclesiastical tension, poverty, disease, personal danger and recent community bereavement.

It can be observed that the principal 'instruments' employed in bringing about a revival are human agents who are so yielded to God that they become channels of His living word. Their preaching is noted for being uncompromising, Christ-centred and demanding of personal commitment. Revivals in Scotland have typically occurred as a result of the arrival of a new, usually young, minister in the area or the preaching of an evangelist or minister from outside the district. Within the Presbyterian tradition, revivals have often been closely associated with Communion seasons; other common avenues through which they are channelled include written reports of a work of grace elsewhere in the nation or world, or more directly from testimonies of individuals who have visited, or have been converted during, a revival in another locality.

Revivals generally, though by no means always, commence during times of declension in the spiritual life of local congregations, or, in the case of a general awakening, of the Church nationally. They have as their focus Christ-centred preaching and the authority of the word of God. Deep conviction of sin (on the part of both believers and non-believers) is a necessary outcome of such focus, followed by genuine repentance, a release of peace and joy, and a marked change in lifestyle (we really have to question the veracity of any claim of evangelical revival that does not have these basic attributes at its core). A deep awareness of the nearness of the divine is another recurring feature of spiritual outpourings. A further important aspect concerns how long they endure. This usually varies from several days to a number of years and is generally dependent upon which of the three models of revival as defined by Kenneth Jeffrey they fall under (see Introduction, page 27).

Experience has proved that in general people are more likely to make commitments of faith during their teens or twenties than at any other period in their lives. This explains the predominance of converts of a younger generation during times of spiritual quickening. Revival converts are also more likely to be female than male, and to come from the working classes rather than the middle or upper echelons of society. Revivals are more common in close-knit communities, such as crofting, mining and fishing neighbourhoods – where there are strong cultural or occupational bonds – than in large towns and cities.

Prayer is invariably regarded as an essential prerequisite to the outbreak of revival in a community, and is indeed one of the most typical features of the revivals documented in this book. Having said that, it is impossible to prove or disprove outright any precise cause and effect pattern; hence unwise to suggest that revival could not possibly occur in a district unless a faithful band of prayer warriors had been interceding for that very event in preceding weeks or months. Nor can we assume that concentrated prayer for revival, even over a considerable time, will automatically lead to that result. Nevertheless, traditionally, prayer and revival have an inextricable inter-connection.

The impact of revivals on the individuals and congregations caught up in them is clearly considerable, and often wholly transforming. They also result in a steady advance in the ordinary work of the Church. Their impact on the wider community, be that temporary or lasting, is often more variable, and will depend on the magnitude of the movement as well as which of the six 'R' levels as outlined in the Introduction (pages 25 and 26) is in operation.

Partly because revivals are unpredictable, messy affairs, they invariably come in for a degree of opposition, both from without, and more commonly (and generally more hurtfully), from within the Church. Such criticism may be on theological grounds, due to denominational rivalry, or because of jealousy of other individuals or churches experiencing blessing. Sometimes church splits have occurred as a result of a work of grace in a community; at other times the formation of a whole new denomination may emerge.

Estimating the number of converts in an awakening is always a precarious task. Historically, Presbyterian commentators did not have the fixation with numbers of converts that we do today, and in any case considered it injudicious to proclaim with any degree of certainty who is and isn't among God's elect. Accessions to church membership are a helpful indicator, though not always an accurate guide. Part of the problem may be in counting as converts everyone who has shown deep interest and even evidence of soul concern, but who are not savingly changed. The decreasing distinction made between these two very different spiritual states over the decades has resulted in much confusion and disappointment. Connected to this is the issue of backsliding, which is sometimes overlooked in the reporting of awakenings, probably because most revival accounts are written while the movement is still in progress. A better assessment might be made a year or two later.

All of these factors are discussed at some length in Part 5 of my book, *Glory In The Glen*, in the chapter entitled 'Revival Considerations', the entirety of which is taken up with analysing both the revivals included in the present volume and those from later periods of Scottish Church history. Indeed, a great many of the spiritual movements documented in *Land of Many Revivals*, as well as many of its chief players, are referred to by name within the 45 pages of that chapter, and the reader is encouraged to turn there for more in-depth assessment of their main characteristics.

Yet another fascinating aspect of revivals is their chronology. As regards those detailed in this book, a very significant portion occurred within less than six decades of one particular century – the nineteenth. This volume considers spiritual outpourings up to 1857. Fresh on the heels of that year a fresh and glorious new awakening spread across the land, not a single county – and in some counties hardly a single community – being left untouched. This was of course the 1858–61 revival which had its genesis in Canada/America, before crossing the Atlantic and sweeping through Ulster, Scotland and other parts of the United Kingdom. Further surges of revival emerged in various parts of Scotland later in the 1860s, and again in 1873–4, the latter as a result of Moody and Sankey's mission to the northern kingdom. During the last two decades of the nineteenth century a host of more localised movements occurred – in the fishing ports of the north-east coast, up and down the Outer Hebrides, and in many other parts of mainland Scotland. These, as well as many later revivals are recounted in *Glory in the Glen*. The 1800s truly was the century of Scottish revivals. Indeed, such was the intensity of revival activity all across the nation in the twenty year period 1858 to 1878 that it requires treatment as a separate work. This will be the subject of a forthcoming book in the chronicling of Scotland's dramatic revival history.

BIBLIOGRAPHY

General

Bardgett, Frank, *North Coast Parish: Strathy and Halladale: A Historical Guide to a Post-Clearance Parish and Its Church*, Strathy 1990

Bebbington, D. W., *Evangelicalism in Modern Britain: A History from the 1730s to the 1980s*, London 1989

Beith, Alexander, *A Highland Tour*, Edinburgh 1874

Blakey, Stephen S., *The Man in the Manse*, Edinburgh 1978

Burgess, Stanley (Ed.), *The New International Dictionary of Pentecostal and Charismatic Movements*, Grand Rapids 2002

Butler, Dugald, *John Wesley and George Whitefield in Scotland, or, The Influence of the Oxford Methodists on Scottish Religion*, Edinburgh 1898

Calder, Walter, *Strathy: An Account of the Parish*, Wick 1897

Campbell, Murdoch, *Gleanings of Highland Harvest*, Stornoway 1953 [reprinted 1989]

Campbell, Thorbjorn, *Arran: A History*, Edinburgh 2007

Chalmers, Thomas (Ed.), *Sermons of John Russel of Muthill*, Glasgow 1826

Cunningham, William (Ed.), *Sermons by the Rev. Robert Bruce, with Collections for his Life, by Robert Wodrow*, Edinburgh 1853

Davenport, Rowland A., *Albury Apostles: The Story of the Body Known as the Catholic Apostolic Church*, Birdlip 1970

Erskine, Thomas, *Letters of Thomas Erskine of Linlathen, from 1800 till 1840*, Edinburgh 1877

Frank, Derek, *The Jeremiah Diagnosis*, Godalming 2000

Fraser, Alexander, *Tarbat, Easter Ross: A Historical Sketch*, Evanton 1988

Gunn, Adam, *Sutherland and Reay Country*, Glasgow 1897

Hasse, E. R., *The Moravians*, London 1912

Henderson, Henry, *The Religious Controversies of Scotland,* Edinburgh 1905

487

Hossack, B. H., *Kirkwall in the Orkneys*, Kirkwall 1900

Hutchison, James, *Weavers, Miners and the Open Book: A History of Kilsyth*, Kilsyth 1986

Irvine, Rev. Alexander, *Substance of a Speech, Delivered Before the Commission of the General Assembly of the Church of Scotland … on the State of Religion and the Necessity of Erecting New Parishes in the Highlands and Islands of Scotland*, Edinburgh 1819

Isaac, Peter, *A History of Evangelical Christianity in Cornwall*, Gerrards Cross 2000

Jeffreys, George, *Pentecostal Rays: The Baptism and Gifts of the Holy Spirit*, London 1923

Kennedy, John & Bonar, Horatius, *Evangelism: A Reformed Debate*, Port Dinorwic 1997

Kirk, John, *Way of Life Made Plain: Being Lectures on Important Propositions*, Kilmarnock 1842

Laidlaw, John, *Robert Bruce's Sermons on the Sacrament*, Edinburgh 1901

Lamb, William, *McCheyne from the Pew, Being Extracts from the Diary of William Lamb*, London 1914

MacLean, Rev. Donald, *Duthil Past and Present*, Inverness 1910

Maclean, Charles, *Island on the Edge of the World*, Edinburgh 1972

Macleod, John, *Memories of the Far North*, Caithness 1919

Macpherson, Dave, *Incredible Cover Up*, Plainfield, N.J. 1975

MacRae, Alexander, *Kinlochbervie: Being the Story and Traditions of a Remote Highland Parish and its People*, Tongue 1932

Miller, Hugh, *Sutherland and the Sutherlanders; Their Religious and Social Condition*, Edinburgh 1844

Scenes and Legends of the North of Scotland; or, The Traditional History of Cromarty, Edinburgh 1869

Moore, R. D., *Methodism in the Channel Islands*, London 1952

Morris, R. J., *Cholera 1832: The Social Response to an Epidemic*, London 1976

Murray, Iain H., *The Puritan Hope: A Study in Revival and the Interpretation of Prophecy*, Edinburgh 1971 (reprinted 1991)

Murray, John, *Collected Writings of John Murray*, Edinburgh 1982

Pytches, David, *Prophecy in the Local Church*, London 1993

Roberts, Richard Owen, *Whitefield in Print: A Bibliographic Record of Works by, for, and against George Whitefield*, Wheaton 1988

Robertson, Rev. A., *A Vindication of the Religion of the Land from Misrepresentation and an Exposure of the Absurd Pretensions of the Gareloch Enthusiasts, in a Letter to Thomas Erskine, Esq., Advocate*, Edinburgh 1830

Robson, Michael, *St Kilda: Church, Visitors and 'Natives'*, Port of Ness 2005

Sands, John, *Out of the World; or, Life in St Kilda*, Edinburgh 1876

Schmidt, Leigh Eric, *Holy Fairs: Scotland and the Making of American Revivalism*, Princeton NJ. 1989

Seton, George, *St Kilda*, Edinburgh 1878 (reprinted 1980)

Sherrill, John L., *They Speak with Other Tongues*, London 1964

Somerville, W. F. (Ed.), *Precious Seed Sown in Many Lands*, London 1890

Steel, Tom, *The Life and Death of St Kilda*, Glasgow 1975

Stewart, Andrew (Ed.), *The "Albatross" Yacht Mission: A Story of Joyous Christian Adventure*, Edinburgh nd

Strachan, Gordon, *The Pentecostal Theology of Edward Irving*, London 1973

Stuart, Rev. Atholl, *Blair Atholl as it Was and Is*, Edinburgh 1857

Thompson, J., *A Brief Account of a Visit to Some of the Brethren in the West of Scotland*, London 1831

Walker, Robert, *Expostulatory Letters to Free Church Ministers, on their Secession from the Church of Scotland*, Dingwall 1846

Warfield, B. B., *Counterfeit Miracles*, London 1972

Westerkamp, Marilyn, *Triumph of the Laity: Scots-Irish Piety and the Great Awakening, 1625–1760*, Oxford 1988

Wilson, James A., *A History of Cambuslang, A Clydesdale Parish*, Glasgow 1929

Wylie, J. A., *The History of Protestantism*, London 1879

Scottish Church History – General

Bebbington, D. W., *The Baptists in Scotland*, Glasgow 1988

Brown, Callum, *Social History of Religion in Scotland since 1730*, London 1987

Brown, Stewart J. & Fry, Michael (Eds), *Scotland in the Age of the Disruption*, Edinburgh 1993

Brown, Thomas, *Annals of the Disruption*, Edinburgh 1893

Buchanan, Robert, *The Ten Years' Conflict: Being the History of the Disruption of the Church of Scotland*, Glasgow 1849

Burleigh, J. S. H., *A Church History of Scotland*, London 1960

Cameron, Nigel M. de S. (Ed.), *Dictionary of Scottish Church History & Theology*, Edinburgh 1993

Escott, Harry, *A History of Scottish Congregationalism*, Glasgow 1960

Ferguson, Fergus, *A History of the Evangelical Union from its Origin to the Present Time*, Glasgow 1876

Fleming, Robert, *The Fulfilling of the Scripture*, vol. 1, Glasgow 1801

Henderson, G. D., *The Church of Scotland: A Short History*, Edinburgh 1939
   Heritage: A Study of the Disruption, Edinburgh 1943

Hetherington, W. M., *History of the Church of Scotland*, Edinburgh 1848

Kirkton, James, *The Secret and True History of the Church of Scotland, from the Restoration to the Year 1678*, Edinburgh 1817

Knox, John, *The Reformation in Scotland*, Edinburgh (1982 edition)

Lindsay, T. M., *The Reformation in Scotland*, Edinburgh 1882 [reprinted 2006]

Lynch, Michael, *Scotland: A New History*, London 1991

Magnusson, Magnus, *Scotland: The Story of a Nation*, London 2000

Mathieson, William L., *Church and Reform in Scotland*, Glasgow 1916

McCrie, Thomas, *The Story of the Scottish Church*, Edinburgh 1874 (reprinted 1988)

McIntosh, John, *Church and Theology in Enlightenment Scotland: The Popular Party 1740–1800*, East Linton 1998

McKerrow, John, *History of the Secession Church*, Edinburgh 1839

McNaughton, William D., *A Few Historical Notes on Early Congregational Independency in Scotland*, Kirkcaldy 2000

Early Congregational Independency in Orkney, Cambridge, 2006

Macpherson, John, *A History of the Church in Scotland From the Earliest Times Down to the Present Day*, Paisley 1901

Murray, Iain H., *A Scottish Christian Heritage*, Edinburgh 2006

Open University, *A History of Scotland*, Milton Keynes 2008

Reid, Harry, *Reformation: The Dangerous Birth of the Modern World*, Edinburgh 2009

Renwick, A. M. & Harman, A. M., *The Story of the Church*, Leicester 1958

Small, Robert, *History of the Congregations of the United Presbyterian Church from 1733 to 1900*, Edinburgh 1904

Smellie, Alexander, *Men of the Covenant: The Story of the Scottish Church in the Years of the Persecution*, London 1903

Stevenson, David, *The Covenanters: The National Covenant and Scotland*, Edinburgh 1988

Struthers, Gavin, *History of the Rise, Progress and Principles of the Relief Church*, Glasgow 1843

Swift, Wesley F., *Methodism in Scotland: The First Hundred Years*, London 1947

Vos, Johannes G., *The Scottish Covenanters: Their Origins, History and Distinctive Doctrines*, Edinburgh 1998

Wodrow, Robert, *The History of the Sufferings of the Church of Scotland, from the Restoration to the Revolution*, vol. 2, Edinburgh 1722

Yullie, Rev. George, *History of the Baptists in Scotland*, Glasgow 1926

Scottish Church History – Regional

Ansdell, Douglas, *The People of the Great Faith: The Highland Church 1690–1900*, Stornoway 1998

Bardgett, Frank D., *Two Millennia of Church and Community in Orkney*, Edinburgh 2000

Brown, J. Wood, *The Covenanters of the Merse*, Edinburgh 1893

Cameron, John K., *The Church in Arran*, Edinburgh 1912

Escott, Harry, *Beacons in Independency: Religion and Life in Strathbogie and Upper Garioch in the Nineteenth Century*, Huntly 1940

Finlay, James T., *The Secession in the North: The Story of an Old Seceder Presbytery [i.e. Buchan], 1688–1897*, Aberdeen 1898

Harcus, Henry, *The History of the Orkney Baptist Churches*, Ayr 1898

Kennedy, John, *Days of the Fathers in Ross-shire*, Edinburgh 1861 (reprinted 1979)

Lawson, Bill, *St Kilda and its Church*, Northton 1993

Lawson, Rev. R., *The Covenanters of Ayrshire*, Ayrshire 1887

Macaulay, Rev. Murdo, *Aspects of the Religious History of Lewis Up to the Disruption of 1843*, Inverness nd

Macdonald, Murdoch, *The Covenanters In Moray and Ross*, Nairn 1875

Macleod, Rev. Calum I. (Ed.), *Pronnagan: Gospel Advent in Barvas Parish*, Barvas 2008

McInnes, John, *Evangelical Movements in the Highlands of Scotland*, Aberdeen 1951

Mackay, John, *The Church in the Highlands*, London 1914

Macleod, John, *By-Paths of Highland Church History*, Edinburgh 1965

Macleod, John, *Banner in the West: A Spiritual History of Lewis and Harris*, Edinburgh 2008

Macleod, K. M., *A Brief Record of the Church in Uig (Lewis) Up to the Union of 1929*, Stornoway 1994

McNaughton, William D., *Early Congregational Independency in the Highlands and Islands and the North-East of Scotland*, Glasgow 2003

Early Congregational Independency in Lowland Scotland, vol. 1, Glasgow 2005

Early Congregational Independency in Lowland Scotland, vol. 2, Glasgow 2007

A Few Historical Notes on Early Congregational Independency in Scotland, Kirkcaldy 2000

Early Congregational Independency in Orkney, Cambridge, 2006

Early Congregational Independency in Shetland, Lerwick 2005

Helensburgh and Alexandria: A Tale of Two Congregational Churches, Glasgow 1996

The Congregational Church in Kirkcaldy and Other Congregational Churches in Fife (From their Beginnings to 1850), Ventura 1989

MacRury, Ewan, *A Hebridean Parish*, Inverness 1950

Meek, Donald E., *Island Harvest: A History of Tiree Baptist Church 1838–1988*, Tiree 1988

Sunshine and Shadow: The Story of the Baptists of Mull, Edinburgh 1991

Munro, Rev. Donald, *Records of Grace in Sutherland*, Edinburgh 1953

Noble, John, *Religious Life in Ross*, Inverness 1909

Sage, Donald, *Memorabilia Domestica*, Wick 1889

Thomson, D. P., *Tales of the Far North West: A Sutherlandshire Miscellany*, Inverness 1955

Various Contributors, *Sketches of Churches and Clergy in the Parishes of Row, Rosneath, and Cardross*, Helensburgh 1889

A Collace Miscellany, Collace 1993

Individual Congregational Histories

Adamson, Thomas, *Free Anderston Church, Glasgow. A Centenary Sketch*, Glasgow 1900

Agnew, Hugh, *United Free Church West, Cumnock: Its History, 1773–1923*, Cumnock 1923

Baird, William, *Sixty Years of Church Life in Ayr: The History of Ayr Free Church from 1836 to 1896*, Ayr 1896

Binnie, Thomas, *Sketch of the History of the First Reformed Presbyterian Congregation, now the Great Hamilton Street Free Church, Glasgow*, Paisley 1888

Couper, W. J., *Kilbirnie West: A History of Kilbirnie West United Free, Formerly Reformed Presbyterian Church, 1824–1924*, Kilbirnie 1923

Crichton, Rev. Alex S., *Annals of a Disruption Congregation in Aberdeenshire: West Church, Inverurie*, Aberdeen 1943

Gage, James, *Historical Sketch of the Congregation: Great Hamilton Street Free Church (formerly Reformed Presbyterian), Glasgow*, Glasgow 1890

Goodwin, John, *History of Free St Peter's Church, Glasgow*, Glasgow 1886

Grant, G. V. R., *Urray & Kilchrist Church of Scotland*, Ross-shire 1998

Grieve, William, *A Short History of Shotts Parish Church*, Shotts 1928

Hillis, Peter, *The Barony of Glasgow: A Window onto Church and People in Nineteenth-Century Scotland*, Edinburgh 2007

Inglis, Rev. Andrew, *Notes of the History of Dudhope Free Church, Lochee Road, Dundee*, Dundee 1890

Laurie, John, *Chronicles of the Evangelical Union Church of Leith*, Edinburgh 1871

Lyall, Francis & William Still, *History of Gilcomston South Church, Aberdeen, 1868–1968*, Aberdeen 1968

Macdonald, Angus, *An Enduring Testimony: Inverness East Church*, Inverness 1998

McGregor, George, *A Short Sketch of the History of Lochee Free Church, now Lochee East Church of Scotland 1846–1946*, Dundee 1946

MacInnes, Rev. David, *Kilmuir Church, North Uist 1894–1994*, Kilmuir 1994

Mackinnon, Donald, *Annals of a Fifeshire Congregation. Being the Story of the Original Associate (Burgher) Church at Kennoway, afterwards the United Original Secession Church at Kennoway, and since 1845 the Free Church at Kennoway, 1800–1945*, Perth 1946

Maclagan, David, *St George's, Edinburgh. A History of St George's Church 1814 to 1843 and of St George's Free Church 1843 to 1873*, London 1876

McNeill, John, *The Baptist Church in Colonsay*, Edinburgh 1914

Martin, John R., *The Church Chronicles of Nigg*, Nigg 1967

Millar, Audrey, *St George's, Dumfries, 1843–1993: The Life of our Church*, Dumfries 1994

Murray, John J., *The Church on the Hill: Oban Free High Church, A History and Guide*, Oban 1984

Murray, Neil, *Chum Fios A Bhi Aig An Al Ri Teachd* ['*Back Free Church*'], Back nd

Niven, Bill, *East Kilbride Old Parish Church: A History of the Christian Faith in East Kilbride*, East Kilbride 2002

Robertson, D., *Blackfriars United Free Church, Glasgow: Being an Historical Sketch of the Church which was Originally 'The Original Burgher Associate Congregation', and Afterwards East Campbell Street Free*, Glasgow 1901

Robbie, William, *Bon-Accord United Free Church Aberdeen. A Retrospect of 100 Years, 1828–1928*, Aberdeen 1928

Thomson, William, *The First Relief Church in the West: An Account of Bellshill West United Free Church*, Glasgow 1913

Tulloch, Robert, *History of Henderson United Free Church, Kilmarnock 1773–1923*, Kilmarnock 1923

Journals, Diaries and Autobiographies

William Arnot – Arnot, William, *The Autobiography of the Rev. William Arnot*, New York 1878

Andrew Bonar – Bonar, Marjory (Ed.), *Andrew A. Bonar: Diary and Life*, Edinburgh 1893 (reprinted 1961)

John Bowes – Bowes, John, *Autobiography or History of the Life of John Bowes*, Glasgow 1872

John Brown – Brown, John, *Brief Account of a Tour in the Highlands of Perthshire, July 1818*, Edinburgh 1818

Dugald Buchanan – Buchanan, Dugald, *The Diary of Dugald Buchanan, with a Memoir of his Life*, Edinburgh 1836.

James Calder – Taylor, William (Ed.), *Diary of James Calder*, Stirling 1875

Duncan Campbell – Campbell, Duncan, *Reminiscences and Reflections of an Octogenarian Highlander*, Inverness 1910

Alexander Cumming – Cumming, Alexander, *Memorials of the Ministry of the Rev. Alexander Cumming*, Edinburgh 1881

James Dodds – Dodds, James, *Personal Reminiscences and Biographical Sketches*, Edinburgh 1888

Niel Douglas – Douglas, Niel, *Journey to a Mission to Part of the Highlands of Scotland, in the Summer and Harvest, 1797*, Edinburgh 1799

Samuel Dunn – Bowes, H. R.(Ed.), *Samuel Dunn's Shetland and Orkney Journal 1822–1825*, Sheffield 1976

Charles G. Finney – Rosell, Garth M. &, Richard A. G. Dupuis (Eds), *The Memoirs of Charles G. Finney*, Grand Rapids 1989

James Garie – Garie, James, *Memoirs of the late Rev. James Garie, Minister of the Gospel in Perth*, Edinburgh 1801

James Haldane – Haldane, James, *Journal of a Tour Through the Northern Counties of Scotland and the Orkney Isles, in Autumn 1797*, Edinburgh 1798

William Haslam – Wright, Chris, *Haslam's Journey: "From Death to Life" and "Yet Not I" (Abridged and Annotated)*, Godalming 2005

Sir Archibald Johnston – Paul, George Morison (Ed.), *Diary of Sir Archibald Johnston of Wariston 1632–1639*, Edinburgh 1911

John Kennedy – Kennedy, Howard A. *Old Highland Days: The Reminiscences of Dr John Kennedy*, London 1901

John Love – Love, John, *Memorials of the Rev. John Love*, vol. 1, Glasgow 1857

Neil Mackenzie – Mackenzie, Neil, *Episode in the Life of the Rev. Neil Mackenzie at St Kilda*, Aberfeldy, privately published 1911

William McKillican – McNaughton, W. D., *Journal of William McKillican*, Glasgow 1994

Alexander Macleod – Macleod, Alexander, *Diary and Sermons, With Brief Memoir by the Rev. D. Beaton, Wick*, Gizborne N.Z., 1961

J. M. Macleod – Macleod, J. M., *Reminiscences and Reflections, Referring to his Early Ministry in the Parish of Row, 1825–31*, London 1873

John Mill – Mill, John, *The Diary of the Reverend John Mill, Minister of the Parishes of Dunrossness, Sandwick and Cunningsburgh in Shetland, 1740–1803*, Edinburgh 1889

Dugald Sinclair – Sinclair, Dugald, *Journal of Itinerating Exertions in Some of the More Destitute Parts of Scotland*, Edinburgh, 1814–17

Biographies

Gustavus Aird – MacRae, Alexander, *The Life of Gustavus Aird, A.M., D.D., Creich, Moderator of the Free Church 1888*, Stirling 1908

Jonathan Ranken Anderson – Cameron, Neil, *Sketch of the Life of Rev. Jonathan Ranken Anderson*, Glasgow 1914

James Blair – Blair, Rev. James, *The Scottish Evangelist. The Life and Labours of the Rev. James Blair, of the Bridge of Allan*, Glasgow 1860

Robert Blair – Row, W.(Ed.), *The Life of Mr Robert Blair*, Edinburgh 1848

Horatius Bonar – Various Contributors, *Horatius Bonar, D.D. – A Memorial*, Edinburgh 1890

Various Contributors, *Memories of Dr Horatius Bonar by Relatives and Public Men*, Edinburgh 1909

Thomas Boston – Morrison, Rev. George H., 'Introduction' to *Memoirs of the Life, Time, and Writings of the Reverend and Learned Thomas Boston*, Edinburgh 1776

Hugh Bourne – Wilkinson, John T., *Hugh Bourne 1772–1852*, London 1952

David Brown – Blaikie, William G., *David Brown: Professor and Principal of the Free Church College*, London 1898

John Brown – Mackenzie, Robert, *John Brown of Haddington*, London 1918 [reprinted 1964]

Robert Bruce – MacNicoll, Duncan C., *Robert Bruce: Minister in the Kirk of Edinburgh*, London 1961

Dugald Buchanan – Sinclair, Rev. A., *Reminiscences of the Life and Labours of Dugald Buchanan, with his Spiritual Songs*, Edinburgh 1875

William Chalmers Burns – Burns, Islay, *Memoir of the Rev. Wm. C. Burns, Missionary to China from the English Presbyterian Church*, London 1870

McMullen, Dr Michael, *God's Polished Arrow: W. C. Burns: Revival Preacher*, Fearn 2000

William H. Burns – Burns, Islay, *The Pastor of Kilsyth, or, Memorials of the Life and Times of the Rev. W. H. Burns, D.D.*, London 1860

Hector Cameron – Macaulay, Rev. Murdo, *Hector Cameron of Lochs and Back*, Edinburgh 1982

Richard Cameron – Grant, Maurice, *The Lion of the Covenant: The Story of Richard Cameron*, Darlington 1977

Duncan Campbell – Macgregor, Duncan, *Campbell of Kiltearn*, Edinburgh 1874

John Campbell – Philip, Robert, *The Life, Times, and Missionary Enterprises of the Rev. John Campbell*, London 1841

John Campbell – Campbell, John, *Missionary and Ministerial Life in the Highlands, Being a Memoir of the Rev. John Campbell, Late Pastor of the Congregational Church, Oban*, Edinburgh 1853

John McLeod Campbell – Campbell, Donald (Ed.), *Memorials of John McLeod Campbell*, London 1877

Donald Cargill – Grant, Maurice, *No King But Christ*, Darlington 1988

Thomas Collins – Coley, Samuel, *The Life of Rev. Thomas Collins*, London 1876

Archibald Cook – Campbell, Norman, *One of Heaven's Jewels: Rev. Archibald Cook of Daviot and the (Free) North Church, Inverness*, Stornoway 2009

David Inglis Cowan – Thomson, D. P., *David Inglis Cowan*, Edinburgh 1961

Robert Craig – Craig, Robert C., *Memorials of the Life and Labours of the Rev. Robert Craig, A.M., Free Church, Rothesay*, Glasgow 1862

John Davidson – Gillon, R. Moffat, *John Davidson of Prestonpans*, London 1938

John Duncan – Moody Stuart, A., *The Life of John Duncan*, Edinburgh 1872 (reprinted 1991)

Brown, David, *The Life of Rabbi Duncan*, Glasgow 1986 (formerly published 1872 as *Memoir of John Duncan*)

Jonathan Edwards – Murray, Iain H., *Jonathan Edwards: A New Biography*, Edinburgh 1987

Elizabeth, Duchess of Gordon – Moody Stuart, Rev. A., *Life and Letters of Elizabeth, Last Duchess of Gordon*, London 1865

Fergus Ferguson – Adamson, William, *The Life of the Rev. Fergus Ferguson, M.A., D.D., Minister of Montrose Street Evangelical Union Church*, London 1900

Robert Findlater – Findlater, William, *Memoir of Rev. Robert Findlater, Together with a Narrative of the Revival of Religion During his Ministry at Lochtayside, Perthshire 1816–1819*, Glasgow 1840

George Gilfillan – Macrae, David, *George Gilfillan: Anecdotes and Reminiscences*, Glasgow 1891

John Gordon – Gordon, M., *John Gordon of Pitlurg and Parkhill, or, Memories of a Standard-Bearer*, London 1885

Hay MacDowall Grant – Mrs Gordon, *Hay MacDowall Grant of Arndilly: His Life, Labours and Teachings*, London 1876

Peter Grant – Mitchell, George. J. *Highland Harvester: Peter Grant's Life, Times and Legacy*, Kilsyth 2013

Thomas Guthrie – Guthrie, David K. & Charles J., *Autobiography of Thomas Guthrie, and Memoir*, 2 volumes, London 1874

Guthrie, C. J. G., *Life of Thomas Guthrie*, Glasgow 1897

Lord Haddo of Aberdeen – Duff, Alexander, *The True Nobility: Sketches of the Life and Character of Lord Haddo, Fifth Earl of Aberdeen*, London 1868

Thomas Halyburton – Halyburton, Thomas, *Memoirs of the Life of the Rev. Thomas Halyburton*, Edinburgh 1847

Patrick Hamilton – Cameron, Alexander (Ed.), *Patrick Hamilton: First Scottish Martyr of the Reformation. A Composite Biography*, Edinburgh 1929

Edward Hammond – Headley, Rev. P. C., *The Reaper and the Harvest: Or Scenes and Incidents in Connection with the Work of the Holy Spirit in the Life and Labours of Rev. Edward Hammond*, New York 1884

James Ballantyne Hay – Walker, I., *Memoir of the Rev. James Ballantyne Hay, Late Minister of the Free Church of Scotland at North Berwick*, Edinburgh 1870

Alexander Henderson – McCrie, Thomas, *Life of Alexander Henderson*, Edinburgh 1846

Stephen Hislop – Smith, George, *Stephen Hislop, Pioneer Missionary & Naturalist in Central India from 1844 to 1863*, London 1888

Edward Irving – Mrs Oliphant, *The Life of Edward Irving*, London 1862

Drummond, A. L., *Edward Irving and His Circle*, Cambridge 1934

Dallimore, Arnold, *The Life of Edward Irving: The Fore-runner of the Charismatic Movement*, Edinburgh 1983

John Kennedy – Auld, Alexander, *Life of John Kennedy*, London 1887

John Kirk – Kirk, H., *Memoirs of Rev. John Kirk D.D.*, Edinburgh 1888

John Knox – McCunn, Florence A., *John Knox*, London 1895

Robert Murray M'Cheyne – Bonar, Andrew, *Memoir and Remains of the Rev. Robert Murray M'Cheyne, Minister of St Peter's Church, Dundee*, Dundee 1844

Smellie, Alexander, *Robert Murray McCheyne*, London 1913

Robertson, David, *Awakening: The Life & Ministry of Robert Murray McCheyne*, Carlisle 2004

Van Valen, L. J., *Constrained By His Love: A New Biography on Robert Murray McCheyne*, Fearn 2002

Prime, Derek, *Travel with Robert Murray McCheyne: In the Footsteps of a Godly Scottish Pastor*, Leominster 2007

Donald Macdonald – Macfarlane, Rev. D., *Memoir and Remains of Rev. D. Macdonald, Shieldaig*, Glasgow 1903

John Macdonald – Kennedy, Rev. John, *The Apostle of the North*, London 1866 [reprinted 1979]

Charles C. Macintosh – Taylor, Rev. W., *Memorials of Rev. C. C. Macintosh*, Edinburgh 1871

Alexander McIntyre – Robinson, J. C., *The Rev. Alexander McIntyre*, Melbourne 1919

Lachlan Mackenzie – Murray, Iain H. (Ed.), *The Happy Man: The Abiding Witness of Lachlan Mackenzie*, Edinburgh 1971

Thomas McLauchlan – Leask, W. Keith, *Dr Thomas McLauchlan*, Edinburgh 1905

John Macleod – Collins, G. N. M., *Principal John Macleod D.D.*, Edinburgh 1951

Norman M'Leod – Macdonald, D. A., *In Memoriam: A Brief Sketch of the Life and Labours of the Rev. Norman M'Leod, M.A. United Free Church Portree*, Edinburgh 1913

Roderick MacLeod – Gillies, Donald, *The Life and Work of the Very Rev. Roderick MacLeod of Snizort*, Skeabost Bridge 1969

Donald McQueen – Ross, James, *Donald McQueen: Catechist in Bracadale*, London 1891

John Macrae – Nicolson, Nicol, *Reverend John Macrae ('Mac-Rath Mor' – 'Big Macrae') of Knockbain, Greenock and Lewis: A Short Account of his Life and Fragments of his Preaching*, Inverness 1924

Jessie McFarlane – G., H. I., *Jessie McFarlane A Tribute of Affection*, London 1872

Duncan Matheson – Macpherson, John, *Life and Labours of Duncan Matheson, The Scottish Evangelist*, London 1871

John Milne – Bonar, Horatius, *Life of the Rev. John Milne of Perth*, London 1869

Alexander Moody Stuart – Moody Stuart, K., *Alexander Moody Stuart: A Memoir*, London 1899.

James Morison – Adamson, William, *The Life of the Rev. James Morison*, London 1898

John Murker – Stark, James, *Rev. John Murker: A Picture of Religious Life and Character in the North*, London 1887

Brownlow North – Moody Stuart, K., *Brownlow North: His Life and Work*, London 1878 (reprinted 1961)

Alexander Patrick – Drake, Rev. John, *The Wallacestone Reformer; or, A Sketch of the Life and Labours of Mr Alexander Patrick, Wesleyan Local Preacher*, Kirkintilloch 1848

Robert Rainy – Simpson, P. Carnegie, *The Life of Principal Rainy*, London 1909

Andrew Reed – Shaw, Ian J., *The Greatest Is Charity: The Life of Andrew Reed, Preacher and Philanthropist*, Darlington 2005

James Robertson – M., M. H., *James Robertson of Newington: A Memorial of his Life and Work*, Edinburgh 1887

David Sandeman – Bonar, Andrew, *Memoir of the Life and Brief Ministry of the Rev. David Sandeman, Missionary to China*, London 1861

Mrs Stewart Sandeman – Barbour, Margaret F., *Memoir of Mrs Stewart Sandeman of Bonskeid and Springland*, London 1883

Charles Simeon – Carus, Rev. William (Ed.), *Memoirs of the Life of the Rev. Charles Simeon*, London 1847

George Smeaton – Keddie, John, *George Smeaton: Learned Theologian and Biblical Scholar*, Darlington 2007

Alexander N. Somerville – Smith, George, *A Modern Apostle: Alexander N. Somerville, D.D. 1813–1889*, London 1890

Alexander Stewart – Stewart, James, *Memoirs of the Late Rev. Alexander Stewart, D.D: One of the Ministers of Canongate, Edinburgh*, Edinburgh 1822

Alexander Stewart – Tomlinson, Glenn, *From Scotland to Canada: The Life of Pioneer Missionary, Alexander Stewart*, Guelph, Ontario, 2008

Robert Story – Story, Robert, *Memoir of the Life of the Rev. Robert Story, Late Minister of Rosneath, Dumbartonshire*, Cambridge 1862

Alexander Thomson – Smeaton, George, *Memoir of Alexander Thomson of Banchory*, Edinburgh 1869

Andrew Thomson – Miller, R. Strang, *Andrew Thomson: A Great Scottish Churchman*, Dunedin 1961

James Troup – Stark, James, *Memoir of Rev. James Troup, M.A., Minister of Helensburgh Congregational Church*, Helensburgh 1897

James Turner – MacHardie, Elizabeth, *James Turner: or, How to Reach the Masses*, Aberdeen 1875

Ralph Wardlaw – Alexander, William Lindsay, *Memoirs of the Life and Writings of Ralph Wardlaw*, Edinburgh 1856

John Watson – Alexander, W. Lindsay, *Memoir of the Rev. John Watson, Late Pastor of the Congregational Church in Musselburgh, and Secretary of the Congregational Union for Scotland*, Edinburgh 1845

John Welsh – Young, Rev. James, *Life of John Welsh, Minister of Ayr*, Edinburgh 1866

John Wesley – Fitchett, W. H., *Wesley and his Century: A Study in Spiritual Forces*, London 1906

Kent, John, *Wesley and the Wesleyans: Religion in Eighteenth-Century Britain*, Cambridge 2002

George Whitefield – Stout, Harry S., *The Divine Dramatist; George Whitefield and the Rise of Modern Evangelicalism*, Grand Rapids 1991

Alexander Wilson – Brisbane, Thomas, *The Life of Alexander Wilson, Insch*, Aberdeen 1867

John Wilson – Smith, George, *The Life of John Wilson*, London 1878

George Wishart – Baird, James W., *Thunder Over Scotland: The Life of George Wishart, Scottish Reformer, 1513–1546*, California 1982

James Wodrow – Wodrow, Robert, *Life of James Wodrow*, Edinburgh 1828

Collective Biographies

Anon., *Sidelights on Two Notable Ministries*, Inverness 1970

Beaton, Donald, *Scottish Heroines of the Faith: Being Brief Sketches of Noble Women of the Reformation and Covenant Times*, London 1909

Some Noted Ministers of the Northern Highlands, Inverness 1929 (reprinted 1985)

Carruthers, R., *Biographies of Highland Clergymen*, Inverness 1889

Collins, G. N. M., *Men of the Burning Heart*, Edinburgh 1983

Cook, Faith, *Hymn Writers and their Hymns*, Darlington 2005

Haldane, Alexander, *The Lives of Robert & James Haldane*, London 1852 (reprinted 1990)

Howie, John, *The Scots Worthies*, Edinburgh 1870 (reprinted 1995)

Hudson, J. H., Jarvie, T. W.& Stein, J., *Let the Fire Burn*, Dundee 1978

Ker, John & Watson, Jean L., *Lives of Ebenezer and Ralph Erskine*, Edinburgh 1882

Kinniburgh, Robert, *Fathers of Independency in Scotland or, Biographical Sketches of Early Scottish Congregational Ministers, A.D. 1798–1851*, Edinburgh 1851

MacCowan, Roderick, *The Men of Skye*, Glasgow 1902

Macfarlane, Norman C., *The 'Men' of the Lews*, Stornoway 1924

Apostles of the North: Sketches of Some Highland Ministers, Stornoway, 1989

MacKinnon, Donald, *Clerical Men of Skye*, Dingwall 1930

Macleod, Principal J., *Donald Munro of Ferintosh and Rogart, with Sketch of Rev. John Graham*, Inverness 1939

Norton, Robert, *Memoirs of James and George Macdonald, of Port-Glasgow*, London 1840

Thomson, A. B., *Sketches of Some Baptist Pioneers in Scotland*, Glasgow 1903

Tweedie, Rev. W. K. (Ed.), *Select Biographies*, Edinburgh 1847

Various Contributors, *Disruption Worthies of the Highlands: Another Memorial of 1843*, Edinburgh 1877

Scottish Divines 1505–1872, Edinburgh 1883

Walker, George, *Craigdam and its Ministers, the Rev. William Brown and the Rev. Patrick Robertson*, Aberdeen 1885

Walker, Patrick, *Six Saints of the Covenant*, vol. 1, London 1901

Wylie, Rev. James, *Disruption Worthies – A Memorial of 1843*, Edinburgh 1881

Books on Revival

Anderson, Jonathan Ranken, *Days in Kirkfield: Being Discourses on a Revival Occasion in Kirkfield Chapel, Gorbals of Glasgow, from 24th November 1839 to 5th January 1840*, Glasgow 1872

Anon., *Narrative of Revival Meetings at Stirling*, Stirling 1840

Anon., *A Narrative of the Surprising Work of God in the Conversion of Souls in Kilsyth, Finnieston, and Cumbernauld, and the Revival of Religion in Anderston and Paisley; with an Account of the Remarkable Occurrences which took Place at the Dispensation of the Sacrament at Kilsyth, on 22nd September, 1839*, Glasgow 1839

Baikie, J. M., *Revivals in the Far North*, Wick nd

Bailie, W. D., *The Six Mile Water Revival of 1625*, Belfast 1976

Burns, James, *Revivals: Their Laws and Leaders*, London 1909

Cairns, E. E., *An Endless Line of Splendour*, Wheaton 1986

Carwardine, Richard J., *Transatlantic Revivalism: Popular Evangelicalism in Britain and America, 1790–1865*, Westport, Connecticut, 1978

Cleveland, Catharine C., *The Great Revival in the West 1797–1805*, Massachusetts 1959

Couper, W. J., *Scottish Revivals*, Dundee 1918

Crawford, M. J., *Seasons of Grace: Colonial New England's Revival Tradition in Its British Context*, New York 1991

Davies, R. E., *I Will Pour Out My Spirit: A History and Theology of Revivals and Evangelical Awakenings*, Tunbridge Wells 1992

Duncan, Mary Lundie, *History of Revivals of Religion in the British Isles, Especially Scotland*, Edinburgh 1836

Edwards, Brian H., *Revival: A People Saturated With God*, Darlington, 1990

Can We Pray for Revival? Darlington 2001

Evans, Eifion, *When He is Come: An Account of the 1858–60 Revival in Wales*, Denbigh 1959

Fawcett, Arthur, *The Cambuslang Revival: The Scottish Evangelical Revival of the Eighteenth Century*, Edinburgh 1971

Ferguson, John, *When God Came Down: An Account of the North Uist Revival 1957–58*, Inverness, 2000

Gillies, John, *Historical Collections of Accounts of Revival*, Edinburgh 1845 (Revised and enlarged 1981)

Jeffrey, Kenneth S., *When the Lord Walked the Land: The 1858–62 Revival in the North East of Scotland*, Carlisle 2002

Johnson, H. N., *Stories of Great Revivals*, London 1906

Jones, D. Geraint, *Favoured With Frequent Revivals: Revivals in Wales 1762–1862*, Cardiff 2001

Lambert, Frank, *Inventing the Great Awakening*, Princeton, N.J., 1999

Lloyd-Jones, Dr Martyn, *Revival—Can We Make It Happen?*, Basingstoke 1986

Lumsden, James, *Sweden: its Religious State and Prospects: with Some Notices of the Revivals and Persecutions which are at Present taking place in that Country*, London 1855

Macaulay, George, *Times of Revival, or The Nature, Desirableness and Means of Revival in Religion*, Edinburgh 1858

Macfarlan, Duncan, *The Revivals of the Eighteenth Century, particularly at Cambuslang*, Edinburgh 1847

MacGillvary, Angus, *Sketches of Religion and Revivals of Religion in the North Highlands During the Last Century*, Edinburgh 1859

McKinnon, L. M., *The Skye Revivals*, printed privately 1995

MacMillan, Douglas (Ed.), *Restoration in the Church: Reports of Revivals 1625–1839*, Glasgow 1839 (reprinted 1989)

Macpherson, John, *Revival and Revival Work: A Record of the Labours of D.L. Moody & Ira D. Sankey, and Other Evangelists*, London, 1875

MacRae, Alexander, *Revivals in the Highlands & Islands in the 19th Century*, Stirling 1906 [reprinted 1998]

The Fire of God Among the Heather; or The Spiritual Awakening of the Highland People, Tongue 1930

Mathews, T. T. (Ed.), *Reminiscences of the Revival of Fifty-Nine and the Sixties*, Aberdeen 1910

Murray, Iain H., *Revival & Revivalism: The Making and Marring of American Evangelicalism 1750–1858*, Edinburgh 1994

Pentecost Today: The Biblical Basis for Understanding Revival, Edinburgh 1998

Nixon, William, *An Account of the Work of God at Ferryden*, London 1860

Orr, J. Edwin, *The Eager Feet: Evangelical Awakenings 1790–1830*, Chicago 1975

Second Evangelical Awakening, London 1949

Presbytery of Aberdeen, *Evidence on the Subject of Revivals Taken Before the Presbytery of Aberdeen*, Aberdeen 1841

Robe, Rev. James, *Where the Wind Blows*, Belfast 1985

Roberts, Dyfed Wyn (Ed.), *Revival, Renewal And The Holy Spirit*, Milton Keynes 2009

Roberts, Richard Owen, *An Annotated Bibliography of Revival Literature*, Wheaton 1987

    Revival, Wheaton 1991

    Scotland Saw His Glory, Wheaton 1995

Sprange, Harry, *Kingdom Kids: Children in Revival*, Fearn 1993

Stewart, James A., *Opened Windows: The Church and Revival*, Asheville, NC 1958

Taylor, Steve, *The Skye Revivals*, Chichester 2003

Various Contributors, *The Revival of Religion: Addresses by Scottish Evangelical Leaders Delivered in Glasgow in 1840*, Edinburgh 1840

Walters, David, *Children Aflame*, South Carolina 1995

Weisberger, Bernard, *They Gathered at the River*, Chicago 1958

Articles in Journals

Andsell, Douglas, 'The 1843 Disruption of the Church of Scotland in the Isle of Lewis', in *SCHSR*, Edinburgh 1992

Dallimore, Arnold, 'Whitefield and the Evangelical Revival in Scotland', in *Banner of Truth*, vol. 79, 1969

Devine, Tom, 'Scotland: The Reformation and the Enlightenment', in *Life and Work*, January 2010

Dickson, Neill, 'Modern Prophetesses', in *SCHSR*, vol. 25, Edinburgh 1993

Jones,, G Penrhyn, 'Cholera in Wales', in *National Library of Wales Journal*, vol. 10/3, Summer 1958

Landsman, Ned, 'Evangelists and their Hearers: Popular Interpretation of Revivalist Preaching in Eighteenth-Century Scotland', in *Journal of British Studies*, vol. 28, 1989

Luker, David, 'Revivalism in Theory and Practice: The Case of Cornish Methodism', in *The Journal of Ecclesiastical History*, vol. 37, no. 4, October 1986

Mackay, W. R., 'Early Evangelical Religion in the Far North: A Kulturkampf', in *SCHSR*, vol. 26, 1996

Macleod, Rev. William, 'The Beginning of Evangelical Religion in Skye', in *Banner of Truth*, Aug/Sept. 1995, volumes 383-4

McNaughton, William D., 'Revival and Reality: Congregationalists and Religious Revival in Nineteenth-Century Scotland', in *SCHSR*, vol. 33, 2003

Mechie, S., The Psychology of the Cambuslang Revival', in *SCHSR*, vol. 10 (1948–50)

Medley, W., 'Horatius Bonar D.D.: A Brief Sketch to Commemorate the Centenary of his Death', in *The Evangelical Library Bulletin*, Spring 1989

Meek, Donald E., 'The Baptists of the Ross of Mull', in *Northern Studies*, vol. 26, 1989

'Falling Down as if Dead: Attitudes to Unusual Phenomena in the Skye Revival of 1841–1842', in *Scottish Bulletin of Evangelical Theology*, vol. 13/4, Autumn 1995

'The Preacher, the Press-gang and the Landlord: the Impressment and Vindication of the Rev. Donald MacArthur', in *SCHSR*, vol. 25 (1995)

'Evangelical Missionaries in the Early Nineteenth Century Highlands', quoted in *Transactions of the Gaelic Society of Inverness*, vol. 56 (1989)

'Dugald Sinclair. The Life and Work of a Highland Itinerant Missionary', in *Scottish Studies*, vol. 30, 1991

Muir, Alex, 'Revivals in Inverness: Robert Bruce, Fire in the North', quoted in *Sword* magazine, vol. 4, no. 5, 2009

'Revival in Scotland: A Personal Perspective', in *Prophecy Today*, vol. 1, no. 4, 1985

'Revivals in Inverness: Robert Bruce, Exiled to Save!', in *Sword* magazine, vol. 4, no. 6, 2009

Muirhead, Andrew T. N., 'A Secession Congregation in its Community: The Stirling Congregation of the Rev. Ebenezer Erskine, 1731–1754', in *SCHCR*, vol. XXII (1986)

Muirhead, Ian A., 'The Revival as a Dimension of Scottish Church History', in *SCHSR*, vol. 20, 1980

Murray, Iain H., 'The Puritans and Revival Christianity', in *Banner of Truth*, Sept 1969.

Reeves, Dudley, 'Charles Simeon in Scotland', in *Banner of Truth*, Jan 1973, vol. 112

Reid, Harry, '1560: The Greatest Year in Scotland's History', in *Life and Work*, January 2010

Robb, George, 'Popular Religion and the Christianization of the Scottish Highlands', in *Journal of Religious History*, vol. 16 (1990)

Roberts, Maurice J., 'John Welsh of Ayr', in *Banner of Truth*, vol. 174, March 1978

'Remembering the 1859 Revival in Scotland', in *Banner of Truth*, vol. 352, January 1993

Roxburgh, Kenneth B. E., 'The Scottish Evangelical Awakening of 1742 and the Religious Societies', in *The Journal of the United Reformed Church History Society*, vol. 5, no. 5, November 1994

Smout, T. C., 'Born Again at Cambuslang: New Evidence on Popular Religion and Literacy in Eighteenth Century Scotland', in *Past and Present*, vol. 97, 1982

Somerset, Rev. D. W. B., 'The Achreny Mission' in *Free Presbyterian Magazine*, 2004/1, vol. 109

Taylor, William, 'The Diary of James Calder', in *Banner of Truth*, vol. 130, July/Aug 1974.

Van Den Berg, Professor Johannes, 'The Evangelical Revival in Scotland and the Nineteenth-Century "Reveil" in the Netherlands', in *SCHSR*, vol. 25 (1995)

Walker, R. B., 'The Growth of Wesleyan Methodism in Victorian England and Wales', in *Journal of Ecclesiastical History*, vol. 24, 1973

Articles in Books

Bebbington, D. W., 'Revival and the Clash of Cultures, Ferryden, Forfarshire, in 1859', in Dyfed Wyn Roberts, (Ed.), *Revival, Renewal, and the Holy Spirit*, Milton Keynes 2009

Blaikie, W. G., 'Memoir of Islay Burns', in Islay Burns, *Select Remains of Islay Burns*, London 1874

MacGregor, Rev. Malcolm, 'Prefatory Memoir', in Rev. William Forbes, *Communion and Other Sermons (partly edited by the late Rev. John Kennedy)*, London 1867

MacInnes, Allan I., 'Evangelical Protestantism', in Graham Walker and Tom Gallacher, *Sermons and Battle Hymns: Protestant Popular Culture in Modern Scotland*, Edinburgh 1990

Meek, Donald E., 'Gaelic Bible, Revival and Mission: The Spiritual Rebirth of the Nineteenth-Century Highlands', in James Kirk (Ed.), *The Church in the Highlands*, Edinburgh 1998

'Religious Life in the Highlands Since the Reformation', in Michael Lynch (Ed.), *The Oxford Companion to Scottish History*, Oxford 2001

Miller, R. Strang, 'Greatheart of China: A Brief Life of William Chalmers Burns, MA, Scottish Evangelist and Revival Leader, and Early Missionary to China', in Various, *Five Pioneer Missionaries*, Edinburgh 1965

Roxburgh, Kenneth B. E., 'Revival, An Aspect of Scottish Religious Identity', in Robert Pope (Ed.), *Religion and National Identity: Wales and Scotland c.1700–2000*, Cardiff 2001

Stout, Harry S., 'George Whitefield in Three Countries', in Mark A. Noll, David W. Bebbington and George A. Rawlyk, *Evangelicalism: Comparative Studies of Popular Protestantism in North America, the British Isles, and Beyond, 1700–1990*, New York 1994.

Talbot, Brian, 'Reserved from Erroneous Views? The Contribution of Francis Johnston as a Baptist Voice in the Scottish Evangelical Debate, in the Mid-Nineteenth Century, on the Work of the Holy Spirit', in Dyfed Wyn Roberts (Ed.), *Revival, Renewal and the Holy Spirit*, Milton Keynes 2009

Unpublished Ph.D. Theses

Bussey, Oscar, *The Religious Awakening of 1858–60 in Great Britain and Ireland*, Ph.D. Thesis, University of Edinburgh, 1947

Brown, Callum Graham, *Religion and the Development of an Urban Society: Glasgow 1780–1914*, Ph.D. Thesis, University of Strathclyde, 1981, vol. 1

Macleod, Roderick, *The Progress of Evangelicalism in the Western Isles, 1800–1850*, Unpublished Ph.D. Thesis, University of Edinburgh, 1977

McNaughton, Arthur, *A Study of the Phenomena of Prostration Arising from Conviction of Sin*, Ph.D. Thesis, University of Edinburgh, 1937

Robertson, George Booth, *Spiritual Awakening in the North-East of Scotland and the Description of the Church in 1843*, Ph.D. Thesis, University of Aberdeen, 1970

Newspapers, Journals and Reports

The Baptist Home Missionary Society Report, 1832, 1833, 1836, 1838–45, 1849–50, 1852, 1855, 1857, 1862

The Congregational Magazine, 1830

The Edinburgh Christian Instructor, April, May 1838

The Edinburgh Review, June 1831

The Free Church General Assembly Report 1901

The Free Church Report on the State of Religion & Morals, 1874, 1884–85

The Free Church of Scotland Monthly Record, 1895, 1918

The Gaelic School Society Report, 43 1844 45

The Highland News, 28/03/1896

The Inverness Advertiser, 1/11/1859

The Oban Times, 24/09/1898

The Scottish Guardian, 21/03/1860, 10/08/1861

The Stornoway Gazette, 15/01/1972; 22/01/1972, 26/02/1972, 04/03/1972, 11/03/1972, 18/03/1972

Other Resources

Macleod, Donald, *Testimony of Strathnaver Clearances* (www.helmsdale.org – accessed 04/11/11)

MacLeod, Principal Donald, *The Gospel in the Highlands*, A lecture given to mark the Centenary of Knockbain Free Church in the Black Isle in 1989 (www.freechurch.org – accessed 08/06/11)

Sage, Rev. Donald, *Testimony of Strathnaver Clearances* (www.chebucto.ns.ca – accessed 04/11/11)

Somerset, Rev. D. W. B., *The Achreny Mission*, Part 3 (www.fpchurch.org.uk – accessed 12/07/11)

Taylor, Steve, *Skye Revival*, CD ROM, 2003

PEOPLE INDEX

PLACES INDEX

Tom Lennie

"Just as Pentecost was desperately needed at the beginning of the Christian era, so another season of God-sent revival is the urgent need of this hour. A careful reading of 'Glory in the Glen' will help in many ways."

Richard Owen Roberts
International Awakening Ministries

Glory in the Glen

A History of Evangelical Revivals in Scotland

1880–1940

Glory in the Glen

by Tom Lennie

No nation on earth has a richer, more colourful, and more long-standing heritage of evangelical awakenings than Scotland – yet most people are unfamiliar with its dramatic legacy. Most historical studies stop at, or before, the Moody & Sankey Revival of 1873-74. It is commonly assumed that very few genuine revivals occurred since that date until the Lewis Revival of 1949-53.

Tom Lennie thoroughly debunks this idea – showing that religious awakenings were relatively common in Scotland between these dates – and provides a comprehensive account of the many exciting revivals that have taken place throughout Scotland. The Awakenings in the Outer Hebrides and North East fishing communities, that had several unique and striking features, are considered in separate sections. Revivals amongst both children / students and Pentecostals are also given separate treatment.

Of particular significance is the first comprehensive account of the 1930's 'Laymen's Revival' in Lewis. This fascinating, but near-forgotten, movement may have been even more powerful and influential than the later Lewis Revival. *Glory in the Glen* tells a thoroughly absorbing, and largely untold, story. It is the result of painstaking research, conducted over more than half-a-decade, from hundreds of source materials as well as personal interviews. Much of the material has never before been published.

ISBN: 978-1-84550-377-2

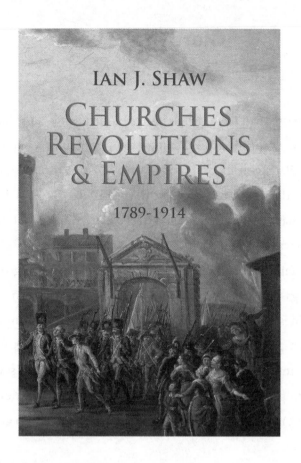

Churches, Revolutions & Empires

by Ian J.Shaw

1789 to 1914 was a time of momentous and often violent change religiously, socially, politically and economically in the western world. The revolutions in the churches and the powerful empires of the day were to have a profound effect upon society at large both then and in the years that followed. In this detailed yet fascinating study, Ian Shaw gives context and understanding to this legacy which has been passed on from that era by providing an expert analysis of the period with a focus on the key leaders, influences and issues.

ISBN: 978-1-84550-774-9